Comparative Programming Languages

Generalizing the Programming Function

Linda Weiser Friedman

Department of Statistics and
Computer Information Systems
Baruch College, City University of New York

PRENTICE HALL, Englewood Cliffs, New Jersey 07632

Library of Congress Cataloging-in-Publication Data

Friedman, Linda Weiser.
    Comparative programming languages : generalizing the programming
    function / Linda Weiser Friedman.
        p.   cm.
    Includes bibliographical references and index.
    ISBN 0-13-155482-4
    1. Programming languages (Electronic computers)   I. Title.
QA76.7.F75 1991
005.13--dc20   90-39893
                                                     CIP

Editorial/ production supervision and interior
  design: Sharen Levine and Joe Scordato
Cover design: Lundgren Graphics
Manufacturing buyers: Linda Behrens and Patrice
  Fraccio
Acquisitions editor: Tom McElwee

TRADEMARK INFORMATION

© 1991 by Prentice-Hall Inc.
A Division of Simon & Shuster
Englewood Cliffs, NJ 07632

Printed in the United States of America

10 9 8 7 6 5 4 3 2 1

ISBN 0-13-155482-4

Prentice-Hall International (UK) Limited, *London*
Prentice-Hall of Australia Pty. Limited, *Sydney*
Prentice-Hall Canada Inc., *Toronto*
Prentice-Hall Hispanoamericana, S.A., *Mexico*
Prentice-Hall of India Private Limited, *New Delhi*
Prentice-Hall of Japan, Inc., *Tokyo*
Simon & Schuster Asia Pte. Ltd., *Singapore*
Editora Prentice-Hall do Brasil, Ltda. *Rio de Janiero*

for Michael J. Weiser

In Memoriam

We miss you.

Contents

APPENDICES 520

INDEX 568

Preface

This is a book for problem solvers working within the programming function, an area that can encompass such diverse tasks as software system design and development, language selection, testing and debugging, documentation, data design, training, and evaluating software products. In this area, language dependence—the narrow mindset we can develop by working within a single programming language, methodology, tool, or environment—stymies and dulls the creative process just as effectively as machine dependence. Given the rapidly changing environment of the programming function, language dependence can also lead rather quickly to programmer obsolescence. In order to step beyond the constraints of a single language, we must develop at least a rudimentary understanding of many different kinds of languages and many different ways of programming solutions. We must understand and generalize the vast conceptual commonalities in programming languages rather than emphasize artificial syntactic differences. The constructs we learn from studying a variety of programming languages and systems are the tools that we can use to solve future problems.

This book is designed to help us become better programmers, program developers, system analysts. Its main objective is to give students the tools with which to generalize their skills within the programming function rather than simply concentrate on learning a particular programming language. As a result, skills learned in a number of computer courses, or from working with a variety of programming languages, may all be applied to any programming task. The student or general reader will then be sufficiently competent and confident to independently learn any new procedural or nonprocedural language, programming environment, or computer package. In the commercial information processing environment, this text will serve to improve the skills required to evaluate software products and make better purchasing decisions.

This book covers the elements common to many programming languages and discusses the features that make many of these languages unique. It is designed to give the reader a passing familiarity with the major programming languages used in commercial applications and an appreciation for the growing interest in the computing community in new programming methodologies, tools, and environments.

The textbook has been organized around a unifying theme, *structure*. Structure, along with its partner, *abstraction*, is the major organizing device available to us in reducing the complexity of systems that are becoming ever more complex. Any programming task must take into consideration program structures, control structures, data structures, and file structures. And any programming language can be studied by examining the language's approach to these elements of structure.

PART 1: ELEMENTS OF PROGRAMMING LANGUAGES

This section introduces and discusses general concepts common to a large number of programming languages, especially elements relating to structure and abstraction at the data, program, and control levels.

PART 2: PROGRAMMING LANGUAGES FOR INFORMATION PROCESSING

This part helps students learn the generality of programming tools by providing a brief introduction to a number of different programming languages. It looks at specific languages in terms of their common structures and serves to illustrate how many of the concepts introduced in Part 1 have actually been implemented.

PART 3: OTHER PROGRAMMING TOOLS AND ENVIRONMENTS

In order to achieve our goal of generalizing the programming function, we go beyond merely examining the commonalities of programming languages and their individual attributes. We also consider programming methcdologies and tools; modern programming environments; fourth-generation, high-productivity programming tools; and the integrated applications-development environment. These topics serve to put Parts 1 and 2 into a practical framework and can serve as a springboard for the in-depth study of the programming function. Written and oral term projects based on these issues are useful adjuncts to a course using this textbook.

The appendices include a current bibliography, a glossary, and some brief guidelines for students conducting term projects. Surprisingly, although a glossary is essential to a textbook in this area, it is often lacking. The computing industry is distinguished by a large quantity of terminology, all of which has come into common usage fairly recently. Much of the terminology will be new and unfamiliar, and the glossary will serve as a handy reference in using the book as a study guide and as a ready source of information that will help in future endeavors and in other computer courses.

This book is intended as required or recommended reading for university students in a one-semester graduate or upper level undergraduate course in an IS, CIS, MIS, or CS program. Coming into the course, a working familiarity with at least two powerful, general-purpose programming languages is ideal; for many students, a prerequisite of one language is sufficient.

This book is also directed at professional readers who wish to broaden their knowledge of programming languages and the spectrum of skills with which they approach problem-solving in the programming function. It will prove to be valuable to anyone who wishes to break free from the constraints of language dependence.

ACKNOWLEDGMENTS

Many people helped in creating this book. David Stephan and Beata Lobert at Baruch College were extremely generous with their time, reading early drafts of this work and discussing at length many aspects with me. Lucy Garnett and Bill Ferns, also of Baruch College, graciously agreed to review selected chapters. I am grateful to Hershey H. Friedman of Brooklyn College for his work on Chapter 15, much of which was written by him. A special thanks is due my students at Baruch College for their valuable suggestions and criticism of earlier drafts of this book, and for their input to the programming illustrations of Part 2 and to the glossary. Colleagues and students alike helped me form many of the ideas expressed in this book. Any errors, however, are my own. Special thank you's are due to Esther Friedman and Pearl Friedman for their timely help with typing and proofreading sections of the manuscript.

Finally, to Esther, Pearl, Sarah, Rachel, and Devorah—many, many thanks for your patience and understanding—and for your love, when you ran out of patience and understanding.

Linda Weiser Friedman

PART 1

Elements of Programming Languages

The next few chapters introduce the reader to the subject of comparative programming languages, and discuss general concepts common to a large number of programming languages, especially those elements relating to structure and abstraction at the data, program, and control levels. These general concepts are not presented in terms of any one particular language syntax. Later, in Part 2, you will see how these ideas are implemented in several real languages.

1

Introduction

A programming language is a notation for expressing instructions to be carried out by a computer. It is a medium of communication between the human and the machine and, often, between one human being and another.

Over the years, computers have become more and more "friendly" to human users. This means that the computer is made to work more like a human and, consequently, the human is required to make less of an effort to "think like a machine." In large measure, this increased friendliness depends on the development of software systems of increasing size and complexity.

As software systems have increased in size and complexity, a large number of programming languages, systems, and methodologies have been developed in an attempt to reduce or, at least, manage this complexity. Consequently, the study of these programming languages, systems, and methodologies is crucial to those of us who are involved in the programming function.

1.1 THE PROGRAMMING FUNCTION IN SYSTEM DEVELOPMENT

The programming function is not an isolated endeavor. Typically, computer systems are designed, developed, and maintained by a large group of individuals working together.

The System Development Life Cycle

Let us examine a "typical" system development life cycle, such as the one pictured in Fig. 1.1, in order to grasp the part played by the programming function. This life *cycle* is indeed cyclical—computer systems, like other organizational entities, become obsolete as new technologies are developed or as the firm's needs evolve. At each step in the life

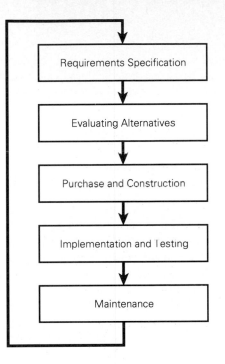

Figure 1.1 The system development life cycle

cycle, consideration is given to every type of system component. These include hardware, software, data, procedures, and personnel.

Requirements specification. This step includes a problem definition as well as analyses of the current system and of the firm's goals in developing the new computer system. The system development group must work closely with other parts of the organization in order to plan for present and future needs.

Evaluating alternatives. A number of alternative systems are designed that satisfy the requirements specified in the previous step. These alternatives are tested for feasibility, including technological feasibility (*Can it be built?*), economic feasibility (*Can we afford it?*), and behavioral feasibility (*Can it be implemented with a minimum of trauma to the firm and its personnel?*).

Purchase and construction. Once management decides on the appropriate system, it must be "built." For hardware this almost always means "purchase," since few firms go to the trouble of building their own computers. The software component of the system, however, can be either purchased or constructed.

Purchase. If the decision is made to purchase "off-the-shelf" software, existing products must be evaluated and the appropriate one(s) purchased. Even ready-made software often must be customized to meet the individual needs of the firm or to integrate different products into a single system.

Construction.   If custom software is to be developed from scratch, a programming language must be selected. Sometimes this includes decisions about an appropriate program development environment or programming methodologies. Then the program(s) are designed and developed.

Implementation and testing.   The various components of the system are integrated and put into working order. The system is tested for errors, and these errors are corrected. At this point, the old system is probably not yet discarded. Often the old and the new are used in parallel for several months, and the results compared for accuracy and adequacy.

Maintenance.   Maintenance operations take place throughout the lifetime of the computer system. A good system will allow for evolution as the firm's needs change over time. Eventually, though, the firm may perceive the need for a new system, and the cycle begins again.

The Programming Function

System development is concerned with hardware, software, data, personnel, and procedures. The programming function is considerably narrower in scope and limited to software and data considerations. Of course, these limited considerations cannot be approached without some concern for the rest of the system. Specific concerns are:

- What hardware will be used (supercomputer, mainframe, minicomputer, microcomputers, independent workstations, distributed system...)?
- What people will use the system (technical or nontechnical)?
- What procedures will the system implement (data processing, report generation, transaction processing, inventory management, missile systems...)?

As you can see from Fig. 1.2, the programming function covers a rich variety of endeavors and requires the talents of capable individuals. Learning to program in one language, even if we learn it exceptionally well, does not give us sufficient breadth to be able to intelligently carry out the programming function. That is why it is better to study

Evaluating software products	Language selection
Data design	Software system design and development
Designing screen/report formats	Prototyping
Consultation/training of nontechnical personnel	Coding
Evaluating/selecting software development tools	Testing, debugging
User documentation	Technical documentation

Figure 1.2   The programming function

numerous programming languages, systems, and methodologies. The knowledge we obtain from one, we can bring to bear in using another. As we grow, we learn to use different tools in creating better systems.

1.2 GENERALIZING THE PROGRAMMING FUNCTION

Many of us are beginning to realize that *language dependence*—dependence on a particular programming language or system—can be just as constraining, just as limiting to a programmer's creativity, education, and maturity, as *machine dependence*. It dulls the creative process just as effectively. The dependence on a particular programming language poses a very real danger to the organization, to the individual programmer, and to the computer industry as a whole.

Language dependence can lead to programmer burnout or, at the very least, low job satisfaction. Given the quickly changing environment of the programming function, language dependence can also lead to programmer obsolescence.

The Problem

Programming myopia is characterized by dependence on one particular programming language. This shortsightedness makes for a very narrow conception of the programming function. Expertise in and dependence on a single programming language means that a programmer can work comfortably in *one* programming paradigm, *one* operating environment, *one* set of data types, *one* set of data structures, *one* set of file structures, *one* set of control structures, *one* method for building programs from smaller units.

When the software engineer or any employee within the programming function is bound by some sort of visceral dependence to a single programming language in which she is an "expert," that individual is constrained by the constructs of the language and, consequently, lacks the sense of perspective necessary to properly evaluate a new language, operating system, package, or computer-aided software engineering (CASE) tool. What's more, she knows it. And that knowledge can be terrifying.

It is this fear of the unknown that keeps language selection in its wrongful place as a phantom phase in the system-development life cycle. This phase is often discussed and covered extensively in textbooks, but true language selection may not exist in the real world. Too often, programmers find themselves working in whatever language they know or are most comfortable with—or whatever language the firm insists on. In addition, besides its obvious importance to language selection, a broad knowledge of programming languages, systems, and methodologies is critical throughout the programming function. For example, when a firm first installs a computer system, or during periodic reviews, it needs qualified people to evaluate system software, including the programming languages to be used. When a firm embarks on a new application development project, it needs qualified people to determine the best programming language and programming style for the application. When a firm is involved in purchasing off-the-shelf software, it needs qualified people to evaluate the different packages available and match them to the company's requirements. It may also have to decide whether a packaged off-the-shelf software product, rather than customizing its own application, is the appropriate choice at all.

How is one to do all that if one is stuck inside of, say, a COBOL mindset? Or a C mindset? Or even a dBASE® mindset?

What will help us make a better decision in language selection or software evaluation? What will make our programmers, analysts, system developers, software engineers, and data processing managers more mature, creative, sophisticated? What will give them this much-needed sense of perspective? What will enable a firm to better satisfy its customers' present and future needs?

We need a broader sense of the programming function, a more universal and less parochial approach to applied programming methodology. We must be able to transcend the specific in order to better address the needs of our customers and the needs of the firm.

The Solution

In order to step beyond language, we must first of all have at least a rudimentary understanding of many different kinds of languages and many different ways of programming solutions. We must understand and generalize the vast conceptual commonalities in programming languages rather than emphasize the artificial syntactic differences. In short, we ought to be comfortable with the *programming function*, not a particular *programming language*, not a particular *implementation*, not a particular *operating system*, not a particular *machine*.

To some extent, structured programming methodology addresses the problem of language dependence. The techniques of structured programming can be implemented using any programming language in the design of any program. Thus, structured programming methodology can be considered an early attempt to generalize the programming function and loosen the hold of specific programming languages over programmers.

Beyond structured programming, many new techniques and language constructs exist at the forefront of software technology. These include fourth-generation languages and tools, CASE tools, data abstraction, object-oriented programming, high-productivity programming tools, integrated program-development environments, and concurrently executing communicating processes. A broad knowledge of constructs in all languages, systems, and methodologies will enhance our expertise in any one of them.

Anything we learn about creating software for computers is an additional building block for the construction of a particular, special-purpose, abstract computing machine. Using a good hardware configuration, a good programming language, and a good implementation (e.g., compiler) solves only some of the problems associated with the design, development, and maintenance of a quality software product. The constructs that the software engineer brings to the problem are also required. These constructs can be learned from the study of a variety of programming languages and subsequently can be applied in the development of a single software system.

The Future of Programming

Some recent trends in software technology clearly illustrate the growing need for language independence in the programming function.

- Programs are getting larger, requiring more effort out of more programmers over longer periods of time. It does not make good sense for managers of software development to limit this sort of effort to a single programming language with its particular language structures.

- Although programming has a tradition of being done "piecemeal," one application at a time (rather like fine artwork), there is simply too much programming being done today to keep it that way. Let's not ask our software engineers to reinvent the wheel every time they sit down to a new applications project. We need to foster a more knowledgeable, more efficient programming function whose members understand the long-term needs of the firm and of the customers it serves. The trend towards the development of reusable code is one step in this process. The ability to use a variety of languages will ensure the best fit for the application.

- The construction of large programs from blocks of relatively independent yet interrelated program code has been popular for a long time. This type of program design has been called *modular decomposition* of programs. Perhaps, the push now ought to be toward the convenient linking of modules that have been coded in different programming languages—again to increase the availability of reusable code.

Is the future of programming language oriented? If the programming function is to continue to satisfy the needs of its customers, it had better not be.

1.3 ABSTRACTION AND STRUCTURE

If we are going to study programming languages with an eye towards universality, we should concentrate on general concepts that are universally applicable. *Abstraction* and *structure* are important in creating a framework for generalizing the programming function. These two related concepts are also involved in the reduction and management of software complexity. Both abstraction and structure, as they apply to programming languages, may be best discussed in terms of *data*, *program*, and *control*. Hence, the organization of Part 1 of this book. Constructs mentioned briefly in this section are discussed in more detail in the referenced chapters.

Abstraction

Abstraction is the means by which we consider only the information that is relevant to the problem at hand, ignoring trivial details and unimportant facts. Abstraction models reality or, at the very least, a chosen view of reality in which irrelevant objects or properties are ignored in favor of streamlining the model, thus making the model simpler conceptually and easier to study or implement. The details that have been ignored are not really gone; they have been relegated to a lower level of consideration.

The general model governing abstraction is the so-called *Black Box model*, adopted from the engineering disciplines. In this model, a set of inputs is mapped to a set of outputs or results by means of a *transform*. This concept is illustrated in Fig. 1.3. To use the transform one need not know how it works only *that* it works. For example, we do

Figure 1.3   The Black Box model

not need to understand much about electricity to know that when we flip the light switch (input), the bulb will light up (output).

Let us consider an example from statistical analysis. The straight line function of mathematics, $y = \alpha + \beta x$, is often used as an abstraction of some real-world (somewhat linear) process in which the value of y depends upon the value of x. In reality, there exist virtually no such simple two-variable relationships, and the regression model that we actually use has the form: $y = \alpha + \beta x + \varepsilon$, in which ε, the error term, represents all the variation in y not accounted for by its dependence on x. In other words, ε contains the aggregate effect of all the other non-x variables that were left out of the original, stated relationship because they were considered unimportant.

Abstract computers.   Abstraction in computing has evolved on many levels and has been going on ever since those first "virtual machines" which led to the "FOR-TRAN machines" and other high-level, automatic coding systems. It has been going on since the first COBOL compiler modeled an abstract machine that understood English-like commands and worked with data files. After all, a computer is a nice little gadget, but it is not exactly a machine, in the sense of doing anything useful, without appropriate software. In that sense, any software provides the computer user with a machine abstraction and, indeed, it has been so taken over the years. Thus, programming languages and their processors become abstract, high-level, even programmer-friendly, "computers," which may be used without regard for such machine-level clerical details as keeping track of memory locations, program instruction counters, etc. [**See CHAPTER 3**]

Even the evolution of programming languages has followed a course of continuing abstraction of these languages and systems away from the level of the machine and towards the level of the human user. [**See CHAPTER 2**]

Data abstraction.   Data-level abstractions include *data types*, which are generally built into the language, and *abstract data types*. An abstract data type facility may be used to implement data structures as true user-defined data types by hiding the details of the implementation (the *how*) behind the wall of a user interface (the *what*). In the object-oriented programming paradigm, the object is a *data abstraction*. The data models of database management systems are *data-level abstractions* as are the models for knowledge representation in artificial intelligence applications. [**See CHAPTER 4**]

Program abstraction.   On yet another level, the use of subprograms for relatively independent tasks in programming is a kind of abstraction. When defining the subprogram, the programmer is intently concerned with *how* to code the algorithm—with the details of its implementation. The subprogram in this case represents an extension to the programming language in the form of a new operation. When invoking the subprogram, the programmer (the same one or, perhaps, someone else accessing it from a library of subprograms) need only be concerned with *what* it does. This program-design approach (i.e., top-down and modular) looks at the subprogram as an information-hiding device. [**See CHAPTER 5**]

Control abstraction.   On this level, we have the structured constructs of the so-called *structured programming revolution*. These structured constructs—simple sequence, selection, iteration—are *control abstractions* that enable us to write statement-oriented programs with a clear, immediately understandable flow of control and to easily discern it in others. Subprogram control constructs are also abstractions, including such models for parallel processing as *message passing* and *dataflow*. Control abstractions in programming often come in the form of a "plan" or a template for a generalized process. These may include the input/process/output-loop plan, a plan for accumulating in a loop, an input-validation plan, a control-break processing plan, etc. Control abstraction in a programming language also depends on the programming paradigm by which the language is defined. [**See CHAPTER 6**]

Structure

When something is confusing and complex, we try to impose structure on it as a means of ordering our universe. For example, when you had a large term project to do for school, you learned to construct an outline first as a device to organize your thoughts and the resulting work. Structure, which may be seen as implementing (or *concretizing*) abstraction, is applied in different ways at each of the levels studied here:

Data-level structure.   A structure at the data level is defined by the relationships among its data elements and by the operations that are acceptable to it. This definition applies to data structures, the logical structures that a program is conceived as working on. It also can be viewed as applying to data types and abstract data types, as well as to the file structures and databases on permanent storage. [**See CHAPTER 4**]

Program-level structure.   At the program level, structures are the *textual units* that make up the program, including words, expressions, statements, and subprograms. The most obvious kind of program-level structure is the subprogram. A top-down modular program is one that has been decomposed into subprograms by means of *stepwise refinement*. [**See CHAPTER 5**]

Control-level structure.   Control structures are specified over operations, statements, and subprograms. Control over statements involves the *structured control constructs* of sequence, selection, and iteration. Control over subprograms involves the "traditional" call as well as such nontraditional control structures as recursion, exception handling, parallel processing, and coroutines. [**See CHAPTER 6**]

1.4 WHY STUDY PROGRAMMING LANGUAGES?

Regardless of your interest or position in the programming function, the study of programming languages serves to give you a sense of perspective that can only enhance the work that you do and your value to your organization. One who has studied only a single programming language, system, or methodology has learned something worthwhile, but his knowledge is still very narrow in scope. To truly grasp the universality of what was learned—to transform the depth of knowledge into a breadth of vision—requires the critical examination of a variety of languages, systems, and programming approaches.

Some additional motivating factors are:

- The ability to form more intelligent, informed decisions in *evaluating and selecting* appropriate languages and other software products.

- Greater ease in *learning a new language* or system. After studying comparative programming languages, most individuals find it easier to approach learning a new language or system without trepidation.

- Such study is important if you are going to be in a position to influence the *design* and/or *implementation* of future programming languages. Although few of us plan to be in such a position, the principles of good language design are important if we are going to use *extensible* languages like FORTH or Smalltalk [see Chapter 13]. These languages allow the programmer to create new language structures that are indistinguishable from the built-in structures. Also, regardless of any intention to design or implement languages, studying programming languages promotes better problem solving by encouraging the use of abstract constructs in software development.

- The *freedom from language dependence*. Constructs learned from the study of a language or system that you will not actually use in practice may often be applied to whatever language you do use. The greater the variety of languages studied, the greater the number of abstract constructs you have to work with in the future.

SUMMARY AND KEY TERMS

Chapter Summary

In this chapter, we have discussed the position of the programming function within the scope of the system-development life cycle. We have argued for generalization of the programming function as opposed to the narrow mindset that results from expertise in a single programming language. The universality of programming languages may be studied by exploring considerations related to abstraction and structure. These were explored at the data, program, and control levels, reflecting the organization of this book. Finally, a number of motivations underlying the study of programming languages were considered.

Chapter 1 Terminology

The following are some terms presented in this chapter. Some of these terms (and many others not listed here) were introduced only briefly in this chapter, and will be discussed in more detail in the chapters that follow.

abstraction   Black Box model
programming language   programming myopia

SUGGESTIONS FOR FURTHER STUDY

Ramamoorthy *et al.* (1984), Blum (1987), and Grant (1985) discuss the programming function in system development.

The problem of language dependence is addressed in papers by Bover and Brayton (1987) and Wells and Kurtz (1989). There are a number of books that assist in generalizing the programming function because they are structured so as to emphasize the corresponding constructs in two or more languages. These include: Baron (1986), Brown (1975), Cohen (1983), Feuer and Gehani (1984), Muldner and Steele (1988), REA (1985), Shammas (1988), Smedema *et al.* (1983), Wiatrowski and Wiener (1987). Also of interest are papers by Wells and Kurtz (1989) and Tello (1984).

Abstraction concerns are the subject of books by Bishop (1986) and Thomas *et al.* (1988) and are addressed in papers by Abbott (1987), Richmond (1986), and Shaw (1980, 1984).

For a general study of programming language concepts see Herriot (1977), and textbooks by Elson (1973), Ghezzi and Jazayeri (1987), Horowitz (1983, 1984), Mac-Lennon (1983), Marcotty and Ledgard (1987), Nicholls (1975), Pratt (1984), Schneider (1984), Sebesta (1989), Sethi (1989), Tucker (1986), Wilson and Clark (1988), and Zwass (1981). Also of general interest are a number of articles by Hoare (1986, 1987, Hoare *et al.* 1987) and Knuth's (1973, 1981, 1982) seminal series of books on computer programming.

2

Perspectives on Programming Languages

While one of the stated objectives of this textbook is to help its readers learn to generalize the programming function by studying the elements common to a large number of languages, it will nevertheless be useful for us to start out by taking the wide view. In this chapter, we will examine and explore the *diversity* in computer programming languages. We will first study how these programming languages evolved, and then look at some ways in which we can classify them in order to emphasize the shared common characteristics of a variety of well-known programming languages and the unique features of each. We will also examine some desirable characteristics of computer programming languages along with techniques for evaluation and selection of an appropriate programming language.

2.1 FROM BABBAGE TO BABEL: A BRIEF HISTORY OF PROGRAMMING LANGUAGES

First, a question: Why should we study the history of computer programming languages?

To study high-level programming languages by examining only the state of such languages as they exist today would be incomplete. We might, for example, miss the fact that the most widely used programming languages today are also the oldest. Why are FORTRAN and COBOL still so popular after surviving several generations of programmers, computer hardware and, yes, programming languages?

Why did high-level languages evolve? Why aren't we still programming in machine code? On the other hand, why haven't we gone further? Early programming languages exerted a profound influence on later, "state-of-the-art" languages, an influence that continues to this day. Is this why so many languages have such similar constructs?

Many students in their first course in computer programming are intrigued by the "why" questions that are left unanswered. They are told, more often than not, that to program a computer one must learn "how," that programming is best thought of as a game, and that one must simply learn the rules of the game. "How" statements are pieced together from expressions, and "how" they are built into programs are legitimate questions in those first courses in computing. Now, as we study the history of programming languages, perhaps we can try to answer some of those "whys."

The literature on the subject of programming language history and evolution is rich and fascinating. Unfortunately, the following overview is necessarily brief. Should you desire to delve more deeply into the subject of programming language history, the references given at the end of the chapter will provide a useful starting point.

Before Electronic Computers

According to Donald Knuth, who has studied the development of mathematical and numerical algorithms from antiquity to the modern era, whereas notations for describing *static* functional relationships, such as the equations used in mathematics, physics and chemistry, evolved over the centuries into a highly sophisticated concise form, notations for *dynamic* processes (i.e., algorithms) did not follow suit. Often, in order to denote an algorithm as an input/output transformation, one would simply express it as $y = f(x)$, where x is the input variable, y is the output variable, and f is the abstract (or, "black box") model, the (possibly numerical) algorithm. To this day, notations for algorithms have not been highly developed and are relatively wordy and imprecise.

The earliest known "computer" is generally acknowledged to be Charles Babbage's design for an Analytic Engine. This device—which provided a changeable sequence of numerical operations and internal storage for data—was, in 1834, so far ahead of the existing technology that it could not be built in his lifetime. However, this did not stop him and his collaborator, mathematician Lady Augusta Ada, Countess of Lovelace (and daughter of the poet Lord Byron), from coding programs for it. Machine-code operations on Babbage's machine were of the form: $v_1 \times v_2 = v_3$, with operations (for example, the multiply operation) and variables (in this case, the subscripts 1, 2, 3) on separate punched cards (*Jacquards*). These cards were to be fed into the machine and would work on internal data (the "store"). The Analytic Engine was designed to accommodate conditional "jumps," that is, branches to instructions out of sequence. This was to be accomplished by a mechanical means in which a band of cards could be physically jumped over. Lady Lovelace postulated that many processes that were composed of repetitive sequences of operations could be coded most efficiently by the execution of a backward jump, which would cause the repetitive execution of a single band of cards. She is thus credited with innovating the *loop*, or *repetition*, construct. A working model of the Analytic Engine has finally been built and stands in the Smithsonian as the first "computer." Just as Babbage is credited as the first computer architect, Lovelace was the first computer programmer.

It wasn't until 1945, with the publication by the University of Pennsylvania of John von Neumann's *First Draft of a Report on the EDVAC*, that the stored-program computer was described and eventually, this time, implemented. The EDVAC (**E**lectronic **D**iscrete

Variable Arithmetic Computer) report describes a configuration in which the processor is tightly coupled to primary storage, primary storage is large enough to store vast amounts of data along with the program code, and operations are executed sequentially without the parallelism that was needed on earlier machines to counteract their extremely limited storage capabilities. This type of configuration, which has since come to be known as the *von Neumann architecture*, has influenced the design of many of the high-level programming languages with which we are so familiar today.

Hardware

It is a good idea for us to review the major innovations of computer hardware so that we can use them as a frame of reference in discussing the concurrent evolution of programming languages. These are presented in Table 2.1, which is annotated.

The table presents a number of innovative experimental computers leading to Remington-Rand's UNIVAC, the first electronic computer produced specifically for commercial use. (The first UNIVAC was purchased by the U.S. Department of the Census.) Thus, the UNIVAC heralded the first generation of computers, characterized by vacuum tubes. Each successive generation of computer hardware is defined and characterized by a new and different technology, namely, *transistors*, *integrated circuits*, and *large-scale integration*.

If the 1951 introduction of the UNIVAC signaled the first generation of our modern-day "computer revolution," then, like other revolutions, it took the experts by surprise. When the UNIVAC I was installed in 1951, experts predicted that all of 12 computers would be in use in the United States by 1975. By 1975 there were 155,000 computers in use, and so it was predicted that 1985 would see as many as 500,000 computers in use. In 1985, there were actually 9 million personal computers in use in offices across the United States and in December 1989 there were altogether 54 million computers in use in the United States.

The Software Ladder

We see that computer hardware can be classified according to "generation," beginning with the UNIVAC I, the first commercially available computer. Similarly, each software generation may be defined so as to represent a different software technology. This is the approach taken in Fig. 2.1. As you can see, each successive software generation provides an additional rung in the ladder and so extends the distance between the human user and the computer. The higher the human user is able to climb, the more useful and pervasive will be the effect of the relatively new discipline of computing.

The first generation of computer software is the era of machine-language programming. It is always difficult to mark the beginning and end of an era. In the case of the first software generation, we date it from the hand-coded programming done on the MARK I computer (pre-first generation machinery) at Harvard University. As to defining the end of this era, it is especially difficult in this case since large numbers of adherents to machine-coded programs continued to resist newer software technologies even until the release of the first FORTRAN compiler and beyond.

TABLE 2.1 ELECTRONIC COMPUTER MACHINERY: SOME MILESTONES

Year	Computer	Technological feature	Designer/ team leaders	Place
1939	ABC prototype	design of the electronic digital computer	John V. Atanasoff Clifford Berry	Iowa State College

The ABC, the Atanasoff-Berry Computer, was designed to automate certain calculations in physics and influenced later work on the ENIAC.

Year	Computer	Technological feature	Designer/ team leaders	Place
1941	Z3	electromagnetic relays	Konrad Zuse	Berlin
1943	MARK I	electromechanical relays	Howard Aiken	Harvard

The MARK I was also known as the Automatic Sequence-Controlled Calculator.

Year	Computer	Technological feature	Designer/ team leaders	Place
1943	Colossus	electronic	Alan Turing	England

The Colossus helped decipher German code during World War II.

Year	Computer	Technological feature	Designer/ team leaders	Place
1946	ENIAC	electronic	J. Presper Eckert John Mauchly	University of Pennsylvania

The ENIAC, which stands for Electronic Numerical Integrator and Computer, was programmed by manually setting jumper connections on the front panel. It took a team of five people at least two days to enter a program into the computer.

Year	Computer	Technological feature	Designer/ team leaders	Place
1949	EDSAC	stored program	Maurice Wilkes	Cambridge University

The EDSAC, which stands for Electronic Delay Storage Automatic Computer, was based on the EDVAC report published in 1945. Wilkes rushed in order to complete his machine before von Neumann's and was successful. The EDSAC is thus credited at being the first stored-program computer.

Year	Computer	Technological feature	Designer/ team leaders	Place
1950	EDVAC	stored program	John von Neumann	University of Pennsylvania

J. von Neumann's innovative report on the EDVAC, or Electronic Discrete Variable Arithmetic Computer, appeared in 1945. It was the first totally sequential electronic computer, with no parallelism.

Year	Computer	Technological feature	Designer/ team leaders	Place
1951	UNIVAC® I	vacuum tubes	Eckert, Mauchly	Remington-Rand

The first computer to be available for commercial sale, the UNIVAC I, an acronym of Universal Automatic Computer, begins the first generation of computer machinery.

The second software generation saw the development of programming aids for the machine-language coding specialist. This is the era of automatic coding, interpretive routines, and symbolic assemblers.

The technology of the third generation of software, beginning with the first FORTRAN report in 1954, is the high-level programming language. Third-generation languages stress expressivity and machine independence and are, for the most part, limited by the von Neumann machine design. Because of their close association with and depen-

TABLE 2.1 (continued)

Year	Computer	Technological feature	Designer/ team leader	Place
[1st generation] 1951–1960		vacuum tubes		

e.g., UNIVAC I; IBM®'s 701, 650; Burroughs' E101; Honeywell's Datamatic 1000

| [2nd generation] 1959–1965 | | transistors | | |

e.g., IBM®'s 1401, 1620; Burroughs' 5000; Honeywell's Model 800

| [3rd generation] 1964–present | | integrated circuits | | |

e.g., IBM® 360

The first "general-purpose" machine, much of the 360 architecture design is credited to Gene Amdahl. Some 360 innovations are microcode and systems programming. Virtual memory came later along with timesharing.

1969	Nova	16-bit minicomputer	Edson de Castro	Data General
1969	PDP-11®	16-bit minicomputer	Ken Olsen	DEC
[4th generation] 1971–present		very large scale integration microprocessors		

e.g., Altair, Apple®, TRS-80

| 1972 | Intel®'s 8008, 8-bit microprocessor | | | |

| 1974 | Radio Electronics article on how to build a MARK 8 (using the 8008 processor), "your personal minicomputer" | | | |

| 1974 | Altair developed at MIT by Roberts; Yates. | | | |

| 1977 | Apple computer marketed by Wozniak, Jobs. | | | |

| [5th generation] present–future | | parallel processing architecture | | |

| 1981 | Japan announces its Fifth-Generation Project based on parallel processors and logic programming. | | | |

dence on the von Neumann concept, third-generation languages are largely *procedural*. Programming in such a language, one must express precisely the individual, detailed instructions that the computer will follow in order to accomplish a task.

Languages with a more natural user interface, beginning with the first statistical packages, are classified as belonging to the fourth-generation. Of course, what is natural to one group of users (say, mathematicians) is not necessarily natural to another (such as managers). For this reason, fourth-generation software is often oriented toward a very specific problem area.

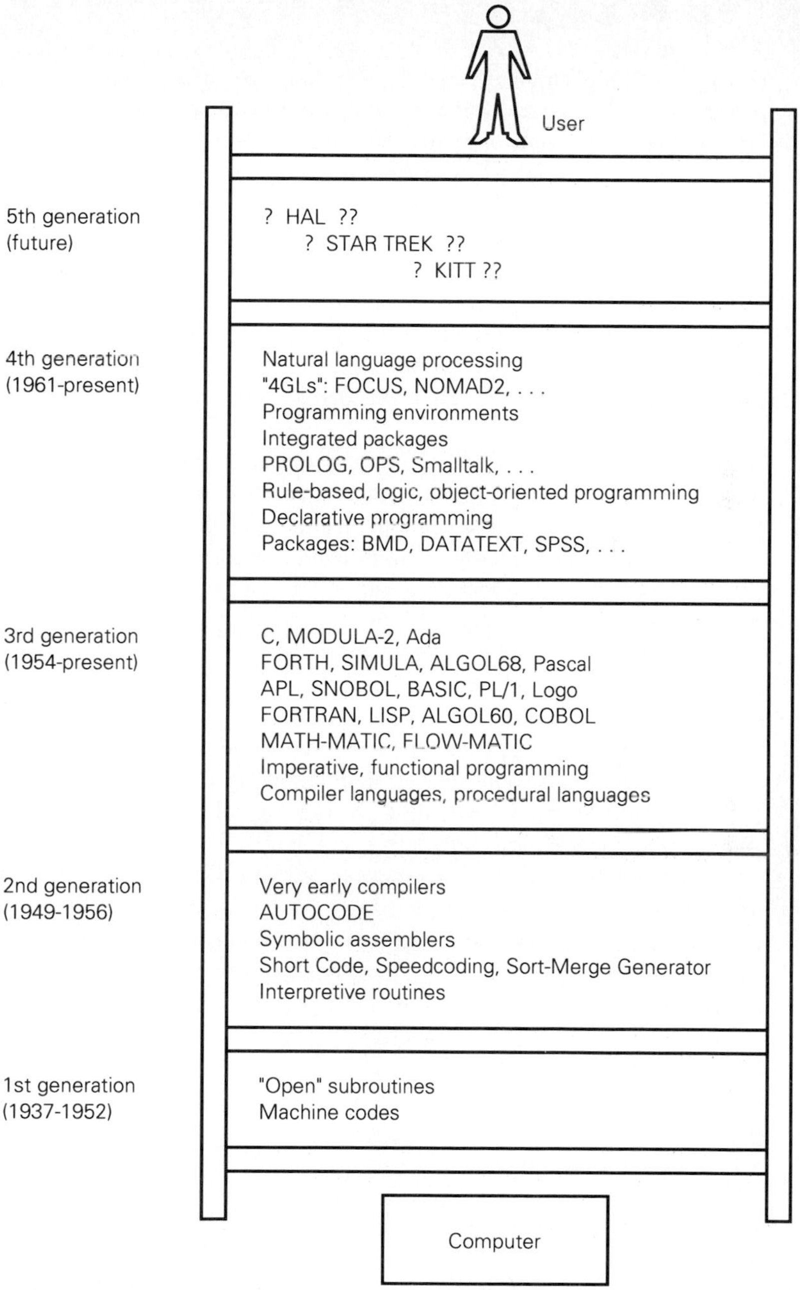

Figure 2.1 The software ladder

The First Generation

During the 1940s and early 1950s, all coding was done in machine language, that is, the computer's own internal (binary-based) instruction set. Machine coding, or "hand coding," remained popular long after that, long after the second-generation coding aids such as automatic code generators, interpretive routines, and assemblers were available, long after—as with many other enterprises in which humans are expected to change their way of doing things—it should have. Every machine has its own built-in code and in this first generation of software every task was coded "from scratch" with little or no opportunity for generalizing from one computer to another or from one program to the next.

The word wasn't *programming* then, but *coding*, and programmers were *coders*. The word *programmer* originated in England, and when it finally crossed the Atlantic in the early 1950s it was, naturally, considered more prestigious to be a programmer than a coder and the term stuck.

There was very little in the way of formal communication among the members of the early coding community. The Association for Computing Machinery (ACM) was first formed in 1947, and did not begin publishing its journals until several years later. On the other hand, there was plenty of informal communication going on in the form of meetings and written correspondence and sharing copies of code. Very little thought was given to ownership or claim and, for this reason, it is often difficult to attribute a programming "first" to a single source.

In 1947, an event occurred that is of special interest to programmers and students of computing. Grace Murray Hopper, in investigating why the MARK II computer was not working properly, discovered a small, dead moth in the machine and removed it with a tweezer. The moth went into her logbook along with a note recording the incident for posterity. From then on, computing errors were called "bugs" and the process of finding and removing them known as "debugging."

Around 1951 Howard Aiken proposed and constructed a "coding machine" for the Mark III. By simply pressing a button on the console of this machine, one or more machine codes such as operators, operands, and signs would be punched on paper tape. This paper tape would later serve to enter the program into the computer. In this way, the human coder would not have to memorize many complicated sequences of binary code. The human brain was now one small step removed from the "thought" processes of the actual computer. Although this was truly a machine, and not an example of early software, it propelled the evolution of programming languages forward by demonstrating the usefulness of a machine as an automatic coder and providing the initial spark for many second-generation computer software designers.

The Second Generation

The second generation of software, the pre-compiler era, saw the development and distribution of *machine-code subroutines*, *interpretive routines*, *automatic code generators*, and *assemblers*. It is a time period marked by many firsts. These, like the first, tentative steps of an infant, may seem too tiny to fuss over from our vantage point as a more sophisticated generation. In order to appreciate the monumental importance of these accomplishments we have to bear in mind, first, that the mindset of the coding establishment was such that anything other than hand coding was considered to be inferior and, second, that those hand-coded, machine-language programs were actually very complex and intricate and did as much, with less storage, as our sophisticated programs do today. For example, the UNIVAC I, with 12K of memory handled Prudential Life's entire premium file and did the payroll for U.S. Steel.

In all fairness, much of the skepticism of the coding establishment about automatic coding systems was warranted. These systems almost always turned out programs that were less efficient and more costly than equivalent hand-coded versions produced by clever, inventive human coders.

At about this time, programmers were no longer necessarily coding an entire program from scratch. Many would now manually copy sections of code, such as routines for floating-point arithmetic and input/output conversion, from one hand-coded program to another. In addition to simply copying, an enterprise already fraught with transcription errors, this involved many manual addition operations that were necessary to make sure that the subroutine was referencing the appropriate machine language storage addresses. And all of this manual work was done in order to operate a machine that was really good at copying and adding and doing it quickly and accurately!

In 1949, John Mauchly proposed and implemented "Short-Order Code" or "Short Code" for the BINAC computer as a set of interpretive subroutines stored in memory. It was thought of as a "pseudocode" for a simulated computer. The BINAC (**BIN**ary **A**utomatic **C**omputer) was a pre-first-generation computer built in 1949 for the Northrop Aircraft Company by J. Presper Eckert and John Mauchly who had left the University of Pennsylvania to form their own company. (This was later bought out by Remington-Rand.) The Short Code system was coded for use on the UNIVAC I in 1950 and revised in 1952. Short Code executed approximately 50 times slower than the equivalent hand-coded program.

The years 1950–1951 saw the emergence of a host of artificial machine languages, or "pseudocodes," for various machines. These instructions would provide for emulation of a hypothetical computer—for example, one that could handle floating-point storage and arithmetic—and would be processed by an interpretive routine. John Backus's 1953 Speedcoding System for the IBM® 701 was an example of this type of programming tool.

In the early 1950s, Betty Holberton's Sort-Merge Generator was a first attempt toward using a computer to write programs, and it inspired a whole family of other program generators. The Sort-Merge Generator accepted as input the specifications for the files to be operated on and automatically produced the sort-merge code.

In 1951, the first textbook on programming came over from England— *The Preparation of Programs for a Digital Computer* by Wilkes, Wheeler, and Gill. The book discussed and contained several fully developed examples of machine-code subroutines and subroutine linkage. The term *assembly routine* was introduced in this book and referred to a piece of code that would combine a set of subroutines and allocate storage as blocks of relocatable addresses called *floating addresses*.

Late in 1951, Grace Murray Hopper, working on Remington-Rand's UNIVAC I, came up with the notion that programs constructed from "pseudocode" instructions, rather than being interpreted, ought to be translated into a complete set of machine-language instructions. For this, she coined a new term: a *compiling* routine.

In November 1952, Millie Coss came out with her "Editing Generator" which produced the code to take data stored in the computer, apply simple arithmetic operations, and edit it appropriately for printed output so that it would be readable by managers and other users. This was the first of the RPG-type of program.

In 1953, Nathan Rochester conceived of and developed an assembler program that could be used to convert the symbolic equivalents of operating codes, operands, and modifiers into the appropriate machine codes.

In 1952, Alick E. Glennie, of England's Royal Armaments Research Establishment, developed his AUTOCODE system, a primitive, highly machine-dependent algebraic compiler that translated algebraic statements into the machine language of the Manchester Mark I. Glennie's system, inspired by Aiken's "coding machine," serves to link the second generation to the third generation of computer software, in which the emphasis is on "compilers" of increasing sophistication and, finally, on the design of compiled, high-level programming languages.

The Early Compilers

Many consider the first, true, working algebraic compiler to be a system developed by J.H. Laning Jr. and N. Zierler for MIT's WHIRLWIND computer. The WHIRLWIND, designed by Jay Forrester and Ken Olsen, was the first 16-bit minicomputer and was capable of parallel processing and real-time computing. This first compiler was demonstrated in the spring of 1953, or possibly even earlier, and the system was up and running by January of 1954.

In Italy, Corrado Bohm's doctoral dissertation, submitted in 1951, describes a system that was unusual and prophetic: It was not only a complete compiler, but was also defined in its own language, a concept that was not to be implemented in a programming language until many years later. In Bohm's language, every statement is a special case of the assignment statement. For example, an unconditional branch to a statement named S would be equivalent to "set the program counter to the value of variable S."

Grace Murray Hopper's programming team at Remington-Rand (UNIVAC) began in 1955 to develop an algebraic programming language that used some English keywords. Released as MATH-MATIC in April of 1957, the original compilers had been known internally as the "A series" (A-0, A-1, A-3, AT-3). MATH-MATIC executed very inefficiently. In 1958, FLOW-MATIC (originally, the "B series" of compilers, B-0, B-1,...) was released, a language that used English words heavily and was geared to business data processing. FLOW-MATIC was an important factor in the subsequent design of COBOL.

The First Programming Languages

In 1945, a theoretical programming language was developed in Germany by Konrad Zuse, called *Plankalkul* (program calculus). This development went virtually unnoticed for a long time by many in the computing community, especially in the United States, and was not published in its entirety until 1972. The language is interesting to us because it was developed completely from the "human" point of view regardless of whether it would ever be implemented on any particular machine. Among its features, Zuse's language provided for hierarchical data structures similar to those that would eventually appear in COBOL. Although it lacked expressivity and was neither easily writable nor easily readable, still it is interesting to see such an early attempt to design a *language*, rather than a *compiler*.

FORTRAN.   In 1954, John Backus led an IBM team of researchers (later named the Programming Research Group) into uncharted territory. The aim: to design and develop an efficient automatic translator of mathematical formulas into IBM® 704 machine code. The group would accept nothing less than a system that would produce programs at least as efficient as their hand-coded counterparts. Due to the prevailing skepticism on the part of the coding establishment about anything that produced automatic code, the overriding concern of the group was the efficiency of the executable code. A highly efficient automatic code generator that was highly efficient would be more likely to be accepted by the coding community. Programming language design, which always embodies a trade-off of sorts between the human's ability to express high-level concepts and the machine's ability to operate efficiently, was all but ignored in the interest of designing and developing a compiler that would optimize as it translated from algebraic notation to machine code. The language design aspects were handled rather quickly, in the manner of a chore that had to be completed before the "real" work (the design of the compiler) could be done.

The group's first report was released in 1954 and described the specifications for a proposed **FOR**mula **TRAN**slating System, or FORTRAN™. A large portion of the 1954 document was devoted to a justification of the system, including the very optimistic expectation that FORTRAN would all but eliminate coding and debugging. Although the original, projected completion time for the compiler was six months, it wasn't until October 1956 that the FORTRAN language reference manual was published and with it a promise to provide the compiler itself by late 1956. IBM finally delivered it in April of 1957. (Some things don't really change.)

Customers did not immediately rush to embrace the new system, but a well-written *Programmer's Primer*, by Grace E. Mitchell, published by IBM in 1957 did a lot for the eventual acceptance of FORTRAN in the computing community. As it turned out, the translator was not only as efficient as the 1954 report had anticipated but, in some cases, it could be shown to produce code more efficient than the equivalent hand-coded program.

Among the innovations to FORTRAN's credit, in addition to its title as the first true programming language, are:

- a language based on variables, expressions, statements;
- the form of the arithmetic-assignment statement;
- conditional and repetitive branching control structures;
- arrays with maximum size known at compile time;
- FORMAT-directed input and output, which eliminated input/output conversions;
- statements such as COMMON and EQUIVALENCE for data sharing;
- provision for comment statements even though FORTRAN code was thought to be thoroughly "self-explanatory";
- the optimized utilization of index registers, based on the expected frequency of execution of different portions of the program.

FORTRAN, like certain other languages designed during this period, was designed for a specific machine. While many of the statements of this original version of FORTRAN were machine dependent and have disappeared from the language as we know it today, certain distinguishing features (such as length of instruction) that remained in the FORTRAN language derived from the IBM® 704 computer for which it was designed.

In 1958, FORTRAN compilers were released for the IBM® 709 and the 650; in 1960, for the 1620 and 7070. These versions were not necessarily identical to the original system, and a program written on one compiler was not guaranteed to produce identical results on another. In 1961, FORTRAN compilers were made available for the UNIVAC and for the Remington-Rand LARC, and an imitation called ALTAC was used on the Philco 2000. In all, by 1964 there were more than 40 different FORTRAN compilers on the market. While every new FORTRAN compiler tried, for the customers' sake, to be somewhat consistent with the original definition of the language, a user could not really be certain that a value computed on one machine would be the same when computed on another machine. The day of the portable, machine-independent language had not yet arrived.

FORTRAN II was released in 1958, followed closely by FORTRAN III and FORTRAN IV (1962). FORTRAN IV was the standard for the language until FORTRAN 77 was released in 1978. It included many enhancements, such as character strings and selection and iteration constructs, learned from other, newer languages and from structured programming methodology.

LISP. LISP, an interactive, functional language was designed for the IBM 704 by John McCarthy at Dartmouth during the years 1956–1958. He began implementing it at MIT in 1959 and the first reference manual was published in 1960. LISP is a language based on lambda calculus and, unlike the algebraic languages that were being developed during the same time period, it was designed for symbolic formula manipulation. Over the years, LISP (**LIS**t **P**rocessor) has become the *lingua franca*, the medium of communication, of the artificial intelligence community. Within that application area, LISP has been used as a publication language for algorithms. Some important innovative features of LISP are:

- the function as the basic program unit;
- the list as the basic data structure;
- dynamic data structures;
- facilities for "garbage collection";
- use of symbolic expressions as opposed to numbers;
- recursion and the conditional expression as control structures;
- the "eval" function for interactive evaluation of LISP statements.

There are many dialects of LISP, including CommonLISP and Scheme.

ALGOL. In 1958, a committee consisting of European and American representatives held meetings in Zurich to design a universal high-level programming language. The European representatives were from GAMM, a German association for applied mathematics and mechanics, and the American delegation was provided by the Association for Computing Machinery. One of the American members of this committee was John Backus, who had led the FORTRAN development group.

One of the stated purposes of this design and development effort was to facilitate the communication and exchange of ideas among the members of the international computing community. In actuality, there was a more practical goal, as well. The European computing community, with the exception of England, did not go through a so-called "second generation" of software consisting of symbolic assemblers and other coding aids. They were still hand-coding programs in machine code and, while one might say that a compiler language was desperately needed, the work progressed on a more theoretical and organized level than did the more pragmatic, "seat-of-the-pants," American programming research efforts. In fact, one of the reasons that a new language was desired, rather than simply adopting FORTRAN, is that FORTRAN was still, at the time, a proprietary language—an IBM product. A recommendation to adopt FORTRAN as the programming language of choice in Europe would have been considered equivalent to a recommendation to purchase only IBM machines. Such a recommendation would have been not only impractical but violently opposed. Many members of the ALGOL committee were specifically interested in curtailing what they felt were IBM's efforts to dominate in Europe as well as in America. For these reasons and because of the international character of the design committee, the language these individuals designed can be said to be independent of both machine and political affiliation.

The language was originally named IAL, for **I**nternational **A**lgebraic **L**anguage, and eventually renamed ALGOL (**ALGO**rithmic **L**anguage); this first version became known as ALGOL58. ALGOL58 was implemented on a number of computers and influenced the development of many subsequent languages. One of these was a language called JOVIAL which, in turn, exerted a significant influence on the development of PL/1.

The committees, meeting again in Paris in 1960 to improve the language and eliminate weaknesses that had been uncovered, revised the language and issued an official ALGOL60 Report. Although revised, ALGOL60 retained many of the distinctive features of ALGOL58. The influence of ALGOL60 on programming language design, and on the development of computer science in general, has been nothing less than profound. Among the many important features of the ALGOL60 Report is the appearance for the first time of the BNF (Backus Normal Form) *meta*language for programming language definition, credited to John Backus and Peter Naur. BNF has earned its own place in computing history: It has influenced and, indeed, created many areas of computer science theory.

In the development of ALGOL (58 and 60), we see the programming language itself as the object of study, rather than simply a means toward an end. ALGOL has been used as a publication language for algorithms, in American publications as well as internationally, although ALGOL was never as widely implemented in the United States as, say, FORTRAN or COBOL. ALGOL60 was widely implemented in Europe. Some of the distinguishing features of ALGOL are:

- block structure and localized data environments;
- nesting of program units;
- free-format program code;
- explicit type declarations;

- dynamic memory allocation;
- parameter passing by value and by name;
- recursion;
- **if/then/else**;
- **begin/end** to delimit a compound statement;
- arrays with dynamic bounds.

ALGOL60 has spawned a host of "ALGOL-like" languages, which contain such features as nested block structures, compound statements, scoping rules, declaration of local variables, and parameters passed by name, value, or reference.

COBOL.   In May 1959, another group met, under the auspices of the U.S. Department of Defense, to discuss the feasibility of developing a "common" programming language, this time for data processing applications. This group, comprising about 40 members, represented computer manufacturers and users from industry, universities, and government and became known as the CODASYL Committee (**CO**nference on **DA**ta **SY**stems **L**anguages). The result, in April 1960, was a language called COBOL (**CO**mmon **B**usiness-**O**riented **L**anguage). It was in the interest of both the computer manufacturers represented and the government (which uses the products of many different manufacturers) to design the language so as not to cater to or become dependent on any one specific machine or machine family. Thus, the language started out relatively machine independent, unlike FORTRAN.

COBOL was influenced by such existing languages as FLOW-MATIC, FORTRAN, ALGOL58, and English. The significance of the use of English language words and constructs must not be underestimated. Remember that first- and second-generation programming was relatively esoteric and poorly understood and was considered by many to be something of a "black art." One of the hardest jobs ahead of the innovators of this COBOL programming language was going to be promoting the language among managers in the data processing community. The heavy reliance on English would not only make programming easier to do and easier to learn, but would serve to demystify the activity of programming and the workings of computers over all. Important and innovative features of COBOL were:

- the record data structure;
- file description and manipulation facilities;
- the machine independence of data and program descriptions;
- the equal emphasis placed on the data descriptions in the Data Division and the operations in the Procedure Division;
- the influence of English in the use of verbs, clauses, sentences, paragraphs, sections, and divisions;
- a relatively natural language style, including noise words for readability;
- the overall effort toward a language that would produce self-documenting program code.

In separating the description of data from program statements, and in giving these two aspects of the programming task equal prominence, COBOL started an important trend in programming. This trend toward data-oriented languages has culminated in the current proliferation of database management systems, query languages, and database-centered, high-productivity programming products.

In addition, the COBOL report described the language in its own distinctive meta-language which, while not as widely used or well known as the BNF of the ALGOL60 report, has found its way into a variety of language descriptions over the years. This COBOL-type of metalanguage is characterized by the use of English, few verbs, and many options.

Not the least significant factor in its eventual acceptance in the data processing community was the widespread availability of COBOL compilers. Shortly after the CODASYL committee completed its design work, the Department of Defense sent a strongly worded letter to all computer manufacturers advising them that if they wanted to continue to sell computers to the Department of Defense (the largest computer contractor and endower of research grants) they had better put a COBOL compiler on it. The COBOL language revision in 1961 was, needless to say, widely implemented.

Major revisions of the COBOL language were standardized and released in 1968, 1974, and 1985.

One of the more interesting phenomena in the history of programming languages is that FORTRAN, COBOL, and LISP, which are three of the four oldest programming languages, and which sparked a tremendous interest in programming language design and motivated the development of a huge number of diverse languages in the 1960s and 1970s, are still the most widely used languages today. The fourth, ALGOL, has until recently been the medium of choice for sharing and communication among computing professionals and scholars (Pascal and C are now also used for this purpose).

Babel

The decades of the 1960s and the 1970s saw a truly amazing proliferation of programming languages. It was this hubbub of activity that Jean Sammet in 1969 likened to the biblical Tower of Babel (or, "babble"). Relatively few of these languages are widely known today. Some were highly specialized languages with a small user following, or were designed for one particular machine, or were used only at one particular installation (such as a university research group). Some rose and shone for a short while, only to be extinguished or replaced. We consider here a small selection of the better-known, third-generation programming languages.

APL. The design of APL began as early as 1957 by Kenneth Iverson at Harvard and continued on through 1960. Iverson did not then intend for the language to be implemented but, rather, intended to design a notation for the expression of concepts for which mathematical notation alone was insufficient (for example, a sorting function). The language was ultimately formally defined and introduced to the public in a 1962 book by Iverson entitled *A Programming Language*. Unnamed for many years, the language eventually took its name from this publication. APL (**A P**rogramming **L**anguage) is a functional, interactive, science-oriented language that assumes the array as the default data structure. One of its most distinguishing features is its unusually large character set requiring the use of a special keyboard. It is suitable for applications with a heavy use of numerical data in large multidimensional arrays. It has also been used successfully in areas that require speedy response to queries and, therefore, also for database management systems. A subset, APL\360 was implemented on the IBM 360 in 1966.

SNOBOL.   SNOBOL, was designed in 1962 by David J. Farber, Ralph Griswold, and Ivan P. Polonsky, working at AT&T Bell Laboratories, as a string manipulation language to be used by researchers as a tool for formula manipulation. It was first implemented in 1963. The language was influenced mainly by early work at Bell Laboratories in string manipulation languages (SCL) and by COMIT, an MIT symbol-manipulation language designed for use by linguists. The 1963 implementation was actually named SEXI (**S**tring **EX**pression **I**nterpreter), but for some unknown reason that name was considered unacceptable. When the developers realized that the language might, in fact, see widespread use someday, they worked hard at coming up with a more appropriate name and have been known to confess that work on the name took more time and effort than designing and implementing the entire language. They finally settled on SNOBOL, a semi-comic, intricate acronym of Stri**N**g **O**riented sym**BO**lic **L**anguage, claiming that the language had the proverbial "snowball's chance." The complexity of the acronym was intended as a humorous jab at an industry with a well-known proclivity for acronyms.

In addition to formula manipulation, various researchers began using the language for graph processing, text processing, and program generation. Among the initial design criteria were conciseness, simplicity, flexibility, and problem orientation (rather than computer orientation). After going through several revisions in 1964, the language finally emerged as SNOBOL4, developed over the years 1966–1968 by Griswold, Jim Poage, and Polonsky. SNOBOL4, released in 1968, was designed for third-generation computer hardware and is a very *different* language from its predecessors. It is used interactively, in a time-shared environment. SNOBOL4 supports a multitude of data types and treats patterns as data objects. There are a large variety of pattern types. The unique feature of the language is its facility for string and pattern matching.

BASIC.   At Dartmouth College in 1963, Thomas E. Kurtz, John Kemeny, and a succession of undergraduate students designed a high-level language with the intention of using it to introduce students in nonscientific disciplines to computing. The first version of BASIC (**B**eginner's **A**ll-purpose **S**ymbolic **I**nstructional **C**ode) ran in May 1964. By the fall of 1964 there were 20 time-shared terminals hooked up to the BASIC system.

Among the influences on the design of the language were FORTRAN, ALGOL, and several earlier, more primitive compilers designed at Dartmouth itself. The major goal was to simplify the user interface. This meant that simplicity was chosen over compiler efficiency; time-sharing was chosen over punched cards; technical distinctions such as integer versus real were eliminated; automatic defaults were provided for variable declarations, variable values, dimensioning arrays, and output formats; clear error messages were provided; and students had "open access" to computer terminals at all times. The third version of the language produced in 1966 was for the first time interactive, with the addition of the INPUT statement. The use of BASIC spread rapidly to universities, high schools, elementary schools, personal use, small businesses, and even industry. Unfortunately, there is no universal BASIC standard—although the American National Standards Institute has published a *minimal* BASIC standard—and many implementations are markedly different from others.

PL/1. In 1963, IBM set out to design an extension to FORTRAN that would run on new IBM computers that were still unannounced and unreleased; an extension that would be sufficiently general, or multipurpose, to bring in more customers in addition to FORTRAN's hard-core faithful engineers. The new equipment was to be the "360-family" of computers and the language would be built to cater to users in the business, scientific, real-time, list processing, and systems programming areas. The design committee, which was for a time referred to internally as the FORTRAN VI Committee (FORTRAN IV had just been released in 1962), drew on design concepts of FORTRAN, COBOL, ALGOL60, and JOVIAL. JOVIAL, developed by the System Development Corporation for the Air Force, was designed soon after the 1958 Zurich meetings as an ALGOL58 extension for command and control applications, and has the distinction of being the first general-purpose programming language.

This "FORTRAN extension" got farther and farther away from the FORTRAN specifications and, in March 1964, the first specifications report for a new programming language was released. Named NPL (New Programming Language, of course), the language was aimed at users in the scientific, data processing, text processing, real-time, and systems programming communities. Unfortunately, the initials NPL conflicted with those of the National Physical Laboratory in England and when the first version was finally ready for distribution—the first compiler for the IBM 360, implemented by an IBM research group in England, was released in August of 1966— it had been renamed PL/1, for Programming Language/one.

PL/1, the "language to end all languages," was not the immediate success that IBM had anticipated. The first compilers were inefficient and unreliable. The language developed a reputation as a "monster" requiring a machine with large amounts of available memory. FORTRAN and COBOL already had a large base of dedicated users with large libraries of trusted subroutines. In addition, while compilers had, up to that point in time, been included at no additional cost when a computer was purchased, the release of the IBM 360 family in 1965 and the release of the first version of the PL/1 language were concomitant with the "unbundling" of software from the hardware purchase. In other words, where FORTRAN and COBOL had previously been provided free of charge, users would have to purchase PL/1 separately and few were willing to make that sort of commitment to a new language.

One of the reasons that PL/1 eventually generated a lot of interest, especially in the academic community, was that it was a state-of-the-art language that contained virtually every conceivable element of language design. It is for this same reason that it has drawn much of its criticism—as a language that is too big, with too many features. From FORTRAN, it inherited much of its expression and statement syntax, shared data, and the external procedure; from COBOL, the language got its data description, record and file handling, and report generation facilities; from ALGOL, its block structure, type declarations, and recursion. In addition, it was the first language to provide:

- multitasking;
- programmer-defined exception (interrupt) handling;
- defaults;
- explicit use of pointers and list processing;

- a wide variety of alternatives for storage allocation—static, automatic, controlled;
- and to consider problems arising from interacting with an operating system.

Logo.   Seymour Papert of MIT, along with a group of researchers and consultants at a Cambridge research firm, developed Logo over the years 1966 to 1968. It was designed specifically for mathematics education and was actually used experimentally in elementary school classrooms in 1967. Papert wanted to find a way to make children more comfortable learning mathematics. He had studied under the mathematician and psychologist Jean Piaget and was very strongly influenced by Piaget's work on childhood development. Papert felt that if mathematics, an abstract discipline, could be made more concrete for children, they could not only learn it more easily but at an earlier stage of development.

Logo is very similar to LISP, relying on the use of functions and list structures. It incorporates "turtle graphics" as a vehicle for teaching geometric principles at a concrete level. The child gives a "turtle" on the screen instructions so that it can create geometric shapes. Logo's memory requirements are quite small, and it is widely available on microcomputers.

FORTH.   During the 1960s, Charles H. Moore strove to develop a language that would be efficient enough for scientific and engineering applications yet allow for faster programming using fewer lines of code than, say, FORTRAN. Due to these two, apparently conflicting goals, the resulting language combines features of both high-level and low-level programming, a feature popularized later in C and MODULA-2. In FORTH, as in LISP, programs are constructed using functions. FORTH's functions are called *words*, and like functions, which are built up on top of other functions, words may be composed of smaller words. Like assembly language, FORTH arithmetic is based on Reverse Polish notation and a stack for processing. FORTH was first used in 1971 at the National Radio Astronomy Observatory.

The name of the language derives from its author's goal to design the first "fourth-generation language." (Moore did know how to spell—the IBM 1103 computer on which he worked allowed no more than five characters in a name.) FORTH cannot be considered a fourth-generation language today. It is highly procedural and requires a great deal of intense effort and computer know-how on the part of a technical programmer. FORTH is not intended for the nontechnical, casual user.

SIMULA™.   Designed in 1962 by Kristen Nygaard and Ole-Johan Dahl at the Norwegian Computing Center under contract with UNIVAC, SIMULA was motivated by a desire to create a programming language for simulation applications—a technique of operations research that has since been successfully used in a large number of diverse application areas—which would also serve as a medium for describing the (simulated) system under study. The SIMULA world view is of activities consisting of interacting processes. SIMULA drew heavily from ALGOL60. SIMSCRIPT™, a language for discrete-event simulation developed in 1963 at the Rand Corporation, had considerable influence on the development of SIMULA, especially with regard to its list processing, time scheduling, and library routines. SIMULA was implemented in 1964 on the UNIVAC 1107 and the language reference manual was published in 1965.

SIMULA67, the 1967 revision of the SIMULA language, was of a more general nature. The *class* concept, an important generalization of ALGOL's block concept, which enables the programming of coroutines, was first incorporated into this version of the language. The class concept of SIMULA67 was an important influence on languages that later provided for data abstraction and object-oriented programming.

ALGOL68. In 1968, the ALGOL committee produced a considerably revised and extended version of ALGOL. ALGOL68 is a huge, general-purpose language, setting it apart from the scientific orientation of ALGOL60. It was, in fact, quite a different language from ALGOL60 and was not well accepted by much of the computing community because it was considered to be overly complicated and impractical, and difficult for compiler writers. Compared to the profound influence ALGOL60 has had on programming language design and on computer science, ALGOL68 casts a pale shadow. In fact, many consider ALGOL68 to be a mere offshoot of its famous ancestor while Pascal carries the tradition. To its credit, ALGOL68 introduced the user-defined data type and the pointer type, both significant features of Pascal.

Pascal. The entire ALGOL committee could not be said to be in favor of the 1968 revision to the language. One of the dissenters, Niklaus Wirth, felt that ALGOL68 was needlessly big and awkward. After having first proposed in 1965 an altogether different "new" ALGOL— which subsequently became known as ALGOL-W—he designed the Pascal programming language, which was first implemented in 1970. Wirth intended to illustrate the direction that ALGOL should have taken. Pascal stands out in opposition to the trend—a trend that began with PL/1 and ALGOL68 and continues to this day with Ada—of enriching a language with so many complicated features that no one user could be expected to know all of it. In fact, Pascal, a true child of ALGOL60, has rapidly supplanted ALGOL68 in prominence.

Named after the seventeenth century French philosopher and mathematician Blaise Pascal, the language is currently the predominant programming language in the academic community. It has also become increasingly popular as the language of choice for developing a wide variety of microcomputer applications. Pascal is a narrowly defined, simple, and elegant language. Among its interesting features are the *case statement*, the facility for *user-defined data types*, the *record structure*.

C. In 1972, Bell Laboratories' Kenneth Thompson and Dennis Ritchie developed the C language for coding the routines of the UNIX® operating system. C was an extension of the B language—also designed by Thompson— which itself drew heavily on an earlier systems programming language, BCPL. (In fact, BCPL had, by a circuitous route, been influenced by ALGOL60.) By 1973, 90% of the UNIX code had been rewritten in C. C, a high-level systems programming language, created the notion of a portable operating system. This benefit is currently contributing to wide and increasing support for UNIX and for C. The language is not without its problems, however. A concise syntax makes C programs difficult to read, understand, debug, and maintain. The language provides no built-in operations for handling composite data objects such as character strings, sets, and lists. Because it is not strongly typed, is rather permissive regarding data conversions, and provides no run time type checking, it is considered by some not only to allow programmer errors but to encourage them. Still, the extreme degree of portability of the language and the ability to code low-level operations in a high-level language make C the language of choice for an increasingly large number of programmers.

MODULA-2. MODULA-2, a direct descendant of Pascal, is another high-level language with facilities for systems programming. Intended for use in large system software design, including real-time and parallel-processing systems, the language supports a high degree of problem decomposition and program abstraction. In 1978, Niklaus Wirth, of Pascal fame, directed the design and development of MODULA-2, drawing heavily from Pascal and MODULA (**MODU**lar **LA**nguage), an earlier experiment with multiprocessing. MODULA-2 was designed in 1978 and released in 1980.

MODULA-2 is characterized by strong typing and syntactic style, and, of course, the *module*, a type of block that can be compiled independently and easily assembled into program libraries. The module facilitates information hiding and the decomposition of a program into subprogram units with relatively well-defined interfaces. This is important for the definition of abstract data types. It is also important for low-level programming in a high-level language since it allows these "dangerous," low-level computations to be encapsulated in clearly delineated pieces of code. A distinguishing feature of the language is the system of library modules that can be provided along with the compiler and which is then added to by the programmer. The module library varies with the implementation.

Ada™. If PL/1 was the 1960s answer to the perceived need for a "language to end all languages" then Ada provides that service two decades later, with about the same degree of success. Named after the first computer programmer Lady Augusta Ada Lovelace, designed according to specifications developed by the U.S. Department of Defense, the Ada language was intended for the programming of embedded computer systems. Specifically, it had to be applicable to systems programming, real-time systems, parallel and distributed processing systems, and the program development environment.

The Department of Defense discovered that it was using about 400 different programming languages, many of them dialects of existing common languages. This situation had evolved over the years as one systems programmer after another had tailored languages to applications in the interest of productivity. Of course, while this increased the productivity of the computer, programmer productivity suffered.

The language requirements stressed the implementation of structured programming methodology and emphasized readability—including clarity, understandability, and modifiability—over writability. The Ada language design effort marks the first time that a completely separate group—not the one to ultimately work on language design and implementation—defined the requirements. Documents describing the language requirements started appearing in 1975 and became progressively more detailed and well defined. The complete language was finally proposed in 1980 as MIL-STD 1815 (the year that Lady Lovelace was born). The final, standardized version appeared in 1983. Working, usable compilers first started to appear on the scene around 1985, so experience with the language is still rather new.

One of the lures of the Ada language, at least in the computing community, is that Ada contains virtually every known state-of-the-art element of programming language design. It contains facilities for exception handling, parallel processing, abstract data

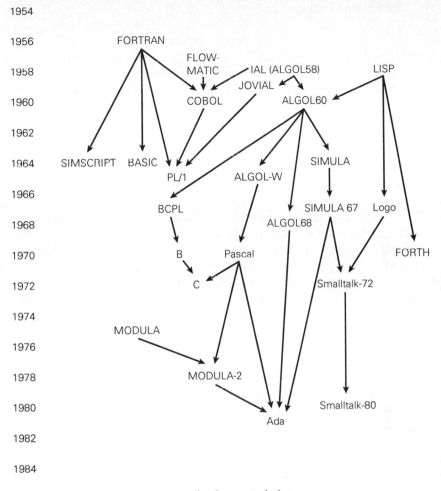

Figure 2.2   Some influences on programming language design

types, and many other features. Whatever we want to study, when it comes to Ada, "it's in there." As with PL/1 and ALGOL68, this is also its major drawback.

The publication of that first FORTRAN report in 1954 triggered a veritable revolution in computing. That revolution was characterized by the development of literally hundreds of programming languages, all with the expressed goal of taming the electronic computer for high-level use by humans in every application area. Fig. 2.2 illustrates some of the influences on programming language design exerted by the "ancestor" languages FORTRAN, COBOL, LISP, and ALGOL on their descendants, culminating in the famous ALGOL family of programming languages. These are third-generation, procedural languages. Other languages of equal importance have not been represented in this figure simply because their lineages are short and simple and their influence over later languages is minimal.

The Fourth Generation

The von Neumann type of computer architecture, while serving as catalyst for a generation of programming languages may also, it appears, be responsible in large part for the degree of stagnation we have seen in the conceptual development of programming language technology. The stored program concept binds computer control directly and intimately with program variables representing memory locations and involves the use of a single counter that controls program flow by a sequence of instructions. Programming language paradigms relying on this underlying computer architecture tend to be statement oriented, assuming the sequential execution of a limited number of operations. Programs written in these languages comprise vast numbers of lines of code. The debugging of a complex program, while a definite improvement over hand-coded machine language versions, is often an arduous and lengthy task. Also, maintenance is time consuming and costly. Third-generation programming languages are largely procedural. This includes imperative, statement-oriented languages like FORTRAN, ALGOL and their descendants and the function-oriented languages like LISP and its progeny, although functional languages are *less procedural* than imperative languages. One might say that while imperative languages were developed because of the von Neumann architecture, functional languages were developed in spite of it. Both, however, rely on the programmer's ability to completely specify *in detail* precisely how the computing is to be done.

A fourth-generation language is *declarative*, in other words, its instructions to the computer concentrate more on *what* is to be done rather than on describing in detail *how* to do it. You may wish to refer again to the illustration of the "software ladder" in Fig. 2.1. Fourth-generation software tends toward an emphasis on high productivity, choosing to optimize human labor over computer time and is frequently aimed at the nontechnical user in a particular application area. Programs are shorter, and easier to code, debug, and maintain. Some of the trends in fourth-generation software include:

- declarative languages;
- packaged software;
- integrated packages;
- user-friendly interactive environments;
- query languages;
- high-productivity programming tools;
- the integration of languages, programming tools (e.g., editor, linker, translators, file handler, etc.), and the user interface within a single interactive system.

Clearly, some of the languages (or systems) labeled as fourth generation are only partly nonprocedural; the classification, as always, is arbitrary.

Packages. We mark the beginning of this fourth generation of software with the development in 1961 of the first statistical package, BMD, at the University of California at Berkeley. BMD (**BioMeD**ical package) was implemented in FORTRAN on the IBM 7090. It was followed soon after by a host of others, including DATATEXT, developed at Harvard University in 1967 under the direction of Arthur S. Couch and aimed at social scientists. Although BASIC, a procedural language whose prime objective was ease of use and a more "natural" user interface, was also developed during this period, it is obvious that an instruction such as, for example:

```
COMPUTE REGRESSION (STATUS ON AGE, IQ, INCOME)
```

would be easier for social scientists (or anyone) than learning how to code solutions to the regression equation in BASIC. While BMD, DATATEXT and other statistical packages such as SPSS™, SPSS-X™, BMD-P, and SAS, undoubtedly contain procedural elements as well, the major thrust is toward a declarative programming orientation. Packaged, off-the-shelf software has continued to proliferate, especially with the advent of the personal computer, and now extends into a large number of application areas.

PROLOG.   PROLOG (**PRO**gramming in **LOG**ic) was developed in 1970 by Alain Colmerauer and Phillipe Roussel of the University of Marseille's artificial intelligence group, in collaboration with Robert Kowalski of the University of Edinburgh. First implemented in 1972 in ALGOL-W, for the purpose of natural-language processing, this logic-oriented language is declarative in nature. It has a firm mathematical basis, grounded as it is in the principles of predicate calculus. A PROLOG program expresses a problem in the terminology of logic, describing the problem in terms of facts and rules, and the system uses deductive reasoning to find possible solutions for the problem. This language has been used for such application areas as natural language processing, building expert systems, building relational databases, and the intelligent querying of such databases. Until the 1980s, it was popular mainly in Europe; in the U.S., LISP, along with its many dialects, is still a strong contender in the artificial intelligence community. Since 1981, when PROLOG became closely associated with Japan's Fifth Generation Project, use of the language has become increasingly widespread both in this country and in the international computing community.

Collaboration between Marseilles and Edinburgh ended at about 1975, but since research into the language continued at both locations, there exist two slightly different versions of the language, M-PROLOG and E-PROLOG. Edinburgh PROLOG has become the *de facto* standard.

OPS.   OPS is a production-system, or rule-based, language used in the field of artificial intelligence. A production is another name for a condition-action rule; a set of these rules is called a *production system*. OPS, named somewhat tongue-in-cheek as the **O**fficial **P**roduction **S**ystem, was developed at Carnegie Mellon University in 1970 and is still maintained there. The latest version, OPS5, was released in 1977 and has been implemented on microcomputers.

Smalltalk.   Smalltalk was designed and implemented in 1972 at Xerox Palo Alto Research Center (PARC) as the software component of Alan Kay's legendary Dynabook, a notebook-sized personal computer for the nontechnical user. This early implementation took the form of a 1000-line BASIC program. Later that year, the system was rewritten in assembly code by Daniel H.H. Ingalls, who is also responsible for later versions of the language.

Smalltalk can actually be considered a language embedded within an environment. Both of these components are composed totally of *objects*, small encapsulated pieces of code that are cousins to MODULA-2's modules and Ada's packages. It is interesting to note that, with its roots in SIMULA67, an imperative language, and Logo, a functional language, Smalltalk created and continues to define the *object-oriented* approach to programming. In this approach, a program is designed as a system of objects that communicate ("talk") with one another and with the human user by sending messages. Although the language can be implemented without the environment, the environment—a user-friendly, interactive interface with multiple overlapping windows, graphical and textual menus, a mouse for selecting and pointing—is an integral part of the Smalltalk approach to program development. In fact, this is a characteristic of most fourth-generation software. That the environment can be implemented without the language was demonstrated by Steve Jobs, then of Apple Computer, when he used it as the basis of the Lisa® and subsequently the Macintosh® operating system.

Smalltalk went through a series of revisions at Xerox PARC, where it was strictly a proprietary product, until 1983 when Smalltalk-80™ was released to the general public. Since then, the language itself has become increasingly popular but, more than that, the distinctive features of Smalltalk—including its object orientation and graphical interface—have profoundly influenced many other languages, software products, and computer science methodology.

High-productivity programming environments. A fourth-generation, high-productivity tool is largely nonprocedural, user friendly, and problem oriented. An integrated package of these high-productivity programming tools, coming together to produce a friendly, often intelligent, programming environment, can significantly speed up the development and implementation of application programs. These systems have been centered around a database and include the components of a database management system, and are fairly "taking over" in the business/data processing community, where they have been referred to for some time as "4GLs" (for **4**th **G**eneration **L**anguage). A "full-function" fourth-generation tool is likely a system that includes:

- a central database and data dictionary;
- a nonprocedural query language;
- a data-definition language;
- a graphics component;
- a statistical or decision-support component;
- an interactive programming environment;
- a report generator.

The full-function fourth-generation tools include FOCUS, NOMAD2, and RAMIS II. Some of the systems in this category are intended for use by programming professionals, but others—equipped with a natural language front-end—are designed so that the nontechnical end user can write applications without professional assistance. [**See Chapter 15.**]

From Yesterday to Today

While the trend in computer hardware evolution has been to produce computers that are increasingly more powerful, smaller, and less costly, the story of computer software evolution began with human beings that were forced to "think" in the code of a specific machine—Grace Murray Hopper tells of accidentally balancing her checkbook in octal—and developed eventually into computer systems that can communicate and "think" much like human beings or, at least, act as if they can.

Virtually all of the languages in wide use today have a long and varied history. Fig. 2.2 summarized the major influences on the *initial* design of some programming languages in wide use today. However, although the oldest languages were first released many years ago and underwent independent research and development efforts at the time, they are all characterized by a lengthy period of development that continues to the current day. The numerous revisions of these programming languages have, over the years, exerted considerable influence over *each other* as much as over the newer languages and dialects. Perhaps that is why they are still so very much alive.

2.2 CLASSIFICATION OF PROGRAMMING LANGUAGES

The proliferation of computer programming languages—the "Tower of Babel"—continues to this very day. There have probably been more than 1000 programming languages designed and implemented, although many of these have been used solely for "in-house" production rather than marketed for commercial use. At any rate, the "traditional" languages, such as FORTRAN, COBOL, BASIC, and Pascal, no longer command the exclusive attention of the computing community.

There are a lot of exciting things happening today in the realm of programming languages:

- the design of *Ada*, a language that represents the culmination of a long line of development beginning with FORTRAN and ALGOL and including such influences as PL/1, Pascal, MODULA-2, and SIMULA67, structured programming methodology, data abstraction, and concurrent processing techniques;
- renewed interest in *artificial intelligence* and LISP;
- PROLOG and commercial *expert systems*;
- user-friendly *integrated packages;*
- *natural language* processing;
- the *high-productivity programming environments* used in business data processing;
- the *object-oriented* programming languages and programming environments that may well carry structured programming methodology and large systems development into the twenty-first century.

Many of these long-awaited advances in software are first possible now because of the ready availability of inexpensive hardware, user-friendly operating systems, and powerful programming environments.

One way to learn about and become familiar with these seemingly diverse programming languages is to try to understand the similarities among them. That is one reason for classifying programming languages. Remember, however, that while all the languages in a particular category share common characteristics, every language has features that make it unique. On the other hand, although we tend to remember languages for their unique distinguishing attributes, they are in fact more similar than they are different.

Programming languages may be classified in many different ways depending on the criterion used. For example, FORTRAN could be called science oriented, imperative, procedural, batch processing, and high level—in addition to a number of other apt descriptors.

General Criteria for Classifying Programming Languages

Programming languages can be classified according to:

- the degree to which they are dependent on the underlying hardware configuration;
- the degree to which programs written in that language are process oriented;
- the data type that is assumed or that the language handles most easily;
- the problems it is designed to solve;
- the degree to which the language is extensible;
- the degree (and kind) of interaction of the program with its environment;
- the programming paradigm most naturally supported.

Low level vs. high level. A *low-level* programming language is considered to be machine oriented since it closely follows the built-in instruction set of the underlying computer (usually taken to be a von Neumann type of computer). Machine codes and assembly languages are highly machine oriented. Even FORTRAN, a high-level language, may be considered *relatively* machine oriented, especially when compared to a functional language such as LISP or to an object-oriented programming language such as Smalltalk. A *high-level* programming language provides for more natural expression of algorithms. It is usually problem oriented, providing the programmer with a high level of abstraction so that the computer actually appears to have been tailored, or "rewired," to fit the problem at hand. It can express the same program as a low-level language, but with less detail and consequently fewer lines of code. This is because the language itself handles much of the detail work.

As you might have guessed, the high/low-level characteristic is actually on a continuum reflecting the degree to which the programming language is dependent on the hardware. In fact, the distinction between high-level languages (compiler languages, for example) and low-level languages (assembly languages, for example) is not as clear as it once was. Today, we have languages like C and MODULA-2, which combine low-level language efficiencies with high-level language structure, abstraction, and portability.

Procedural vs. declarative. In distinguishing between procedural and declarative languages, it helps to think of the "how" versus the "what." *Procedural* languages are process centered; they are concerned with "how." Procedural language statements require the programmer to devise complete, detailed instructions (in other words, "how" to do it) for every step the computer will take in solving the problem. These may include instructions without any real-life counterpart, such as establishing counters, looping, formatting input/output, and initializing variables. *Declarative* languages are more data centered. Declarative language statements enable the programmer to specify "what" is to be done with the data, rather than detailing "how" it is to be accomplished. These languages are generally at a higher level than process-oriented languages and provide a more natural means of programming within a particular problem domain.

To illustrate the difference between the "what" and the "how" let us try the following real-life example. You might declare: "I'm going out for pizza." That's declarative. Or, you might say: "I'm going out the door. Then I'm going across the street. Then I'm going to turn right. Then I'm going to walk two blocks. Then... " You get the idea. Consider a problem closer to home: summing the numbers in a set of data. Many declarative languages might provide a statement such as SUM (dataset). A procedural language would require the program to code the familiar sequence of instructions beginning with: initialize accumulator, ...

Again it is a matter of degree. For one thing, some languages are more procedural than others. LISP, for example, and other functional languages, are less procedural than, say, FORTRAN or COBOL but more so than PROLOG or Smalltalk. Also, most procedural languages allow you to define new program structures (for example, functions, paragraphs, subroutines) and then use them declaratively. Conversely, many declarative languages have some procedural features.

Data type. Some general-purpose programming languages have facilities for a variety of different data types and may handle all (or most) of them equally well. Others assume one default data type and handle it easily and efficiently. Such languages may be distinguished based on this default data type. Examples are *lists* in LISP, *strings* in SNOBOL, and *arrays* in APL. Of course, languages that are identified by the way they handle a particular data type often have facilities for other data types as well. Data types in programming languages will be discussed more fully in Chapter 4.

Problem-orientation. High-level programming languages may frequently be considered problem oriented. That is, they have been designed so as to handle a particular problem or application area efficiently although they can often handle other types of problems equally well. For example, FORTRAN is a general-purpose language that is particularly well suited to problems in the areas of science, engineering, and mathematics. These problems typically require facilities for manipulating large amounts of numerical data. COBOL is a general-purpose language that is particularly well suited to problems in business data processing. These problems typically require high-volume input/output, easy access to permanent storage media, and large printed reports. Both FORTRAN and COBOL, however, may be used for just about any problem area from robotics to database management. However, they are both best suited to the problem areas for which they were designed, and other languages would be better choices for other radically different areas. Very few languages have been designed specifically to handle any problem area as well as another. PL/1 and Ada are examples of true general-purpose languages.

Extensibility. A programming language is *extensible* if the user is able to create new language structures and so "customize" the language for her own specific purposes. Defining subroutines in FORTRAN or functions in Pascal is not quite the same thing, since the language has not been changed. Even storing routines in a library is not true extensibility, since the mechanism for incorporating these routines into a program is not transparent and, again, the language itself has not been altered. A truly extensible programming language evolves as the user changes, and grows along with the knowledge and ability of the user. Languages like MODULA-2 and Ada, that have facilities for data abstraction, may be considered to be somewhat extensible. Smalltalk is a highly extensible language.

Processing environment.   When we use the *processing environment* as a means of classifying programming languages, we are considering the degree to which the application program interacts with its environment during execution. There may be interaction with a human—the programmer or the nontechnical user—as in a man-machine simulation. There may be real-time interaction with physical objects, as in a process-control system such as an automated factory or a space vehicle. And there may be interaction with other programs, as in a multiprogramming operating system.

Programming paradigm.   A programming paradigm is a problem-solving approach. Most programming languages assume a particular programming paradigm as the major organizing principle. By far, the most prevalent paradigm in programming languages today is the *imperative programming paradigm*, in which a program is assumed to be a sequence of detailed statements, instructing the computer exactly how a task is to be accomplished. Indeed, the imperative paradigm is so prevalent, that many people are surprised when they first discover that there are others. An example of another approach to programming is the *functional paradigm* supported by LISP.

Some Classification Hierarchies

Some of the criteria discussed above may be used to produce broad overviews of the programming languages in widespread use today. We will attempt to classify programming languages in four ways according to:

- level of complexity of the language and its software development environment;
- major function or type of problem to be solved;
- the processing environment assumed by the language;
- the major programming paradigm or organizing principle supported by the language.

By level of complexity.   The "software ladder" of the previous section, reproduced here in Fig. 2.3, illustrates the classification of software according to generation. Each successive generation is defined in order to represent some new software technology or approach. Each "step" in the software ladder is built on top of the methods of the previous one. The distinction between software generations is often murky and sometimes arbitrary. Indeed, the years indicated in parentheses on the figure are intended as general guidelines at best. However, while it is not always easy to classify a particular language or software product as belonging in a particular generation, the trend over the past 40 or so years from machine-oriented at the bottom of the ladder to user-oriented at the top is always abundantly clear and continues to this day.

5th generation (future)	? HAL ?? ? STAR TREK ?? ? KITT ??
4th generation (1961-present)	Natural language processing "4GLs": FOCUS, NOMAD2, . . . Programming environments Integrated packages PROLOG, OPS, Smalltalk, . . . Rule-based, logic, object-oriented programming Declarative programming Packages: BMD, DATATEXT, SPSS, . . .
3rd generation (1954-present)	C, MODULA-2, Ada FORTH, SIMULA, ALGOL68, Pascal APL, SNOBOL, BASIC, PL/1, Logo FORTRAN, LISP, ALGOL60, COBOL MATH-MATIC, FLOW-MATIC Imperative, functional programming Compiler languages, procedural languages
2nd generation (1949-1956)	Very early compilers AUTOCODE Symbolic assemblers Short Code, Speedcoding, Sort-Merge Generator Interpretive routines
1st generation (1937-1952)	"Open" subroutines Machine codes

Figure 2.3   The software ladder

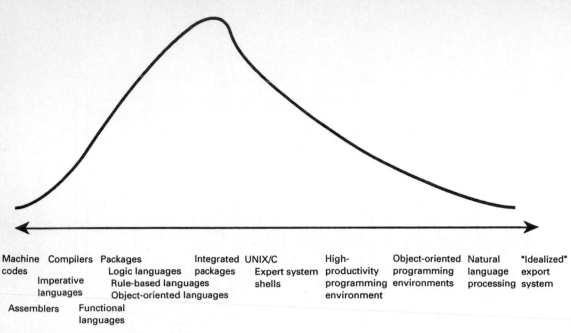

Machine codes	Compilers	Packages		Integrated packages	UNIX/C	High- productivity programming environment	Object-oriented programming environments	Natural language processing	"Idealized" export system
	Imperative languages	Logic languages			Expert system shells				
		Rule-based languages							
		Object-oriented languages							
Assemblers		Functional languages							

Figure 2.4   Continuum of complexity

The first software generation was machine coding. Programs were composed of sequences of binary digits that varied from computer to computer. The second software generation included symbolic assemblers and other machine-code generators. These software products were also (and still are) totally machine dependent. The third software generation encompasses high-level, procedural programming language technology. The general focus of this generation is the language rather than the translator. Important distinguishing features of these languages are their *problem orientation*, their *expressivity* (especially with regard to particular problem areas), and *portability*. At the next step, the software products of the fourth-generation break away from the process orientation and are largely declarative in nature. There is even more expressivity and more of a problem orientation and they are, in general, more user friendly.

As the complexity of software products increases over time, each successive software generation provides an additional rung in the ladder, extending the distance between the human user and the bare computer. The higher the human user is able to climb, the more useful the computer will be to a greater number of people.

In classifying software on the basis of level of complexity, using time as a factor may be deceptive. Certainly, we can see that it forces one to make arbitrary decisions regarding the end of one phase and the beginning of the next. Software generations beginning with the third tend to blur as languages learn from each other and are continually revised and updated. Perhaps it is more reasonable to simply view this criterion as a "continuum of complexity" and attempt to fit software products into their proper (or most appropriate) places on this continuum. This is the approach taken in Fig. 2.4 which illustrates this continuum, complexity increasing along the horizontal axis from left to right. To the left are simple, stand-alone programs that place less of a burden on the machine than on the programmer; to the right are complicated, often intelligent, inte-

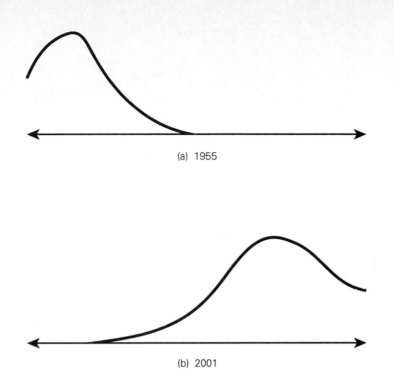

(a) 1955

(b) 2001

Figure 2.5   The changing shape of complexity

grated environments that increase the load on the machine (the "system," really) to the extent that many can be used by nontechnical users. In this figure, an attempt is made to indicate the current popularity of these software products in the computing community, with the height of the curve representing relative frequency of use.

Fig. 2.5 depicts a similar curve for the mid-1950s (a) and a hopeful but realistic projection for the early twenty-first century (b).

The changing shape of this curve is probably more accurate as an indicator of the time factor in classifying languages by level of complexity than the "generations" laid out over the rungs of the software ladder.

By problem-orientation.   Beginning with the third software generation, software became increasingly high level and problem oriented, less machine oriented. Most programming languages (and other related software products such as packages and integrated software systems) could be considered as belonging to a particular problem domain. The tree in Fig. 2.6 defines three broad categories of programming languages with respect to the major function or problem area for which the language was designed. These three major categories are:

1. Languages that are not problem oriented. In other words, these are true general-purpose languages that are intended to work as well for any one problem domain as for another. Very few languages have been designed with this in mind.

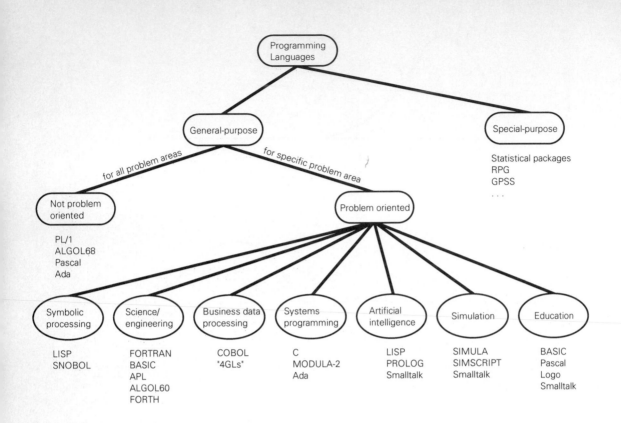

Figure 2.6   Classification by major function

       2. Languages that are general purpose but also problem oriented. In other words, even though they were designed for use in a particular problem domain, they are sufficiently general purpose to be applicable to any other area. However, while certainly feasible, the application of these languages to areas for which they were not designed will probably result in programming and processing inefficiencies.

       3. Languages or systems that are truly special purpose. That is, they cannot be used for any other problem area other than the one for which they were designed. Packages and program generators fall into this category. (GPSS and DYNAMO are simulation languages.)

       By processing environment.   Classification by processing environment indicates the degree to which the program interacts with the environment during execution. The tree in Fig. 2.7 breaks this down according to the type of interaction for which the language was designed.

       The oldest sort of processing environment is one in which there is no interaction of any sort with the executing program. This has been called *batch processing*. In this type of processing environment, user jobs—consisting of code for one or more sequential programs, data, and commands to the operating system—are typically submitted in sequential batches. The languages listed in the batch processing category are representa-

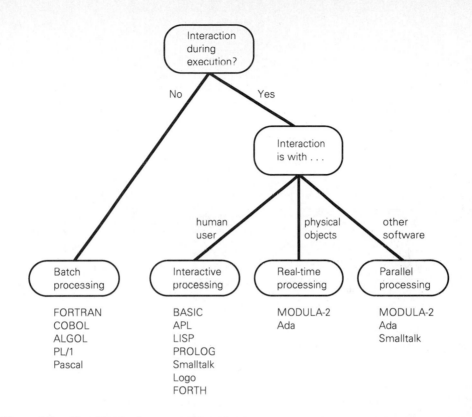

Figure 2.7 Classification by processing environment

tive of those designed to be used with little or no interaction between the user and the job during run time. That is not to say that interaction is impossible, simply that it is not central to the philosophy of the language.

The languages LISP, BASIC, PROLOG, and APL were specifically designed for use in an *interactive processing* environment, under either a single-user (for example, with a stand-alone personal computer) or a time-sharing system. Translators for these languages are often closer to interpreters than to compilers and instructions may be executed immediately. An interactive processing environment is characterized by interaction between the program and its human user/programmer during program execution. Thus, an interactive "session" takes on the character of a dialogue, or conversation, between the human and the computer. The term *time-sharing* implies that the system is able to support several on-line users seemingly simultaneously, enabling each user to interact with the computer at what appears to be the same moment in time.

A *real-time processing environment* is a feature of process-control systems, in which external processes such as physical objects interact with and impose strict time constraints on the responses from executing programs. Such systems, often called *embedded systems*, include those involved in automated production, robotics, automatic pilots, and space vehicles. The programming language Ada was designed for this type of environment.

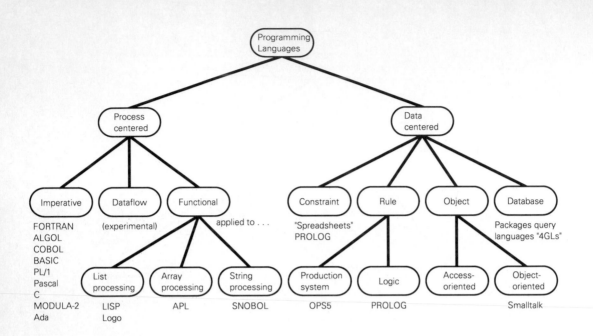

Figure 2.8   Classification by programming paradigm

When a program is expected to communicate with other programs, this is called a *concurrent* or *parallel processing environment*. In such an environment, two or more programs execute simultaneously, may share system resources, and may need to interact with each other to a greater or lesser degree. There may or may not be real-time constraints involved. A multiprogramming operating system is a system-level example of a parallel processing environment. Communicating programs may be executed on a single central processor or over a distributed processing configuration.

By programming paradigm.   A programming paradigm is a world view governing the way a problem is conceptualized, the way the solution is organized and, finally, the design and implementation of the program. It is an approach to programming. The design of a programming language usually assumes a particular programming paradigm from the outset, so it is difficult to separate the programming language from the programming paradigm. In fact, many of the paradigms discussed in this book have their origins in and are defined by the languages in which they first originated. Fig. 2.8 classifies programming languages according to the major programming paradigm or organizing principle that is supported by the language.

Programming paradigms, like the languages that support them, can be classified as either *process centered* or *data centered*. *Process-centered* languages and paradigms are concerned with the details of computing a solution and with the process of problem decomposition. *Data-centered* languages and paradigms support the development of programs by way of the formal specification of the data that will be manipulated.

Most of the languages discussed in this book, and most of the languages in widespread use today, support the *imperative programming paradigm*. These languages promote sharp distinctions between program and data. They are heavily concerned with variables tied to main storage locations and with assignment of values to these variables. Some of the necessary detail work, while meaningful to the computer, is meaningless in the context of the application area. For example: possibly arbitrary initial values for variables, assignment of values to program control variables, control structures such as loops.

In the *dataflow* programming paradigm, a dataflow analysis determines the dependencies among the data, and operations are ordered based on those dependencies. In other words, operations are selected for execution as soon as their operands have been computed, and any possible parallelism is exploited. The dataflow paradigm is not widely used in programming and no major programming language supports this world view. In order to fully exploit the parallelism exposed by the dataflow analysis, dataflow programs are intended to run on data-flow machines, which are still largely experimental.

In *functional programming*, also called *applicative programming*, the major organizing principle is the *function*, a subprogram that returns a single value. A functional program defines an expression whose operands may themselves be expressions (that is, other functions). Programming languages that support the functional programming paradigm are also called *applicative languages*.

A *constraint-oriented language* enables the specification of relationships among a set of data objects. The constraint-satisfaction system then sets about attempting to solve the system so that the relationships are satisfied. Spreadsheet-based systems such as Lotus 1-2-3® and logic programming languages like PROLOG have a constraint orientation.

In the *rule-oriented languages*, facts and rules may be specified about data objects and their interrelationships and the system may then be queried regarding these objects and relationships. The *production-system paradigm*, also called *rule-based programming*, sets up a knowledge base of condition-action rules (productions) and contains a specific mechanism for acting upon those rules. Such a system is expected to generate explanations of program behavior. While the PROLOG language may be and is used to set up databases of rules (knowledge bases) for artificial intelligence applications and so qualifies as a rule-oriented language, it is also a very specific type of constraint-oriented language since it satisfies logical constraints. Thus PROLOG is sometimes considered to follow the *logic programming paradigm*.

In the *object-oriented paradigm*, individual data objects are defined by modules of code, often called *classes*, which encapsulate data declarations and algorithms for the operations, called *methods*, which are necessary for the definition of the data object. Objects communicate with each other by means of messages that serve to invoke execution of methods. Conversely, in *access-oriented programming*, a data object may be monitored and, on its access (a possible change in value), a subprogram is invoked. This programming approach is seldom used for the design of a complete language but, rather, may be used in conjunction with another organizing principle to produce a hybrid or multiparadigm language (or, environment). Access-oriented programming may be used, for example, to program the graphical user interface for a software system. The subject of programming paradigms will be discussed at greater length in Chapter 6.

2.3 CHARACTERISTICS OF PROGRAMMING LANGUAGES

In evaluating a computer programming language, certain key features must be considered. The ideal programming language will be easy to write, easy to read, portable, and efficient in terms of its usage of both computer and human resources. Different languages will have these features in differing degrees. The selection of a programming language for a particular application depends on the degree to which the application requires the presence of each of these programming language characteristics.

Writability. *Does the programming language facilitate the development of clear, concise, error-free programs?*

A programming language with writability will make it easy for the programmer to design, code, test, run, document, and modify programs. Many of the features discussed below contribute to the ease in writing programs. For example, many of the same features that make a program easy to read—such as the support for structured techniques—make the program easier to design and to write as well. A distinguishing feature of a language with writability is its simplicity. It will have few basic language constructs, and those will be similar to each other and easy to learn. Syntax rules will be clear, simple, and consistent. Other features, such as built-in default values, may make a program easier to write but decrease its readability. Writability may contribute to the development of a program containing fewer errors.

Error-checking. *Does the programming language facilitate the development of error-free programs?*

Such a language will not only encourage the development of error-free programs, but it will also contain debugging facilities for finding errors that do occur. Other features of such a language would include type checking and extensive compiler diagnostics.

Readability. *Are programs written in the programming language easy to read?*

Being easy to read assumes that a program will be read and reread by the original programmer and by other programmers who "speak" the same language. It may also assume that the program will be read by other technical personnel who do not know that particular programming language and even by nontechnical personnel such as end users, managers, and auditors. Readable programs are clear, understandable, and easily modifiable; they are characterized by logical clarity in expressions and algorithms. Some languages that have writability are lacking in readability. APL and FORTH, for example, have been called "write-only" languages. Ada, on the other hand, was designed with readability taking priority over writability.

Self-documenting. *Is the source code alone sufficient documentation for the program?*

The extent to which a language facilitates the development of self-documenting programs contributes to its readability. If a language is self-documenting, other forms of documentation usually attached to the source code for the benefit of maintenance programming—for example, structure charts, flowcharts, data dictionaries, I/O formats—do not contribute much more than does reading the source code alone. Some language features that contribute to making a language self-documenting are:

- descriptive names for data and program structures, comments, noise words (is, to, some, and);
- encouraged use of indenting and blank lines;
- support for modularization;
- language constructs supporting structured programming.

Most languages at least provide for comments to communicate the intent of the program to future programmers. One problem with comments is that they may not have been maintained along with the rest of the code. If the working code is itself relatively self-documenting, this may be more reliable than comments for future programmers.

Extensibility. *Can the programmer extend the language by creating new language constructs?*

A language is extensible if it enables the programmer to define new language components, which are then indistinguishable from the language's own built-in primitives. An example of a highly extensible language is Smalltalk. Some less-extensible languages still allow one to think as if the programmer-defined constructs are true extensions to the language even when they are not treated in exactly the same way as built-in language constructs. The feature of extensibility may be critical in the construction of large, complex programs.

Portability. *Is the programming language machine independent?*

This is an important defining characteristic of high-level languages, those of the third software generation and above. In order for a programming language to be considered portable, compilers for it must exist on a number of different computers. In addition, these compilers must ensure that the language works in the same way on these different machines so that a program written in the language and tested on a particular computer will still work and will give similar results on a different machine/compiler. If a so-called high-level language has only a single compiler available so that it can be run on only a single computer, it is considered to be still experimental in nature.

Efficiency. *Is the programming language efficient in its use of computer and human resources?*

One might think that the construction of an efficient, reliable object program is the primary consideration for any programming language, more important than all of the language features mentioned above. It was, in fact, the primary consideration in the design of the FORTRAN language in the early 1950s. However, we have come a long way since FORTRAN. Machine-efficiency considerations relate to the efficient use of memory space (as little as possible) and computer processing time (as fast as possible). These considerations are nearly always at odds with human-efficiency considerations: ease in programming and developing correct programs, in debugging, and in program maintenance.

Over the past several decades marking the information/technological revolution, we have seen several trends:

- more memory concentrated in less physical space;
- increased processor speed;
- decreasing costs for storage and computation;
- increased use of computers in all application areas;
- increased use by nontechnical people;
- increasing costs for good programmers.

There is no doubt that these trends all dictate that we reduce emphasis on the machine-efficiency of languages and systems, sacrificing efficient use of storage space and processor time in order to support human efficiencies. After all, programmer time is currently many times more expensive than machine costs. Also, our applications backlog of the past several years is attributable to human, not machine, considerations.

All other things being equal, of course, efficiencies relating to use of computer resources are then an important consideration in evaluating a programming language. Lack of efficiency can certainly be very costly to the organization. Lately, the trend toward the development of large, complex systems has brought efficiency considerations back into the limelight.

2.4 CHOOSING A PROGRAMMING LANGUAGE

Is it true that language selection is the most frequently omitted step in the program development process? Is it true that most people will simply continue to program in the language that they know best? Is it true that most data processing groups will continue to program in the language that was used for their other applications? Probably.

Of course, there is something to be said for the use of a single programming language for all your programs. Programmers who use a single language get to know it very well and may be able to write programs that are highly efficient. Thus, programs may be written more quickly and may be better than otherwise. Use of a single language may contribute to the production of reusable code. After all, why reinvent the wheel? If a module has already been coded in a particular language, there is no reason to code it again if it can be easily inserted into or linked with a new application. These are some of the reasons behind the recent design effort that resulted in the Ada language.

Language selection then may only sometimes be an important factor in program design and development. At any rate, suppose that, for the reasons listed above, a firm decides to employ a single programming language for all of its programs. Wouldn't that make the evaluation and selection of an appropriate programming language all the more crucial?

Whether evaluating a language for use in a single application program or over several applications, we have many of the same considerations. In addition, software evaluation and selection has probably become more important of late in the evaluation and selection of packaged, off-the-shelf software.

We have looked at some of the ways of classifying programming languages and at desirable characteristics of a programming language. Both of these figure prominently in the evaluation of languages for possible selection. Let us now look at some others:

Features of the Application

It is just as important to evaluate the application in selecting a programming language as to evaluate the language itself. After all, is it feasible to select an appropriate tool before knowing the sort of job it will be used for? Specifically, what sort of work will be done with this language?

Public vs. private computing. *Are programs to be written by a single programmer for his or her own private use or by employees of a firm for use by the organization?*

Private computing is computing done by individuals for their own personal or professional use. In public computing, the kind done by most professional programmers, programs are written and used by many different programmers and program maintenance is an important consideration—so are structured programming techniques; so is documentation.

Complexity. *How big is the job?*

Is the program small enough to be understood and completed by a single programmer? Will the final program be composed of a single module? Perhaps it will instead be composed of several internal, nested subprograms or a large number of independent, external subprograms.

Language vs. package vs. ...? *Do we want a language at all? What are the alternatives?*

If the application is sufficiently similar to other standardized applications, then off-the-shelf software can be successfully applied. If not, customized software may be needed. Alternatively, there may be available off-the-shelf software that can be customized for the particular application.

In any event, do we need a full-blown, high-level language? Will the programming tools provided by some high-productivity, integrated packages be sufficient? Who will do this programming? The size of the company may dictate the answers to these questions.

Features of the Language

In addition to the language characteristics of the previous section—such as writability, readability, portability, and efficiency—we may wish to consider a few others.

Problem-orientation. *How good a "fit" is the programming language for the application area or areas for which the programs will be written?*

The language should provide appropriate built-in data types and data structures for the application area. Choice of control structures will also be a consideration. Language syntax should be a "natural" medium for expressing problems and algorithms. Of course, what is natural to some people is not natural to others and that is exactly what is meant by problem orientation.

Programming environment. *What program development tools are associated with the programming language? Specifically how does the language assist in the programming function?*

A programming environment, also called a *software development environment*, is a set of tools that includes a programming language and serves to aid in program development. Some of the tools that may be contained within a programming environment are a language translator, an editor, a linker, a debugging facility, on-line help. An off-line consideration is the written technical documentation provided.

Learning curve. *How easy will it be for a programmer to learn this programming language?*

Is it a language that many programmers already know? Is it a dialect of such a language? Is it a new language but similar to a familiar language? On the other hand, if you are considering a totally unfamiliar language, are training tools available? What kind of technical skills are required in order to use the language? How good are the user and reference manuals? Are there well-written textbooks available? Where can additional information be obtained (e.g., a user's support group)?

SUMMARY AND KEY TERMS

Chapter Summary

In this chapter, we have discussed the evolution of programming languages from their conception to their modern form. We have stressed the diversity of programming languages as well as their common features. Finally, some general principles for language design and criteria for selecting an appropriate language were discussed.

Chapter 2 Terminology

Some of the terms presented in this chapter may have been new to you. Use this list as a guide in reviewing the chapter. When you review the list, if you come across a term that is unfamiliar to you, go back and review the section that discusses it. Some of these terms were introduced only briefly in this chapter, and will be discussed in more detail in the chapters that follow.

access-oriented language	Ada	ALGOL60
ALGOL68	APL	applicative language
assembler	BASIC	batch processing
C	COBOL	compiler
concurrent processing	constraint-oriented language	data-centered language
data-flow language	declarative language	efficiency
extensibility	FLOW-MATIC	FORTH
FORTRAN	fourth-generation software	functional language
high-level language	imperative language	interactive processing

interpreter	learning curve	LISP
logic programming language	Logo	low-level language
machine code	machine-oriented language	MODULA-2
object-oriented	OPS	parallel processing
Pascal	PL/1	portability
problem-orientation	procedural language	process-centered language
processing environment	production-system language	programming environment
programming paradigm	PROLOG	readability
real-time processing	rule-oriented language	self-documenting
SIMULA	Smalltalk	SNOBOL
timesharing	von Neumann computer	writability

SUGGESTIONS FOR FURTHER STUDY

For further in-depth study of the early history of programming languages, the reader is referred to articles by Landin (1966), Knuth (1972, 1980), Sammet (1972), Cheatham (1972), Rosen (1972), Hoare (1981), Wirth (1985), Strehlo (1986), and Taylor (1987) and books by Morrison and Morrison (1961), Sammet (1969), Metropolis et al. (1980), Wexelblat (1981), Stein (1985), and Burks and Burks (1988). Also of interest are Randall (1973) and articles by Computerworld (1986, 1989) and Rosen (1969) for a more general history of computing. As regards moving from the present into the future, consult Herriot (1977), Winograd (1979), Wasserman (1982), Balzer et al. (1983), Wexelblat (1984), Florentin (1985), Grant (1985) and books by Chorafas (1986a, 1986b) and Martin (1982, 1985, 1986a, 1986b).

Articles by Baron (1986) and Mally (1988) and books by REA (1985) and Baron (1986) are excellent sources for the classification and characteristics of programming languages in widespread use today. Some technical comparisons of various programming languages are contained in Boom and DeJong (1980), Cashin (1988), and Shaw et al. (1981).

Branquart and Wodon (1988) are concerned with good language design. For choosing a programming language, see the paper by Elfring (1985) and the book by Wooldridge (1973).

Books by REA (1985) and Horowitz (1983) provide very different approaches to the study of several programming languages. For more detailed information about the individual languages mentioned in this chapter, refer to Chapters 8 through 13 and to the following selected sources.

Ada.   Books by Bray and Pokrass (1985), Cohen (1983), Feuer and Gehani (1984), Ledgard (1983), Shumate (1983). Articles by Clarke et al. (1980), Ichbiah (1984), Tetewsky (1986, 1987), and Wehrum et al. (1986).

ALGOL.   Books by Dijkstra (1962), and Brailsford and Walker (1979). The reference for ALGOL-W is contained in Horowitz (1983).

APL. Books by Bryson (1982) and Iverson (1962). Articles by Bozman (1989) and Konstam (1985).

BASIC. Books by Kemeny and Kurtz (1981, 1985).

FORTH. A book by Brodie (1987).

LISP. Books by Dybvig (1987) and Touretzky (1984). Articles by Abelson and Sussman (1988), Touretzky (1988), and Winston (1985).

Logo. A book by Harvey (1985).

PL/1. A book by Katzan (1972).

SIMULA. A book by Birtwistle *et al.* (1973).

SNOBOL4. Books by Griswold *et al.* (1971) and Hockney (1986). Article by Shapiro (1985).

3

Language Processors and Related Concepts

Much as we applaud the trend toward greater abstraction in computing, there is little doubt that a basic knowledge of the workings of the low-level machine, along with an understanding of the manner in which our high-level language statements are transformed so that they can operate on that low-level machine, will help us in such high-level pursuits as system development, software evaluation, and program maintenance.

Calling these facilities *translators* has come to be considered "passé." As computer programming languages continue to make programming easier, the relative simplicity of high-level language constructs has been achieved by means of increasingly sophisticated language processors, creating a more usable machine for the human user. This enhanced machine is often referred to as a *virtual computer*.

3.1 THE VIRTUAL COMPUTER

Were it not for software, bare (hardware-only) computers would still be in the realm of the experimental and relegated to research laboratories of universities willing and able to fund such esoteric, theoretical research projects.

Any type of software provides the computer user with a level of machine abstraction. It creates a "new" machine that is more useful within the framework of a particular application area. In fact, users of the early FORTRAN and COBOL compilers often referred to their "FORTRAN machines" or "COBOL machines."

High-level programming languages and their translators transform bare hardware into abstract, high-level computers that may be used without regard for such machine-level clerical details as keeping track of main memory locations or updating program instruction counters. Every level of software provides an additional layer of abstraction,

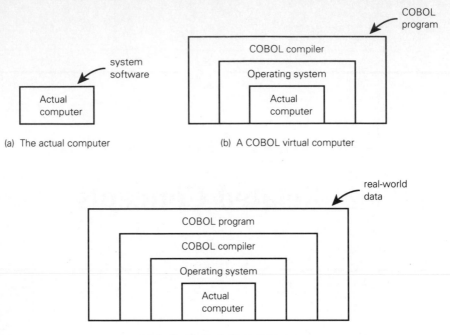

(a) The actual computer

(b) A COBOL virtual computer

(c) An "application" virtual computer

Figure 3.1   Levels of computer abstraction

thereby raising the level of the perceived virtual computer. Fig. 3.1, for example, depicts the COBOL virtual computer and contrasts it with the actual computer. This "actual" computer, of course, can itself be considered an abstraction since it is associated with "firmware" (i.e., microprogramming) that provides it with a machine-language interface so that the computer can be programmed using a machine-language code.

We also see from Fig. 3.1 that a program written in a high-level language may be considered a machine abstraction. It is a virtual computer that has been defined by the applications programmer. Thus, an executing program can be said to transform the bare machine into, say, an "accounts-receivable computer."

This layering of virtual computers on top of the actual computer raises the humble machine so that it is more compatible with the high-level human user. This view is consistent with the trend pictured in the software ladder of Chapter 2: As computers become increasingly "human," the human user is required less and less to learn to think like a machine in order to speak to it, and this makes computer technology available to a broader group of users.

In a sense, what is considered a *program* at one level of abstraction, is recognized as *data* by the program at the level below it. The actual hardware, along with its machine-language interface, operates upon the operating system. The operating system software operates on the high-level language processor which, in turn, operates on the high-level language statements themselves.

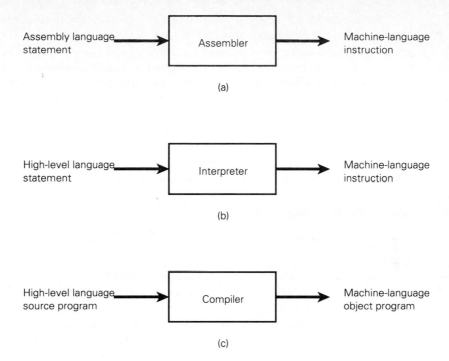

Figure 3.2 Translators

Can a computer be designed to be just like a virtual machine? In other words, can the computer be designed so that it accepts the high-level language statements as *its own* machine-language instructions? Certainly. Symbolics' LISP Machine is such a product. Japan's Fifth Generation Project, announced in 1981, is centered around machines to be built for processing a PROLOG-type of logic programming language. Of course, when a machine is built specifically to process the high-level instructions of a particular language, it is an awkward (at best) enterprise to use it for a different programming language. That is why a computer is usually designed as a low-level machine that depends on the addition of layers of software to raise it to a high-level virtual computer for a particular programming language. This results in a device that is both more efficient and more flexible. Changing the software provides a simple transformation of the machine from one virtual computer to another.

3.2 TYPES OF LANGUAGE PROCESSORS

A translator program, such as the ones pictured in Fig. 3.2, accepts high-level language statements as input and produces the equivalent executable machine-language instruction. Of the three translators pictured in Fig. 3.2, however, the assembler in (a) actually processes rather low-level statements.

An *assembler* is a translator program that translates assembly language to machine language. Assembly language provides a kind of shorthand notation for the actual machine-language instructions and there is a one-to-one correspondence between each assembly-language instruction and its corresponding machine-language instruction. For this reason, assembly languages are highly machine dependent and, in fact, have not been standardized. There is an assembly language for each type of computer (or computer family).

Language processors accept high-level code and are, as a result, significantly more complex than assemblers. These processors, *compilers* and *interpreters*, sometimes convert high-level language statements to an assembly type of code rather than to machine code. This assembly code is then passed through the assembler to be executed.

Compilers and Interpreters

A *compiler* is a translator program which transforms a *source program* composed of high-level language statements into an *object program* consisting of machine-language executable code. The source program is translated completely before any execution takes place. Usually, a major objective of a compiler is to produce highly efficient object code.

Compilation occurs in two broad phases, each of which may encompass a number of steps. The first phase decomposes the source program into small identifiable units and analyzes it for syntactical accuracy. This phase is not, to any large degree, machine dependent, being governed more by the features of the particular programming language under translation than by the details of the actual machine. The second phase takes the machine-code modules associated with the basic units identified in the first phase and uses them to compose the object program. Some compilers also subject the code to a variety of optimizing transformations.

Although some compilers do translate into an object program composed of an assembly-type code (which is then executed by an assembler), a program written initially in assembly language will usually (if well written) run more efficiently than the equivalent compiler-produced assembly program. In addition, there is of course the compile process itself as a user of computer time and storage.

There are two different kinds of compilers that may coexist even for the same programming language on the same machine. These represent the trade-off between speedy execution and speedy compilation. Some compilers translate quickly, employing virtually no optimization techniques, but provide the user with plenty of sophisticated diagnostics including a good error report. These compilers may be used in developing and debugging programs. They are the sort often employed in academic settings, the so-called "teaching" compilers (e.g., WATFIV for FORTRAN or PL/C for PL/1). These translators not only provide excellent feedback for students regarding program errors, but also the speedy compilation essential for student programs: After all, novice programmers must often recompile a program scores of times (if not more) in order to produce a single usable run.

Other compilers take longer to translate because they optimize as well, taking full advantage of all machine-level dependencies and often improving program logic in the process. They work slowly, but produce highly efficient code. These compilers are useful

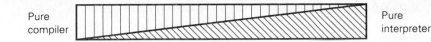

Pure
compiler

Pure
interpreter

Figure 3.3   Spectrum of program translators

for programs that will govern production runs. The source program is translated once, and then the object code is executed repeatedly, often over an extended period.

An *interpreter* processes the source program on a statement-by-statement basis. It translates a high-level language statement and then executes it, one statement at a time. An interpreter does little to alter the structure of the source code. Thus, run time machine-language routines must be present in order to execute the actions implied by the high-level language statements in the program. The action of an interpreter imitates the machine's own instruction cycle, which is: fetch next instruction; decode instruction; execute instruction. The interpreter's instruction cycle is: fetch next statement; translate statement; execute the actions contained in the statement. Thus, the interpreter simulates a machine that cycles over high-level statements rather than over machine instructions. As such, the "translation" or "decoding" step is unobtrusive.

Interpreted programming languages provide an interactive processing environment and immediate results. Also, program errors are easier to locate. These important advantages, however, come along with some costs. Interpreters generally run more slowly than compiled programs. After all, once a program has been compiled, the object program can execute rather quickly. The interpreter, which does not produce machine-executable object code, must continue to translate each statement before executing it, no matter how many times the program is run. Consider the time wasted on a statement inside the body of a loop, which must be translated every time the loop is executed.

In reality, there are very few pure compilers and pure interpreters, that is, translators that follow the strict definitions outlined above. In fact, there is a growing trend to simply consider all of these processors as varieties of compilers. Most translators actually fall somewhere in between the two extremes, residing somewhere on the spectrum shown in Fig. 3.3.

For example, most interpreters do put the program through an initial phase (similar to a compiler's source code analysis) that produces a complete program in an intermediate code that may be similar to assembly code; the program is then executed by a low-level interpreter or by an assembler. On the other hand, most compilers require that some run time routines be present (for example, to handle input and output) in order to execute the object program. Many compilers produce object programs in an internal code rather than in machine code; this internal code is then subjected to a process very similar to an interpreter.

Some programming languages lend themselves more readily to one or the other of these two means of processing. One of the factors that determines whether an interpreter will be used rather than a compiler is the degree to which interactive processing is considered important to the philosophy of the language. Another possible factor is binding time.

Binding and Binding Time

Binding is the association of a particular property with a particular unit of program code. For example, the binding of one or more attributes (such as location, type, or value) with a variable. The *binding time* for a particular association answers the question: When does this binding occur? Binding can occur as early as during the language design process, as late as during an interactive run. For our purposes, it is sufficient to distinguish between binding that occurs before run time (*early*, or *static*, binding) and during run time (*late*, or *dynamic*, binding). An association made by static binding is not changed once established but a dynamic binding can be changed or superseded.

Clearly, binding done by a compiler—for example, binding type to a variable or to an expression—must be static binding. An interpreter, on the other hand leaves variables unbound until execution has already begun. One of the run time routines necessary for the functioning of an interpreter must handle the association of a variable with its type. When a variable declaration statement is used—either because the language demands it or because the programmer chooses it—early binding for that variable is predetermined. On the other hand, a language may be described as "not compilable" if a particular binding cannot be made before run time; it must therefore be interpreted. Thus, binding time may be predetermined by the design of the language.

Programming Language Implementations

A *programming language implementation* is a mechanism for interpreting high-level programs that have been expressed in the stylized formal notation of the programming language. For most high-level languages, this implementation will be some variation of a compiler or an interpreter. The formal notation itself is independent of the decision regarding its implementation.

Because of the forced declaration of all variables in Pascal programs, the language tends to be implemented by a compiler type of translator program. Similarly, COBOL, PL/1, MODULA-2, and Ada are usually compiled. Some languages, which encourage the coding of statements that are extremely concise and powerful, take so long to execute a statement its translation time is irrelevant. These languages are usually interpreted. Also, languages with a simple structure lend themselves more easily to an interpreted implementation. Examples are LISP, APL, and FORTH. Sometimes the implementation is dictated by the philosophy of the language. Most BASICs are interpreted although several compiled versions exist. Some languages, like FORTH and Smalltalk, may be implemented using both a compiler and an interpreter, for different kinds of processing.

Sometimes both a compiler and interpreter are available for a particular programming language. In that case, the interpreter, with its advantages of immediacy and interactive debugging, may be used for the initial development and debugging of a program. The final, error-free program will then be input to the compiler and the resulting efficient object code will be stored and used in production runs.

Just as the design of the language may affect the implementer's choice of a processing mechanism, the language design may also be affected by implementation decision, such as, for example, regarding binding time. For example, the perceived need of a

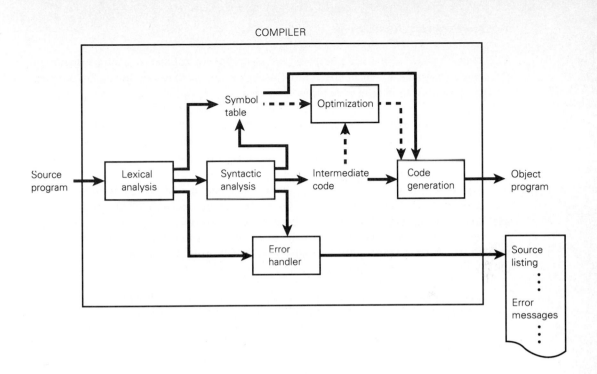

Figure 3.4 The compile process

high-level language programmer to shift binding time for particular associations—say, to delay some bindings until a later stage in the processing of the program—may result in a total restructuring of the type of processor used to implement the language or even in the design of the language itself.

3.3 THE COMPILE PROCESS

A compiler is a complex translator program that is initially involved with breaking down the source program into its components, checking for correct use of the language, and producing intermediate code; finally, a machine-executable object program is produced and, perhaps, optimized. The first phase is relatively machine independent, being more concerned with the programmer's use of high-level language structures than with the efficient use of the underlying hardware. Fig. 3.4 diagrams the steps of the compile process.

The first phase of the compile process encompasses the *lexical analysis* and the *syntactic analysis*, producing the symbol table and intermediate (assembly-level) code. We will call this phase *source program analysis*.

Source Program Analysis

The analysis phase of the compile process dissects the lexical and syntactic structure of the source program. It detects errors to be listed for the user, and produces the program symbol table and the intermediate program code.

Lexical analysis.   Lexical analysis is concerned with the actual text of the program, which is considered to be a meaningful sequence of characters. This module identifies the separate pieces of program text called *tokens*. Tokens are the basic symbols used by the program: identifiers, operators, punctuation, language keywords, constants. Some of these tokens are built-in language elements and are already stored in a permanent *symbol table* within the compiler. Others are programmer-supplied words and are used to create a new symbol table for processing the program.

At this step, the program text is tightened up by eliminating the "redundancy" so important to human scanning of a program but irrelevant to the computer. This includes eliminating blanks and comments.

Syntactic analysis.   Syntactic analysis is concerned with identifying the logical structure of the program in accordance with the rules of grammar governing the high-level language. It is in this step that the program is checked to see whether it uses the language structures correctly. Properties of variables may be identified at this stage and bound to the variables in the symbol table. This step uses a *parse tree* obtained by a manner similar to that employed in parsing a natural language (like English) text. Fig. 3.5 contains a simple parse tree for the COBOL sentence:

```
ADD VALUE TO TOTAL,
IF TOTAL > MAX
      MOVE 0 TO TOTAL.
```

The parse tree, also called a *syntax tree*, contains the hierarchy of operations in the high-level language statements. In this tree, every leaf node contains one of the symbols (tokens) in the statement.

The symbol table.   The symbol table, also called the *dictionary*, maps program symbols such as variables with their properties such as type, size, and relative location. This table is produced by the lexical and syntactic analyses and is used in generating intermediate code and, finally, machine-executable code for the program. The symbol table may be sorted for more efficient access and stored on a DASD (direct-access storage device) to save internal storage space.

To deal with a program's block structure, the symbol table may be segmented as well so that the same name may be used independently for local variables in different blocks.

The error handler.   During the lexical and syntactic analyses, information regarding an error encountered is sent to the error handler module of the compiler, which will arrange to print out a message to the user. It may also attempt some sort of error recovery so that the rest of the program may be analyzed (but not executed) and any other errors uncovered as well.

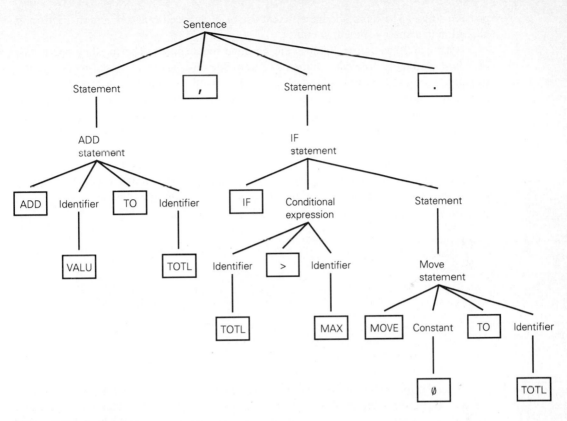

Figure 3.5 A parse tree

Intermediate code generation.   The results of the lexical and syntactic analyses and the information in the symbol table are brought together to produce program
code in some intermediate form similar to assembly-language code. (It may actually be
the machine's own assembly code, which would then be processed by the assembler.)
Statements in this intermediate code may contain four fields: the operation, the symbolic
addresses of the two operands, and the symbolic address of the result. This resembles the
machine instruction format for many actual computers.

Output from the syntactic analysis step, the intermediate code serves as input to the
code generation step. In optimizing compilers, however, this intermediate code is first
subjected to various *optimizing transformations* before the machine language object code
is actually generated.

Optimization

Some optimizing transformations used by compilers to produce efficient code are
machine dependent. They take advantage of machine characteristics that can be coded
into the low-level object program in order to make more efficient use of main storage and

processor time. These include the efficient use of high-speed registers and main memory allocation in a space-efficient manner.

Other optimization techniques are machine independent. That is, they could have been built into the source code in the first place. Sometimes, certain of these optimization techniques are used to correct "bad programming practice," and we can learn from them. Sometimes, however, the source program is purposely developed with a less *efficient* construct in order to make it more elegant, simpler, or more readable from the human perspective. These are laudable goals and should not be automatically ignored in favor of machine efficiency.

One technique calls for detecting code that can be moved out of a loop. This comes under the heading of correcting bad programming practice. Some statements may be placed inside a loop erroneously, as the following Pascal example illustrates.

```
sum := 0;
count := 0;
read (indata, value);
while not eof (data) do
        begin
             sum := sum + value;
             count := count + 1;
             average := sum / count ;
             read (indata, value)
        end
```

Clearly, this piece of code works. It computes the average of a set of input data. Just as clearly, the average of a set of data values ought to be computed only once after the entire data set has been read and summed. The algorithm would be more efficient (and elegant) as follows:

```
sum := 0;
count := 0;
read (indata, value);
while not eof (data) do
        begin
             sum := sum + value;
             count := count + 1;
             read (indata, value)
        end;
average := sum / count
```

By moving that one statement out of the loop we have not only improved the efficiency of the program, but improved its logical structure as well.

Another optimization technique that serves to correct a bad program involves the detection and elimination of dead code. *Dead code* is program code that is inaccessible in the normal processing of the program and will consequently never be executed. Eliminating it tightens up the program so that the space is not allocated unnecessarily. In addition, a message may be printed along with the program output indicating the location of the dead code to signal that a manual check of the program may be called for. Dead code may occur as a result of source program maintenance involving repeated updating and patchwork fix-ups.

In the following piece of COBOL code, the second **IF** statement will not be executed.

```
IF DATA IS LESS THAN MINIMUM
       GO TO TOOLITTL
       ELSE GO TO PROCESSING.
IF DATA IS GREATER THAN MINIMUM GO TO...
```

Of course, had the programmer used the structured branch **PERFORM** rather than the unstructured **GOTO**, this dead code would not exist at all.

Arithmetic expressions can sometimes be computed in a manner making more efficient use of machine resources—if they are reduced to sequences of simpler expressions. By way of illustration, the COBOL statement

```
COMPUTE POWER = X**4.
```

would execute more quickly and more efficiently by reducing the strength of the exponent as in, for instance:

```
COMPUTE POWER = X*X,
COMPUTE POWER = POWER * POWER.
```

Although the latter piece of code is certainly easier on the computer, using the higher exponent is (thankfully) no longer considered poor programming practice since it enhances the readability of a high-level program.

Compiler Output

The most important compiler output is, of course, the machine-executable object program produced at the code generation step. However, this is not the only tangible result of the compile process.

Compilers are also expected to turn out a good deal of sophisticated diagnostics in the form of printed output. The *source listing* reproduces the source program and enhances it with line numbers and other information. Various *error messages* regarding errors detected during the lexical and syntactic analyses may pinpoint the probable causes of these errors in the enhanced source program listing. A *symbol listing*, cross-referenced with the source program listing, provides a list of programmer-defined variables and other identifiers (for example, names of subprograms) along with their attributes. This listing is valuable when a language or its implementation has many built-in defaults for attributes or initial values.

In addition, some compilers have routines that provide for the output of program *statistics and accounting information*. This may include such information as object program size and compiler processing time.

SUMMARY AND KEY TERMS

Chapter Summary

In this chapter we have examined the concept of *computer abstraction*, the virtual computer that is achieved by the layering of software over the actual bare computer. We discussed different types of language processors, such as compilers and interpreters. We looked in some detail at the steps comprised by the typical compiler process.

Chapter 3 Terminology

Some of the terms presented in this chapter may have been new to you. Use this list as a guide in reviewing the chapter. When you review the list, if you come across a term that is unfamiliar to you, go back and review the section that discusses it.

assembler	binding	binding time
compiler	computer abstraction	dynamic binding
early binding	error handling	interpreter
late binding	lexical analysis	object program
optimization	source program	static binding
symbol table	syntactic analysis	tokens
virtual computer		

SUGGESTIONS FOR FURTHER STUDY

For a general treatment of the subject of language processors, the general books by Zwass (1981), Nicholls (1975), and Sebesta (1989) contain quite readable sections. For a more detailed treatment of the specific topics in this chapter, and related information on the implementation of programming languages, consult the books by Aho *et al.* (1977, 1986), Henderson (1980), Harland (1984), Berry (1984), and Gordon (1988).

4

Data-level Structure

Over the past several decades, the way we look at data has undergone changes of revolutionary proportion. The beginnings of this revolution of sorts can probably be traced to the introduction of the first COBOL compiler in 1959. Since then, data has evolved from being simply the stuff on which programs operate to its present status as the reason for keeping those programs at all. The path has not been straight by any means, and it has forked in many different directions. Some of the event markers along the way have been statistical packages, object-oriented programming systems, database management systems, and the high-productivity fourth-generation tools so prevalent in the business computing environment. Further evidence of the vast and ever-increasing importance of data to computing organizations are the pervasive interest in, to cite just a few examples, such topics as data security, data recovery systems and methods, and the continuing debate over centralized versus distributed control.

A programming language is not only a notation for expressing an algorithm, it is also a notation for expressing *data structures*. These two functions come together in the abstract data types of MODULA-2 and Ada as well as in the very high-level languages of fourth-generation software, as we shall see more clearly when we examine PROLOG (Chapter 12), Smalltalk (Chapter 13), and the various alternative programming paradigms discussed in Chapter 6.

Programming languages deal with different kinds of entities. Some of these entities are data-level objects and some are program-level objects. For example, a *constant* is a data-level object, while a *function* is a program-level object. A constant has several characteristics associated with it, including a value, a type, and possibly a name. A function has a name, a type, and a list of parameters (functions are discussed in Chapter 5). These entities might be called programming's static aspects; its dynamic aspects are those that deal with control, the subject of Chapter 6.

4.1 CONSTANTS AND VARIABLES

Constants. A constant is a data item that remains unchanged throughout the execution of the program. Constants may be used *literally* or they may be *named*.

A *literal* is a data value that is used explicitly (or, literally) in a program. We can speak of a *numeric literal* (sometimes called a *numeric constant*) such as 3.33 or .235E − 02. Numeric literals may be made up from the numeric digits 0 through 9 and the special characters +, −, ., and E. A string literal may be composed of any valid characters in the language's character set and is often enclosed in single or double quotations marks, for example, 'NAME THIS QUOTE'.

Some languages have other sorts of literals, such as the logical constants of FORTRAN (**.TRUE., .FALSE.**) and ALGOL-like languages (**true, false**).

Named constants are sometimes termed *symbolic constants* or *figurative constants*. These constants look like variables because they are identified by a name. However, they are permanently bound to their values, which remain unchanged during the run and, in fact, are protected from change the same as literals. Examples may be found in COBOL's use of **SPACE, ZERO, HIGH-VALUE**, and **LOW-VALUE** and anything declared in Pascal's **constant** statement, for example:

```
constant PI = 3.1416
```

Variables. A *variable* is a receptacle for storing data values and each variable is associated with a domain of allowable values. The use of variables enables programmers to construct programs for which the actual data values are not needed until execution.

Most variables are related to the real world and use real-world data values. Some variables, however, have no real-world counterparts. These *control variables* exist only in relation to the executing program or in the context of algorithmic computation and have no relevance whatsoever to the outside world. An example of a control variable is the index variable used in looping, or repetition, constructs. Other examples are record names and file names. Program-level control variables are statement labels and subprogram names, which provide a way of identifying and referencing pieces of program text. In this case, the program text is actually treated as if it were data.

A variable has a name, one or more attributes, a value, and a storage location. Another characteristic of a variable may be its scope. The name and some or all of a variable's attributes are provided implicitly (in other words, just by using it) or by declarations. Some typical attributes are initial value, storage sharing, scope and, of course, type. The type attribute may be the most important since it determines the domain of values that the variable is allowed to take on and the set of operations that may be performed on the variable.

Values may be provided for variables in one of three ways:

1. By initialization when the variable is created. This can occur either by a special initialization statement or by default as, for example, in the case of BASIC, which initializes all variables to zero when program execution begins.

2. By an input operation.

3. By assigning a value in an assignment statement.

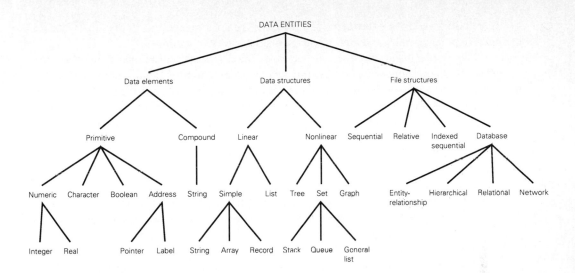

Figure 4.1 Classification of data entities

In the latter case, the variable named on the left side of the assignment operator is the *target*, or receiving field. In other words, it is the variable that is receiving the assigned value. The right side of the assignment operator, even if it also contains a variable (or other reference), represents the value to be imputed to the target. Therefore, a statement such as: $K := K + 1$, which would be considered hopeless in mathematics, is perfectly fine in "computerese." In addition, this is as good a place as any to point out that the assignment operator is definitely *not* an equal sign (which, in mathematics, is a logical operator), not even in FORTRAN, which actually does use an equal sign to denote assignment. (In FORTRAN, by the way, "equal" is denoted by **.EQ.** .)

4.2 CATEGORIES OF DATA

There is no universal agreement about the classification of data-level entities. We will discuss these entities according to the classification tree presented in Fig. 4.1.

The most basic data entity is the *data element*. These data elements may be grouped together to form simple or complex *structures*. The choice of a language often implies the choice of a set of data elements and structures. Of course, special-purpose languages will probably have specialized, built-in structures for particular applications. Examples are SNOBOL's string, LISP's list, SETL's set, and SIMSCRIPT's queue.

Data Elements

Data elements are the building blocks from which complicated data structures and large databases are ultimately composed.

Primitive data elements. Primitive data elements are those that can be directly operated on by machine-language instructions. For example:

Numeric elements such as integers and floating-point real numbers may be operated on by the arithmetic operators. Integers are whole, nonfractional numbers that may be positive or negative. Integers are more restrictive in their domains than are real-valued numbers, and they may be represented as real numbers. For example, the integer 100,000,000 if represented as a floating-point number might look like: $.1 \times 10^9$ or $.1 \text{ E} + 09$.

Boolean, or *logical*, data elements are binary-valued entities operated upon by logical operators such as **and, or, not**. A Boolean data element may take on such values as **false, true** or 0,1.

Characters consist of a single character that may be alphabetic, numeric, or a special character. Character values vary, to some extent, depending on the character set used by the particular language.

Data elements that are addresses. A *label*, while more properly called a *program element* than a data element, is actually the address of a program statement. In this context, however, a label can be thought of as a data element that may be operated on by the **goto** operation.

Pointers also are addresses. Instead of identifying the location of a program element (statement) as does a label, a pointer references or "points to" another (unnamed) data element. Pointers are useful in implementing dynamic data structures and recursive algorithms.

Compound data elements. *Strings*, which are linear sequences of characters, are sometimes considered primitive data elements and sometimes classified as data structures. We will call them *compound data elements* and in doing so place them in a class all by themselves. Strings may be operated on by string functions such as concatenation.

Structures

Data structures are organized collections of data elements that are subject to certain allowable operations. These operations vary from one structure to another and may act on the structure as a whole or on individual (or groups of) component data elements. The description of a data structure must include both a *static aspect*, the description of the relationships among the component data elements, and a *dynamic aspect*, the descriptions of the operations and algorithms for carrying them out. Methods must be set up by which the individual component data elements may be accessed. For example, array components are accessed by means of subscripts and record components are accessed by means of qualified names. Data structures are logical entities in the sense that they are created by programmers to be operated on by high-level programs. These may have little bearing to the physical entities, that is, the storage structures operated on by machine language object code.

The notion of the logical as opposed to the physical is one that will arise many times during the course of your studies and, no doubt, already has. It is easiest if you remember that the *real*, or *physical*, is "what you have." The *logical*, or *virtual*, is "what you think you have." For example, although real main memory is actually limited, in a virtual storage computer system, when a running program needs more memory than is internally available, the system makes use of a high-speed, direct access storage medium instead. The physical size of main memory is what the programmer really has; however, virtual main memory is, from the programmer's point of view, nearly infinite.

It is important at this point to distinguish between data structures and storage structures, and between data structures and file structures.

Storage structures are data structures after they have been mapped to memory. While the data structure is the logical organization of your data, the storage structure represents the way in which your data is physically stored in memory during the execution of your program. For example, suppose you are working with a two-dimensional array. You read values into it, one element at a time, and process it in some way. You access individual elements by the use of two subscripts, one as a row indicator, the other as a column indicator. Your array, say four rows by two columns, is not actually stored in two dimensions in your computer's main memory, but as a linear sequence of elements, probably—since this is the scheme used in most programming languages— in row-major order, e.g.: A(1,1), A(1,2), A(2,1), A(2,2), A(3,1), A(3,2), A(4,1), A(4,2).

To some extent, the data structures as implemented in most programming languages are really (at least, in part) storage structures. This is due to the fact that they derive some of their properties from assumptions about or limitations of storage.

File structures refer to data residing in secondary storage, that is, outside the world of the program. When program execution terminates, the storage structures no longer exist. Neither do the data structures although, in a sense, they never did. Only the file structures survive termination of the program. Some typical file structures are the sequential, random (or direct), indexed sequential, and multikey methods of organization.

4.3 DATA TYPES

A *data type* is composed of a domain of data elements and a set of operations that act on those elements—operations that can construct, destroy, or modify instances of those data elements. Every programming language has some built-in data types. Some of the most common are integer, real (e.g., floating-point), and Boolean. Other types are character (or alphanumeric), string, and pointer. Some languages have built-in structured data types such as lists or records.

In addition, some languages have facilities for the definition of new data types by the user. ALGOL68 and Pascal were the first programming languages to provide the programmer with a means for defining new data types. A *typing system* is a facility for defining new types and for declaring variables to be of such types. A typing system may be used to define a complex data structure such as a record, a multidimensional array, or a file. It may be used to set up a "template" for declaration of several scalar or structured variables that may be described in the same way. This carries with it the advantage that changes to the declaration need be done only once, to the template, no matter how many variables are declared using this template. A typing system may also have the capability for *type checking*, which may be *static* or *dynamic*, depending on whether this checking is done at compile time or during execution.

A *strongly typed programming language* is one in which the types of all variables are determined at compile time. Programs written in a strongly typed language must explicitly declare all programmer-defined words, making them more readable and maintainable and, generally, more reliable. Storage requirements for global and local variables are determined completely during compile time. A strongly typed programming language may include a typing facility for defining new types. Pascal, MODULA-2, and Ada are considered to be strongly typed languages.

With *dynamic typing*, variables are not bound to type at compile time. Languages that allow for dynamic typing of variables utilize dynamic type checking, which requires the presence of run time routines to check types and perform correct operations such as those involving storage mapping and code selection. For example, the expression $A + B$ will be evaluated differently depending on whether the variables A and B are numeric or, say, string. This is often used in interactive languages such as LISP, SNOBOL, and APL. In object-oriented languages like Smalltalk, each data object keeps track of its own allowable operations, so that a separate type checking facility is not needed. For this reason, Smalltalk is often called a "typeless" language.

Declarations

In languages with static type checking, the program must somehow communicate the types of the variables it uses. For obvious reasons, then, this is also sometimes called *lexical type checking*. The way this type checking is done varies from one programming language to another.

Explicit type declarations. Declarations make up the majority of the non-executable statements found in programming languages. They are primarily related to data rather than to control or program structure. However, in some languages, declarations appear in their own program unit (the **DATA DIVISION** in COBOL, the **PREAMBLE** in SIMSCRIPT) and so contribute considerably to the program structure. In certain languages, subprogram units such as procedures and functions are considered to be declarations, that is, the subprogram is described first (nonexecutable) to be invoked later (executable).

Declarations provide information to the compiler as well as to the human readers of the program. There are declarative statements to describe individual variables, files, and structured variables. Some declarations provide information regarding storage allocation (**DIMENSION** in FORTRAN, **CONTROLLED** in PL/1), user-defined types (**type** in Pascal), and the computing environment (the **ENVIRONMENT DIVISION** in COBOL). Declarations allow for early binding of a variable to its attributes, including the type attribute.

Complete knowledge of variable types at compile time leads to a more efficient object program because of:

1. More efficient allocation of storage. As an example, a logical variable can be stored in the same way as an integer, but that would be wasteful when all that is needed is a single bit.

2. More efficient routines at run time. For example, the + operator in the expression $A + B$ is handled differently depending upon whether A and B are integers or real numbers.

Even though many programming languages have the means for explicit declarations of type and other attributes, they do not all handle it in the same way. In COBOL, type declarations are done in the **DATA DIVISION** using such clauses as **PICTURE** and **USAGE**. In Pascal and other ALGOL-like languages, type declarations are placed at the front of the program (and at the front of each procedure for local declarations) using such keywords as **integer**, **real**, and **Boolean**. In SIMSCRIPT, a general-purpose, problem-oriented language for simulation programming, all (global) variable declarations including type declarations are placed in a separate "routine," called a **PREAMBLE**, which must be the first routine in the program. FORTRAN has separate declarative statements for **INTEGER**, **REAL**, and **COMPLEX**. However, these are not the only way of declaring a variable's type in FORTRAN.

Implicit type declarations. In some languages, such as FORTRAN, BASIC, and PL/1, the type of a variable may be implicitly declared simply by using it. Variables with names that begin with the letters I through N are automatically associated with the integer type and storage is allocated accordingly. Variables with names that begin with any other letter are taken to be real-valued. These are defaults that can be overridden by explicit declarations. Not all languages are so flexible and, indeed, any benefits from implicit declarations are widely considered to be outweighed by benefits attributed to explicit declarations, such as increased readability and decreased tendency toward error. In Pascal, for example, a strong typing facility allows no implicit declarations whatsoever: Any variable used anywhere in the program must have been previously declared explicitly.

Scalar Data Types

Fig. 4.2 classifies data types over two dimensions, according to whether they are scalar (simple) or structured types, and whether they are generally built into the language or may be defined by the programmer. This classification will naturally vary slightly from one language to another.

The following are some scalar types commonly found in many programming languages in current use. A scalar data type has a domain composed only of individual primitive data elements.

Numeric types. Numeric-type variables are sometimes known as *computational* since it is reasonable to perform computations with them. Numeric variables are related to or represent quantities in the outside world. However, whereas in the outside world these types may have infinite domains, in the world of computer processing their domains are definitely finite. The domain, or the set of allowable values, for any data type is limited by the size of word storage for the particular computer system. In COBOL, for example, the largest integer possible would be denoted by the figurative constant **HIGH-VALUES**; in Pascal, by the standard identifier **maxint**.

Some numeric types are integer, floating-point, fixed-point, and complex numbers. The operations performed on numeric-type data are the arithmetic operations such as addition (+), subtraction (−), multiplication (*), division (/) and, sometimes, exponentiation (** or ^)—except in the case of Pascal and MODULA-2, which believe that programmers who are silly enough to want to perform exponentiation should be required to

	Scalar	Structured
Built-in	Integer Real Character Boolean	String List Array Record
User-defined	Enumerated Subtype	Stack Queue Abstract data type

Figure 4.2   Data types

code their own functions to do it. Although the operator looks the same (+, −, ...) for different types of numeric operands, the actual arithmetic performed at the machine level can be very different depending on the type of the data being operated on.

Integers, the whole numbers or counting numbers, may be considered a subset of real-valued numbers in the outside world, but that is not the case in computer processing. In the world of the computer they are distinct, separate types, and they are assigned to storage in totally different ways. Sometimes the term "real" is used to refer to noninteger numeric types that are not complex. However, due to limitations on the number of significant digits that can be stored in the computer, real numbers aren't truly real, at least not in the sense used in mathematics. For example, the quantity π in storage will have a different value depending on how storage has been allocated (for example, single precision or double precision) or the number of significant digits declared by the programmer. This will affect the accuracy of the program accessing that value. Integers, too, are not a subset of real values in computer processing, and are not necessarily accurately represented within the "real-valued" domains. For example, the relation J = TRUNC (FLOAT(J)), which compares an integer J to J converted to a real-valued number and then truncated, is not necessarily **true**, although one might initially expect it to be.

Floating-point numbers have two components: a fractional portion, the mantissa, and an exponent, the scaling factor. *Fixed-point numbers* generally have a limited number of significant digits after the decimal point. Some languages have other numeric types. For example, FORTRAN boasts such types as *double precision*, which is floating-point taking up two words in storage for greater accuracy, and *complex*, two floating-point numbers representing the real component and the imaginary component of a complex number.

Logical.   Logical, or Boolean, variables can take on only two values, say, **true** and **false**, which may be represented in the machine as 1 and 0. Conditional expressions also result in logical values. Operations on logical data are performed by the logical operators **and**, **not**, **or**.

Pointer.   A pointer is a reference to an object or data element. A pointer variable is an identifier whose value is a reference to an object. Pointers are used to create and organize data structures. Languages with a built-in pointer data type include Pascal, MODULA-2, and Ada. The pointer type is important for the dynamic allocation of a previously undetermined amount of data and for defining linear and nonlinear relationships among data elements. In addition, pointers permit data to reside on several lists simultaneously.

Pointer variables point to and provide the means for accessing unnamed, or *anonymous*, variables. Consequently, operations on pointers must distinguish between operations on the pointer variable itself and operations on the quantity to which the pointer is pointing. In Pascal, for example, assignment of a location to a pointer variable is denoted by p := q while assignment of a value to the element pointed to by a pointer variable is denoted by p^ := q^. Notation for pointers is far from uniform across programming languages that have such facilities.

Structured Data Types

A *structured data type* has domain elements that are themselves composed of other scalar or structured type elements. Some languages provide special structured types for the purpose of aggregating data elements so that they may be treated as a single unit. Generally, we expect such built-in structured types to allow for access to the entire structure (by a structure-level name) and access to the individual components of the structure (by way of component names or subscripts). Some structured types are strings, lists, arrays, and records.

Strings. A string is an ordered sequence of characters that increases and decreases dynamically (over time). Although a character string may be implemented by the programmer using an array, some languages do provide for a string type. Some operations on strings are concatenation, substring formation, and comparisons. There must also be a way of determining the length of the string since strings, unlike arrays, are dynamic structures that are expected to grow and shrink in size as execution progresses. This is often implemented by the string function **LENGTH**(STRING). String operations may be represented in different ways. For example, concatenation may be represented by the + operator or by the built-in function **CONCAT**(STRING). Notice that in a language that uses the + operator for concatenation as well as for arithmetic addition, type checking of the operands is desirable, to say the least.

Lists. Although a list is sometimes classified as a type of string it is actually quite different. A list is an ordered sequence of components, which may themselves be lists. This means that, while the formal definition appears to be of a linear structure, the result may be anything but linear. We will see an example of this later on in this chapter.

Fig. 4.3 displays a simple list storage structure that might correspond to the LISP list: (Sunday, Monday, Tuesday, Wednesday, Thursday, Friday, Saturday). In LISP, lists are represented as lists of linked pointers to atoms. In LISP, the list type is assumed; it does not need a declaration.

In list processing languages like LISP, the individual components of a list are not directly accessible as they would be in, say, an array. Thus, different methods of processing must be used. Often this takes the form of picking off the first element of the list (the *head*), examining or processing it in some way, and then recursively processing the rest

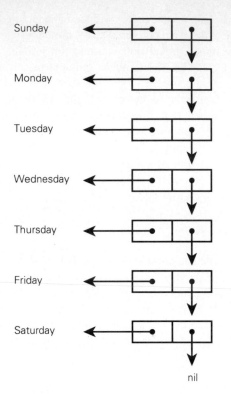

Figure 4.3   List storage structure

of the list (the *tail*) in the same way. In LISP, this is implemented by the famous CAR function (returns the head) and CDR function (returns the tail).

In languages without a built-in list type, lists may be constructed by the programmer using pointer variables to link the components together. The following Pascal declarations define the linked list structure pictured in Fig. 4.4.

```
type DayType = (Sunday, Monday, Tuesday, Wednesday, Thursday, Friday,
                Saturday);
     Link = ^DayRec;
     DayRec = record
         OneDay : DayType;
         NextDay : Link;
         end; {DayList record}
var  DayList : DayRec;
     FirstDay: Link;
```

Arrays.   By its strict, formal definition, an *array* is a fixed-size, ordered collection of data elements all of the same type. Thus, an array variable (sometimes called a *subscripted variable*) has at least two attributes: type and size. The *dynamic arrays* inno-

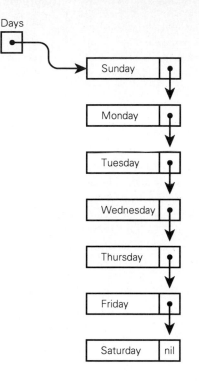

Figure 4.4 Linked list

vated by ALGOL60 relaxed the "fixed-size" restriction of this definition. Access to array components is accomplished by means of subscripts on the array name. For example, for storage to or retrieval from the third sequential component in a one-dimensional array called A, we use the subscripted name A(3). In addition, some languages provide "macro" array operations—operations that are performed on an entire array structure so that the programmer does not have to access each component one at a time (inside of a looping construct). For example, in PL/1, the statement A = B + 1 adds one to every component of the array B and assigns the result to the corresponding component in A. A and B must be declared to be of the same type and size.

Records. The record, also called the *hierarchical* or *structured type*, is an ordered collection of data elements that are not necessarily of the same type. Record components, often called *fields*, are accessed by name rather than by subscript. For example, in COBOL, the first programming language to include this sort of built-in type:

```
01  COMPLEX-NUMBER.
    05  REAL-PART         PICTURE        V99999.
    05  IMAGINARY-PART    PICTURE        V99999.
```

And, in Pascal:

```
type CompNo = record;
            RealPart:                    real;
            ImaginaryPart:               real;
end;    (* CompNo record definition *)
var ComplexNumber:                       Compno;
```

User-defined Types

Some languages, such as ALGOL68, Pascal, and Ada, allow the programmer to define and use new data types. Besides enhancing the readability and clarity of the program text, the capability for user-defined types makes it possible, firstly, to define a complicated data structure once and then create as many instances (variables of that type) of it as necessary and, secondly, to use the language's own type-checking facility—part of the same typing system that enabled the definition of the new type—for input data validation such as range or consistency checking.

Enumerated. This user-defined type provides for the enumeration of the domain of the type by the programmer. The domain values are listed in a declarative statement. For example,

```
type DayType = (Sunday, Monday, Tuesday, Wednesday, Thursday, Friday,
            Saturday);
```

Subtype. This is the specification of the domain as a subrange of another, already existing type. For example, in Pascal,

```
type Digits= 0..9; (* a subtype of integer *)
type Workday = Monday..Friday; (* a subtype of DayType *)
```

The term *user-defined type* is actually a misnomer if we suscribe to the definition of a data type as encompassing domain and operations. The enumerated and subrange definitions do not allow for specification of operations, only domain. A data abstraction facility comes closer to allowing for the definition of a new type, called an *abstract data type*.

Abstract Data Types

Abstract data types are not merely an extension of user-defined types, but a whole new way of computing. The concept of data abstraction arose from the research into structured programming methodology, was implemented in a variety of experimental and nonexperimental languages including MODULA-2 and Ada, and evolved into the *classes* of object-oriented programming languages such as Smalltalk.

Using a data abstraction facility, the domain values of and operations on a new data type may be defined and encapsulated so that the type can be used in many parts of the program and by many different programs (and different programmers) without concern for the details of the implementation. Abstract data types are discussed further in Section 4.6 and Chapter 10.

4.4 DATA STRUCTURES

Data structures are organized collections of data objects. The components of a data structure may be either unstructured data elements or they may themselves be structured. The term *data structures* refers to the logical organization of data and the operations that may be performed on them.

It must be stressed here that a data structure does not necessarily refer to anything physical or concrete. It does not necessarily describe the way data has been organized on magnetic permanent storage (such as a floppy diskette). That would be called a *file structure*. It does not describe the way data is organized in the storage locations of main memory (e.g., RAM) while your program is working on it. That would be called a *storage structure*. A data structure refers purely to the *logical organization* of your data: the way you the programmer like to think about it, or the way it most resembles the data used by humans in the real, outside world.

Data structures may be classified in several different ways such as, for example, linear versus nonlinear or static versus dynamic. A linear, as opposed to nonlinear, data structure is one in which the individual components are an ordered sequence. A *static structure* is one that has no capacity for change, specifically with regard to its size attribute, during the course of execution. Arrays and records are examples of static linear structures. A *dynamic structure* is able to change over time as program execution proceeds.

We saw in the previous section that some programming languages provide built-in data types for certain, frequently used data structures such as strings, arrays, and records. In addition, certain languages allow the programmer to define new data types by specifying their domains. One of the reasons for doing so is to more easily represent and use data structures that have not been built into the language design. Unfortunately, merely defining relationships among data elements is not sufficient. In order to completely specify a data structure one must indicate not only the way the data is organized but also the operations that are allowable on the structure and the detailed algorithms for carrying out those operations. So, for example, the **type** statement of Pascal is not really a good vehicle for completely specifying a data structure. Later in this chapter, we will discuss a concept that enables a programmer to "extend" a programming language to include (for example) data structures that are not part of the original design. This technique is called *data abstraction* and there are already several modern languages that have a facility for defining and implementing abstract data types.

Any data structure may be described by the relationships among the data elements it contains and by the operations that it may receive.

Relationships in Data Structures

The rules by which data elements are organized into structures obviously differ from structure to structure, but they can be generally described in terms of one or more of the following structuring relationships.

Hierarchical.   The hierarchical relationship is the prevalent one in record structures. It can be stated as: *R contains S*, where R is a structure and S is an element or a

Figure 4.5   Linked list

structure. For example, using the following selected **DATA DIVISION** declarations from a COBOL program,

```
01    EMPLOYEE-RECORD.
      05 ID-NUMBER              PICTURE ...
      05 EMPLOYEE-NAME.
          10    LAST-NAME       PICTURE ...
          10    FIRST-NAME      PICTURE ...
          10    MID-INITIAL     PICTURE ...
      05 TITLE                  PICTURE ...
      05 PAY-RATE               PICTURE ...

      ...
```

we can say that EMPLOYEE-RECORD contains EMPLOYEE-NAME and that EMPLOYEE-NAME contains LAST-NAME.

Successor.   The successor relationship is important in all data structures lending themselves toward *linked allocation*, which will be discussed later in this chapter. These include linear structures, such as strings, arrays, and lists, as well as trees and directed graphs. This sort of relationship organizes the data structure by defining an ordering of the data elements, and may be stated as follows: *Q is a successor of P*. The most important question with regard to data structures organized in this way is: what data element is *next*? For example, Fig. 4.5 highlights a section of a generalized linked list in which node Q follows and is pointed to by node P. This successor relationship applied recursively can serve to define the entire structure.

Equivalence.   The equivalence relationship states: *A is equivalent to B*. The equivalence relationship is implied in equality, in other words, if *A* and *B* are equal, they must be equivalent. This relationship is actually more important in testing data structures for certain conditions than in organizing the structure in the first place. Equivalent data structures share a common structure so that element-by-element operations will be carried out correctly. For example, arrays *A* and *B* are equivalent if they both have the same number of rows, columns, etc. The arrays in Fig. 4.6 are equivalent since they are both 2 × 3 arrays. This sort of relationship is important in certain programming languages with powerful array processing capabilities, for example, APL and PL/1. In processing tree structures, the equivalence relation is equally important. For example, the two binary trees of Fig. 4.6 are equivalent since their structure is the same. Two structures may be equivalent, but not *equal*, if they do not contain the same data values.

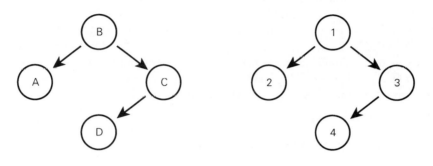

10	40	30
60	20	50

623	99	472
901	344	101

(a) Equivalent arrays

(b) Equivalent binary trees

Figure 4.6   Equivalent data structures

Operations on Data Structures

The relationships described above are concerned with the static part of the definition of a data structure, its *specification*. There must also be a dynamic part to this definition, including algorithms for the specialized operations appropriate to a particular data structure. Each of these operations can usually be considered to belong to one of the following operation categories. For any data structure, we need methods for *creating* (allocating, building up) and *destroying* (deallocating, breaking down) the structures; we need methods for gaining *access* to the values of the individual components of the structure; and we need to be able to perform *tests* for certain conditions. Clearly, all programming languages will not be able to accommodate all the operations necessary for all possible data structures. That is one of the reasons that some languages are better suited for certain applications than are others.

We will use the term *function* repeatedly to describe these operations even though some operations can be more appropriately coded using procedures or subroutines and even though some operations (access to array elements, for example) cannot be appropriately coded into a subprogram at all.

Figure 4.7   A two-dimensional array

Constructors.   Constructor functions create or build up data structures. In PL/1 or SIMSCRIPT, for example, space for a data structure can be dynamically allocated when it is created by explicitly requesting such space using **ALLOCATE** in PL/1 or **RESERVE** in SIMSCRIPT. In Pascal, space for a locally declared (built-in type) data structure is implicitly requested and automatically allocated upon entering the block in which it is declared. An example of a constructor function that creates and builds up an array structure is APL's ρ. The APL statement:

$$2\ 3\ \rho\ 1\ 2\ 3\ 4\ 5\ 6$$

sets up the 2×3 array pictured in Fig. 4.7.

Destructors.   Destructor functions destroy, or break down, data structures. Some destructor functions break a data structure into smaller structures or into its component elements. An example would be the decomposition of a large string into substrings or the stack POP operation. Other destructors deallocate the space that had been reserved for the data structure and return the newly freed storage back to the system. An example is the **FREE** statement in PL/1. Implicit destruction (deallocation) of a locally defined data structure is accomplished in a language like Pascal simply by exiting the block in which the local structure was created.

Access.   Access functions provide access to the individual components and to groups of components of a data structure by means of one of a variety of referencing methods. Access may be accomplished:

1. By qualified name, as in the case of a record structure. As an example of a qualified name, referring to the COBOL record description above, we would be able to refer to EMPLOYEE-NAME **OF** EMPLOYEE-RECORD.
2. By location or subscript, as in the case of an array component. For example, X := A(2).
3. By name, as in the case of array-level operations. For example, in PL/1: A = B, where A and B are equivalent arrays.

Predicates.   These Boolean functions test a data structure for the presence of a particular property. Some commonly used predicates include tests for an empty (or full) structure (**nil** in LISP), for set membership (the $\subset$ operator in APL), and for a particular substring (**INDEX, VERIFY** in PL/1).

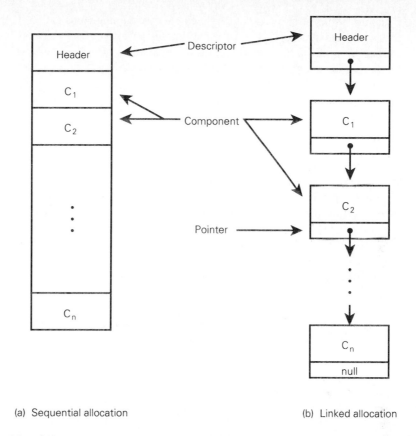

(a) Sequential allocation   (b) Linked allocation

Figure 4.8   Storage structures

Storage Structures

There are two ways in which storage can be allocated for most data structures. These are *sequential allocation* and *linked allocation*. A sequentially allocated structure may be called a *static* structure since it is incapable of change throughout its lifetime. A structure that has been stored by means of linked allocation may be called a *dynamic* structure, implying that change is possible. These structures are able to grow and shrink dynamically as execution progresses. These two allocation methods are represented by the storage structures pictured in Fig. 4.8 which, while they can be used to represent any linear structure, for simplicity of description we will say is a one-dimensional array.

Static structures use *implicit ordering*, in which components are ordered by virtue of their sequential ordering in the structure (i.e., first, second, ...). Dynamic structures employ *explicit ordering*, in which each component contains within itself the address of the next item so that it is in effect "pointing" to its own successor.

Sequential storage allocation is the only method available in languages such as FORTRAN and COBOL, which are capable only of static memory allocation. With sequential allocation, a single block of contiguous storage locations is allocated for the structure. More often than not, the elements are homogenous (all of the same type) so that every element takes up the same amount of space. Thus, access is easily accomplished by use of a base address plus an offset value. The base address is the address of the header or descriptor; the offset value is the relative location (subscript) multiplied by the size of each component.

With linked allocation, each component has two parts: one containing the original data element (or structure) and the other containing a pointer to the next component. The value of this pointer is the address of the next component in the structure. Linked representation is usually used for variable-size dynamic structures such as strings, lists, stacks, and queues (and nonlinear data structures), although it can also be used to represent arrays and records. The entire structure is not allocated at once, but each component is allocated as it is needed from a pool of available storage locations. An example of a dynamic, linked structure is the list structure of LISP. Many languages, including Pascal and Ada, restrict a particular declared pointer variable to point only to elements of the same specific type.

One language that is interesting in its treatment of data structures is SIMSCRIPT. While SIMSCRIPT offers the programmer a variety of data structures, they are all mapped to storage using linked allocation, making this one of the few languages that is capable of handling a so-called "ragged array," pictured in Fig. 4.9. The logical data structure in part (a) of the figure illustrates the idea of, in this case, a two-dimensional array in which some of the cells will not be used and, indeed, do not exist. (Later, in Fig. 4.11, you will see some specialized arrays that could easily and efficiently be represented as ragged arrays.) Fig. 4.9(b) depicts the storage structure for this ragged array, as it would be implemented in SIMSCRIPT. Notice that this unusual data structure is accomplished by the allocation of a one-dimensional array of pointers, each of which points to its own one-dimensional array of some declared length. (These lengths may be read in as data). This allocation method follows the mathematical definition of a two (or more) dimensional array as a vector of vectors.

The disadvantages of static structures as compared to dynamic structures are:

- full storage remains allocated during the entire run or, at least, until the block in which the structure was declared has terminated;
- in order to avoid overflow, static structures are usually allocated more space than they will need, making them even less efficient;
- insertions and deletions to or from the middle of an ordered structure (say, an array) means moving many components in order to maintain the ordering scheme.

The disadvantages of dynamic structures are:

- the extra storage space required for the link or pointer field;
- the longer time required to search the structure; that is, it takes longer to jump from one address to another (to another) than it does to increment a subscript variable and access an array component by subscript.

It is worth noting that the time it takes for the array reference itself is not dependent on either the size of the array or the position referenced.

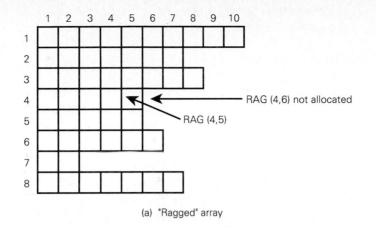

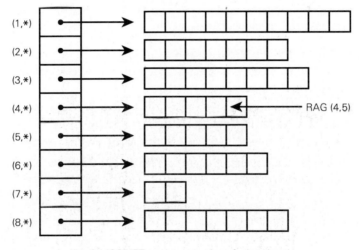

(a) "Ragged" array

(b) SIMSCRIPT storage mapping of ragged array

Figure 4.9 Ragged array

In languages that allow for linked allocation, there is often a choice. You may decide that your data structure is to be mapped to storage in either sequential or linked fashion. The choice is similar to the one between a sequential file organization and a random/direct file organization. In this case, however, sequential allocation provides for direct access to components (by means of subscripts), while linked allocation is capable only of sequential searches over paths provided by the links or pointers. Sequential allocation appears to be more efficient since each component takes up less storage space and searches through the structure are easily accomplished by varying the subscript in a loop. However, they turn out to be much less efficient in cases where the size of the array is not known until the program is already executing or the size of the structure varies over the course of execution.

Linear Data Structures

The linear data structures are those for which the component elements can be said to form an ordered sequence. These include: strings, arrays, lists, stacks, queues, and records. We will see that, while a list is a linear structure, it can also be used to construct a tree that is a nonlinear structure.

Strings.   A string is an ordered set of data elements of dynamically changing size. It follows, then, that a string has at least two attributes: type and length. *Type* refers to the domain for the individual data elements of the string. Typical types for string elements are character, bit, and numeric digit. *Length* refers to the number of elements in the string, and is a dynamic quantity that changes continually as the string is created, modified, and operated on. Most of the time, when we speak of a string, we mean "a character string" or, in other words, a string (ordered sequence) of characters. This is often enclosed in single or double quotation marks, as in: STR = 'FOR SURE'.

Some typical string operations are:

1. **CONCAT**enation, creating a string from smaller strings;
2. **SUBSTR**ing, creating a string from a sequence of elements in a larger string (e.g., by copying the sequence);
3. **INDEX**, a Boolean function that tests for the presence of a substring in a larger string and indicates where the substring begins;
4. **LENGTH**, an integer function that returns the number of components in the string;
5. Text processing operations such as **INSERT, DELETE, REPLACE**, which operate on character strings, or portions of character strings.

There are some specialized programming languages for string handling. SNOBOL is an example. These languages are useful for text processing and formula manipulation, among other applications. List processing languages such as LISP may also be used for string handling, since a list may be used to represent a string. In addition, PL/1 has extensive string processing facilities. COBOL, on the other hand, has a limited ability to manipulate simple string structures; FORTRAN and ALGOL have virtually none. Sometimes, in APL for example, a string may be treated like an array. However, in languages that do not provide dynamic storage allocation (e.g., FORTRAN) this ends up being a very awkward representation since strings by their definition ought to be allowed to increase and decrease in length as execution proceeds. To declare a string structure and allocate storage to it dynamically, we would use, in PL/1:

```
DECLARE STRING CHARACTER (*) CONTROLLED;
...
ALLOCATE STRING CHAR(LENGTH(INPUT));
STRING = INPUT;
...
FREE STRING;
...
```

Arrays.   The array is probably the most familiar data structure since it is highly efficient for use on a digital computer. It also happens to be the simplest data structure.

A one-dimensional array, which we recognize from mathematics as a vector, may be defined as a *fixed-size*, *ordered* set of *homogeneous* data elements. *Fixed-size* means that there is a specified number of elements in the array and that this number does not change over the course of execution of the program. Thus, by this definition, an array is a static structure. Some languages allow for "dynamic" arrays in which this restriction is relaxed. *Ordered* means that the components are arranged so that there is a first, a second, and so on. *Homogeneous* means that all the components of the structure are of the same type. In that sense, the entire array can be said to have a type. While this definition of a one-dimensional array can probably apply loosely to an array of two or more dimensions, such a matrix or multidimensional array can be more formally defined as a vector of vectors—in other words, a vector, or one-dimensional array structure in which the individual components are themselves array structures.

An array structure is called for when it is necessary to keep a large number of data items in storage at the same time and to process them in a uniform manner. Arrays are used for storing tables of constants (look-up tables), for organizing experimental data for subsequent statistical analysis, and for any process that requires the computational methods of matrix algebra. Arrays of two (or more) dimensions are useful for organizing data dependent on two (or more) variables. For example, of the hourly pay rate look-up tables of Fig. 4.10, the two-dimensional table of part (a) shows the rates classified on two dimensions, or characteristics: the length of time an employee has been with the firm and a type of job classification. In Fig. 4.10 (b), the same data has been reclassified on three dimensions to illustrate that job categories 3 and 4 of part (a) were actually management-level job classes.

The *dimensionality* of an array structure refers to the number of directions on which it is defined. An array will have as many subscripts as it has dimensions, that is, one for rows, one for columns, etc. Sometimes it helps to visualize a three-dimensional array as a book containing many two-dimensional matrices of data elements, one on each page of the book. Then, the first subscript represents row number, the second represents column number, and the third represents page number.

In defining an array structure, the important attributes are: the type of the array, meaning the type of the component data elements; the dimensionality of the array; and the number of elements, or the size, in each direction.

Construction of an array structure is often accomplished by simply declaring it in the program or procedure in which it will be used; sometimes not even a declaration is necessary. Similarly, destruction of the array is most often accomplished by termination of the program or procedure. Access to any array component, for purposes of storage and retrieval, is usually done by means of a subscript attached to the array name. Some possible operations on arrays are SEARCHing for a particular stored value and SORTing the array in order by the value stored (or by a key value in the case of an array of records). Sorting techniques for arrays are called *internal sorts* since during execution of the sort algorithm all the data to be ordered is in main memory (*internal* storage) all at the same time.

Certain specialized arrays may present special storage problems if they are to utilize storage space in the most efficient way possible. Some special types of arrays are illustrated in Fig. 4.11. These are (a) the symmetric matrix, (b) the triangular matrix, (c)

Hourly Pay Rate

Tenure with Firm	Job Class			
	1	2	3	4
less than 1 year	13.80	20.70	33.20	40.07
2–5 years	14.98	22.35	36.68	45.03
6–10 years	15.92	25.01	40.03	49.98
11–20 years	16.94	27.06	44.08	54.37
21–40 years	18.06	29.08	49.54	60.04

(a) Two-dimensional pay rate table

Hourly Pay Rate

Tenure with Firm	Non-Management		Management	
	Job Class		Job Class	
	1	2	1	2
less than 1 year	13.80	20.70	33.20	40.07
2–5 years	14.98	22.35	36.68	45.03
6–10 years	15.92	25.01	40.03	49.98
11–20 years	16.94	27.06	44.08	54.37
21–40 years	18.06	29.08	49.54	60.04

(b) Three-dimensional pay rate table

Figure 4.10   Multidimensional Arrays

the band matrix, and (d) the sparse matrix. Cells that are pictured as blank actually contain zeros. Matrices with nonzero elements only on the diagonal (the famous identity matrix is of this type) are a special case of the band matrix. All of these arrays share a problem with space efficiency. If they are simply stored as shown, as complete two-dimensional arrays, there is much wasted storage space. In the case of the symmetric matrix, only half needs to be stored, since the other half is repeated. In the case of the sparse matrix, less than 10 percent of the storage is used for nonzero data values.

The problem of storing these arrays efficiently is an intriguing one, and has been studied in many different ways. One possible solution is to use the "ragged array" structure described previously. Each nonzero data element in the sparse matrix can be efficiently stored as a triplet of values, (row-index, column-index, value). For more on this subject, consult the references at the end of this chapter.

(a) Symmetric matrix

4	2	1	3	8
2	9	0	7	3
1	0	6	4	1
3	7	4	2	1
8	3	1	1	8

(b) Triangular matrix

4	2	1	3	8
	9	1	7	3
		6	4	1
			2	1
				8

(c) Band matrix

4	2			
6	9	1		
	3	6	4	
		7	2	1
			2	8

(d) Sparse matrix

	1					2			
					1	1			
			2						3
1									

Figure 4.11   Specialized arrays

Lists.   A list is a generalized, dynamic, linear data structure, which may be simply defined as an ordered set of components. While these components, called *nodes*, are not necessarily all of the same type, many implementations will insist on homogeneity. An array is sometimes considered to be a specific instance of the list structure.

Lists expand and shrink with the passage of time; that is why they are called dynamic structures. Fig. 4.12 illustrates the ease with which a new node may be inserted into its proper position in a generalized linked list called LIST. Each node (often represented as a record structure) contains an additional field, a pointer, which points to the node's own successor. The pointer field of the last node in the list contains a null value in place of an address; it does not point anywhere. Every list must have an external pointer variable pointing to the first node in the list. An empty list is indicated by a null value for the external pointer. This is a *singly linked list*: it points only in one direction. With a *doubly linked list*, each node contains two pointers: one pointing to the node's successor and one pointing to the node's predecessor in the list. In a doubly linked, or two-directional, list searching can be done both forward and backward.

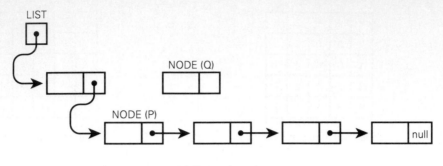

(a) Before insertion

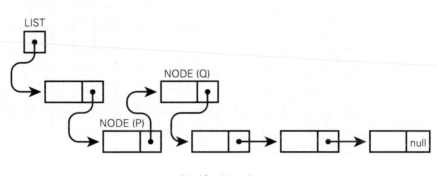

(b) After insertion

Figure 4.12 Node insertion

LIsts and other dynamic structures can be represented in languages that allow only static allocation by using an array to "house" the dynamic structure. When the array is a house for a dynamic structure such as a list, the list is allowed to increase and decrease dynamically inside of the array. The list of Fig. 4.13 could be defined in FORTRAN in the following manner:

```
DIMENSION FRUIT (100), LINK (100)
CHARACTER FRUIT * 10
INTEGER LINK, FIRST
FIRST = 0
```

In COBOL, it would look like this:

```
01   FRUIT-TABLE.
        05   FRUIT-LIST OCCURS 100 TIMES.
             10   FRUIT      PICTURE X(10).
             10   LINK       PICTURE 999.
77   FIRST                   PICTURE  999 VALUE ZERO.
```

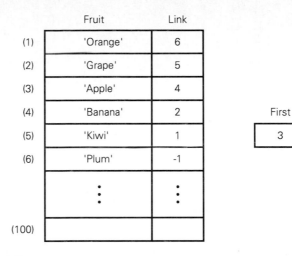

	Fruit	Link
(1)	'Orange'	6
(2)	'Grape'	5
(3)	'Apple'	4
(4)	'Banana'	2
(5)	'Kiwi'	1
(6)	'Plum'	-1
	⋮	⋮
(100)		

First

3

Figure 4.13   A list

Similarly, we can represent other dynamic structures— trees and graphs, for example—as being housed inside sequentially allocated structures.

Operations on a list include:

1. creation/destruction operations;

2. INSERT, which inserts a new component into a specified position in the (possibly ordered) list;

3. REMOVE, which deletes a specified component from the list;

4. SEARCHing a list for a particular value;

5. SORTing a list on a particular key value, although often a list is ordered as it is built up since insertions are easily made into any point in the list;

6. EMPTY, a test for an empty list, usually implemented by testing the external pointer for a null value.

Simple singly linked lists have several specialized forms, among them stacks, queues, and deques. These are pictured in Fig. 4.14. These specialized lists share an important characteristic: The individual nodes that are not at a designated "end" of the list are of absolutely no importance and access to them is not allowed.

A *stack* is an ordered set of items (a list) into which new items may be inserted, and from which items may be deleted, at one end only; that end is called the TOP. Stacks are the most frequently used linear data structure, undoubtedly because they figure so prominently in systems programming (where they are often called "push-down stores"), especially compiler design. Stacks are used for storage management in recursive programming and to implement inherently recursive routines (e.g., the quicksort algorithm) in languages that allow only static memory management. They are used a lot for processing nested program structures such as: bracketed arithmetic/logical expressions; programs

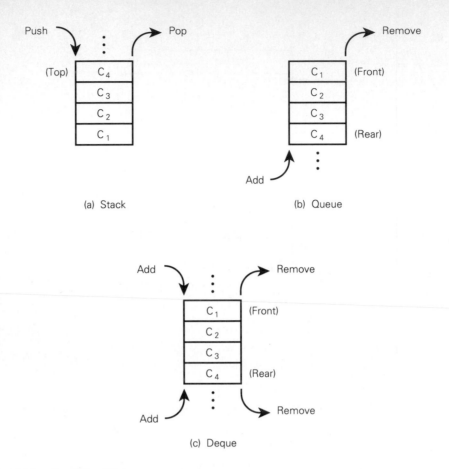

Figure 4.14 Specialized lists

with block structure; statements with matching delimiters such as **if / then / else / end**. Stacks may be used wherever a LIFO-type (last-in first-out) of system is called for. To understand a stack better, picture a stack of trays in a cafeteria: Clean trays come out of the kitchen and are placed on TOP; customers pick up trays from the TOP.

Operations on a stack include

1. creation/destruction operations;

2. PUSH, which inserts (pushes down) a new component onto the TOP of the stack;

3. POP, which deletes (pops off) a component from the TOP of the stack;

4. PEEK, which provides access to the value stored in the TOP location of the stack without POPping it off;

5. EMPTY, a test for an empty stack, usually implemented by testing for TOP = null.

A *queue* is a list into which new items can be inserted at one end only called the REAR (or, sometimes, TAIL) and from which items may be deleted at one end only, the FRONT (or, HEAD). Thus, queue processing requires that a list have two external pointers. Queues are also called *waiting lines* and are appropriate for representing any FIFO-type (first-in first-out) system. Queues are used heavily in simulation programming and are built-in types in such languages as SIMSCRIPT (a general-purpose, simulation language) and GPSS (a highly specialized simulation language). Queues also see heavy use in systems programming, especially job scheduling by the operating system. To understand a queue, picture if you will a line of customers waiting for teller service at a bank.

Operations on a queue include

1. creation/destruction operations;
2. ADD, which inserts a new component at the REAR of the queue;
3. REMOVE, which deletes a component from the FRONT of the queue;
4. EMPTY, a test for an empty queue.

A *deque* is a sort of queue that allows for insertions and deletions at both ends. Deque stands for **D**ouble-**E**nded **QUE**ue. Deques, while not widely implemented, find occasional use in simulation programming and symbol manipulation. An example of a deque is a waiting line (a queue) that allows for priority components: These would be inserted at the FRONT, which might cause the last item in line to be "bumped out" (deletion at the REAR) if the maximum size of the queue has been reached.

Operations on a deque are similar to those on a queue, except that a deque requires two ADD operations and two REMOVE operations—one for the FRONT and one for the REAR .

Multilinked lists.   Each component node of a multilinked list contains two or more pointers and is thus able to reside on several lists simultaneously. Multilinked lists may be used for ordering lists on several different key fields, or for creating and maintaining sublists within a single large list (or, database). Examples of both these uses are shown using the data set in Fig. 4.15 which represents a class of students. The instructor wishes to access this data in various ways: in alphabetic order by name; in order by student identification number; in ascending order of midterm grade; in ascending order of final examination grade. These last two may be for convenient display of minimum and maximum grades, the range, and the median grade. In addition, the instructor wishes to collect information about the students within majors and within classes. Fig. 4.15 illustrates this with three majors and three classes.

A multilinked list is the basis of Study Problem #3 in Chapter 7.

Records.   Records will come up again, specifically in the context of file structures, later in this chapter. However, it is important to understand that the record structure, besides being part of the file structure hierarchy, is a convenient and useful way of organizing data items that are related and yet may be of different types. Perhaps it is to avoid this sort of confusion that some languages with a built-in record type refer to it as a structured type or hierarchical type rather than using the term *record*. As noted above the basic relation inherent in record structures is that of *containment*.

A record as a logical data structure is a fixed-size, ordered collection of possibly heterogeneous components that may themselves be structured. It is desirable to be able to access individual elements, groups of elements, or the entire structure. Fig. 4.16 illus-

	Name		ID	Grade		Major	Class
	Last	First		Midterm	Final		
(1)	Hammett	Dashiel	000780420	75	87	BUSINESS	GR
(2)	Chandler	Raymond	000427241	87	77	BUSINESS	GR
(3)	Parker	Robert B.	101480001	60	90	ENGINERG	SE
(4)	Macdonald	Ross	000531427	99	65	QUANTSCI	GR
(5)	McDonald	Gregory	101481011	55	73	QUANTSCI	SE
(6)	MacDonald	John D.	063485906	94	76	BUSINESS	GR
(7)	Paretsky	Sara	111661010	64	98	BUSINESS	JU
(8)	Kellerman	Faye	111661101	85	79	ENGINERG	JU
(9)	Kellerman	Jonathan	066668003	91	89	ENGINERG	JU
(10)	Spillaine	Mickey	100481111	62	85	ENGINERG	GR
(11)	Stout	Rex	000648888	89	99	QUANTSCI	GR
. . .	. . .	. . .	. . .	. . .	. . .	. . .	. . .
(100)							

(a) The data set

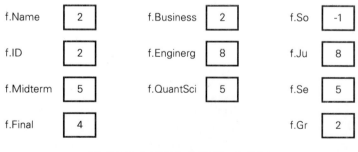

(b) A single node in the list (includes "next" links)

f.Name	2		f.Business	2		f.So	-1
f.ID	2		f.Enginerg	8		f.Ju	8
f.Midterm	5		f.QuantSci	5		f.Se	5
f.Final	4					f.Gr	2

(c) External pointers to first in each list

Figure 4.15 A multilinked list

Contact

Name				Telephone Numbers					
				(1)		(2)		(3)	
Last	First	MI	Ext	Area	Local	Area	Local	Area	Local

Duck	Donald	D	5925	101	1234567	202	2345678	303	3456789

Figure 4.16   A record structure

trates a record structure that may be used as the structure for the individual components in a look-up table represented as a one-dimensional array.

In COBOL, we would define this structure as follows:

```
01   CONTACT.
        05   NAME.
               10   LAST         PICTURE …
               10   FIRST        PICTURE …
               10   MI           PICTURE …
        05   OFFICE-EXT          PICTURE …
        05   TELEPHONE-NUMBERS.
               10 TELEPHONE OCCURS 3 TIMES.
                      15   AREA    PICTURE …
                      15   LOCAL   PICTURE …
```

In Turbo Pascal®:

```
type   String3 = string[3];
       String7 = string[7];
       String4 = string[4];
       String10 = string[10];
       NameRec = record
           Last, First : string10;
           Mid: char;
           end;   {Name record}
       PhoneRec = record
           Area: String3;
           Local: String7;
           end; {Phone record}
       PhoneArray = array[1..3] of PhoneRec;
       ContactRec = record
           Name : NameRec;
           Ext: String4;
           Phone: PhoneArray;
           end; {Contact record}
var Contact: ContactRec;
```

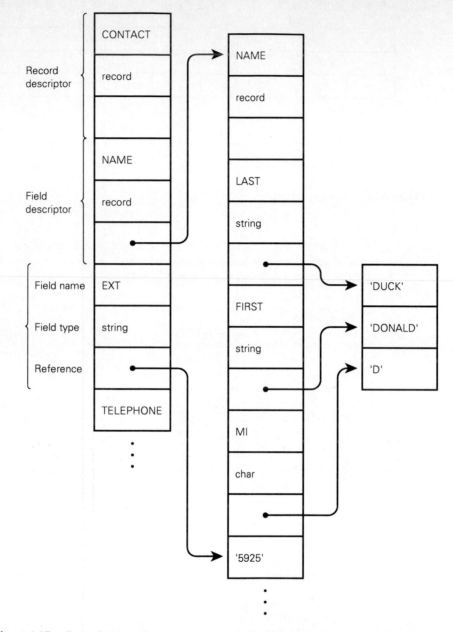

Figure 4.17 Record storage structure

A possible storage structure for a record of this type is depicted in Fig. 4.17.

Although the definition of a record structure includes the fixed-size attribute, there are some exceptions to this rule, for example variant records and variable-length records.

Variant records are records that are allowed to have two or more variations. This means that there will be some fields that are common to all record variations and some

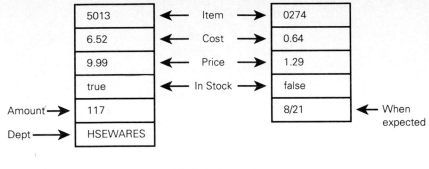

(a) Variant record

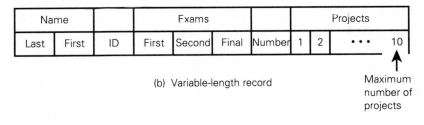

(b) Variable-length record

Maximum number of projects

Figure 4.18 Other kinds of records

fields that are unique to each record variation. In addition, there will be one field that, based on its value, will determine the form that the record will take. Pascal allows declaration of variant records. For example, for the structure depicted in Fig. 4.18 (a):

```
type    String4 = string[4];
        String8 = string[8];
        ItemRec = record
            ItemNumber: String4;
            Cost, Price: real;
        case InStock: boolean of
                false:  (WhenExpected: String4);
                true:   (Amount: integer; Dept: String8);
            end; {ItemRec}
var Item : ItemRec;
```

Variable-length records are similar to variant records. In this case the variation involves the number of a repeated field (which will probably be set up in a table). A specific field on the record will contain the number of components in the repeated field. The structure of Fig. 4.18 (b) can be declared in COBOL as:

```
01   COURSE-DATA.
      05  NAME.
             10   LAST       PICTURE ...
             10   FIRST      PICTURE ...
      05  STUDENT-ID  PICTURE ...
      05  EXAMS.
             10   FIRST      PICTURE 999.
             10   SECOND     PICTURE 999.
             10   FINAL      PICTURE 999.
      05  NUM-PROJECTS       PICTURE 99.
      05  PROJECTS-TABLE.
             10   PROJECTS   OCCURS 10 TIMES DEPENDING ON NUM-PROJECTS
                             PICTURE 999.
```

Nonlinear Data Structures

Sets.   A set is a structure containing an *unordered* collection of *distinct* values. A set is of unspecified size and must be allowed to grow and shrink dynamically as execution proceeds. The characteristic of being unordered distinguishes this structure ·from linear structures such as a list or an array. Since there is no ordering, a set is merely a collection of objects, and so these objects must be distinct in order for the set to be meaningful. Operations on sets include insertion/deletion of individual members; union, intersection, and difference of sets (these are, in a sense, constructor or destructor functions); and tests for membership, subset, superset, etc. The language SETL provides sets as a built-in data structure.

Trees.   A tree is a hierarchical collection of nodes. Each node may be considered the "root" of another tree. There is one node that has no predecessor, called the *root* node. In a tree, the predecessor of a node is called the *parent*, and a successor is called the *child*. Any node with no successor is called a *leaf* node. A collection of trees is sometimes referred to as a *forest*.

A tree can be defined recursively, as a structure in which the individual components are trees or, alternatively, as a list in which the individual components are lists. To illustrate, in Fig. 4.19, the tree structure of part (a) is also represented in part (b) as a LISP-type list structure, corresponding to: (A(B(DE)C(FG))). In this case, while the logical data structure is a tree, the actual storage structure is closer to a list.

Tree structures are useful for representing sequential decisions, game playing, and any branching type of relationship. This includes hierarchical relationships such as organizational management charts, family trees, and record structures. For example, the record structure of Fig. 4.16 can be represented by the tree structure of Fig. 4.20.

Access to a component of this sort of structure can be accomplished by construction of a "path" traversing the tree. The record structure set up in Fig. 4.16 can be accessed in this way. For example, the area code of the second telephone number may be accessed in COBOL by the qualified name AREA **IN** TELEPHONE(2) **IN** CONTACT and in Pascal by the structured name Contact.Telephone.Area[2]. This sort of "hierarchical" name is equivalent to setting up a path along the tree, beginning at the ROOT.

A special type of tree is a *binary tree*, in which each node has at most two children. A *binary search tree* is a binary tree that has been ordered for a binary search, an

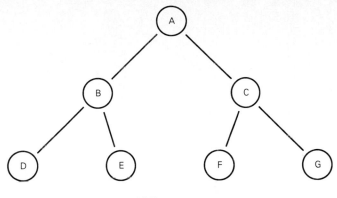

(a) Tree structure

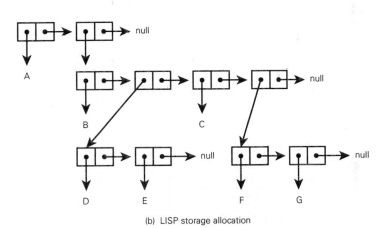

(b) LISP storage allocation

Figure 4.19 Tree represented as list

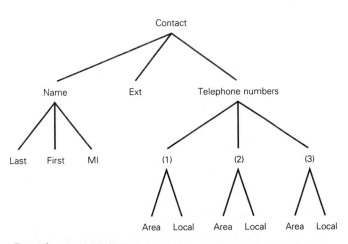

Figure 4.20 Record as tree structure

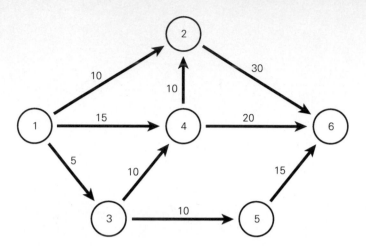

Figure 4.21   PERT network

iterative technique that reduces the size of the data set by one-half at each iteration. For each node of a binary search tree, all nodes in the left subtree precede that node in order and all nodes in its right subtree are ordered after that node. Operations on a binary search tree include

1. CREATion of the tree from an ordered set of data. The data may have to be SORTed prior to construction of the tree;

2. DIRectSEARCH, using the binary search technique;

3. SEQuentialSEARCH using one of several traversal methods. *Traversing* a tree is the process of "traveling" over the branches of a tree in such a way so that each node is accessed once and only once;

4. INSERTing a node into its proper position in the tree;

5. DELETing a node from the tree in such a way as to maintain the ordering scheme.

A binary search tree is the basis of Study Problem #4 in Chapter 7.

Graphs.   A graph is a collection of nodes and edges (lines). The nodes are similar to the nodes in a tree, and the edges are links from one node to another. A graph is the most generalized of the data structures. In fact, most of the other structures can be considered to be special cases of a graph.

The PERT network depicted in Fig. 4.21 is an example of a graph. It is a particular type of directed graph called an *activity graph*. In this case, the edges are "weighted" with information about duration or the length of time (in days) required to complete a specific task. There are a number of ways to represent this graph structure. Fig. 4.22 illustrates a linked graph representation in which each node in the network is represented by a node of information and edges are represented by pointer variables contained within

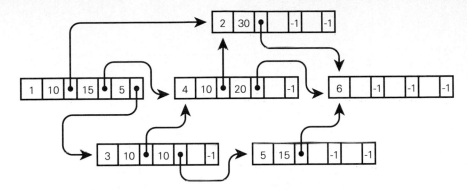

Figure 4.22   Linked graph representation of the PERT network

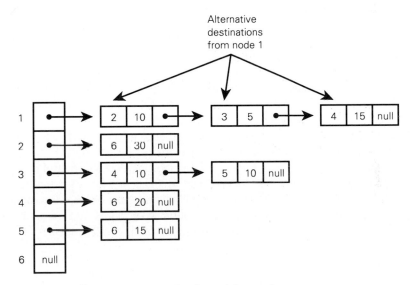

Figure 4.23   Node directory representation for activity graph

the nodes. The pointer value '−1' is an end-of-list designation and is equivalent to null. In this case, each node, as defined, can be linked to at most three possible successor nodes, and information regarding duration is stored within the node rather than within the edge.

Fig. 4.23 depicts what is perhaps a less natural but more flexible representation for this sort of activity graph. With node directory representation, two types of nodes are stored: one type corresponding to the actual nodes in the graph and one corresponding to the edges. This enables storing information about the edges as well as about the nodes. Each node in the node directory is (or contains) an external pointer to a linked list. The linked list represents the edges emanating from that source node.

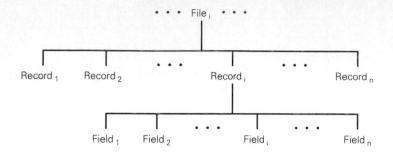

Figure 4.24   The data hierarchy

4.5 FILE STRUCTURES

Of all the structures we study in this book, file structures are the only ones that are not only permanent, but are meaningful in the real world. File structures connect your program to the outside world.

Early computer languages used a variety of input/output operations, each for a specific I/O device. With the advent of COBOL came the concept of hierarchically organized data files as a means of logically defining input/output files in a manner that would be independent of the particular machine configuration used. Any machine dependencies were tied to the **ENVIRONMENT DIVISION**.

It may very well be impossible for language designers to design a programming language that is completely independent of machine characteristics. That is why some widely used languages were designed without any consideration for input/output at all. It is generally felt that this practice helps preserve the purity and simplicity of the language but, on the other hand, also makes it subject to compiler dependencies.

The Data Hierarchy

The *data hierarchy* refers to the logical organization of data that is (probably) stored on secondary or external storage media such as magnetic tape or magnetic drum. As Fig. 4.24 shows, fields are organized into *records*, and records are organized into *files*. Sometimes we speak of files organized into *databases*.

A *file* is a collection of related records, related to a particular application. A *record* is a collection of related data items, or fields, related to a single object of processing. A *field* is a data item, a piece of information, either a data element or a structured data item, that is contained within the record. An example would be a personnel master file in which each record relates to a single employee. A data item of interest on this record might be the employee's name. Such a record is illustrated in Fig. 4.25. A special data item that serves to uniquely identify a particular record is called a *key*. The employee's identification number is an example of a key.

Employee			ID-number	
		Name	Last	
			First	
			MI	
		Address	Street	
			City	
			State	
			Zip	
	Telephones	Phone 1	Area	
			Local	
		Phone 2	Area	
			Local	
		Phone 3	Area	
			Local	
			Job-title	
			Location	
			Department	
			Annual-salary	
			Last-promoted	
			First-employed	

Figure 4.25   Employee record

To define this personnel file in COBOL, we might use the following DATA DIVISION declarations:

```
FD  PERSONNEL-FILE.
    RECORD IS EMPLOYEE-INPUT.
01  EMPLOYEE-INPUT.
    05  ID-NUMBER       PICTURE X(9).
    05  NAME.
        10 LAST         PICTURE X(10).
        10 FIRST        PICTURE X(10).
        10 MI           PICTURE X.
```

```
05  HOME-ADDRESS.
    10  STREET          PICTURE X(15).
    10  CITY            PICTURE X(10).
    10  STATE           PICTURE XX.
    10  ZIP             PICTURE X(5).
05  TELEPHONES.
    10  PHONE OCCURS 3 TIMES.
        15  AREA        PICTURE X(3).
        15  LOCAL       PICTURE X(7).
05  JOB-TITLE          PICTURE X(8).
05  LOCATION           PICTURE X.
05  DEPARTMENT         PICTURE X(4).
05  ANNUAL-SALARY      PICTURE 9(5)V99.
05  LAST-PROMOTED      PICTURE X(4).
05  FIRST-EMPLOYED     PICTURE X(4).
```

Characteristics of Files

A file has several attributes, among them: access mode, processing mode, and file organization method.

Access mode.   The mode, or direction, of access for any particular file is determined by whether the file is to be used for input, for output, or both. An *input* file, or a read-only file, is one in which a majority of accessing operations will be performed to read data from the file. An example is the transaction file input to a file update program. An *output* file, or a write-only file, is one in which a majority of accessing operations will be performed to write data to the file. An example is the report file output from a report writing program and spooled to the printer. An *input-output* file, or a read-write file, is one which will be required to accept input and output operations in the same application. An example is a master file that contains relatively permanent data and must be regularly maintained.

Processing mode.   A file may require processing in one of two ways: batch or query. The processing mode attribute depends on whether records are to be retrieved as part of a group or one at a time, interactively, as needed.

When a file is processed in *batch mode*, the component records of the file are operated on in sequential order, often by the value of an identifying key field on the record. This is sometimes called *report generation* or *scheduled retrieval*. An example is the check-writing program that processes a payroll file.

When a file is processed in *query mode*, an individual record is operated on by accessing it directly from the location in which it has been stored. This is unscheduled or *ad hoc* retrieval. Any type of inquiry-response system could be used as an example: banking's use of automatic teller machines (ATMs), airline reservation systems, inventory systems.

A file's retrieval mode depends on (and influences) its file organization and storage medium.

File organization. The file organization method refers to the organization, in terms of a physical ordering, of the records in a file residing on secondary storage and the appropriate operations for accessing particular records. The file organization attribute depends, to a large extent, on the actual external storage medium used, specifically whether it is a sequential medium such as magnetic tape or a direct-access storage device (DASD) such as magnetic disk or drum, and the retrieval mode.

Three techniques surveyed briefly below are the *sequential*, *relative*, and *indexed sequential* file organizations. In addition to being widely used methods today, these have a rich history, have been thoroughly studied, and are applicable to a wide range of applications.

Operations on Files

Open. The **open** operation serves to cue the operating system so that it will set up the appropriate buffers, allocate the appropriate device to the executing program and, if necessary, set the file-position pointer to the first component record to be accessed. The OPEN operation must specify file name and access mode.

Close. The **close** operation reverses the process of the **open** operation, deallocates the device used, and frees buffer space.

Read. The **read** operation assigns the value of the current or requested component record to a designated record variable or input buffer variable.

Write. The **write** operation creates a new component record at the current position or designated storage location and copies the value of a designated program record variable or output buffer to this new component.

EOF. The EOF operation tests for "end-of-file" and returns a Boolean value. This operation is used on sequential files in conjunction with a **read** operation.

Maintenance. For permanent files requiring regular maintenance, also called *master files*, there are a variety of operations, often kept in the form of utility files and accessed through the operating system. These operations include: SORTing, MERGing, UPDATing, file CREATion, reSTRUCTURing, and BACKUP.

Some Kinds of Files

Sequential files. A sequential file is a linear sequence of records that may be ordered on some key field. There is often the additional restriction that the records must all be of the same type. Sequential files may be accessed in input-only or output-only mode; not in input/output access mode. A *file-position pointer* is a pointer variable associated with sequential files that references the next component record to be accessed (whether it is for input or for output).

The sequential file approach is simple to understand. It is highly efficient when the activity rate of the file is high, but extremely inefficient and uneconomical when the activity rate is low. The *activity rate* of a file is the proportion of file records that are normally processed at once. Since the file may not be used for both input and output at the same time, there is the additional advantage that an automatic backup file is produced whenever the file is modified. Of course, records must be physically sorted if such ordering is important, and this adds to the processing overhead. In addition, since it is more efficient to update this sort of file in batch mode, saving up needed changes until a respectable number of these transactions has accumulated, the data may suffer from a lack of timeliness.

Textfiles.　A textfile is a stream of characters, separated into *lines* by an end-of-line character such as the carriage-return character. A textfile is often taken to be a specific type of sequential file, meaning a file of characters in which the component records are lines. A source program is an example of a textfile.

Relative files.　A relative file is an unordered collection of component records in which each record can be accessed directly by location (absolute or relative), but only if the file has been stored on a direct-access storage device (DASD). Relative files may be processed sequentially (batch) or directly (query mode). Since the records of a relative file need not be physically sorted, batch processing is limited to applications in which the records are processed as a group, but in random order.

In this kind of file organization, the record's location is tied to its key value by some sort of mapping or transform function, R, defined by the relation: LOCATION ← R(KEY). The algorithm used for this function falls into one of three categories: direct mapping, directory look-up, or address calculation.

Direct mapping techniques require that the storage address (absolute or relative) of the record be included as the key value within the record structure itself. This is quite efficient as it does not require additional CPU time to process the record, but it is very machine/device dependent and makes use of a key value that is meaningless to the outside world. A *directory look-up* makes use of a table of paired entries. With this technique, as the file grows, the directory gets larger as well. An *address calculation algorithm* uses arithmetic operations to calculate the address of a storage location from the real-world key value: ADDRESS = R(KEY). Address calculation algorithms are also sometimes called *transform algorithms* or *key-to-address transformation methods*. More commonly, they are known as *hashing* or *hash table methods*.

Relative files are sometimes called *random files* and, sometimes, *direct files*. They are called random files because of the way in which the hashing algorithm appears to randomly assign records to storage locations, that is, without apparent physical ordering of the records in the file. They are called direct because it is possible to access a particular record directly, simply by knowing its key value.

Relative file organization methods provide interactive access to individual records and enable immediate updating of data as new data comes in. Relative files are very efficient with low activity files, but extremely inefficient with high-activity files because of the added processing time necessary to locate each record. Relative files are less efficient in the use of storage space than are sequential files. In fact, some implementations require 30 to 40 percent more storage space in order to minimize the possibility of collisions.

Indexed sequential files.   Indexed sequential files represent a compromise of sorts between sequential and relative files. Files are stored sequentially on a DASD but, in addition, there is an index that allows access directly (or, at least by way of optimized search) to a particular record in the file. In addition, sequential access of the file can begin at any record and not necessarily at the beginning. The index may be stored as a paired table entry (key, address) or as a tree structure set up for optimized searching. Indexed sequential files are used in applications that need to access file data in batch mode, in order by key value, and also in query mode, directly by key value. In banking, for example, customer files are processed in batch mode in preparing quarterly statements and in query mode in processing transactions at ATMs.

Indexed sequential file organization methods try to achieve "the best of both worlds" and are probably most appropriate when file activity is high about as often as it is low. However, no compromise is without its sacrifices. This type of file organization tends to be considerably more wasteful of storage space than others, and access to records is slower using indexes than with address calculation methods.

Databases

A database is a logically interrelated set of data items—sometimes viewed as an integrated set of files—related to a particular application or environment, stored on a large-scale DASD. Both technical and nontechnical personnel may require access to the database, which must be maintained so that its data values are correct and timely and protected from deliberate and accidental damage. A programmer uses a database by "creating," with the aid of a *database management system* (DBMS), a *logical* file of records assembled from the data items stored within the database. The actual *physical* assembly of all the pieces of a data file is no longer necessary.

File processing systems have several disadvantages that database systems attempt to overcome.

1. Since these systems often contain several different physical files that are related—e.g., personnel and payroll files—and these files often have data items in common, the related problems of redundant and inconsistent data arise. *Redundant data* means the same data item is stored in more than one file and is likely to be used by more than one user. When updates occur, it is virtually impossible to ensure that all redundant copies of the same data item are updated to reflect the new information. This leads to *inconsistent data*. A data item will have different values in different files, and there is no way to determine which is correct. In addition, at the very least, redundancy leads to wasted storage space.

2. File processing systems are, by definition, *inflexible* and resistant to change. When the data must be processed in a previously unforeseen manner, a new file must often be created.

3. *Data security* is often less than it should be since many different users need access to the data as it is physically stored. Not all users should be able to access (certainly not update) all data.

4. Since data exists in *isolation* in various independent files, writing new applications often means the collection of data that already exists.

The implementation of a database solves many of these problems while it increases the independence of the data. Data is no longer merely an appendage of, or required input to, a program. A database must provide for:

- *flexibility* in the definition and description of interrelated data items and in their use;
- *consistency* checking;
- *timeliness* of the data due to its increased capacity for immediate updating by the user;
- *extensibility* to new applications;
- a high degree of *data integrity*;
- an orderly approach to *data security*.

Data integrity refers to the vigilant maintenance of the intended values of the data items as they were stored in the database. In order to maintain data integrity, safeguards must be implemented to guard against recording errors (e.g., data-entry errors, physical damage to disk unit, …) and data sharing errors (e.g., two users wishing to update the same data item at the same time). *Data security* refers to safeguards to protect the system from deliberate or accidental physical damage (e.g., flood, fire, power failure, sabotage, …) and from revealing data or software to people without authorized access (e.g., embezzlement, industrial espionage, malicious damage, invasion of privacy, …).

Data models.   Data in databases are structured according to a variety of different data models, the most widely used being:

- the *relational* data model, which represents data as a collection of tables;
- the *hierarchical* data model, which represents data as collections of trees;
- the *network* data model, which represents data as collections of graphs;
- and the *entity-relationship* data model, which views data as a collection of entity sets and relationship sets and specifies constraints to which the data must conform.

In both the hierarchical and network data models, data are represented by collections of records (nodes) and relationships are represented by links between the nodes. In the entity-relationship model, the database can be represented as a collection of tables, one table for each entity set and one for each relationship set.

DBMS.   Often, a database is accessed by means of specialized software called a database management system (DBMS). A DBMS may be looked at as a software interface between the physical storage of the data and the use of the data by humans (both

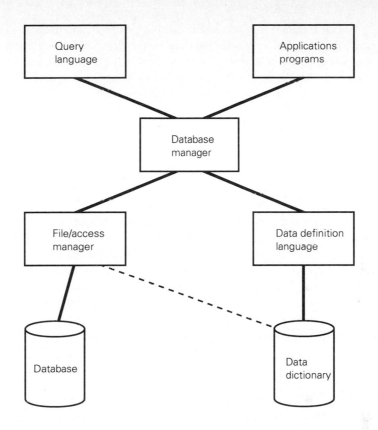

Figure 4.26 A database management system

technical and nontechnical) in various applications. A DBMS is an abstraction in the sense that it hides from both the casual user and the applications programmer the details of the actual physical storage of data items and the implementation of the DBMS operations. There will be more about data abstraction in the next section.

A DBMS can contain the following components, in addition to the database itself. (These are illustrated in Fig. 4.26.)

1. a *data definition language* which is used to specify a database and produces a data dictionary or directory.

2. a *data dictionary* in which information regarding the structure of the database is maintained.

3. a *data manipulation language*, sometimes called a *query language*, which is used to retrieve and/or update data in the database in a manner that is easy for the human and efficient for the machine.

4. a *database manager*, software that acts as liaison between the stored data and the programs which use it.

5. a *file manager*, software that manages the allocation of disk storage space.

A DBMS is not a programming language in itself, but it usually is accompanied by a user-friendly query language that may be powerful enough to allow for sophisticated programming of a procedural or nonprocedural nature. Examples are SQL for System R, Natural for Adabas, and QUEL for the Ingres database system. QBE (Query-By-Example) is the name of both the database and the query language.

4.6 DATA ABSTRACTION

Data abstraction in programming languages generally refers to a language facility that integrates the representation of a programmer-defined data object and the operations that may be performed on that data object into a single syntactic unit.

Although research into data abstraction was initiated during the late 1970s, today we realize that the concept actually dates back to the classes introduced by SIMULA67. The concept of data abstraction is important in database design, large-scale system development, and in object-oriented programming systems. It has representation in some form or another in a variety of programming languages, among them SIMULA67 (classes), Smalltalk (objects), MODULA-2 (modules), and Ada (packages).

Abstraction at the data level is not really a new concept. It is a logical extension of the programming language concepts of:

- built-in primitive types such as integer and floating-point numeric types;
- static structures such as arrays;
- dynamically allocated structures such as those of PL/1;
- user-defined data types such as the ones in Pascal.

In addition, the database management system is a data abstraction since it presents to the user a logical, high-level view of the database consistent with the particular data model employed regardless of how the data is actually stored. In fact, virtually everything we studied in this chapter has figured prominently in the evolution of the data abstraction concept.

It has been said that the user-defined types of ALGOL68 and Pascal were the first significant milestone on the road toward true data abstraction in programming languages. While that may be, remember that this sort of typing facility is not a data abstraction facility. User-defined types provide a limited means for specifying the domain of a "new" type based on some other predefined type, but there is no encapsulation of this definition with the specification of the operations that are allowed on this new type. A true data abstraction facility must, in addition to providing for the definition of a new type domain, enable the programmer to define the operations on those values and package the definition and the descriptions of the algorithms together in a single syntactic unit. Instances of these types may be used (in other programs and by other programmers) but the definitions and descriptions may not be changed.

Data abstraction is implemented by way of two ideas that arose from the structured programming consciousness of the 1970s—modular decomposition and information hiding—both of which are important in building levels of abstraction. Clearly, the line between "data structures" and "program structures" begins to blur. Modular decomposition is discussed in Chapter 5 and encompasses such features as nested subprograms, high cohesion, low coupling, and stepwise refinement. Interaction between modules is limited and highly stylized. Information hiding is a concept that can, among other things, simplify the use of stored subprogram modules. It provides information to the user of the subprogram on a "need to know" basis only. Information regarding *what* the subprogram does is visible; information regarding *how* this is done is hidden.

Defining Abstract Data Types

Rather than providing a confusing abundance of built-in data abstractions (simple types, structured types), a data abstraction facility would enable the programmer to easily define and use new abstractions as needed. Just as built-in primitive and structured data types can be accessed but not altered, data abstraction provides a means for accessing the data objects of some newly defined class while, at the same time, hiding its implementation and thus protecting it from change.

In implementing abstract data types, two kinds of modules are identified: the specification (the "what") and the implementation (the "how"). The specification is visible to the user of the abstract data type and includes information only on a need-to-know basis. The implementation is only accessible to the author of the abstract data type and hides behind its "wall" details of the implementation of the abstract data type that a user of the type does not need to know (for example, local variables, local procedures, and the implementation details of data structures). If the modules defining the abstract data type are stored in a library, any programmer wishing to use the abstract data type can find all the information necessary for its use in the specification module. The specification part provides all the information—the data names, type names, procedure names— necessary if one is to use the class. Some of the specification may also be hidden (e.g., the **private** types of Ada) from the user. Specifically, while the *names* are necessary to the user, the manner in which they are implemented (e.g., the way the types specified are constructed) is not.

It is important to understand that data abstraction involves *encapsulation*. It requires the facility for defining a class of data objects and for defining a group of operations. Many languages provide for one or both of these facilities—separately. This first can be called a user-defined type; the second, a set of subprograms. A data abstraction facility can encapsulate both of these definitions so that they are hidden as much as possible from the user of the abstract data type and protected from inadvertent or unauthorized change. The defined operations may be applied to the defined data objects without regard to how they were implemented.

Example: A Stack

To illustrate a data abstraction mechanism, let us use the stack as defined above in an earlier section. A stack is a linear, dynamic data structure that may be allocated storage sequentially or dynamically. If sequential allocation is used, an array is defined to house the stack—that is, the stack is allowed to grow and shrink dynamically within the confines of the array. Admittedly, this is not a superior means of implementing a stack in languages that do allow for linked allocation of storage, but it enables the use of clearer and simpler algorithms, and that is why we use it here. This picture of a stack is illustrated in Fig. 4.27.

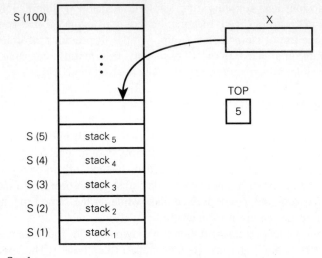

S (5)   stack $_5$

S (4)   stack $_4$

S (3)   stack $_3$

S (2)   stack $_2$

S (1)   stack $_1$

Figure 4.27   Stack

The abstract data type Stack may be defined in Ada in the following manner:

```
package Stack is                 —specification begins here … these
                                  names are exported
     Maxsize: constant := 100;
     type Stack_type is private;
     S: Stack_type;
     procedure PUSH (X:real);
     function POP return real;
private Stack-type
     type is array (1. . maxsize) of real;
end Stack;

package body Stack is            —implementation begins here … these
                                     names are local
     Top: integer range -1. . maxsize;
procedure PUSH (X: real) is
begin
     Top := Top + 1;
     S(Top) := X;
     end PUSH;
function POP return real is
begin
     Top := Top - 1;
     return S(Top + 1);
end POP;
begin                            —initialization begins here
     Top := 0;
end Stack;
```

To use the names and operations defined in the package called Stack, we would need the statements:

```
        ...
            with Stack
            use Stack
        begin
            ...
            PUSH Stack(X);
            ...
            Y := POP();
            ...
```

Or, alternatively,

```
        ...
            with Stack
            use Stack
            procedure PUSHSTACK(X: real) renames STACK.PUSH;
            function POPSTACK return real renames STACK.POP;
        begin
            ...
            PUSHSTACK (X);
            Y := POPSTACK();
            ...
```

Such a Stack type may be defined once and then used repeatedly as if it were truly a part of the built-in language types.

The Class and Object-oriented Programming

A class is, at the same time, the precursor of the abstract data type (in SIMULA67) and an extension of the abstract data type (in object-oriented programming). A class *defines* a set of objects that are instances of the class in much the same way that a type is defined by specifying its domain of values. These abstract data objects receive messages from other parts of the program, and code defined within the class specifies the actions to be taken for each message received. Every class controls its own message protocol or external interface, that is, the set of messages to which objects of the class can respond. The definition of a class is contained within a subprogram structure, consisting of a specification part and an implementation part. The implementation may be hidden from the user so that it cannot be changed simply to suit a particular program in which it is used.

It is interesting to compare the abstract data types of MODULA-2 and Ada with the classes and objects of Smalltalk and C++. This exercise is left to the student.

SUMMARY AND KEY TERMS

Chapter Summary

In this chapter we discussed the data-level entities in programming languages. Structures—data structures, storage structures, and file structures—were defined and differentiated. Using the classification tree of Fig. 4.1, we discussed simple data elements, data structures and their associated storage structures, file structures, and databases.

Many of these entities are provided in programming languages by means of built-in types; sometimes by user-defined typing facilities. A relatively new concept, that of abstract data types, is flexible enough to define any structure, its organization and operations.

Chapter 4 Terminology

Some of the terms presented in this chapter may have been new to you. Use this list as a guide in reviewing the chapter. When you review the list, if you come across a term that is unfamiliar to you, go back and review the section that discusses it. Some of these terms were introduced only briefly in this chapter, and will be discussed in more detail in the chapters that follow.

abstract data type	access mode	array
binary search tree	binary tree	Boolean type
class	constant	data abstraction
database	database management system	data element
data hierarchy	data structure	data type
deque	dimensionality	direct file
dynamic structure	enumerated type	file
file organization	file structure	graph
indexed sequential file	information hiding	key
label	linked allocation	linked list
list	multilinked list	named constant
pointer	processing mode	queue
query language	random file	record
relative file	sequential allocation	sequential file
set	stack	static structure
storage structure	string	strongly typed language
subtype	textfile	tree
typing system	user-defined type	variable
variable-length record	variant record	

SUGGESTIONS FOR FURTHER STUDY

The first and still definitive work on data structures may be found in Chapter 2 of Knuth (1975). Other excellent and more recent texts include Ellzey (1982), Horowitz and Sahni (1983), Tremblay and Sorenson (1984), and Tenenbaum and Augenstein (1981). Also, see Russell (1983). A discussion of the history and evolution of some of this material is in Knuth (1975, pp. 405–406, 456–463). Data types are discussed in the paper by Steensgaard-Madsen (1989). For a complete work on file structures, see Grosshans (1986), and also refer to the paper by Shapiro (1986). Loomis (1983) is a very readable exposition with excellent treatment of data concepts, including both data structures and file structures.

Korth and Silberschatz (1986) discuss database systems in a manner that is both readable and comprehensive. Also see papers by Blaha *et al.* (1988), Chrisman and Beccuc (1986), Elmasri (1985), Feldman and Miller (1986), Newfeld and Cornog (1986), Selinger (1987), Stein (1988), and Wiederhold (1984, 1986).

For more on the subject of data abstraction, see books by Stubbs and Webre (1987), Bishop (1986), Liskov and Guttag (1986), and Thomas *et al.* (1988) and articles by Guttag (1977), Walker and Alexander (1986), and Richmond (1986).

Other related books of interest are: J.J. Martin (1986), Bertsekas and Gallager (1987), Tsichritzis and Lochovsky (1982), and Hanson (1986).

5

Program-level Structure

Any discussion of structures at the program level is naturally concerned with the program text itself: How it is organized and how it looks to us. Program objects, like data objects, may be considered *passive* entities: We can describe them, and we can also describe the operations that may be performed on them (for example, a simple call). In addition, we can use program objects in order to help us describe a particular programming language. In programming, and in programming languages, the *active* entities are the control structures; any and all action takes place at the control level. Control structures will be the subject of the next chapter.

In the following sections we consider a number of topics related to the appearance and organization of units of program text. A classification of many of these program objects is attempted in Fig. 5.1 although, as we shall see, the definition and classification of program object terminology is one of the most elusive of tasks. Some of these terms are rather like moving targets: They change shape and meaning from one context (language, author) to another. In this chapter, we will first examine those elements of programming languages that control the *appearance* of the program text. These include a number of features not under programmer control, such as: How the program text is formatted, the built-in character set of the language, and the symbols and strings used as delimiters. On the other hand, certain features provided by programming languages to affect the appearance of the program text are under programmer control, for example: indenting, comments, and other programming conventions.

Most programming languages in use today follow the imperative, statement-oriented, programming paradigm. This chapter leans toward this bias. The subject of programming paradigms will be discussed in Chapter 6. For a look at two specific paradigms that are radically different from the imperative approach, see Chapters 12 and 13.

We will identify and distinguish among the various *program entities* such as identifiers, expressions, statements, subprograms, and programs. Then we will shift our focus

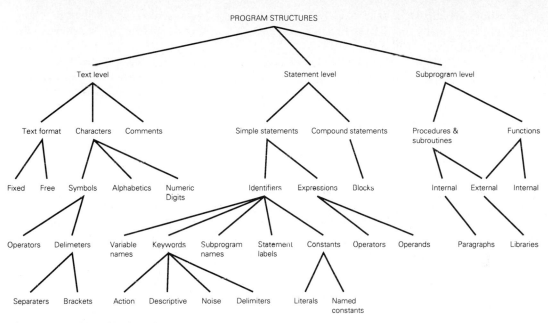

Figure 5.1   Classification of program structures

to take an in-depth look at *subprograms*, the most distinguishable program structure. Certain language facilities for sharing and/or protecting data in subprograms will be discussed, among these: parameters, rules for scope of variables, and global and local variables. Then we will briefly discuss the operations allowable on subprograms. These include the traditional subprogram call and other kinds of control relationships between subprograms leading to specialized kinds of subprograms like exception handlers and parallel processes.

The key question underlying the discussion of a language's program structure is: What does this language *look* like? To list just a few possible considerations: Is the language block-structured? Does it have subroutines? Does it use semicolons? Periods? How are comments handled? ...

Let us take the COBOL language as an example. (You might wish to take a quick peek at the sample COBOL programs listed in Chapter 8.) COBOL programs have a standard appearance. It is a fixed-format, line-based language, although the arrangement of program text is relatively free within the confines of the B margin (characters 12 through 72) of the line, so that indenting is feasible and should be used. There is a main *program*, which may be accompanied by one or more *subroutines*. The program is composed of four *divisions*, and this composition is probably the most distinguishing characteristic of COBOL program structure. The **IDENTIFICATION DIVISION** provides information regarding the name and purpose of the program, the author of the program, the date it was written, etc.; the **ENVIRONMENT DIVISION** provides machine-dependent information concerning the configuration of the particular computer system upon which the program will be run; the **DATA DIVISION** contains declarative statements describing the input data, output data, and temporarily stored data which the program will use; finally, the **PROCEDURE DIVISION** contains the executable statements of the program.

In COBOL, a **DIVISION** may be composed of one or more **SECTION**s, a **SECTION** may be composed of one or more paragraphs, a paragraph is composed of one or more sentences, and a sentence contains one or more statements. A paragraph is invoked with a **PERFORM** statement and execution of the program terminates on encountering a **STOP RUN** statement. Any *statement* is of the form: <keyword> <body>, where the keyword is a COBOL verb. Speaking of keywords, COBOL has several hundred built-in *keywords* for a variety of purposes. These are *reserved*; programmers are not allowed to use them as identifiers. COBOL programs are considered *self-documenting* because of the relative flexibility in constructing descriptive names for variables and paragraphs and the incorporation into the language of "noise" words (**TO, FROM, IS**) added to, of course, the liberal use of comments and indenting. The COBOL character set contains 50 characters, including the letters A through Z, the numeric digits 0 through 9, and the blank space, hyphen, and 12 other special characters.

5.1 PROGRAM TEXT

The *syntax* of any language—including COBOL, Pascal, LISP or, even, English—is a set of rules governing the construction of strings of characters that are grammatically correct. Program text may be considered a string of characters that is ultimately translated into an ordered sequence of machine instructions. We will now examine these characters themselves, the way they are organized into the substrings that make up the pieces of program text, and the way they are arranged over the many lines of code that make up a complete program.

In programming languages, the set of rules governing the way that these characters may be arranged on the line contributes to the appearance of the program and often highlights the unique characteristics of the language used. Some of these rules, such as those regarding the use of comments, blank lines, and indenting, actually result in more rather than less flexibility for the programmer. The programmer is then able to produce a program that is readable by humans as well as (after suitable translation) by the machine. Other rules may be very restrictive in nature and may vary widely from one programming language to another. Some examples are rules governing the allowable character set, the construction and use of delimiters within the program and, on a broader level, the format prescribed for the placement of program text on the input line.

Character Set

A character is a single, distinguishable symbol. While all languages can boast in their character sets the 26 uppercase alphabetic characters (A ... Z), the 10 numeric digits (0 ... 9), and the blank space, and many also contain the 26 lowercase alphabetic characters, languages differ with regard to the remaining symbols used and recognized by the language. Many contain the "standard" arithmetic symbols (+, −, *, /), the relational sym-

FORTRAN

A B C D E F G H I J K L M N O P Q R S T U V W X Y Z
0 1 2 3 4 5 6 7 8 9
blank + - * / . , ' = $ ( )

Algol

A B C D E F G H I J K L M N O P Q R S T U V W X Y Z
a b c d e f g h i j k l m n o p q r s t u v w x y z
0 1 2 3 4 5 6 7 8 9
blank < ≤ = ≥ ∧ ∨ ≡ ~' ⊃
+ - × ÷ ≠ , . ; : ' " ( ) [ ]

PL/1

A B C D E F G H I J K L M N O P Q R S T U V W X Y Z
0 1 2 3 4 5 6 7 8 9
blank $ # @ + = - * / ( ) , . ' % ; : ¬ & | > < _ ?

APL

A B C D E F G H I J K L M N O P Q R S T U V W X Y Z
0 1 2 3 4 5 6 7 8 9
blank " < ≤ = ≥ ≠ ∨ ∧ + - × ÷ ? ; : , . / \ 0 |
( ) [ ] { } □ ˙ ° # ~ _
⊂ ⊃ ∩ ∪ ⊥ ⊤ ∇ ∆ ⌈ ⌊ α ω ε ρ ↑ ↓ ∫ → ⊢ ⊣

PROLOG

A B C D E F G H I J K L M N O P Q R S T U V W X Y Z
a b c d e f g h i j k l m n o p q r s t u v w x y z
0 1 2 3 4 5 6 7 8 9
blank + - * / \ ∧ < > ~ : . ? @ # $ &
= ! % ' ( ) ' | [ ] { } _ ; ,

Ada

A B C D E F G H I J K L M N O P Q R S T U V W X Y Z
a b c d e f g h i j k l m n o p q r s t u v w x y z
0 1 2 3 4 5 6 7 8 9
blank " # % & ' ( ) * + , - . / : ; < = > _ |
! $? @ [ ] \ ∧ ' { } ~

Figure 5.2 Character sets for several programming languages

bols (<, >, =), and the symbols ∧, $, period (.), comma (,), semicolon (;). The character sets built into several widely used programming languages are displayed in Fig. 5.2. APL is unique among programming languages in that it requires its own, specialized keyboard. This is because the large APL character set recognizes many special characters (including Greek letter symbols), which do not appear on standard keyboards.

Two standardized and, by now, international character sets are IBM's EBCDIC (**E**xtended **B**inary **C**oded **D**ecimal **I**nterchange **C**ode) and the American National Standards Institute's ASCII (American Standard Code for Information Interchange). EBCDIC, an 8-bit code capable of representing codes for up to 256 characters, is the older of the two. ASCII, a 7-bit code capable of representing codes for up to 128 characters, has become extremely well known and widely implemented in the context of the microcomputer and data communication explosion.

Strings of one or more characters are used to construct the various identifiers and words that make up the vocabulary of the programming language, as well as the special operators and delimiters used in the language.

Operators

Operators are built-in, value-returning, generic functions. Operator names usually consist of a single character or a string of two characters (called a *compound symbol*). While different languages will naturally have different operations, and often use different symbols for the same operation, many operations and their associated symbols belong to the common heritage of modern programming languages and have, in effect, become industry standards.

The *arithmetic operators* are addition (+), subtraction (−), multiplication (*), division (/) and, sometimes, exponentiation (** or ^). Arithmetic operators work on numeric, or computational, data and form arithmetic expressions. The *relational operators*, used in logical comparisons, are less than (<), less than or equal to (<=), equal to (=), not equal to (<>), greater than or equal to (>=), and greater than (>). Relational operators work on operands of any type and form relational expressions (conditions) that compute to Boolean values. The *logical* operators are and (&), or (|), and not (¬). Logical operators work on Boolean data and relational expressions, which are Boolean. These operator symbols may sometimes be used for other purposes. In addition, some languages provide built-in keywords rather than symbols, as operator names. For example: **and**, **not**, **or**, **.EQ.**, **ADD**, **DIVIDE**, **EQUAL**.

Delimiters

Delimiters are symbols or keywords that serve to separate pieces of program text. They are punctuation for your program. Delimiters may be classified as either separators or brackets.

Separators indicate the end of one program entity and the beginning of the next. A blank space often serves to separate identifiers and expressions within statements. Some languages use a colon (:) to separate a variable name from its type declaration. Many different symbols may be used to delimit the end of one program statement and the beginning of the next, for example: period (.), comma (,), semicolon (;). The **END** statement of FORTRAN is a program delimiter; it indicates the last line of the program text.

Brackets, which may be symbols or keywords, come in matching pairs. A set of brackets is a pair of related delimiters that set off (or, delimit) a program code segment. Examples of frequently used bracketing symbols are: parentheses ( ), square braces [ ], and curly braces {}. ALGOL-like languages contain the familiar **begin/end** pair of keywords for delimiting a compound statement. Other examples of built-in language keywords that delimit programming constructs are: **PROCEDURE/END**, **DO/END**, **while/endwhile**, **if/then/else/endif**.

Fixed vs. Free Format

Fixed-format programming languages have strict rules governing the arrangement of program text on a line. These are, in general, the very early languages that were input via punched cards on unit-record machinery, although the use of punched cards does not really require fixed-format program text. When such languages are used today with terminal input, every line is actually considered to be something of a "card image" and so, in effect, we are treating the line as a "simulated card." If you think this is a little silly, you are not alone. When a fixed-format language becomes popular, and finds itself with a large number of dedicated and tenacious users, upgrades of the language must always be upwardly compatible so that users are able to run all their old programs and subroutines under the new version, using the new translator. This limits the upgrade to some extent and, while a language may evolve and change considerably over several decades, it will still contain vestiges of its earlier forms.

The definitive example of such a programming language is, of course, FORTRAN, a fixed-format language that is fascinating to study not only because of its place in and contribution to the history of programming languages, but also because it is a viable language in current use. In its current form, FORTRAN has incorporated a number of the features of newer languages, many of which were themselves originally inspired by or influenced by FORTRAN.

A fixed format does have several advantages. For one thing, programs have a standard appearance, which means that some errors are easier to detect because they stand out. Also, it is easier for the compiler to scan the text.

A fixed-format language has strictly defined fields on each line (card image) of program text and, perhaps, different types of specially designated lines. A FORTRAN program has several such strictly defined lines: There is the *initial* line of a statement; the *continuation* line, indicated by a continuation mark placed in column 6; the *comment* line, indicated by a C in column 1 instructing the compiler to ignore the entire line; and the *end* line, containing the delimiter **END** to signify the end of the lines of program text. In FORTRAN, the fields of a line (or card) are defined as shown in Table 5.1.

Card columns 73–80 would often contain a short form of the program name plus a sequence number so that, in the all-too-likely event that the box of program cards would fall off of its cart and tumble its contents onto the computer room floor, the cards could be easily reassembled into their proper positions.

Another early language, COBOL, is also fixed format, although it is somewhat more flexible than its predecessor, FORTRAN. The fields on a line of COBOL text are laid out as shown in Table 5.2.

A *free-format* language has no fixed fields. Program text is treated as a stream of characters, and the end of a statement may be indicated by a delimiter built into the language (say, a period or a semicolon). Alternatively, the end of a statement and the beginning of a new statement may be identifiable only "in context." For example, the occurrence of a verb keyword in the program text may indicate the beginning of a

TABLE 5.1

Character (card column)	Used for
1	C for comment
1–5	line number
6	continuation line indicator
7–72	FORTRAN statement
73–80	not read by compiler, this area is often used by programmers for identification and sequencing

TABLE 5.2

Character (card column)	Used for
1–6	sequencing, not used by compiler
7	mark "*" for comment or "–" for continuing word or string
8–12	the A margin, for headers of program units
12–72	the B margin, for statements
73–80	program identification, not used by compiler

new statement. At any rate, the physical end of the unit record (punched card, card image, line) is ignored. Free-format languages originated with the ALGOL language. The design of ALGOL was, you will recall, an international effort, and the resulting high-level programming language was implemented mainly in European computing centers. Thus, the designers of ALGOL were not limited by the artificial boundaries of (IBM) punched cards. In fact, punched paper tape was the assumed input medium, being a popular input medium in Europe and a good choice for a language that was to be independent of any particular machine manufacturer.

Among the advantages of free-format text is, of course, an increased flexibility in program design. Along with this increased flexibility, the appearance of the program text takes on additional importance since it is now in the programmer's realm of control to make a program either more or less readable simply by the arrangement of the pieces of the program text.

Program Text Appearance

There are a number of programming methods and conventions that make the program text easier to read—that is, for the human reader. These techniques, such as indenting and the use of comments and blank lines, are not built into a language except in the sense that a free-format language, being more flexible, is naturally more amenable to them. These techniques are much more than simply a concession to "esthetics." They are capable of making a program easier to read, easier to debug (since errors and omissions may stand out more readily), and easier to maintain.

Indenting.   What's wrong with the following segment of Pascal code?

```
begin sum:=0;n:=0; read(x); while not (x<0) do begin
n:=n+1; sum:=sum+x;read(x) end; a:=sum/n end
```

How about this one?

```
begin sum:=0;n:=0;
   read(x); while
not (x<0) do begin n:=n+1;
   sum:=sum+x;read(x) end; a:=sum/n end
```

The answer: Nothing is wrong.

Nothing, that is, if you are a computer. On the other hand, if you are a human (in which case, phrases like "on the other hand" make a great deal of sense), then the above code segment is pretty difficult to decipher, to say the least. Now, try this, for a change:

```
begin
    sum:=0;
    n:=0;
    read(x);
    while not (x<0) do
       begin
           n:=n+1;
           sum:=sum+x;
           read(x)
       end;
    a:=sum/n
end
```

Better? The moral is: Indenting makes a big difference. This is especially true in free-format languages, since we cannot expect to find particular program entities in particular fields on the line, and since we become accustomed to seeing certain constructs laid out in very specific ways. There are a number of conventions with regard to indenting that are fairly universal and which we are well advised to follow:

1. Subordinate clauses within statements are indented. For example,

```
READ PERSONNEL-FILE
      AT END PERFORM EOJ-RTNE.
```

and,

```
while not eof do
      read data
```

and,

```
if not X <0
      then add 1 to sum.
```

2. Important words or phrases used as delimiters—for example, **if/then/else**—ought to be lined up in some way. The most common conventions for doing this are either to line up these keyword delimiters one beneath the other as in:

```
if  X < 0
        then call negative
else
        call positive.
```

or, to indent each successive keyword beyond the position of the previous one, as in:

```
if X < 0
        then call negative
                else call positive.
```

Blank lines.   Program source code, just like other documents written for communication among human beings, benefits from an abundance of "white space." Some of this is achieved by indenting, some by inserting blank lines into the stream of program text. The insertion of blank lines into strategic spots of the program text can serve to separate program units, highlight pieces of code, or emphasize comments. In languages where a blank line is not allowed, a blank comment line serves the same purpose.

Comments.   While high-level programs are more expressive than machine language code, they still describe algorithms within a fairly rigid, prescribed framework. Within this framework, comments serve to clarify, to humanize, to breathe life into a program. Ideally, comments describe the program's intent in real-world terms and explain the logical methods used in the program. Comments are absolutely necessary for the timely maintenance and evolution of programs. However, they are only valuable to the extent that the comments themselves are maintained so that they are a reliable and correct representation of the algorithm. Comments are provided for in programming languages in a variety of ways and, while important, do not affect the processing of the program. Some languages, such as FORTRAN, relegate a comment to its own line, while others place delimiters around the comment so that it may be inserted anywhere in the program text: **READ** A "description of a", B "description of b", C "description of c".

5.2 PROGRAM STRUCTURES

Program structures relate to each other in what can typically be viewed as a hierarchy. As we saw in the previous chapter, the defining relationship among hierarchical entities is that of *containment*. Looking at a program as a unit that *contains* a sequence of statements is an example of this sort of relationship. Additionally, a statement may *contain* expressions and an expression may *contain* identifiers. Fig. 5.3 depicts this relationship over several levels of program entities. From this figure, the relative independence of the program units may be inferred. Objects at the bottom of the hierarchy have the least autonomy, and the higher a structure, the more independent it is. The program is the most independent, the subprogram is slightly less so, and so on.

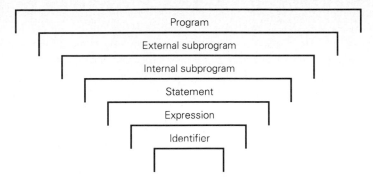

Figure 5.3   Hierarchy of program structures

Identifiers

Identifiers are words that provide access to program and data entities. An example of a program-level identifier is a procedure name. An example of a data-level identifier is a variable name. Some identifiers are supplied by the programmer and some are keywords that have been built into the language. A *reference* is similar to a variable name in that it provides access to data, but a reference must undergo some degree of evaluation first. Examples are a *function reference*, which must invoke a function subprogram, and an *array component reference* in which the subscript variable or expression must be evaluated before the component can be accessed.

Names.   There are a number of user-supplied identifiers required in every program. These are names identifying variables, files, statements, subprograms, or programs. Every programming language has its own set of rules for constructing names. Some differentiate among the different types of names while others make no such distinction— that is, a variable name is constructed by the same rules as a subprogram name and by the same rules as a statement label.

Variable names identify the locations in which data used by the executing program is stored. *Statement labels* serve to identify statements in the program. In some languages, a statement label is a number (a line number, usually an integer) and the program statements are ordered according to this number. In some languages, a statement label is a name that looks a lot like the names of variables. The COBOL paragraph name is, in actuality, a statement label, identifying the first statement following the paragraph name. When a **PERFORM** statement is executed, all the statements, from the one labeled by the paragraph name to the statement preceding the next paragraph name, are executed in sequence. This creates the illusion of a "paragraph" name. A *subprogram name* identifies a segment of code that is treated as a unit. The name is supplied by the author of the subprogram as part of its specification, and used by the author of the main (or calling) program in a call statement.

Keywords.   The keywords of a language constitute a built-in vocabulary for the programmer. Sometimes, as in Pascal, Ada and, most notably, COBOL, these words are considered "reserved." This means that they are off limits to the programmer, who may not use them to denote programmer-supplied words. Reserving certain words for specific purposes may help make programs more readable by humans, and also relieves the compiler of some degree of effort that would otherwise have to go into identifying pieces of text in context. For example, try distinguishing the keywords from the variable names in the following: IF DO>IF THEN IF = DO ELSE ADD=END + PROGRAM. Admittedly, this is a silly example, but it makes the point.

Keywords serve a variety of different purposes. There are the *action keywords*, or *verbs*, that are common to imperative languages: **ADD, GOTO, READ, WRITE, DO, PERFORM**. There are other statement keywords such as **IF, ELSE**. Many of the bracket type of *delimiters* noted earlier in this chapter are statement keywords. There are *descriptive keywords*, such as those used in declarative statements: **INTEGER, REAL, FLOAT, COMMON**. Then there are the "*noise*" keywords, which serve no special purpose except the noble goal of making programs more readable: **TO, THEN, A, AND, SOME, IS, ON, WITH**.

There is a type of keyword called a *named constant*, which identifies a constant and is, thus, protected from change by the program. Named constants may be used in order to make a program more readable or to access values that may be difficult to obtain or are machine dependent. For example, in COBOL, the word **SPACE** is clearly more readable than the literal ' ' and the constant **HIGH-VALUES** may have a different value depending on the underlying machine structure. Some languages, Pascal for example, allow the programmer to supply additional named constants by means of a constant definition statement in the declarative portion of the program. Such programmer-supplied named constants ought to be protected against change as well.

Expressions

Expressions, composed of operators and operands, are sequences of operations to be evaluated. An expression evaluates to a single result and is, thus, very much like a variable except that it does not have a name. Since it bears no unique name, it is not associated with any specially assigned storage location. Expressions, once evaluated, are stored in a temporary location (an *anonymous* variable) that is not accessible to the programmer. Expressions are inherently recursive since one expression may be contained within and defined in terms of another. This means that the result obtained by evaluating one expression may then be used as an operand in evaluating the next. The functional style of programming (à la LISP, APL, SNOBOL) is expression oriented rather than statement oriented. In the functional programming paradigm, the expression is the means by which functions are combined, as opposed to the sequential control of statement-oriented languages.

Statements

In imperative languages, a program is often defined as a collection of statements, in sequence, that accomplish a particular task. This definition of a program, which serves equally well to define a subprogram, highlights the importance of the statement as a program structure. In your first programming course the statement was probably the program entity you encountered first. (The second is usually the variable name.)

There are different kinds of statements. Statements may be classified as either *executable* or *informative* (nonexecutable). Examples of nonexecutable statements are declarations that describe the data used by the program, the first three divisions of a COBOL program, and FORTRAN's **FORMAT** and **END** statements. The executable statements in a program are those that cause an action on the part of the computer.

Simple statements contain a single action. Examples are input/output statements, the **GOTO** or unconditional branch, the subprogram call, and the assignment (or, arithmetic/assignment) statement. In addition to simple statements, some control statements are structured in such a way so that they contain within themselves other statements. For example: **IF** X<0 **THEN** <statement1> **ELSE** <statement2>. Another example: **while not** eof **do** <statement3>. In these examples, statement 1, 2, or 3 may be any executable statement, including another **IF** or **WHILE**.

A *compound statement* is a program structure that is composed of two or more simple statements, often delimited by a pair of matching keywords. The compound statement may be used wherever a single statement is allowed since it is treated, syntactically, as a single statement. Examples of compound statements are ALGOL's and Pascal's **begin/end** and PL/1's **DO/END**. The COBOL sentence, a sequence of statements ending with a period, is also a compound statement.

Subprograms

A subprogram is a block of statements that has the following characteristics: it has a name; it is relatively independent; and it performs specific tasks. The subprogram is the most obvious and varied program structure, and we will discuss it in greater depth and detail later on in this chapter. Paragraphs, procedures, subroutines, and functions are all specific types of subprograms. Due to the myriad ways in which terms such as block, procedure, and subroutine have been defined (see below), we will use the term *subprogram* to express this concept. Subprograms can be classified according to: whether they are internal to the program or external to it; whether they return a single value or any number of values (none, more than one, etc.) to the calling program (functions); the operations that may be performed on them, that is, the control structure used in invoking the subprogram (coroutines, recursion, etc.).

Internal subprograms.   These are named program units that are part of and contained within the text of the program. An internal subprogram is compiled together with the program in which it is called. It may accept arguments from a calling module. Internal subprograms may be nested, but not overlapped, and they may contain their own local declarations. Thus, a set of rules governing the scope of variables declared within nested internal subprograms is required. In ALGOL-like languages, internal subprograms make up the internal block structure of the program. In ALGOL60, these units are not required to have a name. Pascal's internal subprograms are termed either **procedure**s or **function**s.

External subprograms.   These are named program units that are outside the text of the program and may be separately compiled into object modules that are then used as needed. An advantage of this separate compilation is that when changes are made, only those subprograms that were changed need to be recompiled. The way this is implemented varies from FORTRAN, which typically does no type checking over external subprogram boundaries, to MODULA-2, which calls for a very formalized interface between modules (the external subprogram units of MODULA-2) and a high degree of type checking across module boundaries. In some languages (FORTRAN, for example), these external subprograms are called *subroutines*. In Pl/1, external subprograms are termed *external procedures*.

Programs

A program may be loosely defined as an independent program unit that can be executed. A program often has a name and may invoke one or more subprograms, in which case, it might be called the *main program*. A program may accept input data from the outside world and will provide results to be output in some appropriate form to the outside world.

A *job*, not pictured in Fig. 5.3, is a unit that interfaces with the operating system and may contain within it several programs and subroutines that are to be linked together and/or executed in sequence. The job is recognized by the operating system and communicates with it by means of a specialized command language such as, for example, JCL (**Job Control Language**).

5.3 THE SUBPROGRAM AS A PROGRAM STRUCTURE

Over the years, the subprogram has achieved a measure of prominence among program structures. The design and construction of huge, complicated software systems, an enterprise that is more properly called "software engineering" rather than merely "programming," depends to a large extent on the design and construction of smaller, relatively simple subprograms. The methodology of structured programming rests on the conceptual foundations of modular decomposition and the stepwise refinement of modules expressing progressively more of the detail of the total program. This view of programming relies heavily on the subprogram as a program-level abstraction that can be invoked as needed to perform a specific, well-defined task.

A subprogram, like the program itself, contains both informative statements and executable statements. The declarative portion of the subprogram, the subprogram *heading*, contains the informative statements consisting of declarations that pertain to the subprogram, and provides a syntactic interface between the action statements contained in the subprogram and the call from the "main." The subprogram heading contains: the name of the subprogram and the list of parameters, in order, each with its own particular type. The *action* portion of the subprogram contains the executable statements, which, collectively, may be termed the implementation of the subprogram.

In the action portion of the subprogram, one statement is specified as the *entry point*—the point at which execution begins when the subprogram is invoked. Often, this is simply the first executable statement in sequence. PL/1 and COBOL allow for more than a single entry point through the use of an **ENTRY** statement. The *exit point*, or the point at which execution of the subprogram ends before control is returned to the calling program, may be the last statement in the subprogram or an explicit **return** or **exit** statement. If the complete truth must be told, exiting a subprogram can often be accomplished by way of a **goto** or a **stop**, but both of these methods for exiting are discouraged since one produces programs with a confusing control hierarchy, and the other has an "invisible" stopping point. Although there may be more than one possible exit point in a subprogram, and although languages like PL/1 allow for the specification of more than one entry point, program design and maintenance can be greatly simplified by limiting subprograms to a single entry point and a single exit point. This is one of the requirements in the top-down method of designing modular programs, which will be described later in this chapter.

Subprograms may be internal or external. Generally speaking, an external subprogram may be compiled separately while an internal subprogram is compiled along with the program unit in which it is called. Some subprograms, whether internal or external, may be specially designated to return a single value to the calling module; these are known as *functions*.

Internal and external subprograms are both invoked by means of call statements. At each call, or invocation of the subprogram, an *activation record* is created and placed on a run-time stack. This record contains: locally declared variables, the return address for the next instruction in sequence in the calling program, and the address pointing to the action code of the subprogram. When a subprogram terminates, the activation record is popped off the stack and control of execution is transferred to the address indicated for the return. The fact that these activation records are maintained on a stack, a last-in-first-out (LIFO) structure, implies that any currently executing subprogram must terminate before the termination of the subprogram (or program) that called it. This enforces the rule governing nesting of subprograms without overlapping them and, in languages that allow recursion, this controls the execution of repeated recursive calls.

The call statement often takes the form: **call** name (argument-list). When a **call** statement does not require the keyword **call** (or **PERFORM**, or ...), the subprogram name can be chosen so as to make the call statement appear to be a regular language statement. In this way, the subprogram, a unit defined by the programmer, represents an extension to the language in the form of a "new" statement or operation. Ada and ALGOL68 allow procedure names to be constructed using any character in the language's character set and this enables the programmer to define new, more meaningful operators. For example, a subprogram may be named "#" and coded so as to pop the topmost element off a stack.

After the subprogram has been executed, control resumes at the statement following the call.

Varieties of Subprogram

Blocks.   A block is a very general term which, depending on the particular programming language used or textbook studied, may refer to one program structure or another. At times, it is used to refer to any subprogram such as a paragraph, procedure, function, or subroutine. At times, it is used specifically to refer only to subprograms that are part of the stream of program text internal to the program (this would exclude the external subroutine). Sometimes it is used to refer to *unnamed* modules of code such as those found in compound statements; e.g., **if** <condition> **then** <block1> **else** <block2> **endif**. In ALGOL60, PL/1, and C, the term *block* refers specifically to an unnamed program unit activated not by an explicit call statement, but by execution of the normal sequence of instructions in the program.

Procedures, subroutines. The word *procedure* is often used generically to denote any subprogram (even a function, which would then be called a *value-returning procedure* or a *typed procedure*). More often than not, a *procedure* is defined as a named subprogram that is internal to the program—that is, it is physically contained within the stream of text that constitutes the program code. Thus defined, a procedure may have its own local declarations and a specified list of parameters for communication between the calling procedure and the called procedure. Some languages allow procedures to be nested and, in that case, scoping rules are needed to determine the variables that may be referenced—that is, considered global—within each procedure. Pascal defines a procedure in this way, while in PL/1, any named block of code is a procedure. The word *subroutine* is often used to denote an external subprogram—that is, one that is not contained within the confines of the text of the program and which is capable of being independently compiled. This is the only type of subprogram recognized by FORTRAN. Often, the terms procedure and subroutine are used in a more specific context to refer to subprograms (internal or external) that are *not* functions.

Paragraphs. The COBOL paragraph has many features of a procedure. It is an internal subprogram, a named sequence of statements. It is invoked by means of a call statement of the form: **PERFORM** <paragraph-name>. Paragraphs are different from other internal subprograms in that they consist of implementation only. In other words, with the exception of the specification of a name, the paragraph contains only executable statements. It allows for no local definition of variables and no parameters to store data passed specifically to it from the calling module. The only means of communication among paragraphs (including the "main" paragraph) in a COBOL program is by means of global variables declared in the **DATA DIVISION**.

Functions

A function returns a single value. Functions are called simply by using the name of the function (along with any needed arguments) in any place in the program text where a variable name would be allowed. This is called a *function reference*. This is equivalent to storing the value returned from the function in a temporary memory location with the same name as the function itself. So the name of the function may in a sense be considered to be, at the same time, an identifier of a program unit and identifier of a (temporary) data variable. One result of this is that the name of the function must be given a type, and so we come to speak of arithmetic functions (e.g., SQRT), Boolean functions (e.g., EOF), integer functions (e.g., MOD), and string functions. In languages that support the functional programming paradigm, functions are applied to arguments in the same way that expressions are applied to operands. The program itself, then, can be treated like an expression.

In imperative, statement-oriented languages, a *function* may be an internal or external subprogram. In fact, there is really no reason for the special word, function, except for the fact that it has come to be used so frequently and its meaning is clear. However, it is important to remember that a function is not a totally different kind of subprogram, but rather, is a *value-returning subprogram.*

Built-in functions are functions that are supplied along with the compiler and are thus part of the vocabulary of the language. There are many reasons for including built-in functions in a programming language and programmers have come to expect that they will be there. Many built-in functions are those that are used frequently by programmers. Many of the arithmetic functions (SQR, SQRT, EXP, LOG) fall into this category, as does the end-of-file function (EOF, **AT END**). Some built-in functions provide information that would be impossible or difficult to obtain in any other way, for example, the current date or time. A built-in function may be more accurate, more efficient, and more reliable than a programmer-supplied version.

A *generic function* is one whose type depends on the types of the arguments used at the point of call. For example, suppose the function SQRT(X) can be an integer function, a real function, or a double-precision function depending upon the type of the variable X. Some built-in functions are in fact generic functions; many built-in operators are necessarily generic. Ada and Smalltalk provide for the specification of generic functions.

Subprogram Libraries

There are many routine tasks that are regularly required by a variety of problems. These are often coded once, stored on-line (or, sometimes, off-line) as external subprograms, and then reused by means of call statements placed in various programs. Examples of these are arithmetic functions, statistical routines, searching/sorting arrays or files, matching strings, etc. These libraries, collections of external subprograms, extend the programming language and allow each programmer to build on rather than duplicate the work of previous programmers.

Subprogram libraries may be provided along with the compiler (built-in functions, procedures); purchased separately, perhaps from a different vendor; coded and maintained by the programmer(s); or composed of units from any combination of the above sources.

5.4 SUBPROGRAMS AND DATA

A subprogram is a curious conglomeration of data, program, and control considerations. As a program structure, it may be considered a program abstraction in much the same way that a data object is a data abstraction. Construction of a subprogram involves serious consideration of control structures since the algorithm will be constructed differently depending on, say, whether the subprogram will be applied functionally, recursively, or concurrently (in parallel with another), although the most common control structure used in subprograms involves the total control of one program unit over another. Considerations regarding the data used in subprograms fall into one of two categories: *Protecting* it (for example, by the use of local variables) and *sharing* it (for example, by the use of parameters).

Access to Data in Subprograms

When a subprogram is invoked some data, the *global variables*, may already be accessible to it without anything special being done. *Local variables* are made accessible on invocation of the subprogram. The *scope* of a variable, meaning the portion of the program in which a variable name is associated with and accesses a particular value, is often considerably more complex than simply a global/local dichotomy. For example, when internal subprograms are nested, data considered local to one subprogram may be global to another. Also, in languages with dynamic typing, scope is also dynamic. In such cases, a subprogram's access to data is often determined by some sort of scoping rule. In addition to global and local variables, a subprogram has data available in the form of parameters. On invocation, the arguments used at the point of call are evaluated if necessary and passed to the corresponding *parameters* listed in the specification of the subprogram.

When the subprogram completes execution and control returns back to the calling subprogram, local variables are freed, arguments are disassociated from parameters, and, in the case of a function subprogram, a value is returned to the point of call.

Local vs. global variables.   Variables declared within the confines of the subprogram specification are *local variables*. They come to life only when the subprogram is invoked and, once execution of the subprogram is completed, they cease to exist. Local declarations are used in order to limit the scope of a variable. The use of local variables cuts down on the problem of data name clashes. These occur when the same identifier name is used in different subprograms, possibly by different programmers. When these variables are declared and used locally, there is no clash. The name references a different quantity in different parts of the program and the quantity referenced in one part cannot be affected by any processing done in the other part. This affords a degree of protection for your data. Some languages provide for certain designated local variables to retain their values between calls while still remaining inaccessible to the program. These are sometimes called *static variables* since memory is allocated to them statically, that is, permanently for the duration of the program execution. ALGOL60 designates these as **own** variables, PL/1 calls them **INTERNAL** and **STATIC**, and in C they are designated as **static**.

Global variables are declared in the main program, remain in existence throughout the course of execution of the program, and may be accessed in all program units. Global variables are thus subject to change as the result of processing done in a subprogram. For this reason, they are sometimes referred to as implicit parameters and, in fact, they are in many ways similar to input/output parameters. Variables that are global over internal subprograms may be specified implicitly simply by declaring them in the specification of the main program (for example, in ALGOL and Pascal). Variables that are global over external subprograms may be specified by declarations set aside for this purpose, for example, **COMMON** (in FORTRAN) and **EXTERNAL** (in PL/1). In COBOL, all variables must be explicitly declared globally, in the **DATA DIVISION**. In SIMSCRIPT, variables are local by default, and global variables are declared explicitly in the **PREAMBLE**, the program module which is reserved for the declarative statements at the program level.

One programming problem commonly associated with the unbridled use of global variables is that of side effects. A *side effect* is a change to a global variable that occurs as the result of processing carried out in a subprogram. Side effects, sometimes termed *context effects*, may be difficult to detect and are often unanticipated and undesired. At the very least, the use of global variables can lead to sloppy programming, which produces code that is difficult to decipher. For example, in the following code segment, it is not clear (without the comments) that the value of X might print out differently before and after the call to procedure P.

```
var X;         • X is global
print X;       • before change
call P;        • procedure P changes the value of global variable X
print X;       • after change
```

Scope.   The *scope* of a variable refers to the portion of the program in which the variable is associated with and has access to a particular value. For example, the scope of a local variable is the subprogram in which it is declared. Programming languages that allow nesting of internal subprograms must incorporate a means for determining which variables are accessible to each part of the program. Often, this is done by means of the *static scoping rule*, also called the *lexical scoping rule*, since the program text itself is all that is needed to determine scope. This scoping rule is simple to state but sometimes a little tricky to understand: Every variable is accessible to the subprogram in which it is declared and to any subprogram nested inside of it—unless the same variable name is redeclared as a local variable within some inner subprogram—but is not accessible to any subprogram outside or surrounding it.

Consider the program skeleton of Fig. 5.4. The static scoping rule for nested subprograms can probably best be understood by viewing the levels of nested subprograms as levels in a tree structure (see Fig. 5.5). From Fig. 5.4, we see that the scope of variables named A through E and X through Z are shown throughout the program. Variables X, Y, and Z are declared at the program level and are global to the entire program, except for variable X, which is redeclared as a local variable in procedure RedLevel2. This is known as a "hole-in-scope," that is, a global variable that is redefined in an inner block, canceling the previous declaration, until the inner block is finished executing, at which point the previous declaration is once again in effect. A reference to X will access a different value in a different storage location, treating it, in effect, as a different name, depending on where in the program the reference is made. Variables C and D are local to procedure RedLevel1, global to procedure RedLevel2.

An exception to this "hole-in-scope" rule is found in Ada: When a variable name has been redeclared in an inner block, the value referred to by the variable of the same name in the outer block can still be retrieved by means of a qualified name. In our example, we could write:

```
procedure RedLevel2;
    var X;

    ...
    Y := ShowScope.X

    ...
    end RedLevel2;
```

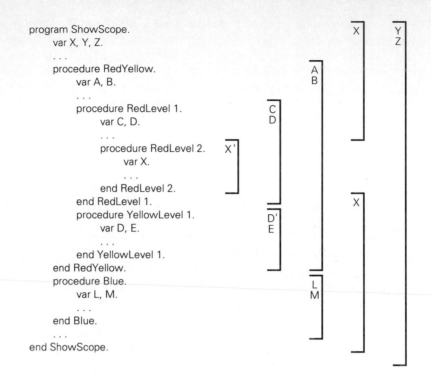

Figure 5.4   The lexical scoping rule

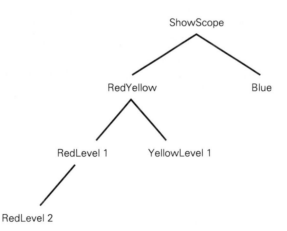

Figure 5.5   Nested subprograms as a tree structure

The data name ShowScope.X is a qualified name meaning "the X declared in ShowScope" and referring to the value stored in the variable named X, which was declared in subprogram ShowScope.

A program designed to take advantage of scoping rules can realize benefits similar to those obtained by the use of local variables. This sort of program will be more easily designed in a modular, top-down fashion, since the possibility of data name clashes is

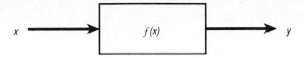

Figure 5.6   Black Box model of a function

minimized and subprograms are thus more independent of one another. In addition, variables will be more often declared close to the program text in which they are used—a practice that promotes the readability of the program.

In dynamic languages supporting a high degree of recursion, such as LISP, APL, SNOBOL, and Smalltalk, a *dynamic scoping rule* is in effect. As the name of this rule implies, the scope of a variable is determined not from examination of the program text but during execution time and may, in fact, change over time as execution proceeds. In this case, the scope of a variable is defined by the most recent occurrence and still active definition of that variable name. Thus, the definition of a variable at any given time during the execution of the program depends solely on which function was the last to use it.

Parameters.   A subprogram, like a program, may be considered to be a mapping of a particular set of values into a particular set of results. In *mathematical* terms, using the square root function as an example, we would say: $y = f(x)$, where f is the square root function, x is a value input to the function, and y is the result of the function, the square root of x. In the Black Box model of programming, it would look like the picture in Fig. 5.6.

Names for these values and results are given in the specification of a subprogram and are collectively referred to as *parameters*. *Input parameters* refer to values that are input to, and operated on by, the subprogram. *Output parameters* receive their values by processing done within the subprogram; these are the results. *Input/output parameters* provide two-way communication between the calling subprogram and the called subprogram: They may be used both for data input to and for results output from the subprogram. Depending on the type of parameter-passing mechanism used, an input/output parameter is somewhat similar to a global variable, without the accompanying problem of possible side effects.

When a subprogram is called, the name of the subprogram is followed by a list of *arguments*, which is often enclosed in parentheses. The arguments correspond in number and order to the parameters listed in the subprogram specification. When a parameter is used for input, the argument provides information to the subprogram. When a parameter is used for output from a subprogram, the argument provides a receiving field ready to accept that output. The parameters (sometimes called *formal parameters* or *dummy arguments*) are specified by the author of the subprogram and are, in effect, data name placeholders, which will be associated with storage locations and with values at the time the subprogram is invoked. Since the parameters are nothing more than placeholders (hence, the term "dummy argument"), the names used for the parameters are not critical. Declaring a subprogram as "**procedure** A (X, Y, Z)" is just the same as declaring it "**procedure** A (W, X, Y)." The change of variables changes nothing since the arguments are associated with parameters simply by their positions in the list. The arguments (sometimes called *actual parameters*) are specified by the author of the calling subprogram, the user of the called subprogram, and are the means by which information is finally passed to or received from the subprogram.

The use of parameters, as opposed to global variables, for sharing and communicating data between the subprogram and the calling program, enables us to generalize the effect of the subprogram.

Parameter Passing Mechanisms

The mechanism by which an argument is transferred to the corresponding parameter of a subprogram is called *parameter passing*. The activity of parameter passing follows that of *parameter evaluation* in which each argument in the calling program is associated with its corresponding parameter in the subprogram, and any necessary computation (for example, in the case of an expression) is carried out. There are two major methods for parameter passing: passing *by location* and passing *by value*. A third, passing *by name,* is not often put to practical use, although it is interesting to study because of its possibilities in some applications. Functional programming languages employ a mechanism known as passing *by need*.

By location.   Call by location is also known as *call by reference* or *call by address*. It is the most widely used means for communicating data to and from subprograms. It is the default method in FORTRAN, COBOL, and PL/1, and is available in Pascal, MODULA, and SIMULA.

When passing an argument to a subprogram during a subprogram call, the calling program (or subprogram) passes a reference, or machine address, for the argument. The parameter, then, is a pointer variable that points to the location of the argument. Rather than sending a value to the subprogram, this method results in the two modules sharing the data residing in some storage location. If the argument is an array, only the location of the first component is passed. The exception to the data-sharing characteristic of call by location is in the event that the argument being passed is an expression. In that case, the expression is evaluated first, and the result stored in a temporary unnamed storage location. It is this location that is then shared with the subprogram. This sort of unnamed location is termed an *anonymous variable*.

Fig. 5.7 shows the memory locations for the arguments and parameters used in the following example. In order to illustrate how call by location works for different kinds of arguments, of the three arguments used in the call statement, one is a scalar variable name, one is a constant, and one is a simple, arithmetic expression.

```
program Passing;
    var A, B, C: integer;
    ...
    procedure Sub(X, Y, Z);
        begin
            ...
            X:= X+Y+Z;
            ...
        end procedure Sub;
```

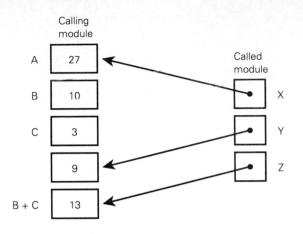

Calling module

A 27

B 10

C 3

9

B + C 13

Called module

X

Y

Z

Figure 5.7   Call by location memory allocation

```
begin
    ...
    A:=27;
    B:=10;
    C:=3;
    call Sub(A, 9, B+C);
    ...
end program Passing;
```

The effect of the data sharing that occurs is that the variable argument passed by location is accessible from the subprogram without limitation. In other words, the statements in the subprogram have access to the data stored in the storage location, both to read from that location and to write into it. When the subprogram terminates, the pointers are freed (deallocated), but any changes that were made to the arguments will, of course, be permanent. Thus, there is very little difference in effect between this and a global variable.

When global variables are used, the data names used in the called subprogram must be exactly the same as the data names used in the calling program. This is the only method for data sharing available in BASIC and COBOL. An advantage of using location parameters rather than global variables, although the effect of the two is the same, is that the data names used for the parameters are independent of those used for arguments. The two modules may easily be written by different programmers at different times without the necessity for coordination.

Here is a warning: Using both global variables and location parameters at the same time can cause some very interesting (and possibly incorrect!) results. Consider the following example:

```
procedure MessyData(A)
A:=A+1                              •   change A
if A=B then A:=A+B                  •   A and B are always the same
end MessyData                           in the subprogram
    ...
```

```
call MessyData(B)
```

In this example, A is a location parameter and B is a global variable. However, B is also bound to the subprogram as an argument to A. As soon as A is incremented, the value of B also changes, since they are actually the same. This is called *aliasing*—that is, two variables, A and B, both accessing the same storage location. Depending on the intent of the programmer, this is probably an error. It is certainly confusing.

By value.   When arguments are passed to parameters by value, the parameters are set up as variables local to the subprogram and initialized to the value of the arguments. In effect, the values of the arguments are copied to locations set aside for the parameters. The storage locations of the arguments are, therefore, protected from change within the subprogram. In ALGOL, these arguments may be declared explicitly using a value statement. Passing parameters by value is also available in Pascal, MODULA, SNOBOL, APL, and SIMULA. In PL/1, location parameters are the default for variables but constants and expressions are passed by value. Thus, call by value can be "forced" for a variable in PL/1 by bracketing the variable name with parentheses, as in: **CALL SUB ((A), 9, B + C)**. A call by value is accomplished in Ada by using **in** parameters: Data are not copied into a new location, but the Ada system does not allow assignments to an argument passed to an **in** parameter.

While location parameters are appropriate for use as input/output parameters, value parameters are used for input only. Sometimes, this use may be called *read-only*.

Important as it is to provide a means for protecting arguments, the disadvantage of passing arguments by value is that an additional storage location is allocated for each argument passed to the subprogram and remains allocated until the subprogram execution terminates. It is a space-inefficient method, especially for arguments requiring a large amount of space such as, say, a 1000-component array. It is also time inefficient. Fig. 5.8, using the same example as above, shows the memory allocation in a call by value. Notice that rather than pointers to locations, the subprogram's parameters now contain actual data values that are copies of the data values in the main program.

Passing arguments by value is the method of choice for function subprograms. By definition, a function is a subprogram that accepts input from the main program and returns a single result. This result is returned by way of the function name itself, which then acts in the same way as a variable identifier. Thus, if, by definition, the function returns only a single result, and if this result does not require the use of a parameter, then it follows that a function's parameters should all be input parameters, or value parameters.

Two variations of call by value are the parameter passing mechanisms of *call by result* and *call by value-result*.

The language Ada provides *call by result*, a little-known parameter passing method that is similar in effect to the result returned by way of the function name at the completion of a function subprogram. In this case, the parameters are set up like local variables but are not initialized to any values taken from the main program. At termination, however, the values stored in the parameters are copied back to the corresponding arguments in the main program. These parameters are output-only.

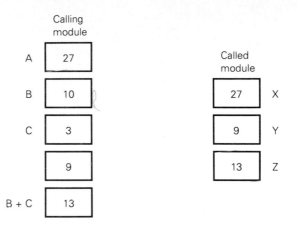

Figure 5.8 Call by value memory allocation

Call by value-result is a variation of passing arguments by value. This is a method that is designed to provide the advantages of both location parameters and value parameters. A parameter that communicates with the main program using call by value-result performs like an input/output parameter. Data values are passed to the subprogram in the manner of call by value and returned to the calling program by result. Thus, the parameter is declared and initialized as a local variable with initial value equal to that of the argument. When the subprogram terminates, the final value of the parameter is copied back to the argument. This is the only time the subprogram can change to the actual storage location of the argument. This sounds like it ought to produce the same effect as call by location, but it doesn't always, as an example below will demonstrate.

By name.   This parameter passing mechanism, introduced by ALGOL60 as its default and available in SIMULA, defers evaluation of each argument until it is actually needed during execution of the subprogram. Instead of passing a value, or a location of a value, to a parameter, we pass a *rule for evaluating the parameter*. It is, conceptually at least, a text replacement mechanism. Each time the parameter name appears in the text of the subprogram it is "replaced" (not really, but the effect is as if it were replaced) by the exact text of the argument. When the subprogram is called, the text at the point of call is replaced by a copy of the text of the subprogram in which parameters are replaced by the arguments, as above. Call by name is thus a very powerful tool for, e.g., producing generalized procedures—but it is also quite inefficient and dangerous if used carelessly. It is dangerous, because it can lead to data name clashes, as Fig. 5.9 demonstrates, and incorrect results. Because of this ever-present possibility of data name clashes, implementation of call by name may incorporate a facility for systematically renaming local variables where necessary. An example of the application of call by name is contained in Fig. 5.10. In this case, no special memory locations are set aside for "parameters" X, Y, Z. Rather, during execution of the subprogram, text substitution is completed first, then the operations are performed on values of A, B, C as if the text had appeared in the main program.

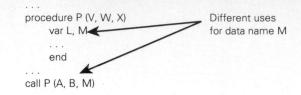

```
    . . .
procedure P (V, W, X)
        var L, M
    . . .
        end
    . . .
call P (A, B, M)
```

Different uses
for data name M

Figure 5.9 Dataname clash with call by name

With call by name, if the argument is a scalar variable, the effect is the same as with call by location; if the argument is an expression, the effect is the same as with call by value. In languages that do not provide for call by name (most of them do not), the effect can sometimes be achieved by passing a subprogram as an argument to the subprogram. After all, the idea of call by name is to pass a rule for evaluating the parameter. Of course, this assumes that the language does allow for arguments that are subprograms.

The use of call by name may be placed in the category of "cute programming tricks." However, while most techniques in this category are motivated by a desire for greater efficiency, this one may be cuteness for its own sake. Most algorithms can be programmed more efficiently and just as elegantly using the other parameter passing mechanisms. There is one classic example, due to K. Jensen, of an algorithm that benefits from the use of call by name. This is known as *Jensen's Device* (Knuth, 1967) and illustrates a generalized subprogram which, depending on the arguments presented to it, will perform slightly different tasks at each call. Jensen's Device looks something like this:

```
real procedure SIGMA (x, k, n);  value n;
      real x; integer k, n;
      begin real s; s:= 0;
      for k:=1 step 1 until n do s:= s+x;
      SIGMA := s
      end
...
SIGMA (A[i], i, 10)
SIGMA (A[i]*B[i],i,10)
SIGMA (SIGMA(C[i,j],i,20),j,30)
...
```

The first call to subprogram SIGMA returns the sum of the elements in the one-dimensional array, A: A[1] + A[2] + A[3] +...+ A[10]. The second call to SIGMA returns the sum of the product of corresponding elements of conformable arrays A and B: A[1] * B[1] + A[2] * B[2] + ... + A[10] * B[10]. The third call, assuming that subprograms are acceptable as arguments and that local variables will be systematically renamed, sums the elements of a 20×30 two-dimensional array, C: C[1,1] + C[1,2] +...+ C[1,30] + C[2,1] +...+ C[2,30] +...+ C[20,30].

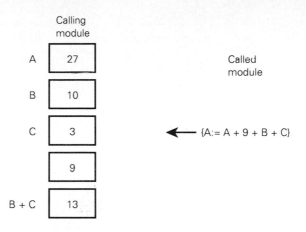

Figure 5.10 Call-by-name "memory allocation"

For an excellent exposition on the call by name mechanism, see Barron (1977, pp. 60–64).

In order to better understand and visualize the different effects of the different methods available for passing arguments to parameters, try the following example:

```
Program Passing;
    var X, Y, Result;
    procedure MakeWork (A, B, C, D, E);
        C:=C-A;
        B:=D+E;
    end;
    …
    X:=3;
    Y:=12;
    Result:=10;
    MakeWork (2, Result, Y, Y, X+Y);
    Write (Result);
    …
end Program Passing;
```

The value output for Result is different depending on the method of passing used. Fig. 5.11 shows how this example would be worked out for each of four parameter passing techniques. The results are shown in Table 5.3.

By need.   In the functional programming paradigm, an expression is evaluated only when some other expression (or function) requires its output. This *lazy evaluation*, or *delayed evaluation*, of arguments translates into a parameter passing mechanism known as *call by need*. The effect of parameter passing by need is very similar to ALGOL's call by name since an argument is evaluated only when its value is needed and not immediately at the point of call.

TABLE 5.3

Passing mechanism	Result
call by location	25
call by value	10
call by value-result	27
call by name	23

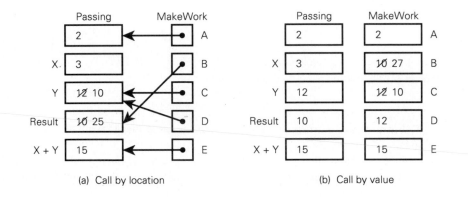

(a) Call by location

(b) Call by value

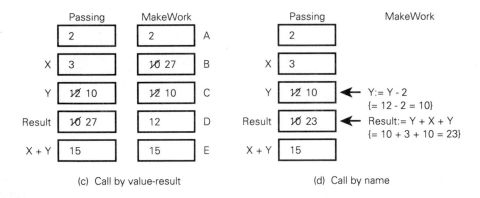

(c) Call by value-result

(d) Call by name

Figure 5.11 A parameter passing example

5.5 RELATIONSHIPS BETWEEN SUBPROGRAMS

Following the example of the previous section, this section might have been entitled, "Subprograms and Control." It is a difficult and futile task to separate program structures from control structures. The definition of a program structure must necessarily include both a description of the entity and the definition of the operations that activate and are performed on it. (We have seen that this is true for data structures as well.) The definition of subprograms based on the relationships that exist among them depends, to a large extent, on the control structure of the program, which is the subject of the next chapter.

The following is a brief overview of control relationships between subprograms. For the most part, the relationships discussed here are control relationships between a calling program (or subprogram) and the called subprogram. These are introduced briefly here, and will be discussed in greater detail in Chapter 6.

Total Control

The traditional subprogram (subroutine, procedure, function) embodies a fairly traditional and constrained control structure: total control of the calling program over the called subprogram. Often, this is called a *master/slave relationship*. The calling program invokes the subprogram, transferring control to it temporarily, so that it can perform a specific task. This is the relationship inherent in the top-down program design approach and the control structure charts (control hierarchy charts) that are utilized in this approach.

When a subprogram is invoked, control of execution branches to the entry point of the subprogram, while the address of the next instruction, the one that will be processed after completion of the subprogram, is saved. When the exit point of the subprogram is encountered during execution, control returns to the calling program and to the instruction corresponding to the address saved at the point of call.

The constraints inherent in this sort of relationship between called and calling modules are:

1. A subprogram *cannot call itself*. If the traditional lines of subprogram control—those represented in pictorial form by top-down control hierarchy charts—are to be maintained, one module, the calling subprogram invokes and has total control over another module, the called subprogram.

2. The subprogram is invoked by means of an *explicit call* statement within the sequence of statements that make up the calling program.

3. Only a *single subprogram has control* of execution at any one time. Thus, two subprograms cannot be invoked to execute concurrently.

4. And, of course, the calling program has *total control* over the subordinate subprogram, as a master to a slave.

If we remove each of these constraints, in turn, we are left with a subprogram which has a different relationship with its calling program and a control structure which is somewhat different from the traditional: 1) a recursive subprogram exerts control over itself; 2) an exception handler is controlled implicitly; 3) concurrent subprograms execute in parallel; and 4) coroutines exert mutual control over one another.

Self Control

A subprogram that can call itself is termed *recursive*. *Direct recursion* involves a direct call by a subprogram to itself from within the action portion of the subprogram. *Indirect recursion* involves a call from subprogram A to subprogram B which, in turn, calls subprogram A. A recursive subprogram may be a function or subroutine, internal or external.

The facility for recursion can sometimes lead to the design of simpler, more elegant algorithms. Some algorithms are inherently recursive and can be described best with a recursive subprogram. Most examples of inherently recursive algorithms come from the areas of mathematics and systems programming; there are relatively few examples from commercial data processing. Some examples are the factorial algorithm, the quicksort algorithm, and the traversal of a binary search tree.

The following is an example of a recursive function that returns the value of the factorial of N, defined as $N! = N(N - 1)(N - 2)...(2)(1)$. This definition is inherently recursive. To illustrate this characteristic, we can restate it as $N! = N(N - 1)!$.

```
function factorial(N);
    if N<2 then
            factorial := 1                          •  return with 1
    else
            factorial := N*factorial(N-1);   •  return with N(N-1)! and keep on
    end;                                                        going!
```

Of course, the relationship involved in that first call to a recursive subprogram is one of total control. As long as control is contained within the subprogram, however, it may call itself.

Implicit Control

When PL/1 was introduced, it defined a new kind of subprogram called an *exception handler*. This is a subprogram that is written by the programmer, interfaces with the operating system, and is invoked only when a specified "exceptional condition" is encountered. An exceptional condition might be an error condition, such as an attempt to divide by zero; it might simply be a condition that occurs infrequently, such as end of input file or end of printed page. This kind of invocation is called an *implicit call*. There is no single explicit call statement transferring control to the subprogram, and there is no other single module controlling the invocation of the exception handler. Ada is another language that has such a facility.

A condition must be specified as *monitored* (or, *enabled*) so that when it occurs, it will *raise an exception*—that is, trigger an implicit call to the exception handler. When this happens, execution of the program is temporarily interrupted and control is transferred to the exception handler subprogram.

Another kind of implicit control is demonstrated by the *scheduled call*, a type of subprogram control important to event-oriented system simulation. In this control mechanism, which we discuss in greater detail in the next chapter, the "call" is simply a scheduling of the subprogram call that is actually to occur at some later time. The subprogram will, at that time, be invoked by the timing routine—a different subprogram from the one that scheduled the call. Once a subprogram has been scheduled to occur, the scheduling subprogram loses all control over it. Both invocation and return are governed by the timing routine.

Parallel Control

When two or more subprograms (processes, tasks, ...) are allowed to operate simultaneously and relatively independently, this is called *parallel processing*, *multitasking*, or *concurrent processing*. Languages with such a facility include PL/1, ConcurrentPascal, MODULA, and Ada. Some mechanisms for addressing the concerns of concurrency in a programming language are monitors, semaphores, and message passing. (These will be discussed in the next chapter.)

The subprogram relationship of parallel control becomes especially important when an algorithm, designed for a problem lending itself toward decomposition into two or more relatively independent subtasks, is to be run on a multiprocessor system configuration. This is not the only configuration that can support concurrency, however. A single central processor may become, in effect, a virtual multiprocessing system and the subtasks may appear to be executing simultaneously when in fact they are not.

Mutual Control

A relationship of mutual control is the operative one on *coroutine subprograms*. Coroutines "call" each other. With coroutines, there is no need for an explicit return to a controlling module; rather, a call from one coroutine to another simply means that execution will resume from the last active point in the subprogram.

Fig. 5.12 depicts a standard control hierarchy chart for the usual subprogram relationship of total control and, along with it, contains slightly "revised" (bastardized) versions of this chart attempting to adapt it to portray the other types of relationships as well. In Fig. 5.12(a), the MAIN module exerts total control over modules P, Q, and R. They are called from the MAIN and when they finish executing they return control to the main. In (b), subprogram R is now recursive and to illustrate this we draw a line of control that originates at R and goes into R (self-control). In (c), R is implicitly controlled by monitoring of a condition that is expected to arise unpredictably and infrequently during the processing of the MAIN. Hence the dotted (implicit) line of control. In (d), Q and R are parallel processes, R having *fork*ed off of Q. When R terminates, it will "return" its control to Q which, when it terminates, will return control to MAIN. In (e), Q and R are coroutines, each exerting a measure of mutual control over the other.

Again, these control relationships between subprograms are presented in greater detail in Chapter 6.

5.6 MODULAR PROGRAMMING AND TOP-DOWN DESIGN

The approach to software engineering in which a large program is designed as a collection of blocks of code (modules) dates back at least as far as the advent of ALGOL with its characteristic block structure. As a matter of fact, it also dates back to COBOL's paragraphs, sections, and divisions. Even further, the FORTRAN subroutine, and the accumulation of libraries of these independently compiled modules was predated, in the early days of computing, by the machine-coded open subroutines which were shared freely among programmers working in the same installation and across the industry.

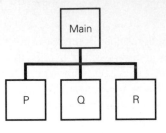

(a) Total control

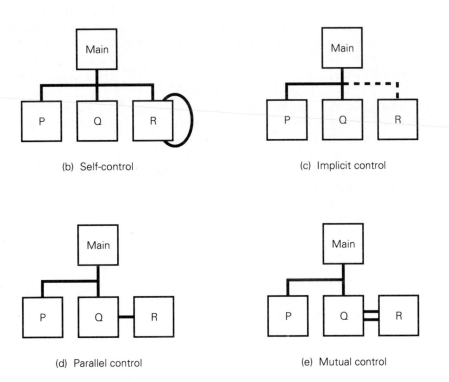

(b) Self-control

(c) Implicit control

(d) Parallel control

(e) Mutual control

Figure 5.12   Relationships between subprograms

More recently, it has become insufficient to simply modularize a problem into a set of subtasks. Problems for computer applications have grown huge and complex, and programs have increased in size accordingly. Programs are no longer—if, indeed, they ever were—written by a single individual to be used once and thrown away. Rather, program design (or, more appropriately, software engineering) has become an enterprise characterized by:

- organization sponsorship;
- large teams of individuals, working together and independently;

Figure 5.13   The Black Box model

- programs overseen and "walked through" by individuals other than those in the development team;
- maintenance and evolution of programs by a totally different team;
- large numbers of users removed from the development process.

In short, the environment of program development is anything but a vacuum.

It is in this environment that a host of programming conventions have arisen, including: user and technical documentation techniques, prototyping, structured walkthroughs and, of course, structured programming. Two concepts of major importance to the programming methodology known as *structured programming* relate to program structure. These are the *modular decomposition* of a program into relatively independent subtasks and *top-down,* or hierarchical, design.

Program Abstraction

Program abstraction involves the creation of a relatively independent program unit for the processing of a specific task. This is done in such a way so that the author of a calling subprogram never needs to know exactly *how* the subprogram accomplishes its goal, only *what* the function is that it performs. The model governing program abstraction is the so-called *Black Box model*, which has been adopted from the engineering disciplines. In this model, a set of inputs is mapped to a set of outputs by means of a *transform* (see Fig. 5.13). To use the transform one need not know how it works only *that* it works (and what it does!). An example is the nonmechanic car owner who regularly fills up the tank with fuel and knows only that when he starts the car it "goes." The Black Box representations of Fig. 5.14 illustrate several familiar program abstractions. In the course of our studies and professional work, we have all certainly encountered many of the abstractions pictured. (The odds are that 5.14(d) is the one most familiar to the largest number of people.)

In a well-structured program, any module may be considered a program abstraction as long as it has a single entry point, a single exit point, and performs a single, clearly defined action. Module, in this context, is a term meaning *a block of program code.* Thus, any code segment is a module, including: program, external subprogram, internal subprogram, block, compound statement, and even a statement.

Modular Programming

Modular programming is a disciplined process involving the identification, definition, and construction of relatively independent subprograms. In a well-constructed program, every subprogram has a single, clearly defined task to perform. Lower level modules will exhibit a greater level of detail and will, necessarily, have a more narrowly defined

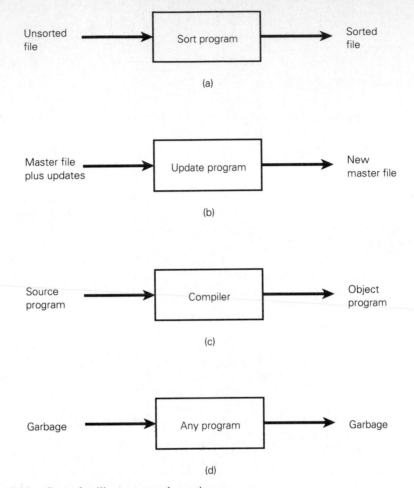

Figure 5.14   Some familiar program abstractions

function. Additionally, a subprogram should have a high degree of *cohesion* and a low degree of *coupling*.

Cohesion in program design means that each subprogram performs only a single function and all statements contained within that subprogram relate only to that function. As the term implies, in a cohesive subprogram, the statements contained within it tend to "stick together"—that is, they are strongly related to each other and to the task that the subprogram was designed to perform.

Coupling refers to the degree of relatedness of subprograms to the rest of the program. The greater the coupling, the less independent a subprogram is from the rest of the program. For example, the use of global variables increases the coupling of a subprogram with the rest of the program. In general, the two characteristics go together—that is, the greater the cohesion, the lower the coupling.

Top-Down Design

The top-down design of a modular program is based upon the process of stepwise refinement. *Stepwise refinement* is the consecutive specification of subprograms over several, progressively more detailed levels of abstraction. This process of stepwise refinement results in the modular decomposition of a program into a hierarchical structure. It works something like this:

First, we identify a module that will describe and govern the overall workings of the program, taking the large view. This module, often called the *main module* (or main program), will also contain the statements to start and stop program execution. We then proceed by breaking down this module into component subtasks, identifying each by function and only in as much detail as is necessary (*what* it does, not *how* it will do it). This is equivalent to saying to yourself, "I know what needs to be done here, but I will defer working out the details to a later time." Once this level of decomposition is complete, we review what we have done and then take each subprogram in turn, breaking it down further into subprograms containing a progressively more detailed algorithm. This process terminates when no subprogram can be broken down any further. Fig. 5.15 depicts the beginning of the step-by-step decomposition of a scheduled-report algorithm. This process of stepwise refinement continues at each level until no subprogram is complex enough to warrant further decomposition.

If you have ever constructed an outline in planning a story, book report, or term paper, you have used this technique. If you are not convinced that an outline resembles a top-down hierarchy, make up an outline of this chapter and then compare it to the corresponding hierarchy chart in Fig. 5.16.

With the top-down design approach a large, complex task is structured into a hierarchy of manageable subtasks. At each level in the hierarchy, low-level decisions and detail work are delayed to be done "later"—that is, when work on a lower level is done.

Contrast this with the approach known as *bottom-up program design*. The programmer begins coding immediately, starting with some low-level modules that are well defined. The programmer is thus forced to make low-level decisions early in the programming process. Concern with low-level details is then very likely to overwhelm the larger problem and draw attention away from the overall objective. Of course, there may be situations in which a combination of top-down/bottom-up techniques would be optimal. It may be difficult to design good reusable code before seeing many examples of how it will be used.

Advantages

The beginning of this section listed some of the trends in program design that are largely responsible for the push toward modular programming. Modular programming, along with the design of a modular program in a top-down fashion, results in many beneficial effects. While some of these benefits are expected, even planned, others are happy side benefits.

Reusable code. As we have seen, the same piece of code may be invoked many times within a single program. It may be used by the same programmer in many different

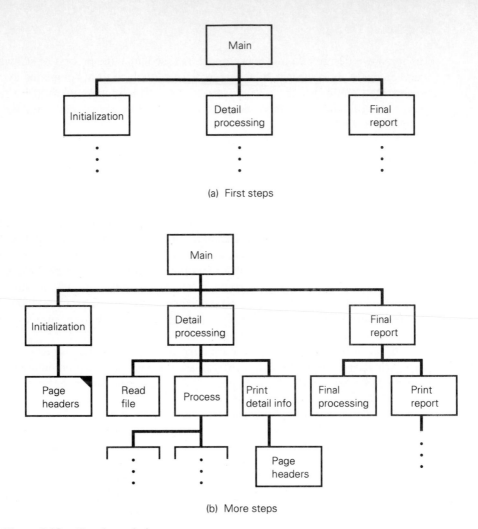

(a) First steps

(b) More steps

Figure 5.15   Top-down design

programs, and it may be used by different programmers who manually insert it into the text of their own programs or access it from subprogram libraries.

Efficient use of programmers.   This benefit is partly due to the availability of reusable code. Also, it is easier and less time consuming to code, test, and debug a program that has been decomposed into tractable subtasks. Additionally, maintenance programmers will require less time to locate areas of the program that require changes.

Efficient use of storage.   When a language that supports dynamic storage allocation is used, data local to each subprogram are allocated only on invocation of the subprogram and released as soon as execution of the subprogram terminates. In that case, designing a program as a collection of a large number of small, cohesive subprograms is

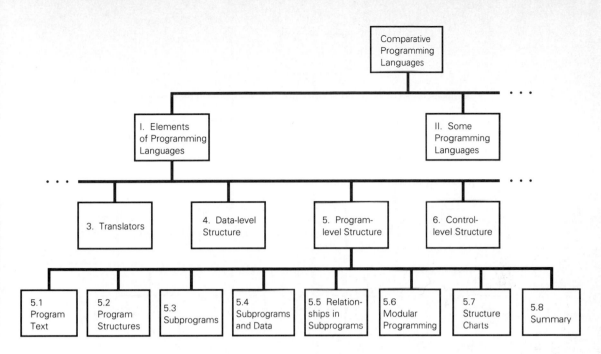

Figure 5.16   Outline as hierarchy chart

space efficient, since only a small fraction of the total amount of space needed by the program must be allocated at any one time. Also, in a multiprogramming, virtual memory environment, a large program may be too large to fit in its entirety into main memory, and some of the program code may have to be stored on a DASD while other parts of the program are executing. A well-designed modular program, with high cohesion and low coupling, reduces the number of swaps required between main memory and the DASD. On the down side, a modular program may result in an algorithm somewhat less efficient albeit more readable.

Local data declarations.   Data may be declared close to the portion of the program text in which it is used. Expressive variable names may be used (or reused) without regard for whether they may have been declared for a different purpose in another distant part of the program. In addition to conserving space, local data declarations serve to enhance the readability and expressive clarity of a program.

Localized debugging.   Testing and debugging the program code are facilitated when subprograms are compiled and tested individually. When each subprogram represents a small subtask, it is easier to locate errors and so the likelihood of implementing a faulty program is reduced.

Language extension.   The concept of the module, or subprogram, as a program abstraction allows us, in effect, to extend the capabilities of the language—by defining new functions, operations, etc.

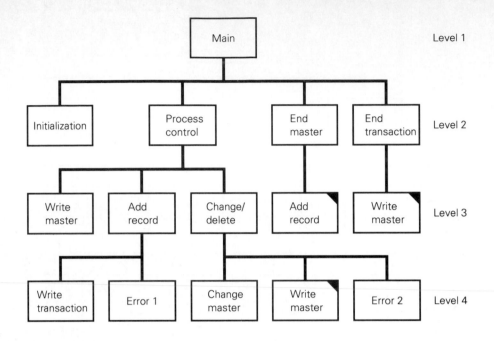

Figure 5.17 Update program hierarchy chart

5.7 CHARTING THE PROGRAM: HIERARCHY CHARTS

Hierarchy charts, also called *control hierarchy charts*, have already been used several times throughout this chapter. A hierarchy chart gives you a "birds-eye view" of the entire modular decomposition of a hierarchical program. You can take in the entire program in a single glance. You have already seen how the hierarchy chart for a hierarchically (top-down) designed program resembles an outline. In fact, this chart is sometimes called a "visual table of contents."

In a hierarchy chart, every subprogram is portrayed as a rectangle with its name and/or function written inside of it. Control between subprograms is indicated by the connecting vertical lines. The subprogram at the top (*the source*) of a vertical connecting line invokes and exerts total control over the subprogram at the bottom (*the destination*). Hierarchy charts are arranged much like trees, in levels. Subprograms on the same level do not communicate with each other. For the most part, all the subprograms on a given level are supposed to have approximately the same level of detail: The lower the level, the greater the detail. At the highest level, there is only a single module, the main module, which contains the starting and stopping points for program execution and describes the overall workings of the program in a very general way.

Fig. 5.17 contains a hierarchy chart for a sequential file update program. (See Study Problem #2 in Chapter 7 for the complete detailed algorithm.) Level 1 contains only the MAIN subprogram that governs the rest of the program. On level 2, the subprograms controlled by the MAIN, we have the PROCESS CONTROL subprogram, which contains the major logic of the update program, and subprograms that will be performed

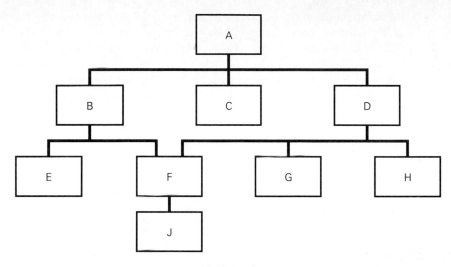

(a) Network

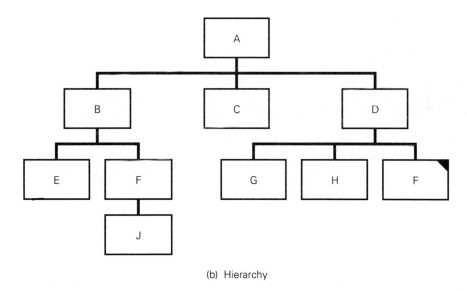

(b) Hierarchy

Figure 5.18   Common subprogram

at the beginning (INITIALIZATION) of the program or toward the end (END of MAS-TER file, END of TRANSACTION file) of the processing. The PROCESS CONTROL subprogram contains level 3 subprograms for processing the updates (adding, changing, deleting records) and, of course, for writing out sequential records to a new master file.

A subprogram that is called more than once from different subprograms in the program (sometimes referred to as a *common function*) may be represented by an additional rectangle for every place in the program from which it is called. In this way, we keep the hierarchy chart looking like a tree, not a network. Compare the two charts in Fig. 5.18. In order to avoid confusion, repetitions of a subprogram are indicated by rectangles with a corner "bitten off," and any subordinate subprograms are not indicated at that point. For example, in the sequential file update program hierarchy chart of Fig. 5.17, notice how the different calls to the subprograms named ADD RECORD and WRITE MASTER are represented.

A word of caution is appropriate at this point: Since these are different calls to the same subprogram, if this subprogram should be changed at some future time, one must make certain that the change is appropriate throughout the program at every point at which the module is invoked.

The subprogram control relationship reflected by the hierarchy chart is one of total control of one subprogram over its subordinate subprograms.

SUMMARY AND KEY TERMS

Chapter Summary

In this chapter, we have discussed program level objects and structures, beginning first with the program text itself represented as a string of characters laid out over several input lines. Program objects were presented as a hierarchy of structures, with identifiers at the lowest level of the hierarchy and the program itself at the highest level.

The remaining portion of the chapter was devoted to the topic of the subprogram as a program unit, including data access and control relationships in subprograms and coverage of the program design techniques of modular decomposition and top-down design. Finally, a charting technique for hierarchical, modular programs was presented.

Terminology

Some of the terms presented in this chapter may have been new to you. Use this list as a guide in reviewing the chapter. When you review the list, if you come across a term that is unfamiliar to you, go back and review the section that discusses it. Some of these terms were introduced only briefly in this chapter, and will be discussed in more detail in the chapters that follow.

activation record	actual parameter	aliasing
anonymous variable	argument	Black Box model
bottom-up design	brackets	call by address
call by location	call by name	call by need
call by reference	call by result	call by value
call by value-result	cohesion	compound statement
coroutine	coupling	delimiter
dynamic scoping rule	entry point	exception handler
exit point	external subprogram	fixed-format
formal parameter	free-format	function

generic function	global variable	hierarchy chart
identifier	implicit control	input parameter
input/output parameter	internal subprogram	job
keyword	lexical scoping rule	local variable
modular programming	module	named constant
output parameter	parallel processes	parameter
program	program abstraction	recursive subprogram
reference	reserved words	scope
separator	side effect	simple statement
static scoping rule	stepwise refinement	subprogram
subprogram call	subprogram library	top-down design

SUGGESTIONS FOR FURTHER STUDY

For more detailed coverage of the material in this chapter, see books by Dijkstra (1976), Gries (1978), and Martin and McClure (1988) and articles by Gries and Prins (1985), Parnas (1972a, 1972b, 1976), McKeeman (1975), and Wirth (1974a). Also, some texts of a general nature have very readable expositions on program structure and modular, top-down programming. These include Zwass (1981) and Barron (1977).

The topic of reusable software libraries is taken up in papers by Goguen (1984), Meyer (1987), and Standish (1984) and in the book by Cox (1986).

6

Control-level Structure

So far, we have discussed *passive* programming language objects, those that don't actually do anything but rather are descriptive in nature. Chapter 4 covered data objects, and Chapter 5 discussed program objects. These objects have been described, each along with its set of appropriate or allowable operations, and relationships among these entities have also been discussed. This is, admittedly, a very passive approach to programming languages and to the *activity* of programming. In this chapter, we take a more active point of view.

Due to a reliance on the von Neumann model of computer architecture, much programming methodology depends on and assumes an underlying machine that is sequential in nature. A single instruction is executed, followed by another, followed by another, and so on. Thus, the default control structure in the majority of programming languages is simply a sequential flow of control. However, as we shall see, the programmer has a great many opportunities to influence the flow of control—that is, the sequence in which the computer will perform the set of operations that make up the program.

From the hierarchy of program structures discussed in Chapter 5, we saw that a program or subprogram may contain a sequence of statements. In imperative, statement-oriented languages, the most important statement—because it is the one that does the major work of the program—is the assignment statement. Assignment statements contain expressions to be evaluated and stored in a named location, and an expression is a way of representing a sequence of operations. Thus, ultimately, all control over program units reduces to control over the elementary operations that we expect the computer to perform. The hierarchical relationship among program structures, while crucial to an in-depth understanding of the programming process and imperative programming languages such as COBOL and Pascal, is not the only meaningful one.

In fact, the relationship characterizing these program units is much closer and more elegant than you might at first perceive. Since a subprogram may be described as an operation and an operation as a subprogram, there is a close, symmetrical relationship between the lowest unit in the program hierarchy and the highest.

Subprogram as operation. We can formally describe an entire subprogram in terms of a single operation or expression. This is the position taken in the top-down program design technique, which creates a hierarchy of program abstractions. Each program abstraction, or subprogram module, has the single-entry/single-exit characteristic and is thought of as performing a single action. Of course, the entire program can be viewed in this way as well.

From a different point of view, a statement represents an operation that may be performed on one or more operands. For example, in the following familiar "operations" the operators are italicized:

```
assign ComputedValue to StoredValue
branch to StatementLabel
input StoredValue
```

Then, since an expression is nothing more than a sequence of operations, the complete subprogram unit is an expression—it contains a sequential collection of operations. It accomplishes its objective by the evaluation of this expression. Thus, a subprogram is an operation that causes the evaluation of a highly complicated expression. This view of subprograms as operations considers input parameters as operands.

Operation as subprogram. We can take the position that an operation is a kind of simple subprogram. Since an operation returns a value, let us think of it as a function subprogram. Then, an expression is evaluated by means of the invocation of some functions in the order specified. For example, the operations contained in the expression 2(a + b) may be invoked in the following manner: Multiply(2, Add(a, b)). If you have trouble with this concept, think of the large number of machine-language instructions necessary to evaluate an ordinary arithmetic expression.

Thus, we see that if we look at the operation as a subprogram, we again reach the conclusion, although by a slightly circuitous route, that a subprogram is nothing more than the evaluation of a high-level expression. The symmetry of this relationship between the smallest and the largest program structure is very appealing.

In this chapter, we will discuss implicit and explicit control structures at the expression level, the statement level, and the subprogram level. *Implicit control structures* are those that the language makes available by default and *explicit control structures* are those imposed by the programmer over the default flow of control. In our discussion of control structures, we will be guided by the classification tree displayed in Fig. 6.1. Control at the expression level is concerned with control over operations, the sequential order of operations to be performed in computing the value of the expression. Control at the statement level is concerned with the ordering of the statements that make up the program—a composition that may be accomplished sequentially, by selection among alternatives, or by iteration. Control at the subprogram level is concerned with subprogram invocation and the relationship between the calling module and the called module. Control over the program is typically not a concern of the programming language but of the operating system that interfaces between user and computer.

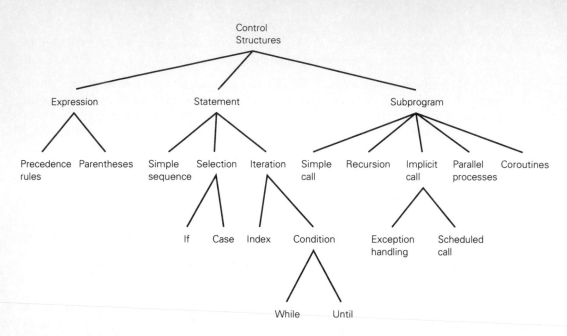

Figure 6.1   Classification of control structures

In addition, the programming world view most pervasive in computing today, the *imperative programming paradigm*, will be discussed in depth along with several alternative programming paradigms: the functional, rule-oriented, logic, and object-oriented programming paradigms. Finally, we will examine charting techniques that can aid in expressing the structured flow of control in well-written programs.

6.1 CONTROL OVER OPERATIONS

Expressions

An *expression* is a formula for computing a value, and it is represented as a formalized sequence of operators, operands, and parentheses. An expression results in a computed value that resides in a temporary storage location until it is used, say, in an assignment operation. Thus, an expression has an implicit type. It might be, for example, arithmetic (integer, real, double, complex), logical (condition or assertion), or string depending on the types of the operands and the particular operations to be performed.

It is indicative of the importance of expressions to computing that the first successful compiler was written entirely for the purpose of efficient expression evaluation (**FOR**mula **TRAN**slating system). This was and is a tremendous advantage over hand coding and assembler language coding because it serves to hide the low-level nature of the underlying machine. An expression, a reasonably clear formalism that is familiar to us from mathematics, specifies and may be translated to a huge number of sequential machine-language instructions. Each of these instructions performs an operation and produces a result that requires a storage location. The value at that storage location is then used as data to be operated on by a future primitive instruction. The execution of an expression keeps these intermediate results anonymous or hidden from the programmer, who is not required to name them or even to devote time to thinking about them. Thus, the expression serves to raise the programming process to a higher, more abstract, level.

An expression is written as a sequence of operators, operands, and parentheses. An *operator* is a primitive function that returns a value and is often represented by a single symbol. An *operand*, which represents a data value and is actually a means of accessing a value, may be a constant, a variable name, a function reference, an array reference, or even another expression. Many languages have a built-in set of rules that establish priorities in the execution of the operations in an expression. The *parentheses* allow the programmer to override these rules.

An operator may be classified as either a *binary operator* having two operands, for example, X + Y, or a *unary operator* having one operand, for example, -X, **not** B. *Arithmetic operators* (+ - * / ^) operate on arithmetic data and form arithmetic expressions. A *mixed-mode expression* is one that contains operands of different types and some conversion is needed in order to evaluate it. For example, the expression 5 / 2.5 is converted to 5.0 / 2.5 and then evaluated as a real-valued arithmetic expression. *Relational operators* (< <= = <> >= >) may operate on virtually all types of data and form conditions. A *condition* is an assertion of a relation that computes to a Boolean value. *Logical operators* (**and or not**) operate on Boolean data and enhance conditions. In most programming languages, operator precedence rules follow, with some variation from one language to another, the following hierarchy. From highest precedence to lowest:

Precedence of Operators
not
* /
+ −
< <= = <> >= >
and or

In addition, sequences of operations on the same level of precedence are usually, but not always, performed left to right. Delimiting an operation or a sequence of operations by parentheses serves to override these rules. Any operation contained within a set of parentheses has the highest level of priority. These rules become mostly irrelevant in functional programming languages such as LISP and APL. LISP has no need for such a hierarchy since all operations are nested within parentheses (see the discussion of Cambridge Polish notation, below). The effect of this is that the programmer sets up her own explicit control structure over all operations. In APL, "unparenthesized" expressions are simply evaluated from right to left, all operations having equal priority.

Conditional expression.   The conditional expression is a form of expression that originated with LISP, made its way into ALGOL60, and is currently used in C. It is a selection construct (see the next section) that, in statement-oriented languages, could possibly replace a sequence of statements and so result in a clearer, more concise expression. For example, the C expression

```
B = (A>B)? A: 0
```

reads this way: If the expression (A > B) is true, then B = A; otherwise B = 0. It is equivalent to the selection construct

```
if (A>B) B=A else B=0.
```

Representation of Expressions

There are a variety of formalized ways with which to represent expressions. This includes the purely mathematical form. Some of the forms will be familiar to you from your work with various high-level programming languages. Others are useful in understanding the underlying control structure in expressions, and still others are important because the expressions may actually be evaluated in that form by the underlying machine. Let us examine some of these different representations, using a relatively simple arithmetic expression presented first in mathematical form:

$$\frac{2(a + b)}{c - d}$$

Parenthesized forms. The standard *parenthesized form* for the representation of expressions is the one most familiar to us and most commonly relied on in programming. In this form, the expression is represented as a linear sequence of operators and operands which is ordered so as to exploit as much as possible the built-in precedence rules of each language. Some parentheses are used, but only when it is necessary to indicate that, for certain operations, the rules do not apply. In parenthesized form, the simple arithmetic expression above would appear as:

```
2*(A+B)/(C-D)
```

Fully parenthesized form does not rely on any precedence rules at all. Instead, all operations are contained within parentheses. For example:

```
((2*(A+B))/(C-D))
```

Functional form. *Functional form* represents all operations as functions; the operands are arguments to these functions. This form is familiar to us from mathematics where it appears as $f(x,y)$. For example, the functional forms for addition and multiplication are Add(X,Y) and Mult(X,Y). Since operands may be functions as well, this form is characterized by repeated application of function on top of function. In our example:

```
Div(Mult(2,Add(A,B)),Subt(C,D))
```

This representation may also be called *applicative form* or *ordinary prefix form*. This last term becomes clearer when we use operator symbols to represent the functions, as in: /(*(2,*(A,B)),... . In other words, the operator appears before its operands. In the same way, the parenthesized forms above are called *infix forms*. (To complete this terminology, Reverse Polish form, described below, is called a *postfix form*.)

Cambridge Polish form is somewhat "cleaner" than standard functional form. It is the type of functional form employed in LISP, which then actually makes use of tree

Figure 6.2   Function represented as a tree

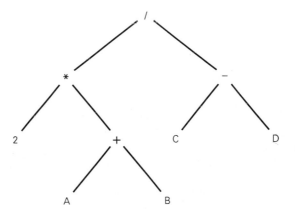

Figure 6.3   Arithmetic expression as a tree

structures in evaluating the expressions. In Cambridge Polish form, the parentheses surround the operator and its associated operands as, in general, (*f x y*) or, for example, (Add X Y). For our simple arithmetic expression, this would appear as:

```
(Div (Mult 2 (Add A B)) (Subt C D))
```

Tree form.   In the tree representation of expressions, the root of each subtree is an operation, and its branches are the operands. Any function can be represented as a tree. This is depicted in general in Fig. 6.2. Leaf nodes are references to data values—that is, they may be constants, variable names, function references, or array references; they are *not* expressions. For example, see Fig. 6.3. The root node of the tree is the location that will contain the result computed by the expression when it has been evaluated. Fig. 6.4 shows how this simple expression might be evaluated using a tree-structure representation.

Parenthesis-free forms.   Trees are fine for human beings and they enhance our understanding of the control structures governing the execution of the operations contained within the expression, but parenthesis-free forms are much easier for the computer to process. Parenthesis-free forms were introduced by a Polish mathematician-logician named Lukasiewicz and have come to be known as "Polish" forms. As the "parenthesis-free" implies, the sequence of operators and operands alone are sufficient to indicate the order of operations desired by the programmer, and no parentheses are needed.

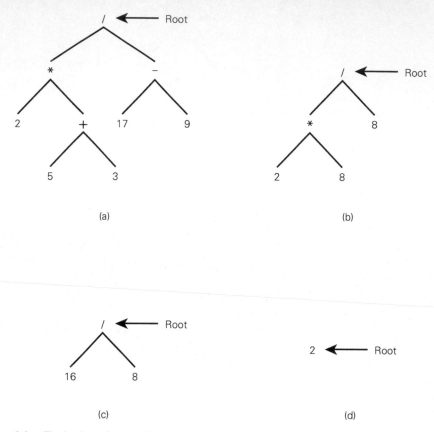

Figure 6.4 Evaluation of expression in a tree

In ordinary *Polish form,* the convention is to write the operator before the operands, in *prefix form.* This is an efficient means of representing an expression since a stack may then be used in its evaluation. However, the number of operands expected by each operator must be known and not subject to change. The simple arithmetic example above represented in Polish notation would look like this:

```
/*2+AB-CD
```

Reverse Polish notation, used in the language FORTH, is a *postfix form* of notation for representing expressions, which is easier to evaluate than ordinary Polish. In Reverse Polish notation, the operator follows its operands. For example:

```
AB+2*CD-/
```

Fig. 6.5 illustrates how this expression, represented in Polish form or Reverse Polish form, would be evaluated to produce the correct value. Stacks would be used in both cases, to store the sequence of operator symbols and operands and to evaluate the operations. In the case of Polish notation, we repeatedly pop items off the stack until two operands followed by an operator have been popped. Then we evaluate that subexpression and push it back onto the stack. In the case of Reverse Polish, as each component of

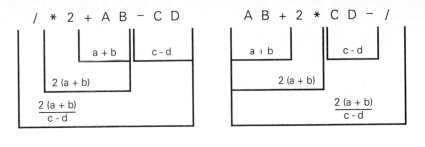

(a) Polish   (b) Reverse Polish

Figure 6.5   Parenthesis-free forms

the expression comes in on the input stream, operands are pushed onto the stack. When an operator is encountered, the top two (or other appropriate number) operands are popped off the stack, and the result is pushed onto the stack. It is not necessary to assume that all the operators are binary operators, but you can see why Polish notation demands that the number of operands expected by each operator be fixed.

It need hardly be noted that all these forms for representing expressions are superior to machine coding the sequence of operations. Using a fictitious assembler-type code, the expression would look something like this:

```
LOAD    T1   A
ADD     T1   B
MULT    T1   2
LOAD    T2   C
SUBT    T2   D
DIV     T1   T2
```

Fig. 6.6 contains another example. This one is a slightly more complicated arithmetic expression, depicted first in mathematical form and then using the various representations discussed here.

6.2 CONTROL OVER STATEMENTS

There are a variety of statements commonly found in many computer programming languages. Most of us, in fact, first learned programming one statement at a time. Every programming language statement can be placed in one of the following categories:

- assignment statement
- input/output statements (**read, get, write, print,** ...)
- decision statements (**if**)
- branching statements (**goto**)
- subprogram call statement (**call**)
- looping statements (**do**)

Some languages also include a **return** statement for exiting from a subprogram and a **stop** statement for stopping execution at the program level.

$$\frac{X^3 + 5XY + 6}{3(X-Y)^2}$$

(a) Mathematical form

(X^3+5*X*Y+6)/(3*(X–Y)^2)

(b) Parenthesized form

(((X^3)+((5*(X*Y))+6))/(3*((X–Y)^2)))

(c) Fully parenthesized form

DIV (ADD (UP (X,3), ADD (MULT (5,MULT (X,Y)), 6)), MULT (3, UP (SUBT (X,Y), 2)))

(d) Functional form

(DIV (ADD (UP X 3) (ADD (MULT 5 (MULT X Y)) 6)) (MULT 3 (UP (SUBT X Y) 2)))

(e) Cambridge Polish form

/ + ^ X 3 + * 5 * X Y 6 * 3 ^ – X Y 2

(f) Polish form

X 3 ^ 5 X Y * * 6 + + 3 X Y – 2 ^ * /

(g) Reverse Polish form

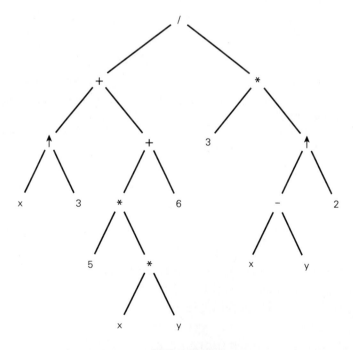

(h) Tree form

Figure 6.6   Representations of expression

Most of the languages in use today employ the imperative programming paradigm, discussed more fully in Section 6.4. These languages take a statement-oriented approach to programming and the most important of these statements is the assignment statement. If you think about it for a moment you will realize that the assignment statement is the only one that does any real, productive work! The assignment statement retrieves a value using instructions on the right side of the assignment operator and stores that value in the memory location named on the left side of the assignment operator. Whatever it is that the program actually accomplishes, it does by way of the assignment statement. With the exception of input/output statements, which are, after all, only there because it is necessary for the computer to communicate with the outside world, all the other statement categories listed above are involved in control over execution. If we consider these control statements as "management," then the assignment statement is "production."

The simplest control structure is called *simple sequence*; it is the default. In this structure, individual statements are executed one after another in the order they appear in the program. Of the methods that are available for altering this built-in structure, the simplest and most dangerous is the unconditional *branch*, also called a *jump* or a *transfer*, which most frequently uses the keyword **goto**. The **goto** statement transfers control of execution to another part of the program, and execution picks up sequentially from there with no return to the point of the transfer. The decision statement, often called the **if** statement since that is the keyword most frequently used, exerts control over execution by a process called *selection*. One body of statements or another will be executed depending on the value computed by the conditional expression contained in the statement. Another form of selection that allows for more than two alternatives is the **case** *construct*. Finally, the most complicated, powerful, and varied control structure is the loop, often called *iteration*. It is a means of repeating a section of code and can take on a variety of forms.

Simple Sequence

A program is often defined as a collection of statements *ordered in a particular sequence* to accomplish a specific goal. The sequence of statements is crucial: Change it and you have very likely changed the meaning and effect of the program. *Simple sequence*, also called *sequential composition*, may be represented in flowchart form by the flowchart diagram in Fig. 6.7 or as:

```
statement1;
statement2;
statement3;

...
```

The compound statement is a language construct representing simple sequence. In many languages, a compound statement is a sequence of statements, delimited by paired keywords such as **begin** and **end**, which may be used anywhere in the program that a single statement is expected.

Often, simple sequence alone is insufficient for expressing the necessary computation. This may occur, for example, when a section of code must be repeated several times. Simply writing the group of statements in that section of code over and over again is time consuming and obscures the intent of the program. It may also be infeasible since

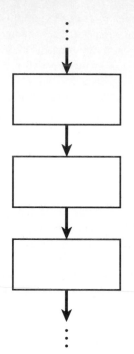

Figure 6.7   Simple sequence

the number of times to repeat the section of code may not be known until run time. The simple sequence control construct is also inappropriate when a group of statements is to be executed only if a particular condition is met (or, not met).

The goto Controversy

The **goto** is a low-level control instruction available in most high-level languages. It mimics the machine-language branch instruction, which transfers control of execution forward or backward to a nonsequential instruction. The **goto** instruction is the simplest means by which a programmer can exert control over the order of execution of the statements in a program. This statement is most often denoted by the keyword **goto** and a statement identifier such as a statement number, an alphanumeric label, or a paragraph name. For example: **goto** Identifier. A general unconditional **goto** statement is represented in flowchart form in Fig. 6.8 (a) along with a conditional branch in 6.8 (b), its most common use in conjunction with a decision.

Although the **goto** has been called the most powerful sequence control structure, it is actually the least powerful. Power is defined in terms of the number of machine-level instructions to which a high-level construct must be translated. For any programming language, the greater the ratio of machine-level instructions to high-level instructions—the fewer high-level statements are necessary to code the program—the more powerful is the language. A single **goto** statement translates to a single machine-level branch instruction.

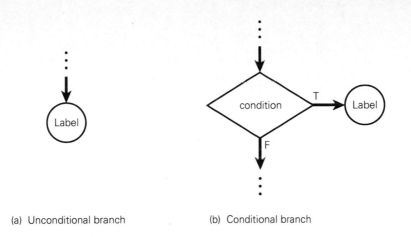

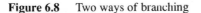

(a) Unconditional branch   (b) Conditional branch

Figure 6.8   Two ways of branching

The 1970s and 1980s saw a great deal of discussion regarding the use of this controversial control statement. There is no doubt that it is an important statement. There is no doubt that it is a dangerous statement and can easily lead you to code confusing and error-prone programs. There is also no doubt that it is important to learn why this simple construct has been so maligned and which other constructs may be, but are not always, better.

Just because the **goto** statement mimics an instruction found in the machine's own instruction set is no reason to use it. It may, in fact, be a reason not to use it. Ever since we gave up on hand-coding programs in machine languages in favor of second-, third-, and fourth-generation software, we have been striving toward more and more abstraction in programming. A high-level language ought to enable us to use a high level of abstraction in expressing algorithms instead of resorting to the use of a statement that has no meaning of any kind outside of the limited world of the computer. It is interesting to note that even in systems programming, which is generally considered to be a low-level endeavor, the trend is toward programming in high-level languages (C, EUCLID, BLISS, MODULA-2, Ada).

Objectively, the very worst thing you can say about the **goto** as a control structure is that it is a low-level construct that does not provide for any degree of abstraction at the control level. It is not, however, a poor construct; it is certainly not an evil construct. It is simply a tool; one that will be used well by a good programmer and badly by a bad programmer. It is this capacity for abuse that has thrown the **goto** into the center of a hot and mostly one-sided controversy. The ways in which the **goto** provides a means by which a poor programmer can write bad programs is by now well known. If you have the capability to branch arbitrarily to another part of a program, you can branch to many different statements and never return; you can branch willy-nilly forward and backward until the program's control flow comes to resemble a plate of spaghetti, and it thus becomes very difficult to grasp what a program does (or, is supposed to do) simply by reading the code. For example, consider the following program segment, written by an exceptionally bad programmer who wishes to remain anonymous. What does this code segment do?

```
      …
10    print "headings"
20    goto 50
30    print i
40    goto 200
50    i = 1
60    goto 30
80    i = i + 1
100   if i>1 then goto 30
200   if i=100 then stop
210   goto 80
      …
```

Your first response might be to say that this particular piece of code does nothing but jump backward and forward without producing anything constructive. Your second response might be that if it does accomplish anything, it probably does it wrong. However, if you examine it a little bit more you will find that this program segment actually prints out all the whole numbers between 1 and 100. Aha! you exclaim. Why wasn't it simply written as:

```
      …
print "headings"
do i=1 to 100
print i
      …
```

You see that you have already been conditioned to think in terms of high-level abstractions instead of designing an algorithm by examining one simple statement at a time. Clearly, the **goto** statement is not the culprit here. The true culprit is the programmer who abuses it. This programmer who is so fond of **goto**s ought to keep a wary eye out for the boss—who might well tell the programmer where to goto …

It has been shown that if constructs for selection and iteration are available, then any program can be written without the use of the **goto** statement. These constructs provide for abstraction at the control level and allow—some would say, force—a programmer to think more in terms of *what* is to be done rather than *how* to get to the statement that does it. When a language does not provide these constructs, a good programmer will use the **goto** judiciously to create them and work with them conceptually.

For example, consider the somewhat facetious example above. We eliminated the **goto**s by using an indexed loop construct. What if such a construct were not available? Would we be required to accept the first version of the program? Not at all. A good programmer would code it this way:

```
      …
print "headings"
i = 1
10    print i
i = i + 1
if i <= 100 then goto 10
      …
```

```
for j := 1 to 1000 do                    for j := 1 to 1000 do
    if A(j)=X then jsave := j                if A(j)=X then go to Out
A(jsave) := Y                        Out:   A(j) := Y


(a) Without goto statement            (b) With goto statement
```

Figure 6.9   Early exit from within a loop

Obviously, even if such high-level control abstractions such as the indexed loop construct are not explicitly provided by the language, these abstractions are capable of promoting clarity of thought and expression throughout the algorithm.

Whether or not explicit language constructs for selection and iteration are available, you would be well advised to make minimal use of branching instructions for the control of execution. Some benefits of this policy are: a more disciplined program design process; increased modularity in programs; more readable programs; algorithms with greater expressive clarity. In addition, it will be easier for the compiler to optimize code since the flow of control is clearly delineated.

A few programming languages have banned the use of the **goto** altogether and do not even provide facility for an unconditional branch at all. These include the languages BLISS, MODULA-2, and EUCLID. Some languages, like Ada, tried to eliminate the statement but found that its use was necessary or, at least, expedient in certain situations.

What kinds of situations could possibly require the use of the **goto** statement as the most appropriate control structure? There are at least two:

1. Early exit may be required from a loop. For example, take a look at the two search algorithms in Fig. 6.9. Algorithm 6.9(a) does not use a **goto** statement. The loop must run through the full range of the index variable even if the "target" is found on the first iteration. Also, an additional variable is required in order to save the location of the target. Algorithm 6.9(b) uses a **goto** statement judiciously and results in more efficient code. Of course, efficient code may or may not be a critical design criterion.

2. Other constructs may not enable you to construct the algorithm in the most natural manner. For example, consider the two read-and-process algorithms in Fig. 6.10. You have by now seen a form of the algorithm in 6.10(a) many times. Perhaps (especially you younger programmers) it is the only form of the "read-and-process" algorithm you have ever seen. Think about it. There is redundant code in it due to the structure of the while/do which required a "priming" read outside of the loop. The body of the loop seems to get things backwards, processing and then reading when what we really want to do is read and process. What we really want to do is described by the algorithm in 6.10 (b). Now, *that* looks like a read-and-process algorithm.

How do different programming languages handle these situations? For the first situation, some, like Ada, provide an **exit** statement to be used in place of a **goto**. The **exit** statement is reserved explicitly for branching out of a loop to the very first statement following the loop. The second situation is not often addressed, since it varies from one algorithm to another. For the specific example used here, the **AT END** clause on COBOL's **READ** statement works well.

```
print "prompt for input"                    do
input X                                          print "prompt for input"
while X <> sentinel do                           input X
    process_X                                    if X = sentinel then go to Out
    print "prompt for input"                     process_X
    input X                                  end do
end while                                 Out:
```

(a) Without goto statement   (b) With goto statement

Figure 6.10   A read-and-process loop

It appears that even though, theoretically, all programs can be coded using only the control structures of simple sequence, selection, and iteration, this is not sufficient reason to eliminate the **goto** from the programmer's arsenal. In some situations, it may be the most elegant tool to use. The total elimination of **goto** statements from the syntax of programming languages in order to prevent its abuse by poor programmers is akin to the extraction of a full set of teeth in order to prevent tooth decay. While the objective will be achieved, the surgery seems a bit extreme.

Selection

Selection, also called *selective composition*, is a type of programming construct employed when a programmer wishes to choose among two or more alternative statements (or, groups of statements). The **if/then/else** construct is used to choose between two alternative code segments. The more recent **case** construct is used for selection among any number of alternatives.

    if.   The use of an **if** statement in conjunction with a **goto** (or its equivalent) is one of the oldest high-level statements and, at the same time, one of the most primitive since it is a high-level representation of the machine-level conditional branch instruction. We are more concerned here with a "structured" form of the **if** statement, which we call the *two-way selection construct* or the **if/then/else**. This construct is illustrated in flowchart form in Fig. 6.11. It is characterized by the keyword **if** followed by a conditional expression that computes to a Boolean value; a "then" clause consisting of a statement or a group of statements to be executed in the event that the condition evaluates to true; an "else" clause consisting of a possibly empty group of statements to be executed in the event that the condition is false. Many languages have some means of indicating that the **if** construct has ended (the junction indicated by a circle in Fig. 6.11): in COBOL, it is the period ending the sentence; in ALGOL-like languages it is the semicolon ending the statement or separating it from the next statement; in some other languages, a keyword delimiter such as **endif** may be used.

    Depending on the language, the **if/then/else** statement might look something like this:

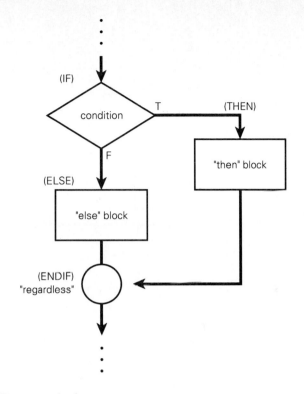

Figure 6.11   Two-way selection

```
if (condition)
        then
            statement
            statement
            ...

        else
            statement
            statement
            ...

    endif
```

It is important to note that this form of the **if** statement differs from the **if/goto** in that it has only a single entry point and a single exit point. Compare the two diagrams in Fig. 6.12. No matter what statements are contained within the "then" block and the "else" block, control of execution ultimately arrives at a juncture of the two alternatives. The very next statement following this juncture may be called the "regardless" statement since it is executed regardless of whether the condition on the **if** statement is true or false.

The "then" or "else" block may contain *any* executable statement, including another **if** statement. Two forms of such nested-if statements are illustrated in the flowchart of Fig. 6.13. Flowcharts (a) and (b) contain the **if** statement nested inside of the

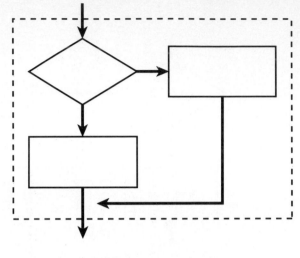

(a) Single entry/single exit

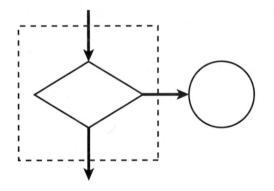

(b) Single entry/multiple exit

Figure 6.12 Two forms of the "if" statement

"then" block. This can result in some pretty confusing code. The following code segment would correspond to Fig. 6.13(b):

```
if (condition1)
        then if (condition2)
                then if (condition3)
                        then statementT3
                        else statementE3
                else statementE2
        else statementE1
endif
```

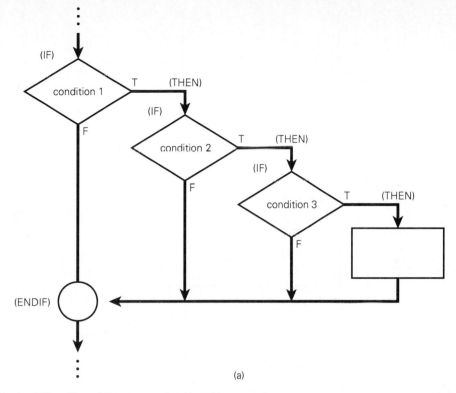

(a)

Figure 6.13 Nested-if statement (continued next page)

This code would be totally unintelligible without the indenting, which serves to line up the **else**'s within their respective **if**'s. Even so, it is rather hard to figure out which statement gets executed when. The flowchart in Fig. 6.13 (c) shows the case of **if**'s nested in the **else** block. This results in code that is more readable and has more logical clarity, as the following code indicates:

```
if (condition1)
        then statementT1
        else if (condition2)
                then statementT2
                else if (condition3)
                        then statementT3
                        else statement E3
endif
```

case. The **case** statement, designed as an answer to **goto** diehards, can sometimes take the place of a sequence of nested-if statements of the form of Fig. 6.13(c). It is represented in flowchart form in Fig. 6.14. One of several alternative code segments will be selected, depending on the value of the selector variable (or, sometimes, expression) named on the **case** statement. Some languages also provide for an "otherwise" or "else" clause in the event that the value of the selector variable does not match any of the

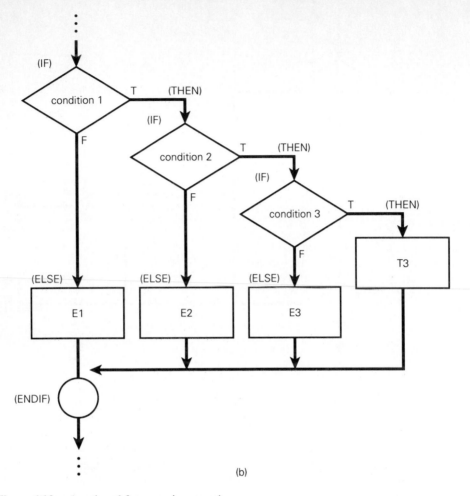

(b)

Figure 6.13   (continued from previous page)

choices listed (for example, an input error). The **case** structure might be coded as follows:

```
case Selector of
      value1:     statementT1
      value2:     statementT2
      value3:     statementT3
else  statementE3
endcase
```

The case structure is similar to the **if/then/else**. However, the **if/then/else** can
accommodate any sequential decision process, not merely one that tests the same selector
variable on equality conditions.

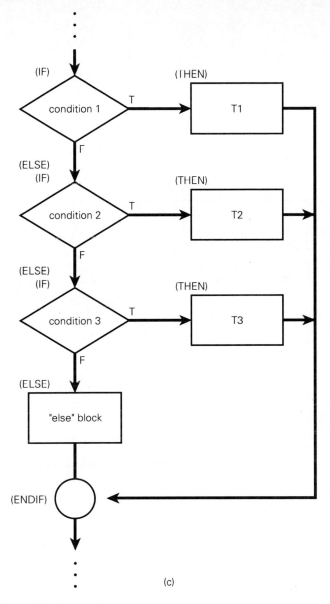

(c)

Figure 6.13   (concluded)

Iteration

The *iteration* type of construct is sometimes called *repetition*, sometimes called *iterative composition,* and sometimes simply called a *loop*. Lady Ada Lovelace, the first computer programmer (see Chapter 2), is credited with "inventing" the loop. She discovered that a branching instruction, in addition to skipping forward over a group of statements, may

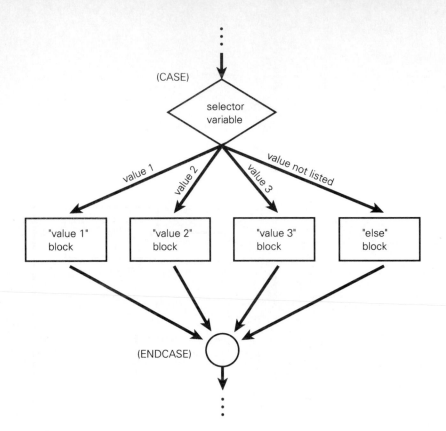

Figure 6.14 Case structure

also be used to branch *backward* in order to repeat the execution of a group of statements that would otherwise have to be input again.

There are three basic looping constructs: the *counting* or *indexed* loop, the *test-before* loop, and the *test-after* loop. All have the desirable feature of a single entry point and a single exit point.

Indexed loop. The indexed loop, sometimes called a counting loop, a **do** loop, or a **for/do** loop, is the iteration construct we use when we wish to execute a code segment (the body of the loop) a countable number of times. It may be two times or a 100 times or N times. An index variable, or counter variable, is initialized when the loop is first entered and then, with each iteration, incremented and tested against a final value. Two ways of flowcharting this construct are illustrated in Fig. 6.15. Notice that they are equivalent since flowchart (a) is actually reduced to flowchart (b) by the translator program. This is the structure underlying FORTRAN's **DO**, Pascal's **for/do**, and BASIC's **FOR/NEXT**. From Fig. 6.15 (b), it is clear that while this is a high-level construct, it reduces to rather simple instructions:

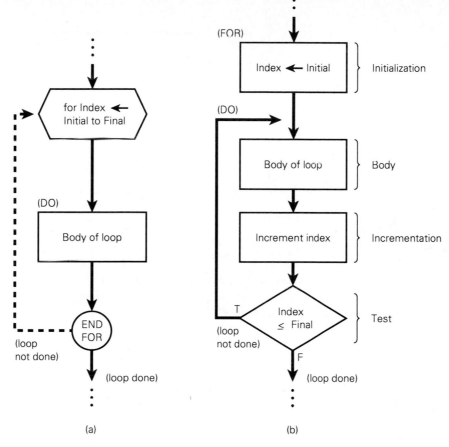

Figure 6.15   Indexed loop

- an *initialization* statement to set the index variable to its initial value;
- the *body* of the loop;
- the *incrementation* (or, sometimes, *decrementation*) statement to provide the index variable with its value for the next iteration;
- the *test* to determine whether to perform another iteration or exit from the loop.

Errors may arise when one is allowed to branch into such a loop since the index variable will not have been initialized but, then, this practice is discouraged in any case.

Test-before loop.   This construct is often called a **while/do** or a **do/while** loop (or, simply, a *while* loop) and may be represented by the flowchart in Fig. 6.16 or the statement: **while** (condition) **do** \<body\>, where \<body\> may be a single statement, a group of statements (such as in a compound statement), or a call to a subprogram. In this

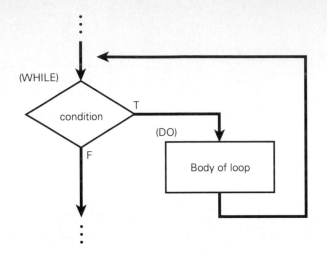

Figure 6.16 Test-before loop

construct, the statements in the body of the loop are iterated as long as a particular condition is true. This condition is tested before each iteration. The result of this structure is that it is possible that the loop will not even be executed one time. This is because, if the condition is false the first time, the body of the loop will be totally and immediately bypassed.

Test-after loop. This construct is often called the **repeat/until** or **do/until** loop. (In COBOL, it is a **PERFORM/UNTIL**.) It is similar to the **while/do** as the flowchart in Fig. 6.17 illustrates. The major difference between these two, condition-based iteration constructs is that the statements contained within the body of the test-after loop will always be executed at least once regardless of whether the condition tested is true or false the first time around.

Any program can be constructed by using only the structured constructs of simple sequence, selection, and iteration. The use of these constructs does not depend on the syntax of the particular programming language used. These are control abstractions that may be used with any high-level or low-level procedural language, or even, to some extent, a declarative language.

Control Abstraction

The very stylized, structured control constructs of simple sequence, selection, and iteration are actually *control abstractions*. They are neat, little packages—more tools for our toolbox that we can call on as needed in the programming process. These control abstractions enable a programmer to think in terms of high-level abstractions instead of low-level machine instructions.

To some extent, a programmer who is limited to building a program out of these structured building blocks will be forced to think a bit more about *what* the algorithm is supposed to do rather than simply step-by-step *how* it might be done.

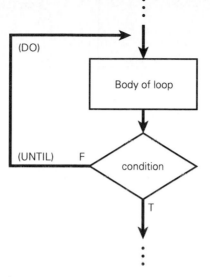

Figure 6.17   Test-after loop

The requirement of single-entry/single-exit is necessary if we are to think of each construct as an abstraction unit, performing a single action. This is equivalent to the single-entry/single-exit requirement in subprograms, which also facilitates abstraction—program abstraction. The Black Box Model is, as usual, an excellent device for visualizing abstraction. Structured programming methodology makes full use of this model, as we shall see in Chapter 14.

6.3   CONTROL OVER SUBPROGRAMS

As the size and complexity of a program increases, so will the number of subprograms it comprises. It is simply good programming practice. Of course, when you construct a program using subprograms as building blocks, you are presented with the additional problem of deciding on the control structures that will govern those program units. Subprograms may be invoked by other subprograms in a variety of ways, but the simplest and most widely used control structure over subprograms—both internal and external subprograms—is the simple call.

Simple Call

The *simple call* reflects a highly constrained control structure. With it, the calling subprogram exerts total control over the called subprogram. We have previously described this as a master/slave relationship. Generally speaking, the top-down design techniques and structure charts discussed in Chapter 5 assume this underlying control mechanism. The simple call is illustrated in Fig. 6.18. At any invocation, an *activation record* is created that represents not only the subprogram as a textual entity, but also the environment of

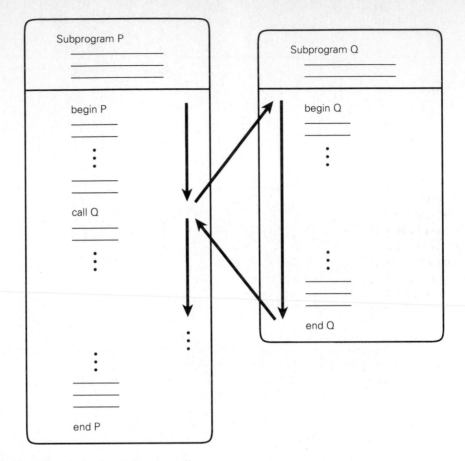

Figure 6.18 A simple subprogram call

the subprogram at the time of the call. Thus, each call to a particular subprogram causes the creation of a new and different activation record. The activation record contains locally declared variables, subprogram parameters, a pointer to the executable subprogram code, and the return address for the next instruction in sequence in the calling program. The activation record, once created, is placed on a run time stack; when the subprogram is terminated, it is popped off the stack and destroyed. When we picture these activation records maintained on a stack, we see why subprograms may be nested but not overlapped. Any subprogram must complete executing (and its activation record will then be popped off the stack) before the subprogram that called it can terminate.

We might infer from Fig. 6.18 that we can describe the effect of the simple call in the following manner: It is *as if* the text of the called subprogram were inserted into the text of the calling subprogram at the point of call (**call** Q). This is called the *copy rule*. Of course, we have to allow for the (imaginary) change of some data names in order to avoid data name clashes in passing arguments to parameters and in assignments to local variables. Describing the relationship between two program units by means of the copy rule is very limiting. It allows only for the simple-call control structure, assuming all of the constraints of the master/slave relationship, namely:

1. A subprogram cannot call itself. Not only would this violate the traditional lines of control in a hierarchical program, but the copy rule becomes quite unwieldy and confusing when we try to imagine inserting a copy of the subprogram text into itself an indefinite number of times.

2. There is an explicit call statement in the appropriate place in the calling subprogram. If there is no explicit call, or if the call simply preschedules a future invocation of the subprogram, where do we copy the subprogram text?

3. A subprogram cannot be invoked to execute concurrently with any other subprogram. The copy rule, like the master/slave relationship, assumes temporary suspension of the calling subprogram when control is passed to the called subprogram.

4. The called subprogram is in a subordinate position and must complete execution before returning control to the calling subprogram. The copy rule places the entire text of the called subprogram into place in the calling subprogram. This obviously does not allow for the possibility of mutual control between the two program units.

The suspension of these constraints provides a variety of structures for control over subprograms:

1. *Recursion* is a control structure characterized by a subprogram calling itself.

2. *Exception handling* refers to the implicit invocation of subprograms to handle exceptional conditions. A *scheduled call* provides for the invocation of a subprogram at some future time during execution of the program.

3. *Parallel processing* allows for the simultaneous or concurrent execution of subprogram units.

4. *Coroutines* are characterized by a relationship of mutual control.

Used alone or in combination, these are very powerful tools for the construction of programs.

Recursion

When a subprogram calls itself, it is said to be *recursive*. Recursion can sometimes lead to the development of algorithms that are more concise and elegant than their nonrecursive counterparts, but the price is paid in a run that will very likely be less efficient with regard to both time and space considerations. Recursion is only a programming technique and, while some algorithms are inherently recursive, its effect may be achieved in other ways. For example, consider once again the factorial algorithm of the previous chapter.

The factorial of a positive integer N is defined as $N! = N(N - 1)(N - 2)...(2)(1)$. That this definition is recursive may be seen more clearly when it is rewritten as: $N! = N(N - 1)!$. An algorithm to compute the factorial of any positive integer N may be written as:

```
function Fact (N)
      Fact := 1
      if N>1 then
            for J := 2 to N do
                  Fact := Fact * J
end Fact
```

This is the nonrecursive version. It uses iteration, specifically, an indexed loop. The recursive version follows:

```
function Fact(N)
        if N<2  then Fact := 1
                else Fact := N * Fact(N-1)
end Fact
```

Both of these algorithms perform correctly for N equal zero as well as for N equal any positive integer, since the factorial of zero is, by definition, 1.

Notice that each time a recursive subprogram is called, the problem is made simpler by a small amount and is thus that much closer to solution. Eventually, then, the problem is so simple that it is directly solvable without further recursion. This is called a *primitive problem*. At this point the original problem can also be solved. Thus, the recursive approach to programming involves partitioning a problem into a solvable portion and another, simpler problem of the same form.

Recursion, like iteration, must not be allowed to proceed indefinitely; there must be a way of determining when the problem is solvable. In the factorial function above, it is when the argument N is less than 2, since 1! =1 would be the final step in the computation of N! for any N. In general, a recursive algorithm will be of the form:

```
if problem is primitive
      then
            return with solution
      else
            process
            call yourself
end
```

At each call to a recursive subprogram, an activation record is created and placed on the central run time stack directly on top of the activation record of the previous call. Each of these activation records may have its own local declarations, and all the activation records point to the same unit of executable code. When a subprogram terminates, control is transferred to the activation record directly beneath it and when that one terminates, ... Well, you get the idea. The activation record for the first call to the recursive subprogram is the last to be released. This ensures that there will be no overlapping of the lifetimes of the subprogram calls, and that subprogram execution will be completely nested within that of the calling subprogram. It is clear that a stack models recursion very well and, indeed, algorithms that are inherently recursive—such as the tree traversal algorithm presented in Chapter 7—may be coded using stacks in languages that do not support recursion or to increase run time efficiency.

In order to help you understand exactly how a recursive algorithm is solved, Fig. 6.19 displays successive "snapshots" of the run time stack of activation records for the recursive factorial algorithm.

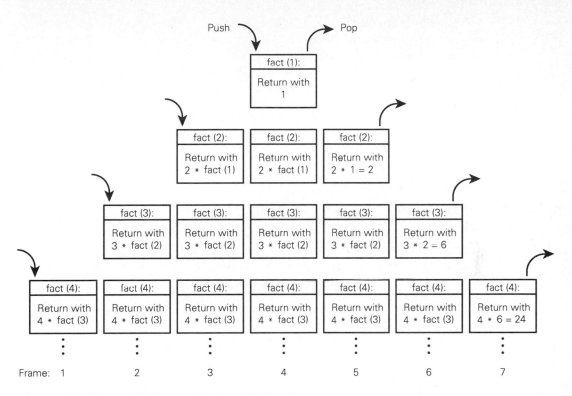

Figure 6.19 Evaluation of a recursive factorial algorithm

Although the activation records of a recursive subprogram all point to the same piece of executable code, the effect is as if many complete copies of this subprogram were available in memory, each with its own parameters, local definitions, etc. Some would say, then, that in recursion the "copy rule" is invoked dynamically. While this use of pointers may represent a considerable saving of storage space, still the memory space required by a recursive routine can be burdensome. After all, new storage space is needed for every activation record, at every level of recursion. Besides the actual magnitude of the storage space needed, the total amount of storage required is not known before the onset of execution. Thus, in order for a language to support recursion, the facility for dynamic memory management must be available.

In LISP, recursion is an important control structure that takes the place of iteration. In PL/1, it must be explicitly declared, as in: FACTORIAL: **PROCEDURE** (N) **RECURSIVE**; . FORTRAN and COBOL with static memory management, do not support recursion; all the memory required for a program is allocated before execution begins.

Implicit Calls

An implicit call is performed when a subprogram causes another subprogram to be invoked but does not call it directly.

Exception handling. An exception handling facility gives the programmer control over exceptional conditions such as errors that might otherwise cause premature termination of execution. Exceptions may be *raised* by the interrupt capability of the underlying machine or operating system, or by programmer-defined conditions. An *exception* is an event that occurs unexpectedly, infrequently, and at random intervals. Examples of exception conditions are: end of input file, divide by zero, and subscript out of range. Exception handlers may also be used for tracing a program during the testing and debugging stage. While the PL/1 language is often credited with introducing the exception handler, actually PL/1 defined it as a major, extensive part of the language, bringing more of the system under programmer control. However, we do see exception handling in COBOL on a simple level. For example:

READ PERSONNEL-FILE **AT END PERFORM** END-OF-JOB-ROUTINE.

An exception handler is a subprogram that is designed to "handle" a particular exceptional condition. It is not invoked with an explicit call. The subprogram is identified with a particular exception condition which may then be enabled or disabled. An *enabled* condition is monitored for occurrence. When the condition occurs, it will raise an exception. *Raising an exception* involves: noticing that the exception condition has occurred; causing program execution to be interrupted, or temporarily suspended; and invocation of the exception handler. A *disabled* condition is not monitored.

The programmer may define a condition to be monitored by giving it a name. The exception handler subprogram itself does not need a name since it is not explicitly called by the program. It may contain local declarations and executable statements for handling the exception. The code for the exception handler may be placed directly into the subprogram in which the exception is expected to occur or it may be in a more remote location.

PL/1 and Ada have exception handling facilities.

Scheduled call. A scheduled call is typical of the type of subprogram control used in event-oriented simulation programs. Control over some subprograms is managed by a timing mechanism, a subprogram that may be built into the programming language or coded by the programmer.

For example, suppose subprogram A "calls"—that is, preschedules—subprogram B with a particular activation time. (In a simulation program, this usually refers to simulated time, not real time.) An activation record is created for subprogram B and inserted into a queue maintained in ascending order by activation time. The timing routine periodically examines the first record in this queue; when its activation time matches the current simulated time, the record is removed from the queue, placed on the run time stack, and the subprogram is invoked. Subprograms may also be scheduled to occur not at an explicit time, but "as soon as possible." This might occur when the subprogram depends on the availability of a particular resource or the completion of another subprogram. In that case, an activation record is created and stored on another queue of activation records that are all waiting in first-come-first-served order for the same resource or occurrence. When the resource becomes available, the timing routine removes the first activation record from this "as soon as possible" queue, places it on the run time stack, and invokes the appropriate subprogram code.

Fig. 6.20 presents a pictorial overview of a timing routine and some other relevant subprograms that might be used in simulating, say, customers arriving and being served

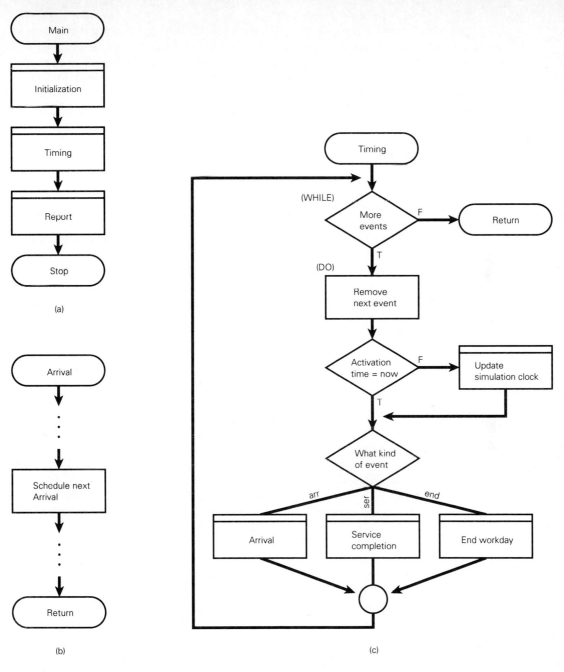

Figure 6.20 Scheduled call

in a bank, and coded in any general-purpose programming language such as FORTRAN or Pascal. In a special-purpose simulation language, this timing routine would be invisible (transparent) to the programmer and "schedule next Arrival" would be the only visible "call" to subprogram Arrival.

SIMSCRIPT and GPSS are simulation languages that provide for scheduled calls to subprograms and a built-in timing routine that hides the invocation of these subprograms. For example, if you were to code the simulation program of Fig. 6.20 in SIMSCRIPT, you would need to supply the following modules: MAIN, INITIALIZATION, REPORT, ARRIVAL, SERVICE.COMPLETION, and END.WORKDAY. Anything connected with timing, the simulation clock, or calling event subprograms is handled by the language itself.

Parallel Processing

Parallel processing, also called *concurrent processing*, refers to the concurrent execution of two or more subprograms (processes, tasks) in order to solve a specific problem. Parallelism may be *real*, that is, executing simultaneously in real time on multiple processors, or *virtual*, simulated parallelism on a single central processor. Although the von Neumann machine concept contains only a single processor that can execute only one instruction at a time, we are no longer completely constrained by this limitation. This greater flexibility is partly reflected in different hardware configurations—for example, a distributed processing system with common memory—and partly in software systems—for example, a mainframe, multiprogramming system.

While we focus here on the concurrent execution of tasks within a single program, it is instructive to note that at the system level, parallelism has been with us for a long time. Some examples are multiprogramming operating systems (which actually *simulate* concurrency) and the overlapping of input/output operations with CPU-bound operations. More recently, multiprocessing systems and distributed processing systems contain multiple processors set up so that they can operate independently and simultaneously. A *multiprocessing system* is composed of multiple processors that all share a common memory unit. A *distributed processing system* is a network of multiple processors, each with its own memory unit, that communicate with each other and access shared peripherals. When two or more processes execute concurrently, each on its own processor, and do not share a common database or need to communicate with one another in any way, that is parallelism at the system level. While such processes do operate in parallel, they are totally *asynchronous*. We are more concerned here with processes that are part of a single program, share a common resource such as a database, and may communicate with or in some way depend on each other.

There are a number of specific features that are required if a programming language is to support this kind of subprogram control structure. Languages with such a facility include PL/1, Ada, MODULA-2, and ConcurrentPascal. Some application areas for parallel processing include systems programming, real-time applications, and simulation.

Parallel control is illustrated by Fig. 6.21. The "fork" statement or its equivalent invokes subprogram B while at the same time allowing subprogram A to continue its own processing uninterrupted. Since A initiated the call to B, it may not be able to terminate until B has completed its processing.

In designing programs with parallel control, a programmer must consider several important problems, including synchronization, deadlock, and mutual exclusion around critical regions. These will be approached differently depending on the programming language employed since there is very little standardization in this area.

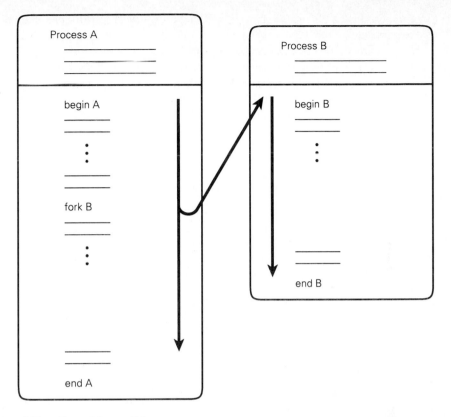

Figure 6.21   Control in parallel processes

Critical region.   Suppose a process requires access to a stored variable that it shares with other processes. Then, the critical region is that section of the subprogram code that contains the sequence of statements referring to the shared variable. There may be more than one critical region.

Mutual exclusion.   Two parallel processes must be able to access a common resource such as a database but, at the same time, that access must be limited in some way so that the data is protected from an unintentional loss of integrity. In general, once one process has accessed a variable, it "controls" it so that other processes cannot access the same variable until control is relinquished.

Synchronization.   When concurrently executing processes must communicate with each other, we have the problem of synchronization. Often one process must wait for the completion of or a signal from another process. If several processes make requests from a process, they may have to be queued in some manner.

Deadlock.   A concern related to synchronization and mutual exclusion is *deadlock*, in which two processes cannot continue or terminate because they remain indefinitely in a state in which each is waiting for the other. For example, suppose process A requires variables x and y at the same time that process B needs access to these variables.

Suppose that A gets *x*; B gets *y*. Now each process must wait for one variable and neither can proceed without it.

Parallel processing can be implemented in a number of ways, including shared memory models such as semaphores and monitors; the message passing model; the dataflow model. The *dataflow programming paradigm* is a general approach to programming that takes advantage of the inherent parallelism in an algorithm and is intended to run on parallel architecture machinery. We discuss dataflow programming in Section 6.4.

Semaphores. Semaphores are employed to control access to a shared resource. The semaphore mechanism provides for mutual exclusion in critical regions. Semaphores were implemented in ALGOL68.

A semaphore is a Boolean variable with two operations: *wait* and *signal*. These operations may be coded as:

```
Wait(s):         if S = 1 then S := 0 else InsertQueue(process)
Signal(s):       if not EmptyQueue then RemoveQueue(process) else S := 1
```

Both of these operations are constrained to complete without interruption. The effect of the wait operation is to temporarily "put the process to sleep" if the data required is being used by another process. The signal operation causes the first waiting process to be "awakened" and allowed access to the data. Typically, these operations surround the critical region:

```
...
Wait(S)
...
access shared data
...
Signal(S)
...
```

Monitors. A monitor, which is itself a named subprogram, contains a collection of concurrent processes all of which share some data. Since these are all packaged together, the monitor technique is not particularly appropriate for use on a multiprocessing system. It is often used to simulate concurrency. The monitor controls access to the shared data much as a traffic cop controls access to an intersection. This mechanism is provided in Concurrent Pascal and MODULA-2.

```
monitor Name
    begin
        declarations of data local to monitor Name
        subprogram process1
        ...
        subprogram processN
        initialization of local data
    end Name
```

Message passing. The message passing mechanism simulates a distributed processing system. This model allows for the exchange of information among communicating processes. Processes communicate with each other (e.g., for synchronization) by

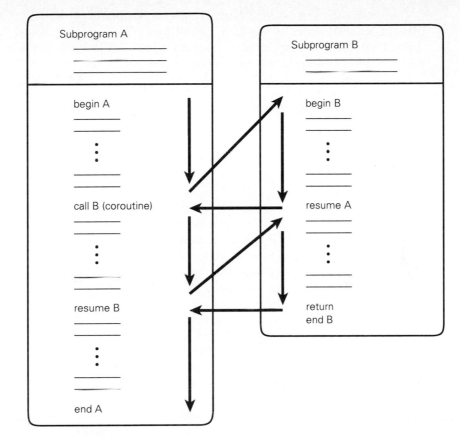

Figure 6.22 Coroutines

means of messages. For example, within process A may be a statement sending a message to process B:

```
B! MessageType(<argument>)
```

Although not specifically designed for parallel processing, Smalltalk uses message passing to invoke subprograms and may easily be employed for concurrent subprogram control.

Coroutines

Two subprograms that are *coroutines* exert mutual control over one another. They can each call the other. A "call" by, say, B to A actually transfers control to the point in subprogram A where A last "called" B. A different keyword, such as **resume**, may be used in place of **call**. In effect, subprogram B invokes A and waits for a call back in order to resume execution. This is illustrated in Fig. 6.22. Notice that the activation records of coroutines must be maintained between "resume"s.

Application areas for coroutines are simulation and real-time processing. Coroutines are supported by SIMULA, MODULA-2, and ConcurrentPascal. There is no standard coroutine mechanism. Such considerations as data scoping and parameter passing are handled differently from one language to another.

6.4 PROGRAMMING PARADIGMS

The control structures available in a given high-level language are very much dictated by the programming paradigm followed by that language. Of course, regardless of the language or its approach to programming, the fundamental control construct is the application of operations to operands. However, the way in which an individual can combine operations to produce a program may differ widely from one group of languages to another. The approach to programming as dictated by the programming language is often what we mean when we refer to a programming paradigm.

A *programming paradigm*, or world view, is an approach to solving programming problems. In practice, this approach may be dictated more by the particular programming language used than by the orientation of the programmer except, perhaps, in the programmer's choice of a language. In a sense, given the history of the major programming paradigms, they may be considered abstractions based on the features of the particular programming languages in which they arose. If this sounds rather haphazard, it was, and is. To some extent, the "Tower of Babel" described in Chapter 2 can be characterized as many different languages doing the same thing. Often, however, we find ourselves bumping up against a small number of radically different languages that do things in quite different ways. Still, if there is at least one unifying concept in all paradigms, it is that *operations* are ultimately applied to *operands*. The differences lie in the ways in which the operations and operands may be organized and described.

A classification of programming paradigms is presented in Fig. 6.23. Languages listed are associated with a particular programming paradigm as the major organizing principle. Some of the languages listed are not widely known and, in fact, may be somewhat esoteric. Others are experimental. (Sources are given at the end of the chapter.) Each of these programming orientations represents not just a different way of coding a program, but often a totally different way of approaching a problem conceptually and organizing the solution before any coding takes place. As we saw in Chapter 2, the orientation of a programming language may be more procedural (concerned with *how*) or more declarative (concerned with *what*); it may be more process-centered or more data-centered. And, among the data-centered languages, the programming world view will differ drastically depending upon the form of the data in question.

You will note that most of the traditional, widely known languages and most of the languages discussed in this book, are classified under the imperative paradigm, all in one branch of the classification tree. In a sense, then, this tree is deceptive. Although many different paradigms exist or have been studied, most languages in current use are still imperative languages in the FORTRAN line of descent. That is why the imperative branch of the classification tree is relatively heavy with representative languages while the rest of the tree is rather sparsely populated. The organization of the topics covered in

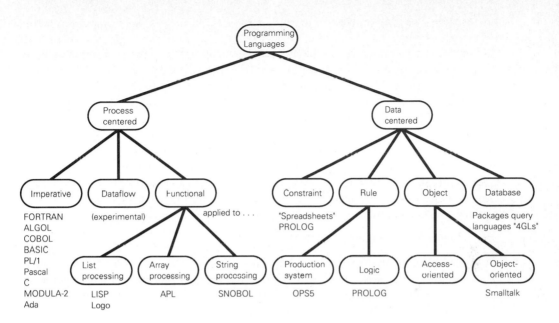

Figure 6.23 Programming paradigms

Part 1 of this book reflects this preoccupation with the imperative programming paradigm. This is partly due to the preoccupation of the industry with this type of programming approach, and to the predominance of programming languages that subscribe to this approach. Another reason is that the imperative programming paradigm lends itself to the detailed decomposition and separate analysis of the various structures that make up a program and are facilitated by a programming language, namely: the data-level structures, the program structures, and the control structures.

In some other paradigms, the distinction among these various types of structures is not as clear. For example, in the object-oriented programming paradigm, data abstraction, program abstraction, and control abstraction are all contained within the same structure.

From a theoretical point of view, the choice of an appropriate programming paradigm for a particular application is independent of the language used to implemented it and, in fact, may or may not precede the selection of an appropriate programming language. Of course, in reality, the programmer will be more than a little limited by the organizing principle of the particular programming language used. However, it is sometimes possible to design a solution using one world view and then mold a programming language with a different organizing principle to that world view. The language should be highly extensible and, naturally, the fit would never be complete. In addition, there are some languages available and others under development that support more than one programming paradigm. Some of these, for example, C++ and LOOPS will be discussed at the end of this section. In fact, much of the research going on today in the area of programming paradigms involves efforts to make several of these approaches available in a single programming language or environment.

Imperative Programming

The imperative programming paradigm is a statement-oriented approach reflected in all the languages that have their roots in FORTRAN, COBOL, and/or ALGOL. Clearly, then, many languages take this approach. These languages are also known as *algorithmic languages*, because they facilitate the construction of programs as *algorithms*, or as sequences of instructions for computing.

The imperative world view supports sequential *imperatives* that effect changes to the contents of internal storage locations by assignment. Here, the word imperative (a noun) means *command*. It may also be used as an adjective, meaning *in the manner of a command* (e.g., an *imperative statement*). The imperative approach is perhaps seen most clearly in COBOL statements, each of which begins with an action verb (that is, a command). For example:

```
READ, WRITE, PERFORM, COMPUTE, DIVIDE.
```

The most important elements of imperative languages are *variables*, the *assignment operator*, and *procedures*. The imperative programming paradigm, the most commonly used programming world view, draws its major characteristics from the most prevalent machine architecture, the von Neumann architecture.

The von Neumann machine. The statements of imperative languages are closely related to the built-in instruction set of the underlying machine. Even high-level imperative statements translate in a fairly simple, straightforward manner into low-level machine code. Imperative statements reflect an assumption of and dependence on the von Neumann type of computer architecture—namely, a central processor that executes one primitive instruction at a time tied very closely to an internal memory unit containing a large number of unique addressable storage locations that may be retrieved one at a time, and a one-word bus for transporting data between the two components. Thus, this architecture and consequently these languages are fairly low level and highly variable dependent.

Imperative programming languages are characterized by their variables, the assignment operation, and the iteration control construct. Other paradigms are typically characterized by the absence of these features.

Variables. Programmer-defined variables correspond to, and are used to access, individual storage locations containing values. Changes are made by explicit assignment of values to variables. The values of the collection of variables represent the state of computation: as assignments are made to these variables over the course of program execution, so the state of the program changes over time. Thus, an imperative program is *history sensitive*, meaning that the result of the program depends a great deal on the state of computation when execution starts up. Another criticism of this programming approach is that too much programmer effort is spent keeping track of individual variables. This includes naming conventions and the detail work of managing every change by assignment.

Assignment. The most important statement in an imperative language is the assignment statement, since it is the only one that does any real, productive work. The assignment statement, which is often of the form <var> := <expression>, retrieves a value using instructions on the right side of the assignment operator and stores that value in the memory location designated by the variable named on the left side of the assignment operator. Thus, what the program actually accomplishes, it does by means of the assignment statement. With the exception of input/output statements—which are, after all, only there because it is necessary for the computer to communicate with the outside world—all the other types of imperative statements are involved in control (management) not assignment (production).

Iteration.   An imperative program will typically execute a statement or sequence of statements repeatedly. This repetition may be controlled by a counter or index variable. The iteration control construct itself contains a branching instruction (a **goto**), which is also a characteristic of the imperative programming paradigm.

Procedures.   Procedures represent an enhancement to imperative programming language statements. In the procedural programming paradigm, statements may be grouped together into a module that serves as an abstraction device. Thus, control abstraction is facilitated by modules forming the sequence, selection, and iteration constructs. Program abstraction is built by modular decomposition and stepwise refinement. Data abstraction may be provided by specialized modules encapsulating data and procedure description. When procedures and modules can be nested, static scoping rules are important. These languages are often called block structured languages.

Examples of imperative languages are COBOL, Pascal, MODULA-2, and Ada. BASIC is an imperative language that is not typically procedural.

Imperative programming languages are still the most efficient ones on von Neumann-type machines, and this type of computer architecture is still the most prevalent today. Indeed, the other programming paradigms that we will discuss are typically compiled to low-level imperative programs in the interest of efficient execution.

Functional Programming

The *functional programming paradigm* involves the mathematical specification of the solution to a programming problem. In mathematics, the major organizing principle is the function and, in programming, this mathematical entity is translated as a subprogram returning a single value. A complete functional program defines an *expression* which, when used with specific operands, solves a particular problem. The use of functions to construct programs can often result in an elegant, concise algorithm.

In a functional programming language, a program is a function that is built up from smaller functions. The functional programming paradigm allows a programmer to solve a programming problem by means of a hierarchy of functional abstractions, in other words, with top-down functional decomposition by stepwise refinement. Functions are combined, producing more powerful functions. Functional programming languages, also called *applicative languages*, achieve their major effect by the application of functions to arguments, which may themselves be functions. This is easily distinguished from imperative programs, in which state transitions are accomplished by means of assignment statements.

Functional programming languages are characterized by powerful data structuring capabilities. These languages are not constrained by variables tied to storage locations. A large, and often complicated, data structure is treated simply as if it were a single value.

Data in these languages are often organized into such structural forms as lists, strings, and arrays.

There are three major control constructs used to build up functional programs:

- *Functional composition* is used to define a function in terms of other functions that are the operands.
- The *conditional expression* is used for selecting a function based on the value of another (possibly Boolean) function.
- *Recursion* is used in much the same manner as it is in mathematics, replacing the iteration construct of imperative languages.

Both functional and imperative languages allow specification and application of functions. The difference is that, in an imperative language, a function is merely another type of subprogram and, as such, allows assignment of values to parameters and to global variables. Along with the problems of side effects, then, imperative functions lack referential transparency.

Referential transparency.   An important distinguishing feature of functional programming, referential transparency may be described as follows: The value of a function is a unique value that is determined solely by the values of the arguments to the function. This corresponds to the mathematical definition of a function. Thus, two applications of the same function using the same arguments must produce exactly the same result. In other words, the solution is unique. This may be characterized as a many-to-one transformation. Imperative languages, with their high degree of dependence on sequential assignments of values to variables, are history sensitive and not referentially transparent. Relational and rule-based languages, on the other hand (PROLOG, for example), do not have referential transparency because they are characterized by the many-to-many transformation.

Lazy evaluation.   In the functional programming paradigm, an expression or function is evaluated only when some other expression needs its output. Since a functional program is implemented as a series of functions applied to arguments, this "lazy," or delayed, evaluation of expressions is translated into a parameter-passing mechanism known as *call by need*, very much like ALGOL's call by name, in which an argument is evaluated only when its value is needed and not immediately at the point of call. This provides the advantages of both call by name and call by value—since when an argument's value is not required, it is not evaluated; and if it is required it is evaluated once only without the possibility of unwanted changes.

The oldest functional programming language, in fact, the archetype for functional languages, is LISP. The mathematical foundation of LISP is in lambda calculus, and the unifying data structure (and program structure) is the list. LISP is not a "pure" functional programming language since, in the interests of efficiency, it was augmented early on with some features of imperative languages, for example, variables and the assignment operation. Over the years, there have been a number of derivatives of LISP, for example, SCHEME, CommonLISP, and Flavors. APL, although it does have an assignment operation, may be considered a functional programming language due to its heavy reliance on expressions combining powerful functions.

In order to implement a functional approach in an imperative language, we would need to: Avoid the use of global variables and side effects and use call by value exclusively as a parameter-passing mechanism.

Functional languages provide many benefits. Since variables are not a feature of the functional paradigm, there is greater control over the flow of data, there is no threat from "side effects," and programs are referentially transparent. In addition, it may be possible to mathematically prove program correctness. However, functional languages are not based on the von Neumann architecture and are inefficient on most of today's computing machinery. Specialized computers (such as LISP machines) may be required.

Rule-oriented Programming

In the rule-oriented paradigms, one may: specify facts and rules about objects and their relationships; query the system regarding these objects and relationships; combine facts to express them as a single rule; easily integrate new facts and rules into a program. This approach is important in artificial intelligence in which it is used to build knowledge bases. A knowledge base is simply a database composed of facts and rules.

A *rule* is a condition-action statement, also called a *production*, that may be of the form: if <condition> then <action>. Rule-oriented programming has two personas: *Production-system programming* views knowledge as a production system, a rule base composed of independent rules. A rule-based system must be able to deal with uncertainty and explain itself as well. *Logic programming* is grounded in the mathematical basis of predicate calculus. Its rules are in a more restrictive form. This approach does not attempt to deal with uncertainty (too informal) and does not include an explainer facility as part of its definition. Logic programming seeks to satisfy a goal along with its subgoals. Production-system programming, with its less formal underpinning, is able to look for a second-best or "good enough" solution. Logic programming is referentially transparent; production-system programming is referentially opaque. Both approaches share a number of features.

A distinguishing feature of the rule-oriented paradigms is the explicit and complete separation of data and control elements in the program. The knowledge base is a separate unit operated on by the control component. This control mechanism differs in the logic and rule-based paradigms. The data is not only independent of the control element, but there is a large degree of independence within the database as well. Rules (or, at least, groups of rules) are independent of each, and can be added to the knowledge base incrementally or modified as new knowledge becomes available, without modifying the control elements of the program. Clearly, this type of system would be a never-ending nightmare to implement and maintain in conventional imperative languages.

Both logic programming and production-system programming call for a decision regarding a reasoning mechanism and a search strategy. (Of course, this "decision" may be part of the language design and, as such, out of the hands of the programmer.) The reasoning mechanism can move either forward (i.e., inductive) or backward (i.e., deductive), referring to the order in which the rules are examined. The search strategy may be either depth-first or breadth-first.

The *backward-chaining* reasoning mechanism begins with a solution or goal and tries to prove it correct. Backward-chaining systems are also called *top-down* or *goal-directed systems*. The system selects one goal at a time and sets about trying to prove it.

Each goal may consist of a number of subgoals, each of which must be proven in order for the hypothesis to be correct. *Forward chaining* begins with the facts and rules at hand and uses that as a starting point to search for a solution. Forward-chaining systems are also described as *bottom-up*, *data-driven*, or *event-driven*. In this case, the system examines one data item at a time, making whatever inferences it can from it. After analyzing some facts in this manner, the system may query the user for other facts it needs in order to reach a conclusion. Of the two reasoning mechanisms, backward chaining is more efficient and is more commonly applied, although the two may sometimes be combined. Backward chaining is appropriate when the solutions are known, and there are not too many of them. Forward chaining works better when the number of starting points is small relative to the number of possible solutions.

A *search strategy* is employed to search the knowledge base. The *depth-first* search strategy is the most commonly used. This is a search along a single search path resulting in ever-increasing detail. The search continues to a possible goal before attempting to explore another path leading to another goal. The *breadth-first* strategy searches across paths, examining all rules on a given level, eliminating as many as possible, before going to the next, more detailed, level. It does not commit the system to completely examine only a single goal before looking at any other goal.

The rule-oriented programming paradigms represent a "many-to-many" transformation, i.e., there is a *set* of solutions for a particular application. For example, if Jennifer, Donna, and Mary have been defined as sisters, the query Sister<Donna> might produce as a response either Mary or Jennifer, and either response would be correct.

For more on programming with rules, see Chapters 12 and 16.

Production-system programming. A production is a condition-action rule. A set of such rules, called a *production system,* is the oldest way of representing human knowledge to the computer. Production systems, first formulated by Allen Newell and Herbert Simon at Carnegie-Mellon University as models of human cognition, are sets of independent knowledge modules containing these condition-action rules, which represent knowledge. Today, they are commonly called *knowledge bases*. Since the rules (or, at least, groups of rules) are independent, it is possible for such systems to "learn" incrementally. This provides the basis for the production-system programming paradigm, which is perhaps more commonly known as the *rule-based programming paradigm*.

The elements of a rule-based system are:

- the production system, equivalent to a program structure;
- working memory, containing values that are the system's state of current knowledge and are thus somewhat like global data; and
- the inference engine, which is the interpreter and provides the control structures for the system.

The *control mechanism* of a rule-based system is its key distinguishing characteristic. The inference engine works on a match-select-execute cycle.

Match: The inference engine finds all the rules that meet a match to the goal—that is, the left-hand side evaluates to true. All rules meeting this condition are maintained in a conflict set.

Select:	One rule is selected from the conflict set according to a particular conflict resolution mechanism.
Execution:	The interpreter processes the clauses of the right-hand side of the selected rule to modify working memory.

The inference engine cycles over these processes until the conflict set is empty.

Explanation module.   An important part of a rule-based system is the "explainer" facility, which keeps track of which rules have been satisfied, and can output to the user the specific chain of reasoning that led to the particular conclusion reached and action taken. In this way it is said to generate explanations of program behavior.

The first production-system programming language, and still the definitive language for this programming paradigm, is OPS (named, somewhat tongue in cheek, as the **O**fficial **P**roduction **S**ystem), designed at Carnegie Mellon in 1970. The current version is OPS5.

Logic programming.   The rules of the logic programming paradigm are *Horn clauses*. These are more restrictive than the productions of the rule-based paradigm: the left-hand side of the rule may contain at most a single clause. This reduces the search space, improving the efficiency of the system.

In the logic programming paradigm, the programmer provides a description of a problem in the form of predicate logic statements. The system then is interpreted by a mechanism based on resolution logic. Logic programming languages may be used to set up databases of rules called *knowledge bases* and, therefore, they fall under the rule-oriented paradigm. In fact, the logic programming approach may be considered to be a more formal subset of the rule-based paradigm.

A logic program evaluates theorems to see if they are true. Constraints of a problem are specified rather than the algorithm for solution. A logic program is composed of:

- a knowledge base, the program structure;
- a goal to be proved, often, in the form of input data; and
- an inference mechanism, or control structure.

The inference mechanism is built into the language or system used.

Logic programming languages suffer from a "closed world" view. In other words, any fact not in the knowledge base is automatically not true. This means that if a relation is disproved it may not in reality be false; it may simply be absent from the program.

The prototypical logic programming language is PROLOG; others are, for the most part, extensions and enhancements of this language. The particular approach taken by PROLOG is also a very specific type of constraint-orientation (see below) since it satisfies logical constraints. Since the rules of PROLOG are relations, it is also sometimes classified as a relational language (along with query languages like SQL, which are used to access data from relational databases).

Object-oriented Programming

Object-oriented programming makes good on the promise of structured programming. It implements in a very practical way the principles of program decomposition, data abstraction, and information hiding. It ties together and provides a framework for abstraction and structure at all levels: data, program, and control. As such, it is the natural culmination of everything we have studied in Part 1 of this book.

Object-oriented programming picks up where structured programming methodology leaves off. Dijkstra's concept of structured programming, Wirth's stepwise refinement, and Parnas's information hiding all contributed to a software development milieu that promised to become increasingly systematic and scientific. Object-oriented programming, to a great extent, fulfills that promise. It takes the concepts of data abstraction, modular decomposition, and information hiding and refines them into a cohesive world view in which the organizing principle is the data object. In this world view, data objects are active entities. Instead of passing data to procedures, the user asks data objects to perform operations on themselves. A complex problem is viewed as a network of objects that communicate with each other.

Large programming projects have problems of complexity that structured programming alone cannot alleviate. Structured programming methodology appears to break down when applications exceed about 100,000 lines of code. At that point, the assumption that the programmer will be able to "get it right the first time" is no longer valid. Bugs abound, programmer productivity plummets, and the term "software maintenance" becomes about as popular as "plague." Furthermore, as applications increase in size and complexity, even getting it right the first time is no longer good enough since these applications are frequently evolutionary in nature. The object-oriented programming paradigm promotes and facilitates software evolution.

The object-oriented approach provides a natural framework for easily modularizing programs and data, eliminating much of the headache of structured-design techniques. Programming can be carried out in an incremental fashion. In a very real sense, an object-oriented program is a simulation of the real world. It is therefore a relatively natural way to program. In object-oriented programming, we would:

- identify objects and their attributes;
- identify operations on the objects;
- establish the interfaces between objects.

An *object* is a bundle of data and related functions. In an object-oriented programming language, every data element is an object. This includes literals and all sorts of data structures. Objects are defined by a hierarchy of *classes* capable of *inheritance*. Objects communicate with each other by passing *messages*. The object receiving the message activates a *method* corresponding to that message and may, in turn, send messages to other objects.

A *class* is an independent program module representing a class of data object, much in the same way that Ada's package implements an abstract data type. However, the class concept, which originated with SIMULA, goes beyond data abstraction. A class encapsulates the data declarations, called *instance variables*, and the function specifications, called *methods*, necessary for the definition of the data object. An *object* is an instance of a class. There may be many instances of the same class coexisting at any moment in time. A class, then, may be viewed as a template for generating objects. An object's data is private to it, and the only way to access that data is to ask the object to invoke one of its methods

Methods are operations defined within the class. A method is invoked when an object receives an appropriate *message* (which may contain arguments and typically returns a value to the sender of the message). Objects communicate with each other by means of *message passing*. A message is a request to the object to carry out an operation and is roughly (very roughly) equivalent to a subprogram call. The operation must be contained in the group of procedures in the definition of the object. These methods are given in the class definition and specify how objects of the class will respond to any particular message. Thus a method is similar to a function specification and a message is equivalent to a function call. Every object is associated with a *class protocol* as specified in its class definition. This is the external interface and contains the messages to which the object can respond, and for which the object has matching methods.

The state of an individual object is maintained and represented by its *instance variables*, which are not deallocated when execution of a method terminates. This differentiates method invocation from a standard subprogram call. Instance variables are roughly equivalent to the **STATIC** variables of PL/1. Only the methods, akin to local procedures, can directly manipulate this data. This is the implementation of the principle of information hiding that is important in all modular programming in reducing the interdependencies between modules. Objects do have the capability to declare purely local variables, called *temporary variables*, that only exist during execution of the method subprogram. *Class variables* contain common data values, which may be shared by all objects of the class.

If we were going to draw a very rough comparison between the features of object-oriented programming and imperative programming, we would say that an object is somewhat equivalent to a record, a class to a record type or an abstract data type, an instance variable to a field on the record, and a message to a subprogram call. This comparison is not terribly accurate but it is close enough to be a good starting point for a programmer grounded in the imperative paradigm to cross over to object-oriented programming. For example, defining a class in ObjectPascal is very much like a Pascal-type definition:

```
type
        ClassName = object(SuperclassName)
        <instance var declarations>
        <method header declarations>
end;
```

One key characteristic that separates classes from abstract data types is *inheritance*. Classes and their objects are organized into a hierarchy. The variables and methods of a class are inherited by its subclasses and do not have to be recoded in the subclass definitions. The subclasses then need code only for the structure and behavior that is unique. Thus, a class may be seen as a specialization of a superclass and may either override or provide additional definition to its superclass. This makes for reusable code, since common structures and methods do not need to be recoded from scratch for each new class of objects, only that which is different from the existing class. Inheritance relationships enable the customizing of objects to a user's specific needs without costly and time-consuming coding of custom software.

Fig. 6.24 gives an example of a class hierarchy structure for a registration and record-keeping system in a particular (hypothetical) university. Each class contains infor-

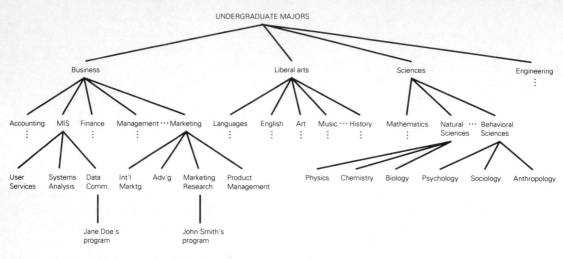

Figure 6.24   Classification of objects

mation, such as required and elective courses, specific to its own majors. The class MIS contains information important to all MIS majors, such as required MIS core courses. Jane Doe is a data communication major. Jane Doe's program is an object, a class instance. Any student's program is a specific instance of a major. Each class inherits all the characteristics from the one above it and then adds its own particulars. MIS majors must take the required business core curriculum, and there may be certain core requirements across all undergraduate majors.

The concepts of class and inheritance implement two special relationships called is-a and a-kind-of. The *is-a* relationship relates an object to its defining class and the *a-kind-of* relationship relates a class to a superclass. For example, from Fig. 6.24, John Smith's program *is-a* MarketingResearch major's program; MarketingResearch is *a-kind-of* Marketing major, which is *a-kind-of* Business major.

Dynamic binding, also called *late binding*, means that the association of a data element with a particular property occurs during run time, rather than at compile time (that would be *early binding*). Thus, for example, stack definition may be used for integers, characters, or records. This is true data abstraction. With late binding, the same name can be used for similar operations (methods) on different kinds of objects. This is called *polymorphism*. A polymorphic operation may be applied to a variety of different types of data objects. The message looks the same but it invokes a different method depending on the type of object receiving the message. Traditional languages call this *operator overloading*. This tends to eliminate a lot of selection constructs from the control structure of the program.

A *garbage collection* facility, which originated fairly early on with LISP, automatically reclaims storage that is no longer needed by the program. This eliminates the need for programmer control over memory management and may represent a large savings in a large, complex application. However, garbage collection facilities are often time consuming and space inefficient and thus serve to increase the overhead in a large software system. One method of garbage collection, which is used in Smalltalk-80, is *reference counting*. In the reference-counting method of garbage collection, the system automatically keeps track of the number of pointers to each object in the system. When the number of pointers drops down to zero, the object is deallocated, and the space may be used for another object. Another garbage collection method, called *mark and sweep*, works in this way: When the system runs out of memory, a two-pass procedure is triggered. The "mark" pass traces and marks all objects that are not garbage. The "sweep" pass reclaims storage space from everything else.

The archetyal object-oriented programming language is Smalltalk, designed at the Xerox Palo Alto Research Center (PARC) in the early 1970s. Object-oriented methodology has also been incorporated into and combined with a range of different languages, producing ObjectPascal, ObjectiveC, C++, LOOPS.

Some of the benefits of object-oriented programming are probably obvious. There is a high degree of modularity in object-oriented programs. Since objects are relatively self-contained and encapsulate data and related code segments together in a single package, the object-oriented world view is better equipped to handle complexity in a natural manner and can be better for the design of very large programs. Also, objects are less susceptible to the kind of programming error that occurs when a data structure or its component is changed. When code is changed, it only has to be changed in one place in the program. The inheritance characteristic means that object-oriented programs will have a great deal of reusable code. This too reduces the chance of programming error. And then, there is the naturalness and readability that goes along with polymorphism. Finally, the object-oriented approach is well suited for such control mechanisms as parallel processing and coroutines.

On the negative side, object-oriented programming is often inefficient due to dynamic binding and garbage collection. In addition, message passing requires more processing time than does calling subprograms. In general, with this approach, the emphasis will be on greater programmer productivity at the (possible) expense of machine efficiency.

Other Paradigms

The programming paradigms discussed so far are the most widely used as organizing principles for coding programs. They are represented by established languages that are not experimental and have an experienced user base. There are also a number of programming paradigms that are not as widely known or used. Some of these are experimental or used primarily in conjunction with another paradigm.

Access-oriented programming. Access-oriented programming is, in some respects, a refinement of object-oriented programming. It has historical roots in the language SIMULA and "attached procedures."

In this approach to programming, accessing data, either storing or retrieving, from variable locations in storage can cause procedures or methods to be invoked. As compared to the object-oriented paradigm, in which an object may receive a message to change its own state, in the access-oriented paradigm, whenever the state of an annotated object changes (on *access*), a message is sent to invoke a procedure. The access-oriented paradigm is often considered the "dual" of object-oriented programming. Access-oriented programming involves the specification of "side effects," sometimes called "demons," which are attached to the manipulation of variables. A "demon" is a program triggered by specific conditions. Access-oriented programming provides a mechanism for monitoring these conditions.

This approach is based on a value called an *annotated value*, which associates annotations with data objects. A kind of annotated value is an *active value*, which monitors a data object and, on its access, triggers the invocation of the appropriate method (demon). There is no need for explicit function calls. Active values are objects and have their own variables for saving state. An active value may be considered to be an abstraction that transforms a variable access to a method invocation. Another kind of annotated value is a *property annotation*, which maintains property lists for data values. The property list can change dynamically over the course of execution and can be used, for example, to store a history of value changes.

One application of access-oriented programming is run time type checking. It is also appropriate for game playing and simulation applications and to implement the windows and iconic menus often found in an interactive user interface.

The access-oriented paradigm is not used on its own in language design, but it may be combined with other world views.

Constraint-oriented programming.

In the constraint-oriented programming paradigm, the programmer specifies a set of relations among a set of data objects. The constraint-satisfaction system, then, attempts to find a solution that satisfies the relations. For example, if the system specified is simply $A + B = 27$, and a value for A is also specified, the system will find the value of B. If a value of B is given, the system will find the value of A. The one relation alone is sufficient to do both types of analyses and no additional coding is necessary. Thus stating that $A = 3$ is the same as $3 = A$.

A constraint system is a set of constraints on data objects. These constraints may be specified in any sequence. The system is satisfied as long as all of the constraints in the set are satisfied. Constraints may be identified as *basic* or *unconditional* constraints (these are equations), *complex* constraints (which may be reduced to basic constraints), *conditional* constraints, *constraint generators*, and *nested* constraints.

In this type of system, a data object may be defined implicitly based on its relationship with another specified object.

PROLOG is a (very specific) type of constraint-oriented language: It satisfies logical constraints. Constraint-oriented programming is the paradigm of spreadsheet applications. This approach is also used in the areas of graphics, engineering, and knowledge representation.

Some numeric constraint-oriented languages are Sketchpad, designed as early as 1963 by Ivan Sutherland, Juno (Nelson 1985), IDEAL (Van Wyk 1982), VIVID (Maleki 1987), ThingLab (Borning 1987), and TK!Solver (Konopasek and Jayaraman 1985).

Dataflow programming.

The dataflow programming paradigm specifies the flow of data through a network of operations. In this respect, it is similar to the dataflow analysis at the larger system analysis and design level. Strictly speaking, dataflow programs are intended to run on dataflow machines. True dataflow machines, however, are a rarity and still experimental.

Dataflow analysis determines dependencies among data and the order of execution is in turn determined by these dependencies. Operations are selected for execution once their operands have been computed. For example in the following instruction set:

1. X = Y + Z

2. Y = 3 + 5 / 8

3. Z = 9 - 8

statement 1 must wait for results from statements 2 and 3, both of which may be executed independently and in parallel. Thus, it is the flow of data between operations, rather than statement number, that actually constitutes the "control structure" of the program.

Once the flow of data between statements is examined, operands necessary for several (>1) operations may be available simultaneously, and the program's inherent parallelism is exposed. The program may, in fact, be executed on a dataflow-oriented machine that takes advantage of the parallelism thus exposed to speed up execution. This is sometimes called a paradigm for multiprocessing since it provides an approach to organizing multiple processors to work together on a single program.

The dataflow program is translated from a dataflow graph, which is a directed graph. The nodes of the graph represent operators; the arcs represent the flow of data between successive operators. The basic operators are illustrated by the nodes in Fig. 6.25. The value generator node is used to insert constants into the data flow. The switch and merge nodes are used together to conditionally select blocks of code. The input to these nodes, "control," is a Boolean value.

Data values are not stored in variables but are either used as they are computed (called *data driven*) or computed as they are needed (called *demand driven*). Therefore, the dataflow paradigm does not have the problem of side effects.

True dataflow languages are largely experimental since they are intended to run on dataflow architecture machines, which are themselves still experimental. Some dataflow languages are VAL (Dennis *et al.* 1984), LUCID (Ashcroft and Wadge 1977), and Id (Arvind and Gostelow 1982).

Multiparadigm Languages

Through most of the evolution of computer programming languages, one paradigm of programming, the imperative programming paradigm, has been prominent. Will the future of programming belong to one of the others?

A good case can probably be made for the abandonment of imperative programming in favor of, say, object-oriented programming. This is unlikely to occur, however, for reasons of economy, efficiency, and inertia. A far more likely (and, perhaps, even more optimistic) scenario is that an object orientation will be integrated into a variety of imperative languages. This is, in fact, occurring to a large degree. One of the most promising areas of research into programming methodology is in the area of multiparadigm programming systems. That this is not purely an experimental area is evident: Many languages, some of these quite well known and widely used, already combine the features of two or more programming paradigms.

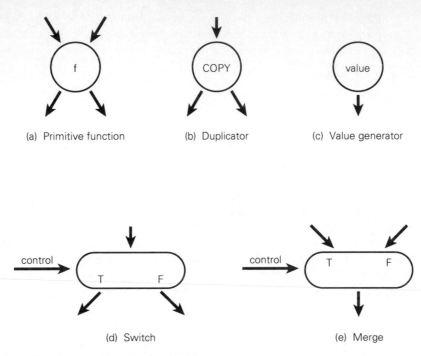

Figure 6.25   Operators in a dataflow graph

TurboPascal Version 5.5 has object-oriented features. Plans are currently under way for the introduction of object-oriented features into the next ANSI standard of COBOL. C++ is object-oriented C, developed at Bell Laboratories. ObjectPascal, developed jointly by Apple Computer and Niklaus Wirth, is object-oriented Pascal.

LOOPS, used in developing knowledge-based systems, combines the functional paradigm of traditional LISP programming with features supporting the object-oriented, rule-oriented, and access-oriented world views. LOGLISP, developed at Syracuse University about 1980, provides the PROLOG languages within a LISP environment.

Expert systems, the driving force in much programming research today, are sometimes developed so that object-oriented programming is used for representing basic concepts, rules are used to specify inferences, access-oriented programming drives the graphics display, and procedures are used for the overall control structure.

6.5 CHARTING AT THE CONTROL LEVEL

Chapter 5 introduced the structure chart for charting at the program level. This chart illustrates function, not logic flow, and is useful for defining a hierarchy of program abstractions. Useful as it is, at some point we have to set the *what* of high-level program abstraction aside and settle down to the *how* of the detailed program logic. This section presents two techniques for charting the flow of control in a program unit: flowcharts and N-S charts. First, however, we will briefly review a nonpictorial method of expressing program logic flow: pseudocode.

Pseudocode, flowcharts, and N-S charts all share some important characteristics:

- they are concerned with control of statement execution;
- they provide a clear, relatively natural presentation of the flow of control in the algorithm;
- they are machine independent;
- they are programming language independent;
- they allow the programmer to concentrate on logic flow without the need to worry about syntax.

Pseudocode

Pseudocode refers to the expression of algorithms in a natural, yet formalized, manner. Other terms for pseudocode are *structured pseudocode* and *structured English*. Pseudocode is important in its own right as a natural means of expressing algorithms, but it is also important because of its use to describe the contents of charting symbols.

There is no single "standard pseudocode." That would be virtually a contradiction in terms for a methodology that draws its strength from being natural, machine independent, and language independent. Every programmer has his own personal style of pseudocode. The important thing is to be clear, precise, and consistent. There is no universal pseudocode style; still certain keywords representing certain control structures are universally accepted (if, while, case). After all, if everyone were to create new keywords, pseudocode would hardly be useful as a means of communication.

One of the most important pseudocode devices for communicating the levels of nesting and scope in control structures is indenting. Indenting is also the single largest indicator of the author's personal pseudocode style. For example, the two-way selection control construct might look like this in pseudocode:

```
if condition then
        then-part
else
        else-part
endif
```

Or, it might look like this:

```
if condition
        then then-part
        else else-part
endif
```

The important thing is to be consistent.

Flowcharts

Flowcharts were first introduced in 1947 by H.H. Goldstine and J. von Neumann in an attempt to represent algorithms in a precise notation that would be at a higher level than machine language. Although this date may make the flowchart seem ancient to some, still, to paraphrase Mark Twain, the reports of the flowchart's death have been greatly

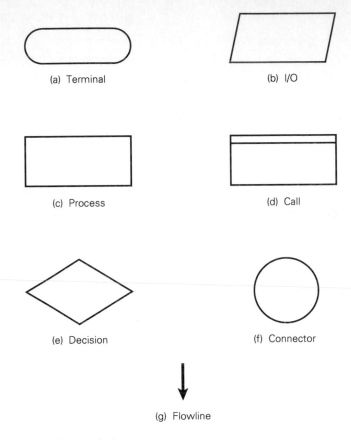

(a) Terminal

(b) I/O

(c) Process

(d) Call

(e) Decision

(f) Connector

(g) Flowline

Figure 6.26   Flowchart symbols

exaggerated. Since flowchart symbols are simple pictures, they provide a universal means of communicating algorithms, albeit at a fairly low level.

There are six basic flowchart symbols. These are displayed in Fig. 6.26. The oval is the *terminal* symbol and is used to represent the beginning or end of program (or subprogram) execution. The parallelogram is the *I/O* symbol and is used to represent input or output operations. The rectangle is the *processing* symbol and is used to represent assignment to variables of possibly computed values. The rectangle with the horizontal bar across the top (sometimes represented instead by two vertical lines, one down either side of the rectangle) is the *call* symbol representing a simple call to a subprogram. The diamond is the *decision* symbol and is used to represent a Boolean expression. The circle is the *connector* symbol and is used to represent a branch to another named part of the flowchart. Finally, the arrow, or *flowline* is used to indicate flow of control through the program (flowchart).

Since flowcharts are at a fairly low level, as indicated by the presence of the low-level branch, they must be used by the programmer in a disciplined, structured manner. The structured control constructs discussed in this chapter are depicted in flowchart form in Fig. 6.27.

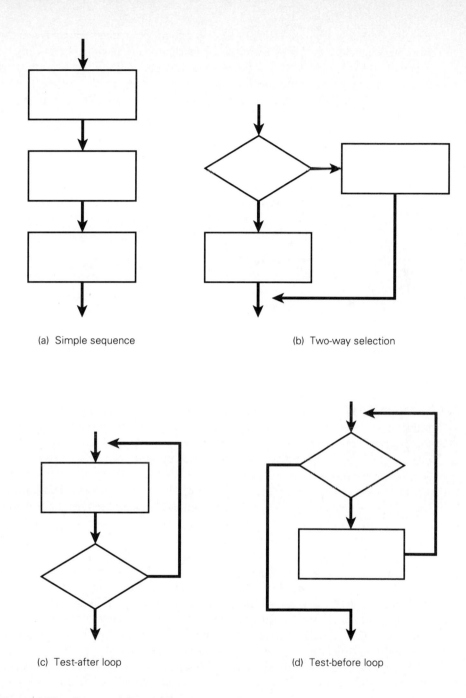

(a) Simple sequence

(b) Two-way selection

(c) Test-after loop

(d) Test-before loop

Figure 6.27 Structured flowcharts

It is clear that once we begin nesting control structures, these flowcharts can get large very quickly. Fig. 6.28 displays a flowchart representation of the nested control structures that we used earlier in the chapter. Clearly, while flowcharts are conducive to thinking through the logic of a program requiring a very small amount of nesting, it is easier to view the larger picture, especially in a structured program with pseudocode:

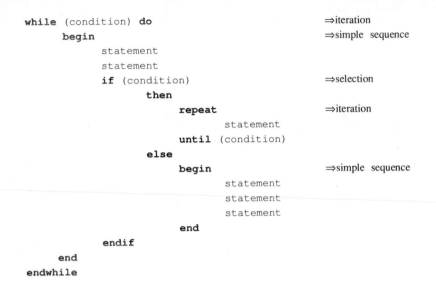

```
while (condition) do                              ⟹iteration
    begin                                         ⟹simple sequence
            statement
            statement
            if (condition)                        ⟹selection
                then
                        repeat                    ⟹iteration
                            statement
                        until (condition)
                else
                        begin                     ⟹simple sequence
                            statement
                            statement
                            statement
                        end
            endif
        end
    endwhile
```

Flowcharts are not only useful tools for communicating algorithms, but their flexibility makes them ideal tools to use (along with others) in developing algorithms, using the pictorial control abstractions of Fig. 6.27 as a conceptual aid. These structured flowchart constructs illustrate that a well-structured program can be written in any language, from the very lowest to the very highest, whether specific syntax elements such as the **while** or **case** statements are available or not. The necessary tools need not be built into the programming language: They must be built into the programmer's education.

N-S Charts

Introduced by I. Nassi and B. Shneiderman in 1973, Nassi-Shneiderman charts are rectangular nested flowcharts that "force" structured control constructs onto the algorithm. N-S charts bear a strong resemblance to pseudocode and are, in fact, the pictorial equivalent of pseudocode. (Some say that the easiest way to construct N-S charts is to first write out the algorithm in pseudocode and then draw the appropriate shapes around it. The question then arises: Is this truly a charting technique?)

Figs. 6.29 and 6.30 illustrate some structured control constructs represented as N-S charts. Nesting of control structures in an N-S chart is shown in Fig. 6.31. It is clearly more compact than the flowchart version and even more compact than the pseudocode version, since all those nested "**end**s" are not necessary.

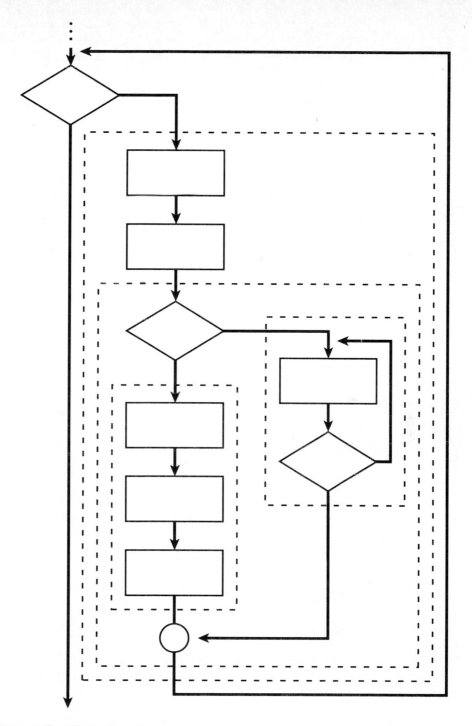

Figure 6.28   Nesting control constructs

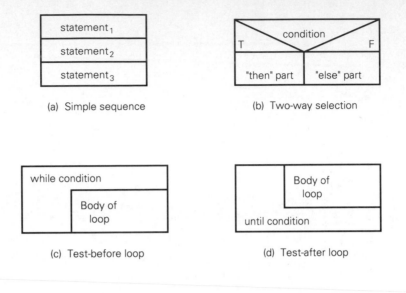

(a) Simple sequence   (b) Two-way selection

(c) Test-before loop   (d) Test-after loop

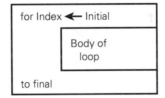

(e) Indexed loop

Figure 6.29   Some control constructs

Large modules with several layers of nesting fare as poorly with N-S charts as with flowcharts. Since well-done N-S charts will be restricted to a single page, programmers find that they either have to write very, very small or keep program modules at a relatively manageable size.

SUMMARY AND KEY TERMS

Chapter Summary

In this chapter, we have examined control structures at the expression, statement, and subprogram levels. We have also looked at different approaches to programming that affect the control structures employed. These include the imperative, functional, production-system, logic, and object-oriented programming paradigms. Finally, charting at the control level was discussed, including flowcharts, N-S charts and, a nongraphical technique, pseudocode.

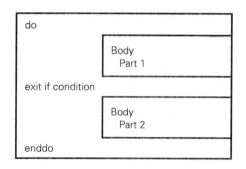

(a) Nested-if

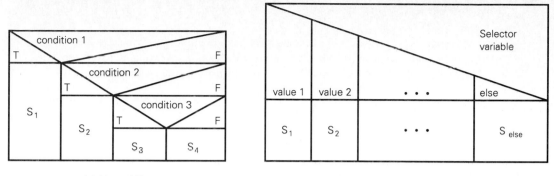

(b) Multiway selection

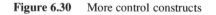

```
do
              Body
                Part 1

exit if condition

              Body
                Part 2

enddo
```

(c) General loop

Figure 6.30   More control constructs

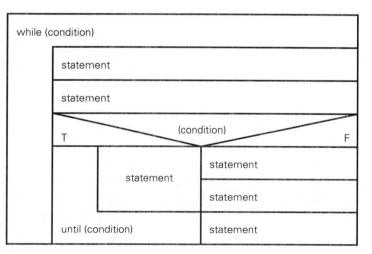

Figure 6.31   Nested control constructs

Terminology

Some of the terms presented in this chapter may have been new to you. Use this list as a guide in reviewing the chapter. When you review the list, if you come across a term that is unfamiliar to you, go back and review the section that discusses it.

activation record	arithmetic operators	asynchronous programming
concurrent processing	control abstraction	coroutine
critical region	deadlock	disabled condition
enabled condition	exception	exception handler
expression	flowchart	functional programming
goto-less programming	imperative programming	implicit call
indexed loop	iteration	iterative composition
logical operators	logic programming	message passing
modularization	monitors	mutual exclusion
N-S chart	object-oriented programming	operand
operation	parallel processing	precedence rules
programming paradigm	pseudocode	raising an exception
recursion	recursive subprogram	relational operators
repetition	scheduled call	selection
selective composition	semaphores	sequential composition
simple call	simple sequence	structured control constructs
structured English	structured programming	synchronization
top-down design		

SUGGESTIONS FOR FURTHER STUDY

Many of the control constructs discussed in this chapter are given excellent treatments in books by Elson (1973), Pratt (1984), and Holt *et al.* (1978) and papers by Morgan (1988), Goodenough (1975), Krajewski (1985), Obermeier (1988), Paseman (1985), and Thomsen and Knudsen (1987). For material regarding the controversy surrounding the use of the goto instruction, see papers by Knuth (1974), Dijkstra (1968), and Wulf (1977). For thoughts about recursion and other matters, the book by Hofstadter (1979) is a fascinating read.

Research in the area of programming paradigms is rich and dynamic. For more detailed examination of the material presented here, see Backus (1978), Eisenback and Sadler (1985), Allen and Pokrass (1987), Swaine (1988), and Luker (1989). For material on the individual programming paradigms covered in this chapter, refer to the following selected sources:

Functional. Books by Glaser *et al.* (1984) and Henderson (1980). Articles by Harrison and Khoshnevisan (1985) and Henderson (1986).

Logic.   Books by Lazarev (1989) and Sterling and Shapiro (1986). Articles by Bic and Lee (1987), Genesereth and Ginsberg (1985), Cohen (1985), Komorowski and Maluszynski (1987), and Kowalski (1979, 1985, 1988).

Production-system.   Articles by Fickas (1987), Hayes-Roth (1985), and Moskowitz (1986).

Object-oriented.   Books by Cox and Hunt (1986), Harland (1984), Krasner (1983), Pinson and Wiener (1988), Shlaer and Mellor (1988), and Tello (1989). Articles by Anderson (1988), Bach (1989), Bailin (1989), Blaha *et al.* (1988), Booch (1986), Bulman (1989), Burns and Morgeson (1988), Cioch (1989), Cook (1986), Cox (1984, 1986), Danforth and Tomlinson (1988), Gardner (1988), Kurtz *et al.* (1989), Wechsler and Rine (1988), Wegner (1986, 1987). Also see the August 1981, May 1985, and August 1987 issues of *Byte* magazine.

Dataflow.   Articles by Barzel and Salesin (1986), Clarke *et al.* (1989), Doman (1981), Gaudiot (1986), Kavi *et al.* (1986), Lee and Messerschmitt (1987), and Motteler and Smith (1985).

Constraint.   Articles by Borning (1987), Borning *et al.* (1987), Dansforth (1988), Ege (1988), and Konopasek and Joyaraman (1985) and the book by Leler (1988).

For more on multiparadigm systems see the January 1986 issue of *IEEE Software* and other articles by Adelsberger *et al.* (1986), Amsterdam (1988), Bellia *et al.* (1986, 1988), Bobrow (1985), Daniel (1988), Darlington (1987), Eilbert and Satter (1986), Gabriel (1989), Goguen and Meseguer (1986), Grimshaw (1987), Koschmann and Evens (1988), Lassez (1987), Loucopoulos and Karakostas (1989), Ruiz-Mier and Talavage (1987), Stefik *et al.* (1986a, 1986b).

The book by Martin and McClure (1988) provides an overview of many different structured and charting techniques. Also see Schneyer (1984).

PART 2

Programming Languages for Information Processing

INTRODUCTION TO PART 2

The following six chapters each present the specific language structures of a particular computer programming language. These languages were chosen for a variety of reasons:

- COBOL (Chapter 8) because of its hardiness; because it is still the major programming language for practical business applications; because many database management systems and "4GLs" have borrowed to a lesser or greater extent from COBOL concepts.
- Pascal (Chapter 9) because of the simplicity of and uniformity of its syntax; because of its ubiquity in academic environments; and because of its influence on later languages like MODULA-2 and Ada.
- MODULA-2 (Chapter 10) because of its importance as a high-level, Pascal-like (and therefore ALGOL-like) systems programming language; and because it is oriented toward programming in a real-time environment with concurrency.
- C (Chapter 11) because, like MODULA-2, it is a high-level systems programming language; because of its burgeoning popularity in the microcomputer/UNIX environment; and because many programs aimed at Ada are now actually programmed in C instead.
- PROLOG (Chapter 12) because of its position of importance as the implementation language of choice for expert systems, an increasingly important application area in information processing.
- Smalltalk (Chapter 13) because it defines the object-oriented programming paradigm, which promises to be an important trend in the further development and evolution of new and current programming languages.

These chapters all share a common organization and structure. This was done to emphasize those aspects of the languages that are the same or similar in concept, although the syntax used for implementing these concepts may be radically different from one language to the next.

The purpose of these chapters is clearly *not* to train expert programmers in any (certainly not *all*) of these languages. At best, a good programmer in another language might be able to use one of these chapters as an introduction to the study of a second or a third programming language. It is relatively simple to find a particular structure in a language already known to the programmer and then look up the syntax of the equivalent structure (should one exist) in the new language. Certainly, if one is to become expert in the new language, further in-depth study will be required. Just as certainly, these chapters are not appropriate as introductions to the study of a *first* programming language.

Rather, the intention of Part 2 of this book is to familiarize you with the actual programming language concepts and structures as implemented in several, widely used computer programming languages. These chapters collect and summarize information regarding the data-level structures, program structures, and control structures of five widely used programming languages. The chapters are set up in such a way as to relate these real language structures to the theoretical, generalized concepts presented in Part 1 and, I hope, to facilitate a comparison of these languages. Some of the syntactic details and advanced or optional features of these languages are, of necessity, left out.

7

Sample Programming Problems

The next few chapters will introduce you (or, in some cases, *re*introduce you) to a variety of programming languages, their syntax and application. It will help if we develop a few study problems so that, when you study the sample programs presented in these chapters, you will be able to concentrate on language syntax rather than confounding the problem at that time by forcing you to work through the logical solution to a brand-new problem each time. Four problems for study will be presented here, all of which can use data from the fictitious personnel file described in the following section. These four problems are:

1. a bubble sort,
2. a sequential file update,
3. maintaining multiple lists, and
4. binary search tree processing.

These study problems are presented in such a way as to make them relatively independent. This, it turns out, involves some redundant I/O of files and/or huge temporary arrays. This is done so that each problem can be approached separately as an independent unit, rather than as a small part of a large operation. For example, the logic flow of Study Problem #3 for maintaining multiple sublists within an ordered list of data could be easily incorporated into the structure of the sequential file update program (Study Problem #2) and might, indeed, make more sense to us that way than the relatively independent way it is treated here.

In an attempt to maintain language independence as much as possible in this chapter, algorithms are depicted in flowchart form. For some of you, the COBOL programs in Chapter 8 or the Pascal programs in Chapter 9 will be more comfortable as a starting point.

Employee			ID-number	
		Name	Last	
			First	
			MI	
		Address	Street	
			City	
			State	
			Zip	
	Telephones	Home-1	Area	
			Local	
		Home-2	Area	
			Local	
		Emergency	Area	
			Local	
			Job-title	
			Location	
			Department	
			Annual-salary	
			Last-promoted	
			First-employed	

Figure 7.1 Employee Record

7.1 THE DATA SET

The data set we will work with in the study problems presented here is a personnel file, organized sequentially and consisting of 100 fictitious employee records. Each record looks like the one outlined in Fig. 7.1. Aside from annual salary (real), and the last-promoted and first-employed fields (dates), all other fields are stored as character strings. The key field is the 9-digit employee identification number (e.g., social security number).

The entire set of data for the personnel file, called *NMPERSNL* as it has been ordered alphabetically by employee *name*, is presented in Fig. 7.2. Of course, since name is not the key field of this record (name is not a unique identifier), the file may need to be sorted on the employee identification number before it is used in a file-processing context.

The bubble sort algorithm presented in the following section will be used to transform the data set into an ordered sequential file, in order by employee ID number. This new sorted file, called *IDPERSNL*, will then be used in, for example, the sequential file update problem of Section 7.3.

7.2 STUDY PROBLEM #1: BUBBLE SORT

Sorting, the process of ordering a list of data, is an important, required subtask in many problems. Study Problem #2, for example, the sequential file update, requires that the two files used for input, the master file and the transaction file, both be ordered on the same key and in the same direction. Study Problem #4, the binary search tree problem, requires that data be sorted first so that the tree can be constructed in the best way to search through an ordered set of data. Even Study Problem #3, the multiple lists problem, benefits from an ordering scheme of some sort.

The bubble sort is a frequently used type of exchange sort. An *exchange sort* is an internal sort in which key values of pairs of records are compared and, if they are not in the correct relative positions, the records are exchanged. While the bubble sort is not the most efficient of the exchange sorts, it is nevertheless often employed—perhaps because of the logical clarity of the algorithm or, perhaps, because of its memorable name. The *bubble sort* algorithm allows each key to float to its proper position through a series of pairwise comparisons and exchanges with *adjacent* key values. Fig. 7.3 (p. 222) illustrates the general exchange sort in (a) and the bubble sort in (b).

As the example in Fig. 7.4 (p.222) illustrates, each pass results in "bubbling" at least one (often more) record to its final position in the sorted list. Thus, each pass requires (and gets) at least one less comparison than the previous pass. Or, in other words, the *ith* pass requires at most $n - i$ comparisons (where n is the size of the list or the number of records to be sorted), since i records are already in sorted order.

The list of integers in Fig. 7.4 finds its way to its final sorted form after four passes through the bubble sort algorithm. After the first pass, the largest number, 8, is already at its final position at the bottom of the list. As this example demonstrates, although the "standard" bubble sort is allowed to go through $n - 1$ passes, we like to take advantage of the fact that the list may be sorted way before the $n - 1$th pass. The algorithm ends after the first pass that resulted in no exchanges.

```
859673715 ARCHER     LEW         101 ROSS ST      NOTOWN    NY 10031
583532918 BERGERAC   CYRANO    D 1 PARIS ST       PERSONTOWN NY 30005
007511852 BOND       JAMES       122 GOLDFINGER   PERSONTOWN NY 30022
853600995 BOURNE     JASON       418 AMNESIA ST   METROPOLIS NY 20045
892369626 BRAGG      PETER       340 MODEST ST    PERSONTOWN NY 30025
783563314 BURKE      AMOS        114 BARRY ST     NOTOWN    NY 10024
501620748 BUTLER     RHETT       44 WIND ST       METROPOLIS NY 20012
250141546 CANNON     FRANK       22 DIET ST       NOTOWN    NY 10040
351453116 CARTER     NICK        400 MASTER ST    METROPOLIS NY 20016
584836738 CARTWRIGHT HOSS        5 PONDEROSA LA   PERSONTOWN NY 30003
431815949 CARTWRIGHT BEN         5 PONDEROSA LA   PERSONTOWN NY 30003
096283018 CHAMBERS   DIANE       100 BAR ST       NOTOWN    NY 10011
986141483 CHAMBERS   PAT         14 HAMMER ST     METROPOLIS NY 20024
525042311 CHAN       CHARLIE     10 MOTT ST       NOTOWN    NY 10023
360475339 CHARLES    NICK        10 PEEPER ST     PERSONTOWN NY 30022
117308423 CHARLES    NORA        10 PEEPER ST     PERSONTOWN NY 30022
606984917 CLOUSSEAU  INSPECTOR   21 MEENKY ST     METROPOLIS NY 20014
412074985 DIAMOND    RICHARD     36 TYLER ST      NOTOWN    NY 10004
513789593 DILLON     MATT        14 MARSHALL ST   PERSONTOWN NY 30015
547247690 DIPALMA    LOUIE       30 SLEAZE ST     METROPOLIS NY 20003
940476548 DRAKE      JOHN        24 AGENT ST      NOTOWN    NY 10005
053939677 DREW       NANCY       42 NOSY ST       PERSONTOWN NY 30006
782667746 ED         MISTER      10 OAT ST        METROPOLIS NY 20025
097366399 FAWLTY     BASIL       13 TOWER ST      NOTOWN    NY 10007
412122593 FIELDING   DAN         18 COURT ST      PERSONTOWN NY 30028
629195747 FLETCHER   IRWIN     M 2 CHASE ST       METROPOLIS NY 20021
156533413 FLYNN      FRANCIS   X 8 HERB ST        NOTOWN    NY 10017
560874087 GOODWIN    ARCHIE      12 WOLF ST       PERSONTOWN NY 30010
513351904 GUNN       PETER       25 MANCINI ST    METROPOLIS NY 20007
744146916 HARRISON   CHIP        36 BLOCK ST      METROPOLIS NY 20014
812815428 HAMMER     MIKE        1 SPILLANE ST    NOTOWN    NY 10013
165245544 HARDY      FENTON      30 SNOOP ST      PERSONTOWN NY 30019
279319399 HART       JENNIFER    10 POWERS ST     METROPOLIS NY 20014
422375009 HAVELOCK   MICHAEL     22 LUDLUM ST     NOTOWN    NY 10029
532859964 HELM       MATT        13 HAMILTON ST   PERSONTOWN NY 30014
109094977 HOLCROFT   NOEL        10 HUNTER ST     METROPOLIS NY 20012
623541383 HOLMES     MYCROFT     18 CLUB ST       NOTOWN    NY 10017
315551263 HOLMES     SHERLOCK    221B BAKER ST    PERSONTOWN NY 30021
900619229 HOPE       MATTHEW     246 ATTORNEY ST  METROPOLIS NY 20013
909295632 IGNATOWSKI JIM         13 DREAM ST      NOTOWN    NY 10038
525416210 IRONSIDE   ROBERT    T 10 EARL ST       PERSONTOWN NY 30023
897176599 JONES      BARNABY     4 HILLBILLY ST   METROPOLIS NY 20015
243634844 KEATON     ALEX      P 34 ELITE ST      NOTOWN    NY 10018
018647329 KENT       CLARK       20 KRYPTON ST    PERSONTOWN NY 30029
358928785 KIRK       JAMES     T 100 TREK ST      METROPOLIS NY 20028
027602435 KRAMDEN    ALICE       20 HONEYMOON ST  NOTOWN    NY 10031
999410773 KRAMDEN    RALPH       20 HONEYMOON ST  NOTOWN    NY 10031
197340858 LANE       LOIS      L 28 SUPER ST      PERSONTOWN NY 30032
993610980 MADISON    OSCAR       22 SLOB ST       METROPOLIS NY 20013
```

Figure 7.2 Personnel file, in order by name (continued next page)

312	6436808			312	2826590	ANALYST	A	R&D	41876.00	0186	0980
513	7435589			513	2553233	ANALYST	B	MIS	48999.00	0381	0576
513	3759007			513	7486007	CLERK	B	R&D	31246.00	0188	1085
112	2590381			112	8915116	DESIGNER	C	MIS	48267.00	0187	1178
513	4995195	513	4995196	513	9962302	MANAGER	D	R&D	52800.00	0287	0381
316	3763580			316	9191504	CLERK	A	MIS	24643.00	0586	0174
112	9413335			112	6253207	ANALYST	B	PROD	41278.00	0687	0782
312	3666323			312	3723835	MANAGER	C	MIS	63200.00	0186	0180
112	3451665			118	2305018	CLERK	D	PROD	25198.00	0786	0279
412	6225101			513	2778316	ANALYST	A	R&D	40008.00	0288	0282
412	6225101			513	2778316	DESIGNER	B	MIS	48809.00	0188	0976
316	8585109			312	7781993	MANAGER	C	PROD	67000.00	0186	0382
112	3757148			112	3462108	ANALYST	D	PROD	42080.00	1186	0983
312	2385240			312	9416121	CLERK	C	MIS	38828.00	0887	0580
513	9631621			513	2721892	MANAGER	B	R&D	67890.00	0587	1179
513	9631621			513	2721892	DESIGNER	A	PROD	57240.00	0388	0580
118	3385183			118	3846843	ANALYST	D	MIS	39980.00	0386	0678
316	8379150			316	2567791	CLERK	C	R&D	23400.00	0482	0979
412	4676448			412	7734323	MANAGER	B	PROD	78877.00	0387	0883
112	2513133			118	2753446	DESIGNER	A	MIS	43729.00	0787	0986
312	5962806			316	2827538	ANALYST	D	R&D	32316.00	0787	0784
412	2356038			513	4980553	CLERK	C	PROD	29658.00	0787	0983
118	9658222			112	4633260	MANAGER	B	MIS	50005.00	0385	0680
312	7732288			316	8586385	ANALYST	A	PROD	42010.00	0288	0185
412	4494500	412	2826768	513	2564539	CLERK	D	MIS	37645.00	0286	0880
112	3737266			118	8278452	MANAGER	C	R&D	63087.00	0387	0878
316	4698991			312	7451490	DESIGNER	B	PROD	48523.00	0187	0379
513	6380415			412	8212730	ANALYST	A	MIS	33246.00	0387	0485
118	6297109			112	9222706	CLERK	D	R&D	24126.00	0286	0681
112	4620061			112	7824088	ANALYST	D	PROD	37037.00	0187	0281
312	9537297	312	9537298	312	4966165	CLERK	C	MIS	27246.00	0486	0676
513	4696338			513	5749676	MANAGER	B	R&D	78000.00	0487	0177
110	7457425			118	5315667	DESIGNER	A	PROD	57453.00	0388	0776
316	3841838	316	3861521	316	3665332	ANALYST	D	MIS	45144.00	0387	0676
412	6800304			412	7480765	CLERK	C	R&D	37820.00	0387	0582
112	3889521			112	6223982	MANAGER	B	PROD	65152.00	0188	0579
312	9227385			316	7780875	DESIGNER	A	MIS	56249.00	0388	0883
513	4344908			513	7738267	ANALYST	D	R&D	43891.00	0784	0682
118	8755200	118	7687008	118	4991983	CLERK	C	PROD	37323.00	0388	0681
312	2575228			312	9349059	MANAGER	B	MIS	51000.00	0580	0877
412	7897801			412	4392120	DESIGNER	A	R&D	55550.00	0585	0176
112	9347516			112	3427953	ANALYST	D	PROD	41200.00	0185	0280
316	8563006			316	9196045	CLERK	C	MIS	21350.00	0586	0684
513	6482699			513	7633871	MANAGER	B	R&D	62045.00	0387	0483
118	6461204			118	9967241	DESIGNER	A	PROD	50100.00	0487	0185
312	7685967			312	8590276	ANALYST	D	MIS	42186.00	0187	0280
312	7685967			312	8590276	CLERK	C	R&D	33320.00	0186	0481
412	2728075			412	7733625	MANAGER	B	PROD	60010.00	0386	0782
112	3390296			112	4552585	DESIGNER	A	MIS	43051.00	0388	0681

Figure 7.2 (continued next page)

```
439348245 MAGNUM       THOMAS        201 ALOHA ST     NOTOWN     NY 10019
847258657 MALONE       SAM           100 CHEERS ST    PERSONTOWN NY 30008
686944932 MARLOWE      PHILIP        12 CHANDLER ST   METROPOLIS NY 20014
961008182 MARPLE       JANE        A 14 PARLOUR ST    NOTOWN     NY 10009
454768105 MARTIN       ANGEL         2 ROCKFISH ST    PERSONTOWN NY 30016
297000324 MASON        PERRY         12 ATTORNEY ST   METROPOLIS NY 20017
154574105 MAVERICK     BRETT         173 GAMBLE ST    NOTOWN     NY 10031
966456476 MCCOY        LEONARD       2 ENTERPRISE ST  PERSONTOWN NY 30026
796681101 MCGEE        TRAVIS        20 FLUSH ST      METROPOLIS NY 20023
594184602 MCMILLAN     SALLY         120 HUDSON ST    NOTOWN     NY 10016
144936551 MUDD         HARRY         1 STAR ST        PERSONTOWN NY 30031
519251496 MUNROE       JESSICA       42 AUTHOR ST     METROPOLIS NY 20003
426743441 NASHE        HAMILTON      23 OXFORD ST     NOTOWN     NY 10038
045828304 NORTH        JERRY         14 MARTINI ST    PERSONTOWN NY 30004
761736932 NORTH        PAM           14 MARTINI ST    PERSONTOWN NY 30004
467287118 NORTON       EDWARD        15 TRIXIE ST     METROPOLIS NY 20016
336345414 OHARA        SCARLET       10 TARA LA       NOTOWN     NY 10008
048111007 OLSEN        JIMMY         300 CUB ST       PERSONTOWN NY 30017
764319959 PEEL         EMMA          111 AVENGER ST   METROPOLIS NY 20015
575504962 PERRIN       REGINALD      100 GROT ST      NOTOWN     NY 10001
098480250 PETERSON     NORM          20 VERA ST       PERSONTOWN NY 30011
406725718 POIROT       HERCULE       22 INSPECTOR ST  METROPOLIS NY 20019
498634876 POPPINS      MARY          25 MAGIC ST      PERSONTOWN NY 30035
766688163 QUIXOTE      DON           111 WINDMILL ST  NOTOWN     NY 10015
671920794 RANDALL      JOSH          56 BOUNTY ST     METROPOLIS NY 20017
678466125 REAGER       ALEX        J 74 ADVISOR ST    NOTOWN     NY 10038
949326445 REDDY        JASON         17 SECURITY ST   NOTOWN     NY 10013
129275576 RHODENBARR   BERNIE      L 22 CROOK ST      PERSONTOWN NY 30027
676865001 ROCKFORD     JAMES       T 33 TRAILER ST    METROPOLIS NY 20029
740350623 SCUDDER      MATTHEW       12 ALCOHOL ST     METROPOLIS NY 20003
373603340 SHAYNE       MIKE          21 SURF ST       NOTOWN     NY 10026
751645142 SING         HOP           153 COOK ST      PERSONTOWN NY 30005
885034483 SKYWALKER    LUKE          500 FORCE ST     METROPOLIS NY 20015
739096328 SMALL        DAVID       R 777 CLERGY ST    NOTOWN     NY 10003
742201761 SPADE        SAM         S 179 FALCON ST    PERSONTOWN NY 30011
265522806 SPENSER      HAWK          33 BEACON ST     METROPOLIS NY 20016
071918464 STEED        JOHN          18 BOWLER ST     NOTOWN     NY 10010
164669628 STEELE       REMINGTON   R 15 ALIAS ST      PERSONTOWN NY 30013
231081163 STREET       DELLA         580 DELLA ST     METROPOLIS NY 20023
634950378 TANNER       EVAN          300 SLEEPER ST   NOTOWN     NY 10013
602407060 TEMPLAR      SIMON         96 SAINT ST      PERSONTOWN NY 30007
989000740 TORTELLI     CARLA         35 ZENA ST       METROPOLIS NY 20017
434606028 UNGER        FELIX         240 HONK ST      NOTOWN     NY 10031
175666707 VADER        DARTH         13 SPACE ST      PERSONTOWN NY 30032
875490775 VANCE        PHILO         111 NEW YORK ST  METROPOLIS NY 20029
750855555 WALKER       AMOS          165 DETROIT ST   NOTOWN     NY 10015
815520270 WATSON       JOHN        H 93 MEDICAL ST    PERSONTOWN NY 30011
382547177 WEISER       MARION      N 17 IMA ST        NOTOWN     NY 10003
107908321 WHITE        PERRY         28 CHIEF ST      METROPOLIS NY 20011
081956797 WINE         MOSES         12 HIP ST        METROPOLIS NY 20017
337510916 WOLFE        NERO          608 ORCHID ST    NOTOWN     NY 10023
```

Figure 7.2   (continued next page)

```
316 6331827                   316 8332633 DESIGNER D R&D    51182.00 0287 0883
513 8366666                   513 4998860 ANALYST  C PROD   37213.00 0486 0279
118 8549401 118 8549405 118 7631562 CLERK    B MIS    24463.00 0286 0580
312 9531735                   312 2887553 MANAGER  A R&D    70000.00 0388 0781
412 3845600                   412 8914331 DESIGNER D PROD   44440.00 0684 0479
112 2824380                   112 8750020 ANALYST  C MIS    49534.00 0885 0379
316 7453258                   316 8537123 CLERK    B R&D    36631.00 0287 0285
513 6464670                   513 9466005 MANAGER  A PROD   73385.00 0184 0380
118 3895432                   118 3831987 DESIGNER D MIS    55640.00 0286 0682
312 9633065                   316 6429088 ANALYST  C R&D    47251.00 0587 0879
412 4498858                   412 8591265 CLERK    B PROD   24976.00 1184 0182
112 9536380                   112 6047506 MANAGER  A MIS    83927.00 0188 0580
312 4533284 312 7825473 312 7982174 DESIGNER D R&D    47208.00 0388 0285
513 2665096                   513 7454965 DESIGNER D R&D    48282.00 1186 0575
513 2665096                   513 7454965 ANALYST  C PROD   48276.00 0588 0383
118 4867454                   118 3841197 CLERK    B MIS    28976.00 0586 0379
316 3732006                   316 2090232 MANAGER  A R&D    79896.00 0388 0979
513 2573708                   513 2372302 DESIGNER D PROD   53218.00 0286 0783
112 4973476                   112 2844022 ANALYST  C MIS    50000.00 0588 0383
312 2253437                   312 9461974 CLERK    B R&D    30002.00 0384 0179
412 3316213                   412 3314217 MANAGER  A PROD   73208.00 0387 0676
118 6220826                   118 7688259 DESIGNER D MIS    53854.00 0183 0380
412 8585462                   513 3361957 CLERK    D PROD   30000.00 0187 0480
316 7352643 316 7827324 312 6493467 ANALYST  C R&D    43333.00 0284 0181
112 6475759                   112 9982723 ANALYST  A R&D    35278.00 0982 0577
312 6333178                   312 8366761 CLERK    D PROD   20993.00 0884 0583
312 2665706 312 2665707 312 7460709 ANALYST  D MIS    49994.00 0386 0283
513 7483123                   513 4491925 MANAGER  C MIS    53807.00 0987 0486
118 3722142                   118 7832068 DESIGNER B R&D    53080.00 0583 0280
118 7682789                   112 8363377 MANAGER  D R&D    53276.00 0386 0183
316 7696660                   316 8913926 DESIGNER C PROD   48725.00 0387 0684
412 4358705                   412 3772930 ANALYST  B MIS    37456.00 0886 0382
112 3761000                   112 8573213 CLERK    A R&D    27241.00 0387 0580
316 8586972                   316 8712321 ANALYST  A PROD   39898.00 0983 0480
412 7747951                   412 7712472 CLERK    D MIS    24936.00 0181 0879
112 4984277                   112 2520567 MANAGER  D R&D    77776.00 1187 0381
312 5747168                   312 9468252 DESIGNER C PROD   47365.00 0286 0281
513 2307100 513 8573003 412 6366900 ANALYST  B MIS    33241.00 0787 0378
118 2510223                   118 2362863 CLERK    A R&D    27346.00 0886 0583
316 3981525                   316 2414738 MANAGER  D PROD   73296.00 0286 0183
412 5314579 412 5312580 513 6257977 DESIGNER C MIS    59806.00 0388 0279
112 8912212                   112 8914187 ANALYST  B R&D    31978.00 0886 0981
312 2820482                   312 3724385 CLERK    A PROD   39999.00 0983 1080
412 7485968                   412 8360320 MANAGER  D MIS    50001.00 0380 1175
118 6251426                   118 6253991 DESIGNER C R&D    47199.00 0382 0577
316 3874093                   316 7742466 ANALYST  B PROD   37219.00 0585 0779
412 4558010                   412 5962693 CLERK    A MIS    34265.00 0386 0978
312 2593137 312 8535544 312 8312726 MANAGER  D R&D    84999.00 0588 0178
112 6049648 112 6046472 112 7481735 MANAGER  C PROD   56273.00 0386 0684
118 4030038                   118 4032736 ANALYST  B MIS    49928.00 0388 0977
312 8340306                   312 9195078 CLERK    A R&D    27329.00 0183 1078
```

Figure 7.2 (concluded)

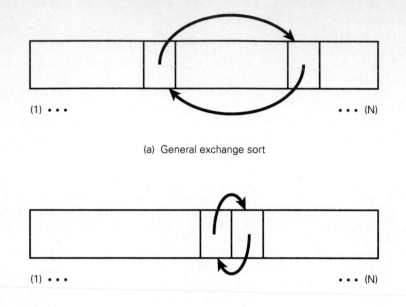

(a) General exchange sort

(b) Bubble sort

Figure 7.3   Exchange sort

Unsorted list	Pass 1	After Pass 1	Pass 2	After Pass 2	Pass 3	After Pass 3	Pass 4	After Pass 4	Pass 5
2	2	2	2	2	2	2	~~2~~ 1	1	1
4	4	4	4	4	~~4~~ 1	1	2	2	2
8	~~8~~ 5	5	~~5~~ 1	1	~~4~~ 3	3	3	3	3
5	~~8~~ 1	1	~~5~~ 3	3	4	4	4	4	4
1	~~8~~ 3	3	5	5	5	5	5	5	5
3	~~8~~ 7	7	~~7~~ 6	6	6	6	6	6	6
7	~~8~~ 6	6	7	7	7	7	7	7	7
6	8	8	8	8	8	8	8	8	8

Remarks:	1st pass orders: 8	2nd pass orders: 7						5th pass No exchanges

Figure 7.4   A bubble sort

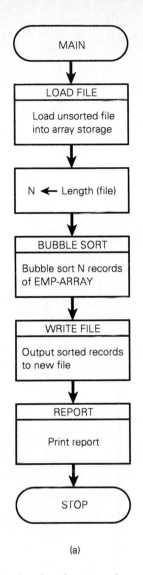

(a)

Figure 7.5   Bubble sort algorithm (continued next page)

We will use the form of the bubble sort algorithm depicted in flowchart form in Fig. 7.5. Notice that since *n*, the number of records to be sorted, is assumed to be a global variable, its value is saved by assignment to a local variable (LIMIT), which is then manipulated in order to control the length of the list to be sorted at each pass. The same effect would be accomplished by passing the value of *n* to the bubble sort subprogram as a value parameter.

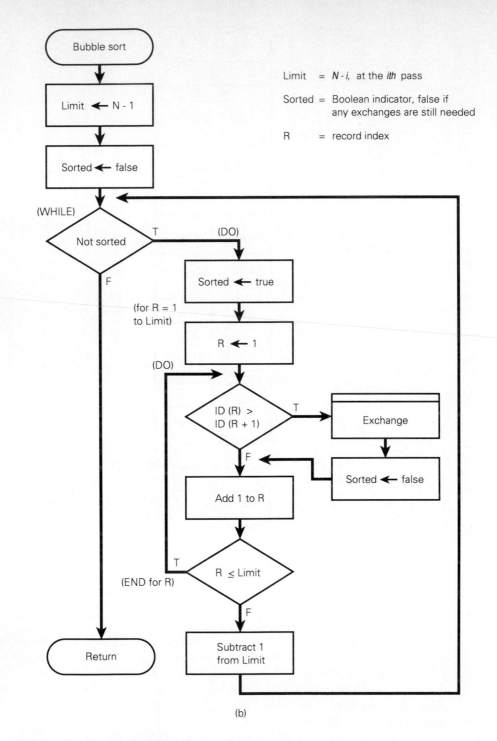

Limit = $N-i$, at the ith pass

Sorted = Boolean indicator, false if any exchanges are still needed

R = record index

(b)

Figure 7.5   (continued next page)

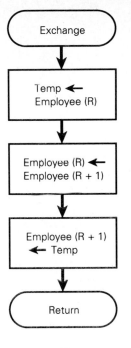

(c)

Figure 7.5   (concluded)

When this algorithm is implemented, the data set of personnel records is input via the main program into an array. The array entries are then sorted in ascending order by key value (employee ID number) and output to another sequential file. The first 10 records of this new file are listed in Fig. 7.6. The printed (or screen) output layout for this study problem is displayed in Fig. 7.7 (p. 227).

7.3 STUDY PROBLEM #2: SEQUENTIAL FILE UPDATE

The diagram of Fig. 7.8 (p. 227) illustrates a sequential file update at the system level. Notice that a backup file is produced automatically simply by virtue of the fact that the records have been stored in a sequential file and updating may not occur in place. The magnetic tape symbol has been used to represent the master file in this diagram to emphasize the sequential nature of the file, although it is certainly true that a sequential file may be stored on a direct-access medium as well. The file of transactions, or updates, to the master file has been sorted in the same order as the master file and may be on

```
007511852BOND        JAMES      122 GOLDFINGER PERSONTOWNNY300225133759007
018647329KENT        CLARK      20 KRYPTON ST  PERSONTOWNNY300295136482699
027602435KRAMDEN     ALICE      20 HONEYMOON STNOTOWN    NY100313127685967
045828304NORTH       JERRY      14 MARTINI ST  PERSONTOWNNY300045132665096
048111007OLSEN       JIMMY      300 CUB ST     PERSONTOWNNY300175132573708
053939677DREW        NANCY      42 NOSY ST     PERSONTOWNNY300064122356038
071918464STEED       JOHN       18 BOWLER ST   NOTOWN    NY100103125747168
081956797WINE        MOSES      12 HIP ST      METROPOLISNY200171184030038
096283018CHAMBERS    DIANE      100 BAR ST     NOTOWN    NY100113168585109
097366399FAWLTY      BASIL      13 TOWER ST    NOTOWN    NY100073127732288
098480250PETERSON    NORM       20 VERA ST     PERSONTOWNNY300114123316213
107908321WHITE       PERRY      28 CHIEF ST    METROPOLISNY200111126049648

. . .
```

Figure 7.6   Sorted personnel file (continued next page)

```
                        Bubble Sort Report
          -----------------

          Number of records read from input file --
          NMPRSNEL File --  100

          Number of records written to output file --
            IDPRSNEL File --  100
```

Figure 7.7   Bubble sort report

magnetic tape as well, or the transactions may be input interactively one at a time from the keyboard. In the diagram, they are represented by punched cards in order to indicate the transitory nature of this set of records, at least relative to the semipermanent nature of the master file. Fig. 7.9 lists the transaction file records that will be used.

Each transaction record contains a key value corresponding to the key value on the master file record to be updated, and a code that indicates the type of transaction or update to be processed. In general, transaction records are of three basic, coded types:

1. ADD a new record when a new employee is hired
2. DELETE a record when employment is discontinued
3. CHANGE an existing record as, say, when an employee moves, gets a raise, etc.

The master file we will use is the *IDPERSNL* file output from Study Problem #1. We will still require the bubble sort in this problem for ordering transaction file records. The major logic of the sequential file update is illustrated in Fig. 7.10 (p. 230)—it involves repeatedly comparing "current" keys from each of the transaction and master files and proceeding as indicated. For example, if the key value of the current transaction file record is smaller than that of the current master file record, the only possible update

```
         5137486007CLERK    BR&D   312460001881085
         5137633871MANAGER BR&D   620450003870483
         3128590276ANALYST DMIS   421860001870280
         5137454965DESIGNERDR&D   482820011860575
         5132372302DESIGNERDPROD 532180002860783
         5134980553CLERK    CPROD 296580007870983
         3129468252DESIGNERCPROD 473650002860281
         1184032736ANALYST BMIS   499280003880977
         3127781993MANAGER CPROD 670000001860382
         3168586385ANALYST APROD 420100002880185
         4123314217MANAGER APROD 732080003870676
1126046472112748173SMANAGER CPROD 562730003860684
```

Figure 7.6   (concluded)

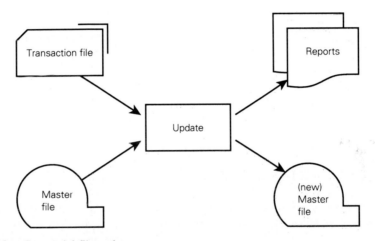

Figure 7.8   Sequential file update

(transaction) is an ADD. In other words, the transaction record comes before the master file record in sequence, and it must be written out to the new master file in its proper order. Therefore, the code of the transaction record must be an ADD, or it must be an error. Notice that we are assuming that there is at most a single update record per key value. This implies relatively frequent updating. The update algorithm itself is depicted in the large by the control hierarchy chart of Fig. 7.11 and by the detailed flowchart of Fig. 7.12. In some places, efficiency has been sacrificed in favor of the expressive clarity of the algorithm.

Fig. 7.13 lists the first 10 records of the updated master file. The printed outputs produced as a result of the update program provide job completion information such as the number of transactions processed and a report listing errors discovered by the update

```
018647329MAN          SUPER       20 KRYPTON ST  PERSONTOWNNY300295136482699
090666491HOPPER       GRASS       609 KUNG FU LA NOTOWN   NY100313123234589
097366399FAWLTY       BASIL       13 TOWER ST    NOTOWN   NY100073127732288
320007177WISER        H.FRED      171 ALIAS AVE  NOTOWN   NY100073128591989
412122593FIELDING     DAN         100 SLEAZY CT  PERSONTOWNNY300284124494500
560874087GOODWIN      ARCHIE      12 WOLF ST     PERSONTOWNNY300105136380415
583532918BERGERAC     CYRANO      D1 PARIS ST    PERSONTOWNNY300055137435589
676029444BAILEY       GEORGE      1 CAPRA ST     PERSONTOWNNY300107121234567
676865010
766688163JUAN         DON         111 WINDMILL STNOTOWN   NY100153167352643
859673715ARCHER       LEW         101 ROSS ST    NOTOWN   NY100313126436808
892369626BRAGG        PETER       340 MODEST ST  PERSONTOWNNY300255134995195
999966010KNIGHT       WHITE       30 ARTHUR ST
```

Figure 7.9   Transaction file (continued next page)

program. The output format for this error report is displayed in Fig. 7.14 (p. 236). There are at least three kinds of errors to look for:

1. attempting to insert a record as "new" when it already exists

2. attempting to delete a record that does not exist

3. attempting to change a record that does not exist.

7.4 STUDY PROBLEM #3: MULTIPLE LISTS

Chapter 4 describes a type of dynamic data structure called a *multilinked list*. One of the purposes to which a structure of this sort may be put is the maintenance of sublists within a larger list of data without having to actually duplicate records or physically store them in separate files. Pointer variables are set up, one for each sublist to be maintained. These are stored within the record structure itself. In this way, for example, a college registrar can keep track of the students registered for particular classes, as well as the classes taken by each individual student, using the same set of data. This information may be used, on the one hand, to print out class rosters and grade sheets and also to send students an official transcript of their grades at the end of the term.

For our problem, we would like to produce a report listing, separately, all employees holding a particular *JobTitle*, all employees working in a particular company *Location*, and all employees working in a particular *Department*, for all possible JobTitles, Locations, and Departments. The format for this sort of printed report is presented in Fig. 7.15 (p. 237).

```
             5137633871MANAGER BR&D   620450003870483C
             5139968300MANAGER DMIS   486130001890189A
             3168586385ANALYST APROD  420100002880185B
             1126629300ANALYST BPROD  150000001890189A
   41228267685132564539CLERK   DMIS   376450002860880C
             4128212730ANALYST AMIS   332460003870485D
             5132553233ANALYST BMIS   554980001890576C
             3122822201ANALYST AR&D   418760001890189
                                           0 0
   31678273243126493467ANALYST CR&D   433330002840181C
             3122826590ANALYST AR&D   556000001890980C
   51349951965139962302MANAGER DR&D   528000002870381D
                                              A
```

Figure 7.9   (concluded)

Fig. 7.16(a) (p. 238) illustrates the revised record (or, *node*) structure that will be required. The format of this revised record, called *EmpNode*, is obtained by attaching to the *Employee* record of our personnel file the necessary pointers for maintaining the lists of interest. In addition, we will need the external pointers to the beginning of each list, including one for the "master" list of all records in sorted order (by employee identification number). These are shown in Fig. 7.16(b).

The first part of this problem (Part A) involves "creation" of the (logical) sublists as part of the master list. The creation algorithm (Fig. 7.17 on p. 239) uses the same ADD procedure that will be used to add new employees to the data set when it is updated.

The second part of this problem (Part B) involves updating this "master" multi-linked list. Updates are done when new employees are hired (ADD), when employees leave or are fired (DELETE), and when employees are promoted or transferred to another location and/or department (CHANGE). The updates to be used in testing this program are taken from the transaction file of Study Problem #2. The update algorithm is illustrated by the flowchart of Fig. 7.18 (p. 241). To keep things simple, we can assume no errors in update records.

Perhaps some clarification of the variable names used is in order. Variables beginning with the "prefix" *F* are external pointers to the beginning (the *First* node) of a list. There is one for every list or sublist. These are the pointer arrays *Fjob* (1 to 4), *Floc* (1 to 4), and *Fdept* (1 to 3) for the sublists of interest, and *Fnode* as the external pointer to the "major list" of all employees. Variables beginning with the "prefix" *S* are internal pointers or links and appear as part of the revised record *EmpNode* of Fig. 7.16. Each points to its successor, or the next node in order in the list or sublist. These are *Sjob*, *Sdept*, and *Sloc* for the sublists and *Snode* for the major list. The pointer variables *NEXT* and *FIRST* of the INSERT algorithm are parameters, or place-holders, for the internal and external pointers, respectively, of a particular list or sublist.

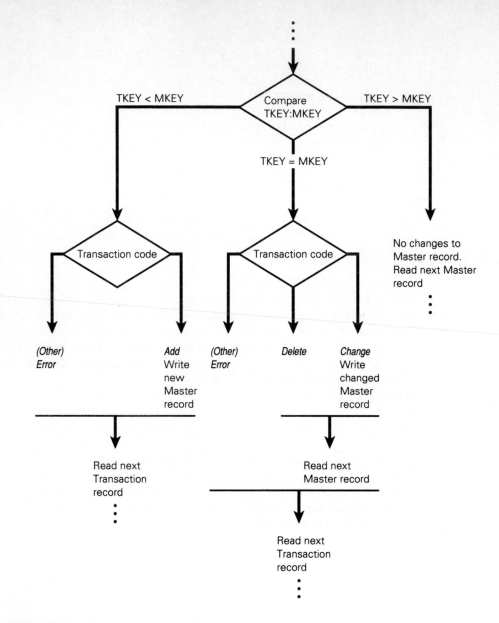

Figure 7.10   Overview, sequential file update

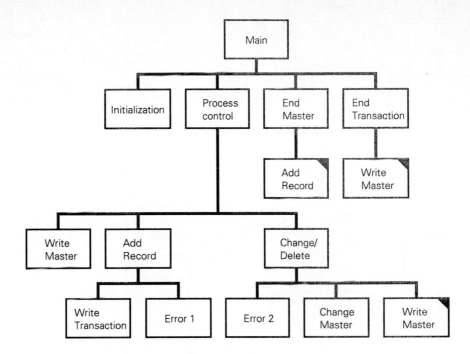

Figure 7.11 Update program hierarchy chart

Normally, in REMOVing a node from a singly linked dynamic structure, the storage space allocated for that node will be freed or deallocated within the REMOVE subprogram. However, in this example, the node must be REMOVEd from several lists before it can be freed. The REMOVE subprogram is invoked four times from the DELETE subprogram—one time for each of the four lists maintained. Then the node is finally freed using the node pointer, which was "returned" as an output parameter from the REMOVE subprogram.

7.5 STUDY PROBLEM #4: BINARY SEARCH TREE

A *binary search tree* is a binary tree that is ordered for a binary search such that, for each node, all nodes in its left subtree precede that node in the ordered list, and all nodes in its right subtree come after that node in the ordered list (see Fig. 7.19 on p. 244). In other words, the value at the node itself is exactly in the middle in order. In our problem, the nodes of the tree will be constructed by adding two pointer fields to our *Employee* record: a RIGHT pointer and a LEFT pointer.

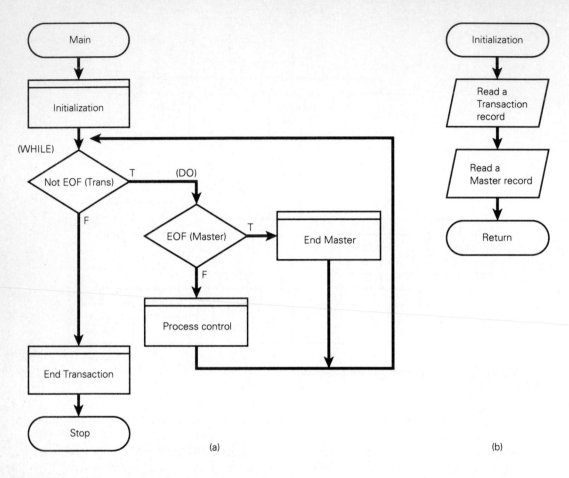

Figure 7.12   Update program (continued next page)

In order to ensure that the tree is balanced, and that subsequent search and retrieval is more efficient, creation of a binary search tree should be performed on an already ordered set of *n* records. Thus, the flowchart for creating a binary search tree, shown in Fig. 7.20 (p. 245), may also assume that the set of records has already been sorted, perhaps by a main program invocation of the bubble sort.

Traversal is the process of going through a tree in such a way that every node is accessed once and only once. *In-order* traversal of a binary tree occurs like this:

1. traverse the left subtree of the current node

2. process the current node

3. traverse the right subtree of the current node.

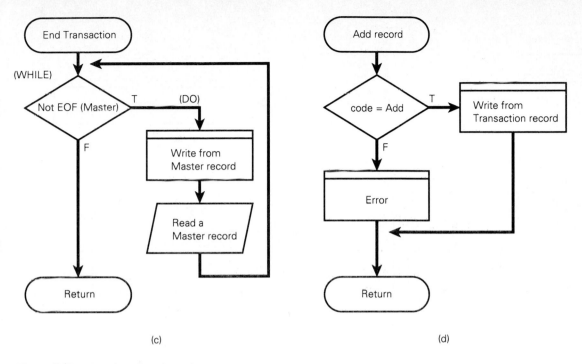

(c)

(d)

Figure 7.12 (continued next page)

In-order traversal maintains the sorted order of the tree and can be used whenever all nodes must be processed in sorted order; for example, in printing a detailed report from the data. It is obvious that this in-order traversal algorithm is inherently recursive, and it is quite simply represented for coding by the flowchart of Fig. 7.21 (p. 247).

A tree may also be processed without using recursion. In that case, as always, stacks are used in order to simulate recursion. In fact, a nonrecursive algorithm is often used even in languages that allow for dynamic memory management and recursion. This is because the nonrecursive algorithm is often more efficient than its recursive counter-part. The advantage of recursion is obvious from a comparison of the recursive and nonrecursive algorithms presented in this chapter: Recursion sometimes facilitates the design of simpler, more elegant algorithms. Algorithms for nonrecursive creation and in-order traversal of a binary search tree are contained in Ellzey (1982) and Loomis (1989). "Play computer" or desk trace with these algorithms, using a small amount of simple test data.

For our problem, the main program would consist simply of two call statements invoking CREATE and InPrint(ROOT) in sequence.

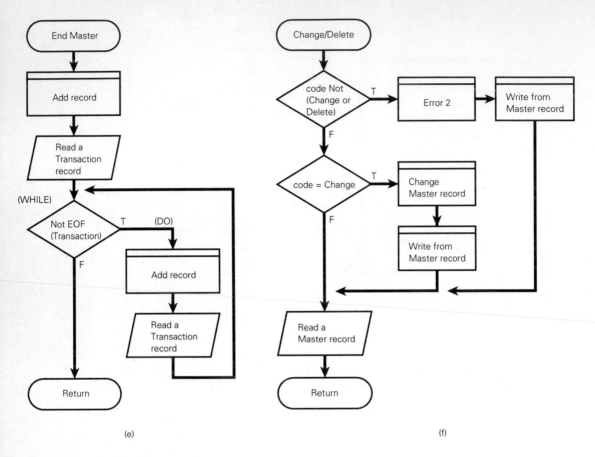

Figure 7.12   (continued next page)

```
007511852BOND      JAMES      122 GOLDFINGER PERSONTOWNNY300225133759007
018647329MAN       SUPER      20 KRYPTON ST  PERSONTOWNNY300295136482699
027602435KRAMDEN   ALICE      20 HONEYMOON STNOTOWN     NY100313127685967
045828304NORTH     JERRY      14 MARTINI ST  PERSONTOWNNY300045132665096
048111007OLSEN     JIMMY      300 CUB ST     PERSONTOWNNY300175132573708
053939677DREW      NANCY      42 NOSY ST     PERSONTOWNNY300064122356038
071918464STEED     JOHN       18 BOWLER ST   NOTOWN     NY100103125747168
081956797WINE      MOSES      12 HIP ST      METROPOLISNY200171184030038
090666491HOPPER    GRASS      609 KUNG FU LA NOTOWN     NY100313123234589
096283018CHAMBERS  DIANE      100 BAR ST     NOTOWN     NY100113168585109
097366399FAWLTY    BASIL      13 TOWER ST    NOTOWN     NY100073127732288
098480250PETERSON  NORM       20 VERA ST     PERSONTOWNNY300114123316213

   . . .
```

Figure 7.13   Updated master file (continued next page)

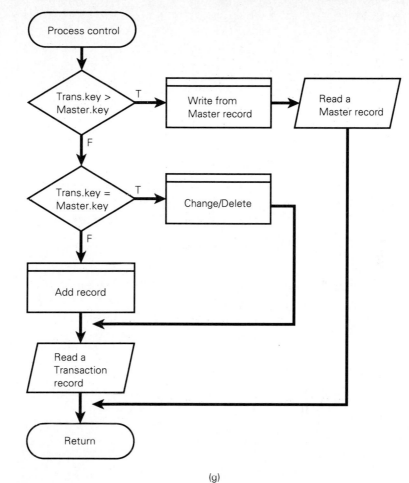

(g)

Figure 7.12 (concluded)

```
5137486007CLERK    BR&D   312460001881085
5137633871MANAGER BR&D    620450003870483
3128590276ANALYST DMIS    421860001870280
5137454965DESIGNERDR&D    482820011860575
5132372302DESIGNERDPROD   532180002860783
5134980553CLERK    CPROD   296580007870983
3129468252DESIGNERCPROD   473650002860281
1184032736ANALYST BMIS    499280003880977
5139968300MANAGER DMIS    486130001890189
3127781993MANAGER CPROD   670000001860382
3168586385ANALYST APROD   420100002880185
4123314217MANAGER APROD   732080003870676
```

Figure 7.13 (concluded)

```
                    Sequential File Update
                    Personnel File Maintenance

-----------------------------------------------------------

    Total Number of transactions  =     13
    Transactions processed successfully =    10

The following transactions could not be processed
due to errors

  ID Number Trans.Code   Error
  --------- ----------   -----

  097366399 B            Transaction Code is not C or D
  676029444              Transaction Code is missing
  676865010              Transaction Code is missing


-----------------------------------------------------------


   3 records added to Master File

   2  records deleted from Master File

   5 records changed
```

Figure 7.14   Update program output

```
           Multiple Sublists

        Listing for Jobtitle Analyst
        ------------------------

          027602435 KRAMDEN ALICE
          081956797 WINE MOSES
          097366399 FAWLTY BASIL
           .  .  .
           .  .  .


           Multiple Sublists

        Listing for Jobtitle Clerk
        ------------------------

          007511852 BOND  JAMES
          053939677 DREW  NANCY
          144936551 MUDD  HARRY
           .  .  .
           .  .  .


           Multiple Sublists

        Listing for Jobtitle Designer
        ------------------------

          045828304 NORTH JERRY
          048111007 OLSEN JIMMY
          071918464 STEED JOHN
           .  .  .
           .  .  .


           Multiple Sublists

        Listing for Jobtitle Manager
        ------------------------

          018647329 KENT  CLARK
          096823018 CHAMBERS DIANE
          098480250 PETERSON NORM
           .  .  .
           .  .  .


           Multiple Sublists

        Listing for Location A
        ------------------------

          097366399 FAWLTY BASIL
          098480250 PETERSON NORM
          117308423 CHARLES NORA
           .  .  .
           .  .  .
```

Figure 7.15   Report, multiple lists problem

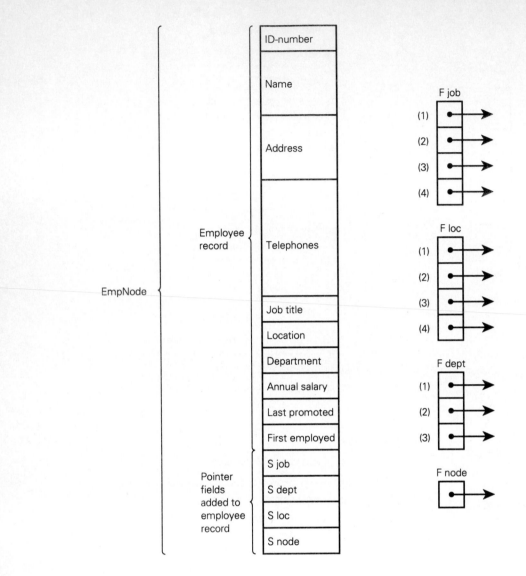

	ID-number
	Name
	Address
Employee record	Telephones
	Job title
	Location
	Department
	Annual salary
	Last promoted
	First employed
Pointer fields added to employee record	S job
	S dept
	S loc
	S node

EmpNode

F job
(1)
(2)
(3)
(4)

F loc
(1)
(2)
(3)
(4)

F dept
(1)
(2)
(3)

F node

(a) Node   (b) External pointers

Figure 7.16   Multilinked list structures

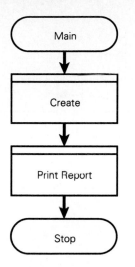

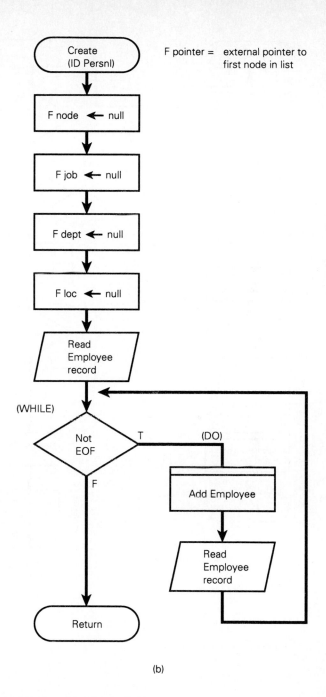

(a)   (b)

Figure 7.17   Creating a Multilinked list (continued next page)

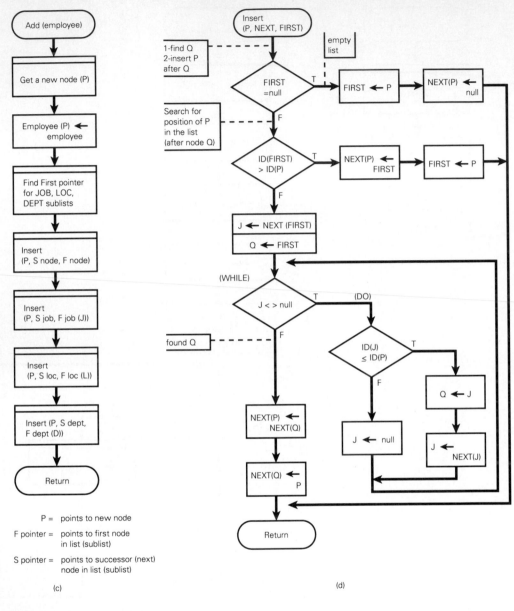

Figure 7.17 (concluded)

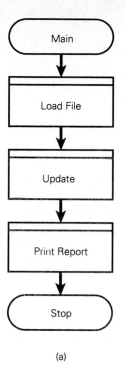

(a)

Figure 7.18   Multilinked list update (continued next page)

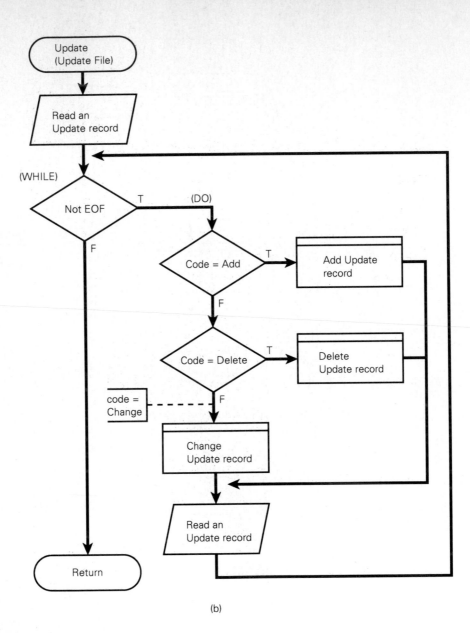

(b)

Figure 7.18   (continued next page)

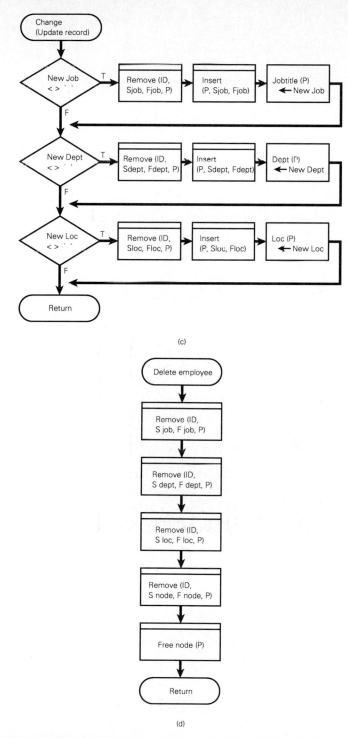

(c)

(d)

Figure 7.18   (continued next page)

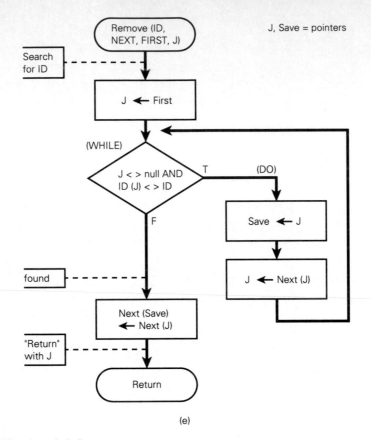

Figure 7.18   (concluded)

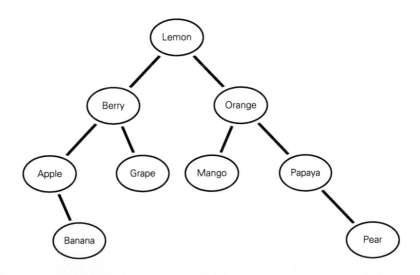

Figure 7.19   A binary search tree

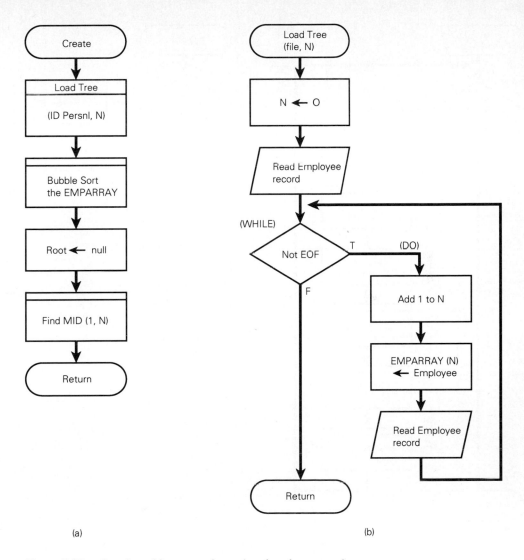

(a)

(b)

Figure 7.20 Creating a binary search tree (continued next page)

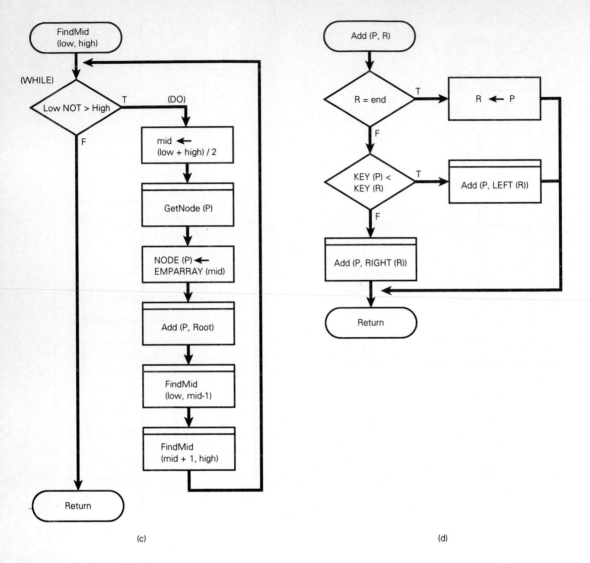

(c)

(d)

Figure 7.20 (concluded)

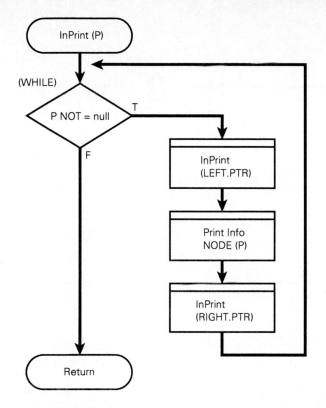

Figure 7.21   In-order traversal

8

COBOL Language Elements

COBOL (COmmon Business-Oriented Language), designed in answer to the business community's rapidly developing computing needs has, since the 1960s, maintained its position of prominence in commercial data processing. The oldest programming language for business applications, it is still the most widely used. However, its position in first place is by no means absolutely secure. Recent developments such as query languages, integrated packages, and "4GLs"—many of these, in fact, derivatives of COBOL—have been chipping away at the COBOL bastion. One feature these products share—a strong reliance on a database nucleus—can be traced back to COBOL's innovative treatment of data descriptions as separate from and equal to executable program instructions.

8.1 A BRIEF OVERVIEW OF COBOL

COBOL is a supremely eadable language characterized by an English-like notation, four distinct program divisions, a simplistic approach to arithmetic computation, hierarchical data structures, and a powerful file-handling capability. Although COBOL programs are not exactly known for their terseness, still, the wordiness of the language—a distinct disadvantage if you are counting keystrokes—often results in code that is self-documenting and easily read by nontechnical users and managers.

History and Development

In the year after the design of ALGOL (then called IAL) by a committee of European and American computer scientists, another committee proposed another group programming language development effort. Roughly 40 representatives of computer manufacturers, industry, academia, and government met in May 1959, calling themselves the **CO**nference on **DA**ta **SY**stems **L**anguages (CODASYL), for the purpose of developing a common programming language for commercial data processing applications. The committee's work was supported—though not initiated—by the U.S. Department of Defense. Since the language was intended for industry-wide acceptance and not targeted for a particular computer manufacturer (unlike FORTRAN), the group's mandate was to develop a high-level, machine-independent language. The language's only lack of generality was to come from its orientation towards data processing applications. The CODASYL group responded to an anticipated difficulty in promoting the new language among managers in the commercial data processing community, by designing a language syntax heavily rooted in a language the managers already knew—English. The result of this group effort was the design in April 1960 (an early version appeared in December 1959) of the COBOL language: a high-level, machine-independent, business-oriented, English-like programming language.

In addition to English, the design of COBOL was influenced by FORTRAN, IAL (ALGOL58), and FLOW-MATIC—a language, developed by Grace Murray Hopper's team at Remington-Rand, that used English keywords and was geared toward business data processing.

Revised in 1961, COBOL soon became widely implemented. The language was revised in 1965 and standardized by the American National Standards Institute (ANSI) in 1968 and then again in 1974. Work on a new COBOL standard began again in the late 1970s (labeled COBOL 198x) accompanied by widespread industry complaints at the anticipated evolutionary changes in a language that had become comfortable. This latest version of the language (COBOL 1985) is still not widely available.

Application Areas

COBOL is the definitive programming language for business applications. Business data processing applications are characterized by high-volume input and output, permanent external file maintenance, and relatively simple algorithms, especially when compared with languages developed for applications in science or engineering. Some language features that distinctly support business data processing are I/O file description and manipulation facilities, an English-like syntax, the facility to edit data for output, the Report Writer facility for report generation, and a variety of features that together serve to promote the construction of source programs that are relatively self-documenting.

Classification

Software generation: Third
Procedural/declarative: Procedural
Translator: Compiled
Processing environment: Batch
Programming paradigm: Imperative

8.2 STUDY PROBLEM #1—BUBBLE SORT PROGRAM

Before examining COBOL language structures in detail, it is instructive to first look at a complete COBOL program. Fig. 8.1 lists the bubble sort program that was described in Chapter 7. It should be noted that COBOL has a built-in bubble sort routine available simply by using the SORT statement. This program is presented here for illustrative purposes only.

Notice the four distinct divisions in a COBOL program: the **IDENTIFICATION DIVISION**, which identifies the program to the system; the **ENVIRONMENT DIVISION**, which describes the hardware configuration such as the computer and any I/O devices used; the **DATA DIVISION**, which defines and describes all the data used by the program; and the **PROCEDURE DIVISION**. Of these four divisions, only the **PROCEDURE DIVISION** contains any executable (action) statements. Thus, the **PROCEDURE DIVISION** statements in Fig. 8.1 correspond to the algorithms laid out for this problem in Chapter 7.

This program was run on an IBM mainframe using OS/VS COBOL (1982).

8.3 DATA: TYPES, FILES, AND DATA STRUCTURES

COBOL recognizes the importance of data in the business data processing environment. In fact, if we examine the bubble sort program we see that equal emphasis is placed on the data descriptions in the **DATA DIVISION** and on the operations in the **PROCEDURE DIVISION**. Both are needed for proper processing of the program, and both are independent of the particular computer or I/O devices used. Other data-level features that make COBOL distinctive are its highly flexible hierarchical data structure (a logical record structure) and its powerful file-definition facility. Memory management in COBOL is static.

Constants

Literals. COBOL supports the use of numeric and nonnumeric literals in program code. A *numeric literal* represents a numeric value and is composed of a string of characters that may include the digits 0–9 and the special characters + , - , . (decimal point). The upper limit for the number of digits in a numeric literal is 18. An example of a numeric literal in COBOL is: -127.5

A *nonnumeric literal* is a character string that may contain any valid EBCDIC characters and is enclosed in quotation marks. It may contain up to 120 characters. An example of a nonnumeric literal is: "I AM A LITERAL".

Named constants. Some COBOL words represent constant values. These words, called *figurative constants*, may be used in a program in the same way as any literal. These words, like other language-defined words are *reserved*, which means that they may not be used in any other way by the programmer. The following are some figurative constants provided by COBOL:

```
//  JOB
// EXEC COBUCLG,PARM.COB=STATE
//COB.SYSIN DD *
      *********************************
      *                               *
       IDENTIFICATION DIVISION.
      *                               *
      *********************************
       PROGRAM-ID. BUBBLE.
      *                               *
      *********************************
      *                               *
       ENVIRONMENT DIVISION.
      *                               *
      *********************************
       CONFIGURATION SECTION.
       SOURCE-COMPUTER. IBM-370.
       OBJECT-COMPUTER. IBM-370.
       INPUT-OUTPUT SECTION.
       FILE-CONTROL.
           SELECT INFILE  ASSIGN TO UT-S-CPLNAME.
           SELECT PRINTOUT  ASSIGN TO UT-S-SYSOUT.
           SELECT OUTFILE ASSIGN TO UT-S-CPLNUMB.
      *                               *
      *********************************
      *                               *
       DATA DIVISION.
      *                               *
      *********************************
       FILE SECTION.
       FD  INFILE
           LABEL RECORDS ARE STANDARD
           BLOCK CONTAINS 10 RECORDS
           RECORD CONTAINS 121 CHARACTERS
           DATA RECORD IS INLINE.
       01  INLINE PIC X(121).
       FD  PRINTOUT
           LABEL RECORDS ARE OMITTED
           RECORD CONTAINS 133 CHARACTERS
           DATA RECORD IS OUTLINE.
       01  OUTLINE.
           05  FILLER     PIC X.
           05  PRINTLINE  PIC X(132).
       FD  OUTFILE
           LABEL RECORDS ARE STANDARD
           BLOCK CONTAINS 10 RECORDS
           RECORD CONTAINS 121 CHARACTERS
           DATA RECORD IS FILELINE.
       01  FILELINE PIC X(121).
```

Figure 8.1   Bubble sort program (continued next page)

```
*
WORKING-STORAGE SECTION.
*
01   ARRAY-STORAGE.
     05   EMPLOYEE OCCURS 100 TIMES.
          10   EMP-ID          PIC X(9).
          10   OTHER-DATA   PIC X(112).
01   PROGRAM-COUNTERS.
     05   N-LENGTH        PIC S9(3) VALUE ZEROS.
     05   LIMIT-N         PIC S9(3).
     05   XCOUNT          PIC S9(3) VALUE ZEROS.
     05   RECORD-COUNTER  PIC S9(3) VALUE ZEROS.
     05   R               PIC S9(3) VALUE ZEROS.
     05   NEXT-R          PIC S9(3).
01   TEMP                 PIC X(121) VALUE SPACES.
01   EOF-INDICATOR        PIC X(3)    VALUE 'NO'.
     88   END-OF-FILE          VALUE 'YES'.
*---------------------------------------*
*                                       *
*     R E P O R T   F O R M A T         *
*---------------------------------------*
01   REPORT-HEADING-1.
     05   FILLER          PIC X(10) VALUE SPACES.
     05   FILLER          PIC X(20)
          VALUE 'BUBBLE  SORT  REPORT'.
     05   FILLER          PIC X(103) VALUE SPACES.
01   REPORT-HEADING-2.
     05   FILLER          PIC X(10) VALUE SPACES.
     05   FILLER          PIC X(20)
          VALUE '--------------------'.
     05   FILLER          PIC X(103) VALUE SPACES.
01   REPORT-LINE-1.
     05   FILLER          PIC X VALUE SPACE.
     05   FILLER          PIC X(40)
          VALUE 'NUMBER OF RECORDS READ FROM INPUT FILE--'.
     05   FILLER          PIC X(92) VALUE SPACES.
01   REPORT-LINE-2.
     05   FILLER          PIC X(5) VALUE SPACES.
     05   FILLER          PIC X(16)
          VALUE 'NMPERSNL FILE --'.
     05   FILLER          PIC X(8) VALUE SPACES.
     05   RECORD-COUNTER-I PIC ZZ9.
     05   FILLER          PIC X(101) VALUE SPACES.
01   REPORT-LINE-3.
     05   FILLER          PIC X VALUE SPACE.
     05   FILLER          PIC X(42)
          VALUE 'NUMBER OF RECORDS WRITTEN TO OUTPUT FILE--'.
     05   FILLER          PIC X(90) VALUE SPACES.
```

Figure 8.1   (continued next page)

```
01   REPORT-LINE-4.
     05   FILLER           PIC X(5) VALUE SPACES.
     05   FILLER           PIC X(16)
          VALUE 'IDPERSNL FILE --'.
     05   FILLER           PIC X(8) VALUE SPACES.
     05   RECORD-COUNTER-O PIC ZZ9.
     05   FILLER           PIC X(101) VALUE SPACES.
01   REPORT-LINE-5.
     05   FILLER           PIC X VALUE SPACE.
     05   FILLER           PIC X(35)
          VALUE 'BUBBLE SORT COMPLETED SUCCESSFULLY.'.
     05   FILLER           PIC X(97) VALUE SPACES.
01   REPORT-LINE-6.
     05   FILLER           PIC X VALUE SPACE.
     05   FILLER           PIC X(37)
          VALUE 'BUBBLE SORT COMPLETED UNSUCCESSFULLY.'.
     05   FILLER           PIC X(95) VALUE SPACES.
*                            *
*********************************
*                            *
 PROCEDURE DIVISION.
*                            *
*********************************
*------------------------------------------------------------*
* RECORDS ON FILE ARE LOADED INTO A TABLE CALLED EMPLOYEE    *
* THE LENGTH OF FILE IS COUNTED AND STORED AS N-LENGTH.      *
*------------------------------------------------------------*
 MAIN-PROGRAM.
     PERFORM INITIALIZATION.
     PERFORM LOAD-FILE VARYING R FROM 2 BY 1
          UNTIL END-OF-FILE.
     PERFORM BUBBLE-SORT.
     PERFORM WRITE-FILE VARYING  R FROM 1 BY 1
          UNTIL R > N-LENGTH.
     PERFORM PRINT-REPORT.
     PERFORM CLOSING.
     STOP RUN.
*
 INITIALIZATION.
     OPEN INPUT INFILE  OUTPUT OUTFILE, PRINTOUT.
     READ INFILE INTO EMPLOYEE(1)
         AT END MOVE 'YES' TO EOF-INDICATOR.
*
 LOAD-FILE.
     ADD 1 TO N-LENGTH.
     READ INFILE INTO EMPLOYEE(R)
         AT END MOVE 'YES' TO EOF-INDICATOR.
```

Figure 8.1   (continued next page)

```
*----------------------------------------*
*                                        *
*      B U B B L E    S O R T            *
*----------------------------------------*
*----------------------------------------------------------*
* SINCE THE # OF RECORDS SWITCHED DURING THE BUBBLE SORT *
* WILL NOT EXCEED THE TOTAL NUMBER OF RECORDS, THE        *
* LIMIT OF POSSIBLE EXCHANGES IS CONTROLLED BY LIMIT-N.   *
* LIMIT-N IS REDUCED BY 1 AFTER EACH PASS.                *
*----------------------------------------------------------*
 BUBBLE-SORT.
     COMPUTE LIMIT-N = N-LENGTH - 1.
     MOVE 1 TO XCOUNT.
     PERFORM SORTER UNTIL XCOUNT = 0.
*
 SORTER.
     MOVE 0 TO XCOUNT.
     PERFORM PROCESS VARYING R FROM 1 BY 1
             UNTIL R > LIMIT-N.
     SUBTRACT 1 FROM LIMIT-N.
*
 PROCESS.
     COMPUTE NEXT-R = R + 1.
     IF EMP-ID(R) > EMP-ID(NEXT-R)
         THEN PERFORM EXCHANGE, ADD 1 TO XCOUNT.
*
 EXCHANGE.
     MOVE EMPLOYEE(R) TO TEMP.
     MOVE EMPLOYEE(NEXT-R) TO EMPLOYEE(R).
     MOVE TEMP TO EMPLOYEE(NEXT-R).
*----------------------------------------*
*                                        *
*     W R I T E   T O   D I S K   F I L E  *
*----------------------------------------*
 WRITE-FILE.
     MOVE EMPLOYEE(R) TO FILELINE.
     WRITE FILELINE.
     ADD 1 TO RECORD-COUNTER.
*----------------------------------------*
*                                        *
*      P R I N T E D    R E P O R T      *
*----------------------------------------*
 PRINT-REPORT.
     WRITE OUTLINE FROM REPORT-HEADING-1 AFTER PAGE.
     WRITE OUTLINE FROM REPORT-HEADING-2.
     WRITE OUTLINE FROM REPORT-LINE-1 AFTER 3.
     MOVE N-LENGTH TO RECORD-COUNTER-I.
```

Figure 8.1   (continued next page)

```
                WRITE OUTLINE FROM REPORT-LINE-2 AFTER 2.
                WRITE OUTLINE FROM REPORT-LINE-3 AFTER 3.
                MOVE RECORD-COUNTER TO RECORD-COUNTER-O.
                WRITE OUTLINE FROM REPORT-LINE-4 AFTER 2.
                IF RECORD-COUNTER = N-LENGTH
                    THEN WRITE OUTLINE FROM REPORT-LINE-5 AFTER 3
                    ELSE WRITE OUTLINE FROM REPORT-LINE-6 AFTER 3.
        *
           CLOSING.
                CLOSE INFILE  OUTFILE,  PRINTOUT.
  /*
  //GO.SYSIN DD *
  //GO.CPLNAME DD DSN=WYL.BB.LWF.CPLDATIN,
  //           DISP=(OLD,CATLG)
  //GO.SYSOUT DD SYSOUT=A
  //GO.CPLNUMB  DD DSN=WYL.BB.LWF.CPLDATOU,DISP=(NEW,CATLG),
  //           VOL=SER=CNY004,SPACE-(1210,10),UNIT=SYSDA,
  //           DCB=(LRECL=121,BLKSIZE-1210,RECFM=FB)
  //
```

Figure 8.1   (concluded)

Word	Meaning
ZERO	The numeric value 0 or the character value 0
ZEROS	(repeated to fit the size of the field), depends
ZEROES	on the context in which it is used.
SPACE	One or more blanks.
SPACES	
HIGH-VALUE	The highest possible value.
HIGH-VALUES	
LOW-VALUE	The smallest possible (positive) value.
LOW-VALUES	

If you look at the bubble sort program in Fig. 8.1 you will see **ZERO** and **SPACE** used repeatedly to initialize variables described in the **DATA DIVISION**.

User-defined constants.   COBOL does not provide a facility for programmer-defined named constants. The programmer can, of course, define words in the **DATA DIVISION** with particular initial values and use them in place of named constants in the program. However, care must be taken with this approach since these words are treated like any other user-defined variable, and they are not protected by the system from unintentional change.

Variables

Variables are programmer-defined words (data-names) representing data values that may be changed by the executable statements of the program.

Variable declaration.   In COBOL, all variables must be completely described in the DATA DIVISION. This includes both permanent file I/O data and temporary data that are internal to the program.

Explicit declaration.   In the **DATA DIVISION**, data-names used in input or output file structures are defined within the **FILE SECTION**; program variables not used on file I/O are declared within the **WORKING-STORAGE SECTION**. A variable declaration contains, at minimum, a level-number and a programmer-supplied data-name, and ends with a period. It can also contain one or more optional clauses that serve to bind additional attributes, such as type and size, to the data-name. A level-number is a 2-digit numeric code taken from the following: 01 to 49, 66, 77, 88. The 77 level indicates an elementary (nonstructured) data item. The 88 level indicates a condition-name (discussed below). The 66 level is used for the **RENAMES** clause, which renames and may regroup data items already defined. The levels 01 to 49 group data items into a hierarchical (record) structure and may be used to define higher order structured data in a very flexible manner. Sometimes, data items are grouped to enhance the documentation of the source code. For example:

```
01    PROGRAM-COUNTERS.
      J                        PICTURE 9(2).
      K                        PICTURE 9(2).
```

Implicit declaration.   There is no implicit declaration of variables in COBOL. All programmer-supplied names used in the program must have been previously declared in the **DATA DIVISION**. Certain attributes do have implicit default values; for example, file access mode is assumed to be sequential if not declared otherwise.

Initialization.   Variables may be given initial values in the **DATA DIVISION** description by adding a **VALUES** clause, as in: COUNTER **PICTURE** 9(2) **VALUE ZERO**. They may also, of course, be initialized by means of assignment statements in the **PROCEDURE DIVISION**. There are no implicit or default initial values for data-names.

Built-in types.   Types are declared in the **PICTURE** clause of **DATA DIVISION** entries.

Numeric data is indicated by a string of 9s in the **PICTURE** definition. COBOL is somewhat unusual in this regard for the number of digits must be declared, even for integers. For example, **PICTURE** 99999 would represent a 5-digit integer. The same description could be shortened using a repetition factor: **PICTURE** 9(5). **PICTURE** strings for numeric data may make use of the digit 9, an S to represent signed data, and a V to indicate the position of the (implied) decimal point. For example a data value such as -729.50 may be stored in a variable declared with the definition: SOME-NUMBER **PICTURE** S9(3)V99. In addition to using the V in the **PICTURE** string, a true real-valued numeric type may be declared with the **USAGE IS COMPUTATIONAL-1** clause.

Alphabetic data are indicated by As in the **PICTURE** clause: **PICTURE** A(20). Variables declared as alphabetic may contain only the characters A through Z and the space (blank) character.

Alphanumeric data or, in other words, a character string, are indicated by an X: for example, EMPLOYEE-NAME **PICTURE** X(20). When numeric data has been *edited* for output using edit characters, the resulting data field is considered alphanumeric. For example, before printing the value of SOME-NUMBER in a report, it may be assigned to an output-edited variable declared as: SOME-NUMBER-OUT **PICTURE** $ZZ9.99.

COBOL does not support *Boolean* data as such, although conditional expressions will of course compute to Boolean results in program control statements. In addition, an 88 level-number may be used in the **DATA DIVISION** in order to describe a condition-name that will result in a Boolean value (that is, it will be either true or false). For example:

```
01   EOF-INDICATOR        PICTURE 9  VALUE ZERO.
     88   FILE-IS-ENDED   VALUE  1.
01   TRANSACTION-CODE     PICTURE X(3).
     88   VALID-CODES     VALUE  'ADD',  'DEL', 'CHG'.
01   LINE-COUNTER         PICTURE 99 VALUE ZERO.
     88   END-OF-PAGE     VALUE 50.
```

In the first example, EOF-INDICATOR has been initialized to 0 and the name FILE-IS-ENDED is equivalent to the condition (relational expression) EOF-INDICATOR = 1. In the second example, the name VALID-CODES is equivalent to the condition (TRANSACTION-CODE = 'ADD' **OR** TRANSACTION-CODE = 'DEL' **OR** TRANS-ACTION-CODE = 'CHG').

User-defined types.   There is no COBOL language facility for programmer-defined data types.

Structured Data

There are primarily two methods for structuring data in COBOL: in tables using the **OCCURS** clause, and in a hierarchy using level numbers to group elementary data items into a grouped data item.

Arrays.   The **OCCURS** clause indicates that a specified number of fields is defined in exactly the same way and may be referenced by the same (subscripted) name. Groups of identical fields must be grouped under a group-name defined with a lower level-number. For example:

```
01   DATA-TABLE.
     05 DATA-VALUE     PICTURE 9(5)V99
                       OCCURS 100 TIMES.
```

Then we can access a particular cell of the table with a subscripted data-name, such as DATA-VALUE (36) or DATA-VALUE (S). Expressions, even simple ones like (S + 1), are not valid subscripts in array references.

In order to initialize a table used simply for lookup, we might either use assignment statements in an initial module in the **PROCEDURE DIVISION**, or we might provide the table elements with initial values by using the **REDEFINES** clause, as follows:

```
01   JOBTITLE-VALUES.
     05   FILLER          PICTURE X(8) VALUE 'ANALYST'.
     05   FILLER          PICTURE X(8) VALUE 'MANAGER'.
     05   FILLER          PICTURE X(8) VALUE 'DESIGNER'.
01   JOBTITLE-TABLE       REDEFINES JOBTITLE-VALUES.
     05   JOBTITLE        PICTURE X(8)
                          OCCURS 3 TIMES.
```

The **REDEFINES** clause is a way of taking storage space that has already been described in one way and redefining the same allocation in a different way.

A two-dimensional array containing marketing information regarding the number of users and nonusers of a product by region may be defined as follows:

```
01   TWO-WAY-FREQUENCY-TABLE.
     05   ROW-REGION      OCCURS 4 TIMES.
          10   USAGE-DATA OCCURS 2 TIMES
                          PICTURE 9(3).
```

When referring to a cell in this 4 by 2 table, we use two subscripts. The first indicates the row that the cell is in and the second indicates the column. USAGE-DATA(3,2) refers to the number of nonusers of the product in Region 3.

Arrays may be declared with a maximum of three dimensions.

Records.   Just as elementary data items can be combined under a single group name in order to describe the records in a file, data items not contained in an external file may be grouped together to form the hierarchical data structure known as a *logical record*. This use of level numbers in order to group data under a common name is so flexible that many different combinations of record and array structures may be envisioned. We can build records within arrays, arrays within records, and so on. For example, if the employee records containing the data set listed in Chapter 7 were to be stored in a temporary table while the program was executing, this structure might be difficult to declare in another language, but it can be completely described by the COBOL declarations displayed in Fig. 8.2.

Lists.   Since memory management is static in COBOL, true lists are not supported. For applications requiring dynamic structures such as generalized linked lists, stacks, or queues, the programmer is required to simulate dynamic storage allocation using arrays of integer pointers.

Strings.   Character strings are considered elementary data items. They are declared in the **DATA DIVISION** using the X in the **PICTURE** clause with a repetition factor equal to the size of the string. For example,

```
05   NAME            PICTURE X(25).
```

```
01 EMPLOYEE-TABLE.
   05 EMPLOYEE   OCCURS 100 TIMES.
      10 EMP-ID   PIC X(9).
      10 EMP-NAME.
         15 LAST-NAME  PIC X(10).
         15 FIRST-NAME PIC X(10).
         15 MI    PIC X.
      10 EMP-ADDRESS.
         15 STREET  PIC X(15).
         15 CITY   PIC X(10).
         15 STATE  PIC XX.
         15 ZIP   PIC X(5).
      10 TELEPHONES.
         15 PHONE-NO  OCCURS 3 TIMES.
         20 AREA-CODE PIC X(3).
         20 LOCAL   PIC X(7).
      10 JOBTITLE   PIC X(8).
      10 LOCATION  PIC X.
      10 DEPARTMENT  PIC X(4).
      10 ANNUAL-SALARY  PIC 9(5)V99.
      10 LAST-PROMOTED  PIC X(4).
      10 DATE-EMPLOYED  PIC X(4).
```

Figure 8.2   Mixing arrays and records

Notice that strings, like other data structures, are static in COBOL.

Sets.   Sets are not supported in COBOL.

Abstract Data Types

There is no COBOL language facility for abstract data types.

I/O File Structures

The structure of files used for input to or output from the program must be described fully in the **FILE SECTION** of the **DATA DIVISION**. A file has a file-name and contains a set of records. Each record has a record-name and contains a set of fields. In addition, the file organization and access mode must be declared in the **ENVIRONMENT DIVISION**. File organization can be sequential, indexed, or random; access mode can be sequential or random.

An input or output file stored on disk may be described in the **DATA DIVISION** in this way:

```
FD   FILE-NAME
     LABEL RECORDS ARE STANDARD
     BLOCK CONTAINS 25 RECORDS
     RECORD CONTAINS 105 CHARACTERS
     DATA RECORD IS RECORD-NAME.
```

```
01    RECORD-NAME.
      05   FIELD1          PICTURE   X(20).
      05   FIELD2          PICTURE   X(15).
      05   FIELD3          PICTURE   9(6)V99.
      05   FIELD4          PICTURE   9(4).
      05   FIELD5          PICTURE   X(50).
      05   FIELD6          PICTURE   X(8).
```

If the same file were to be output to the line printer in order to preserve it in hard copy form, the **DATA DIVISION** declarations might appear this way:

```
FD    PRINT-FILE
      LABEL RECORDS ARE OMITTED
      RECORD CONTAINS 133 CHARACTERS
      DATA RECORD IS LINE-OUT.
01    LINE-OUT.
      05   FILLER          PICTURE X VALUE SPACE.
      05   FIELD1-OUT      PICTURE   X(20).
      05   FILLER          PICTURE   X(5)   VALUE SPACES.
      05   FIELD2-OUT      PICTURE   X(15).
      05   FILLER          PICTURE   X(5)   VALUE SPACES.
      05   FIELD3-OUT      PICTURE   $ZZZZ99.99.
      05   FILLER          PICTURE   X(5)   VALUE SPACES.
      05   FIELD4-OUT      PICTURE   9(4).
      05   FILLER          PICTURE   X(5)   VALUE SPACES.
      05   FIELD5-OUT      PICTURE   X(50).
      05   FILLER          PICTURE   X(5)   VALUE SPACES.
      05   FIELD6-OUT      PICTURE   X(8).
```

FILLER is a COBOL reserved word that means that we do not need to uniquely name the field because it will not be referenced in the program. It must be part of a hierarchical (record) structure. The data fields of the record have been renamed because all data-names used in program statements (e.g., assignment: **MOVE** FIELD1 **TO** FIELD1-OUT) must be unique. One way of ensuring that they are unique is to rename them all as this example demonstrates. Another way is to leave the original names but to refer to data items by qualifying them by the grouped name as, for instance: FIELD1 **OF** RECORD-NAME or FIELD1 **IN** LINE-OUT. The keywords **OF** and **IN** are synonyms. If nonunique identifiers are used they must be contained inside a grouped data item. In that case, we can also assign all fields of the input record to all fields with the same name in the output record by using the **CORRESPONDING** option of the **MOVE** statement: **MOVE CORRESPONDING** RECORD-NAME **TO** LINE-OUT.

Notice also in this example that editing characters have been used in the **PIC-TURE** description of FIELD3-OUT. Some of these editing characters—like the dollar sign and real decimal point (as opposed to the implied decimal point V description for numeric data)—add extra physical characters to the printout (and must be accounted for if the record is limited to 133 characters). The Z instructs the computer to print a blank in that position rather than a zero. If the value of FIELD3 is 00056123, FIELD3-OUT will print as $ 561.23.

In addition to these **DATA DIVISION** entries, for each file specified, a statement must appear in the **ENVIRONMENT DIVISION** defining the physical I/O device and/or file to be associated at run time with the logical file-name in the program. For example,

```
SELECT FILE-NAME ASSIGN TO <device-name>-DISKFILE.
```

The <device-name> would refer to such physical devices as card reader, card punch, line printer, magnetic tape drive, magnetic disk drive, etc. These devices have different code names for different computer systems. The programmer-supplied name DISKFILE is the actual name of the file on a secondary storage medium.

A program may specify multiple input files and multiple output files, each with its own **FD** file-name, 01 record-name, and **SELECT** and **ASSIGN** clauses. Statements in the **PROCEDURE DIVISION** would direct the computer to **READ** from a particular input file or to **WRITE** to a particular output file. For example, in the bubble sort program, there was one input file, on disk, and two output files, one on disk—the sorted diskfile—and one for the line printer to produce the printed report.

8.4 PROGRAM STRUCTURES

Probably, the feature of COBOL program structure that one would notice first is the use of four distinct divisions for different parts of the program code. The second, then, would be the influence of the English language in COBOL's use of:

- a relatively natural language style;
- synonyms and noise words for readability;
- virtually self-documenting source code;
- verbs, clauses, sentences, paragraphs, sections, and divisions.

The first three divisions contain informative code only. The **IDENTIFICATION DIVISION** identifies the program to the system, giving it a name. Also, it may optionally contain other information—such as the programmer's name and the date it was written—which serves to document the source code for future maintenance. The **ENVIRONMENT DIVISION** is the machine-dependent portion of a COBOL program. It names the computers and other equipment used by the program. It establishes connections between the logical, that which is seen and acted upon by the program, and the physical, that which exists in the real world. The **DATA DIVISION** contains formal declarations for all data used by the program whether external data (**FILE SECTION**) or internal data (**WORKING-STORAGE SECTION**). The **PROCEDURE DIVISION** contains all the executable statements necessary for the processing of the program by the computer.

The Program Text

Character set.   The COBOL character set consists of the following 51 characters: the 26 uppercase alphabetic letters, the 10 numeric digits, and

	blank	*	asterisk	>	greater-than
.	period	)	right parenthesis	=	equal sign
<	less-than	;	semi-colon	"	quotation mark
(	left parenthesis	-	hyphen	+	plus sign
/	slash	$	dollar sign	,	comma

Text formatting. COBOL program text has the appearance of written English although it is, of course, much more formalized.

Free vs. fixed format. COBOL program text is not fixed-format to the extent of, say, FORTRAN, but each line does contain several distinct fields. Each line is an 80-character card image. COBOL program code is written from characters 8 through 72. Anything past 72 characters on a line is not read by the compiler and may be used to document or identify the program to the human eye. Characters 1–6 may be used for line sequence numbers if desired; they are not necessary. When sequence numbers are used, they identify each card image to be compiled. Character 7 on the line is used to indicate a comment line (*) or continuation (-) of a word or literal begun on the previous line. Characters 8 through 11 form "area A" and is reserved for certain items. Characters 12 through 72 form "area B." We may consider program text within the B margin to be free format. This fixed-field format is depicted in Fig. 8.3.

Certain items must begin in area A. These include paragraph names, section names, division names, 01 level **DATA DIVISION** entries, and **FD** headers for file definitions. Certain items must be contained within area B (that is, they may not begin before character 12). These include clauses, sentences, and continuations.

Indenting. Indenting is allowed and encouraged within the B margin.

Comments. A comment line is indicated by an asterisk (*) or a slash (/) in character 7. The entire line is then ignored by the compiler and may contain any valid EBCDIC character.

Blank lines. Blank lines are allowed anywhere in the program.

Punctuation. Every sentence (or entry) is required to end with a period. One blank space is required to separate the words and symbols of text. Optionally, wherever a blank space may be used, we are also allowed to insert a comma, a semicolon, or more spaces. Parentheses may also be used to delimit expressions or subscripts. Quotation marks are used to delimit alphanumeric literals.

Words

COBOL programs contain three kinds of words. *System words* communicate with the system. These system words are codes that identify particular computers, languages, or functions. *Reserved words*, COBOL keywords, make up the built-in vocabulary of the language. These words are protected from change and may not be used by the programmer for any other purpose, including as a variable name. There are over 300 reserved words in COBOL. *User-defined words* are the identifiers specified by the programmer and defined and characterized in the **DATA DIVISION**.

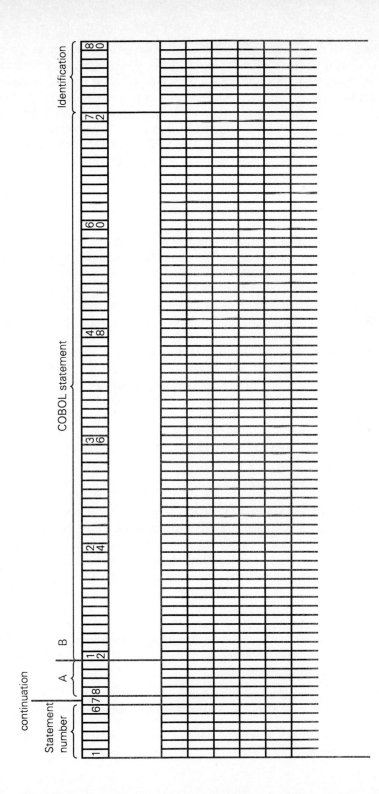

Figure 8.3 COBOL text formatting

263

Identifiers. The programmer supplies identifiers for data-names, paragraph names, section names, and one to name the program itself. Names are limited to a maximum of 30 characters in length (not much of a limit!), and may be composed of virtually any combination of alphabetic characters, numeric digits, and the hyphen (-). The hyphen must not be used for the first or the last character in a name. For variable names, at least one character in the name must be alphabetic. The program name, specified in the **PROGRAM-ID** paragraph of the **IDENTIFICATION DIVISION**, is constructed in the same way with the additional caveat that the first eight characters be unique so that the program will not be confused with other programs (or subprograms) in the system. Two additional rules apply only to program names: the first character must be alphabetic, and no hyphen may appear in the first eight characters.

Keywords. In COBOL, the keywords making up the built-in vocabulary of the language are all reserved words. These names may not be used for any other purpose and may not be "redefined" in the **DATA DIVISION** (the compiler would reject such an attempt). *Descriptive keywords* are those used in the **DATA DIVISION**, for example, **PICTURE, OCCURS, REDEFINES, VALUE**. *Action keywords* are those used in **PROCEDURE DIVISION** statements, for example, **ADD, SUBTRACT, COMPUTE, READ, WRITE, PERFORM**. There are no *delimiter keywords* (e.g., Pascal's begin/end); special punctuation symbols are used as delimiters. COBOL has a special kind of keyword, the *noise keyword*, which doesn't do anything important for the processing of the program—it is useful to humans because it makes the program more readable. **IS, TO, THEN**, and **THAN** are examples of COBOL noise keywords.

In addition COBOL sometimes uses *synonyms*, two or more keywords that mean the same thing and may be used interchangeably. Some examples of synonyms are: **ZERO, ZEROS, ZEROES**; **SPACE, SPACES**; **IN, ON** (for a qualified data-name).

Statements

In the **ENVIRONMENT** and **DATA DIVISION**s, words are combined to form clauses. Clauses combine to form entries, each entry ending with a period. In the **PROCEDURE DIVISION**, words are combined to form statements, and one or more statements form a sentence. Each sentence ends with a period. Both clauses and statements contain specific optional phrases. Paragraphs and sections are composed of sequences of clauses, entries, statements, and/or sentences.

Declarative statements. These are called *entries*. Every entry in the **DATA DIVISION** defines and describes a particular data item, contains a series of one or more clauses, each specifying an attribute of the entry, and ends with a period. An example of an entry for an input data file name is:

```
FD   IN-FILE LABEL RECORDS ARE STANDARD BLOCK CONTAINS
10 RECORDS RECORD CONTAINS 140 CHARACTERS RECORD NAME IS IN-RECORD.
```

The entry contains four clauses and ends at the period. For readability they are usually lined up (in area B) as follows:

```
FD   IN-FILE
     LABEL RECORDS ARE STANDARD
     BLOCK CONTAINS 10 RECORDS
     RECORD CONTAINS 140 CHARACTERS
     RECORD NAME IS IN-RECORD.
```

Executable statements.   **PROCEDURE DIVISION** statements are executable statements: They cause some action on the part of the computer. One or more statements in a series (separated optionally by a comma) form a sentence, ending with a period. Every statement begins with a COBOL verb (an action keyword). The verb defines the type of statement and the choice of available options within the statement.

Assignment.   The assignment verb is **MOVE**. This is clearly a misnomer since the assignment operation performs a copy rather than actually moving data around. The **MOVE** operation includes automatic type conversion, which becomes very useful in formatting data for output. Some examples of **MOVE** statements are:

```
MOVE DATA-VALUE-IN  TO  DATA-VALUE-OUT.
MOVE CORRESPONDING RECORD-IN  TO  RECORD-OUT.
MOVE ZERO TO SUB-TOTAL.
```

Arithmetic.   Most of COBOL's available arithmetic/assignment statements perform a single arithmetic operation, using verbs such as: **ADD**, **SUBTRACT**, **MULTIPLY**, and **DIVIDE**. Some examples:

ADD 1 **TO** J.	**MULTIPLY** A **BY** B **GIVING** C.
ADD A, B **GIVING** C.	**DIVIDE** A **BY** B **GIVING** C.
SUBTRACT 1 **FROM** J.	**DIVIDE** A **BY** B **GIVING** C **ROUNDED**.

The **COMPUTE** statement is similar to the traditional arithmetic/assignment statement familiar to us from other languages. The equal sign is used for assignment, and the expression specified on the right side of equal sign is computed and assigned to the receiving field named on the left side. For example:

```
COMPUTE TOTAL-3-NUMBERS = X + Y + Z.
```

Two options may be included on all five arithmetic statements: **ROUNDED** and **ON SIZE ERROR**. When the result of an arithmetic operation might need to be truncated in order to fit into the specified size of the receiving field (for example, as the result of a divide operation), the **ROUNDED** option causes the result to be rounded instead of truncated before assignment. The **ON SIZE ERROR** option allows the programmer to specify a block of code to be executed in the event that the result is too big (in significant digits) to fit into the receiving field (this can easily happen as the result of a multiply operation). For example:

```
COMPUTE NEW-VALUE ROUNDED = A - B  * OLD-VALUE/(N - 1).

ADD DATA-VALUE-IN TO VALUE-TOTAL
        ON SIZE ERROR PERFORM ERROR-MESSAGE-PARA.
```

Input/output. The verbs **OPEN** and **CLOSE** are used for, respectively, opening and closing files previously defined in the **ENVIRONMENT** and **DATA DIVISION**s. The verbs **READ** and **WRITE** are used, respectively, for input and output of one record at a time to or from an external data file. The **READ** statement syntax calls for specification of a file name, defined in the **FILE SECTION** of the **DATA DIVISION** at the **FD** level. The **WRITE** statement syntax calls for a record name, declared at the 01 level. Examples:

```
OPEN INPUT IN-FILE,
    OUTPUT OUT-FILE.
CLOSE IN-FILE, OUT-FILE.

READ IN-FILE AT END PERFORM EOJ-PARAGRAPH.
WRITE LINE-OUT AFTER ADVANCING 3 LINES.
```

The **AT END** phrase on the **READ** statement indicated action to be taken if the statement reads the end of file character (may be /*). The **AFTER ADVANCING** phrase on the **WRITE** statement may be used to control vertical spacing on the line printer. Both of these phrases are optional.

The **ACCEPT/FROM** and **DISPLAY/UPON** statements are used to transfer low-volume data (not in files) to or from the computer console or some other I/O device. For random access files, the verb **REWRITE** may be used to write over a record in place and **DELETE** to remove a record from the file.

Control. The default sequence control construct is simple sequence. Verbs used for controlling statement execution alter this default control mechanism. These are: **IF**, **GO**, **PERFORM**, **CALL**, and **STOP RUN**. These will be discussed further in the section on control structures below.

Subprograms

COBOL's subprogram structures are relatively primitive when compared to those of other programming languages, especially some of the newer languages. Although modular decomposition is possible to a limited degree, in a large program it may result in somewhat awkward or inefficient code.

Types of subprograms. COBOL provides for a limited form of internal subprogram with the **PERFORM** verb and for external subprograms with the **CALL** verb.

Internal subprograms. The closest thing to an internal subprogram in COBOL is its paragraph (or section). Like internal subprograms in other languages, paragraphs and sections identify and delimit a block of code internal to the program, specify a name, and provide a mechanism (**PERFORM**) for invoking the block of code from a different part of the program. Unlike other internal subprograms, COBOL's paragraphs cannot declare local variables and they cannot specify parameters to accept arguments from the point of invocation. Since these structures cannot be coded in a general manner—for instance, to do the same actions for different data names passed to subprogram parameters—programs often appear wordy and repetitious, rather than concise and elegant.

External subprograms.   COBOL subroutines are external programs, compiled separately from the "main" or calling program, that are invoked by means of a **CALL** statement. They are able to declare their own local variables and receive parameters from the calling program. These external subprograms must have the same basic structure as the calling program, that is, the four divisions. In addition, the **USING** clause on the **PROCEDURE DIVISION** header lists parameters for sharing data with the calling program and the **LINKAGE SECTION** in the **DATA DIVISION** fully describes these shared data items. Although different names may be used by these shared variables, the declarations must be the same.

Functions.   The function program structure is not defined in COBOL.

Sharing data.   The internal and external subprograms in COBOL are very different with regard to the limiting and facilitating of access to shared data items. Internal subprograms, paragraphs and sections, share all data. All data are global, declared in the **DATA DIVISION**; no local variables may be declared. External subprograms recognize no global data as such: All shared data must appear in the parameter list of the **USING** clause.

Global variables.   All variables within a COBOL program are global. They must all be declared in the **DATA DIVISION**. Paragraphs and sections cannot declare their own internal local variables, but only have access to the same **DATA DIVISION** variables as the rest of the program. A called subprogram does not automatically access the data declared in the **DATA DIVISION** of the calling program.

Local variables.   Internal subprograms do not declare local variables. When a subroutine structure is used, variables may be declared local to the subroutine by placing them in a **WORKING-STORAGE SECTION** within the subroutine.

Parameters.   When calling and called subprograms share data, the data to be shared must be declared within the **LINKAGE SECTION** of the subroutine's **DATA DIVISION**. The subroutine's **PROCEDURE DIVISION** header must contain a **USING** phrase listing data names for the variables to be accepted from the calling program in the order in which they are to be passed. The calling program's **CALL** statement must include a **USING** option listing the variables to be passed to the called program. The names on the two **USING** lists need not be the same; correspondence is positional. Parameters are passed by reference.

Scope of variables.   Does not apply since internal subprograms do not have facility for declaring local variables.

Subprogram libraries.   Facilities for creating, accessing, and maintaining subprogram libraries are very limited in COBOL.

Built-in subprograms.   The **SORT** and **MERGE** statements provide the programmer with access to two subprograms used frequently in file maintenance. The **REPORT GENERATOR** feature also can be considered in this category.

Subprogram libraries available.   Not available.

Building a subprogram library. There is no facility for building a subprogram library in COBOL. However, the **COPY** statement can be used to take previously stored pieces of program code and insert them directly into the stream of COBOL statements.

Program Abstraction

Due to the noted limitations in COBOL's subprogram structures, its capacity for program abstraction is also limited.

Modular decomposition. Modular decomposition of programs into hierarchical structures is facilitated by the **PERFORM** and **CALL** statements.

Information hiding. Information hiding is not well supported in COBOL, if it can be said to be supported at all. Internal subprograms have no such facility. Although external subprograms can declare their own local variables, they have the additional limitation that **PICTURE** clauses for parameters must exactly match those for the calling program's arguments. This makes for a lot of necessary cross-checking when changes are made to the program.

Self-Documenting Features

A number of COBOL's features encourage and facilitate the development of a self-documenting program.

The use of English. It relies on English-language structures for its syntactical notation.

Descriptive identifier names. A word length of up to 30 characters and the use of the hyphen in creating names means that extensive comments about data names are not necessary to document the source code.

Program organization. The first three divisions, while adding to the characteristic wordiness of a COBOL program, serve to greatly enhance its self-documenting quality as well. Also, organizing the **PROCEDURE DIVISION** into paragraphs and sections is a good way of imposing structure on a large problem, subdividing it into individual, tractable subtasks and naming each subtask in a descriptive manner.

Comments. Comments are somewhat limited only because each must be keyed on its own line. However, they are nevertheless easy to use.

Program text formatting. The use of blank lines and indenting conventions certainly helps to promote the readability of programs.

8.5 CONTROL STRUCTURES

Since one of the characteristics of business data processing applications is simplicity of algorithm, COBOL's mathematical computing is not high-powered. There are no built-in mathematical or statistical functions, nor any capability for programmer-defined ones.

There appears to have been a built-in assumption that most arithmetic instructions will contain a single arithmetic operation. Expressions, while available and used in COBOL, are not of major importance. Statement control structures are adequate but, at least in the case of iteration constructs, these are sometimes awkward. Iteration is accomplished by the **PERFORM** statement, the same structure used for control over internal subprograms (paragraphs and sections).

Operators

Operators used to form expressions in COBOL may be special symbols or built-in language keywords.

Arithmetic operators. The arithmetic operators act on numeric operands. These operators include: + (add), - (subtract), * (multiply), / (divide), ** (exponentiate), as well as the unary operators + and - which mean, respectively, multiplication by positive or negative 1.

Relational operators. The relational operators act on any type of operand in conditional expressions. These include the symbols < (less than), > (greater than), = (equal to), and the keywords: **LESS, GREATER, EQUAL**. Also useful in forming readable relational expressions are noise words that are acceptable in the source program code but are stripped by the compiler before processing: **IS, THAN**. For example, DATA-VALUE **IS GREATER THAN** MAX is the same as DATA-VALUE > MAX.

Logical operators. The logical operators operate on Boolean data. This type of data is found in computed results of relational or conditional expressions. The only type of data-name in COBOL that is similar to a Boolean data declaration is a name declared with an 88 level-number. The logical operators include: **NOT, OR, AND**. When the logical operator **NOT** is combined with the relational operators they extend the realm of possible conditions for which to test. For example, A **NOT** = B . The combination **NOT** < is the same as "greater than or equal to" and the combination **NOT** > can be used to represent the condition "less than or equal to."

String operators. COBOL's string-handling facility is fairly weak. Concatenation may be done using the **STRING** statement, and a string may be broken down with the **UNSTRING** statement.

Expressions

Arithmetic expressions may be used in **COMPUTE** statements, as well as incorporated into the conditional expressions of the sequence control statements, **IF** and **PERFORM**. A *conditional expression* can incorporate arithmetic, relational, and logical operators along with variable names and condition names. It is used in such control statements as **IF** and **PERFORM** to choose alternative paths in executing the program code.

Expressions are represented in infix, parenthesized form. Operands enclosed within parentheses are evaluated first. Parentheses are used to alter the default sequence control mechanism for evaluating expressions.

According to the rules of precedence for the language:

1. parentheses are, of course, evaluated first

2. unary operators

3. exponentiation

4. multiplication and division

5. addition and subtraction

6. the relational operators, = , < , >

7. **NOT**

8. **AND**

9. **OR**

For a series of operations at the same level of precedence, the processing follows a left-to-right sequence of evaluation.

Control Statements

The default statement level control structure is a simple sequence: statements are executed in the sequence in which they are written in the source program. The following statements may alter this default or in some way control the execution of program statements.

Unconditional branch.   The **GO TO** statement is a simple unconditional branching instruction that transfers control to the paragraph named. For example,

```
GO TO END-JOB-PROCESSING.
GO TO ERROR-ROUTINE.
```

Actually, the statement verb is **GO**; the keyword **TO** is an optional noise word.

Selection.   The selection control construct may be coded using a variety of different statements.

Two-way selection.   The primary language construct for two-way selection is the **IF/THEN/ELSE** statement. The general form of this statement is:

```
IF <conditional-expression> THEN <statement1> ELSE <statement2> .
```

This implements the two-way selection construct pictured in Fig. 8.4. The keyword **THEN** is an optional noise word. Notice that the period (.) ends this construct. The statement immediately following the period—an implicit "return" if it is the end of a called paragraph or section—is the "regardless" statement, executed *regardless* of whether the condition after the **IF** was true or false.

Since statements may be grouped together using a blank space separator rather than a period, the COBOL **IF** statement proves to be quite flexible in implementing blocks of code in <statement1> or <statement2>. Here are some examples of **IF** statements.

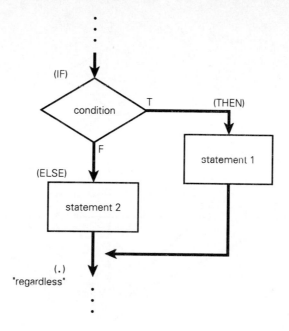

Figure 8.4   Two-way selection

```
IF ERROR COND WRITE OUTLINE FROM ERROR-LINE.

IF CODE = "YES"
     THEN PERFORM DO-IF-TRUE
     ELSE PERFORM DO-IF-FALSE.

IF CODE = "YES"
     THEN    MOVE YES-LINE-OUT TO PRINT-LINE
             WRITE PRINT-LINE
     ELSE    MOVE NO-LINE-OUT TO PRINT-LINE
             WRITE PRINT-LINE.
```

Multiway selection.   COBOL does not have a built-in case structure, but we can simulate the case structure using either the nested-**IF** construct or the **DEPENDING** option of the **GO TO** statement. For example, the case structure pictured in Fig. 8.5 can be coded using either a nested-**IF** structure or a "computed" **GO TO** with the **DEPEND-ING** option.

Here is how it would look as a nested-**IF** statement. In the following, as soon as a condition is true, the indicated paragraph is called and the rest of the statement (until the period) ignored. If no match is found for REGION-CODE, a paragraph is called which probably prints out some sort of error message.

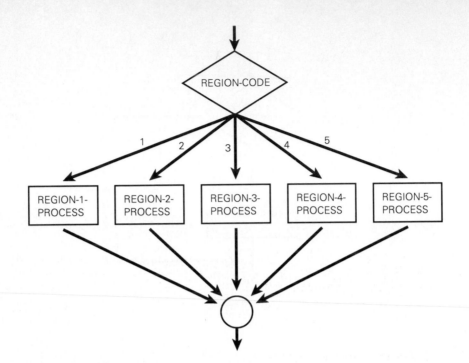

Figure 8.5   Multiway selection

```
IF REGION-CODE = 1
      THEN PERFORM REGION-1-PROCESS
      ELSE IF REGION-CODE = 2
            THEN PERFORM REGION-2-PROCESS
            ELSE IF REGION-CODE = 3
                  THEN PERFORM REGION-3-PROCESS
                  ELSE IF REGION-CODE = 4
                        THEN PERFORM REGION-4-PROCESS
                        ELSE IF REGION-CODE = 5
                              THEN PERFORM REGION-5-PROCESS
                              ELSE PERFORM ERROR-OUTLINE.
```

Here is how the same construct would look as a **GO TO/DEPENDING ON**:

```
      GO TO   REGION-1-PROCESS
              REGION-2-PROCESS
              REGION-3-PROCESS
              REGION-4-PROCESS
              REGION-5-PROCESS
              DEPENDING ON REGION-CODE.
COME-BACK.   <regardless statement>
      . . . . .
REGION-1-PROCESS.
      . . . . .
      GO TO COME-BACK.
REGION-2-PROCESS.
      . . . . . .
```

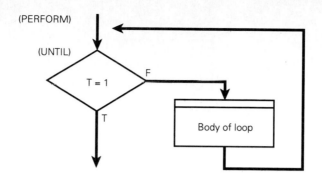

(PERFORM)

(UNTIL)

T = 1

F

T

Body of loop

Figure 8.6   PERFORM/UNTIL

Iteration.   Iteration is controlled by the **PERFORM** statement, naming a para-graph (or section) name as the body of the loop to be performed and one or more options for controlling execution of the loop. This sometimes results in awkward code (e.g., one sentence or otherwise small paragraphs) and a control structure that is not immediately apparent since one is forced to look elsewhere for the code of the body of the loop.

Test-before loop.   Although the test-before loop is usually coded as a do/while, in COBOL it calls for the **UNTIL** option. The following **PERFORM** statement corre-sponds to the loop pictured in Fig. 8.6:

```
PERFORM BODY-OF-LOOP UNTIL T = 1.
```

Test-after loop.   A "repeat/until" type of looping structure is not available in COBOL.

Indexed loop.   The indexed loop construct is implemented by the **TIMES** option. The following statement is equivalent to Fig. 8.7:

```
PERFORM BODY-OF-LOOP N TIMES.
```

Another type of iteration structure implemented in COBOL is the **PER-FORM/VARYING**. In this structure, an explicit index variable is set up by the program-mer to control the loop, initial and step values are specified, and a final condition is given for ending the loop. The following example corresponds to the diagram in Fig. 8.8 (p. 275).

```
PERFORM BODY-OF-LOOP VARYING I FROM 1 BY 1 UNTIL I > N.
```

Notice the difference between the execution of the **PERFORM/TIMES** and the **PERFORM/VARYING**.

Control over subprograms.   Statements that control execution of internal and external subprograms include **PERFORM, CALL, GOBACK,** and **EXIT PROGRAM**.

Call.   The **PERFORM** statement is used to invoke internal subprograms. The **CALL** statement is used to invoke external subprograms.

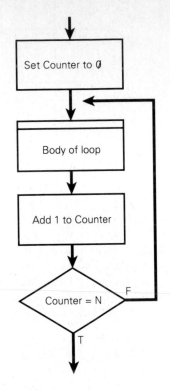

Figure 8.7 PERFORM with TIMES option

Return. There is no explicit statement that returns control from a called internal subprogram (e.g., a paragraph) to the calling paragraph. An explicit return statement—either **GOBACK** or **EXIT PROGRAM**—is required in external subprograms.

Control over program execution. The program starts with the first executable statement after the **PROCEDURE DIVISION** header and the paragraph or section name following that header. There is no explicit statement for beginning the execution of the program. The **STOP RUN** statement halts execution of the program and transfers control to the operating system.

Subprogram Control Structures

COBOL's subprogram structures are rather primitive. Its paragraphs and sections cannot control their own data names in any way and cannot selectively share data with each other. Its external subprogram facility first appeared in the 1974 standard.

Simple call. For COBOL's own variations of the internal subprogram—paragraphs and sections—the **PERFORM** statement without options simply executes the paragraph (or section) named one time. For example:

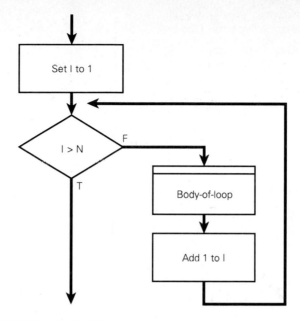

Figure 8.8 PERFORM/VARYING

```
PERFORM INITIALIZATION.
PERFORM PRINTED-REPORT.
```

The invocation of the subprogram is explicit, using the **PERFORM** verb. The return to the point of call is implicit, occurring automatically when the paragraph named is finished executing (that is, a new paragraph name is encountered).

For external subprograms, the **CALL/USING** statement must be used to invoke, and either a **GOBACK** or **EXIT PROGRAM** statement must explicitly appear to return control to the calling program. Fig. 8.9 gives the skeletal structure of a COBOL program using an external subroutine.

Recursion.   Recursion is not available in COBOL.

Implicit call.   There is limited facility for implicit invocation of subprograms. The options **AT END** and **ON SIZE ERROR** test for special conditions to see whether or not to invoke a block of code. These are called special conditions and may be considered exception conditions. Also the programmer may specify a set of paragraphs (or sections) at the start of the **PROCEDURE DIVISION** that are to be executed only on occurrence of a particular monitored I/O error.

Parallel processing.   Parallel processing is not available in COBOL.

Coroutines.   Coroutines are not available in COBOL.

```
IDENTIFICATION DIVISION.
PROGRAM-ID.  CALLING-PROGRAM.

ENVIRONMENT DIVISION.
...

DATA DIVISION.
...

WORKING-STORAGE SECTION.
01 A  PIC ...
01 B  PIC ...
01 C  PIC ...
...

PROCEDURE DIVISION.
...
...

CALL 'SAMPLE-SUB' USING A, B, C.
...
...

**  THIS IS THE CALLED SUBPROGRAM **
 IDENTIFICATION DIVISION.
 PROGRAM-ID.  SAMPLE-SUB.

 ENVIRONMENT DIVISION.
**  NO I/O -- ENVIRONMENT DIVISION IS NULL **

 DATA DIVISION.
 WORKING-STORAGE SECTION.
**  LOCAL VARIABLES    **
 01 J  PIC ...
 01 K  PIC ...
 LINKAGE SECTION.
**  PARAMETERS    **
 01 X  PIC ...
 01 Y  PIC ...
 01 Z  PIC ...

 PROCEDURE DIVISION USING X, Y, Z.
 ...
 ...

 SUB-EXIT.
  EXIT PROGRAM.
```

Figure 8.9   COBOL subroutine call

8.6 PROGRAM DEVELOPMENT

Despite its wordiness and some other disadvantages noted above, COBOL is still the language of choice in many commercial data processing facilities. This popularity cannot be attributed solely to inertia. In developing large-scale COBOL programs, each installation may design its own coding conventions, require particular charting techniques, and institute procedures for managing a programming project (e.g., prototyping, structured walkthroughs).

Several tools are provided by COBOL to facilitate some kinds of processing that occur frequently in business-oriented programming.

- The SORT/MERGE facility allows the programmer to perform a complex operation, one that would normally require preprocessing by another separate program, by simply specifying a single verb.
- Voluminous reports are common in business applications, and the REPORT generator provides a facility for generating fast, preformatted reports using a variety of options.
- The COPY statement is a compiler directive that allows the direct insertion into a program of a prewritten module of COBOL text stored in a Source Program Library. Frequently there are multiple application programs that share a common set of external data files. The use of the COPY statement is often used to save the sort of tedious and error-prone activity involved in repeatedly coding the same DATA DIVISION entries for all programs.
- The DEBUG facility. COBOL's DEBUG module is used to trace execution during program development and to dump the intermediate values of stored variables during execution. Some implementations provide extensive listings to the user in the event of an aborted run.

8.7 MORE SAMPLE PROGRAMS

Fig. 8.10 contains the listing of the sequential file update program. The program follows the algorithm as described in Chapter 7.

The multiple list creation program, Study Problem #3 (Part A), is listed in Fig. 8.11. Part B is left as an exercise for the reader.

EXERCISES

1. Do Study Problem #3 (Part B) in COBOL.
2. Do Study Problem #4 in COBOL.

SUGGESTIONS FOR FURTHER STUDY

Manuals. ANSI (1974, 1981), IBM (1981).

Books. Feingold (1978), Philippakis and Kazmier (1982, 1983), Schneyer (1984).

Chapters in Books. Pratt (1984), Chapter 13: "COBOL," pp. 378–400; Tucker (1986), Chapter 4: "COBOL," pp. 102–160.

Articles. Sammet (1981).

```
//  JOB
// EXEC COBUCLG,PARM.COB=STATE
//COB.SYSIN DD *
      *******************************
      *                             *
       IDENTIFICATION DIVISION.
      *                             *
      *******************************
       PROGRAM-ID. UPDATE.
      *******************************
      *                             *
       ENVIRONMENT DIVISION.
      *                             *
      *******************************
       CONFIGURATION SECTION.
       SOURCE-COMPUTER. IBM-370.
       OBJECT-COMPUTER. IBM-370.
       INPUT-OUTPUT SECTION.
       FILE-CONTROL.
           SELECT MASTER-FILE ASSIGN TO UT-S-MASTER.
           SELECT TRANSACTION-FILE ASSIGN TO UT-S-TRANS.
           SELECT NEW-MASTER-FILE ASSIGN TO UT-S-NEWMASTR.
           SELECT ERROR-REPORT ASSIGN TO UT-S-SYSOUT.
      *******************************
      *                             *
       DATA DIVISION.
      *                             *
      *******************************
       FILE SECTION.
       FD  MASTER-FILE
           LABEL RECORDS ARE STANDARD
           BLOCK CONTAINS 10 RECORDS
           RECORD CONTAINS 121 CHARACTERS
           DATA RECORD IS MASTER-REC.
       01  MASTER-REC            PIC X(121).
       FD  TRANSACTION-FILE
           LABEL RECORDS ARE STANDARD
           BLOCK CONTAINS 10 RECORDS
           RECORD CONTAINS 122 CHARACTERS
           DATA RECORD IS TRANSACTION-REC.
       01  TRANSACTION-REC       PIC X(122).
       FD  NEW-MASTER-FILE
           LABEL RECORDS ARE STANDARD
           BLOCK CONTAINS 10 RECORDS
           RECORD CONTAINS 121 CHARACTERS
           DATA RECORD IS NEW-MASTER-REC.
       01  NEW-MASTER-REC        PIC X(121).
```

Figure 8.10 Update program (continued next page)

```
      FD   ERROR-REPORT
           LABEL RECORDS ARE OMITTED
           RECORD CONTAINS 133 CHARACTERS
           DATA RECORD IS PRINTLINE.
      01   PRINTLINE.
           05   FILLER                    PIC X.
           05   LINEOUT                   PIC X(132).
      *
      WORKING-STORAGE SECTION.
      *
      01   EOF-MASTER                     PIC X(3) VALUE 'NO'.
           88   MASTER-FILE-IS-ENDED      VALUE 'YES'.
      01   EOF-TRANS                      PIC X(3) VALUE 'NO'.
           88   TRANS-FILE-IS-ENDED       VALUE 'YES'.
      01   PROGRAM-COUNTERS.
           05   COUNTER-ERROR             PIC S9(3) VALUE ZEROS.
           05   COUNTER-OK                PIC S9(3) VALUE ZEROS.
           05   COUNTER-TRANS             PIC S9(3) VALUE ZEROS.
           05   COUNTER-DELETES           PIC S9(3) VALUE ZEROS.
           05   COUNTER-CHANGES           PIC S9(3) VALUE ZEROS.
           05   COUNTER-ADDS              PIC S9(3) VALUE ZEROS.
           05   N                         PIC 9(3)   VALUE ZEROS.
      01   BLANK-LINE                     PIC X(133) VALUE SPACES.
      01   MESSAGE1                       PIC X(30)
           VALUE 'TRANSACTION CODE IS MISSING   '.
      01   MESSAGE2                       PIC X(30)
           VALUE 'TRANSACTION CODE IS NOT A     '.
      01   MESSAGE3                       PIC X(30)
           VALUE 'TRANSACTION CODE IS NOT C OR D'.
      01   MASTER-INPUT-AREA.
           05   MASTER-KEY                PIC X(9).
           05   FILLER                    PIC X(112).
      01   TRANSACTION-INPUT-AREA.
           05   TRANS-KEY                 PIC X(9).
           05   FILLER                    PIC X(112).
           05   TRANSACTION-CODE          PIC X.
                88   CHANGE-OR-DELETE     VALUE 'C', 'D'.
      *----------------------------------------*
      *                                        *
      *   R E P O R T   F O R M A T            *
      *----------------------------------------*
      01   REPORT-HEADING-1.
           05   FILLER                    PIC X(16)    VALUE SPACES.
           05   FILLER                    PIC X(22)
                    VALUE 'SEQUENTIAL FILE UPDATE'.
           05   FILLER                    PIC X(95)  VALUE SPACES.
      01   REPORT-HEADING-2.
           05   FILLER                    PIC X(14)   VALUE SPACES.
           05   FILLER                    PIC X(26)
```

Figure 8.10   (continued next page)

```
                     VALUE 'PERSONNEL FILE MAINTENANCE'.
        05  FILLER                    PIC X(93) VALUE SPACES.
    01  UNDERLINE-LINE.
        05  FILLER                    PIC X(6)    VALUE SPACES.
        05  FILLER                    PIC X(45)
          VALUE '---------------------------------------------'.
        05  FILLER                    PIC X(82) VALUE SPACES.
    01   REPORT-HEADING-3.
        05  FILLER                    PIC X(15) VALUE SPACES.
        05  FILLER                    PIC X(30)
                    VALUE 'TOTAL NUMBER OF TRANSACTIONS: '.
        05  FILLER                    PIC X(3) VALUE SPACES.
        05  COUNTER-TRANS-OUT         PIC ZZ9.
        05  FILLER                    PIC X(82).
    01   REPORT-HEADING-4.
        05  FILLER                    PIC X(8) VALUE SPACES.
        05  FILLER                    PIC X(37)
             VALUE 'TRANSACTIONS PROCESSED SUCCESSFULLY: '.
        05  FILLER                    PIC X(3) VALUE SPACES.
        05  COUNTER-OK-OUT            PIC ZZ9.
        05  FILLER                    PIC X(82).
    01  REPORT-HEADING-5.
        05  FILLER                    PIC X    VALUE SPACES.
        05  FILLER                    PIC X(49)
          VALUE 'THE FOLLOWING TRANSACTIONS COULD NOT BE PROCESSED'.
        05  FILLER                    PIC X(83) VALUE SPACES.
    01  REPORT-HEADING-6.
        05  FILLER     PIC X VALUE SPACES.
        05  FILLER     PIC X(14) VALUE 'DUE TO ERRORS:'.
        05  FILLER     PIC X(118) VALUE SPACES.
    01  COLUMN-HEADER-1.
        05  FILLER                    PIC X    VALUE SPACES.
        05  FILLER                    PIC X(47)
          VALUE 'ID NUMBER    TRANS. CODE              ERROR'.
        05  FILLER                    PIC X(85) VALUE SPACES.
    01  COLUMN-HEADER-2.
        05  FILLER                    PIC X    VALUE SPACES.
        05  FILLER                    PIC X(35)
          VALUE '---------    -----------    -----'.
        05  FILLER                    PIC X(25)
          VALUE '-----------------------'.
        05  FILLER                    PIC X(72) VALUE SPACES.
    01  ERROR-LISTING-ARRAY.
        05  REPORT-LINE   PIC X(133) OCCURS 100 TIMES.
    01  MESSAGE-LINE.
        05  FILLER      PIC X     VALUE SPACES.
        05  ID-NUMBER   PIC X(9).
```

Figure 8.10   (continued next page)

```
              05   FILLER          PIC X(10)  VALUE SPACES.
              05   CODE-OUT        PIC X.
              05   FILLER          PIC X(10)  VALUE SPACES.
              05   MESSAGE-OUT        PIC X(30) VALUE SPACES.
              05   FILLER          PIC X(72) VALUE SPACES.
         01   REPORT-FOOTER-1.
              05   FILLER             PIC X(11)    VALUE SPACES.
              05   COUNTER-ADDS-OUT   PIC ZZ9.
              05   FILLER             PIC X(2)     VALUE SPACES.
              05   FILLER             PIC X(29)    VALUE
                   'RECORDS ADDED TO MASTER FILE.'.
              05   FILLER             PIC X(88)    VALUE SPACES.
         01   REPORT-FOOTER-2.
              05   FILLER             PIC X(11)    VALUE SPACES.
              05   COUNTER-DELETES-OUT PIC ZZ9.
              05   FILLER             PIC X(2)     VALUE SPACES.
              05   FILLER             PIC X(33)    VALUE
                   'RECORDS DELETED FROM MASTER FILE.'.
              05   FILLER             PIC X(84)    VALUE SPACES.
         01   REPORT-FOOTER-3.
              05   FILLER             PIC X(11)    VALUE SPACES.
              05   COUNTER-CHANGES-OUT PIC ZZ9.
              05   FILLER             PIC X(2)     VALUE SPACES.
              05   FILLER             PIC X(16)    VALUE
                   'RECORDS CHANGED.'.
              05   FILLER             PIC X(101)   VALUE SPACES.
     *
     *******************************
     *                         *
      PROCEDURE DIVISION.
     *                         *
     *******************************
      MAIN-PROGRAM.
          PERFORM INITIALIZATION.
          PERFORM PROCESS-CONTROL UNTIL TRANS-FILE-IS-ENDED.
          PERFORM END-TRANSACTION.
          PERFORM PRINT-REPORT.
          PERFORM CLOSING.
          STOP RUN.
     *
      INITIALIZATION.
          OPEN INPUT   MASTER-FILE
                       TRANSACTION-FILE
               OUTPUT  NEW-MASTER-FILE
                       ERROR-REPORT.
          PERFORM READ-TRANS-RECORD.
          PERFORM READ-MASTER-RECORD.
```

Figure 8.10   (continued next page)

```
*----------------------------------------*
*                                        *
*  R E A D I N G   1   R E C O R D        *
*----------------------------------------*
READ-TRANS-RECORD.
     READ TRANSACTION-FILE INTO TRANSACTION-INPUT-AREA
          AT END MOVE 'YES' TO EOF-TRANS.
     ADD 1 TO COUNTER-TRANS.
*

READ-MASTER-RECORD.
     READ MASTER-FILE INTO MASTER-INPUT-AREA
          AT END MOVE 'YES' TO EOF-MASTER.
*----------------------------------------*
*                                        *
* M A I N   P R O C E S S   C O N T R O L *
* F O R   U P D A T E   P R O G R A M     *
*----------------------------------------*
PROCESS-CONTROL.
     IF MASTER-FILE-IS-ENDED
          THEN PERFORM END-MASTER
          ELSE PERFORM PROCESS.
*

PROCESS.
     IF TRANS-KEY > MASTER-KEY
          THEN PERFORM WRITE-MASTER-RECORD
               PERFORM READ-MASTER-RECORD
          ELSE IF TRANS-KEY = MASTER-KEY
                    THEN PERFORM CHANGE-DELETE
                         PERFORM READ-TRANS-RECORD
                    ELSE
*                       * (TRANS-KEY > MASTER-KEY) *
                         PERFORM ADD-RECORD
                         PERFORM READ-TRANS-RECORD.
*

ADD-RECORD.
     IF TRANSACTION-CODE = 'A'
          THEN PERFORM WRITE-TRANS-RECORD
               ADD 1 TO COUNTER-ADDS
          ELSE PERFORM ERROR1.
*

CHANGE-DELETE.
     IF NOT CHANGE-OR-DELETE
          THEN PERFORM ERROR2
               PERFORM WRITE-MASTER-RECORD
          ELSE IF TRANSACTION-CODE = 'C'
                    THEN PERFORM CHANGE-RECORD
                         PERFORM WRITE-MASTER-RECORD
                              ADD 1 TO COUNTER-CHANGES
                    ELSE
```

Figure 8.10   (continued next page)

```
*              * (TRANSACTION-CODE = 'D') DO NOTHING *
                    ADD 1 TO COUNTER-DELETES.
     PERFORM READ-MASTER-RECORD.
*
 CHANGE-RECORD.
     MOVE TRANSACTION-INPUT-AREA TO MASTER-INPUT-AREA.
*
*---------------------------------------*
*                                       *
*  W R I T I N G   1   R E C O R D      *
*---------------------------------------*
 WRITE-TRANS-RECORD.
     WRITE NEW-MASTER-REC FROM TRANSACTION-INPUT-AREA.
*
 WRITE-MASTER-RECORD.
     WRITE NEW-MASTER-REC FROM MASTER-INPUT-AREA.
*---------------------------------------*
*                                       *
*  E R R O R   R O U T I N E S          *
*---------------------------------------*
 ERROR1.
     ADD 1 TO COUNTER-ERROR.
     MOVE TRANSACTION-CODE TO CODE-OUT.
     MOVE TRANS-KEY TO ID-NUMBER.
     IF TRANSACTION-CODE = ' '
         THEN MOVE MESSAGE1 TO MESSAGE-OUT
         ELSE MOVE MESSAGE2 TO MESSAGE-OUT.
     MOVE MESSAGE-LINE TO REPORT-LINE(COUNTER-ERROR).
*
 ERROR2.
     ADD 1 TO COUNTER-ERROR.
     MOVE TRANSACTION-CODE TO CODE-OUT.
     MOVE TRANS-KEY TO ID-NUMBER.
     IF TRANSACTION-CODE = ' '
         THEN MOVE MESSAGE1 TO MESSAGE-OUT
         ELSE MOVE MESSAGE3 TO MESSAGE-OUT.
     MOVE MESSAGE-LINE TO REPORT-LINE(COUNTER-ERROR).
*---------------------------------------*
*                                       *
*  FINISH UP WHEN MASTER FILE IS ENDED  *
*---------------------------------------*
 END-MASTER.
     PERFORM ADD-N-READ UNTIL TRANS-FILE-IS-ENDED.
*
 ADD-N-READ.
     PERFORM ADD-RECORD.
     PERFORM READ-TRANS-RECORD.
```

Figure 8.10   (continued next page)

```
*----------------------------------------*
*                                        *
*  FINISH UP WHEN TRANSACTION FILE       *
*      IS  ENDED                         *
*----------------------------------------*
 END-TRANSACTION.
      PERFORM FINISH-MASTER UNTIL MASTER-FILE-IS-ENDED.
*
 FINISH-MASTER.
      PERFORM WRITE-MASTER-RECORD.
      PERFORM READ-MASTER-RECORD.
*----------------------------------------*
*                                        *
*   P R I N T E D   R E P O R T          *
*----------------------------------------*
 PRINT-REPORT.
      WRITE PRINTLINE FROM REPORT-HEADING-1 AFTER PAGE.
      WRITE PRINTLINE FROM REPORT-HEADING-2.
      WRITE PRINTLINE FROM UNDERLINE-LINE.
      SUBTRACT 1 FROM COUNTER-TRANS.
      MOVE COUNTER-TRANS TO COUNTER-TRANS-OUT.
      WRITE PRINTLINE FROM REPORT-HEADING-3 AFTER 3.
      COMPUTE COUNTER-OK = COUNTER-TRANS - COUNTER-ERROR.
      MOVE COUNTER-OK TO COUNTER-OK-OUT.
      WRITE PRINTLINE FROM REPORT-HEADING-4.
      WRITE PRINTLINE FROM REPORT-HEADING-5 AFTER 3.
      WRITE PRINTLINE FROM REPORT-HEADING-6.
      WRITE PRINTLINE FROM COLUMN-HEADER-1 AFTER 3.
      WRITE PRINTLINE FROM COLUMN-HEADER-2.
      WRITE PRINTLINE FROM BLANK-LINE AFTER 2.
      PERFORM PRINT-DETAIL VARYING N FROM 1 BY 1
           UNTIL N > COUNTER-ERROR.
      WRITE PRINTLINE FROM UNDERLINE-LINE AFTER 5.
      MOVE COUNTER-ADDS TO COUNTER-ADDS-OUT.
      WRITE PRINTLINE FROM REPORT-FOOTER-1 AFTER 5.
      MOVE COUNTER-DELETES TO COUNTER-DELETES-OUT.
      WRITE PRINTLINE FROM REPORT-FOOTER-2 AFTER 2.
      MOVE COUNTER-CHANGES TO COUNTER-CHANGES-OUT.
      WRITE PRINTLINE FROM REPORT-FOOTER-3 AFTER 2.
*
 PRINT-DETAIL.
      WRITE PRINTLINE FROM REPORT-LINE(N).
*
 CLOSING.
      CLOSE        MASTER-FILE
                   TRANSACTION-FILE
                   NEW-MASTER-FILE
                   ERROR-REPORT.
```

Figure 8.10   (continued next page)

```
/*
//GO.MASTER DD DSN=WYL.BB.LWF.CPLDATOU,UNIT=SYSDA,
//           DISP=(OLD,CATLG),VOL=SER=CNY004
//GO.TRANS DD DSN=WYL.BB.LWF.CPLTRANS,UNIT=SYSDA,
//           DISP=(OLD,CATLG),VOL=SER=CNY004
//GO.NEWMASTR DD DSN=WYL.BB.LWF.CPLUPDAT,DISP=(NEW,CATLG),
//            VOL=SER=CNY004,SPACE=(1210,15),UNIT=SYSDA,
//            DCB=(LRECL=121,BLKSIZE=1210,RECFM=FB)
//GO.SYSOUT DD SYSOUT=A
//
```

Figure 8.10   (concluded)

```
// JOB TIME=5
// EXEC COBUCLG,PARM.COB=(BATCH,STATE)
//COB.SYSIN DD *
CBL
      *********************************
      *                               *
       IDENTIFICATION DIVISION.
      *                               *
      *********************************
       PROGRAM-ID. MULTLIST.
      *********************************
      *                               *
       ENVIRONMENT DIVISION.
      *                               *
      *********************************
       CONFIGURATION SECTION.
       SOURCE-COMPUTER. IBM-370.
       OBJECT-COMPUTER. IBM-370.
       INPUT-OUTPUT SECTION.
       FILE-CONTROL.
           SELECT INFILE ASSIGN TO UT-S-INMASTR.
           SELECT MULTILIST-FILE  ASSIGN TO UT-S-OUTMASTR.
           SELECT PRINTFILE ASSIGN TO UT-S-SYSOUT.
      *********************************
      *                               *
       DATA DIVISION.
      *                               *
      *********************************
       FILE SECTION.
       FD  INFILE
           LABEL RECORDS ARE STANDARD
           RECORD CONTAINS 121 CHARACTERS
           BLOCK  CONTAINS 0 RECORDS
           DATA RECORD IS EMPLOYEE.
```

Figure 8.11   Multiple lists creation program (continued next page)

```
01   EMPLOYEE.
     05   EMP-ID                    PIC X(9).
     05   EMP-NAME                  PIC X(21).
     05   FILLER                    PIC X(62).
     05   JOB                       PIC X(8).
     05   LOC                       PIC X.
     05   DEPT                      PIC X(4).
     05   FILLER                    PIC X(16).
FD   MULTILIST-FILE
     LABEL RECORDS ARE STANDARD
     RECORD CONTAINS 133 CHARACTERS
     BLOCK CONTAINS 0 RECORDS
     DATA RECORD IS OUTREC.
01   OUTREC.
     05   EMPLOYEE-IN-REC.
          10   EMP-ID               PIC X(9).
          10   EMP-NAME             PIC X(21).
          10   FILLER               PIC X(62).
          10   JOB                  PIC X(8).
          10   LOC                  PIC X.
          10   DEPT                 PIC X(4).
          10   FILLER               PIC X(16).
     05   LINKS-TO-NEXT-IN-LIST.
          10   S-REC                PIC 9(3).
          10   S-JOB                PIC 9(3).
          10   S-LOC                PIC 9(3).
          10   S-DEPT               PIC 9(3).
FD   PRINTFILE
     LABEL RECORDS ARE OMITTED
     RECORD CONTAINS 133 CHARACTERS
     DATA RECORD IS OUTLINE.
01   OUTLINE.
     05   FILLER    PIC X.
     05   PRINTLINE PIC X(132).
*------------------------------*
*                              *
WORKING-STORAGE SECTION.
*                              *
*------------------------------*
01   EOF                      PIC X(3) VALUE 'NO'.
     88 DATA-IS-ENDED    VALUE 'YES'.
01   PROGRAM-COUNTERS.
     05   N                        PIC S9(3) VALUE ZEROS.
     05   I                        PIC 9(3) VALUE ZERO.
     05   P                        PIC S9(3) VALUE ZEROS.
01   PROGRAM-CONSTANTS.
     05   NULL                     PIC 9(3)   VALUE ZERO.
```

Figure 8.11   (continued next page)

```
01  EXTERNAL-POINTERS-TO-FIRST.
    05  F-REC                          PIC 9(3) VALUE ZERO.
    05  F-JOB-TABLE.
        10  F-JOB           OCCURS 4 TIMES PIC 9(3).
    05  F-LOCATN-TABLE.
        10  F-LOC           OCCURS 4 TIMES PIC 9(3).
    05  F-DEPT-TABLE.
        10  F-DEPT          OCCURS 3   TIMES PIC 9(3).
01  MASTER-TABLE.
    05  EMPLOYEE-IN-TABLE   OCCURS 100 TIMES.
        10  T-EMP-ID        PIC X(9).
        10  T-EMP-NAME      PIC X(21).
        10  FILLER          PIC X(62).
        10  T-JOB           PIC X(8).
        10  T-LOC           PIC X.
        10  T-DEPT          PIC X(4).
        10  FILLER          PIC X(16).
01  TABLES-FOR-LINKS-TO-NEXT.
    05  NEXT-RECORD-TABLE.
        10  NEXT-REC            OCCURS 100 TIMES PIC 9(3).
    05  NEXT-JOB-TABLE.
        10  NEXT-JOB            OCCURS 100 TIMES PIC 9(3).
    05  NEXT-LOCATN-TABLE.
        10  NEXT-LOC            OCCURS 100 TIMES PIC 9(3).
    05  NEXT-DEPT-TABLE.
        10  NEXT-DEPT           OCCURS 100 TIMES PIC 9(3).
01  TABLES-FOR-NAMES-OF-SUBLISTS.
    05  JOBTITLE-VALUES.
        10  FILLER          PIC X(8) VALUE 'ANALYST'.
        10  FILLER          PIC X(8) VALUE 'CLERK'.
        10  FILLER          PIC X(8) VALUE 'DESIGNER'.
        10  FILLER          PIC X(8) VALUE 'MANAGER'.
    05  WHAT-JOB-TABLE      REDEFINES JOBTITLE-VALUES.
        10  WHAT-JOB            PIC X(8)
                               OCCURS 4 TIMES.

    05  LOCATION-VALUES.
        10  FILLER          PIC X VALUE 'A'.
        10  FILLER          PIC X VALUE 'B'.
        10  FILLER          PIC X VALUE 'C'.
        10  FILLER          PIC X VALUE 'D'.
    05  WHAT-LOC-TABLE      REDEFINES LOCATION-VALUES.
        10  WHAT-LOC           PIC X
                               OCCURS 4 TIMES.

    05  DEPARTMENT-VALUES.
        10  FILLER          PIC X(4) VALUE 'MIS'.
        10  FILLER          PIC X(4) VALUE 'R&D'.
        10  FILLER          PIC X(4) VALUE 'PROD'.
    05  WHAT-DEPT-TABLE      REDEFINES DEPARTMENT-VALUES.
    10  WHAT-DEPT           PIC X(4)
                               OCCURS 3 TIMES.
```

Figure 8.11   (continued next page)

```
      *----------------------------------------*
      *                                         *
      *  R E P O R T   F O R M A T        *
      *----------------------------------------*
      01  REPORT-HEADING.
          05  FILLER                    PIC X(26)    VALUE SPACES.
          05  FILLER                    PIC X(22)
                    VALUE ' MULTIPLE  SUBLISTS  '.
          05  FILLER                    PIC X(85)  VALUE SPACES.
      01  SUBLIST-HEADING.
          05 FILLER                     PIC X(24)  VALUE SPACES.
          05  FILLER                    PIC X(12)
                    VALUE 'LISTING FOR '.
          05  FILLER                    PIC X        VALUE SPACE.
          05  HEADING-FILLIN            PIC X(8).
          05  FILLER                    PIC X        VALUE SPACE.
          05  WHAT-LST                  PIC X(8).
          05  FILLER                    PIC X(79)  VALUE SPACES.
      01  UNDERLINE-LINE.
          05  FILLER                    PIC X(16)    VALUE SPACES.
          05  FILLER                    PIC X(45)
            VALUE '--------------------------------------------'.
          05  FILLER                    PIC X(72)  VALUE SPACES.
      01  BLANK-LINE                    PIC X(133)  VALUE SPACES.
      01  DETAIL-LISTER.
          05  FILLER                    PIC X(1)     VALUE SPACES.
          05  EMP-ID-LST                PIC X(9).
          05  FILLER                    PIC X(3)     VALUE SPACES.
          05  EMP-NAME-LST              PIC X(21).
          05  FILLER                    PIC X(3)     VALUE SPACES.
          05  LST-INFO1                 PIC X(8).
          05  FILLER                    PIC X(3)     VALUE SPACES.
          05  LST-INFO2                 PIC X(8).
          05  FILLER                    PIC X(74)  VALUE SPACES.
      *********************************
      *                             *
       PROCEDURE DIVISION.
      *                             *
      *********************************
       MAIN-PROGRAM.
           PERFORM INITIALIZATION.
           PERFORM CREATE UNTIL DATA-IS-ENDED.
           MOVE P TO N.
           PERFORM WRITE-FILE VARYING P FROM 1 BY 1 UNTIL P > N.
           PERFORM PRINT-REPORT.
           PERFORM CLOSING.
           STOP RUN.
      *
```

Figure 8.11   (continued next page)

```
      INITIALIZATION.
          OPEN INPUT   INFILE
               OUTPUT MULTILIST-FILE
                      PRINTFILE.
          PERFORM CLEAROUT VARYING P FROM 1 BY 1 UNTIL P > 100.
          MOVE ZERO TO P.
          PERFORM CLEARFJOB VARYING I FROM 1 BY 1 UNTIL I > 4.
          PERFORM CLEARFLOC VARYING I FROM 1 BY 1 UNTIL I > 4.
          PERFORM CLEARFDEPT VARYING I FROM 1 BY 1 UNTIL I > 3.
          READ INFILE AT END MOVE 'YES' TO EOF.
      CLEAROUT.
          MOVE ZERO TO NEXT-REC(P).
          MOVE ZERO TO NEXT-JOB(P).
          MOVE ZERO TO NEXT-LOC(P).
          MOVE ZERO TO NEXT-DEPT(P).
      CLEARFJOB.
          MOVE ZERO TO F-JOB(I).
      CLEARFLOC.
          MOVE ZERO TO F-LOC(I).
      CLEARFDEPT.
          MOVE ZERO TO F-DEPT(I).
  *
      CREATE.
          PERFORM ADD-EMPLOYEE.
          READ INFILE AT END MOVE 'YES' TO EOF.
  *
      ADD-EMPLOYEE.
          ADD 1 TO P.
          MOVE EMPLOYEE TO EMPLOYEE-IN-TABLE(P).
          CALL 'LINKUP' USING P, F-REC, NEXT-RECORD-TABLE, MASTER-TABLE.
          PERFORM SEARCH-JOB VARYING I FROM 1 BY 1 UNTIL
                      WHAT-JOB(I) = T-JOB(P).
                  CALL 'LINKUP' USING P,F-JOB(I), NEXT-JOB-TABLE,
                                   MASTER-TABLE.
          PERFORM SEARCH-LOC VARYING I FROM 1 BY 1 UNTIL
                      WHAT-LOC(I) = T-LOC(P).
                  CALL 'LINKUP' USING P, F-LOC(I), NEXT-LOCATN-TABLE,
                                   MASTER-TABLE.
          PERFORM SEARCH-DEPT VARYING I FROM 1 BY 1 UNTIL
                      WHAT-DEPT(I) = T-DEPT(P).
                  CALL 'LINKUP' USING P, F-DEPT(I), NEXT-DEPT-TABLE,
                                   MASTER-TABLE.
      SEARCH-JOB.
      SEARCH-LOC.
      SEARCH-DEPT.
```

Figure 8.11   (continued next page

```
*----------------------------------------*
*                                        *
*  W R I T I N G   A   R E C O R D        *
*----------------------------------------*
 WRITE-FILE.
     MOVE EMPLOYEE-IN-TABLE(P) TO EMPLOYEE-IN-REC.
     MOVE NEXT-REC(P) TO S-REC.
     MOVE NEXT-JOB(P) TO S-JOB.
     MOVE NEXT-LOC(P) TO S-LOC.
     MOVE NEXT-DEPT(P) TO S-DEPT.
     WRITE OUTREC.
*----------------------------------------*
*                                        *
*   P R I N T E D   R E P O R T          *
*----------------------------------------*
 PRINT-REPORT.
     PERFORM LISTING-BY-JOBTITLE
         VARYING I FROM 1 BY 1 UNTIL I > 4.
     PERFORM LISTING-BY-LOCATION
         VARYING I FROM 1 BY 1 UNTIL I > 4.
     PERFORM LISTING-BY-DEPARTMENT
         VARYING I FROM 1 BY 1 UNTIL I > 3.
*
 LISTING-BY-JOBTITLE.
     MOVE 'JOBTITLE' TO HEADING-FILLIN.
     MOVE WHAT-JOB(I) TO WHAT-LST.
     PERFORM PRINT-HEADINGS.
     MOVE F-JOB(I) TO P.
     PERFORM JOB-DETAIL-LINE UNTIL P = NULL.
*
 JOB-DETAIL-LINE.
     MOVE T-EMP-ID(P) TO EMP-ID-LST.
     MOVE T-EMP-NAME(P) TO EMP-NAME-LST.
     MOVE T-LOC(P) TO LST-INFO1.
     MOVE T-DEPT(P) TO LST-INFO2.
     WRITE OUTLINE FROM DETAIL-LISTER.
     MOVE NEXT-JOB(P) TO P.
*
 LISTING-BY-LOCATION.
     MOVE 'LOCATION' TO HEADING-FILLIN.
     MOVE WHAT-LOC(I) TO WHAT-LST.
     PERFORM PRINT-HEADINGS.
     MOVE F-LOC(I) TO P.
     PERFORM LOC-DETAIL-LINE UNTIL P = NULL.
*
 LOC-DETAIL-LINE.
     MOVE T-EMP-ID(P) TO EMP-ID-LST.
     MOVE T-EMP-NAME(P) TO EMP-NAME-LST.
```

Figure 8.11   (continued next page)

```
              MOVE T-JOB(P) TO LST-INFO1.
              MOVE T-DEPT(P) TO LST-INFO2.
              WRITE OUTLINE FROM DETAIL-LISTER.
              MOVE NEXT-LOC(P) TO P.
     *
       LISTING-BY-DEPARTMENT.
              MOVE 'DEPTMENT'  TO HEADING-FILLIN.
              MOVE WHAT-DEPT(I) TO WHAT-LST.
              PERFORM PRINT-HEADINGS.
              MOVE F-DEPT(I) TO P.
              PERFORM DEPT-DETAIL-LINE UNTIL P = NULL.
     *
       DEPT-DETAIL-LINE.
              MOVE T-EMP-ID(P) TO EMP-ID-LST.
              MOVE T-EMP-NAME(P) TO EMP-NAME-LST.
              MOVE T-LOC(P) TO LST-INFO1.
              MOVE T-JOB(P)  TO LST-INFO2.
              WRITE OUTLINE FROM DETAIL-LISTER.
              MOVE NEXT-DEPT(P) TO P.
     *
       PRINT-HEADINGS.
              WRITE OUTLINE FROM REPORT-HEADING AFTER PAGE.
              WRITE OUTLINE FROM SUBLIST-HEADING AFTER ADVANCING 5.
              WRITE OUTLINE FROM UNDERLINE-LINE AFTER ADVANCING 2.
              WRITE OUTLINE FROM BLANK-LINE AFTER ADVANCING 2.
     *
       CLOSING.
              CLOSE        INFILE
                           MULTILIST-FILE
                           PRINTFILE.
   CBL

       *******S*U*B*********************
       *                              *
         IDENTIFICATION DIVISION.
       *                              *
       ********************************
         PROGRAM-ID. LINKUP.
       ********************************
       *                              *
         ENVIRONMENT DIVISION.
       *                              *
       ********************************
         CONFIGURATION SECTION.
         SOURCE-COMPUTER. IBM-370.
         OBJECT-COMPUTER. IBM-370.
       ********************************
```

Figure 8.11   (continued next page)

```
*                                    *
 DATA DIVISION.
*                                    *
**********************************
*
 WORKING-STORAGE SECTION.
*
 01  J                 PIC 9(3) VALUE ZERO.
 01  Q                 PIC 9(3)  VALUE ZERO.
 01  NULL              PIC 9(3)  VALUE ZERO.
*
 LINKAGE SECTION.
*
 01  P                 PIC 9(3).
 01  FIRST-PTR              PIC 9(3).
 01  MASTER-TABLE.
     05  EMPLOYEE-IN-TABLE   OCCURS 100 TIMES.
         10  T-EMP-ID       PIC X(9).
         10  T-EMP-NAME     PIC X(21).
         10  FILLER         PIC X(62).
         10  T-JOB          PIC X(8).
         10  T-LOC          PIC X.
         10  T-DEPT         PIC X(4).
         10  FILLER         PIC X(16).
 01  NEXT-PTR-TABLE.
     05  NEXT-PTR     OCCURS 100 TIMES     PIC 9(3).
*
**********************************
*
 PROCEDURE DIVISION USING P, FIRST-PTR,
                       NEXT-PTR-TABLE, MASTER-TABLE.
*
**********************************
 INSERT-SUB.
     IF FIRST-PTR = NULL
        THEN MOVE P TO FIRST-PTR
            MOVE NULL TO NEXT-PTR(P)
        ELSE IF T-EMP-ID(FIRST-PTR) > T-EMP-ID(P)
                THEN MOVE FIRST-PTR TO NEXT-PTR(P)
                    MOVE P TO FIRST-PTR
                ELSE MOVE NEXT-PTR(FIRST-PTR) TO J
                    MOVE FIRST-PTR TO Q
                    PERFORM SEARCH-FOR-INSERT-POINT-Q
                                    UNTIL J = NULL
                    MOVE NEXT-PTR(Q) TO NEXT-PTR(P)
                    MOVE P TO NEXT-PTR(Q).
```

Figure 8.11   (continued next page)

```
        *
        SEARCH-FOR-INSERT-POINT-Q.
            IF T-EMP-ID(J)   >   T-EMP-ID(P)
               THEN MOVE NULL TO J
               ELSE MOVE J TO Q
                    MOVE NEXT-PTR(J) TO J.
        *
        SUBPROG-EXIT.
            EXIT PROGRAM.
/*
//GO.SYSIN DD *
//GO.INMASTR DD DSN=WYL.BB.LWF.CPLDATIN,
//            DISP=(OLD,CATLG)
//GO.SYSOUT DD SYSOUT=A
//GO.OUTMASTR DD DSN=WYL.BB.LWF.CPLMLIST,DISP=(OLD,CATLG)
//
```

Figure 8.11   (concluded)

9

Pascal Language Elements

Pascal, named after the seventeenth-century French philosopher and mathematician Blaise Pascal, is currently the predominant programming language in the academic community. It is the language most frequently used to teach introductory structured programming in universities, and it is also frequently used in advanced computer courses as a notation for expressing algorithms. With the growing popularity of the personal microcomputer, Pascal has become increasingly widespread as the language of choice for developing applications in a wide variety of different areas.

Heavily influenced by ALGOL60, Pascal was offered up in competition with ALGOL68 for the mantle of acceptance as the true heir of ALGOL60, and did ultimately win that acceptance. It was, in turn, a strong influence on the design of MODULA-2 and Ada.

9.1 A BRIEF OVERVIEW OF PASCAL

Pascal is characterized by simplicity, elegance, and uniformity. It is a block-structured language that has incorporated structured programming methodology into its language structures. Consequently, it facilitates the development of structured programs.

History and Development

Niklaus Wirth, a member of the ALGOL committee, was upset with the direction that ALGOL68 had taken. He felt that the new language was needlessly cumbersome—that a state-of-the-art programming language did not have to contain every language concept known to man. ALGOL68 is, in fact, a huge language with many varied features, and implementers have found it quite difficult to develop compilers for it. Wirth went off and designed a new language, Pascal, as a minority, dissenting opinion to the ALGOL68 report. In this design effort, Wirth intended specifically to illustrate the direction that he felt ALGOL68 should have taken.

In the end, Pascal, a true child of ALGOL60, has rapidly supplanted ALGOL68 in prominence. Later "ALGOL-like" languages—some, in fact, prefer the term "Pascal-like"—have certainly been influenced more by Pascal than by ALGOL68. Pascal is a narrowly defined, simple, and elegant language. Pascal stands out in opposition to the trend—a trend that began with PL/1 and ALGOL68, and continues to this day with the design of Ada—of enriching a language with so many complicated features that no one could be expected to know all of it.

First implemented in 1970, the official definition of the Pascal language was published in 1971. The language was revised in 1973 and standardized in 1983.

Pascal's current popularity is probably also due to its acceptance by the microcomputer community. There are a number of enhanced and extended versions of the language available for microcomputers, notably UCSD Pascal and Turbo Pascal (Borland International), which is quickly becoming the new industry "standard" for the Pascal language.

Application Areas

Pascal is a general-purpose programming language that is simple enough for teaching introductory programming concepts, yet powerful enough to use for real applications in such areas as mathematical/scientific computation, data processing, systems programming, artificial intelligence, and simulation.

Like ALGOL60 before it, Pascal has been used extensively as a publication language for publishing algorithms in scholarly journals and textbooks.

Classification

Software generation: Third

Procedural/declarative: Procedural

Translator: Compiled

Processing environment: Batch

Programming paradigm: Imperative

9.2 STUDY PROBLEM #1: BUBBLE SORT PROGRAM

Before studying Pascal language structures in detail, let us first examine a complete Pascal program. Fig. 9.1 contains the listing of the bubble sort program, described as Study Problem #1 in Chapter 7.

Notice the distinctive block structure, the declaration of global and local variables, and the use of parameters.

The program was run on an IBM® PC/XT using Borland International's Turbo Pascal. Turbo Pascal is quickly becoming the standard microcomputer version of Pascal due in large part to Borland's innovative pricing policy and support for educational programs, along with its consequent widespread use in academic settings.

```
program BubbleSortProgram (ByNameFile, ByIDFile, Output);

    (**********************************************************)
    (****           GLOBAL       DECLARATIONS         ****)
    (**********************************************************)
const
    Space                   =    ' ';
    MaxNumRecords           =    100;
type
    IndexType               =    1..MaxNumRecords;
    EmployeeRecType         =    record
        ID                  :    string[9];
        OtherInfo           :    string[112]
    end; (* EmployeeRecType *)
    EmployeeArrayType       =    array [IndexType] of EmployeeRecType;
var
    N                       :    IndexType;
    Employee                :    EmployeeArrayType;

    (**********************************************************)
    (*   LOAD  INPUT  FILE  INTO  ARRAY  FOR  SORTING    *)
    (**********************************************************)
procedure LoadFile (var N : IndexType; var Employee : EmployeeArrayType);
var
  ByNameFile              :    text;
  EmployeeInRec           :    EmployeeRecType;

   procedure ReadEmployeeRecord;
   begin
       with EmployeeInRec do
           readln(ByNameFile, ID, OtherInfo);
   end;

begin
    assign (ByNameFile, 'A:NMPRSNEL.DAT');
    reset (ByNameFile);
    N := 0;
    ReadEmployeeRecord;
    while not eof (ByNameFile) do begin
            N := N + 1;
            Employee [N] := EmployeeInRec;
            ReadEmployeeRecord;
          end;   {while}
    close (ByNameFile)
end;
```

Figure 9.1   Bubble sort program (continued next page)

```
(**********************************************************)
(****      SORT   ARRAY   BY   EMPLOYEE   ID   NUMBER      ****)
(**********************************************************)
procedure BubbleSort (var N: IndexType; var Employee: EmployeeArrayType);
var
   Limit, R            :   IndexType;
   Sorted              :   boolean;


   procedure Exchange (var Record1, Record2 : EmployeeRecType);
   var
       Temp                 :    EmployeeRecType;
   begin
       Temp := Record1;
       Record1 := Record2;
       Record2 := Temp;
   end;

begin
   Limit := N - 1;
   Sorted := false;
   while not Sorted do begin
             Sorted := true;
             for R := 1 to Limit do
                 if Employee[R].ID > Employee[R+1].ID
                    then begin
                              Exchange (Employee[R], Employee[R+1]);
                              Sorted := false
                         end;
             Limit := Limit - 1
        end   {while}
end;

   (**********************************************************)
   (*****     WRITE   SORTED   RECORDS   TO   OUTPUT   FILE     ****)
   (**********************************************************)
procedure WriteFile (var N : IndexType; var Employee : EmployeeArrayType);
var
   ByIDFile            :    text;
   EmployeeOutRec      :    EmployeeRecType;
   R                   :    IndexType;

   procedure WriteEmployeeRecord;
   begin
       with EmployeeOutRec do
             writeln (ByIDFile, ID, OtherInfo);
   end;
```

Figure 9.1   (continued next page)

```
begin
     assign (ByIDFile, 'A:IDPRSNEL.DAT');
     rewrite (ByIDFile);
     for R := 1 to N do begin
             EmployeeOutRec := Employee [R];
             WriteEmployeeRecord;
         end;   {for R}
     close (ByIDFile);
end;

     (************************************************************)
     (*****          PRINTED               REPORT        *****)
     (************************************************************)

procedure PrintReport (var N : IndexType);
     Var
     LstrFile : text;
begin
     assign (LstrFile, 'CON:');
     reset (LstrFile);
     writeln (LstrFile, ' ':20, 'Bubble Sort Report':20);
     writeln (LstrFile, ' ':20, '------------------':20);
     writeln (LstrFile);
     writeln (LstrFile, ' ':5, 'Number of records read from input file -- ');
     writeln (LstrFile, ' ':10, 'NMPRSNEL File --  ':20, N:5);
     writeln (LstrFile);
     writeln (LstrFile, ' ':5, 'Number of records written to output file -- ');
     writeln (LstrFile, ' ':10, 'IDPRSNEL File --  ':20, N:5);
     writeln (LstrFile);
end;

     (************************************************************)
     (** M A I N **  BubbleSortProgram execution begins here  **)
     (************************************************************)

begin
     LoadFile (N, Employee);
     BubbleSort (N, Employee);
     WriteFile (N, Employee);
     PrintReport (N);
end.
```

Figure 9.1   (concluded)

9.3 DATA: TYPES, FILES, AND DATA STRUCTURES

Pascal's treatment of data is characterized by a strong, static type-checking facility operating within the framework of its internal block structure. All identifiers—including variable names, procedure names, even statement labels—must be declared explicitly. Storage requirements for global and local variables are determined completely during compile time, implying early binding of variables to attributes. There is late binding to location as local variables are allocated to storage dynamically on entry to the procedure.

Memory management is dynamic, storage being allocated and freed based on the program's block structure.

While it may seem like an awfully cumbersome imposition on the programmer's time to require so many declarative statements, the resulting programs are more readable, easier to maintain, and self-documenting to a greater degree.

Constants

Constants can be inserted directly into the program text as literals, or they may be predefined and given identifier names in a constant declaration statement. Like all data used in Pascal programs, constants have a type. However, in this case, the type need not be declared; the compiler automatically determines the type of a literal or user-defined (named) constant used within the program code.

Literals.   A *numeric literal* represents a numeric value, either real or integer, for example: -127.5. A *string literal* is a character string enclosed within quotation marks. The string literal may contain any character in the Pascal character set (this is sometimes implementation dependent). An example of a string literal is: '--- Report ---'. A *set literal* is a list of scalar, ordinal values delimited by square brackets [ ] and represents a collection of values of an ordinal type. A set literal may be operated on by set operators. For example:

```
if Answer not in ['n', 'N', 'y', 'Y'] then …
```

Named constants.   There are some named constants that are built into the Pascal language and are therefore reserved words. For example, the Boolean values **false** and **true**, and the pointer (non-)value **nil**. The largest integer value **maxint** is a built-in constant whose value may differ depending on the implementation.

User-defined constants.   Pascal provides a facility for programmer-defined named constants that can be used as synonyms for the specified literal. This is the **const** declarative statement. Constants declared in this way are true constants: They are treated just like literals. This means that they are protected from change and, once declared, may *not* be modified in any way later on in the program. Some sample constant declarations are:

```
const
    Space = ' ';
    EmptyString = '';
    ArraySize = 100;
```

Used effectively, programmer-defined constants can enhance the readability of a program.

Variables

Variables are programmer-defined identifiers representing data values that are subject to change by the executable statements of the program.

Variable declaration.   All programmer-defined identifiers, including variable names, must be declared prior to use.

Explicit declaration.   All variables must be explicitly declared before they may be used. The declaration specifies, at minimum, a name and a type. The scope of a variable is determined by the static scoping rule and depends on the block in which the variable is declared. Other attributes may include the number and type of the component elements, as in the case of a structured variable. No default attributes may be assumed.

Variable declarations are accomplished by means of the **var** statement. The general form of this statement is:

```
var <name> : <type>
```

The type may be any built-in or previously defined type.

Implicit declaration.   There is no implicit declaration of variables in Pascal. As noted above, the type of a constant is declared implicitly simply by using it. For example, the numeric literal 100 is an integer since it is not in quotation marks (hence, numeric) and does not contain a decimal point (hence, integer).

Initialization.   Standard Pascal assumes no default initial values for variable names and no provision is made for initializing variables in the declarative portion of the program. Variables may be initialized only in executable statements.

Types.   Pascal's potential for creativity is probably greatest in the area of data types. Pascal supports many different types of data and provides a flexible facility for user-defined data types. This facility is used in three ways:

1. To define a totally new type by specifying its domain of values.
2. To declare a complex data structure such as a record, array, or file.
3. To set up a sort of "template" for the declaration of several variables that may be described in the same way.

Thus, any changes to the description of these variables need only be done once, in the type definition statement. The types available to Pascal programmers are laid out in Fig. 9.2.

Built-in types.   Pascal has several built-in scalar and structured types. The *structured* types are used for building logical data structures and for describing file structures. Structured types are described below. The *scalar* types are:

- **integer**, which represents signed whole numbers;
- **real**, which represents floating point data values;
- **boolean**, limited to the values **true** or **false**;
- **char**acter, a single character from Pascal's character set, enclosed in quotation marks.

Some examples follow:

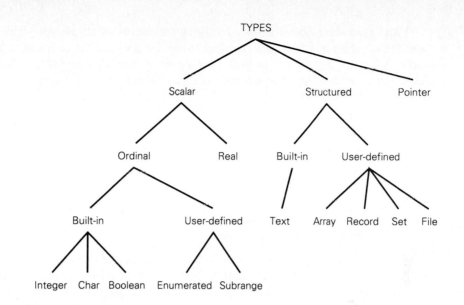

Figure 9.2   Data types in Pascal

```
var
      A:   integer;
      B:   char;
      X:   real;
      S:   boolean;
...
A := 2026;
B := '*';
X := 196.52;
S := false;
...
```

Integer, **boolean**, and **char** are ordinal types. Values of ordinal types can be defined in terms of a *successor* (next) value and a *predecessor* (previous) value. Thus, although real is also a scalar built-in type, it is actually in a class all by itself (as is the pointer type). Boolean-type data is ordinal since **false** is stored as 0 and **true** as 1.

In standard Pascal, strings must be constructed by setting up an array of characters. Some microcomputer versions of Pascal provide a nonstandard built-in type for string manipulation. For example, in Turbo Pascal, a variable called Name may be declared as:

```
var Name: string [20]
```

User-defined types.   One of the unique features of Pascal is its facility for programmer-defined variable types. Scalar user-defined types include enumerated and subrange types. These are also considered ordinal types. Types are defined with a **type** declarative statement.

An *enumerated* type is defined by listing the domain of all possible values for the type. These values may look like character strings but they are not enclosed in quotation marks. A *subrange* type is specified as a subset of any already existing (built-in or user-defined) ordinal type. The subrange is specified with lower and upper bounds separated by two periods. For example:

```
type
      (* * * enumerated type * * *)
      CarType = (COMPACT, SUBCOMPACT, SPORT, SEDAN, WAGON, VAN);

      (* * * subrange types * * *)
      GradeType = 'A'..'F';
      Digit = 0..9;

      (* * * subrange of CarType * * *)
      BigCarType = SEDAN..VAN;
```

The values in an enumerated-type list are considered to be ordered so that, for example, COMPACT is less than SUBCOMPACT, etc. In storing values of enumerated-type data, each value is associated with an integer, beginning with 0. This integer is the *ordinal value* of the enumerated value. For CarType, the ordinal value of COMPACT is 0, of SPORT, 2, and of VAN, 5.

Variable declarations can refer to user-defined types, for example:

```
var
      Car1, Car2 :  CarType;
      FamilyCar :  BigCarType;
      SemesterGrade :  GradeType;
...
Car1 := SEDAN;
Car2 := VAN;
...
SemesterGrade := 'B';
...
if Car1 <  Car2 then  ...
...
```

User-defined types are limited to internal program processing. They cannot be used for input or output. Some advantages of defining new types in a program are:

1. The program can be made more readable, more self-documenting. For example, in the above declarations, the variable Car may be used as a subscript for an array (e.g., Sales[Car] or Sales[COMPACT]) or as an index on a **for** statement (e.g., **for** Car := COMPACT **to** VAN **do**). Also, without user-defined types, a programmer must use coded variables, representing, say, COMPACT with the integer 1, SUBCOMPACT with 2, etc. This makes the program much less readable and requires many lines of comments to document the program.

2. Pascal's own type-checking facility can be used to produce automatic range checking. For example, a SemesterGrade other than one of those declared in GradeType would be invalid.

Structured Data

Pascal provides for the construction of arrays, records, files, and sets with its typing facility. The built-in pointer type is used for the construction of dynamic structures such as linked lists. There is no limitation to the manner in which these data structures may be combined. For example, an array can consist of an ordered sequence of records, each of which may be composed of other records and/or arrays.

Arrays. An array may be declared using the **array** keyword on a variable declaration statement. For example, to declare an array of 100 real-valued elements, X:

```
var   X  :  array [1..100] of real;
```

An array may be composed of elements of any type, including another array (or any other structured type).

Several arrays of the same description may be described by first defining the array as a type and then declaring the array variables as that type. For example:

```
type
      TwoWayFrequencies = array [1..5,1..5] of integer;
...
var
      RateByUsage,
      RegionByUsage    :       TwoWayFrequencies;
```

Records. A record structure may be used either as a logical data structure for grouping data together or as an input/output variable. It is declared as a type using the **record** keyword and then naming fields on the record along with their descriptions. For example:

```
type Date = record
      Month, Day,Year :  integer
end;
...
var
      Previous, Current : Date;
...
```

Notice that the field variables Month, Day, and Year do not have to be declared on a **var** statement; they have already been declared as part of the record type definition. The individual fields of the record may be accessed using a qualified name, for example:

```
if Current.Month <= Previous.Month then ...
```

Alternatively, the individual fields of the record may be accessed using the **with** statement as in, for example:

```
with Current do begin
      Month := 01;
      Day := 01;
      Year := 89
end
```

A field may be declared as being of any type, including a structured type. Pascal's type definitions are a very flexible way of building complex data structures. For example, if the employee records containing the dataset listed in Chapter 7 (and used in the bubble sort program) were to be stored in a temporary array during processing, this structure may be completely described by the definitions and declarations in Fig. 9.3.

Lists.　Dynamic data structures are facilitated in a very natural manner by Pascal's built-in pointer type. The following declarations set up a linked list. ("Info" may contain any number of fields.)

```
type
      NodePointer = ^Node;
      Node = record
            Info :   <some-type>;
            Next : NodePointer
      end;
var
      First, Current := NodePointer;
```

Notice that this is the one instance in which Pascal allows us to use a name (in this case, Node) that has not yet been formally declared. Notice too that we do not declare any variable(s) of type Node. For example, Current^ is the way we refer to the Node pointed to by Current; Current^.Next is the Node pointed to by Next—that is, the next node in the list.

Strings.　Standard Pascal does not provide a built-in type for character strings, although Borland's TurboPascal does. For example, the TurboPascal declaration

```
var
      ID    :    string[9];
```

would have to be constructed in standard Pascal using an array.

Sets.　A set is an unordered collection of distinct, homogeneous units. In Pascal, these units may be any scalar ordinal type, including a user-defined type. For example:

```
type
      PossibleValues = set of ('A', 'M', 'P', 'R', 'W');
var
      ValidValues : PossibleValues;
...
if  InputValue  in  ValidValues  then ...
```

Abstract Data Types

Standard Pascal does not have a data abstraction facility. Simply providing for user-defined types is not data abstraction; the types are defined by their domains, but there is no encapsulation of this definition with the operations that may be performed on the new data type. Certain language extensions, for example, ConcurrentPascal, do provide this facility.

```
const
    MaxNumRecords        =   100;

type
    EmployeeIndex        =   1..MaxNumRecords;

    Name                 =      record
        Last             :   string[10];
        First            :   string[10];
        MidInit          :   char
    end;  (*Name*)

    Address              =      record
        Street           :   string[15];
        City             :   string[10];
        State            :   string[2];
        Zip              :   string[5];
    end;  (*Address*)

    Phone                =      record
        Area             :   string[3];
        Local            :   string[7]
    end;  (*Phone*)

    Date                 =      record
        Month,
        Year             :      integer
    end;  (*Date*)

    Employee             =      record
        IDnumber         :   string[9];
        EmpName          :   Name;
        EmpAddress       :   Address;
        Telephones       :   array [1..3]  of Phone;
        JobTitle         :   string[8];
        Location         :   char;
        Department       :   string[4];
        AnnualSalary     :   real;
        LastPromoted,
        FirstEmployed    :   Date
    end;  (*Employee*)

var
    Employees            :   array [EmployeeIndex] of Employee;
```

Figure 9.3 Defining complex data structures

I/O File Structures

Standard Pascal supports two types of serial files that may be read from sequentially and are written to sequentially, each new record appended to the end of the file. These two types of files are *textfiles* and *binary files*. Random files are not supported in standard Pascal, but may be implemented in some enhanced versions of the language.

A *textfile* is a sequential file of characters, grouped into units called lines, each line ending with a carriage return. There is a built-in type called **text** for declaring textfiles. There are two built-in files of type **text**. These are named input and output and are associated with commonly-used, line-oriented devices such as the keyboard, screen, printer, etc.

Binary files are sequential files of records stored in internal data format. They are not ASCII files and cannot be edited by a word processor. Only another Pascal program can edit or display binary files created by a Pascal program.

Let us use a binary file definition as an example of how we may use Pascal's typing facility to set up a "template" for declaring similar variables. To declare the input and output in, say, a sequential file update program:

```
type
     EmployeeRec = record
        ...
     end;
     EmployeeFile = file of EmployeeRec;
...
var
     MasterFile, NewMasterFile: EmployeeFile;
     MasterRec, NewMasterRec : EmployeeRec;
     Transactions : text;
...
```

9.4 PROGRAM STRUCTURES

Pascal is a block-structured language and a Pascal program is composed of an arbitrary number of possibly nested blocks, subprograms, called procedures and functions. There is a single main program that may contain within it one or more definitions for procedures or functions. Each of these may, in turn, contain nested blocks. Programs, procedures, and functions are all coded in the same manner (with the exception that a function name must have a declared type). Each block contains (optionally) its own local definitions and declarations and a sequence of executable statements delimited by the keywords **begin** and **end**. The block header contains:

- a keyword indicating the kind of block (**program, procedure, function**);
- the name of the block;
- and any parameters to be associated with arguments at the point of call.

Any block may be set up like this:

```
<header>;
const
     <constant declarations>;
type
     <type definitions>;
var
     <variable declarations>;
```

```
procedure
    <procedure declaration>;
…<more procedure declarations> …
begin
    <executable statements>
end.
```

The Program Text

Character set. The Pascal character set consists of the 52 upper- and lower-case alphabetic characters, the 10 numeric digits, and at least the following 17 special characters:

+	plus sign	<	less than sign
-	hyphen	>	greater than sign
*	asterisk	=	equal sign
/	slash	^	up arrow
;	semicolon	:	colon
.	period	,	comma
[ ]	square brackets	( )	parentheses
'	quotation mark		blank

Text formatting. The most distinctive feature of a Pascal program is its block structure. Certain features of the program text—like indenting, comments, and blank lines—can be used to enhance or emphasize this block structure.

Free vs. fixed format. Pascal program text is totally free-format.

Indenting. As in all free-format languages, indenting is allowed and encouraged. Indenting serves to highlight the internal block structure of the program in the same way that it highlights all pieces of program text that are internal or subservient to others.

Comments. Comments are enclosed within the paired delimiters (* and *). In some implementations, curly braces, { and }, may also be used. Comments may be inserted anywhere in the program.

Blank lines. Blank lines may be used anywhere in the program.

Punctuation. The semicolon (;) *separates* successive statements (that is, it is not an end-of-statement delimiter). At least one blank space separates the words and symbols of program text. Commas are used to separate items in a list. Quotation marks delimit string literals. Parentheses, ( ), delimit parameter lists and are used in arithmetic expressions. Square brackets, [ ], are used to delimit array subscripts and sets. The keywords **begin** and **end** are used as delimiters enclosing a compound statement.

Words

The words used in the program may be predefined (language keywords) or programmer supplied (identifiers).

Identifiers. The programmer supplies identifiers for variables, types, named constants, labels, procedures, functions, and for the program itself.

Rules for the construction of identifiers are as follows: Names are composed of any number and combination of alphanumeric characters, the only restriction being that the name begin with a letter. On some implementations it may be important for the first eight characters of the name to be uniquely specified. Since Pascal's character set contains both uppercase and lowercase letters, names can be created to be quite descriptive. For example, compare the variable name AccountsReceivableFile with, say, ACCRCVBL.

Keywords. In Pascal, the keywords that make up the built-in vocabulary of the language are reserved words. There are 35 reserved words in standard Pascal.

Descriptive keywords. These define attributes of variables, for example: **integer**, **real**, **char**, **boolean**, **array**, **set**, **record**, **file**, **text**. The keywords **const**, **label**, **type**, and **var** are used to identify descriptive statements.

Action keywords. These are found on executable statements. In Pascal these are used mostly to define conditional control, for example: **if**, **then**, **else**, **case**, **for**, **do**, **while**, **repeat**, **until**, **with**.

Delimiter keywords. The keywords **begin** and **end** delimit a compound statement.

Noise keywords. There are none.

Statements

Statements may be either executable or nonexecutable. The nonexecutable statements are descriptive in nature: They provide information to the compiler.

Declarative statements. Pascal's wide assortment of nonexecutable statements provides for definitions and declarations of the identifiers that will be encountered later in the program. These are the **const**, **label**, **type**, and **var** statements. Also, to some extent, the entire procedure/function definition may be considered to be strictly descriptive until such time as the subprogram is invoked and execution control enters the executable portion of the block. In other words, the entire subprogram code is descriptive—only the "call" statement (invocation) can activate it.

Executable statements. Action statements in Pascal's language definition may be characterized as either assignment statements or control-related statements.

Assignment. Assignment statements are denoted by the assignment operator := . The general format of an assignment statement is: <variable-identifier> := <expression>

On execution, the expression given on the right-hand side is computed and the resulting value stored in the variable named on the left. Thus, the left- and right-hand sides of the assignment operator must be type-compatible.

Arithmetic. There are no specially designated arithmetic statements in Pascal. Arithmetic instructions are coded within an arithmetic expression on the right side of an assignment statement. The arithmetic symbols (+ - * /) have their traditional meanings;

there is no exponentiation operator. In addition, there are several built-in arithmetic functions such as sqrt and abs.

Input/output. There are no built-in I/0 statements in the Pascal language definition. Language implementors provide some standard built-in procedures for these operations. For input from and output to an external file or device, the standard procedures read (<filename>, <variable-list>) and write (<filename>, <variable-list>) may be used. If the <filename> designation is omitted, then a standard built-in file is assumed, for example, **input** on a read or **output** on a write. These built-in files may refer to such I/O devices as keyboard, console, or screen. The procedures readln (<filename>, <variable-list>) and writeln (<filename>, <variable-list>) may be used only with textfiles. They are similar to read and write except that, after the appropriate I/O operation, there is a "go to the next line" operation. This may be implemented by reading (or writing) the carriage return and/or linefeed characters.

Pascal also relies on built-in procedures to open and close files used in processing the program. To open input and output files, the standard procedures reset (<filename>) and rewrite (<filename>) are, respectively, used. The close (<filename>) standard procedure closes a file.

Control. The default control construct is simple sequence. To alter the default control mechanism, one of the following statements may be used: **go to** for unconditional transfer of control; **if** or **case** for selection among two or more alternatives; **while**, **for**, or **repeat** for iteration. Sometimes, simple sequence must be explicitly defined and a compound statement is used for that purpose. A compound statement is a sequence of statements separated by semicolons, the entire sequence delimited by the keyword **begin** at the beginning and **end** at the end. A compound statement may be used anywhere a simple statement is called for, for example, following the keywords **then** and **else** on an **if** statement. Procedure invocation is another mechanism for altering the standard flow of control. Control structures will be discussed more fully below.

Subprograms

While Pascal is a true block-structured language, its subprogram structure may be considered quite simplistic since it is completely contained within the framework of a single main program. There is no provision for calls to separately compiled program units.

Types of subprograms. There are only two kinds of subprograms available to the Pascal programmer. These, called *procedures* and *functions*, are both internal subprograms.

External subprograms. Pascal does not provide for separately compiled subprograms or subprogram libraries.

Internal subprograms. Procedures and functions are internal subprograms. A procedure is defined within the block (program, procedure, function) that calls it. The procedure definition consists of a header, local definitions and declarations, and a compound statement (delimited by a **begin/end** pair) containing the executable statements of the procedure. The procedure header names the procedure and lists its parameters and their types. For example FindMax, defined to compute the maximum of three values, has the header:

```
procedure FindMax (A, B, C : real; var Maximum : real);
```

Procedures are invoked by a call statement which, for FindMax, might look like this:

```
FindMax (X, Y, Z, Max);
```

Functions. A function is defined in exactly the same manner as a procedure. There are very few differences between a procedure and a function. The most important difference is that a function returns a scalar value. Therefore, the function header must specify a type for the function as well as for any parameters it accepts. For example, FindMax can be defined as a real-valued function (let's rename it Max), instead of a procedure:

```
function Max (A, B, C : real) : real;
```

The name Max must be assigned a value within the action block of the function definition (Max := ...) . The function itself would be invoked by simply referencing the function name within another statement. For example:

```
Result := Max(X, Y, Z) - Max (P, Q, R)
```

Sharing data. Since Pascal recognizes only internal subprograms, the rules for data sharing are extremely simple. They depend wholly on the (static) scoping rule and the use of parameters.

Global variables and *local variables* are determined completely by the static scoping rule defined in Chapter 5. The *scope of a variable* (or any identifier) is that part of the program text in which an occurrence of the identifier refers to the same object as in the definition or declaration. Any identifier (variable, type, constant, label) declared in a particular block is local to that block, global to any block defined within it, and unknown to any outer block. Identifiers declared in the descriptive statements of the main program are global (accessible) throughout the program.

Parameters. The default parameter passing mechanism is call by value. Thus, unless the programmer specifies otherwise, parameters are treated as input parameters (called *value parameters*). This works well for function subprograms, which ought, by definition, to accept only input parameters. Many procedures need to pass data back to the calling program, and this is provided for by the use of call by reference, or variable, parameters. A *variable parameter* (input/output parameter) is indicated explicitly on the procedure header by placing the keyword **var** before the parameter declaration. In procedure FindMax defined above, the parameter Maximum is a variable parameter because the maximum is computed within the procedure and that information must be transferred back to the point of call.

Subprogram libraries. *Built-in subprograms*: There are various predefined, built-in procedures and functions available to the Pascal programmer. These are called *standard procedures* and *standard functions*. Some standard functions are show in Table 9.1:

TABLE 9.1

	Type of X	Result
Integer functions:		
ord (X)	any ordinal type	ordinal value of X
trunc(X)	real	integer portion of X
round(X)	real	X rounded to an integer
abs(X)	integer	absolute value of X
sqr(X)	integer	X-squared
Real functions:		
abs(X)	real	absolute value of X
sqr(X)	real	X-squared
sqrt(X)	real or integer	square root of X
ln(X)	real or integer	natural log of X
exp(X)	real or integer	e raised to the power of X
sin(X)	real or integer	sine of X
cos(X)	real or integer	cosine of X
arctan(X)	real or integer	arctangent of X
Boolean functions:		
odd(X)	integer	true if X is odd
eof(X)	any file type	true if X is at end of file
eoln(X)	textfile	true if X is at end of line
Character Function:		
chr(X)	integer	the character represented by the ASCII value X
Ordinal functions:		
pred(X)	any ordinal type	the value preceding X in order
succ(X)	any ordinal type	the value succeeding X in order

Some standard procedures are:

```
read (<filename>, <variable-list>)        reset (<filename>)
readln (<filename>, <variable-list>)      rewrite (<filename>)
write (<filename>, <variable-list>)       close (<filename>)
writeln (<filename>, <variable-list>)     new (<pointer-variable>)
                                          dispose (<pointer-variable>)
```

Subprogram libraries. There is no facility in standard Pascal for building a Pascal subprogram library since subprogram definitions must be included within the text of the main program.

Program Abstraction

Pascal supports program abstraction well as long as programs are small and can be contained within a single unit.

Modular decomposition. Features such as nested subprograms, descriptive subprogram names, and a simple call statement syntax all facilitate modular decomposition.

Information hiding. Programmers can take advantage of local variable declarations, the static scoping rule defining the scope of identifiers, and value and variable parameters in order to implement information hiding.

Self-Documenting Features

Although Pascal program text cannot be called English-like, and it is not a "natural" language, it contains many features that may be called self-documenting.

The flexible rules for formatting program text—the use of comments, blank lines, etc.—do not guarantee that a Pascal program will be self-documenting but do go a long way toward allowing a good programmer to write a good, readable, maintainable program. The same holds true for the construction of descriptive variable names.

Although programmers (especially beginning programmers) may find the extensive required definitions and declarations to be cumbersome and tedious, they eliminate the need for a lot of comments containing a "data dictionary" and, in the process, force the programmer to document data and other identifiers as part of the program.

Finally, the syntax of the procedure call statement—not having a keyword such as call or perform—allows the programmer to temporarily extend the language itself. The invocation can be coded to look like a built-in language keyword.

9.5 CONTROL STRUCTURES

Pascal control structures are generally what one would expect from an algorithmic, imperative, block-structured language. The one limitation is the lack of a facility for external subprograms.

Operators

Operators are symbols used to form expressions on assignment statements and on conditional control statements.

Arithmetic operators. The arithmetic operators act on numeric operands. These operators include: + (add), - (subtract), * (multiply), / (divide). There is no exponentiation operator. There are keywords for integer division: **div** and **mod**. In addition, references to built-in arithmetic functions may be used. These include such typical functions as sqr, sqrt, abs, sin, etc.

Relational operators. The relational operators act on any scalar-type operand. These include: < (less than); <= (less than or equal to); = (equal to); < > (not equal to); >= (greater than or equal to); > (greater than).

Logical operators. The logical operators operate on Boolean operands. Logical operators include the keywords **and**, **or**, **not**.

String operators. There are no string operators in standard Pascal. Implementations that have extended the language to include a string data type do provide for some rudimentary string manipulation.

Set operators. These operate on sets and include + (set union), - (set difference), * (set intersection) and **in** (set membership test). Set operators can sometimes be used to simplify coding and enhance readability. For example, compare

```
if Answer in ['n', 'N', 'y', 'Y'] then …
```

with

```
if (Answer = 'n') or (Answer = 'N') or
   (Answer = 'y') or (Answer = 'Y') then …
```

Expressions

Expressions are represented in infix, parenthesized form. Operands enclosed within parentheses are evaluated first. Parentheses are used to alter the default sequence control mechanism for evaluating expressions.

According to the rules of precedence for the language:

1. parentheses are of course evaluated first
2. function references
3. * / **and**
4. + - **not or**
5. the relational operators

For a series of operators at the same level of precedence, the processing follows a left-to-right sequence of evaluation.

Control Statements

The default statement-level control structure is simple sequence: Statements are executed in the sequence in which they are written in the source program. Although this is the default, there are times when a simple sequence must be explicitly expressed using a compound statement. Certain statements may alter the default control mechanism or in some way control the execution of program statements.

Unconditional branch. Pascal provides a **go to** statement for unconditional transfer of control to a nonsequential statement. The general form of this statement is:

```
go to <label>
```

In keeping with the general rule that all identifiers must be declared before they may be used, statement labels too must be declared. The declarative statement reserved for this purpose is the **label** statement.

Just because a statement is available does not mean it must be used. In fact, the **go to** statement is used very rarely in Pascal—because the wide variety of structured control constructs built into the language make the use of the unconditional branch virtually unnecessary and largely obsolete.

Selection.　The selection control construct is used to choose one of two or more alternative pieces of code.

Two-way selection.　The primary language structure for two-way selection is the **if** statement. It takes the form:

```
if <conditional-expression> then <statement1> else <statement2>
```

Statement1 and statement2 may contain: a single statement, a procedure invocation, sequences of statements delimited by a **begin/end** pair. The clause **else** <statement2> is optional.

Multiway selection.　The **case** statement is used for selection from among more than two alternatives. It has the general form:

```
case <selector-variable> of
    value1 : statement1;
    value2 : statement2;
    ...
    valueN : statementN
end
```

The selector variable must be of a scalar, ordinal type (not real or structured). The values listed must cover all possible values for the selector variable. Standard Pascal does not provide an else or otherwise clause to account for values not listed (for example, invalid data values), but some enhanced versions of the language do.

Iteration.　There are three language structures for controlling iteration. These correspond to the test-before, test-after, and indexed looping constructs and implement them in a straightforward manner.

Test-before loop.　The test-before loop is implemented with the **while** statement. It takes the form: **while** <boolean-expression> **do** statement. The Boolean expression may contain arithmetic, relational, and logical operators and computes to a Boolean value (**true** or **false**). The <statement> may, as usual, be coded as a single statement, a procedure call, or a compound statement (if the body of the loop contains more than a single statement).

Test-after loop.　The test-after loop is implemented with the **repeat/until** structure. It takes the general form:

```
repeat
    statement1;
    statement2;
    ...
until <boolean-expression>
```

Since the **repeat/until** structure assumes that the body of the loop may contain more than a single statement, the **begin/end** keywords are not needed.

Indexed loop. The indexed loop is implemented with the **for** statement, which takes one of the two following forms:

```
for <index-variable> := <initial-value> to <final-value> do statement
```

or

```
for <index-variable> := <initial-value> downto <final-value>
    do statement
```

Control over subprograms.

Call. A procedure is invoked by a "call" statement that contains only the procedure name and any arguments to be associated with the parameters contained within the procedure definition. There is no statement keyword such as call, invoke, or perform. Some sample procedure invocations are:

```
readln (A, B, C);
FindMax (A, B, C, Max);
writeln (Lst, 'Report Heading');
writeln (Lst, 'Maximum value is ', Max);
FindSum (ArrayOfReals);
WriteToDisk (NewFile);
```

This form of the procedure call has the advantage of making it look as if a well-named subprogram had actually defined a new language structure. The call statement can then appear to be using a built-in language structure rather than calling a programmer-defined subprogram. In fact, the "I/O statements" are actually the predefined (standard) procedures read, readln, write, and writeln.

A function is invoked by referring to it in another statement. A function reference may be used anywhere that a variable of the same type may be used.

Return. In both procedures and functions, return of control to the calling block is implicit at the end of the subprogram. Control is returned when the subprogram is terminated; the subprogram is terminated when it runs through the last executable statement.

Control over program execution.
Program execution begins after the delimiter **begin**. There is no explicit "start" statement for beginning program execution. The program terminates when it runs through the final delimiter **end**. There is no explicit stop statement for terminating program execution.

Subprogram Control Structures

Simple call. Once defined, subprograms may be invoked explicitly: procedures by a call statement, functions with a function reference. Return is implicit once subprogram execution is terminated.

Recursion. Procedures and functions may be used recursively; they need not be specially declared as recursive routines. Direct and indirect recursion are acceptable.

Implicit call. There is no implicit invocation of subprograms in Pascal.

Parallel processes. Parallel processing is not available in Pascal.

Coroutines. Coroutines are not available in Pascal.

9.6 PROGRAM DEVELOPMENT

Pascal is ideal for developing structured programs. It implements structured programming methodology in a simple, elegant manner. This includes top-down design, modular decomposition, and structured control constructs.

Pascal is limited in its applicability to very large programs, however, since it provides no facility for storing and invoking a library of relatively independent, separately compilable modules.

9.7 MORE SAMPLE PROGRAMS

Fig. 9.4 contains the listing for the Sequential file update program, coded in Turbo Pascal. The algorithm was discussed as Study Problem #2 in Chapter 7.

Fig. 9.5 lists the program for Study Problem #3 (Part A), the creation of a multi-linked list.

EXERCISES

1. Complete Study Problem #3 (Part B) in Pascal.
2. Do Study Problem #4 in Pascal.

```pascal
program FileUpdate (MasterFile, TransFile,NewMasterFile, LstFile);

    (*******************************************************)
    (*                                                     *)
    (*            GLOBAL        DECLARATIONS               *)
    (*                                                     *)
    (*******************************************************)

const
    MaxTrans                    =    50;
    Space                       =    ' ';

type
    CodeType                    =    char;
    EmployeeRecType             =    record
        Key                     :    string[9];
        OtherInfo               :    string[112];
    end;  {EmployeeRecType}
    TransRecType                =    record
        Rec                     :    EmployeeRecType;
        Code                    :    CodeType
    end;  {TransRecType}
    ErrorlineType               =    record
        ID                      :    string[9];
        Code                    :    CodeType;
        Error                   :    string[10];
    end;  {ErrorlineType}

var
    LstFile                     :    text;
    Ntrans, Nerrors, NumOK      :    integer;
    Nadds, Ndeletes, Nchanges   :    integer;
    MasterRec                   :    EmployeeRecType;
    MasterFile,NewMasterFile    :    text;
    Trans                       :    TransRecType;
    TransFile                   :    text;
    Errorline                   :    array [1..MaxTrans] of ErrorlineType;

    (*******************************************************)
    (*                                                     *)
    (*         R E A D   1   R E C O R D                   *)
    (*                                                     *)
    (*******************************************************)

procedure ReadMasterRecord;
begin
    with MasterRec do
        readln (MasterFile, Key, OtherInfo);
end;
```

Figure 9.4   Update program (continued next page)

```pascal
procedure ReadTransRecord;
begin
    with Trans do begin
        with Rec do
            read (Transfile, Key, OtherInfo);
        readln (Transfile, Code);
    end; {with Trans}
    Ntrans := Ntrans + 1
end;
    (*****************************************************)
    (*                                                 *)
    (*          W R I T E   1   R E C O R D            *)
    (*                                                 *)
    (*****************************************************)

procedure WriteFrom (NewRecord : EmployeeRecType);
begin
    with NewRecord do
        writeln (NewMasterFile, Key, OtherInfo)
end;

    (*****************************************************)
    (*                                                 *)
    (*          I N I T I A L I Z A T I O N            *)
    (*      OPEN FILES, INITIAL VALUES, INITIAL READS  *)
    (*                                                 *)
    (*****************************************************)

procedure Initialize;
begin
    assign (LstFile, 'LST:');                    {LST: for printer}
    reset (LstFile);                             {CON: for console}
    assign (MasterFile, 'A:IDPRSNEL.DAT');
    assign (TransFile, 'A:TRANS.DAT');
    assign (NewMasterFile, 'A:UPDATE.DAT');
    reset (MasterFile);
    reset (TransFile);
    rewrite (NewMasterFile);
    Ntrans := 0;
    Nerrors := 0;
    Nadds := 0;
    Nchanges := 0;
    Ndeletes := 0;
    ReadMasterRecord;
    ReadTransRecord
end;
```

Figure 9.4   (continued next page)

```
(******************************************************)
(*                                                    *)
(*        ADD, CHANGE, DELETE   A   RECORD            *)
(*                                                    *)
(******************************************************)
procedure ErrorInA;
begin
    Nerrors := Nerrors + 1;
    with Errorline [Nerrors] do begin
            ID := Trans.Rec.Key;
            Code := Trans.Code;
            if Trans.Code = ' '
                then Error := 'missing'
                else Error := 'not A '
        end  {with}
end;

procedure ErrorInCD;
begin
    Nerrors := Nerrors +1;
    with Errorline [Nerrors] do begin
            ID := Trans.Rec.Key;
            Code := Trans.Code;
            if Trans.Code = ' '
                then Error := 'missing'
                else Error := 'not C or D'
        end  {with}
end;
procedure AddRecord;
begin
    if Trans.Code = 'A'
        then begin
                WriteFrom (Trans.Rec);
                Nadds := Nadds + 1
            end
        else ErrorInA
end;

procedure ChangeOrDelete;

    procedure ChangeRecord;
    begin
        MasterRec := Trans.Rec
    end;

begin
    if not (Trans.Code in ['C', 'D'])
        then begin
                ErrorinCD;
```

Figure 9.4   (continued next page)

```
                    WriteFrom (MasterRec)
              end
        else if Trans.Code = 'C'
                then begin
                            ChangeRecord;
                            WriteFrom (MasterRec);
                            Nchanges := Nchanges + 1
                      end
                else Ndeletes := Ndeletes + 1;
      ReadMasterRecord
end;  {ChangeOrDelete}

    (*****************************************************)
    (*                                                   *)
    (*    U P D A T E   P R O C E S S   C O N T R O L   *)
    (*                                                   *)
    (*****************************************************)

procedure ProcessControl;
begin
    if Trans.Rec.Key > MasterRec.Key
       then begin
                WriteFrom (MasterRec);
                ReadMasterRecord
            end
        else begin
                if Trans.Rec.Key = MasterRec.Key
                   then ChangeOrDelete
                   else AddRecord;            {ie, Tkey > Mkey}
                ReadTransRecord
            end
end;

    (*****************************************************)
    (*                                                   *)
    (*          E N D   P R O C E S S I N G             *)
    (*                                                   *)
    (*****************************************************)

procedure EndTrans;
begin
    while not eof(MasterFile) do begin
            WriteFrom (MasterRec);
            ReadMasterRecord
        end   {while}
end;

procedure EndMaster;
```

Figure 9.4   (continued next page)

```
begin
      while not eof(TransFile) do begin
               AddRecord;
               ReadTransRecord
           end   {while}
end;

      (**********************************************************)
      (*                                                       *)
      (*            P R I N T E D    R E P O R T               *)
      (*                                                       *)
      (**********************************************************)

procedure PrintReport;

const
      Underline            =   '-------------------------------------------';
      MsgLit               =   'Transaction Code is ';

var   J                    :   integer;

      procedure SkipLines (N: integer);
      begin
          for J := 1 to N do
               writeln (LstFile)
      end;

begin
      Ntrans := Ntrans - 1;
      NumOK := Ntrans - Nerrors;
      writeln (LstFile, ' ':15, 'Sequential File Update');
      writeln (LstFile, ' ':13, 'Personnel File Maintenance');
      writeln (LstFile, ' ':5, Underline);
      SkipLines (2);
      writeln (LstFile, ' ':14, 'Total number of transactions = ', Ntrans:5);
      writeln (LstFile, ' ':7, 'Transactions processed successfully = ', NumOK:5);
      SkipLines (2);
      writeln (LstFile, ' ':2, 'The following transactions could not be processed ');
      writeln (LstFile, ' ':2,  'due to errors:');
      SkipLines (2);
      writeln (LstFile, 'ID Number':12, 'Trans. Code':15, 'Error':10);
      writeln (LstFile, '---------':12, '-----------':15, '-----':10);
      SkipLines (2);
      for J := 1 to Nerrors do
          with Errorline[J] do
               writeln (LstFile, ID:12, Code:8, ' ':10, MsgLit, Error);
      writeln (LstFile, ' ':5, Underline);
      SkipLines (4);
      writeln (LstFile, ' ':10, Nadds:5, '   records added to Master File');
```

Figure 9.4   (continued next page)

```
        SkipLines (2);
        writeln (LstFile, ' ':10, Ndeletes:5, '   records deleted from Master File');
        SkipLines (2);
        writeln (LstFile, ' ':10, Nchanges:5, '   records changed');
end;

        (****************************************************)
        (*                                                *)
        (*              C L O S I N G                     *)
        (*                                                *)
        (****************************************************)

procedure Closing;
begin
        close (MasterFile);
        close (TransFile);
        close (NewMasterFile);
end;

        (*******************************************************)
        (*                                                   *)
        (*  M A I N   P R O G R A M    EXECUTION  BEGINS  HERE   *)
        (*                                                   *)
        (*******************************************************)

begin
        Initialize;
        while not eof (TransFile) do
                if eof (MasterFile)
                    then EndMaster
                    else ProcessControl;
        EndTrans;
        PrintReport;
        Closing;
end.
```

Figure 9.4 (concluded)

```
program MultiLinkedList (EmployeeFile, ListerFile);

        (**************************************************)
        (*                                                *)
        (*   G L O B A L    D E C L A R A T I O N S       *)
        (*                                                *)
        (**************************************************)

type
                                    (* values used for "next" pointers *)
    ListType                =   (EMPLIST, JOBLIST, LOCLIST, DEPTLIST);
                                    (* values used for "first" pointers *)
    SubListType             =   (EMPLOYEE,
                                 ANALYST, CLERK, DESIGNER, MANAGER,
                                 A, B, C, D,
                                 MIS, PROD, RAND);
    JobTitleType            =   ANALYST..MANAGER;
    LocType                 =   A..D;
    DeptType                =   MIS..RAND;
    EmployeeRecType         =   record
        ID                  :   string[9];
        Name                :   string[21];
        OtherInfo1          :   string[62];
        Job                 :   string[8];
        Loc                 :   string[1];
        Dept                :   string[4];
        OtherInfo2          :   string[16]
    end; {EmployeeRecType}
    EmployeeNodePointer     =   ^EmployeeNodeType;
    EmployeeNodeType        =   record
        Employee            :   EmployeeRecType;
        NextIn              :   array [ListType] of EmployeeNodePointer;
    end; {EmployeeNode}

var
    List                    :   ListType;
    SubList                 :   SubListType;
    JobTitle                :   JobTitleType;
    Location                :   LocType;
    Department              :   DeptType;
                                        (* pointer to "current" node *)
    P                       :   EmployeeNodePointer;
                                    (* external pointers head sublists *)
    FirstIn                 :   array [SubListType] of
                                EmployeeNodePointer;
```

Figure 9.5   Multiple lists creation program (continued next page)

```
          (***************************************************)
          (*                                               *)
          (*      I N I T I A L I Z A T I O N S            *)
          (*                                               *)
          (***************************************************)
procedure  InitializeEmptyLists;
begin
     FirstIn [EMPLOYEE] := nil;
     for JobTitle := ANALYST to MANAGER do
         FirstIn [JobTitle] := nil;
     for Location := A to D DO
         FirstIn [Location] := nil;
     for Department := MIS to RAND do
         FirstIn [Department] := nil;
end; {InitializeEmptyLists}

          (***************************************************)
          (*                                               *)
          (*  I N S E R T   N O D E   I N  A  L I S T     *)
          (*                                               *)
          (***************************************************)
procedure Insert (P: EmployeeNodePointer; List: ListType; SubList: SubListType);
var
   J, Q                :   EmployeeNodePointer;

begin
     if FirstIn[SubList] = nil
        then begin                                    (* insert into empty list *)
            FirstIn[SubList] := P;
            P^.NextIn[List] := nil
        end {then}
        else if FirstIn[SubList]^.Employee.ID   P^.Employee.ID
                then begin                            (* insert in front of list *)
                    P^.NextIn[LIst] := FirstIn [SubList];
                    FirstIn [SubList] := P
                end  {then}
                else begin                            (* find insertion point Q *)
                    J := FirstIn[Sublist]^.NextIn[List];
                    Q := FirstIn[SubList];
                    while J > nil do
                        if J^.Employee.ID > P^.Employee.ID
                           then J := nil
                           else begin
                               Q := J;
                               J := J^.NextIn[List]
                           end; {else}
                                                      (* insert P after Q *)
```

Figure 9.5   (continued next page)

```
                        P^.NextIn[List] := Q^.NextIn[List];
                        Q^.NextIn[List] := P
                end; {else}
end; {Insert}

        (****************************************************)
        (*                                                *)
        (*  A D D   N O D E  -  PLACE IN ALL SUBLISTS    *)
        (*                                                *)
        (****************************************************)


procedure AddEmployee (EmployeeInRec:  EmployeeRecType);

    function JobTitle (EmployeeInRec : EmployeeRecType) : JobTitleType;
    begin
        Case EmployeeInRec.Job[1] of              (* It happens that all *)
                                                  (*  "Job"s begin with *)
            'A'  :   JobTitle := ANALYST;         (* a different first letter *)
            'C'  :   JobTitle := CLERK;
            'D'  :   JobTitle := DESIGNER;
            'M'  :   JobTitle := MANAGER;
        end;
    end;

    function Location (EmployeeInRec : EmployeeRecType) : LocType;
    begin
         case EmployeeInRec.Loc of
                 'A'  :  Location := A;
                 'B'  :  Location :- B;
                 'C'  :  Location := C;
                 'D'  :  Location := D;
             end; {case Loc}
     end;  {Location}

     function Department (EmployeeInRec : EmployeeRecType) : DeptType;
     begin
             case EmployeeInRec.Dept[1] of         (* It happens that all *)
                                                   (* "Dept"s begin with *)
                 'M'  :  Department := MIS;         (* a different first letter *)
                 'P'  :  Department := PROD;
                 'R'  :  Department := RAND;
             end {case Dept}
      end; {Department}
begin
     new(P);
     P^.Employee := EmployeeInRec;
     Insert (P, EMPLIST, EMPLOYEE);
     Insert (P, JOBLIST, JobTitle (EmployeeInRec) );
     Insert (P, LOCLIST, Location (EmployeeInRec) );
     Insert (P, DEPTLIST, Department (EmployeeInRec) );
end; {AddEmployee}
```

Figure 9.5   (continued next page)

```
                 (**************************************************)
                 (*                                                *)
                 (*      C R E A T E    MULTILINKED   L I S T       *)
                 (*                                                *)
                 (**************************************************)
procedure CreateLists;
var
   EmployeeInRec         :      EmployeeRecType;
   EmployeeFile          :      Text;

      procedure ReadInputRecord;
      begin
          with EmployeeInRec do
              readln (EmployeeFile, ID, Name, OtherInfo1,
                                    Job, Loc, Dept, OtherInfo2);
      end; {ReadInputRecord}

begin
      assign (EmployeeFile, 'A:NMPRSNEL.DAT');
      reset (EmployeeFile);
      ReadInputRecord;
      while not eof (EmployeeFile) do begin
            AddEmployee (EmployeeInRec);
            ReadInputRecord;
      end; {while}
      close (EmployeeFile);
end; {CreateLists}

                 (**************************************************)
                 (*                                                *)
                 (*          P R I N T E D    R E P O R T           *)
                 (*                                                *)
                 (**************************************************)
procedure PrintReport;
const
   Tab               =    ' ';
   UnderLine         =    '---------------------------------------------';

type
   String8           =    string[8];
   String4           =    string[4];

var
   ListerFile        :      text;

    procedure SkipLines (N: integer);
    var J             :      integer;
    begin
        for J := 1 to N do
            writeln (ListerFile)
    end;
```

Figure 9.5   (continued next page)

```
function JobTitleOut     (JobName: JobTitleType): String8;
begin
    case JobName of
        ANALYST  :   JobTitleOut     := 'Analyst';
        CLERK    :   JobTitleOut     := 'Clerk';
        DESIGNER :   JobTitleOut     := 'Designer';
        MANAGER  :   JobTitleOut     := 'Manager'
    end
end; {JobTitleOut}

function LocationOut (LocName: LocType): char;
begin
    case LocName of
        A    :   LocationOut := 'A';
        B    :   LocationOut := 'B';
        C    :   LocationOut := 'C';
        D    :   LocationOut := 'D'
    end
end; {LocationOut}

function DepartmentOut (DeptName: DeptType): String4;
begin
    case DeptName of
        MIS  :   DepartmentOut := 'MIS';
        PROD :   DepartmentOut := 'Prod';
        RAND :   DepartmentOut := 'R&D'
    end
end; {DepartmentOut}

procedure PrintHeadings (ListHead, SubList : String8);
begin
    SkipLines(5);
    writeln (ListerFile, Tab:30, 'Multiple Sublists');
    SkipLines(3);
    writeln (ListerFile, Tab:25, 'Listing for ', ListHead, Tab, SubList);
    writeln (ListerFile, Tab:15, UnderLine);
    SkipLines(2)
end;

procedure PrintDetailLines (List: ListType; SubList: SubListType);
var P            :   EmployeeNodePointer;
begin
    P := FirstIn [SubList];
    while P > nil do begin
        with P^.Employee do
            writeln (ListerFile, Tab:10, ID, Tab:10, Name);
        P := P^.NextIn [List];
    end {while}
end;
```

Figure 9.5   (continued next page)

```
begin
    assign (ListerFile, 'LST:');          {CON: for console, LST: for printer}
    reset (ListerFile);
    for JobTitle := ANALYST to MANAGER do begin
        PrintHeadings ('Jobtitle', JobTitleOut (JobTitle) );
        PrintDetailLines (JOBLIST, JobTitle);
    end; {for JobTitle}
    for Location := A to D do begin
        PrintHeadings ('Location', LocationOut (Location) );
        PrintDetailLines (LOCLIST, Location);
    end; {for Location}
    for Department := MIS to RAND do begin
        PrintHeadings ('Deptment', DepartmentOut (Department) );
        PrintDetailLines (DEPTLIST, Department);
    end {for Department}
end; {PrintReport}

        (**************************************************)
        (*                                              *)
        (*      MAIN PROGRAM EXECUTION BEGINS HERE       *)
        (*                                              *)
        (**************************************************)
begin
    InitializeEmptyLists;
    CreateLists;
    PrintReport;
end.
```

Figure 9.5   (concluded)

SUGGESTIONS FOR FURTHER STUDY

As recently as 1977, the only textbook on the Pascal language was the 1974 edition of Jensen and Wirth's *User Manual and Report*. About five years later the academic community was beginning to accept Pascal as the language of choice for teaching programming skills. Today, the market is awash in Pascal textbooks, for both standard Pascal and also many microcomputer implementations, especially USCD Pascal and Turbo Pascal.

Manuals.   IEEE (1983), Jensen and Wirth (1984), Borland (1987d, 1989a, 1989b, 1989c).

Books.   Cooper and Clancy (1985), Koffman (1985, 1986), Reges (1987), Shelly *et al.* (1987), Tennenbaum and Augenstein (1981), Welsh and Elder (1982), Wirth (1973).

Chapters in Books.   Pratt (1984), Chapter 15: "Pascal," pp. 426–456; Smedema *et al.* (1983), Chapter 2: "Pascal," pp. 14–38; Tucker (1986), Chapter 2: "Pascal: Heir to the ALGOL Tradition," pp. 16–62.

Articles.   Wirth (1971b, 1975).

10

Modula-2 Language Elements

MODULA-2 (**MODU**lar **LA**nguage-2), designed for large systems programming, is becoming increasingly popular in academic circles where it is, to some extent, replacing Pascal, its direct ancestor. It is being used by educators as a medium to illustrate such principles as structured programming, data abstraction, information hiding and encapsulation, as well as hardware-level programming methodology. Just as Pascal, in the early 1970s, stood out as a sleek counterpoint to ALGOL68, MODULA-2 goes head to head with Ada as a tool for high-level structured programming of embedded real-time systems.

Although MODULA-2 is similar to Pascal, there are a number of significant differences that go beyond syntactic details and MODULA-2's additional types. MODULA-2's conceptual differences with Pascal are reflected in such features as separate compilation, opaque types, low-level processing capability, coroutines, interrupt handling, and support for abstract data types. The key difference, of course, lies in the *module* structure through which many of these features are implemented.

10.1 A BRIEF OVERVIEW OF MODULA-2

MODULA-2 is a high-level programming language that may be used for both high-level and low-level programming. Considering this dual nature, the language syntax is remarkably parsimonious—there are only about 40 reserved language keywords. Its flexibility and structural uniformity are both due to its central organizing concept—the "module"—which allows the programmer to operate at any of several levels of abstraction and provides for the hiding, or encapsulating, of programmer-defined, low-level operations.

History and Development

In 1977, Niklaus Wirth began a research project to design a single-user computer work-station that would later become known as the Lilith system. It was to be an integrated computer system, with hardware and software designed at the same time by the same team. It was to be programmed totally in a single, high-level programming language. This language would have to be appropriate for systems programming (for example, an operating system) and for applications programming and would therefore have to provide features to support both high-level and low-level programming activities.

In addition to calling for a mix of high-level language features and low-level processing capability, the design goals of MODULA-2 included support for large systems programming, real-time processing, and parallel processing. In designing this language, Wirth drew heavily on Pascal and MODULA, a language he had designed in 1975 in an experiment with programming on multiprocessor systems. In a sense, MODULA-2 may be considered a superset, of Pascal, with enhancements including:

- separately compiled subprograms;
- use of the "module" for data abstraction;
- low-level programming capability;
- parallel processing; and
- even stricter type checking than Pascal.

The MODULA-2 language was first defined in 1978, first implemented in 1979, and first released in March 1980. It has not yet been standardized. The *de facto* standard is the description contained in Wirth's 1985 text, *Programming in Modula-2*.

Application Areas

MODULA-2 is a programming language that is particularly well suited for development of large systems—for example, operating systems and embedded systems. It has facilities for parallel processing and real-time processing, and for maintenance of reusable modules of code in libraries. It has also found advocates in the academic community because of the simplicity with which it implements and its usefulness in teaching abstract data types.

Classification

Software generation: Third

Procedural/declarative: Procedural

Translator: Compiler

Processing environment: Batch processing, real-time processing

Programming paradigm: Imperative

10.2 STUDY PROBLEM #1: BUBBLE SORT PROGRAM

Let us begin by examining a complete MODULA-2 program. Fig. 10.1 contains the listing of the bubble sort program coded in MODULA-2. You will notice that, superficially at least, it does not look much different from the Pascal version presented in Chapter 9. Keywords must appear in uppercase characters (MODULA-2, as opposed to Pascal, is case sensitive). Procedures must end with

```
END <procedurename>;
```

The program must end with

```
END <programname>.
```

Functions are declared simply as "typed" procedures. The main program is contained within a program module.

Perhaps the most obvious syntactic difference is in the input/output statements. In Pascal, I/O is handled by "standard," flexible procedures that are compiled along with the program. In MODULA-2, these procedures are part of the library (usually provided with the implementation and, thus, to some degree implementation dependent) of separately compiled modules. These procedures must be called like any other procedures with the appropriate number and type of arguments. This may make input and output appear somewhat cumbersome. Other syntactical differences from Pascal, as well as many of MODULA-2's unique features, are not illustrated by this program.

This and the other illustrative programs in this chapter were run on an IBM PC/XT using TopSpeed Modula-2 from Jensen and Partners, International.

10.3 DATA: TYPES, FILES, AND DATA STRUCTURES

Like Pascal, MODULA-2 is a strongly typed language. It provides the same data-level language structures as Pascal does—notably its treatment of data types—and also contains some features that are unique. Like Pascal, MODULA-2 is strict in its requirement that all programmer-defined identifiers be declared explicitly before they are used. Since MODULA-2 expects to be used by programmers building up libraries of modules, this feature is not only "easy" on the compiler but also useful in that it enforces a documentation standard within the source code.

Memory management is dynamic, within the framework of a nested internal block structure. A variable is considered local to and has scope within the block in which it is declared. Variables imported from library modules are considered global, static variables. They remain allocated as long as the program executes.

Constants

Constants can be inserted directly into the program text as literals, or they may be predefined (named) in a constant declaration statement. A constant has an implied type that is automatically determined by the compiler when it appears in the program text.

```
MODULE Bubble;

        (***************************************************)
        (*                                                 *)
        (*          IMPORTS FROM LIBRARY MODULES           *)
        (*                                                 *)
        (***************************************************)

FROM FIO IMPORT File, EOF,
               Open, Close, Create,
               RdStr, WrStr, WrLn, WrCard, WrCharRep;
FROM Str IMPORT Compare;

        (***************************************************)
        (*                                                 *)
        (*    G L O B A L   D E C L A R A T I O N S        *)
        (*                                                 *)
        (***************************************************)

CONST  MaxNumRecords         =    100;

TYPE
   IndexType              =    [1..MaxNumRecords];
   EmployeeRecType        =    RECORD
        ID                 :        ARRAY [1..9] OF CHAR;
        OtherInfo          :        ARRAY [1..112] OF CHAR;
                                END;
   EmployeeArrayType      =    ARRAY IndexType OF EmployeeRecType;

VAR
   N, Nout                :    IndexType;
   Employee               :    EmployeeArrayType;

        (***************************************************)
        (*                                                 *)
        (*    L O A D   I N P U T   F I L E                *)
        (*                                                 *)
        (***************************************************)

     PROCEDURE LoadFile (VAR N : IndexType; VAR Employee : EmployeeArrayType);
     VAR
       ByNameFile          :    File;
       EmployeeInRec       :    EmployeeRecType;

         PROCEDURE  ReadEmployeeRecord;
         VAR endlin         :    ARRAY [1..50] OF CHAR;
         BEGIN
             WITH EmployeeInRec DO
                 RdStr (ByNameFile, ID);
                 RdStr (ByNameFile, OtherInfo);
                 RdStr (ByNameFile, endlin);
             END;
         END ReadEmployeeRecord;
```

Figure 10.1   Bubble sort program (continued next page)

```
BEGIN
    ByNameFile := Open ("A:NMPRSNEL.DAT");
    N := 0;
    ReadEmployeeRecord;
    WHILE NOT EOF DO
        N := N + 1;
        Employee [N] := EmployeeInRec;
        ReadEmployeeRecord;
    END; (* while*)
    Close (ByNameFile)
END LoadFile;

(***************************************************)
(*                                             *)
(*          B U B B L E   S O R T             *)
(*                                             *)
(***************************************************)
PROCEDURE BubbleSort (VAR N : IndexType; VAR Employee : EmployeeArrayType);
VAR
    Limit, R          :    IndexType;
    Sorted            :    BOOLEAN;

    PROCEDURE Exchange (VAR Record1, Record2 : EmployeeRecType);
    VAR Temp          :    EmployeeRecType;
    BEGIN
        Temp := Record1;
        Record1 := Record2;
        Record2 := Temp;
    END Exchange;

BEGIN
    Limit := N - 1;
    Sorted := FALSE;
    WHILE NOT Sorted DO
        Sorted := TRUE;
        FOR R := 1 TO Limit DO
            IF Compare (Employee[R].ID, Employee[R+1].ID) = 1
                THEN
                    Exchange (Employee[R], Employee[R+1]);
                    Sorted := FALSE;
                END;
        END; (*for*)
        Limit := Limit - 1;
    END; (* while *)
END BubbleSort;
```

Figure 10.1   (continued next page)

```
(****************************************************)
(*                                                  *)
(*      W R I T E    T O    D I S K          *)
(*                                                  *)
(****************************************************)

PROCEDURE WriteFile (VAR N : IndexType; VAR Employee : EmployeeArrayType);
VAR
    ByIDFile            :    File;
    EmployeeOutRec      :    EmployeeRecType;
    R                   :    IndexType;

    PROCEDURE WriteEmployeeRecord;
    BEGIN
        WITH EmployeeOutRec DO
            WrStr (ByIDFile, ID);
            WrStr (ByIDFile, OtherInfo); WrLn (ByIDFile);
        END;
    END WriteEmployeeRecord;

BEGIN
    ByIDFile := Create ("A:IDPRSNEL.DAT");
    FOR R := 1 TO N DO
        EmployeeOutRec := Employee[R];
        WriteEmployeeRecord;
    END;
    Close (ByIDFile);
END WriteFile;

(****************************************************)
(*                                                  *)
(*        P R I N T E D    R E P O R T       *)
(*                                                  *)
(****************************************************)

PROCEDURE PrintReport (VAR N : IndexType);
CONST
    Space               =    ' ';
VAR
    Lstr                :    File;

    PROCEDURE SkipLines (L : SHORTCARD);
    VAR  R              :    SHORTCARD;
    BEGIN
        FOR R := 1 TO L DO
            WrLn (Lstr);
        END;
    END SkipLines;

BEGIN
    Lstr := Open ('CON');       (* can change to 'PRN' *)
    SkipLines(5);
```

Figure 10.1   (continued next page)

```
           WrCharRep(Lstr, Space,20); WrStr(Lstr,'Bubble Sort Report');WrLn(Lstr);
           WrCharRep(Lstr, Space,20); WrStr(Lstr,'------------------');WrLn(Lstr);
           SkipLines(2);
           WrCharRep(Lstr, Space,5);
           WrStr(Lstr,'Number of records read from input file -- ');WrLn(Lstr);
           WrCharRep(Lstr, Space,10); WrStr(Lstr,'NMPRSNEL File -- ');
           WrCard(Lstr,N,5);WrLn(Lstr);
           SkipLines(2);
           WrCharRep(Lstr, Space,5);
           WrStr(Lstr,'Number of records written to output file -- ');WrLn(Lstr);
           WrCharRep(Lstr, Space,10); WrStr(Lstr,'IDPRSNEL File -- ');
           WrCard(Lstr,N,5);WrLn(Lstr);
           SkipLines(2);
           WrCharRep(Lstr, Space,5);
           WrStr(Lstr,'Bubble Sort completed successfully');WrLn(Lstr);
           Close (Lstr);
       END PrintReport;

       (*************************************************)
       (*                                               *)
       (*    M A I N   P R O G R A M    EXECUTION BEGINS *)
       (*                                               *)
       (*************************************************)
BEGIN
       LoadFile (N, Employee);
       BubbleSort(N, Employee);
       WriteFile (N, Employee);
       PrintReport (N);
END Bubble.
```

Figure 10.1   (concluded)

Literals.   Literals may be values taken from any built-in or user-defined data type. Numeric literals denote real-valued numbers or whole numbers (integers). A *real literal* is a sequence of numeric digits containing a decimal point. There must be at least one digit to the left of the decimal point. The real literal may also optionally contain a scale factor to represent a value in scientific notation. Examples of real literals are -127.5 and 1.275E + 2.

Whole-numbered literals are represented by decimal, octal, or hexadecimal literals. A *decimal literal* represents a base 10 integer, for example, 127. An *octal literal* is a sequence of octal (base 8) digits followed by a B, for example: 177B (= 127 in base 10). A *hexadecimal literal* is a sequence of hexadecimal (base 16) digits followed by an H, for example 7FH (= 127 in base 10). Sometimes a leading 0 is affixed to a hexadecimal literal since it must begin with a 0 through 9 or it would look like an identifier. For example, the hexadecimal literal B4H would be written as 0B4H.

A *string literal* is a sequence of characters enclosed within single or double quotation marks, for example: '---Report---' or "Execution terminated successfully." A string literal of length one is a *character literal*. A character literal may also be written as an octal value (its ASCII-coded value) followed by a C. This is a convenient method for representing unprintable characters. For example, the literal 7C denotes the bell (^G) and the literal 15C denotes the carriage return.

A *set literal* is a list of scalar, ordinal values delimited by curly braces ({ }) and denotes a collection of values of that ordinal type. A set literal is operated on by set operators. For example: **IF** Answer **IN** CHAR {'n', 'N', 'y', 'Y'} **THEN** ....

Literals may also represent *Boolean* or programmer-defined *enumerated* types.

Standard constants.   Some named constants are universally implemented and may be assumed to be part of the MODULA-2 language. These include the Boolean values FALSE and TRUE and the pointer value NIL. In addition, every implementation provides its own set of predefined named constants.

User-defined constants.   MODULA-2's **CONST** declarative statement is an enhanced version of the Pascal **const** statement. As with Pascal, **CONST** may be used to declare programmer-defined named constants which can be used as synonyms for the specified literal. These constants are *true* constants. They are protected from change and, once declared, may not be modified in any way later on in the program. These programmer-defined constants can enhance the readability of a program. Some examples are:

```
CONST
    Space    =    ' ';
    MaxNums  =    100;
    Pi       =    3.14159
```

In addition, MODULA-2's **CONST**ant declaration may be used to define and name constant expressions. For example:

```
    Ratio    =    360.0 / (2.0 * Pi);
    ArraySize =   MaxNums - 1;
```

Variables

Variables are programmer-defined identifiers representing data values that are subject to change by the executable statements of the program.

Variable declaration.   All programmer-defined identifiers, including variable names, must be explicitly declared prior to use.

Explicit declaration.   All variables must be explicitly declared—that is, given a name and a type—before they may be used. Other attributes may include the number and type of the component elements in a structured variable. MODULA-2 assumes no default attributes for variables. Variables are declared with the **VAR** statement. The general form of this statement is:

```
    VAR   <name>    :    <type> ;
```

The type may be any built-in or previously defined type.

Rules for scope of variables are the same as in Pascal, covering nested procedures and modules. In addition, global variables **IMPORT**ed from a library module are accessible throughout the duration of program execution.

	Scalar	Structured	Other	
Built-in	REAL	BITSET	ADDRESS	PROC
	LONGREAL			
	Ordinal:			
	BOOLEAN			
	CHAR			
	CARDINAL			
	INTEGER			
	LONGINT			
User-defined	enumeration	ARRAY	POINTER	PROCEDURE
	subrange	RECORD		
		SET		

Figure 10.2   Data types in MODULA-2

Implicit declaration.   There is no implicit declaration of variables in MODULA-2. A constant, however, although it does have a type, may be declared implicitly simply by using it in the program.

Initialization.   No default initial values for variables are assumed, and no provision is made for initializing variables in a declarative statement. Variables may be initialized only in executable statements.

Types.   Just about everything that can be said of Pascal's data types and typing facility is also true of MODULA-2 . The facility may be used to:

1. define a totally new type by specifying its domain of values;
2. declare a complex data structure such as a record, array, or file;
3. set up a sort of "template" for the declaration of several variables that may be described in the same way; then, any changes to the description of these variables need only be done once, in the type definition statement.

The types available to MODULA-2 programmers are shown in Fig. 10.2. In addition to providing for some types not present in Pascal, MODULA-2's *module* facility enables the specification of an unlimited variety of programmer-defined simple and structured types via data abstraction.

Pointer and procedure types are both indirect references: Pointer variables reference anonymous variables while procedure variables reference procedures. Both are addresses: pointer variables are certainly addresses; the value of a procedure variable is the starting address of the procedure's object code. Pointer types are discussed together with structured data later on in this section. Procedure types are discussed in the next section.

MODULA-2's type checking, even more rigorous than that of Pascal, varies depending on the context. The three kinds of type checking, from most stringent to weakest, are: type equivalence, type compatibility, and assignment compatibility. *Type equivalence* is required for arguments passed to variable parameters. Two types are equivalent only if they have the same name or were derived from the same type name. *Type compatibility* is required for operands in expressions, for **CASE** labels and **CASE** expressions, and for the entities on a **FOR** statement. Two types are type-compatible if they are equivalent or if one is a subrange of the other or if they are both subranges of the same base type. *Assignment compatibility* is required for assignment statements, index variables and the declared array index type, value parameters, and the value on a **RETURN** statement with the declared function type. Two types are assignment-compatible if they are type-compatible or if they are CARDINAL and INTEGER types or subranges of these types.

Built-in types.   MODULA-2's *scalar* types are:

- INTEGER, signed whole decimal numbers;
- LONGINT;
- CARDINAL, unsigned (assumed positive) integers;
- REAL, floating-point numeric data;
- LONGREAL, double-precision floating-point numeric data;
- CHAR, a single (ASCII) character enclosed within quotation marks;
- BOOLEAN, limited to the values TRUE or FALSE.

Some examples are:

```
VAR
        A    :    INTEGER;
        B    :    CARDINAL;
        C    :    CHAR;
        X    :    REAL;
        S    :    BOOLEAN;
...
A := 2026;              (* A is   INTEGER and may take on a sign *)
B := 2026;              (* B is CARDINAL and may not take on a sign *)
C := '*';
X := 196.52;
S := FALSE;
...
```

The largest and smallest values that may be stored using these types is, naturally, highly dependent on the machine and particular implementation used. The standard functions MAX and MIN are provided to determine what these values are. For example, MAX(INTEGER) is equivalent to Pascal's standard constant, **maxint**. One advantage of CARDINAL type over INTEGER is seen when we consider that, for example, in a 16-bit machine, the largest integer is only 32,767 while MAX(CARDINAL) is 65,535. Also, if a variable is known not to go negative, declaring it as CARDINAL eliminates the need for range checking.

All the scalar types except the reals are *ordinal types*, meaning that their values can be defined in terms of a successor (next) value and a predecessor (previous) value. The BOOLEAN value FALSE is stored as 0 and TRUE as 1.

Among MODULA-2's low-level entities is the data type WORD, which is used to represent any value (INTEGER, CARDINAL, BITSET, etc.) that can be stored in a single word in memory. Clearly, this is somewhat dependent on the machine and compiler used. WORD is compatible with all types stored in one word. Although the only operation allowed on WORD-type data is assignment, a variable of this type can be and is primarily used as a parameter to which any type data that is stored in a word may be transmitted.

User-defined types.   Scalar, user-defined types are specified by enumeration or by taking a subrange of an ordinal base type. Enumerated and subrange types are also stored as ordinal types. These are defined with the **TYPE** statement.

An *enumerated type* is defined by listing the domain of all possible values for the type. A *subrange type* is specified as a subset of any already existing (built-in or user-defined) ordinal type. The subrange, enclosed by square brackets, is specified with lower and upper bounds separated by two periods. The name of the base type may be specified as well—especially for documentation purposes—although that is not always necessary. For example, the following two definitions of the subrange type Sub are equivalent:

```
Sub   =   CARDINAL [1..100];
Sub   =   [1..100];
```

When a lower bound specified is negative, for example [-1..99], the assumed base type is INTEGER.

Some examples of user-defined types follow:

```
TYPE
      (*  enumerated type *)
      CarType   =   (COMPACT, SUBCOMPACT, SPORT, SEDAN, WAGON, VAN);

      (* subrange types *)
      GradeType =   CHAR ['A'..'F'];
      Digit     =   CARDINAL [0..9];

      (* subrange of CarType *)
      BigCarType   =   CarType [SEDAN..VAN];

VAR
      Car1, Car2   :   CarType;
      FamilyCar    :   BigCarType;
      SemesterGrade : GradeType;

...
Car1 := SEDAN;
Car2 := VAN;
SemesterGrade := 'B';
...
IF Car1 < Car2 THEN ...
...
```

The values in an enumerated-type list are considered to be ordered so that, for example, COMPACT is less than SUBCOMPACT, etc. Enumerated-type values are associated with integers in storage, beginning with 0. This integer is the *ordinal value* of the enumerated value. The CarType, the ordinal value of COMPACT is 0, of SPORT, 2, and of VAN, 5.

User-defined types may be used for internal processing only; there is no facility provided for input or output of these values.

Structured Data

The **ARRAY**, **RECORD**, and **SET** keywords may be used to construct "custom-made" structured data types. There is no built-in text type or file constructor in MODULA-2. The built in **POINTER** type is used for the construction of dynamic structures such as linked lists. The PROC type allows a procedure to be passed as a parameter to another procedure.

Arrays. An array may be declared using the **ARRAY** keyword on a variable declaration statement. For example, to declare an array of 100 real-valued elements, X:

```
VAR    X  :   ARRAY [1..100] OF REAL;
```

An array may be composed of elements of any type, including another array (or any other structured type).

Several arrays of the same description may be described by first defining the array as a type and then declaring the array variables as that type. For example:

```
TYPE
      TwoWayFrequencies = ARRAY [1..5],[1..5] OF INTEGER;
...
VAR
      RateByUsage,
      RegionByUsage  :  TwoWayFrequencies;
```

Records. A record structure may be used either as a logical data structure for grouping data (as, for example, in constructing a linked list) or as an input/output variable. It is declared as a type using the **RECORD** keyword and then naming fields on the record along with their descriptions. For example:

```
TYPE
      Date = RECORD
                Month, Day,Year :  INTEGER
             END;
...
VAR
      Previous, Current : Date;
...
```

The field variables Month, Day, and Year do not have to be declared on a **VAR** statement; they have already been declared as part of the record type definition. The individual fields of the record may be accessed using a qualified name, for example:

```
IF Current.Month <= Previous.Month THEN …
```

Alternatively, the individual fields of the record may be accessed using the **WITH** statement. With this construct, the record name is given once, and then field names may be used unqualified. For example:

```
WITH Current DO
     Month := 01;
     Day := 01;
     Year := 89
END;
```

A field on a record may be declared as being of any type, including a structured type. There is no limitation to the way these data structures may be combined. For example, an array can consist of an ordered sequence of records, each of which may be composed of other records and/or arrays.

The following example illustrates the way MODULA-2's declarations may be used in building complex data structures: If the employee records containing the data set listed in Chapter 7 were to be stored in a temporary array during processing, this structure may be completely described by the definitions and declarations in Fig. 10.3.

Lists. Dynamic data structures are facilitated in a very natural manner by MODULA-2's built-in POINTER type. A value of type POINTER "points" to an anonymous variable that was created during program execution. Each pointer type is bound to some other type and is consequently constrained with regard to the type of "variable" to which it may point.

The following declarations set up a linked list. ("Info" may contain any number of fields.)

```
TYPE
     NodePointer = POINTER TO Node;
     Node = RECORD
               Info :  <some-type>;
               Next : NodePointer
            END;

VAR
     First, Current := NodePointer;
```

Notice that this is the one instance in which MODULA-2 allows a forward reference—that is, the use of a name (in this case, Node) that has not yet been formally declared. Notice too that we do not declare any variable(s) of type Node. For example, Current^ is the way we refer to the Node pointed to by Current; Current^.Next is the Node pointed to by Next—that is, the next node in the list.

The standard procedures NEW(pointer) and DISPOSE(pointer) are used for allocating and freeing memory space of anonymous variables pointed to by pointer variables. These standard procedures use the procedures ALLOCATE and DEALLOCATE, which must be imported from the standard library module Storage. The multilinked list program, in Section 10.7, illustrates the use of pointers and lists in MODULA-2.

```
CONST
   MaxNumRecords  =  100;

TYPE
   EmployeeIndex  =  [1..MaxNumRecords];

   Name        =  RECORD
                     Last    :  ARRAY [1..10] OF CHAR;
                     First   :  ARRAY [1..10] OF CHAR;
                     MidInit :  CHAR
                  END;  (*Name*)
   Address     =  RECORD
                     Street :  ARRAY[1..15] OF CHAR;
                     City   :  ARRAY[1..10] OF CHAR;
                     State  :  ARRAY[1..2] OF CHAR;
                     Zip    :  ARRAY[1..5] OF CHAR;
                  END;  (*Address*)
   Phone       =  RECORD
                     Area   :  ARRAY [1..3] OF CHAR;
                     Local  :  ARRAY [1..7] OF CHAR
                  END;(*Phone*)
   Date        =  RECORD
                     Month,
                     Year   :  INTEGER
                  END;  (*Date*)
   Employee    =  RECORD
                     IDnumber      :  ARRAY[1..9] OF CHAR;
                     EmpName       :  Name;
                     EmpAddress    :  Address;
                     Telephones    :  ARRAY [1..3]  OF  Phone;
                     JobTitle      :  ARRAY[1..8] OF CHAR;
                     Location      :  CHAR;
                     Department    :  ARRAY[1..4] OF CHAR;
                     AnnualSalary  :  REAL;
                     LastPromoted,
                     FirstEmployed :  Date
                  END;  (*Employee*)
VAR
   Employees   :  ARRAY EmployeeIndex OF Employee;
```

Figure 10.3   Defining complex data structures

It should be pointed out here that there is a standard, predefined pointer type called ADDRESS used to designate specific, actual locations in memory. This is one of MODULA-2's low-level processing features and is defined in the library module System as:

TYPE ADDRESS = **POINTER TO** WORD

ADDRESS is compatible with all pointer types.

Strings. Strings are not built into the MODULA-2 language definition. Strings may be constructed as arrays of CHAR. For example,

```
VAR    ID :    ARRAY [1..9] OF CHAR;
```

The implementation may provide a library module of procedures for processing strings declared in this manner.

Sets. A set is an unordered collection of distinct, homogeneous units. In the standard language definition, the base type of a set may be an enumeration type or a subrange of CARDINAL. However, most MODULA-2 implementations have extended this definition to include many (if not most) ordinal scalar types. Because of the way in which set variables are stored, the maximum allowable number of elements in a set is the number of bits in a machine word.

For example:

```
TYPE
     CarSet = SET OF [COMPACT..SEDAN];   (* subrange of CarType *)
VAR
     Car1 : CarType;
...
IF  Car1  IN  CarSet  THEN ...
```

There is a built-in (standard) set type, BITSET. This high-level data type is used for low-level programming. The base type of BITSET is a subrange of CARDINAL, from 0 to $W - 1$, where W is the word length of the underlying machine (say, 16 or 32). The BITSET type is used for low-level programming since it allows access to the individual bits of a word. For example, the BITSET value {0,3,9,15} denotes a word containing ones in positions 0, 3, 9, and 15 and zeros elsewhere. Any of the set operators may be used on BITSET values, enabling the programmer to perform bit-level operations. For example, an array of, say, 96 Boolean values can be more efficiently stored if the Boolean values are placed in bits. If the word size is 16 bits (2 bytes), then we would need a 6-component **ARRAY** of BITSET. In general, for N bits, we would need an array with (N **DIV** 16 + 1) components.

Abstract Data Types

The typing facilities of Pascal and MODULA-2 do not implement data abstraction. User-defined types provide a limited means for specifying the domain of a "new" type based on some other predefined type, but there is no encapsulation of this definition with the specification of the operations that are allowed on this new data type. As we shall see, MODULA-2's module does facilitate just this sort of encapsulation, using information hiding to achieve the level of abstraction desired. The specification of abstract data types is useful in the processing of, for example, stacks, strings, and files.

I/O File Structures

The MODULA-2 language definition totally ignores input/output and file structures. There is no built-in file type. Most implementations will provide a library module containing a file type definition and procedures for file handling, such as open, close, read, write, append, etc.

10.4 PROGRAM STRUCTURES

The module is certainly the most identifiable MODULA-2 program structure. There are four basic kinds of modules. *Program modules* are complete programs. An *internal*, or local, *module* is nested within some other module. *Definition modules* and *implementation modules* are stored in libraries. The separate compilation of library and program modules supports problem decomposition and team programming of large projects. It allows partitioning of a large program into smaller units with well-defined interfaces. Although the module is a conceptually simple entity, using it (as opposed to misusing it) may prove to be more difficult than you might expect.

The Program Text

Character set. The MODULA-2 character set consists of the 52 upper- and lowercase alphabetic characters, the 10 numeric digits, the blank space, and at least the following 24 special characters:

+	plus sign	<	less than sign
-	hyphen	>	greater than sign
*	asterisk	=	equal sign
/	slash	^	up arrow
#	pound sign	&	ampersand
~	tilde	|	vertical bar
;	semicolon	:	colon
.	period	,	comma
[ ]	square brackets	( )	parentheses
'	single quotation mark	{ }	curly brackets
"	double quotation mark		

Text formatting. Certain features of the program text—like indenting, comments, and blank lines—can be used to enhance or emphasize the internal nested block structure of a MODULA-2 program or library module.

Free vs. fixed format. MODULA-2 program text is totally free-format, with the "usual" restriction that words and literals be contained on a single line.

Indenting. As in all free-format languages, indenting is allowed and encouraged. Indenting serves to highlight the internal block structure of the program in the same way that it highlights all pieces of program text that are internal or subservient to others.

Comments. Comments are enclosed within the paired delimiters (* and *). Comments, which may be inserted anywhere in the program, are treated as "white space," much like a blank, tab, or return. Comments may be nested. This feature is useful when enclosing a portion of a program so that it will be ignored during testing. Nested comments are no problem, and do not have to be removed.

Blank lines.   Blank lines may be used anywhere in the program.

Punctuation.   The semicolon (;) separates successive statements. Since MODULA-2 accepts an "empty statement," there is no problem with using the semicolon as a statement terminator. In fact, this practice is encouraged since it makes programs easier to modify. At least one blank space separates the words and symbols of program text. Commas are used to separate items in a list. Quotation marks (' or ") delimit string literals. Parentheses, ( ), delimit parameter lists and are used in arithmetic expressions. Square brackets, [ ], are used to delimit array indexes and to define subranges. Curly braces, { }, are used to delimit set literals.

Words

The words used in the program may be reserved words, standard (built-in) identifiers, or programmer supplied identifiers. In this chapter, only reserved language keywords appear in boldface.

Identifiers.   The programmer supplies identifiers for variables, types, named constants, labels, procedures, functions, and the program itself.

Rules for the construction of identifiers are as follows: Names are composed of any number and combination of alphanumeric characters, the only restriction being that the name begin with a letter. Names can be created to be quite descriptive, using both uppercase and lowercase letters. For example, compare the variable name AccountsReceivableFile with, say, ACCRCVBL. MODULA-2, unlike Pascal, is *case sensitive*. This means that it does differentiate between upper- and lowercase characters in a name. Thus, the name ACCOUNT is taken to be different from the name Account and Accountrecord is different from AccountRecord.

Keywords.   There are 40 reserved language keywords in the MODULA-2 language definition. Reserved words make up the core of the language and cannot be redefined by the programmer. The reserved words of MODULA-2 are listed as follows:

AND	ELSEIF	LOOP	REPEAT
ARRAY	END	MOD	RETURN
BEGIN	EXIT	MODULE	SET
BY	EXPORT	NOT	THEN
CASE	FOR	OF	TO
CONST	FROM	OR	TYPE
DEFINITION	IF	POINTER	UNTIL
DIV	IMPLEMENTATION	PROCEDURE	VAR
DO	IMPORT	QUALIFIED	WHILE
ELSE	IN	RECORD	WITH

In addition, there are about 30 *standard identifiers* with predefined meanings that we may as well consider to be reserved language keywords. Standard identifiers are words that have been predefined and can be redefined (as identifiers) by the programmer.

However, this practice is discouraged for obvious reasons. The standard identifiers include types (INTEGER, REAL), constants (TRUE, FALSE, NIL), and built-in functions (ABS, MAX, MIN, ORD).

The following are some of the different kinds of keywords provided.

Descriptive keywords. These define attributes of variables, for example: CARDINAL, INTEGER, LONGINT, REAL, LONGREAL, CHAR, BOOLEAN, **ARRAY**, **SET**, BITSET, **RECORD**, PROC. The keywords **CONST**, **TYPE**, and **VAR** are used to identify descriptive statements.

Action keywords. These are found on executable statements, mostly to define conditional control, for example: **IF**, **THEN**, **ELSE**, **ELSEIF**, **CASE**, **FOR**, **DO**, **WHILE**, **REPEAT**, **UNTIL**, **LOOP**, **WITH**.

Delimiter keywords. The keywords **BEGIN** and **END** delimit the executable statements in a module. The keyword **END** punctuates record definitions and control structures.

Noise keywords. There are none.

Statements

Statements may be either executable or nonexecutable. The nonexecutable statements are descriptive in nature: They provide information to the compiler.

Declarative statements. MODULA-2's nonexecutable statements provide for definitions and declarations of the identifiers that will be encountered later in the program. These are the **CONST**, **TYPE**, and **VAR** statements. Also, the definition module, discussed later in this chapter, is descriptive in nature. Similarly, to some extent, an entire procedure definition may be considered to be strictly descriptive until such time as the subprogram is invoked and execution control enters the executable portion of the block. In other words, the entire subprogram code is descriptive—only the "call" statement (procedure invocation) can activate it.

Executable statements. Since MODULA-2 is an imperative language, most of its eleven action statements may be characterized as either assignment statements or control-related statements. The exception is the **WITH** statement.

Assignment. Assignment statements are denoted by the assignment operator (:=). The general format of an assignment statement is : <variable-identifier> := <expression>. The <variable-identifier> may also be an array reference, a field on a record, or an anonymous variable pointed to by a pointer variable.

On execution, the expression given on the right-hand side is computed and the resulting value stored in the variable named on the left. Thus, the left- and right-hand sides of the assignment operator must be assignment-compatible, which is a little weaker than type-compatible.

Arithmetic. There are no specially designated arithmetic statements in MOD-ULA-2. Arithmetic instructions are coded within an arithmetic expression on the right side of an assignment statement. The arithmetic symbols (+ - * /) have their traditional meanings; there is no exponentiation operator. In addition, most implementations will supply some standard arithmetic functions (such as ABS) and many provide a library module containing a large assortment of arithmetic functions and procedures (such as trigonometric functions).

Input/output. There is no standard for input/output in the MODULA-2 language definition. It must be handled by implementation-dependent procedures contained in library modules. Therefore, an input/output procedure must be called like any other procedure, having a fixed number of parameters of specific types. Thus, input/output procedures typically allow one value input or output at a time, which can produce somewhat awkward code. There may be different procedures for specific I/O devices, including "standard" devices such as the console, keyboard, or screen. The MODULA-2 language definition does not support file or text types. Typical procedures for input/output include ReadChar(char), ReadInt(integer), ReadStr(string), WriteStr(string), and WriteLn.

Control. The default control construct is simple sequence. To alter the default control mechanism, one of the following statements may be used: **IF** or **CASE** for selection among two or more alternatives; **WHILE, FOR, LOOP,** or **REPEAT** for iteration. There is no **goto** statement in the language definition, although a number of implementations have provided this "extension." The **EXIT** and **RETURN** statements provide for specific forms of unconditional branch in specific places in a program. There is no explicit structure denoting a compound statement in MODULA-2. Instead, control statements are assumed to contain sequences of statements; therefore, these structures are required to close with the **END** keyword. Procedure invocation is another mechanism for altering the standard flow of control. Control structures will be discussed more fully below.

Subprograms

A module is a "permanent" entity, as opposed to a procedure, which is temporary in nature. A module is a collection of types, constants, variables, and procedures. It is used to group procedures that share common variables, types, constants, and other procedures. It is also used to create abstract data types. The module is a solution to the problem of large program development. It supports the well-designed, very large program. It is also, as we shall see later, the way the language implements its version of concurrency.

Types of subprograms. There are four kinds of modules in MODULA-2. These are: Program modules, definition modules, implementation modules, and internal modules. The main program is contained in a *program module*, which is a unit capable of execution. The program module may contain nested internal procedures and modules and may **IMPORT** for use external procedures from library modules. Program modules never **EXPORT** their procedures for use by other modules. The following is a skeleton of a program module:

```
MODULE <name>;
    …    (* import lists go here *)
    …    (* declarative statements go here *)
BEGIN
    …    (* action statements go here *)
END <name>.
```

An *internal module* (also called a *local module*) may be defined within a program module. Its primary purpose is to control the visibility of identifiers within a program. It encapsulates the data and procedures hidden within its walls and allows the main program access only to those entities it explicitly EXPORTs. In addition, an internal module must explicitly IMPORT what it needs from the main program. An internal module may be set up something like this:

```
MODULE main;
    …                    (* import lists go here *)
    …                    (* declarative statements go here *)
MODULE local;
        IMPORT …    (* import entities from main *)
        EXPORT …    (* export entities to main *)
        …            (* local declarations go here *)
BEGIN
    …                    (* Local module action statements go here. These
                         are executed before those of the main. *)
END local;

BEGIN
    …                    (* main action statements go here *)
END main.
```

Library modules are stored as pairs: Each has a *definition module* and an *implementation module*. Library modules are a convenient way to store related entities such as constants, types, variables, and procedures. A library module that provides entities for use by another module is called a "server"; a module that uses such entities is called a "client." In this way, the module acts as a wall, hiding unnecessary or irrelevant information from client modules. Modules that use entities from other modules must explicitly **IMPORT** them. Import lists are given in the declarative portion of the module. For example,

```
FROM <module-name> IMPORT <entity-list>;
```

All the entities in a module may be **IMPORT**ed by using the form of the statement:

```
IMPORT <entity-list>;
```

Then, references to module entities must be qualified by the module name, much like a field on a record must be preceded by the record name. For example, we would write InOut.WriteLn or FileIO.Close. The construction of library modules, definition and implementation parts, is discussed more fully below.

External subprograms.　　External procedures are contained in library modules, which are compiled separately. Modules are not called; their procedures are imported to other modules where they are invoked. Although these external procedures are compiled separately, once they are imported they are treated just as if they had been declared locally.

Internal subprograms.   Internal procedures are those declared within the program module or are local to another procedure. A procedure is defined within the block (program module or another procedure) that calls it. The procedure definition consists of a header, local definitions and declarations, and a sequence of executable statements (delimited by a **BEGIN/END** pair). The procedure header names the procedure and lists its parameters and their types. For example FindMax, defined to compute the maximum of three values, would have the header:

```
PROCEDURE FindMax (A, B, C : REAL; VAR Maximum : REAL);
```

Procedures are invoked by a call statement, which, for FindMax, might look like this:

```
FindMax (X, Y, Z, Max);
```

A function, a value-returning procedure, is defined in exactly the same manner as a procedure. A function returns a scalar value, and the function header must specify a type for the procedure as well as for any parameters it accepts. For example, FindMax can be defined as a real-valued function (let's rename it Max) instead of a procedure:

```
PROCEDURE Max (A, B, C : REAL) : REAL;
```

The function is assigned a value within the function body by means of a **RETURN** statement, which indicates the value returned. The function itself would be invoked by simply referencing the function name within another statement. For example:

```
Result := Max(X, Y, Z) - Max (P, Q, R);
```

Sharing data.   For internal subprograms, the rules for data sharing are extremely simple. They depend wholly on the (static) scoping rule and the use of parameters.

Global variables and *local variables* are determined completely by the static scoping rule defined in Chapter 5. The *scope of a variable* (or any identifier) is that part of the program text in which an occurrence of the identifier refers to the same object as in the definition or declaration. Any identifier (variable, type, constant, label) declared in a particular block is local to that block, global to any block defined within it, and unknown to any outer block. Identifiers declared in the descriptive statements of the main program are global (accessible) throughout the program.

Parameters.   The default parameter passing mechanism is call by value. Thus, unless the programmer specifies otherwise, parameters are treated as input parameters (called *value parameters*). This works well for function subprograms, which ought, by definition, to accept only input parameters. Many procedures need to pass data back to the calling program, and this is provided for by the use of call by reference, or variable, parameters. A *variable parameter* (input/output parameter) is indicated explicitly on the procedure header by placing the keyword **VAR** before the parameter declaration). In procedure FindMax defined above, the parameter Maximum is a variable parameter because the maximum is computed within the procedure and that information must be transferred back to the point of call.

Other kinds of parameters are open arrays and procedures. An open array can be a one-dimensional array of any specified type with no specific bounds. For example, the following might be used to construct a procedure for computing the mean of an unspecified number of real numbers:

```
PROCEDURE mean (X : ARRAY OF REAL) : REAL;
...
RETURN sum/n;
END mean;
```

When a parameter is specified as WORD, it accepts any data type allocated to a single word in memory. An open **ARRAY OF** WORD will accept anything stored in one or more words in memory. This allows the program to access values of different types and is one mechanism by which MODULA-2 enables movement across several levels of abstractions.

In MODULA-2, a procedure may be passed as an argument to another procedure, just as if it were a variable. Procedure types allow us to supply a procedure as a parameter to another procedure. This is not the same thing as, say, using as an argument (actual parameter) a function reference that evaluates to the same type as the formal parameter. There is one built-in procedure type, PROC. This denotes a proper procedure (not a function) that has no parameters. Standard (built-in) procedures may not be used as procedure values. For example, RealFunction := ABS would be an illegal assignment even if RealFunction is defined in exactly the same manner as ABS.

Subprogram libraries. MODULA-2's set of library modules is implementation dependent. It facilitates programming at several levels of abstraction by hiding low-level, machine-dependent details behind the wall of the module. The library stores reusable procedures that will be imported by client modules.

Built-in subprograms. There are various predefined, built-in procedures available. These are called *standard procedures* and *standard functions*. For example, VAL(T,X) is a standard function used for converting variable X to some type T. Some other standard functions are outlined in Table 10.1

In addition, the name of any built-in type can be used as a function name. This is called a *type transfer function*, with which a value of any data type can be treated as if it were of the named data type. An important restriction is that the two types must take up the same amount of storage, and this feature is clearly implementation dependent. For example, to treat an integer variable *i* as a BITSET variable so that it may be assigned to *b* (a true BITSET variable), we can write:

```
b := BITSET (i);
```

No type conversion is actually done, and there is no change in data representation. The same value in storage (in this case, the binary representation of the integer variable *i*) is simply looked at differently (as a WORD of bits). Type transfer functions are sometimes necessary because of MODULA-2's rigorous type-checking mechanism.

TABLE 10.1

	Type of X	Result
INTEGER functions:		
TRUNC (X)	real	integer portion of X
ABS (X)	any integer type	absolute value of X
MAX (X)	any integer type	the maximum value of X's type
MIN (X)	any integer type	the minimum value of X's type
CARDINAL functions:		
ORD (X)	any ordinal type	ordinal value of X
MAX (X)	any integer type	the maximum value of X's type
TRUNC (X)	real	X converted to CARDINAL
REAL functions:		
ABS (X)	real	absolute value of X
FLOAT (X)	CARDINAL or nonnegative INTEGER	X converted to REAL
BOOLEAN functions:		
ODD (X)	integer or CARDINAL	true if X is odd
CAP (X)	CHAR	uppercase character corresponding to X
CHAR function:		
chr (X)	integer	the character represented by the ASCII value X

Among the standard procedures is the HALT for premature termination of a program. The INC and DEC standard procedures accept ordinal arguments and replace Pascal's **pred** and **succ** standard functions. If i is an integer or cardinal type, INC(i) is equivalent to the assignment $i := i + 1$. If i is another ordinal type, INC(i) replaces the value of i with its successor, so it is equivalent to Pascal's succ(i). INC (i,n) replaces the value of i with the *nth* value following it in sequence. DEC(i) land DEC(i,n) accomplish similar actions, but in reverse. The set procedure INCL (EXCL) adds (removes) an element to (from) a set.

Subprogram libraries available. The standard functions and procedures (such as those noted above) are contained in library modules. The library modules facilitate program portability. Information regarding low-level machine dependencies is hidden behind module walls. Some typical library modules handle memory allocation, input/output, file input/output, string processing, process scheduling, and mathematical functions.

Every implementation of MODULA-2 ought to contain a library module called System, which contains entities for low-level programming. These include such entities as the data types ADDRESS and WORD, type transfer functions, and a set of low-level procedures. For example, the function ADR (x) returns the actual machine address of x.

There ought also be a module called Processes for implementing coroutines (logical concurrency), and a library module containing arithmetic functions such as SQRT and the trigonometric functions for mathematical processing.

Since MODULA-2 has not been standardized, there may be significant differences among implementations with regard to these "standard" library modules. Care must be taken in porting programs from one system to another.

Building a subprogram library. In addition to those library modules provided as "standard," a programmer can define new ones and build up an extensive library of modules to suit a particular application or set of applications. If well done, this leads to reusable code. These library modules are compiled separately for later use. Every component of the library is actually stored as two separate modules: a definition module and an implementation module. This splits the information necessary for the user and the implementer (producer) of a module. The definition module merely *specifies* the entities the module will export for use by other modules. These are the data elements and procedures to be externally visible. The source code of this module is available to users of the module and contains information relevant to its use. The implementation module contains the executable code (the "implementation") for the module and any entities not specifically exported. It hides from the user of the module the details of the implementation and other information that is not relevant to its use. The definition module specifies *what* is done; the implementation module specifies *how* it is done.

The **DEFINITION** module is laid out as follows:

```
DEFINITION MODULE <name>;
    FROM <module> IMPORT <import-list>;    (* if necessary *)
    EXPORT QUALIFIED <export-list>;        (* optional: all entities
                                              listed are exported *)
    ...  (* declarations for constants, types, variables exported*)
    PROCEDURE <heading>;                   (* only the heading is
                                              listed here *)
    ...  (* more procedure headings *)
END <name>.
```

Data types declared in a definition module may be opaque. An *opaque type* is one in which the type name is exported and may be used in other modules, but its structure is hidden within the implementation module. This promotes data abstraction. In fact, an abstract data type should always be defined as an opaque type. For example, the definition module may contain the definition: **TYPE** IntegerStack; The full declaration would be in the implementation module only, hidden from the user.

The **IMPLEMENTATION** module is laid out as follows:

```
IMPLEMENTATION MODULE <name>;
    FROM <module> IMPORT <import-list>;    (* if necessary *)
    EXPORT QUALIFIED <export-list>;        (* optional: all entities
                                             are exported *)
    ...         (* declarations *)
    ...         (* full procedure declarations *)
```

```
BEGIN
    ...     (* action statements, if any. These statements are executed
            only once, when the module is imported. They are used to
            initialize variables, invoke initialization procedures,
            etc. *)
END <name>.
```

Program Abstraction

MODULA-2 contains powerful features that support program abstraction. These include: definition and implementation modules, separate compilation, opaque types, and nested internal procedures.

Modular decomposition. Like Pascal, such features as nested subprograms, descriptive subprogram names, and a simple call statement syntax all facilitate modular decomposition of programs. However, the main feature supporting modular decomposition is the module. MODULA-2's modules provide for program entities that have a high degree of cohesion and low coupling. Interaction between modules, which are separately compiled, is limited. The definition modules may be defined early on in the course of a large systems development project and the implementation left to others.

Information hiding. Programmers can take advantage of local variable declarations, the static scoping rule defining the scope of identifiers, and value and variable parameters in order to implement information hiding. Modules facilitate information hiding by protecting, behind the wall of the implementation module, such irrelevant details as the structure of internal variables and procedures and the implementation details of data structures. All the information that a programmer using library modules could possibly need is provided in the definition module. We might say that the separation of definition from implementation modules provides for information on a "need-to-know" basis. Information hiding is also facilitated by MODULA-2's import lists and opaque types.

Self-Documenting Features

MODULA-2 contains many features that encourage writing self-documenting programs.

The flexible rules for formatting program text—the use of comments, blank lines, etc.—do not guarantee that a program will be self-documenting but do go a long way toward allowing a good programmer to write a good, readable, maintainable program. The same holds true for construction of descriptive variable names.

Although programmers (especially beginning programmers) may find the extensive required definitions and declarations to be cumbersome and tedious, they eliminate the need for a lot of comments containing a "data dictionary" and, in the process, force one to document data and other identifiers as part of the program. This applies to import lists as well. The definition module provides documentation for the individual pieces of a large program, and the import lists help to define how these pieces fit together.

Finally, the syntax of the procedure call statement—not having a keyword such as call or perform—allows the programmer to temporarily extend the language itself. The invocation can be coded to look like a built-in language keyword.

10.5 CONTROL STRUCTURES

MODULA-2 inherited virtually all Pascal's control structures—with the notable exception of the **goto** statement—and contains a rich variety of additional control mechanisms. These include a generalized looping structure, external subprograms, separate compilation, coroutines, and interrupt handling.

Operators

Operators are symbols used to form expressions on assignment statements and on conditional control statements.

Arithmetic operators. The arithmetic operators act on numeric operands. These operators include: + (add), - (subtract), * (multiply), / (real division). There are keyword operators for integer division: **DIV** and **MOD**. There is no exponentiation operator. Also, references to standard arithmetic procedures and procedures imported from mathematical library modules may be used. These include such typical functions as: ln, sqrt, abs, sin, etc.

Relational operators. The relational operators act on any scalar-type operand. These include: < (less than); <= (less than or equal to); = (equal to); < >, # (not equal to); >= (greater than or equal to); > (greater than). The set-membership keyword operator **IN** operates only on sets of data.

Logical operators. The logical operators operate on Boolean operands. Logical operators include the keywords **AND**, **OR**, **NOT** and the symbols & and ~ (synonyms for **AND** and **NOT**).

String operators. There are no string operators in MODULA-2. Instead, most implementations provide a library module containing string handling procedures for strings declared as arrays of CHAR.

Set operators. These operate on sets and include + (set union), - (set difference), * (set intersection), and the relational operators **IN** (set membership test), = (equal), # (not equal), <= (subset). Set operators can sometimes be used to simplify coding and enhance readability. For example, compare

```
IF Answer IN {'n', 'N', 'y', 'Y'} THEN …
```

with

```
IF (Answer = 'n') OR (Answer = 'N') OR (Answer = 'y') OR
   (Answer = 'Y') THEN …
```

Expressions

Due to MODULA-2's strong typing facility, expressions are characterized by type. *Arithmetic expressions* result in REAL, INTEGER, or CARDINAL values; *Boolean expressions* result in BOOLEAN values; *set expressions* result in set values.

Constant expressions contain only operands that are constants and result in constants. They may be used wherever a constant is expected, for example: … = **ARRAY**

[1..3 * End - 1] OF ... where End has been previously defined in a **CONST** definition statement.

Mixed-mode expressions are not allowed in MODULA-2. The values combined in an expression must be compatible. This gives the programmer more responsibility and at the same time more control over the data contained within expressions. For example, CARDINAL and INTEGER types must not be mixed. Also, CARDINAL expressions are not allowed to compute to a negative value. Values of a subrange type may be mixed with values of its base type. When mixing types in an expression, there are several standard functions for type conversion. For example, FLOAT converts CARDINAL or nonnegative INTEGER to REAL; TRUNC converts REAL to CARDINAL; ORD converts INTEGER to CARDINAL; and the more general VAL (T,X) returns the value of X converted to any type T.

Expressions are represented in infix, parenthesized form. Operands enclosed within parentheses are evaluated first. Parentheses are used to alter the default sequence control mechanism for evaluating expressions.

There are four levels of precedence in the language. Parentheses are of course evaluated first, and then:

1. **NOT ~**
2. *** / DIV MOD AND &**
3. **+ − OR**
4. the relational operators and **IN**

For a series of operators at the same level of precedence, the processing follows a left-to-right sequence of evaluation. In relational expressions (conditions), evaluation stops as soon as a condition is found that determines the value of the whole expression. This is sometimes called "short-circuit" evaluation of expressions. For example, in the following **IF** statement, if the value of X is 0, the entire condition is TRUE and the rest of the condition need not be evaluated.

```
IF (X=0) OR (A<B) THEN ...
```

Control Statements

The default statement-level control structure is simple sequence: Statements are executed in the sequence in which they are written in the source program. Although this is the default, there are times when simple sequence must be explicitly expressed using a compound statement. Certain statements may alter the default control mechanism or in some way control the execution of program statements.

Unconditional branch. MODULA-2 does not support the generalized unconditional branch, so there is no provision for a **goto** statement or statement label definition. Although some implementations do contain these features as language enhancements, the wide variety of structured control constructs built into the language make the use of the **goto** virtually unnecessary and largely obsolete.

There are some restricted branching statements. These can all be classified as forward branches. The **EXIT** statement is used to break out of a **LOOP** structure. The

RETURN statement can be used to return from a called procedure prematurely. The **HALT** procedure is used to terminate a program, usually when an error is detected.

Selection. The selection control construct is used to choose one of two or more alternative pieces of code.

Two-way selection. The primary language structure for two-way selection is the **IF** statement. It takes the form:

```
IF <conditional-expression> THEN <statement1> ELSE <statement2> END;
```

Statement1 and statement2 may contain a single statement, a procedure invocation, or a sequence of statements. The clause **ELSE** <statement2> is optional. The keyword **ELSE** may be replaced by **ELSEIF**. Using **ELSEIF** "cleans up" the nested-if structure because it eliminates the need for the additional **END** that would be required for each **IF** statement.

Multiway selection. The **CASE** statement is used for selection from among more than two alternatives. It has the general form:

```
CASE <selector-variable> OF
      value1 : statement1; |
      value2 : statement2; |
      ...
      valueN : statementN;
ELSE          statementE;
END
```

The selector variable must be of a scalar, ordinal type (not real or structured). The **ELSE** is used to trap unspecified **CASE** values.

Iteration. There are four language structures for controlling iteration. These correspond to the test-before, test-after, indexed, and generalized looping constructs and implement them in a straightforward manner.

Test-before loop. The test-before loop is implemented with the **WHILE** statement. It takes the form: **WHILE** <boolean-expression> **DO** statement. The Boolean expression may contain arithmetic, relational, and logical operators and computes to a Boolean value (TRUE or FALSE). The <statement> may, as usual, be coded as a single statement, a procedure call, or a sequence of statements (if the body of the loop contains more than a single statement).

Test-after loop. The test-after loop is implemented with the **REPEAT/UNTIL** structure. It takes the general form:

```
REPEAT
      statement1;
      statement2;
      ...
UNTIL <boolean-expression>
```

Indexed loop. The indexed loop is implemented with the **FOR** statement, which takes the following form:

```
FOR <index-variable> := <initial-value> TO <final-value> BY
    <increment>
DO … <statement-sequence> …
END
```

The index variable must be of ordinal type. The increment may not be a variable, it must be a constant or a constant expression. It can be a negative value, in which case the final value ought to be smaller than the initial value. This is less restrictive than Pascal's **for** statement and eliminates the need for the **downto** form.

Other. The LOOP statement is used to form an endless (or, generalized) loop that must be terminated with an **EXIT** statement. The **EXIT** statement terminates the **LOOP** structure in which it appears. The **LOOP** structure looks like this:

```
LOOP
…
IF <loop-terminating-condition> THEN EXIT
…
END;
```

The **LOOP** may be used for situations in which neither a test-after nor a test-before is called for, but where a middle-loop exit is more logical or natural. It is also appropriate for looping constructs that call for multiple exit points. In addition, system-level programming sometimes calls for true endless loops such as code controlling the system clock or monitoring accesses to a variable.

Control over subprograms. All procedures used must be either local procedures contained within the program module or explicitly **IMPORT**ed from the library module in which they were defined.

Call. A procedure is invoked by a "call" statement that contains only the procedure name and any arguments to be associated with the parameters contained within the procedure definition. There is no statement keyword such as call, invoke, or perform. Some sample procedure invocations are:

```
FindMax (A, B, C, Max);
FindSum (ArrayOfReals);
WriteToDisk (NewFile);
```

This form of the procedure call has the advantage of making it look as if a well-named subprogram had actually defined a new language structure. The call statement can then appear to be using a built-in language structure rather than calling a programmer-defined subprogram. In fact, all "I/O statements" are actually procedures defined within I/O library modules.

A function is invoked by referring to it in another statement. A function reference may be used anywhere that a variable of the same type is used.

Return. Return of control to the calling block is implicit at the end of the subprogram. Control is returned when the subprogram is terminated, when it runs through the last executable statement. Also, one or more **RETURN** statements may be used for premature or multiple termination of a procedure. The **RETURN** is also used to return a value from a function procedure.

Control over program execution. Program module execution begins after the delimiter **BEGIN**. There is no explicit "start" statement for beginning program execution. The program terminates when it runs through the final delimiter **END** <program-name>. The **HALT** standard procedure is provided in place of an explicit "stop" statement for terminating program execution.

Subprogram Control Structures

The module structure, along with a variety of library modules usually provided as standard, provide for a powerful array of subprogram control mechanisms.

Simple call. Once defined, subprograms may be invoked explicitly: procedures by a call statement, functions with a function reference. Return may be implicit at termination of the subprogram or explicit with a **RETURN** statement.

Recursion. All procedures and functions may be invoked recursively; they need not be specially declared as recursive subprograms. Both direct and indirect recursion are allowed.

Implicit call. Although the language does not explicitly provide for user-defined run-time interrupts, they may be handled by coroutines programmed as exception handlers. This is done using the standard procedure IOTRANSFER, which installs a coroutine as an interrupt handler for a particular interrupt and then allows the interrupted coroutine to resume. Basically, the exception handler coroutine is suspended until the interrupt occurs at which time it is (re-)activated. This may be done in the following way: The main program creates a coroutine (using the StartProcess procedure); control is TRANSFERred from the main program to the interrupt handler, which may perform initialization statements or procedures; IOTRANSFER is invoked to suspend the interrupt handler until the particular interrupt occurs. The arguments to IOTRANSFER specify the kind of interrupt and the coroutine (process) to resume after the interrupt is "handled."

Parallel processing. Although MODULA-2, through its low-level processing facilities, could be used to implement true concurrency (on a multiprocessing system, for example), the language was designed for use on a single processor. Therefore, the major form of concurrency supported by MODULA-2 is actually quasi-concurrency (multitasking). This is implemented by the coroutine structure. A common source of confusion here is terminology, since the use of the term "process" in the MODULA-2 language definition actually refers to a coroutine.

Coroutines. Coroutines are modules that are executed quasi-concurrently. This is also called "logical" concurrency. Here, there is no "master/slave" relationship. Only one coroutine may have the use of the processor at any one time.

A "process" is defined as a procedure that has a name, no parameters, code, and its own work area, which is static over successive calls ("resume") to the process. This work area will contain the state of the coroutine when it is suspended, local variables, and the coroutine's stack used for procedure calls done while the coroutine is in execution state. It also has a status (executing, suspended, waiting, terminated) and may have a priority. Transfer of control from one coroutine to another is handled explicitly with the TRANS-FER procedure.

The library module Processes exports procedures and other entities (e.g., the SIGNAL type) necessary for programming with coroutines. This module makes use of the low-level facilities of the System library module. The procedure StartProcess uses a programmer-defined procedure to create, initialize, and transfer control to a new process. The procedure SEND (VAR s: SIGNAL) sends a signal to s that all is clear and a waiting coroutine may now resume. The procedure WAIT (VAR s: SIGNAL) suspends the coroutine until another process sends a signal to s. The function AWAITED (VAR s: SIGNAL): BOOLEAN returns the value TRUE if a coroutine is waiting for a signal to s.

The SIGNAL type and its associated procedures, SEND(signal) and WAIT(signal), enable implicit transfer of control between coroutines and also provide a mechanism for control over mutual exclusion. A program module containing coroutines that communicate by means of SEND and WAIT is the MODULA-2 implementation of the "monitor" concept discussed in Chapter 6. As we saw earlier, coroutines may be used to handle run time interrupts.

10.6 PROGRAM DEVELOPMENT

MODULA-2 is a very powerful language with a simple, elegant, and uniform syntactic structure. It is very easy to use, especially for those trained originally in Pascal. The module, while a powerful language structure, is relatively easy to use. Unfortunately, it is also easy to misuse. Care must be taken, for example, in decisions regarding the visibility of entities exported from library modules. Similarly, the structure of types operated on by procedures in library modules ought to be chosen so that they are useful to the largest number of users.

10.7 MORE SAMPLE PROGRAMS

Fig. 10.4 contains the listing of the MODULA-2 solution to Study Problem #2, the sequential file update program, as described in Chapter 7.

The multiple lists creation program, Study Problem #3 (Part A), is listed in Fig. 10.5. Part B is left as an exercise for the reader.

EXERCISES

1. Complete Study Problem #3 (Part B) in MODULA-2.
2. Do Study Problem #4 in MODULA-2.

```
MODULE Update;

    (*******************************************************)
    (*                                                     *)
    (*        IMPORTS FROM LIBRARY MODULES                 *)
    (*                                                     *)
    (*******************************************************)

FROM FIO IMPORT File, EOF,
            Open, Close, Create,
            RdStr, WrStr, WrLn, WrCard, WrChar, WrCharRep;
FROM Str IMPORT Compare;

    (*******************************************************)
    (*                                                     *)
    (*    G L O B A L    D E C L A R A T I O N S           *)
    (*                                                     *)
    (*******************************************************)

CONST
    MaxTrans                     =    50;

TYPE
    IDType                       =    ARRAY [1..9] OF CHAR;
    CharSet                      =    SET OF CHAR;
    CodeType                     =    CHAR;
    EmployeeRecType              =    RECORD
        Key                      :      IDType;
        OtherInfo                :      ARRAY [1..112] OF CHAR;
                                      END;
    TransRecType                 =    RECORD
        Rec                      :      EmployeeRecType;
        Code                     :      CodeType
                                      END;
    ErrorlineType                =    RECORD
        ID                       :      IDType;
        Code                     :      CodeType;
        Error                    :      ARRAY [1..10] OF CHAR;
                                      END;
    EndOfFile                    =    RECORD
        Master                   :      BOOLEAN;
        Transaction              :      BOOLEAN;
                                      END;

VAR
    Eof                          :    EndOfFile;
    Ntrans, Nerrors, NumOK       :    CARDINAL;
    Nadds, Ndeletes, Nchanges    :    CARDINAL;
    MasterRec                    :    EmployeeRecType;
    MasterFile,NewMasterFile     :    File;
    Trans                        :    TransRecType;
```

Figure 10.4 Update program (continued next page)

```
TransFile                       :   File;
Errorline                       :   ARRAY [1..MaxTrans] OF ErrorlineType;

    (****************************************************)
    (*                                                *)
    (*       R E A D   1   R E C O R D               *)
    (*                                                *)
    (****************************************************)

PROCEDURE ReadMasterRecord;
VAR endlin                      :   ARRAY [1..50] OF CHAR;
BEGIN
    WITH MasterRec DO
        RdStr (MasterFile, Key);
        RdStr (MasterFile, OtherInfo);
    END;
    RdStr (MasterFile, endlin);
    IF EOF THEN
       Eof.Master := TRUE
    END;
END ReadMasterRecord;

PROCEDURE ReadTransRecord;
VAR endlin                      :   ARRAY [1..50] OF CHAR;
BEGIN
    WITH Trans DO
        WITH Rec DO
            RdStr (TransFile, Key);
            RdStr (TransFile, OtherInfo);
        END;
        RdStr (TransFile, Code);
    END;
    RdStr (TransFile, endlin);
    Ntrans := Ntrans + 1;
    IF EOF THEN
       Eof.Transaction := TRUE
    END;
END ReadTransRecord;

    (****************************************************)
    (*                                                *)
    (*       W R I T E   1   R E C O R D             *)
    (*                                                *)
    (****************************************************)

PROCEDURE WriteFrom (NewRecord : EmployeeRecType);
BEGIN
    WITH NewRecord DO
        WrStr (NewMasterFile, Key);
        WrStr (NewMasterFile, OtherInfo);
```

Figure 10.4   (continued next page)

```
        END;
        WrLn (NewMasterFile);
END WriteFrom;

    (****************************************************)
    (*                                                  *)
    (*        I N I T I A L I Z A T I O N               *)
    (*   OPEN FILES, INITIAL VALUES, INITIAL READS     *)
    (*                                                  *)
    (****************************************************)

PROCEDURE Initialize;
BEGIN
        MasterFile := Open ("A:IDPRSNEL.DAT");
        TransFile := Open ("A:TRANS.DAT");
        NewMasterFile := Create ("A:UPDATE.DAT");
        Eof.Master := FALSE;
        Eof.Transaction := FALSE;
        Ntrans := 0;
        Nerrors := 0;
        Nadds := 0;
        Nchanges := 0;
        Ndeletes := 0;
        ReadMasterRecord;
        ReadTransRecord
END Initialize;

    (****************************************************)
    (*                                                  *)
    (*        A D D    A    R E C O R D                 *)
    (*                                                  *)
    (****************************************************)

PROCEDURE AddRecord;

    PROCEDURE ErrorInA;
    BEGIN
        Nerrors := Nerrors + 1;
        WITH Errorline [Nerrors] DO
            ID := Trans.Rec.Key;
            Code := Trans.Code;
            IF Trans.Code = ' '
                THEN Error := 'missing'
                ELSE Error := 'not A '
            END; (* if *)
        END; (* with *)
    END ErrorInA;

    BEGIN
```

Figure 10.4   (continued next page)

```
        IF Trans.Code = 'A' THEN
            WriteFrom (Trans.Rec);
            Nadds := Nadds + 1
        ELSE
            ErrorInA
        END;
END AddRecord;

    (**************************************************)
    (*                                              *)
    (*   C H A N G E / D E L E T E    R E C O R D   *)
    (*                                              *)
    (**************************************************)

PROCEDURE ChangeOrDelete;

    PROCEDURE ErrorInCD;
    BEGIN
        Nerrors := Nerrors + 1;
        WITH Errorline [Nerrors] DO
                ID := Trans.Rec.Key;
                Code := Trans.Code;
                IF Trans.Code = ' '
                    THEN Error := 'missing'
                    ELSE Error := 'not C or D'
                END;
            END  (* with *)
    END ErrorInCD;

    PROCEDURE ChangeRecord;
    BEGIN
        MasterRec := Trans.Rec
    END ChangeRecord;

BEGIN
    IF NOT (Trans.Code IN CharSet {'C', 'D'})
        THEN
            ErrorInCD;
            WriteFrom (MasterRec)
        ELSE IF Trans.Code = 'C'
                THEN
                    ChangeRecord;
                    WriteFrom (MasterRec);
                    Nchanges := Nchanges + 1
                ELSE
                    Ndeletes := Ndeletes + 1;
            END;
    END;
    ReadMasterRecord
END ChangeOrDelete;
```

Figure 10.4   (continued next page)

```
(******************************************************)
(*                                                    *)
(*  U P D A T E    P R O C E S S    C O N T R O L     *)
(*                                                    *)
(******************************************************)

PROCEDURE ProcessControl;

BEGIN
    IF Compare (Trans.Rec.Key , MasterRec.Key) = 1
        THEN
            WriteFrom (MasterRec);
            ReadMasterRecord
        ELSE
            IF Trans.Rec.Key = MasterRec.Key
                THEN ChangeOrDelete
                ELSE AddRecord;          (* ie, Tkey < Mkey *)
            END;
            ReadTransRecord
    END;
END ProcessControl;

    (******************************************************)
    (*                                                    *)
    (*          E N D    P R O C E S S I N G              *)
    (*                                                    *)
    (******************************************************)

PROCEDURE EndTrans;
BEGIN
    WHILE NOT Eof.Master DO
        WriteFrom (MasterRec);
        ReadMasterRecord
    END; (* while *)
END EndTrans;

PROCEDURE EndMaster;
BEGIN
    WHILE NOT Eof.Transaction DO
        AddRecord;
        ReadTransRecord
    END; (* while *)
END EndMaster;

    (******************************************************)
    (*                                                    *)
    (*          P R I N T E D    R E P O R T              *)
    (*                                                    *)
    (******************************************************)

PROCEDURE PrintReport;
```

Figure 10.4 (continued next page)

```
CONST
    Space               =   ' ';
    Underline           =   '-----------------------------------------------';
    MsgLit              =   'Transaction Code is ';

VAR
    Lstr                :   File;
    J                   :   CARDINAL;

    PROCEDURE SkipLines (N: CARDINAL);
    BEGIN
        FOR J := 1 TO N DO
            WrLn (Lstr)
        END;
    END SkipLines;

    PROCEDURE CR;
    BEGIN
        WrLn (Lstr);
    END CR;

    PROCEDURE Tab (N: CARDINAL);
    BEGIN
        WrCharRep (Lstr, Space,N)
    END Tab;

BEGIN
    Lstr := Open ('CON');              (* can change to 'CON' or 'PRN' *)
    Ntrans := Ntrans - 1;
    NumOK := Ntrans - Nerrors;
    Tab(15); WrStr (Lstr, 'Sequential File Update');CR;
    Tab(13); WrStr (Lstr, 'Personnel File Maintenance'); CR;
    Tab(5); WrStr (Lstr, Underline);CR;
    SkipLines (2);
    Tab(14); WrStr (Lstr, 'Total number of transactions = ');
    WrCard (Lstr, Ntrans, 5);CR;
    Tab(7); WrStr (Lstr, 'Transactions processed successfully = ');
    WrCard (Lstr, NumOK, 5); CR;
    SkipLines (2);
    Tab(2); WrStr (Lstr,
               'The following transactions could not be processed ');CR;
    Tab(2); WrStr (Lstr, 'due to errors:');CR;
    SkipLines (2);
    WrStr (Lstr, 'ID Number   Trans. Code    Error    '); CR;
    WrStr (Lstr, '---------   -----------    -----    '); CR;
    SkipLines (2);
    FOR J := 1 TO Nerrors DO
        WITH Errorline[J] DO
            WrStr (Lstr, ID); Tab(8);
            WrChar (Lstr, Code); Tab(10);
```

Figure 10.4   (continued next page)

```
              WrStr (Lstr, MsgLit);
              WrStr (Lstr, Error);CR;
        END;
      END;
      Tab(5); WrStr (Lstr, Underline);CR;
      SkipLines (4);
      Tab(10); WrCard (Lstr, Nadds,5);
      WrStr (Lstr, '   records added to Master File'); CR;
      SkipLines (2);
      Tab(10); WrCard (Lstr, Ndeletes,5);
      WrStr (Lstr, '   records deleted from Master File'); CR;
      SkipLines (2);
      Tab(10); WrCard (Lstr, Nchanges,5);
      WrStr (Lstr, '   records changed');CR;
   END PrintReport;

   (*****************************************************)
   (*                                                 *)
   (*              C L O S I N G                      *)
   (*                                                 *)
   (*****************************************************)

PROCEDURE Closing;
BEGIN
      Close (MasterFile);
      Close (TransFile);
      Close (NewMasterFile);
END Closing;

   (*****************************************************)
   (*                                                 *)
   (*    M A I N   P R O G R A M   EXECUTION BEGINS   *)
   (*                                                 *)
   (*****************************************************)

BEGIN
      Initialize;
      WHILE NOT Eof.Transaction DO
          IF Eof.Master
              THEN EndMaster
              ELSE ProcessControl;
          END;
      END;
      EndTrans;
      PrintReport;
      Closing;
END Update.
```

Figure 10.4   (concluded)

```
MODULE MultList;

                (****************************************************)
                (*                                                  *)
                (*          IMPORTS FROM LIBRARY MODULES            *)
                (*                                                  *)
                (****************************************************)

FROM FIO IMPORT File, EOF,
                Open, Close,
                RdStr, WrStr, WrLn, WrCharRep;
FROM Str IMPORT Compare;
FROM Storage IMPORT ALLOCATE;

                (****************************************************)
                (*                                                  *)
                (*    G L O B A L    D E C L A R A T I O N S        *)
                (*                                                  *)
                (****************************************************)

TYPE
                                        (* values used for "next" pointers  *)
        ListType                =   (EMPLIST, JOBLIST, LOCLIST, DEPTLIST);
                                        (* values used for "first" pointers *)
        SubListType             =   (EMPLOYEE,
                                     ANALYST, CLERK, DESIGNER, MANAGER,
                                     A, B, C, D,
                                     MTS, PROD, RAND);
        JobTitleType            =   [ANALYST..MANAGER];
        LocType                 =   [A..D];
        DeptType                =   [MIS..RAND];
        EmployeeRecType         =   RECORD
            ID                  :       ARRAY [1..9] OF CHAR;
            Name                :       ARRAY [1..21] OF CHAR;
            OtherInfo1          :       ARRAY [1..62] OF CHAR;
            Job                 :       ARRAY [1..8] OF CHAR;
            Loc                 :       CHAR;
            Dept                :       ARRAY [1..4] OF CHAR;
            OtherInfo2          :       ARRAY [1..16] OF CHAR;
                                    END;
        EmployeeNodePointer     =   POINTER TO EmployeeNodeType;
        EmployeeNodeType        =   RECORD
            Employee            :       EmployeeRecType;
            NextIn              :       ARRAY ListType OF EmployeeNodePointer;
                                    END;
VAR
        List                    :   ListType;
        SubList                 :   SubListType;
        JobTitle                :   JobTitleType;
        Location                :   LocType;
```

Figure 10.5   Multiple lists creation program (continued next page)

```
Department                     :    DeptType;
                                              (* pointer to "current" node *)
P                              :    EmployeeNodePointer;
                                          (* external pointers head sublists *)
FirstIn                        :    ARRAY SubListType OF EmployeeNodePointer;


        (****************************************************)
        (*                                                *)
        (*         I N I T I A L I Z A T I O N S          *)
        (*                                                *)
        (****************************************************)
PROCEDURE InitializeEmptyLists;
BEGIN
    FirstIn [EMPLOYEE] := NIL;
    FOR JobTitle := ANALYST TO MANAGER DO
        FirstIn [JobTitle] := NIL;
    END;
    FOR Location := A TO D DO
        FirstIn [Location] := NIL;
    END;
    FOR Department := MIS TO RAND DO
        FirstIn [Department] := NIL;
    END;
END InitializeEmptyLists;

        (****************************************************)
        (*                                                *)
        (*   I N S E R T   N O D E   IN  A  L I S T       *)
        (*                                                *)
        (****************************************************)

PROCEDURE Insert (P: EmployeeNodePointer; List: ListType; SubList: SubListType);
VAR
   J, Q                :    EmployeeNodePointer;

BEGIN
    IF FirstIn[SubList] = NIL
       THEN                                    (* insert into empty list *)
           FirstIn[SubList] := P;
           P^.NextIn[List] := NIL
       ELSE IF Compare (FirstIn[SubList]^.Employee.ID,  P^.Employee.ID) = 1
               THEN                            (* insert in front of list *)
                   P^.NextIn[List] := FirstIn [SubList];
                   FirstIn [SubList] := P
               ELSE                            (* find insertion point Q *)
                   J := FirstIn[SubList]^.NextIn[List];
                   Q := FirstIn[SubList];
                   WHILE J <> NIL DO
```

Figure 10.5   (continued next page)

```
                        IF Compare (J^.Employee.ID, P^.Employee.ID) = 1
                            THEN J := NIL
                            ELSE
                                Q := J;
                                J := J^.NextIn[List]
                        END;
                  END;
                                                    (* insert P after Q *)
                  P^.NextIn[List] := Q^.NextIn[List];
                  Q^.NextIn[List] := P
            END;
        END;
END Insert;

        (***************************************************)
        (*                                               *)
        (*  A D D   N O D E  -  PLACE IN ALL SUBLISTS    *)
        (*                                               *)
        (***************************************************)

PROCEDURE AddEmployee (EmployeeInRec:  EmployeeRecType);

    PROCEDURE JobTitle (EmployeeInRec : EmployeeRecType) : JobTitleType;
    BEGIN
        CASE EmployeeInRec.Job[1] OF       (* It happens that all "Job"s*)
                                           (* begin with                *)
            | 'A'  :    RETURN  ANALYST;   (* a different first letter  *)
            | 'C'  :    RETURN CLERK;
            | 'D'  :    RETURN DESIGNER;
            | 'M'  :    RETURN MANAGER;
        END;
    END JobTitle;

    PROCEDURE Location (EmployeeInRec : EmployeeRecType) : LocType;
    BEGIN
        CASE EmployeeInRec.Loc OF
            | 'A'  :    RETURN A;
            | 'B'  :    RETURN B;
            | 'C'  :    RETURN C;
            | 'D'  :    RETURN D;
        END;
    END Location;

    PROCEDURE Department (EmployeeInRec : EmployeeRecType) : DeptType;
    BEGIN
        CASE EmployeeInRec.Dept[1] OF       (* It happens that          *)
                                            (* all "Dept"s begin with   *)
            | 'M'  :    RETURN MIS;         (* a different first letter *)
            | 'P'  :    RETURN PROD;
            | 'R'  :    RETURN RAND;
        END;
    END Department;
```

Figure 10.5   (continued next page)

```
BEGIN
     NEW(P);
     P^.Employee := EmployeeInRec;
     Insert (P, EMPLIST, EMPLOYEE);
     Insert (P, JOBLIST, JobTitle (EmployeeInRec) );
     Insert (P, LOCLIST, Location (EmployeeInRec) );
     Insert (P, DEPTLIST, Department (EmployeeInRec) );
END AddEmployee;

          (****************************************************)
          (*                                                  *)
          (*     C R E A T E    MULTILINKED    L I S T        *)
          (*                                                  *)
          (****************************************************)

PROCEDURE CreateLists;
VAR
   EmployeeInRec        :    EmployeeRecType;
   EmployeeFile         :    File;

     PROCEDURE ReadInputRecord;
     VAR endlin        :    ARRAY [1..50] OF CHAR;
     BEGIN
          WITH EmployeeInRec DO
               RdStr (EmployeeFile, ID);
               RdStr (EmployeeFile, Name);
               RdStr (EmployeeFile, OtherInfo1);
               RdStr (EmployeeFile, Job);
               RdStr (EmployeeFile, Loc);
               RdStr (EmployeeFile, Dept);
               RdStr (EmployeeFile, OtherInfo2);
               RdStr (EmployeeFile, endlin);
          END;
     END ReadInputRecord;

BEGIN
     EmployeeFile := Open ("A:NMPRSNEL.DAT");
     ReadInputRecord;
     WHILE NOT EOF DO
          AddEmployee (EmployeeInRec);
          ReadInputRecord;
     END;
     Close (EmployeeFile);
END CreateLists;
```

Figure 10.5   (continued next page)

```
        (****************************************************)
        (*                                                  *)
        (*          P R I N T E D   R E P O R T             *)
        (*                                                  *)
        (****************************************************)

PROCEDURE PrintReport;
CONST
    Space               =   ' ';
    UnderLine           =   '-------------------------------------------';

TYPE
    String8             =   ARRAY [1..8] OF CHAR;
    String4             =   ARRAY [1..4] OF CHAR;

VAR
    Lstr                :   File;

    PROCEDURE JobTitleOut    (JobName: JobTitleType): String8;
    BEGIN
        CASE JobName OF
            | ANALYST  :   RETURN 'Analyst';
            | CLERK    :   RETURN 'Clerk';
            | DESIGNER :   RETURN 'Designer';
            | MANAGER  :   RETURN 'Manager'
        END
    END JobTitleOut;

    PROCEDURE LocationOut (LocName: LocType): CHAR;
    BEGIN
        CASE LocName OF
            | A  :    RETURN 'A';
            | B  :    RETURN 'B';
            | C  :    RETURN 'C';
            | D  :    RETURN 'D'
        END;
    END LocationOut;

    PROCEDURE DepartmentOut (DeptName: DeptType): String4;
    BEGIN
        CASE DeptName OF
            | MIS  :   RETURN 'MIS';
            | PROD :   RETURN 'Prod';
            | RAND :   RETURN 'R&D'
        END
    END DepartmentOut;

    PROCEDURE SkipLines (N: CARDINAL);
    VAR J               :   CARDINAL;
    BEGIN
        FOR J := 1 TO N DO
```

Figure 10.5   (continued next page)

```
                    WrLn (Lstr)
            END;
        END SkipLines;

        PROCEDURE Tab (N : CARDINAL);
        BEGIN
            WrCharRep (Lstr, Space, N);
        END Tab;

        PROCEDURE CR;
        BEGIN
            WrLn (Lstr)
        END CR;

        PROCEDURE PrintHeadings (ListHead, SubList : ARRAY OF CHAR);
        BEGIN
            SkipLines(5);
            Tab(30); WrStr (Lstr, 'Multiple Sublists'); CR;
            SkipLines(3);
            Tab(25); WrStr (Lstr,'Listing for '); WrStr (Lstr, ListHead);
                    Tab(1); WrStr (Lstr, SubList); CR;
            Tab(15); WrStr (Lstr, UnderLine); CR;
            SkipLines(2)
        END PrintHeadings;

        PROCEDURE PrintDetailLines (List: ListType; SubList: SubListType);
        VAR P              :    EmployeeNodePointer;
        BEGIN
            P := FirstIn [SubList];
            WHILE P <> NIL DO
                WITH P^.Employee DO
                    Tab(10); WrStr (Lstr, ID); Tab(10);
                    WrStr (Lstr, Name); CR;
                END;
                P := P^.NextIn [List];
            END;
        END PrintDetailLines;

BEGIN
    Lstr := Open ('PRN');              (* CON for console, PRN for printer *)
    FOR JobTitle := ANALYST TO MANAGER DO
        PrintHeadings ('Jobtitle', JobTitleOut (JobTitle) );
        PrintDetailLines (JOBLIST, JobTitle);
    END;
    FOR Location := A TO D DO
        PrintHeadings ('Location', LocationOut (Location) );
        PrintDetailLines (LOCLIST, Location);
    END;
    FOR Department := MIS TO RAND DO
        PrintHeadings ('Deptment', DepartmentOut (Department) );
```

Figure 10.5   (continued next page)

```
          PrintDetailLines (DEPTLIST, Department);
       END;
    END PrintReport;


          (*************************************************)
          (*                                             *)
          (*       MAIN PROGRAM EXECUTION BEGINS HERE    *)
          (*                                             *)
          (*************************************************)
BEGIN
    InitializeEmptyLists;
    CreateLists;
    PrintReport;
END MultList.
```

Figure 10.5   (concluded)

SUGGESTIONS FOR FURTHER STUDY

Manuals.   There is no universally accepted standard language definition, but the *de facto* standard is contained in Wirth's *Programming in Modula-2* (1985). The Top-Speed Modula-2 manuals are JPI (1988) and King (1988).

Books.   Adams *et al.* (1988), Cooling (1988), McCracken and Salmon (1987), Moore and McKay (1987), Stubbs and Webre (1987), Thomas *et al.* (1988), Wiatrowski and Wiener (1987), Wiener and Sincovec (1984).

Chapters in Books.   Smedema *et al.* (1983), Chapter 3: "Modula," pp. 39–65; Tucker (1986), Chapter 14: "Modula-2," pp. 507–548.

Articles.   Wirth (1979, 1984). Also, see the entire August 1984 issue of *Byte*.

— 11 —

C Language Elements

C is a high-level systems programming language. The name C does not "stand for" anything, but simply indicates that this language was derived from another systems programming language called B. The 1970s and 1980s have witnessed the ever-increasing popularity of microcomputers; along with it, the enthusiasm for a portable operating system (UNIX) and for its programming language (C) has increased in lockstep.

C bears some resemblance to MODULA-2 in that it is also a small, high-level systems programming language. The similarity, however, ends there. C, which predates MODULA-2, was developed at about the same time as Pascal and was not influenced by it. If C and MODULA-2 are at all syntactically similar it is probably because they share a common ancestor in ALGOL60.

11.1 A BRIEF OVERVIEW OF C

C is a concise language—it has only about 30 keywords—and it encourages concise code. Programs written in C cannot, by any stretch of the imagination, be called self-documenting.

C is flexible, powerful, and well suited for programming at several levels of abstraction. Programs written in C may be, like assembly, extremely economical and, unlike assembly, highly portable.

C is a modular language. The function is the primary program structure, but functions may not be nested. The C programmer depends on a library of functions, many of which have become part of the standard language definition. There is a preprocessing step that provides for text substitution for macros, inclusion of functions in other files (similar to MODULA-2's IMPORT), and conditional compilation (similar to conditional assembly).

374

C is weakly typed, allowing quite a bit of data conversion and providing minimal run time checking. As such it does not protect programmers from themselves. It is not "dummy-proof" and definitely not for the novice programmer. Even for professional programmers, the learning curve for C is relatively slow.

History and Development

Although the history of C is closely tied to that of the UNIX operating system, C's line of development as a programming language can be traced all the way back to ALGOL60. In 1967, Martin Richards, in Cambridge, developed the systems programming language BCPL, which was heavily influenced by CPL (developed in 1963), which in turn had been influenced by ALGOL60. BCPL (British Combined Programming Language) was designed as a "typeless" language—that is, the basic data type was the machine word, and operations relied heavily on address arithmetic. Meanwhile UNIX was designed in 1969 at Bell Laboratories as an alternative to the Multics operating system for the DEC® PDP-7, and was coded in assembler.

In 1970, Bell Laboratories' Ken Thompson designed the language B, basing it on BCPL; B was also a "typeless" language. The UNIX system was then written in B. In 1972, Dennis Ritchie enriched B with many of the data types and high-level operations of ALGOL that had been removed from the language. The resulting programming language, called (naturally) C, was implemented in 1972 on a PDP-11. In 1973, an extended and improved UNIX system was recoded, over 90 percent of it in C language code. This made UNIX the first "portable" operating system.

As the microcomputer revolution of the 1970s gained momentum, many new computers were brought quickly to market, and many of these computer manufacturers found the UNIX operating system very appealing. Applications for the UNIX environment increased, and C's close ties to UNIX meant that its popularity was on the rise as well. In the mid 1970s, C received an additional boost when UNIX was introduced to the academic computing environment at a number of universities, and the C compiler was included free of charge.

The book written by Kernighan and Ritchie in 1978, *The C Programming Language*, served for years as the *de facto* C language standard (Kernighan and Ritchie 1978, 1988). An ANSI committee was formed in 1983 to produce a standard machine-independent language definition that would still retain the spirit of C while eliminating some of its more glaring problems. This committee produced a draft standard language definition in 1987 (ANSI 1988), which was approved in 1988.

Application Areas

Although C is a general-purpose language, it is primarily used for systems programming. And, although compilers are available for a wide variety of computers, C is primarily used for microcomputer applications. This emphasis may be shifting slightly now, as more mainframe- and supercomputer-based systems come into the UNIX/C brood. C is very popular for the development of packaged, off-the-shelf application software including database, text processing, and various numerical applications. For example: the SAS and dBase III packages are coded in C; some of the computer-animated sequences in the

Star Wars and Star Trek movies were coded in C. The C language is also used for real-time processing systems.

Classification

Software generation: Third

Procedural/declarative: Procedural

Translator: Compiler

Processing environment: Batch processing

Programming paradigm: Imperative

11.2 STUDY PROBLEM #1: BUBBLE SORT PROGRAM

Let us now examine a complete C program. Fig. 11.1 contains the listing for the bubble sort program coded in C. Notice that comments are contained within the paired delimiters /* and */ and a compound statement is contained within a set of curly braces, { }. A semicolon terminates every statement. All subprograms are functions and must therefore have a declared type. A function that does not return any value (called a procedure in some other languages) is typed as **void**. There must be in every program one function named **main**. This is the entry point for program execution.

The preprocessor definitions at the beginning of the program are used in place of the constant declaration facilities of Pascal and MODULA-2. The **#define** causes one character string in the program text to be consistently replaced by another during translation.

As in MODULA-2, a C program handles input and output by means of library I/O functions. These are defined in the "stdio.h" header file. I/O in C is at least as cumbersome as it is in MODULA-2, perhaps even more so.

This program and the others presented in this chapter were run using Borland International's Turbo C™ on an IBM PC/XT.

11.3 DATA: TYPES, FILES, AND DATA STRUCTURES

C is a weakly typed language. Although declarations must be explicit, the language provides the programmer a great deal of leeway in data conversion and pointer assignment and arithmetic. Type checking or any run time checking is minimal, if present at all. In C, the programmer is in complete control. Compared to the more restrictive nature of, say, Pascal or MODULA-2, this can be a very heady experience. In the hands of a good programmer, the code produced can be concise and efficient; in less careful hands, this freedom can give a programmer just enough rope to hang himself.

Memory management is dynamic. Besides declaring variables as simply global or local, there are four storage classes in C: external, automatic, static, and register.

```
/****************************************************
**                                                **
**    B U B B L E   S O R T   P R O G R A M    **
**                                                **
****************************************************/

/*   Include Files   */

# include "stdio.h"
# include "string.h"

/*   Preprocessor Definitions   */

# define TRUE    1
# define FALSE   0
# define MAXRECS 150

/*   Global Declarations   */

typedef struct {
          char ID[10];
          char OtherInfo[113];
        } EmpRec;
EmpRec Employee[MAXRECS];

/*   Function Prototypes   */

int LoadFile();
void Swap (int Indx1, int Indx2);
void BubbleSort (int N);
void WriteFile (int N);
void SkipLines (FILE *Listr, int L);
void PrintReport (int N);


/****************************************************
**                                                **
**    F U N C T I O N    L O A D F I L E        **
**                                                **
**    reads the input file into an array          **
**                                                **
**    returns N, 1 less than the # records read,  **
**    i.e., records are indexed from 0 to N-1     **
**                                                **
****************************************************/

int LoadFile()
{
    FILE *ByName;
    char endlin[];
      int N=0;
    ByName = fopen ("A:NMPRSNEL.DAT", "rt");
      fgets (Employee[N].ID, 10, ByName);
      while (!feof(ByName))    {
          fgets (Employee[N].OtherInfo, 113, ByName);
```

Figure 11.1 Bubble sort program (continued next page)

```
                fgets (endlin, 10, ByName);
                N++;
                fgets (Employee[N].ID, 10, ByName);
                }
        fclose (ByName);
        N--;
        return (N);
}    /*  End LoadFile */


/***************************************************
**                                               **
**   P R O C E D U R E    B U B B L E S O R T    **
**                                               **
**   uses procedure Swap                         **
**                                               **
***************************************************/

void Swap (int Indx1, int Indx2)
{
        EmpRec Temp = Employee[Indx1];
        Employee[Indx1] = Employee[Indx2];
        Employee[Indx2] = Temp;
}    /*   end Swap   */

void BubbleSort (int N)
{
        int R, Limit = N-1;
        int Sorted = FALSE;
        while (!Sorted) {
            Sorted = TRUE;
            for (R=0; R; R++)
                if (strcmp (Employee[R].ID, Employee[R+1].ID) > 0 ) {
                    Swap (R, R+1);
                    Sorted = FALSE;
                    }
            Limit--;
            }
}    /* end BubbleSort   */


/***************************************************
**                                               **
**   P R O C E D U R E    W R I T E F I L E      **
**                                               **
**   writes sorted records to a disk file        **
**                                               **
***************************************************/

void WriteFile (int N)
{
```

Figure 11.1   (continued next page)

```
    FILE *ByID;
    int R;
    ByID = fopen ("A:IDPRSNEL.DAT", "wt");
    for (R=0; R <= N; R++) {
        fputs (Employee[R].ID, ByID);
        fputs (Employee[R].OtherInfo, ByID);
        fputs ("\n", ByID);
        }
    fclose (ByID);
}    /*   end WriteFile   */


/*************************************************
**                                             **
**   P R O C E D U R E   P R I N T R E P O R T  **
**                                             **
**   uses procedure SkipLines                  **
**                                             **
*************************************************/

void SkipLines (FILE *Listr, int L)
{
    int R;
    for (R=1; R<L; R++)
        fprintf (Listr, "\n");
}    /*   end SkipLines   */

void PrintReport(N)
{
    FILE *Listr;
    char Space = ' ';

    Listr = fopen ("CON", "w");       /*  CON or PRN  */
    SkipLines(Listr,5);
    fprintf (Listr, "%20c Bubble Sort Report \n", Space);
    fprintf (Listr, "%20c ------------------ \n", Space);
    SkipLines(Listr,2);
    fprintf (Listr, "%5c Number of records read from input file -- \n", Space);
    fprintf (Listr, "%10c NMPRSNEL File -- %5d\n", Space, N+1);
    SkipLines(Listr,2);
    fprintf (Listr, "%5c Number of records written to output file -- \n", Space);
    fprintf (Listr, "%10c IDPRSNEL File -- %5d\n", Space, N+1);
    SkipLines(Listr,2);
    fprintf (Listr, "%5c Bubble Sort completed successfully \n", Space);
    SkipLines(Listr,5);
    fclose (Listr);
}    /*   end PrintReport   */
```

Figure 11.1   (continued next page)

```
/*****************************************************
**                                                 **
**          M   A   I   N                          **
**                                                 **
**     program execution begins here               **
**                                                 **
*****************************************************/
void main ()
{
    int N;
    N = LoadFile();
    BubbleSort (N);
    WriteFile (N);
    PrintReport(N);
}    /*  End Program   */
```

Figure 11.1   (concluded)

Constants

Literals.   Literals may be values of a wide variety of numeric and nonnumeric types. A *numeric literal* may be an integer or a floating-point number.

An *integer literal* consists of a sequence of digits and an optional plus or minus sign. If followed by an L, the integer is designated as *long*. If prefixed by zero or 0X, it is designated as an *octal* or *hexadecimal integer*, respectively. For example, the following shows a number of ways that the decimal integer 127 might be used as a literal in a program:

```
integer                 127
long integer            127L
octal integer           0177
hexadecimal integer     0X7F
```

A *floating-point literal* is represented by a sequence of integers and, optionally, a plus or minus sign, a decimal point, and/or an E. A floating-point number can be represented by a decimal integer or by such literals as 127.5 or 1.275E + 2. Such a floating-point literal would be stored using double precision. To specify singly, an F is suffixed to the numeric literal.

A *nonnumeric literal* may be a single character or a character string. A *character literal* is represented by a single character (usually, from the ASCII character set) enclosed in single quotation marks, for example, 'c'. Certain nonprintable characters may also be represented, using the backslash as an escape character, for example: '\n' (newline); '\t' (tab); '\0' (Null); '\b' (blank); '\r' (return); '\f' (formfeed). A *string literal* is a sequence of one or more characters enclosed in double quotation marks. For example, "I am a string literal".

If an *enumerated* type variable is declared, values from that type may also be used as literals.

Named constants. The C language definition contains no symbolic constants. Some are, however, predefined in the standard library header files using the #define preprocessor directive.

User-defined constants. The preprocessor directive #define may be used to define constants in C. This is similar to but not exactly the same as Pascal's const statement. Using this facility, a constant identifier and its value may be defined, and the C compiler will perform text substitution everywhere the constant name is used. For example,

```
#define    FALSE    0
#define    TRUE     1
#define    PI       3.1416
```

The library header file stdio.h may be expected to contain some predefined symbolic constants, such as #define EOF -1 and #define NULL 0. NULL is used by C much as nil is in Pascal to indicate an uninitialized pointer.

Variables

Variables are programmer-defined identifiers that represent data values and are subject to change during execution of the program. Much of what is said about variables in C may also be applied to functions. For example, functions have an identifier name, a type, a storage class, and they may be explicitly declared.

Variable declaration. Variable names must be declared prior to use.

Explicit declaration. Variables may be declared in explicit declaration statements, which indicate type and storage class and, optionally, an initial value. These statements, which may be within a block or outside of any function in a file, take the form:

```
<storage class> <type> <variable list>;
```

Implicit declaration. A variable declared outside of any function is taken to have storage class external (global); a variable declared within a function is, by default, automatic (local). Statement labels may be used without declaration. Functions may be declared implicitly.

Initialization. There are no default initial values for variables and uninitialized variables will not be flagged either at compile or run time. Variables may be initialized either by simple assignment statements or when they are declared as, for example:

```
int K = 0;
```

A program or function that uses several accumulators may initialize all of them in a multiple assignment statement such as:

```
V = W = X = Y = Z = 0;
```

Storage classes. There are four possible storage classes in C. These are **automatic**, **static**, **register**, and **external**.

External variables are allocated permanent storage and retain their values throughout program execution. They are somewhat equivalent to global variables in other languages. Any variable declared outside of any function in a file is by default considered to be external to the functions in the file and need not be explicitly declared as such.

The other three storage classes may be considered three variations of local variables. *Automatic* is the default storage class for variables declared within the function or block in which it is used. *Static* variables are similar to local variables except that they are allocated permanent storage. They retain their values throughout execution of the program even between calls to the function in which they are declared. A variable declared as *register* is a request to storage in a fast register. This request may not be granted if no such register is available, but in that case, the storage class reverts to automatic. Register variables may be declared as **int** or **char** only.

Built-in types. The basic types of C are **int**eger, **float**ing point, and **char**acter. Integer type may be further qualified as **short**, **long**, or **unsigned** (assumed positive). There is also **double** precision for floating-point data. The size of the storage allocation for these different types varies depending on the underlying machine being used. Since the manner in which these types are stored is, to a large extent, machine dependent, the **sizeof** operator may be used when necessary to determine the actual storage size of any field.

Here are some examples of how these types may be used:

```
int A;
unsigned int B;
char C;
float X;
...
A = 2018;        /* A may contain a + or - sign */
B = 2018;        /* B may not be used for negative numbers */
C = 'Z';
X = 127.5;
```

There is no *Boolean* type in C. In expressions that are expected to compute to a Boolean value (for example, on control statements such as **if** or **while**), a zero is taken to mean false, and any other value is taken to mean true.

Pointer variables are more important in C than in other languages. The ability to understand and work with pointer variables and pointer arithmetic is critical to good C programming. Certain things we take for granted in other languages—like formatted input, strings, arrays, and parameter passing by reference—require an understanding of how pointers work. A pointer variable contains the machine address and thus "points to" an anonymous variable created during program execution. Every pointer variable is declared as a pointer to a particular type of data. The indirection operator (*) is used in C to declare and reference such an anonymous variable pointed to by a pointer variable. For example,

```
int i;          /*   i is an integer variable  */
int *ip;        /*   ip is a pointer variable; it points to an integer
                     location  */
...
i = 1;          /*   i is assigned the value 1  */
*ip = 10;       /*   ip points to the value 10  */
ip = &i;        /*   ip points to the value of i    */
```

The address operator (&) is used to determine the address of a variable, which may then be assigned to a pointer variable.

When allocating memory space for anonymous variables pointed to by pointer variables, the standard library function malloc, which takes as its argument the size of the location being allocated, is used. In general, if P points to an anonymous variable of type Ptype, we would allocate memory in this way:

```
P = (Ptype *) malloc(sizeof (Ptype));
```

This construct is equivalent in function to Pascal's new (P) procedure. Since malloc returns an address of no specific type it must be converted so that it will conform to the pointer variable to which it is assigned. That is the reason behind the "prefix" (Ptype *). This is called *type casting*.

To deallocate storage, we can use the standard library function: free (P);

The standard library functions malloc, free, and other memory allocation functions are defined in the header file, stdlib.h.

User-defined types.   C has a limited facility, compared to Pascal and MODULA-2, for user-defined data types. There is an enumerated "type" but no way of defining subrange type data.

There is a **typedef** facility that may be used for simplifying the declaration of complicated data structures or for defining a named type once, which may then be used to declare a number of variables locally, within functions. The **typedef** keyword may also be used for "defining" types mainly for better program structure and documentation. This facility does not actually create a new type—it just declares a new name (a synonym) for an existing type. This can be an excellent feature for producing relatively self-documenting code.

An *enumerated*-type variable is declared by listing the domain of all possible values for the variable. These values are called *enumeration constants*. Each value is automatically stored along with an integer equivalent to its position in the list, beginning with 0, and may be used in place of repeated #define directives. For example, the following declaration is equivalent to defining FALSE to mean 0 and TRUE to mean 1:

```
enum Boolean {FALSE, TRUE};
```

It may also be possible, depending on the implementation, to explicitly assign these integers, possibly in a more meaningful way. For example, the definition

```
enum {COMPACT, SUBCOMPACT, SPORT, SEDAN, WAGON, VAN} Car1, Car2
```

would be the same as

```
enum   {
       COMPACT=0,
       SUBCOMPACT=1,
       SPORT=2,
       SEDAN=3,
       WAGON=4,
       VAN=5
}  Car1, Car2;
```

Explicit assignment of the integers with which enumeration constants are stored can result in more meaningful code, as in:

```
enum Weekdays {
       SUNDAY    =1,
       MONDAY    =2,
       TUESDAY   =3,
       WEDNESDAY =4,
       THURSDAY  =5,
       FRIDAY    =6,
       SATURDAY  =7
};
```

This can also be expressed by assigning the first integer only and then allowing the compiler to continue the progression:

```
enum Weekdays {
       SUNDAY=1,
       MONDAY,
       TUESDAY,
       WEDNESDAY,
       THURSDAY,
       FRIDAY,
       SATURDAY
};
```

Enumerated type data is used for internal processing only—enumerated type variables cannot be directly input or output.

To illustrate the use of the **typedef** declaration, an enumerated variable, such as Car1 or Car2 above, may be first declared as a type and then used to declare variables of that type:

```
typedef enum {COMPACT, SUBCOMPACT, SPORT, SEDAN, WAGON, VAN} CarType;
...
CarType  Car1, Car2;
...
Car1 = VAN;
if (Car2 == Car1)...
```

Structured Data

When it comes to declaring structured variables in C, there are many ways to do the same thing. For example, a structured variable may be described in a single declarative statement or first defined as a type. A string may be declared as a char array or as a list (constructed with pointers). C has the ability to declare and build such data structures as arrays, records, lists, and strings. C also has a facility for declaring unions, a special kind of structure that may be used to form variant records.

Arrays.   Unlike other languages, in C arrays, subscripts must always start at 0. Thus, the declaration **int** X[50] creates and allocates storage for a one-dimensional integer array of 50 elements, indexed from X[0] to X[49]. This may take some getting used to, especially when "looping through" an entire structure. The array name itself is a pointer—that is, it references a storage location.

A multidimensional array is declared as an array whose elements are arrays. For example, **int** X [10][50]. We must remember, in this case, that X[1][3] references the element in the *second* row, *fourth* column.

Records.   A record structure, called simply **structure** in C, may be used as a logical data structure for grouping data (as, for example, in constructing a linked list) or as an input/output variable. For example, the following declares two variables, Previous and Current, to be structures each composed of three integers.

```
struct   {
        int Month;
        int Day;
        int Year;
} Previous, Current;
```

The only way to access the individual members of the structure in C is by qualified name, e.g., Previous.Month = 1; Current.Year = 90;... Another way of declaring the same two structured variables is by first assigning a tag name to the structure, as in:

```
struct   Date   {
        int Month;
        int Day;
        int Year;
};
struct Date Previous, Current;
```

Alternatively, a **typedef** declaration may be used:

```
typedef   struct   {
                  int Month;
                  int Day;
                  int Year;
        } DateType;
DateType Previous, Current;
```

```
struct {
  char ID[10];
  struct  {
       char Last [11];
       char First [11];
       char MI;
  } Name;
  struct {
       char Street [16];
       char City [11];
       char State [3];
       char Zip [6];
  } Address;
  struct {
       char Area [4];
       char Local [8];
  } Phone [3];
  char Jobtitle [9];
  char Location;
  char Department [5];
  float Annual Salary;
  struct {
       int Month;
       int Year;
  } LastPromoted, First Employed;
} Employee [100];
```

Figure 11.2   Data structures in C

There is no limitation on the manner in which arrays and structures may be combined. For example, an array can consist of an ordered sequence of structures, each of which may be composed of other structures and/or arrays.

In order to illustrate the way you might build complex data structures in C, consider the data set in Chapter 7. If the employee records listed there are to be stored in a temporary array during processing, this structure may be completely described by the declarations in Fig. 11.2.

Unions.   C supports a type of structure called a **union**, which may be considered a *generic variable* and may be used to construct *variant records*. The type of a variable declared as a **union** can be different at different points during execution of the program. The syntax of a **union** is similar to that of a **structure**, namely:

```
union   {
       <variant1>;
       <variant2>;
       ...

}
```

A union-type variable is stored in a memory unit large enough to hold the largest variant. This device may sometimes be used as a space-saving measure, say, for different variables that are never used at the same time. For example,

```
union IntOrChar {
        int INT;
        char CHAR;
}  X;
...
X.INT = 27;
```

Actually, C does not directly support variant records. A variant record would be considered a *discriminated union*—that is, a union in which the variants have common elements. A variant record may be declared in something of the following manner:

```
struct Record {
      struct common {
            ... /* declarations of elements common to both variants */
      }
      union variants {
            struct variant1 {
                  ... /* elements unique to variant 1 */
            }
            struct variant2 {
                  ... /* elements unique to variant 2 */
            }
      }
};
```

This declaration can be considerably "cleaned up" by first declaring the individual structures and unions in separate **typedef** statements and using type names in declaring the structure Record.

Lists.   Pointers and structures are used in combination in order to build up a linked list. The following declarations may be used to set up a linked list in which the individual nodes contain some information, called Info, which may be scalar or structured data.

```
struct ListNode   {
        <some-type> Info;
        struct   ListNode   *Next;
}  *First, *Current;
```

First is a pointer to the first node in the list; *Current refers to the node pointed to by Current. Current->Next is the node pointed to by Next—that is, the next node in the list.

Strings.   In C, a string is stored within an array of characters, with a special terminating character (\0) used to indicate the end of the string. Standard library functions for string handling generally depend on the presence of this terminating character.

Therefore, the size of the array constructed to hold the string must always be one more than the expected maximum length of the string.

A string may be declared as a character array or as a pointer to character. The following alternative definitions will both set up and allocate memory for a string S of maximum length 80 characters:

```
char   S[81];
             /*  or  */
char   *S;                  /*  S is a pointer to (the first) char  */
S = malloc (81);            /*  to allocate enough memory for the
                                entire string  */
```

If we wish, we can use the typedef facility to set up our own string "type," for example:

```
typedef char *STRING;
STRING S;
S = malloc (81);
```

The individual characters stored in a string variable may be accessed by array subscripting (remember, the first element is subscripted 0). The standard library has several string functions for manipulating strings and for input/output. These are described in a header file called string.h.

Sets.   There is no facility for declaring or manipulating sets in C.

Abstract Data Types

C is flexible enough so that a good programmer can create abstract data types as well as other forms of "reusable" code. This might be done by declaring function names for the operations on the abstract data type in a separate header file available to the user of the ADT. The actual implementation of the data type would be "hidden" in an object file. For this purpose it is a good idea to follow the syntax and programming conventions of MODULA-2, for example its DEFINITION MODULE (i.e., header file) and IMPLE-MENTATION MODULE (i.e., program file).

I/O File Structures

Like MODULA-2, input/output in C is handled by a standard library of functions. The #include <stdio.h> preprocessor directive links a user program with this library. If the stdio.h header file is included in a program file, three standard files are automatically opened when the program begins. Usually, these are defined as stdin (the keyboard), stdout (the screen), and stderr (the screen).

Some of these predefined I/O functions access a single character at a time (getchar or putchar), a string at a time (gets, puts), or any number of variables accessed according to a format string argument (scanf, printf).

There are also definitions and functions for processing external data files. For example, the function fopen opens a specified file for a specified mode (e.g., reading, writing, appending) and returns a file pointer, which may be assigned to a variable, in the following manner:

```
FILE *InputFile;
InputFile = fopen ("myfile.dat","r");
```

11.4 PROGRAM STRUCTURES

The major program structure in C is the function. All subprograms are called functions, whether or not they return a value, and whether or not the value returned is actually used at the point of call.

The Program Text

Character set. The C character set consists of the 52 upper- and lowercase alphabetic characters, the 10 numeric digits, and at least the following special characters.

	blank	!	exclamation pt.	@	"at" symbol
#	pound sign	$	dollar sign	%	percent sign
^	up arrow	&	ampersand	*	asterisk
+	plus sign	=	equal sign	-	hyphen
_	underscore	~	tilde	<	left arrow
>	right arrow	/	slash	\	backslash
'	single quote	"	double quote	:	colon
;	semicolon	.	period	,	comma
( )	parentheses	[ ]	sq. brackets	{ }	curly braces

Text formatting. The formatting of the program text is imposed solely by the programmer and becomes extremely important in constructing C programs that are readable and modifiable. The use of indenting, comments, and blank lines can serve to emphasize and enhance the program's logical structure, which may not otherwise be clearly visible due to C's heavy reliance on operator symbols and concise code.

Free vs. fixed format. C program text is totally free-format. Identifiers and constants are limited to a single line. Preprocessor directives—statements beginning with a #—are limited to a single line. Long preprocessor directives such as macros may be continued on successive lines by placing a backslash at the end of each line before the last.

Indenting. Indenting is allowed and encouraged, although there is no standard convention for indenting C programs. In particular, subservient statements within such control statements as **if, switch**, and **while** should, as usual, be indented. Statements within a block should be indented.

Comments. Comments may be placed anywhere except within identifiers and literals. Comments are delineated by the paired symbols /* and */. Comments may not be nested.

Blank lines.   Blank lines may be used anywhere in the program.

Punctuation.   Unlike Pascal and MODULA-2, the semicolon (;) *terminates* a statement rather than separating successive statements. Thus, every statement, even the last one in a block, must be terminated by a semicolon. At least one blank space separates the words of program text. Commas are used to separate items in a list. Single quotation marks delimit character literals; double quotation marks delimit character strings. Parentheses, ( ), delimit parameter lists and are used to impose explicit control over expressions. Square brackets, [ ], delimit array subscripts. Curly braces, { }, delimit lists of constants for initializing enumerated and structured variables.

The C preprocessor.   Statements beginning with # control the C compiler preprocessor, which modifies the source file before the compile process is initiated. These statements, which are placed at the beginning of the source file, govern such tasks as inclusion of other files in the stream of text of the source file, text replacement for constant and macro definition, and conditional compilation. These directives may be collected in a separate header file, which may then be included in the program file with the #include directive. This is ideal for defining symbolic constants and macros which may be used by more than one program file.

Consider the following example of the use of the #define preprocessor directive:

```
#define AREA(R) (PI * R * R)
```

As you can see, this definition facility is more powerful than simply defining constants. It is a text-substitution facility that can accept "arguments" and thus serves as a macro facility. The parentheses in the last example are necessary because simple text substitution is done: If AREA is used as part of a larger arithmetic expression, the parentheses will ensure that PI * R * R is evaluated together. Macros, especially if they are small, may sometimes be preferred to functions. Execution will be considerably faster since there is some overhead associated with each function reference. On the other hand, a macro uses more memory since a complete copy of the code is placed everywhere the macro name is used.

Words

C is not a very wordy language. It has only about 30 reserved words, but it relies a great deal on special characters as operator symbols. This makes C code very concise, even for very large programs. An advantage of this is that fewer keystrokes are required to enter a C program and, of course, a C expert can quickly read obtuse C code just as easily as a novice can follow a COBOL program.

The words used in a C program may be reserved language keywords, programmer-supplied identifiers, or identifiers that are predefined in the library files. In this chapter, only reserved language keywords appear in boldface.

Identifiers.   The programmer supplies identifier names for variables, types, labels, and functions.

Names may consist of any number and combination of alphabetic characters, numeric digits, and the underscore. The first eight characters must be unique. The name must begin with a letter or an underscore. Note that C is *case sensitive*—that is, it differentiates between upper- and lowercase alphabetic characters used in identifiers. This means that the names DATAVALUE, Datavalue, and DataValue are all different. (Note that because C is case sensitive, DATAVALUE and DATAVALUES are the same.)

Keywords. There are about 30 reserved language keywords in the C language definition. These reserved words make up the core of the language and cannot be redefined by the programmer. They are:

auto	double	if	static
break	else	int	struct
case	entry	long	switch
char	extern	register	typedef
continue	float	return	union
default	for	short	unsigned
do	goto	sizeof	while

The following are some of the different kinds of keywords in the language.

Descriptive keywords. These are used to describe attributes of variables, for example: **int, char, float, double, unsigned, long, short, extern, register, static, auto**.

Action keywords. These are words used in executable statements, to define conditional control, for example: **if, else, for, do, while, switch, case, break, goto, return**.

Delimiter keywords. There are no delimiter keywords in C. The curly braces, { }, are used instead of the begin/end of other languages to delimit blocks.

Noise keywords. There are none.

Statements

Statements may be either executable or nonexecutable. The nonexecutable statements are those that are descriptive in nature; they provide information to the compiler, but do not directly cause actions during run time processing.

Declarative statements. The nonexecutable statements of C include declaration of scalar and structured variables, **typedef** and enum definitions, and function declarations, also called function prototypes. These are similar to the "forward" declarations of other languages (e.g., Pascal).

The entire function definition—type, name, parameter list, local action block—may be considered strictly descriptive in nature, until such time as the function is invoked and control is transferred to the first executable statement in block. Function definitions may appear in any order in a program file. However, if a function is called at a point preceding its definition, the compiler will impute to it the type **int**. This may cause critical errors during processing. A *function declaration*, or *function prototype*, placed at the beginning of the program file ensures that the compiler will recognize the function, its type, and its argument list when it is called.

Header files are composed entirely of such nonexecutable, declarative statements. These may also contain preprocessor compiler directives such as #define used for constant and macro definition and #include for inclusion of other header files.

Executable statements.   The executable statements of C include an expression statement and a variety of control-related statements.

Expression.   The expression statement is a very general structure that describes the "catchall" workhorse statement of C. An expression statement may be a function reference; an arithmetic/assignment expression that looks like an assignment statement of a more traditional (say, FORTRAN) language; a simple increment (X++) or decrement (X– –) of a single variable. Any expression is transformed into a statement by placing a semicolon at the end of it.

Assignment.   Assignment in C is denoted by the equal sign (=) and is just one operator that may be found within an expression statement. Thus, an assignment statement may be considered a special case of the expression statement. Because of this, multiple assignment makes sense, for example: A = B = C = 0. When this expression statement is evaluated, zero is assigned to C, the result of that operation (0) is assigned to B, and so on. In C, any binary operator may be combined with the assignment operator to create "shorthand" expressions. For example, the expression Sum = Sum + X may be shortened to Sum += X.

Arithmetic expression.   Arithmetic instructions are coded within arithmetic expressions and may be used in conjunction with the assignment operator. The arithmetic symbols (+ - * /) have their traditional meanings. There is no exponentiation operator. Various standard arithmetic functions, such as the trigonometric functions, are built into the C function library and described in the header file math.h.

Conditional expression.   The tertiary operator ?: denotes a conditional expression. This takes the form (<E1>)?<E2>:<E3> and reads this way: If expression E1 evaluates to a nonzero result (i.e., it is "true"), then evaluate expression E2, ignoring E3; otherwise evaluate E3, skipping E2. One common use of the conditional expression is assigning one of two alternative values to a variable, for example: B = (A > B)? A : 0. This is equivalent to the selection construct: **if** (A > B) B = A **else** B=0.

Input/output.   There are no input/output statements in the C language definition. Since I/O is the most machine-dependent feature of any language, the extraction and isolation of these features in the function library files have helped to establish C's reputation as a portable language. In fact, the input/output functions are provided in the library files and have become virtually standard over implementations.

Control.   The default control construct is, of course, simple sequence. To alter the default control mechanism, one of the following statements may be used:

- **if** or **switch** for selection among two or more alternative pieces of code;
- **goto**, **continue**, or **break** for branching to a nonsequential location, say, out of a loop;
- **return** to the point of call, with or without a result, from within a function;
- **for**, **while**, and **do** for iteration.

Control structures will be discussed more fully below.

Compound statement. Most of the conditional control statements, such as **if** or **for**, expect a single statement to be executed depending on the result of the condition. For example,

```
if (condition) <statement1> else <statement2>;
```

If more than a single statement is needed, a function call may be used. Alternatively, a block of code may be substituted for any single statement. The *block* is similar to the compound statement of Pascal, but is actually closer to the ALGOL60 concept of a block. A block, delimited by a pair of curly braces, may contain local declarations and executable code.

Subprograms

Most C programs are composed of a large number of functions, each of which performs a particular task. This serves to reduce the complexity of the programming task and to facilitate the reuse of code. The functions referenced by a program may all reside in the same physical program file or may be dispersed over several physical files in the function library and compiled separately.

Types of subprograms. C provides internal (but not nested) subprograms and external subprograms separately compiled in library files.

Internal subprograms. There is no nesting of functions in C. This means that a function may not be defined within the block of another function. However, the functions that reside within a single physical file are compiled together.

External subprograms. Functions residing in library files are compiled separately and may thus be termed external subprograms. These functions, although they have been *defined* in a library file, may be called from within any other program file, as long as the function is first *declared* (with a function prototype) prior to use. Generally, each library file will have associated with it a header file containing function prototypes and other declarations necessary for the use of the functions in the library file. This header file, in addition to providing information for the user of the library functions, may be copied into the user program file with the #include compiler preprocessor directive.

Functions. A function definition has a type, a name, a list of parameters, and a block of statements. The type of the function reflects the type of the value it returns. This type may be **void**, in which case the function does not return any value to the point of call. A function of type **void** is equivalent to a procedure in other languages. The function's parameters are listed each with its own type, separated by commas. The parameter list may be empty, if the function does not require any arguments. The block is delimited by curly braces, { }, and may contain both declarative and executable statements. One of the executable statements is a **return** statement, which indicates the value to be returned to the point of call.

The following is a skeletal definition of a function called Max, which returns the maximum of three real numbers:

```
float Max (float A, float B, float C)
{
        /* implementation of Max */
}
```

This function would be invoked within an expression by simply referencing the function name along with its arguments. For example:

```
Result = Max (X,Y,Z) - Max (P,Q,R);
```

The following function, FindMax, does the same thing, but it is coded as a procedure, that is, a function of type **void**, and so requires an output parameter to return the maximum value to the calling function. Since output parameters must be accessible by the program or subprogram at the point of call, parameter passing by reference must be simulated. We will discuss this shortly.

```
void FindMax (float A, float B, float C, float *Maximum)
{
        /* implementation of FindMax */
}
```

Functions, whether they return a value or not, are invoked in expression statements, either as part of an expression, or as the expression itself (a statement). Even for functions that do return values, those values may be used or ignored. The function FindMax would be called in the following way:

```
FindMax (X,Y,Z, &Max);
```

Not all functions require parameters. Even in such a case, however, C requires the parentheses surrounding an empty list of parameters. For example, the function declaration

```
void Initialize()
```

may refer to a function that accepts no arguments from the calling function and returns no value but simply collects all program statements that are done when the program begins executing.

Sharing data.   The following are some of the ways that C limits and facilitates access to data shared by two or more functions.

Global variables.   Global variables, called *external* in C, are those declared outside any function in the program file. The storage class **extern** may be used to explicitly declare a global variable.

Local variables.   Local variables, called automatic in C, are those declared within a function definition, or even within any unnamed block delimited by a pair of curly braces, { }. The storage class may be explicitly declared to be **auto** (the default), **static**, or **register**.

Scope of variables.   Since functions may not be nested in C, the lexical scoping rule does not, in general, apply. The scope of variables may usually be described very simply as either global (outside of functions) or local (within functions). However, C allows the use of an unnamed *block*, delimited by curly braces { }, which may contain both local variable declarations and local action code. Blocks *may* be nested and, thus, variables described within blocks may be determined by the static scoping rule.

Parameters. In C, arguments may only be passed to parameters by value. Thus, parameters are treated strictly as input-only parameters. This works well for true functions, which ought, by definition, to accept only input parameters and return a single output value, using the name and type of the function itself. The array appears to be an exception to the call by value rule: The entire array is not copied into the local storage allocation of the function; instead, the address of the array is passed to the function. This is because the array name does not store a data value but a pointer to the first location of the array. When an output parameter is required, for example, because a function must pass more than a single data value back to the point of call, parameter passing by reference (address) may be simulated in C by declaring a parameter to be a pointer to the required data value rather than to the value itself.

For example, one frequently coded function accepts two data elements and exchanges them. Often named Swap, this would look something like:

```
void Swap (int A, int B)
{
    int temp;
    temp = A;
    B = A;
    A = temp;
}
```

Unfortunately, this great-looking piece of code would not do the job. This is because the call to Swap, say Swap (X, Y), would pass arguments to parameters *by value* and any change to swap's parameters A and B would not affect the values of the calling function's X and Y. The effect would be as if the exchange never took place. We need a mechanism to pass the two "new" values back to the calling function. This could be done if A and B could be passed references (addresses) instead of values, like the "variable" parameters of ALGOL60, Pascal, and MODULA-2. If the swapping function is set up so as to expect the addresses of the values to be swapped, instead of the values themselves, we are actually simulating the reference parameters known to other languages. We would declare the parameters to be pointers and pass arguments to them that are addresses. For example, the swap procedure could be written as:

```
void Swap (int *A, int *B)
{
    int temp;
    temp = *A;
    *B = *A;
    *A = temp;
}
```

Then, the call to Swap must pass the addresses of the values to be swapped:

```
Swap (&X, &Y)
```

A function—the entire function definition, not simply the value returned from a function reference—can be passed to another function as an argument. This is done by declaring the parameter in question as a pointer to function. For example, in the following function header, the first parameter declares f as a pointer to a function of type **double**.

```
double Summation (double (*f) (), int n)
```

Subprogram libraries.   The C function library is built around a core of standard library functions. Several of these function definitions are machine dependent. This increases the portability of user programs since the machine-dependent code has been abstracted out of the program. The library also serves as a storage receptacle for reusable programmer-defined functions, which are compiled separately and may be linked to other user programs in which they are invoked.

Built-in subprograms.   All functions are contained within the function library and, however much the library is "standard" over all implementations, these functions are not considered to be part of the language definition.

Subprogram libraries available.   The standard C function library contains mathematical functions declared in the math.h header file. These include the trigonometric functions, natural log, $\log_{10}$, exponentiation, etc. Input/output functions for standard I/O devices and for user data files are declared in the stdio.h header file. String manipulation functions are declared in the string.h header file. Functions for memory manipulation may be declared in the stdlib.h header file.

Building a subprogram library.   In addition to those library modules provided as standard, a programmer can define new ones and build up an extensive library of modules to suit a particular application or a set of applications. If well done, this leads to a library of reusable code, often referred to as a set of packages. These library modules are compiled separately for later use.

The best way to structure a library is to group related functions into a file. Function declarations and any other external declarations related to this group of functions would be stored separately in a header file. The header and object files would have the same external file name but different file extensions. This header file would be "included" into the text of the program file using the #include compiler preprocessor directive. The function library does not need to be set up in this way. In fact, you may have noticed that this method borrows two key program structuring ideas from MODULA-2: the DEFINITION MODULE and the IMPLEMENTATION MODULE. Structuring the library in this way splits the information necessary to the user of the library function from the information necessary only to the implementor (author) of the function. It hides irrelevant details of the *implementation* from the user, allowing only *specifications* to be externally visible. In short, the header file describes *what* you are doing when you use a library function; the program file defines *how* the function actually works.

Program Abstraction

The implementation of program abstraction in C is totally up to the programmer. The language imposes virtually no rules regarding the design or structure of programs and enforces nothing at all. This is not a "dummy-proof" programming language, and it is certainly not for beginners. It is also not a hospitable environment for poor programmers. In the hands of experts, however, the C language can be an excellent medium for constructing reusable packages of code and building large, complex systems around them.

Modular decomposition.   Modular decomposition is facilitated in C. Its capability for separately compiled library functions encourages the decomposition of programs into relatively small functional units.

Information hiding.   The expert programmer can employ information hiding in C. By building function libraries in such a way that the specification is accessible in a header file, with the implementation present only in an object file, irrelevant details regarding the implementation of library functions will be hidden from the user, and only the information that the user really needs will be visible.

Self-Documenting Features

It has been said that C combines the power of assembler with the readability of assembler. At any rate, C cannot be considered a self-documenting language. To convince yourself that this is so, compare the texts of a C program and a COBOL program.

A C program is about as far from being "English-like" as you can get. Extensive comments are required. It cannot be easily followed by a nonexpert, making structured walkthroughs difficult to manage.

Nevertheless, there are certain features of C that do assist the programmer in creating a fairly readable program. These include the facility for creating descriptive variable and function names, flexible rules for formatting program text such as those allowing flexibility in indenting, comments, and blank lines, and the compiler preprocessor directive which allows replacement text (#define). All these features encourage the development of programs that are readable and maintainable, although they cannot ensure this result. Also the declarations, which may be contained in a separate header file, for such program entities as variables, types, structures, and functions add considerably to the self-documenting character of a C program.

11.5 CONTROL STRUCTURES

The control structures of C include a rich variety of operators for a powerful, concise formulation of expressions. Control structures at the statement level include those for conditional selection of code and several forms of iteration. Finally, there is the function call, recursion, and separate compilation of library functions.

Operators

Operators are symbols used to form expressions and conditions on control-oriented statements. C has a very large selection of operators (about 40), some of which have no counterparts in other programming languages. The following are descriptions of some of the many operators in C.

Arithmetic operators. The arithmetic operators act on numeric operands. These include: + (add), - (subtract), * (multiply), / (divide), % (modulus). There is no exponentiation operator. In addition, there are a large number of useful mathematical functions contained in the standard library and specified in the math.h header file. These include the trigonometric functions and functions for such common operations as ln, $\log_{10}$, abs, exp, sqrt.

Relational operators. The relational operators act on any scalar-type operand. These include: < (less than), <= (less than or equal to), == (equal to), != (not equal to), >= (greater than or equal to), > (greater than).

Logical operators. The logical operators operate on Boolean (two-valued, false or true) operands. In C, although there is no Boolean type, the integer 0 is assumed to represent false and any other result defaults to true. The logical operators include ! (not), && (and), || (or).

Bit operators. The bit operators are used for machine-level programming. These include: ~ (one's complement), << (left shift), >> (right shift), & (bitwise and), | (bitwise inclusive or), ^ (bitwise exclusive or).

Expressions

Expressions are represented in infix, parenthesized form. Operands enclosed within parentheses are evaluated first. Parentheses are used to alter the default sequence control mechanism for evaluating expressions.

The precedence rules in C are fairly complicated, due partly to the large number of operators and the relative freedom in constructing expressions. Fig. 11.3 displays the operators of C by level of precedence. Even for a sequence of operators at the same level of precedence, the processing is sometimes conducted left-to-right, sometimes right-to-left. This is why a C program may sometimes be identified by the large number of parentheses it contains.

In complex relational expressions (conditions) containing logical operators, evaluation stops as soon as a condition is found that determines the value of the whole expression. This is sometimes called "short-circuit" evaluation of expressions. For example, in the following **if** statement, if the value of A is less than the value of B, the entire condition evaluates to "true" and the rest of the condition may be ignored.

```
if (X==0 || A<B) ...
```

Constant expressions contain only operands that are constants and result in constants. Constant expressions are expected in certain places, for example, in dimensioning of arrays.

Since C is a weakly typed language, *mixed-mode expressions* present no great problem. Proper data type conversion (also called *type coercion*) is left up to the responsibility of the programmer. Type conversion may be explicit or implicit. Implicit type conversion is done whenever you construct a mixed-mode expression. Just about any type data may be combined in expressions, with sometimes surprising results. Explicit type conversion is accomplished on a temporary basis by means of the *type casting* operation. For example,

Level	Operator	Description	Associativity
1	()	function reference	left to right
References	[]	array reference	
	->	pointer to structure-member reference	
		structure member reference	
2	+ -	unary plus, minus	right to left
Unary Operators			
	++ --	increment, decrement	
	!	*logical not*	
	~	one's complements	
	* &	indirection, address	
	sizeof		
	(type)	type cast	
Binary Operators			
3	* /	multiply, divide	left to right
	%	modulus	
4	+ -	add, subtract	left to right
5	<< >>	shift left, right	left to right
6	< <=	less than (or equal)	left to right
	> >=	greater than (or equal)	
7	!= ==	(not) equal	left to right
8	&	bitwise and	left to right
9	^	bitwise xor	left to right
10	|	bitwise or	left to right
11	&&	logical and	left to right
12	||	logical or	left to right
Tertiary operator			
13	?:	conditional expression	right to left
Assignment operators			
14	=	assignment	right to left
	op=		
Other			
15	,	comma operator	left to right

Figure 11.3   Precedence of operators in C

```
float X; int J;
...
X = (float) J; /* J type cast to float */
```

The *conditional expression* is a selection construct at the expression level. It uses the tertiary operator ?: as in, in general, (<exp1>)?<exp2>:<exp3>. This is somewhat equivalent to **if** <exp1> **then** <exp2> **else** <exp3>. This kind of expression may be used in conjunction with assignment as, for example, B = (A>B)?A:0.

Control Statements

The default statement-level control structure is simple sequence: Statements are simply executed in the sequence in which they are written in the source program. Although this is the default, there are times when simple sequence must be explicitly expressed using a compound statement, or *block* in C. Certain statements may alter the default control mechanism or in some way control the execution of program statements.

Unconditional branch. There is a **goto** statement in C. It takes the form **goto** <label>;. Labels do not have to be declared. The **break** statement is a specialized form of the **goto**. It provides for premature exit from a loop and is critical when used in conjunction with the **switch** structure, as we will soon see. The **continue** statement provides a means by which to ignore the remainder of the body of a loop but still go on to the next iteration. The *return* statement can be used to return from a called function prematurely.

Selection. The selection control construct is used to choose one of two or more alternative statements, which may be compound statements (blocks).

Two-way selection. The primary language structure for two-way selection is the conditional (**if**) statement, although as we have seen, the conditional expression (using the ?: operator) provides a limited form of this construct. The **if** statement takes the form:

```
if (<condition>) <statement1> else <statement2>;
```

Statement1 and statement2 may each contain a single statement, a function reference, or a block of statements. The else clause is optional. An **else** is always associated with the closest previous "free" **if**.

Multiway selection. The switch statement is used for selection from among more than two alternatives depending on the result of an integral selector expression. It takes the general form:

```
switch (<selection expression>) {
    case <value1> : /* sequence of statements,
                         possibly ending with break; */
    case <value2> : /* sequence of statements,
                         possibly ending with break; */
    ...
    case <valuek> : /* sequence of statements,
                         possibly ending with break; */
    default       : /* sequence of statements */
};
```

Values 1 through k must be constants or constant expressions. Although only one value, not a range of values, may be represented in each **case** clause, execution of statements continues until it falls through to the next **case**. That is why the **break** statement is needed as an escape from the switch structure. Otherwise one runs the risk of all alternative sequences of code being executed regardless of the value of the selector expression. For example, consider the following:

```
switch (DayNum) {
      case 1 :   do_weekend(); break;
      case 2 :
      case 3 :
      case 4 :
      case 5 :
      case 6 :   do_workday(); break;
      case 7 :   do_weekend(); break;
      default : error_fn (DayNum);
}
```

Iteration.   There are three language structures for controlling iteration. These are the **while, do/while**, and **for** statements.

Test-before loop.   The test-before loop is implemented with the while statement. It takes the form: **while** (<expression>) <statement>. As long as the expression evaluates to true (a nonzero value), the iteration continues. The statement may be a single statement or a block.

Test-after loop.   The test-after loop is implemented in C with the **do/while** structure. It takes the form: **do** <statement> **while** (<expression>).

Indexed loop.   The indexed loop in C is implemented as a specific case of the **for** statement. For example, to print out the integers between one and ten the following loop may be used:

```
for (i=1; i<=10; i++) some_printing_fn(i);
```

The processing of this loop in C is not typical of an indexed loop as described in Chapter 6; it is closer to COBOL's PERFORM/VARYING/UNTIL. If, in general, the indexed for loop is written as **for** (var = init; var <= final; var += step) S, then this may be coded without loss of meaning as a while loop, as follows:

```
var = init;
while (var <= final) {
      S;
      var += step;
}
```

Since an indexed loop is usually used to access the elements of an array, and since array subscripts in C begin at zero, the indexed **for** loop will typically look more like this:

```
for (j=0; j<10; j++) some_printing_fn(A[j]);
```

Other.   The **for** statement of C is actually a more general structure than simply an indexed loop. In general, it takes the form:

```
for (<exp1>; <exp2>; <exp3>) <statement>;
```

The expressions may or may not control an index variable. Any or all of the expressions may be missing. Frequently, the statement is missing and the loop is contained in one of the expressions. For example, in the following, as soon as EOF is reached the loop terminates.

```
for (j=0; A[j]=getchar()!=EOF; j++);
```

Control over subprograms

Call.   A function is invoked by referencing it in an expression. Or, the function call can *be* the statement all by itself. For example,

```
n = LoadArray(Infile);
WriteToDisk;
FindSum (ArrayOfReals);
```

Return.   Return of control to the calling function is done when a return statement is encountered. It takes the form **return** (value) or, simply, **return** for functions of type **void**. One or more **return** statements may appear in a function definition for possible premature (or multiple) termination of a function.

Control over program execution.

Program execution begins at the first executable statement contained within the definition of the function called *main*. The program terminates when it runs through the last executable statement in main. Alternatively, a **return** statement may be used to terminate program execution.

Subprogram Control Structures

C has a limited assortment of structures for control over function invocation.

Simple call.   As described above, C's only subprogram structure is the function. A function reference may be treated as a variable access—like the functions in other languages—or as a statement by itself—like procedures in other languages—in which case, the value returned, if any, would be ignored.

Recursion.   Any function may be referenced recursively; it need not be specially declared as recursive. Both direct and indirect recursion are allowed.

Implicit call.   There is no implicit invocation of functions in the C language definition. Facilities for very limited exception handling are contained in standard library functions declared in the signal.h header file. These functions may vary depending on the particular implementation used.

Parallel processing.   Parallel processing is not directly supported in C.

Coroutines.   Coroutines are not directly supported in C.

11.6 PROGRAM DEVELOPMENT

C programs have a characteristic conciseness. They are cryptic amalgams of operators, parentheses, and curly braces. It is not an easy language to learn. But C generally produces efficient code.

The implementation often supplies an editor, a debugging facility, and other program-development tools. When C is used within the UNIX system, the program development environment is considerably different from when used as simply another language.

11.7 MORE SAMPLE PROGRAMS

The sequential file update program for Study Problem #2 is listed in Fig. 11.4.

The multiple linked lists creation program, Study Problem #3 (Part A), is listed in Fig. 11.5. Part B, multi-linked list maintenance, is left to the reader as an exercise.

EXERCISES

1. Complete Study Problem #3 (Part B) in C.
2. Do Study Problem #4 in C.

SUGGESTIONS FOR FURTHER STUDY

Manuals. Since its publication in 1978 the *de facto* standard C language definition has been Kernighan and Ritchie (1978), now into its second edition (1988). The language has since been standardized by the American National Standards Institute (ANSI 1988). For Turbo C, Borland (1987a, b, c, d).

Books. Barclay (1989), Feueur and Gehani (1984), Kelley and Pohl (1984), Muldner and Steele (1988), Sessions (1989), Shammas (1988), Swartz (1989), Wiatrowski and Wiener (1987).

Chapters in Books. Tucker (1986), Chapter 10: "C," pp. 412–454.

Articles. Cashin (1988), Tello (1984), and the August 1983 issue of *Byte*.

```
/*****************************************************
**                                                 **
**   F I L E   U P D A T E    P R O G R A M   **
**                                                 **
*****************************************************/

/*   Include Files    */

# include "stdio.h"
# include "string.h"

/*   Preprocessor Definitions    */

# define TRUE  1
# define FALSE 0
# define MAXTRANS 50

/*   Global Declarations    */

typedef struct {
            char Key[10];
            char OtherInfo[113];
        } EmpRec;

typedef struct {
            EmpRec Rec;
            char Code;
        } TransRec;

typedef struct {
            char ID[10];
            char Code;
            char Error[11];
        } ErrorlineStruct;

int Ntrans, Nerrors, NumOK;
int Nadds, Ndeletes, Nchanges;
EmpRec MasterRec;
TransRec Trans;
FILE *MasterFile, *TransFile, *NewMasterFile;
ErrorlineStruct Errorline[MAXTRANS];
struct {
    int Master, Transaction;
    } Eof;

/*   Function Prototypes    */

void ReadMasterRecord();
void ReadTransRecord();
void WriteFrom (EmpRec NewRecord);
void Initialize();
void ErrorInA();
void AddRecord();
```

Figure 11.4   Update program (continued next page)

```
void ErrorInCD();
void ChangeRecord();
void ChangeOrDelete();
void ProcessControl();
void EndTrans();
void EndMaster();
void SkipLines (FILE *Listr, int L);
void PrintReport();

/**************************************************
**                                              **
**     R E A D    1     R E C O R D        **
**                                              **
**************************************************/

void ReadMasterRecord()
{
    char endlin[];
    fgets (MasterRec.Key, 10, MasterFile);
    if (feof(MasterFile))
            Eof.Master = TRUE;
    else     {
            fgets (MasterRec.OtherInfo, 113, MasterFile);
            fgets (endlin, 10, MasterFile);
        }
}    /*   end ReadMasterRecord   */

void ReadTransRecord()
{
    char endlin[];
    fgets (Trans.Rec.Key, 10, TransFile);
    if (feof(TransFile))
            Eof.Transaction = TRUE;
    else     {
            fgets (Trans.Rec.OtherInfo, 113, TransFile);
            Trans.Code = fgetc (TransFile);
            fgets (endlin, 10, TransFile);
            Ntrans++;
            }
}              /*   end ReadTransRecord   */

/**************************************************
**                                              **
**     W R I T E    1     R E C O R D      **
**                                              **
**************************************************/

void WriteFrom (EmpRec NewRecord)
{
```

Figure 11.4   (continued next page)

```
        fputs (NewRecord.Key, NewMasterFile);
        fputs (NewRecord.OtherInfo, NewMasterFile);
        fputs ("\n", NewMasterFile);
}    /*   end WriteFrom   */


/****************************************************
**                                                **
**       I N I T I A L I Z A T I O N              **
**                                                **
**  initial values, open files, initial reads     **
**                                                **
****************************************************/

void Initialize()
{
        Ntrans = Nerrors = NumOK = 0;
        Nadds = Ndeletes = Nchanges = 0;
        MasterFile = fopen ("A:IDPRSNEL.DAT", "rt");
        TransFile = fopen ("A:TRANS.DAT","rt");
        NewMasterFile = fopen ("A:UPDATE", "wt");
        Eof.Master = Eof.Transaction = FALSE;
        ReadMasterRecord();
        ReadTransRecord();
}    /*   end Initialize   */


/****************************************************
**                                                **
**       A D D   A   R E C O R D                  **
**                                                **
**       uses procedure ErrorInA                  **
**                                                **
****************************************************/

void ErrorInA()
{
        strcpy (Errorline[Nerrors].ID, Trans.Rec.Key);
        Errorline[Nerrors].Code = Trans.Code;
        strcpy (Errorline[Nerrors].Error, ((Trans.Code == ' ')?
                "missing" : "not A"));
        Nerrors ++;
}    /*   end ErrorInA   */

void AddRecord()
{
        if (Trans.Code == 'A') {
                WriteFrom (Trans.Rec);
                Nadds++;
                }
        else
                ErrorInA();
}    /*   end AddRecord   */
```

Figure 11.4   (continued next page)

```
/**************************************************
**                                              **
**    C H A N G E / D E L E T E    R E C O R D   **
**                                              **
**      uses procedure ErrorInCD                **
**                                              **
**************************************************/

void ErrorInCD()
{
    strcpy (Errorline[Nerrors].ID, Trans.Rec.Key);
    Errorline[Nerrors].Code = Trans.Code;
    strcpy (Errorline[Nerrors].Error, ((Trans.Code == ' ')?
            "missing" : "not C or D"));
    Nerrors++;
}    /*   end ErrorInCD   */

void ChangeRecord()
{
    MasterRec = Trans.Rec;
}    /*   end ChangeRecord   */

void ChangeOrDelete()
{
    switch (Trans.Code) {
            case 'C' :
                    ChangeRecord();
                    WriteFrom (MasterRec);
                    Nchanges++;
                    break;
            case 'D' :
                    Ndeletes++; break;
            default :
                    ErrorInCD();
                    WriteFrom (MasterRec);
                    break;
        }
}    /*   end ChangeOrDelete   */

/**************************************************
**                                              **
** U P D A T E   P R O C E S S   C O N T R O L **
**                                              **
**************************************************/

void ProcessControl()
{
    if (strcmp (Trans.Rec.Key, MasterRec.Key) > 0) {
            WriteFrom(MasterRec);
            ReadMasterRecord();
            }
```

Figure 11.4   (continued next page)

```
        else  {
            if (strcmp (Trans.Rec.Key, MasterRec.Key) == 0) {
                ChangeOrDelete ();
                ReadMasterRecord ();
                }
            else
                AddRecord ();               /*  ie, Tkey< Mkey   */
            ReadTransRecord ();
            }
}     /*  end ProcessControl   */

/*************************************************
**                                            **
**       E N D    P R O C E S S I N G         **
**                                            **
*************************************************/

void EndTrans ()
{
        while (!Eof.Master) {
            WriteFrom (MasterRec);
            ReadMasterRecord ();
            }
}       /*   end EndTrans   */

void EndMaster ()
{
        while (!Eof.Transaction) {
            AddRecord ();
            ReadTransRecord ();
            }
}       /*   end EndMaster   */


/*************************************************
**                                            **
**       C L O S E    F I L E S               **
**                                            **
*************************************************/

void CloseFiles ()
{
        fclose (MasterFile);
        fclose (TransFile);
        fclose (NewMasterFile);
}       /*   end CloseFiles   */
```

Figure 11.4   (continued next page)

```
/***************************************************
**                                              **
**       P R I N T E D   R E P O R T            **
**                                              **
***************************************************/

void SkipLines (FILE *Listr, int  L)
{
    int R;
    for (R=1; R<L; R++)
        fprintf (Listr, "\n");
}   /*   end SkipLines   */

void PrintReport ()
{
    int J;
    FILE *Listr;
    char Space = ' ';
    char *Underline = "-------------------------------------------";
    char *MsgLit = "Transaction Code is ";

    Listr = fopen ("CON", "wt");                    /*  CON or PRN  */
    SkipLines (Listr, 5);
    NumOK    = Ntrans - Nerrors;
            /**************************
            **        Heading        **
            **************************/
    fprintf (Listr, "%15cSequential File Update \n", Space);
    fprintf (Listr, "%13cPersonnel File Maintenance \n", Space);
    fprintf (Listr, "%5c%s \n", Space, Underline);
    SkipLines (Listr, 2);
    fprintf (Listr, "%15cTotal number of transactions = %5d \n", Space,
            Ntrans);
    fprintf (Listr, "%7cTransactions processed successfully = %5d \n",
            Space, NumOK);
    SkipLines (Listr, 4);
            /**************************
            ** Error Detail Listing **
            **************************/
    fprintf (Listr, "%2cThe following transactions could not be
            processed \n", Space);
    fprintf (Listr, "%2cdue to errors: \n", Space);
    SkipLines(Listr, 2);
    fprintf (Listr, "ID Number   Trans. Code      Error      \n");
    fprintf (Listr, "---------   -----------      -----      \n");
    SkipLines (Listr, 2);
    for (J=0; J<Nerrors; J++)
        fprintf (Listr, "%s%8c%c%10c%s%s\n", Errorline[J].ID, Space,
            Errorline[J].Code, Space, MsgLit, Errorline[J].Error);
```

Figure 11.4   (continued next page)

```
        fprintf (Listr, "%5c%s\n", Space, Underline);
        SkipLines (Listr, 4);
                /**************************
                **      Summary Info       **
                **************************/
        fprintf (Listr, "%10c%5d    records added to Master File \n", Space,
                Nadds);
        SkipLines (Listr, 2);
        fprintf (Listr, "%10c%5d    records deleted from Master File \n",
                Space, Ndeletes);
        SkipLines (Listr, 2);
        fprintf (Listr, "%10c%5d    records changed \n", Space, Nchanges);
        SkipLines (Listr, 2);
        fclose (Listr);
}       /*  end PrintReport   */


/**************************************************
**                                              **
**                  M A I N                     **
**                                              **
**      program execution begins here           **
**                                              **
**************************************************/

void main()
{
        Initialize();
        while (!Eof.Transaction)
                if (Eof.Master)
                        EndMaster();
                else
                        ProcessControl();
        EndTrans();
        CloseFiles();
        PrintReport();
}       /*  end program File Update   */
```

Figure 11.4   (concluded)

```
/*********************************************************
**                                                     **
**   M U L T I L I N K E D   L I S T    PROGRAM        **
**                                                     **
*********************************************************/

/*   Include Files   */

# include "stdio.h"
# include "string.h"
# include "alloc.h"

/*   Preprocessor Definitions   */

# define TRUE 1
# define FALSE 0
# define NLISTS 4
# define NJOBS 4
# define NLOCS 4
# define NDEPTS 3

/*   Global Declarations   */

                                    /* values used for "next" pointers  */
typedef enum {EMPLIST, JOBLIST, LOCLIST, DEPTLIST} ListType;
                                    /* values used for "first" pointers */
typedef enum { EMPLOYEE,
               ANALYST, CLERK, DESIGNER, MANAGER,
               A, B, C, D,
               MIS, PROD, RAND
     } SublistType;
typedef struct {
               char ID[10];
               char Name[22];
               char OtherInfo1[63];
               char Job[9];
               char Loc;
               char Dept[5];
               char OtherInfo2[17];
     } EmpRec;
typedef struct EmployeeNode {
                    EmpRec Employee;
                    struct EmployeeNode *NextIn [NLISTS];
     } EmpNode, *EmpNodePointer;

SublistType Sublist;
                                    /*  external pointers head sublists */
EmpNodePointer     FirstIn [1 + NJOBS + NLOCS + NDEPTS];

/* Function Prototypes */
```

Figure 11.5   Multilinked list program (continued next page)

```c
void InitializeEmptyLists ();
void Insert (EmpNodePointer P, ListType List, SublistType Sublist);
SublistType whatJob (EmpRec EmployeeInRec);
SublistType whatLoc (EmpRec EmployeeInRec);
SublistType whatDept (EmpRec EmployeeInRec);
void AddEmployee (EmpRec EmployeeInRec);
int ReadInputRecord (EmpRec *Emp,FILE *EmpFile);
void CreateLists();
void SkipLines (FILE *Listr, int L);
char *JobtitleOut (SublistType JobName);
char *LocationOut (SublistType LocName);
char *DepartmentOut (SublistType DeptName);
void PrintHeadings (FILE *Listr, char *ListHead, char *SubList);
void PrintDetailLines (FILE *Listr, ListType List, SublistType Sublist);
void PrintReport ();

/**********************************************************
**                                                      **
**          I N I T I A L I Z A T I O N                 **
**                                                      **
**********************************************************/

void InitializeEmptyLists()
{
    for (Sublist = EMPLOYEE; Sublist <= RAND; Sublist++)
                  FirstIn [Sublist] = NULL;
}    /*   end InitializeEmptyLists   */


/**********************************************************
**                                                      **
** I N S E R T   N O D E   IN   A   L I S T             **
**                                                      **
**********************************************************/

void Insert (EmpNodePointer P, ListType List, SublistType Sublist)
{
    EmpNodePointer J, Q;

    if (FirstIn [Sublist] == NULL) {
            FirstIn [Sublist] = P;                  /* insert into empty list */
            P -> NextIn [List] = NULL;
            }
    else {
            if (strcmp(FirstIn[Sublist]->Employee.ID, P->Employee.ID) > 0) {
                                                    /* insert in front of list */
                    P -> NextIn[List] = FirstIn[Sublist];
                    FirstIn[Sublist] = P;
                    }
        else {                                      /* find insertion point Q */
```

Figure 11.5 (continued next page)

```
                            J = FirstIn[Sublist]->NextIn[List];
                            Q = FirstIn[Sublist];
                            while (J != NULL) {
                                    if (strcmp (J->Employee.ID, P->Employee.ID) > 0)
                                            J = NULL;
                                    else {
                                            Q = J;
                                            J = J-NextIn[List];
                                            }
                                    }
                            P->NextIn[List] - Q->NextIn[List];
                            Q->NextIn[List] = P;
                            }
                    }
}    /*   end Insert    */


/*******************************************************
**                                                   **
**    A D D    N O D E  -  PLACE IN ALL SUBLISTS      **
**                                                   **
**        uses functions to find sublists            **
**                                                   **
*******************************************************/

SublistType whatJob (EmpRec EmployeeInRec)
{
    switch (EmployeeInRec.Job[0]) {
        case 'A' : return ANALYST;
        case 'C' : return CLERK;
        case 'D' : return DESIGNER;
        case 'M' : return MANAGER;
        }
}    /*   end whatJob   */

SublistType whatLoc (EmpRec EmployeeInRec)
{
    switch (EmployeeInRec.Loc) {
        case 'A' : return A;
        case 'B' : return B;
        case 'C' : return C;
        case 'D' : return D;
        }
}    /*   end whatLoc   */

SublistType whatDept (EmpRec EmployeeInRec)
{
    switch (EmployeeInRec.Dept[0]) {
        case 'M' : return MIS;
        case 'P' : return PROD;
        case 'R' : return RAND;
        }
```

Figure 11.5 (continued next page)

```
}    /*    end whatDept    */

void AddEmployee (EmpRec EmployeeInRec)
{
    EmpNodePointer P;
    P = (EmpNode *)malloc (sizeof (EmpNode));
    P->Employee = EmployeeInRec;
    Insert (P, EMPLIST, EMPLOYEE);
    Insert (P, JOBLIST, whatJob(EmployeeInRec));
    Insert (P, LOCLIST, whatLoc(EmployeeInRec));
    Insert (P, DEPTLIST, whatDept(EmployeeInRec));
}    /*    end AddEmployee    */

/*******************************************************
**                                                   **
**     C R E A T E    MULTILINKED   L I S T          **
**                                                   **
**            from input file data                   **
**                                                   **
*******************************************************/

int ReadInputRecord(EmpRec *Emp, FILE *EmpFile)
{
    char endlin[10];

    fgets (Emp->ID, 10, EmpFile);
    if (feof(EmpFile))
        return TRUE;
    else {
        fgets (Emp->Name, 22, EmpFile);
        fgets (Emp->OtherInfo1, 63, EmpFile);
        fgets (Emp->Job, 9, EmpFile);
        Emp->Loc = fgetc (EmpFile);
        fgets (Emp->Dept, 5, EmpFile);
        fgets (Emp->OtherInfo2, 17, EmpFile);
        fgets (endlin, 10, EmpFile);
        return FALSE;                           /* not eof */
        }
}    /*    end ReadInputRecord    */

void CreateLists()
{
    EmpRec EmployeeInRec;
    FILE *EmployeeFile;

    EmployeeFile = fopen ("A:NMPRSNEL.DAT", "rt");
    while (!(ReadInputRecord(&EmployeeInRec,EmployeeFile)))
        AddEmployee (EmployeeInRec);
    fclose (EmployeeFile);
}    /* CreateLists    */
```

Figure 11.5   (continued next page)

```
/*********************************************************
**                                                     **
**           P R I N T E D   R E P O R T               **
**                                                     **
*********************************************************/

void SkipLines (FILE *Listr, int L)
{
    int R;
    for (R=1; R<L; R++)
        fprintf (Listr, "\n");
}    /*   end SkipLines    */

char *JobtitleOut (SublistType JobName)
{
    switch (JobName) {
        case ANALYST  : return "Analyst";
        case CLERK    : return "Clerk";
        case DESIGNER : return "Designer";
        case MANAGER  : return "Manager";
        }
}    /*   end JobtitleOut   */

char *LocationOut (SublistType LocName)
{
    switch (LocName) {
        case A  : return "A";
        case B  : return "B";
        case C  : return "C";
        case D  : return "D";
        }
}    /*   end LocationOut   */

char *DepartmentOut (SublistType DeptName)
{
    switch (DeptName) {
        case MIS  : return "MIS";
        case PROD : return "Prod";
        case RAND : return "R&D";
        }
}    /*   end DepartmentOut   */

void PrintHeadings(FILE *Listr, char *ListHead, char *SubList)
{
    char Space = ' ';
    char *Underline = "------------------------------------------";

    SkipLines (Listr, 5);
    fprintf (Listr, "%30cMultiple Sublists \n", Space);
    SkipLines (Listr, 3);
    fprintf (Listr, "%25cListing for %s%c%s\n", Space, ListHead, Space, SubList);
```

Figure 11.5   (continued next page)

```
        fprintf (Listr, "%15c%s\n", Space, Underline);
        SkipLines (Listr,2);
}    /*   end PrintHeadings   */

void PrintDetailLines (FILE *Listr, ListType List, SublistType Sublist)
{
    char Space = ' ';
    EmpNodePointer P;

    P = FirstIn [Sublist];
    while (P != NULL) {
        fprintf (Listr, "%10c%s%10c%s\n", Space,P->Employee.ID, Space,
                P->Employee.Name);
        P = P->NextIn [List];
        }
}    /*   end PrintDetailLines   */


void PrintReport ()
{
        FILE *Listr;
    SublistType Jobtitle, Location, Department;

    Listr = fopen ("CON","wt");              /* CON or PRN */
    for (Jobtitle = ANALYST; Jobtitle <= MANAGER; Jobtitle++) {
        PrintHeadings (Listr, "Jobtitle", JobtitleOut (Jobtitle));
        PrintDetailLines (Listr, JOBLIST, Jobtitle);
        }
    for (Location = A; Location <= D; Location++) {
        PrintHeadings (Listr, "Location", LocationOut (Location));
        PrintDetailLines (Listr, LOCLIST, Location);
        }
    for (Department = MIS; Department <= RAND; Department++) {
        PrintHeadings (Listr, "Department", DepartmentOut (Department));
        PrintDetailLines (Listr, DEPTLIST, Department);
        }
}    /*   end PrintReport   */

/*********************************************************
**                                                     **
**   M A I N  -  program execution begins here         **
**                                                     **
*********************************************************/

void main ()
{
    InitializeEmptyLists ();
    CreateLists ();
    PrintReport ();
}    /*   end program MultilinkedList   */
```

Figure 11.5 (concluded)

12

PROLOG Language Elements

PROLOG (**PRO**gramming in **LOG**ic) is a high-level, declarative programming language that has become very closely associated with the building of expert systems. It was not widely known in the United States, even in the arena of artificial intelligence, before the 1980s. Currently, the language enjoys ever-growing popularity in several application areas. This may be attributed to at least two factors. First, the most important impetus for the use of PROLOG in this country was the announcement in 1981 of the Japanese Fifth Generation Computer Systems Project, which proposed the development of a new generation of intelligent computing machinery based on the principles of logic programming. Second, Borland International's Turbo PROLOG, an affordable, efficient microcomputer version of the PROLOG language, has made "logic programming" available to a large number of users who would not otherwise have had access to it.

There are some differences between Turbo PROLOG and the so-called "standard" (Edinburgh) version, the most obvious of which is the typing system of Turbo PROLOG. The illustrations in this chapter were coded in Turbo PROLOG and, therefore, the discussions in the chapter more accurately reflect the syntax of Turbo PROLOG than Edinburgh PROLOG.

This chapter follows the same general organization as do the other chapters in Part 2. This makes it easy to compare PROLOG to other languages you have learned or worked with. However, if you are learning about PROLOG for the first time, you might want to give the entire chapter a quick first reading followed by a more thorough second reading. Some of the ways in which PROLOG processes programs—namely, unification and backtracking—are first discussed in Section 12.5.

12.1 A BRIEF OVERVIEW OF PROLOG

PROLOG is a declarative language. A PROLOG program may state a number of facts and rules and then accept queries regarding those facts and rules. The procedural, or control, aspects of the language are hidden within the processing done by the system (interpreter or compiler). PROLOG programs are generally short and concise, and often they are difficult to read without good documentation.

PROLOG takes a "goal-oriented" approach to problem solving. The goal may be, for example, a query made to a knowledge base of facts and rules. Some goals are satisfied only by satisfying a set of subgoals (a subprogram, in procedural terms). If any subgoal fails, the PROLOG system must backtrack to find an alternative solution, if one exists. PROLOG is based on the principles of predicate calculus, and has become closely identified (if not synonymous) with logic programming. However, due to the practical considerations of computation and efficiency, PROLOG is not "pure" logic programming. Rules and goals that are not part of pure logic programming are sometimes called "metalogical."

History and Development

PROLOG was developed at the University of Marseilles in the early 1970s by Alain Colmerauer and his Artificial Intelligence Group, which included Phillipe Roussel. They collaborated with Robert Kowalski of the University of Edinburgh. The language was first implemented in 1972 in ALGOL-W, but a more efficient version was subsequently implemented in FORTRAN in 1975. The original purpose of the AI Group was to develop a system for natural language question-answering, and this the system was actually implemented in 1972.

Collaboration between Marseilles and Edinburgh ended at about 1975 (funding ran out), and research into the language has since diverged at the two locations. The two versions, sometimes called M-PROLOG and E-PROLOG, have slight syntactic differences. At the University of Edinburgh, David H.D. Warren designed the Edinburgh version of the PROLOG syntax. Although many versions of the language exist today, Edinburgh PROLOG has become the *de facto* standard. The definitive source for this standard PROLOG syntax is the book *Programming in Prolog* by Clocksin and Mellish (1984).

Although PROLOG spread quickly through Europe, it did not immediately become popular with the artificial intelligence community in the United States. Here LISP, and its variants, was the language of choice. Since 1981, when PROLOG was identified as the basis for Japan's Fifth Generation Project, PROLOG has become increasingly popular in this country and in the international computing community.

Application Areas

Logic programming in general, and PROLOG in particular, have applications in the areas of natural language processing and theorem proving. PROLOG is probably best known for its use in the development of *expert systems*, the most commercial branch of artificial intelligence. Recently, there has been much work done in the application of PROLOG to relational database management systems (RDBMS).

Classification

> *Software generation*: Fourth
>
> *Procedural/declarative*: Declarative
>
> *Translator*: PROLOG is usually assumed to be run in an interpreted environment.

However, many compiled versions (including Turbo PROLOG) exist.

> *Processing environment*: Interactive
>
> *Programming paradigm*: Rule-oriented, logic, constraint-oriented

12.2 STUDY PROBLEM #1: BUBBLE SORT PROGRAM

Since PROLOG knowledge bases generally consist of facts and rules expressed in a very formalized style, and the data set we have been working with is in the form of a textfile, the first sample PROLOG program is merely an input-output program designed to get the data "into shape" for PROLOG processing. The program listed in Fig. 12.1 converts the textfile data set of Chapter 7 into a PROLOG-type database (or, knowledge base) and saves it to disk for future processing. Each resulting PROLOG fact is equivalent to a record in the original data set. The first few facts (records) in this knowledge base are listed in Fig. 12.2.

The objective of a PROLOG program is to satisfy one or more goals. In this program, the goal—run—is satisfied only after its subgoals are satisfied. One of these subgoals—readinput—is itself a clause with its own subgoals. In this way PROLOG can support modular decomposition and stepwise refinement. The built-in predicate *frontstr* splits the specified number of characters off the front of a string. The built-in predicate *assert* adds a fact to the named database; the built-in predicate *save* stores the database on a diskfile.

Fig. 12.3 contains the listing for the bubble sort program—Study Problem #1—coded in PROLOG. There is an important caveat here. The bubble sort algorithm is not a natural manner of sorting in PROLOG. Since PROLOG is a language based on recursion as one of its major control mechanisms, a recursive sorting algorithm (e.g., quicksort) would be more appropriate. Furthermore, we used a list structure in this program since it is the data structure that most closely resembles an array. A more appropriate data structure for sorting in PROLOG is the tree—but that wouldn't be a bubble sort. For comparison, see the binary search tree program listing in Section 12.7.

12.3 DATA: TYPES, FILES, AND DATA STRUCTURES

In a sense, data is all there is to a PROLOG program. The "world" as it is known to the PROLOG system is described through a series of clauses representing facts and rules. The system may then be queried regarding this information.

One major difference between Edinburgh PROLOG and Turbo PROLOG is that the latter is compiled and strongly typed. The domains of all data objects, facts, and rules must be declared prior to use.

```
/****************************************
*     Create Personnel Database         *
*          from text file               *
****************************************/

domains
     stringlist = string*
     file = infile
     ID, Name, Address, Phones,
          Jobtitle, Location, Dept,
          Salary, LastPromoted, FirstEmployed = string

database - PersonnelBase
     employee (ID, Name, Address, Phones, Jobtitle, Location, Dept,
          Salary, LastPromoted, FirstEmployed)

predicates
     run
     readinput (stringlist)

goal
     run.

clauses
     run :-
          openread (infile, "A:NMPRSNEL.DAT"),
          readdevice (infile),
          readinput (_),
          save ("A:NMBASPRO.DAT", PersonnelBase),
          closefile (infile).

     readinput ([OneEmployee | Remainder]) :-
          readln (OneEmployee),
          frontstr (9, OneEmployee, ID, RestRec),
          frontstr (21, RestRec, Name, RestRec1),
          frontstr (32, RestRec1, Address, RestRec2),
          frontstr (30, RestRec2, Phones, RestRec3),
          frontstr (8, RestRec3, Jobtitle, RestRec4),
          frontstr (1, RestRec4, Location, RestRec5),
          frontstr (4, RestRec5, Dept, RestRec6),
          frontstr (8, RestRec6, Salary, RestRec7),
          frontstr (4, RestRec7, LastPromoted, RestRec8),
          frontstr (4, RestRec8, FirstEmployed, _),

          assert (employee(ID, Name, Address, Phones, Jobtitle, Location,
                    Dept, Salary, LastPromoted, FirstEmployed), PersonnelBase),
          !, readinput (Remainder).

     readinput ([]).
```

Figure 12.1   Data set transformation

Memory management is dynamic in PROLOG. Variables are bound dynamically; in other words, they have dynamic scope. This makes working with PROLOG very different from working in languages in which static scoping is the rule.

Constants

Literals. Literals are symbols or numbers and may be values of any valid domain. If it is not enclosed in quotation marks, a symbol—a nonnumeric constant— ought to begin with a lowercase letter in order to distinguish it from a variable, which must begin with an uppercase letter. For example,

```
person (susie)      /*  susie is a constant  */
person (Who)        /*  Who is a variable    */
```

User-defined constants. Although there are no built-in named constants, user-defined constants may be declared in Turbo PROLOG in a **constants** section.
For example:

```
constants
    one = 1
    pi = 3.1416
    Area = (Length * Width)
```

The program is preprocessed (much like a C program) and one string of text is substituted for the other everywhere it occurs.

Variables

Variables are identifiers that must be bound to data objects sometime during the processing of the program. Variables may be considered to have two states: *bound*, when they are bound to a value or instantiated; *free*, when they are not bound to a value. Variables cannot be used to permanently store information in PROLOG, because a bound variable is freed as soon as a query is satisfied.

Variable declaration. In PROLOG, a variable is always "declared" implicitly by simply using it. For example, in the following piece of code, the variables Id, Name, Job, and Department are implicitly declared as symbols since they are used where symbols are expected:

```
predicates
    employee (symbol, symbol, symbol, symbol)
clauses
    employee (Id, Name, Job, Department)
```

Built-in types. Most implementations of PROLOG provide at least **integer** and **symbol** as standard domains. Turbo PROLOG provides **integer**, **real**, **char**, **string**, and **symbol**. *Integers* are whole numbers from −32,768 to 32,767. *Reals* are floating-point numbers such as 127.5 or 1.259e + 17. *Chars* are single characters enclosed in single quotation marks. *Strings* are sequences of one or more characters delimited by double

```
employee("859673715","ARCHER      LEW        ","101 ROSS ST      NOTOWN     NY10031","3126436808
employee("583532918","BERGERAC    CYRANO  D","1 PARIS ST       PERSONTOWNNY30005","5137435589
employee("007511852","BOND        JAMES      ","122 GOLDFINGER PERSONTOWNNY30022","5133759007
employee("853600995","BOURNE      JASON      ","418 AMNESIA ST METROPOLISNY20045","1122590381
employee("892369626","BRAGG       PETER      ","340 MODEST ST   PERSONTOWNNY30025","5134995195
employee("783563314","BURKE       AMOS       ","114 BARRY ST     NOTOWN     NY10024","3163763580
employee("501620748","BUTLER      RHETT      ","44 WIND ST       METROPOLISNY20012","1129413335
employee("250141546","CANNON      FRANK      ","22 DIET ST       NOTOWN     NY10040","3123666323
employee("351453116","CARTER      NICK       ","400 MASTER ST   METROPOLISNY20016","1123451665
employee("584836738","CARTWRIGHTHOSS       ","5 PONDEROSA LA PERSONTOWNNY30003","4126225101
employee("431815949","CARTWRIGHTBEN        ","5 PONDEROSA LA PERSONTOWNNY30003","4126225101
employee("096283018","CHAMBERS    DIANE      ","100 BAR ST       NOTOWN     NY10011","3168585109
. . .
```

Figure 12.2   PROLOG database (continued next page)

quotation marks. *Symbols* are names made up of sequences of letters, numbers, and underscores, the first character being a lowercase letter. A symbol that must have embedded blanks or begin with an uppercase letter may be enclosed in double quotation marks. Thus strings and symbols are virtually indistinguishable in Turbo PROLOG and, in fact, are interchangeable.

For example,

```
predicates
     student (string, string, symbol, integer, real)
clauses
     student ("123456789", "Doodle, Yankee", math, 12, 3.54)
```

User-defined types.   The **domains** section is used to define domains for simple or compound data objects. This is often done simply for the purpose of program documentation and readability. For example,

```
domains
     id, name = string
     major = symbol
     credits = integer
     index = real
predicates
     student (id, name, major, credits, index)
clauses
     student ("123456789", "Doodle, Yankee", math, 12, 3.54)
```

Structured Data

PROLOG syntax is remarkably consistent with regard to the organization of data. Every manner of structuring data can be shown to be a special case of the PROLOG *structure*. Structures are identified by *functor name* and *arity*. The functor name is the name outside the parentheses, and the arity is the number of data objects contained within the structure.

```
              3122826590","ANALYST ","A","R&D ","  4187600","0186","0980")
              5132553233","ANALYST ","B","MIS ","  4899900","0381","0576")
              5137486007","CLERK   ","B","R&D ","  3124600","0188","1085")
              1128915116","DESIGNER","C","MIS ","  4826700","0187","1178")
    51349951965139962302","MANAGER ","D","R&D ","  5280000","0287","0381")
              3169191504","CLERK   ","A","MIS ","  2464300","0586","0174")
              1126253207","ANALYST ","B","PROD","  4127800","0687","0782")
              3123723835","MANAGER ","C","MIS ","  6320000","0186","0180")
              1182305018","CLERK   ","D","PROD","  2519800","0786","0279")
              5132778316","ANALYST ","A","R&D ","  4000800","0288","0282")
              5132778316","DESIGNER","B","MTS ","  4880900","0188","0976")
              3127781993","MANAGER ","C","PROD","  6700000","0186","0382")
```

Figure 12.2   (concluded)

Arrays.   Arrays are not directly supported in PROLOG. If arrays are ever necessary, the list structure is more appropriate to PROLOG-type processing and can be used
to simulate an array.

Structures.   Structures are compound objects or, in other words, objects that
contain other objects. For example,

```
employee ("123456789", "Donald D. Duck", cqo, "01/08/52")
```

The object outside the parentheses, employee in this example, is the *functor*. The
number of objects inside the parentheses, four in this example, is the *arity*. The objects
contained within the structure may be constants, variables, or other structures. For example,

```
employee ("123456789", name("Duck", "Donald", 'D'), cqo, date
          ("01","08","52"))
```

Structures are used to represent facts. They may be used to store records of data,
much like in a traditional language. For example, consider the data set in Chapter 7. If
this structure were translated to a PROLOG knowledge base, each record would translate
to a fact that would be completely described by the declarations listed in Fig. 12.4.
Structures are similar to records and, in fact, may be constructed so as to represent
several alternative structures in a manner similar to variant records. For example,

```
domains
    annual_salary, hourly_rate = real
    month, year = integer
    employment =  full_time (annual_salary, date_employed(month,year)) ;
                  part_time (hourly_rate) ;
                  unemployed ()
```

```
/****************************************
*         Bubble Sort Program          *
****************************************/

domains
     file = dbasfile
     id, name, address, phones,
          jobtitle, location, dept,
          salary, lastPromoted, firstEmployed = string
     factlist = person*
     person = employee (id, name, address, phones,
                     jobtitle, location, dept,
                     salary, lastPromoted, firstEmployed)

database - PrsnlBas
     employee (id, name, address, phones,
                  jobtitle, location, dept,
              salary, lastPromoted, firstEmployed)

predicates
     run
     readinput (factlist, file)
     bubblesort (factlist, factlist,integer)
     swap (factlist, factlist,integer,integer)
     newdbase (factlist)

goal
     run.


clauses
/****************************************
*               Main                   *
****************************************/
     run :-
          openread (dbasfile, "A:NMBASPRO.DAT"),
          readdevice (dbasfile),
          readinput (PersnelList, dbasfile),
          bubblesort (PersnelList, Sorted, 1),
          newdbase (Sorted),
          save ("A:IDBASPRO.DAT", PrsnlBas).

/****************************************
*   Read Database into a List          *
****************************************/
     readinput ([employee (ID, Name, Address, Phones,
                  Jobtitle, Location, Dept,
                  Salary, LastPromoted, FirstEmployed) | Remainder], dbasfile) :-
          readterm (PrsnlBas, employee (ID, Name, Address, Phones,
                  Jobtitle, Location, Dept,
```

Figure 12.3   Bubble sort program (continued next page)

```
                    Salary, LastPromoted, FirstEmployed) ),
          !, readinput (Remainder, dbasfile).

     readinput ([], dbasfile).

/***************************************
*       Bubble Sort Section           *
***************************************/

     bubblesort (ToSort, Sorted, Nswaps) :-
          Nswaps  0,
          swap (ToSort, Intermediate,0, NS),
          !, bubblesort (Intermediate, Sorted, NS).

     bubblesort (Sorted, Sorted,Nswaps) :-
          Nswaps = 0.

     swap ([employee (ID1,Name1,Address1,Phones1,Jobtitle1,Loc1,Dept1,
                    Salary1,Lprom1,Femp1),
            employee (ID2,Name2,Address2,Phones2,Jobtitle2,Loc2,Dept2,
                    Salary2,Lprom2,Femp2) |Tail],
           [employee (ID2,Name2,Address2,Phones2,Jobtitle2,Loc2,Dept2,
                    Salary2,Lprom2,Femp2),
            employee (ID1,Name1,Address1,Phones1,Jobtitle1,Loc1,Dept1,
                    Salary1,Lprom1,Femp1) |Tail1], S, Nswaps) :-
          ID1 > ID2,
          NS = S + 1,
          swap ([employee (ID1,Name1,Address1,Phones1,Jobtitle1,Loc1,Dept1,
                       Salary1,Lprom1,Femp1)|Tail],
               [employee (ID1,Name1,Address1,Phones1,Jobtitle1,Loc1,Dept1,
                       Salary1,Lprom1,Femp1)|Tail1],NS,Nswaps).

     swap ([Fact|Tail],[Fact|Tail1],S, Nswaps) :-
          swap (Tail,Tail1, S, Nswaps).

     swap ([],[],Nswaps, Nswaps).


/***************************************
*          Pick apart List -          *
*       Store facts in Database       *
***************************************/

     newdbase ([employee(ID,Name,Address,Phones,Jobtitle,Loc,Dept,Salary,
                  Lprom,Femp) | Remainder]) :-
          assert (employee(ID,Name,Address,Phones,Jobtitle,Loc,Dept,Salary,
                  Lprom,Femp), PrsnlBas),
          !,newdbase (Remainder).

     newdbase ([]).


/*    end Program BubbleSort     */
```

Figure 12.3 (concluded)

```
domains
    id, last, first, mid, street, city, state, zip = symbol
    emp_name = name (last, first, mid)
    emp_address = address (street, city, state, zip)
    area, local = symbol
    phone1, phone2, phone3 = phone (area, local)
    jobtitle, location, dept = symbol
    salary = real
    month, year = symbol
    lastPromoted, firstEmployed = date (month, year)
predicates
    employee (id, emp_name, emp_address,
        phone1, phone2, phone3,
        jobtitle, location, dept, salary,
        lastPromoted, firstEmployed)
```

Figure 12.4   PROLOG structures

The semicolon as it is used here is not simply punctuation; it means *or*. The empty set of parentheses after the functor unemployed is not needed.

Lists.   A list is a predefined structure in PROLOG. It contains an ordered sequence of components, all of the same type. These components may be simple objects, structures, or lists. Lists are delimited by square brackets and must be declared in the **domains** section of a Turbo PROLOG program. For example,

```
domains
    day = symbol
    daylist = day*
    ...
clauses
    ...[sun,mon,tues,wed,thus,fri,sat]...
```

Lists can be processed by breaking them down into a head and a tail, separated by a vertical bar. The *head* is its first component; the *tail* is the rest of the list. For example,

```
[sun | [mon,tues,wed,thus,fri,sat]]
```

or,

```
[OneDay | RestofWeek]
```

Trees.   Unlike other languages, where pointers must be used to build up a tree, a tree may be defined in PROLOG as a recursive data structure. For example, a binary tree may be defined as follows:

```
domains
    info = string
    bin_tree = tree (info, bin_tree, bin_tree); nil
```

This defines a binary tree (bin_tree) as a tree that stores some information in the form of a string and contains a binary tree (a structure just like itself) on its left branch as well as one on its right branch. The name bin_tree may represent tree, a functor with three objects as arguments; or, alternatively, it may represent the functor nil (with no arguments), in which case the tree must be empty.

Strings. A string is a sequence of characters denoted by double quotation marks. Turbo PROLOG supports string processing, providing a number of built-in predicates for processing strings in a manner similar to lists.

Sets. Sets are not supported in PROLOG.

Abstract Data Types

There is no data abstraction facility in PROLOG.

I/O File Structures

PROLOG allows you to create and access sequential files stored on disk by providing a set of standard predicates for opening, closing, reading, and writing files. For example,

```
domains
        file = infile; outfile
clauses
        ...
        openread (infile, "old.dat"), /* associates infile with a
                                              DOS filename */
        readdevice(infile),           % redirects standard input
        readln (Line),                % reads a char string until eoln
        ...
        openwrite (outfile, "new.dat"),
        writedevice(outfile),
        write (X),
        ...
```

Dynamic databases. Although much of a PROLOG program consists of data in the form of facts, sometimes we want to access this data dynamically, during the course of execution, without having to go into and modify the source code of the program itself.

In Turbo PROLOG, these facts can be saved in an *internal database* if their predicates are first declared in a **database** section. This internal database can be accessed with standard predicates such as assert, for adding a fact to the database, or retract, for deleting a fact from the database. The database as a whole can be saved to or retrieved from a diskfile with such standard predicates as save, consult, or readterm.

For large databases, using an internal database may require more memory than is available. In that case, Turbo PROLOG provides an *external database* facility. An external database can be accessed from a file or from memory. Unlike an internal database it is saved in binary form.

12.4 PROGRAM STRUCTURES

One of the ways in which Turbo PROLOG differs from standard PROLOG is in its requirement that all domains used in a program be either one of the standard domains or else declared in the domains declaration section at the head of the program. Turbo PROLOG programs can contain these six program sections:

- The **domains** section for declaring domains of objects used in the program;
- the **constants** section for specifying "constant" definitions;
- the **database** section for declaring an internal dynamic database with its own specific predicates;
- the **predicates** section for declaring the form that facts and rule headers in the clauses section will take;
- the **goal** section for specifying an internal goal to be resolved by the system;
- the **clauses** section for listing facts and rules belonging to the world of the PROLOG program.

The Program Text

Character set.   The PROLOG character set consists of the 52 upper- and lowercase alphabetic characters, the 10 numeric digits, and at least the following special characters:

	blank		underscore	'	single quote
+	plus sign	,	comma	"	double quote
-	hyphen	;	semicolon	%	percent sign
*	asterisk	.	period	|	vertical line
/	slash	:	colon	!	exclamation point
\	backslash	<	left arrow	( )	parentheses
=	equal sign	>	right arrow	[ ]	square brackets

Text formatting.   Although the formatting of PROLOG program text is solely at the discretion of the programmer, the use of such formatting conventions as indenting, comments, and blank lines is crucial in PROLOG programs, which are naturally concise and not very readable.

Free vs. fixed format.   PROLOG text is totally free-format.

Indenting.   Indenting may be used in order to make programs more readable.

Comments.   Comments may be enclosed between the paired delimiters /* and */ and inserted anywhere in the program, although they may not be nested. The percent symbol (%) may be used to indicate single-line comments or comments that extend to the end of the physical line. For example:

```
/* This
is
a
comment    */

% This is also a comment.

/* comment-1 */     employee (id , name, title, salary)     % comment-2
```

Blank lines.   Blank lines may be used anywhere in the program.

Punctuation.   Periods are used to end clauses and goals. Commas are used to separate items in a list. Single quotation marks delimit character literals. Double quotation marks delimit strings. Parentheses, ( ), delimit the objects in a clause. Square brackets, [ ], delimit list structures.

Words

The words of a PROLOG program are called *terms*. A term may be a constant or a variable. Constants may be numbers, such as 127, or symbols, such as employee or nancy or "Nancy".

Identifiers.   Variable names may be composed of alphabetic characters, numeric digits, and the underscore. The first character of a variable name must be an uppercase letter or an underscore. An anonymous variable, denoted by an underscore, is something of a "wild card." It indicates that you "don't care" what the value is, so no name is necessary. For instance, if a query wishes merely to determine whether Bob has a sister, but there is no need to determine who she is:

```
sister (_, bob)
```

Objects like the symbols bob and sister in this example are created with letters, numeric digits, and the underscore. The first character must be a lowercase letter so that the symbol will not be confused with a variable. If necessary, a symbol can contain blanks and start with an uppercase letter as long as it is contained within double quotation marks.

Keywords.   Turbo PROLOG has a few language keywords, used mainly to label the sections of the program and for declaration of objects in the **domains** and **predicates** sections. For example: **integer**, **real**, **symbol**. The keyword **if** may be used in place of the operator :- which separates the head and body of a rule. Similarly, the keyword **and** may be used in place of the comma, and the keyword **or** may be used in place of the semicolon as a logical operator. The keyword **fail**, used to induce backtracking, is probably the closest word PROLOG has to an action keyword. There are no noise keywords in PROLOG.

Statements

Because of the nature of a PROLOG program, we might say that all PROLOG statements are descriptive rather than executable. That is because the entire program is simply a description of a "world" of data, which may then be queried. The query, or goal, might then be considered the only truly executable statement because it is the only one that causes action on the part of the computer. This phenomenon is part and parcel of the declarative mode of programming in which PROLOG participates. The executable "statements" are hidden within the workings of the PROLOG system.

Every PROLOG statement takes a form similar to that of a structure. Statements may be facts, clauses, rules, or goals, and are found in the **clauses** and **goals** sections of the program. Each of these statements is terminated with a period.

A *fact* is an unconditional assertion, representing a relation between objects. Its objects are constants. Facts are also called *ground clauses*. *Clauses* are facts or rules. They may contain unbound variables and, if so, will need to be matched to ground clauses for resolution. Clauses may also be metalogical. In other words, some clauses are used for purposes other than pure logical programming. Examples are clauses for reading and writing. *Rules* are then/if relations of the form: <head> **if** <body>. The head of a rule looks like a simple fact, and its body may be composed of a number of facts. A rule represents the relationship between a fact (the head) and a set of subgoals (the body), which must be satisfied if the fact is to be true. *Goals* are queries that the system attempts to satisfy. A goal may consist of a set of subgoals. Goals take the same form as do facts.

Descriptive statements.   Descriptive, nonexecutable statements in the sense in which they are used in imperative languages—that is, statements that provide information to the compiler regarding types, variables, etc.—are not part of the PROLOG language definition. They are, however, necessary in Turbo PROLOG because it is a strongly typed language. The **domains**, **database**, and **predicates** sections contain this sort of descriptive statement.

Variables do not need to be declared prior to use. The PROLOG system binds variables dynamically during program execution.

Executable statements.   The work done by executable statements in other languages is handled almost completely by the PROLOG system (interpreter or compiler). There are some predicates available for metalogical operations—that is, those that do not arise from pure logic programming but rather are a matter of computational convenience or efficiency.

Assignment.   In truth, there should not be assignment at all in PROLOG, since assignment is an artifact of imperative languages. Variables in PROLOG are not like those in other programming languages. In PROLOG, free variables are bound to values when they are matched to constants in clauses, and they do not stay bound permanently. Therefore, a variable is not a very useful device for storing information.

The equal operator (=) either tests for equality or binds a free variable. That is, the system attempts to constrain the relation to equality and thus resolve the clause. So, for example, the clause $Y = A + B$ is not really an assignment statement although it may look like one superficially. It is really a relation expressed with the equal predicate as an infix operator. If A, B, and Y are all bound to values, this is an equality test that may succeed or fail depending on those values. If A and B are bound but Y is not, Y is then bound to the value of A plus B.

Notice the difference dynamic binding makes in that stock-in-trade of imperative languages, the accumulation statement. This type of statement usually takes one of the following forms, both totally inappropriate in PROLOG:

```
N = N + 1
Sum = Sum + X
```

Such a statement would fail in PROLOG. Using the first clause as an example, since N is already bound to a value, the predicate is tested for equality and, since N can never be equal to N + 1, it fails. The second clause would fail for a similar reason. If, for some reason, one finds it necessary to sum up a sequence of numbers in PROLOG, it can be done this way:

```
totaldata (N, Sum) :-
        readreal (X),
        NewSum = Sum + X,
        NewN = N + 1,
        totaldata (NewN, NewSum).
totaldata (N, Sum) :-
        /*  write out values of N and Sum here  */
```

When the first totaldata clause fails (perhaps because of an input error), the system backtracks and looks for another possible match. It finds it in the second totaldata clause. Besides writing out the values of N and Sum, this clause ensures that the program will not be terminated with failure.

Input/output.   Input and output operations are provided in Turbo PROLOG by a variety of standard predicates like readln, readint, and write.

Control.   Although most of the control structures in PROLOG are hidden within the processing, there are some predicates that allow a programmer to alter the default control mechanism. These are the cut (!) and **fail** predicates.

Subprograms

PROLOG is not a block-structured language. The nested block structure in the ALGOL/Pascal line of descent is necessary precisely because imperative programs require many detailed commands, and there is a resulting need to control complexity. However, even PROLOG programs can get large and unwieldy. For large programs, Turbo PROLOG offers separate compilation of modules.

Types of subprograms.   Although the PROLOG language definition does not provide for subprograms *per se*, a rule may be viewed as somewhat similar to an internal subprogram. Also, Turbo PROLOG does support external subprograms by way of its separate compilation feature.

Internal subprograms.   The PROLOG rule, with its objects taken as arguments, is somewhat similar to the internal subprograms in other languages, but the control mechanisms governing calls to these predicates are vastly different. As we see from the illustrations in this chapter, a goal matched to a rule is satisfied only when a set of subgoals (equivalent to the body of a subprogram) is satisfied. In fact, a PROLOG program can be designed by stepwise refinement, with the clauses at one level calling on the clauses of a lower, more detailed level.

External subprograms.   Turbo PROLOG's project facility allows the programmer to break up a large program over several modules. The project definition file is specified as a record of what modules make up the program.

Functions.   Functions are not supported by the PROLOG language.

Sharing data.   When we speak of sharing data in imperative languages, we generally refer to values stored in variables. In PROLOG, however, since variables are not used for storing information, they are useless for sharing it. In addition, since variables are bound dynamically and cannot store values permanently, the problem of side effects is eliminated.

Global names.   In medium or large programs, sometimes the need arises to share names (of objects, structures, etc.) across modules. In Turbo PROLOG, these modules are stored in files and compiled separately. Shared data must be declared global in each module using global declaration sections such as the **global domains** section, the **global database** section, and the **global predicates** section. A convenient and useful way to do this is to collect the relevant global declarations into a separate file and then to include this file, using the include compiler directive, at the beginning of every module that uses these declarations.

Local names.   All names are local in PROLOG. This includes domains and predicate names.

Scope of variables.   Scope in PROLOG is dynamic. A bound variable remains bound only until the query is satisfied. Then it is freed, even if the system continues to search for other possible solutions.

Parameters.   Parameters are not used to pass information across external modules. Predicates specify parameters that may be used as input or output parameters.

Subprogram libraries.   Turbo PROLOG contains a large number of standard predicates, many of which serve to extend the PROLOG language.

Also, using the facilities for separately compiled modules, project definition, global declarations, and include files, one can build up a personal library of reusable program segments.

Program Abstraction

Although program abstraction is not PROLOG's long suit, the language is continually evolving. Many of the applications for which PROLOG is ideally suited—for example, expert systems and relational database management systems—result in large complex programs that will benefit from the principles of program abstraction.

Modular decomposition.   For large-scale programs, modular decomposition can be achieved in Turbo PROLOG by means of separately compiled modules and global declarations. These modules can then be organized into a program unit by project definition and include files. Since the problem of side effects is not relevant to PROLOG's declarative mode of programming, modular decomposition can be cleaner than in other languages. On a small scale, PROLOG rules can be designed in a modular, top-down manner similar to top-down design in procedural languages.

Information hiding. Since all names are, by default, local in PROLOG, all information is automatically hidden inside its module. Names must be explicitly declared as global in order to be shared.

Self-Documenting Features

PROLOG is not going to win any awards as a self-documenting language. The appeal of the language is not its readability. On the contrary, the features that make this language appealing also tend to make it obtuse: concise code, recursive clauses and structures, backtracking, succinct syntax. In addition, there is the infrequent use of keywords and the lack of noise words.

That Turbo PROLOG requires declarations means that programs are forced to contain at least some measure of documentation. In addition to this, every PROLOG program requires plenty of comments, as well as indenting and blank lines, in order to enhance its readability.

12.5 CONTROL STRUCTURES

The control mechanisms by which PROLOG sets about satisfying goals is mostly hidden from the programmer, tucked away within the layers of the PROLOG virtual computer. A major control consideration is that unless there is a goal to be satisfied, nothing happens. In Turbo PROLOG, goals may be *external goals*, meaning interactive queries, or *internal goals*, part of the program code itself. The major difference in the way internal and external goals are processed is that external goals are satisfied by trying to find all possible alternative solutions while internal goals are satisfied with a single solution. The way PROLOG tries to satisfy a goal is by a matching process called unification.

Unification involves attempting to match a goal or subgoal with a clause in the program. The clauses are examined in order, looking for a match. The procedure for this matching works something like this: First, the predicate of the goal is matched with the predicate of the clause, seeking the same functor (name) and arity (number of arguments). If this match succeeds, then the arguments of the goal are matched with those of the clause. Any free variables are bound to the corresponding objects, whether these objects are constants or are also free variables. If this match succeeds we say that the goal has been unified with the clause. If this clause is a rule, then its subgoals will have to be satisfied in order to claim success. And so, the unification process proceeds.

For example, consider the following program segment:

```
domains
    id, name = string
    job, dept = symbol
    salary = real
```

```
predicates
    employee (id, name, job, dept, salary)
clauses
    employee ("012345678", "First, Who ", manager, acctg, 58590).
    employee ("123456789", "Second, What ", clerk, mis, 27670).
    employee ("234567890", "Abbott, Bud", manager, mis, 62740).
    employee ("345678901", "Costello, Lou", analyst, mis, 38500).
```

Suppose the goal is: employee (_, Name, manager, mis, _). In effect this is equivalent to the English language query: "Who is the manager of the MIS department?" Whoever the manager is, we want the system to respond with his name only. The values of identification number and salary are irrelevant and are indicated by the anonymous variables.

In order to satisfy this goal, the system will begin the unification process with the first clause. But acctg does not match mis, so it continues. The system then tries the second clause, but clerk does not match manager, so it continues. At the third clause, both manager and mis find a match and Name is bound to the string "Abbott, Bud". Success: the goal is unified with the clause. If this were an external goal, the variable Name would then be freed and the search would continue for other possible solutions. In this case, only one solution is possible, but consider the goal: employee(_, Name, manager, _, _). If this is an internal goal, this query translates to: "Name anyone who is a manager," and the search ends at the first manager discovered. If this goal is external, then the translation would read "Name all the managers," and the system would list two possible alternative solutions, the mis manager and the acctg manager.

Backtracking refers to the process by which the PROLOG system attempts to satisfy a goal again by finding an alternative solution, even when unification has already succeeded. This becomes critical when there are several subgoals to be satisfied. If one subgoal fails, then the system backs up to the previous goal to try to find an alternative solution, if one exists. Then unification proceeds again from that point. When a subgoal fails, the backtracking mechanism searches for an alternative solution beginning at the last subgoal that succeeded. A *placemarker* had been placed there previously by the system for just this purpose.

Operators

Operators in PROLOG are equivalent to functors except that they are used in infix form. Some PROLOG operators follow.

Arithmetic operators.   Arithmetic operators expect to act on numbers. The arithmetic operators are: + (add), - (subtract), * (multiply), / (divide), div (integer division), and mod (modulus). Also, Turbo PROLOG provides a number of standard predicates for mathematical functions, including random number generation and the trigonometric functions.

Relational operators.   Relational operators are < (less than), <= (less than or equal to), = (equal), >= (greater than or equal to), > (greater than), <> (not equal), and >< (not equal).

Sometimes, cuts are used to satisfy this last requirement and improve the efficiency of programs.

Test-after loop. The repeat/until loop may be modeled in PROLOG by means of a device that makes the system think there is an infinite number of backtracking possibilities. In the following example, backtracking will bring the system back to the repeat predicate every time, and the repeat predicate is coded to look like it always has alternative solutions.

```
repeat.
repeat :- repeat.

repeat_loop :-
        repeat,
        body_of_loop,
        /* the until condition goes here */ .

body_of_loop :- …
```

Test-before loop. The following skeletal outline of a rule illustrates the way we would model a while loop in PROLOG:

```
while_loop (<argument-list>) :-
        /*  the while condition goes here  */  ,
        …
        while_loop (<argument-list>).
```

The body of this rule is processed only if the while condition is met. Of course, it should be noted that the program will fail as soon as the while condition is not met. If there is still processing to be done a terminating clause needs to be specified:

```
while_loop (<argument-list>) :-
        /*  the while condition goes here  */  ,
        …
        while_loop (<argument-list>).
   while_loop (<argument-list>).
```

The second while_loop clause succeeds when matched since there is no condition to make it fail, but it is encountered only on failure of the first.

Indexed loop. The indexed loop construct can be modeled in PROLOG as a variant of the (also simulated) while loop. Consider, first, that any indexed loop can be transformed into a while loop. In pseudocode,

```
index <- 1
while index <= final do
        BodyofLoop
        index <- index + 1
```

We can model this in PROLOG as a tail-recursive rule:

```
indexed_loop (Final, Result) :-
        do_loop (1, Final, Result).
```

The goal overpaid(Name) would se *ut* predicate, written !, is used to prevent f
found, then the two subgoals of the body is a predicate with no arguments, and it a
the match could be said to have succeeded a cut, the placemarkers for backtrackin

Multiway selection. One of the i track to subgoals that were before it or try
program several alternative clauses for th matches. If the cut were to be translated
match with the first, or if the body of the ar, you're okay—don't look for any more s
The result of this is that we can write
alternative definitions of the same subpro ory, especially when combined with recurs
the rules until it finds one that matches owing it to proceed may not affect the logic
subgoals that succeed. This feature, togeth ell damage its efficiency. The program may
late the case construct. Consider the follov ometimes, a well-placed cut is the differen
that does not.

```
predicates
    case (integer)
goal
    ...
    case (X),
    ...
clauses
    case (1) :- !
        /*  subgoals for case
    case (2) :- !
        /*  subgoals for case
    case (4) :- !
        /*  subgoals for case
    case (_) :-
        /*  subgoals for "else
```

e unconditional goto of imperative languages.
ver the system's internal processing, and it ofte
t to comprehend. In fact, the use of this predicat
as the goto statement has.
ative meaning of the program are called *green*
time efficiency, cutting down on both processing
ould still be the same with or without the cut. If
that is called a *red cut.* In that case the cut is
the program, and removing it would probably
s for an obtuse, often unreadable, program and

nce control constructs as selection and iteration
age, but there are situations in which they might
constructs can be simulated.

The cut in each of the first three cla
checking for more matches." The use ewhat like the if/then construct. The head of the
case(_), means "If you got this far, I do y succeed. For example, let us do some more
cases listed." Clearly, the ordering of t beginning of this section. Adding the rule over-
construct.

Iteration. Iteration is not suppor
simulated using recursion or backtrack
because the logic of the program dema
simply eat up too much memory. The pr
Turbo PROLOG compiler, in the intere ept, salary)
recursion—called tail recursion—into an

Tail recursion. This is a term th rst, Who ", manager, acctg, 58590).
itself as the very last step. In that case, tl cond, What ", clerk, mis, 27670).
to be saved since when the call is over, $ ott, Bud", manager, mis, 62740).
this, Turbo PROLOG does not impleme tello, Lou", analyst, mis, 38500).
call is saved on a stack—but as iteratio
recursive, it not only has to call itself as i' _, Salary),
markers that would necessitate the savi

```
do_loop (Index, Final, Result) :-
        Index <= Final,
        body_of_loop (Result),      /* this subgoal matches a value to
                                       Result */
        NewIndex = Index + 1, !,    /* the cut inhibits unnecessary
                                       backtracking */
        do_loop (NewIndex, Final, Result).
do_loop (Index, Final, Result) :-
        Index > N.

body_of_loop (Result):-
        ...
```

Control over subprograms.   If we think of clauses as subprograms, then the typical control structures are

Call.   A clause can call another clause if it specifies that clause as one of its subgoals.

Return.   If the called clause succeeds, the "caller" can then go on to process other subgoals. If it fails, the calling clause also fails.

Control over program execution.   In Turbo PROLOG, program execution may be initiated either during an interactive session, using external goals, or without interaction, using an internal goal defined within the program. The illustrations in this chapter use internal goals.

Subprogram Control Structures

Let us keep in mind that rules are somewhat similar to subprograms. In fact, some rules are more similar to subprograms than others. For example:

```
print_report (OutputInfo) :-
        write_headings,
        write_details (OutputInfo),
        ...
```

In PROLOG, the only subprogram-level control structure that is familiar to us from our work with other languages is recursion. Recursion and backtracking account for most of the control features of the language.

Simple call.   Goals or subgoals are meant to be satisfied. Technically, this is not a true call as we are used to it, since the copy rule does not apply.

Recursion.   Recursion is the major control structure in PROLOG. It is applied frequently, especially in the processing of recursive data structures such as lists and trees. All structures and predicates may be used recursively without specially identifying them as recursive.

Implicit call.   Turbo PROLOG provides some exception-handling capability with the trap and exit predicates.

Parallel processing. Concurrency is not supported in Edinburgh PROLOG or Turbo PROLOG. However, the language does not specifically exclude it and some concurrent versions do exist.

Coroutines. Coroutines are not supported by the PROLOG language definition.

12.6 PROGRAM DEVELOPMENT

Logic programs are, as expected, incredibly easy to write in a language designed specifically for **PRO**gramming in **LOG**ic. Thus, PROLOG is a very natural medium as long as one is coding an appropriate application.

It is easier to learn PROLOG as a first language, rather than after you are used to the procedural mode of programming. To the experienced procedural programmer, PROLOG may seem extremely difficult. Bear in mind, however, that children have been able to learn the language easily as their first programming language.

The implementation may supply a set of program development tools, including a window- and menu-based editor or an on-screen help facility. Turbo PROLOG provides these and also provides facilities for separately compiled program segments and for interfacing with Turbo C subprograms.

12.7 MORE SAMPLE PROGRAMS

Fig. 12.5 contains the listing for the multiple list creation program, Study Problem #3 (Part A), coded in PROLOG.

Fig. 12.6 lists the binary search tree program, corresponding to Study Problem #4.

EXERCISES

1. Complete Study Problem #3 (Part B) in PROLOG.

2. Update the personnel database using the transaction file. See how close you come to the form of Study Problem #2.

SUGGESTIONS FOR FURTHER STUDY

Manuals. Borland (1988a, 1988b).

Books. Clocksin and Mellish (1984), Goble (1989), Lazarev (1989), Lucas (1988), Nath (1986), Sterling and Shapiro (1986), Teft (1989).

Chapters in Books. Sebcsta (1989), Chapter 14: "Logic Programming Languages," pp. 428–455; Sethi (1989), Chapter 8: "Logic Programming," pp. 296–341; Tucker (1986), Chapter 11: "PROLOG," pp. 382–411; Wilson and Clark (1988), Chapter 10: "Logic Programming," pp. 281–300.

Articles. Cashin (1988), Clocksin (1987), Cohen (1985, 1988), Kowalski (1985, 1988).

```
/***************************************
*       Multiple Lists Program        *
***************************************/

domains
    id, name, address, phones,
        jobtitle, loc, dept,
        salary, lastPromoted, firstEmployed = string
    lineoutlist = lineout*
    lineout = line (id, name)

database - PersonnelBase
    employee (id, name, address, phones,
                jobtitle, loc, dept,
                salary, lastPromoted, firstEmployed)

predicates
    job (jobtitle)
    location (loc)
    department (dept)
    run
    joblists
    loclists
    deptlists
    writeheadings (string,string)
    writeline (id, name)
    writelast

goal
    run.

clauses
    job ("ANALYST ").
    job ("CLERK   ").
    job ("DESIGNER").
    job ("MANAGER ").
    location ("A").
    location ("B").
    location ("C").
    location ("D").
    department ("MIS ").
    department ("PROD").
    department ("R&D ").

/***************************************
*                Main                 *
***************************************/
    run :-
        writedevice (printer),
        consult ("A:IDBASPRO.DAT", PersonnelBase),
```

Figure 12.5   Multiple lists creation program (continued next page)

```
        joblists,
        loclists,
        deptlists,
        writelast.

/****************************************
*        Print all Sublists            *
****************************************/

    joblists :-
        job (JobTitle),
        writeheadings ("Jobtitle", JobTitle),
        employee (ID, Name, _,_, JobTitle, _,_,_,_,_),
        writeline (ID, Name),
        fail.
    joblists.

    loclists :-
        location (Loc),
        writeheadings ("Location", Loc),
        employee (ID, Name, _,_,_, Loc,_,_,_,_),
        writeline (ID, Name),
        fail.
    loclists.

    deptlists :-
        department (Dept),
        writeheadings ("Department", Dept),
        employee (ID, Name, _,_,_,_,Dept, _,_,_),
        writeline (ID, Name),
        fail.
    deptlists.

    writeheadings (What, Which) :-
        nl,nl,nl,nl,nl,nl,nl,
        write ("                    Multiple Lists"),
        nl,nl,nl,
        write ("              Listing for ", What, "  ", Which),nl,
        write ("--------------------------------------------------"),nl,
        nl.

    writeline (ID, Name) :-
        write ("        ",ID,"             ",Name),nl.

    writelast :-
        nl,nl,nl,nl,nl,
        write ("       End of multiple lists listing."),nl.

/*    end Multiple Lists Program      */
```

Figure 12.5   (concluded)

```
/***************************************
*     Binary Search Tree Program       *
***************************************/

domains
    file = dbasfile
    id, name, address, phones,
        jobtitle, location, dept,
        salary, lastPromoted, firstEmployed = string
    person = employee (id, name, address, phones,
                            jobtitle, location, dept,
                            salary, lastPromoted, firstEmployed)
    binarytree = tree (person,binarytree,binarytree) ; nil

database - PrsnlBase
    employee (id, name, address, phones,
                jobtitle, location, dept,
                salary, lastPromoted, firstEmployed)

predicates
    run
    createtree (binarytree, binarytree)
    insert (person, binarytree, binarytree)
    traverse (binarytree)

goal
    run.

clauses
/***************************************
*              Main                    *
***************************************/

    run :-
        openread (dbasfile, "A:NMBASPRO.DAT"),
        readdevice (dbasfile),
        createtree (nil, PersnelTree),
        traverse (PersnelTree),
        save ("A:IDBASPRO.DAT", PrsnlBase).

/***************************************
*    Create Binary Search Tree         *
*                                      *
*   Read items and insert into tree    *
*         in order by ID               *
***************************************/
    createtree (InTree, OutTree) :-
        readterm (PrsnlBase, employee (ID,Name,Address,Phones,Job,Loc,Dept,
                            Sal,Lprom,Femp)),
        insert (employee (ID,Name,Address,Phones,Job,Loc,Dept,Sal,Lprom,
                Femp), InTree, WorkTree),
        !,createtree (WorkTree, OutTree).
```

Figure 12.6 Binary search tree program (continued next page)

```
      createtree (OutTree, OutTree).

    insert (employee (IDin,Namein,Addressin,Phonesin,Jobin,Locin,Deptin,
             Salin,Lpromin,Fempin), nil,
               tree (employee (IDin,Namein,Addressin,Phonesin,Jobin,Locin,Deptin,
                     Salin,Lpromin,Fempin), nil, nil)) :- !.

    insert (employee (IDin,Namein,Addressin,Phonesin,Jobin,Locin,Deptin,
             Salin,Lpromin,Fempin),
               tree (employee (ID,Name,Address,Phones,Job,Loc,Dept,Sal,Lprom,
                     Femp), Left, Right),
               tree (employee (ID,Name,Address,Phones,Job,Loc,Dept,Sal,Lprom,
                     Femp), NewLeft, Right)) :-
          IDin  ID, !,
          insert (employee (IDin,Namein,Addressin,Phonesin,Jobin,Locin,Deptin,
                 Salin,Lpromin,Fempin), Left, NewLeft).

    insert (employee (IDin,Namein,Addressin,Phonesin,Jobin,Locin,Deptin,
             Salin,Lpromin,Fempin),
               tree (employee (ID,Name,Address,Phones,Job,Loc,Dept,Sal,Lprom,
                     Femp), Left, Right),
               tree (employee (ID,Name,Address,Phones,Job,Loc,Dept,Sal,Lprom,
                     Femp), Left, NewRight) ) :-
          insert (employee (IDin,Namein,Addressin,Phonesin,Jobin,Locin,Deptin,
                 Salin,Lpromin,Fempin), Right, NewRight).


/***************************************
*   Traverse tree, stating facts       *
***************************************/
    traverse (tree (employee (ID, Name, Address, Phones, Jobtitle, Loc, Dept,
                         Salary, Lprom, Femp), Left, Right)) :-
        traverse (Left),
        assert (employee (ID, Name, Address, Phones, Jobtitle, Loc, Dept,
                     Salary, Lprom, Femp),PrsnlBase),
        traverse (Right).

    traverse (nil).

/*    end Program Binary Search Tree      */
```

Figure 12.6   (concluded)

13

Smalltalk Language Elements

Smalltalk is the computer programming language that invented, and continues to define, the object-oriented programming paradigm. Some so-called object-oriented languages may offer less than full-featured object orientation (MODULA-2, Ada); some languages are experimental and not widely known or available (ACTOR®, EIFFEL™). A full programming language with object orientation and an integrated interactive programming environment, Smalltalk was first released to the general public in 1983. Its impact is just now in the early 1990s beginning to spread. Whether the language itself will become as widespread as say, BASIC, is doubtful. What we are seeing, however, is the Smalltalk approach being incorporated into other languages and systems; for example, C++, Objective-C™, Object Pascal, LOOPS. Borland's TurboPascal Version 5.5 incorporates object-oriented programming features, and software development efforts have begun on several fronts to attempt the same for the next COBOL standard. Certainly, Smalltalk is credited with permanently changing the "face" of personal computing. Such features as multiple overlapping windows, pull-down menus, iconic menus, scrolling bars, integration of graphics and text, and mice for pointing, which are virtually standard today, are all innovations that have their roots in Smalltalk.

Smalltalk gets its name in part from all the "talking" that goes on in the Smalltalk program. Program (or system) *objects* communicate by sending *messages* to each other; programmers also communicate with these program objects by sending messages to them. Some people mistakenly assume that the Smalltalk system is a small one, or that it works on very small machines, or that programs written in it are small. Actually the name Smalltalk was chosen by its developer Alan Kay in order to avoid appearing pretentious about this totally new way of looking at computing. In other words, talk "small," and no one will be disappointed. As one computer novice was overheard to remark, "Oh, Smalltalk...I guess it's not much to talk about."

13.1 A BRIEF OVERVIEW OF SMALLTALK

Smalltalk is a very high-level programming language embedded inextricably within an interactive environment. The *object* is the central organizing concept throughout the language and system environment, thus imbuing Smalltalk with uniformity, simplicity, and elegance. The object is a well-protected module with a clean interface. Modules can be added and removed easily without compromising the integrity of the system. This high degree of modularity means that large programs can be developed incrementally and that low-level objects are easily replaced or recoded for portability to other hardware systems. Thus, too, Smalltalk is a highly extensible language. The individual programmer or organization adds constructs as needed. These constructs are not simply used once and stored away for possible retrieval and reuse; they actually become part of the system, which changes and grows along with the organization.

Smalltalk's main program structure, its class, is inherited from SIMULA 67. Much of its syntax can be traced back to ALGOL, by way of SIMULA. Its dynamic binding of data and functional application give it much of the character of LISP. And, much of its graphics capability, including turtle graphics, was learned from Logo. Some of Smalltalk's features are unique, for example, its use of messages for procedure invocation, the constraint that all language elements are defined as objects, and its distinctive, interactive graphical user interface.

Although Smalltalk itself is hardly widespread, its user interface, or environment, has transformed personal computing. On a visit to Xerox PARC in the 1970s Steve Jobs, then of Apple Computer, recognized that while the Smalltalk language could not easily be separated from its environment, the Smalltalk environment could be used separately for other applications. He brought back these ideas for the Lisa (and, subsequently, the Macintosh) graphical user interface, a screen representing a desktop with icons, a mouse for pointing and selecting, overlapping windows, scroll bars, etc. Some or all of these features have been implemented in virtually every personal computing system in use today.

History and Development

Although many people are responsible for the development of Smalltalk as we know it today, and many more are responsible for maintaining and developing it further, the history of the system began with a single individual and a personal vision of the future of computing.

In the late 1960s—during the era of bulky mainframes governed by FORTRAN, COBOL, and PL/1—while a graduate student at the University of Utah, Alan Kay conceived of the computer of the future as a powerful, notebook-size personal computer. This model of a computer, called first the FLEX machine and later the Dynabook, would be designed for the nontechnical computer user. The main application area would be education, specifically, the teaching of creative thinking. The user would be able to create new constructs for the computer, so that the computer's capability grows along with the knowledge of the user. The software component of this proposed machine Kay called FLEX, for **FL**exible **EX**tensible language. The model for this legendary vision was laid out by 1969 in Kay's master's and doctoral theses.

Kay soon joined Xerox's Palo Alto Research Center (PARC) and launched the Learning Research Group to research and develop the Dynabook. The software component of this system, called Smalltalk, was first implemented in October 1972 by means of a 1000-line BASIC program written by Kay. The version known as Smalltalk-72 finally came out two months later written in assembly code. Smalltalk-72 features were drawn from FLEX, SIMULA, and Logo. This version and the ones that followed it were implemented by Daniel H.H. Ingalls.

The language was revised at Xerox PARC in approximately two-year cycles, resulting in Smalltalk-74, Smalltalk-76, and Smalltalk-78. These early versions, each named for the year in which it was designed, were strictly Xerox proprietary products and were implemented on the Xerox Alto computer. In 1979, the Learning Research Group began work on the next revision, inviting outside licensees, and for the first time addressing the problems of portability and dissemination of information about the language. Smalltalk-80™ was the first version of the language to be made available to non-Xerox users. It is still the most recent version of the system and provides the standard on which all Smalltalk products are based. This standard is described in books by Goldberg (1984) and Goldberg and Robson (1989).

In 1981, Kay left Xerox and the Learning Research Group became the Software Concepts Group. In May 1983, Smalltalk-80 was released for general licensing. In 1986, Xerox formed a subsidiary, ParcPlace Systems, headed by Adele Goldberg, in order to market Smalltalk-80 to the non-Xerox world as a general-consumption software system. Versions of Smalltalk are being developed by a number of companies for a variety of different computers.

Smalltalk/V is the version of Smalltalk developed by Digitalk for the IBM PC family of computers under MS-DOS™ and is the version used for the examples in this chapter. The first version of Smalltalk/V® was created by Jim Anderson and George Bosworth about 1985 under the name Methods. There is very little difference between Smalltalk/V and the Smalltalk-80 standard.

Application Areas

Smalltalk was originally conceived as an education tool. The system was not motivated by a desire to develop computer-assisted instruction or drills, although it can be used for these systems as well, but rather to foster creativity and encourage students to learn how to think. The system grows along with the student as new constructs are created.

System simulation is another fertile application area for Smalltalk. After all, the language is heavily based in SIMULA, a simulation language, and simulation programs often use objects as the basic modeling unit. Object-oriented technology in general, and Smalltalk in particular, have other areas of application that are appropriate. These include: database management systems, factory management, computer-aided design, graphics systems, and artificial intelligence.

Classification

Software generation. Fourth
Procedural/declarative: Declarative

Translator: Compiler
Processing environment: Interactive
Programming paradigm: Object-oriented

13.2 OBJECT-ORIENTED PROGRAMMING CONCEPTS

Let us review the major features found in an object-oriented programming language. Then, in the following sections, you will see how these features are implemented in Smalltalk.

Objects. The object is an extension of the abstract data type. It encapsulates data and program structures. An object contains private data along with pieces of code called *methods* that enable the object to respond appropriately to messages. A message may require that an object act on itself, for example, to change its state, or act upon other objects by further message passing. An object is an *instance* of a class.

Classes. A class is the template by which objects are defined. A set of similar objects are described and instantiated by their class. The objects differ only in the values of the private data, called *instance variables*. A class has a name, class variables, named or indexed instance variables, and a set of methods. Class variables are named variables that are shared over all the instances of the class. Instance variables are private, local data that serve to customize instances of the class. The interface between the objects of a class and the rest of the system is known as the *class protocol*; this is, at minimum, the set of messages that instances of the class can accept and act on (because there are matching methods for them).

Methods. A method is a procedure defined as part of the class description. The methods of a class specify how its objects—instances of the class—will respond to any particular message. The message selector matches the name given in the heading of the method. Since the method is encoded within the wall of the class description, this explains how different objects can respond to the same message in different ways. This is called *polymorphism*, explained below.

Messages. The message is the basic control structure in object-oriented programs. It is the means by which programmers communicate with objects and objects communicate with each other. If the method is similar to the specification of a procedure in traditional languages, the message is similar to the invocation. The kind of invocation it most resembles is a function call. A message is a request for action sent to the object on which the action is to be carried out. For example, the message expression

```
queue add: newCustomer
```

might be a request to an object called queue to invoke a method called **add:** presumably to add the object newCustomer to the rear of the queue. In this message expression, queue is the receiver, **add:** is the message selector, and newCustomer is the argument.

Class hierarchy.   Classes are organized hierarchically. A class passes down its structure to all its descendants. The root class provides the necessary structure for all classes.

Inheritance.   A subclass inherits the properties—variables and methods—of its superclass. If the superclass itself has superclasses, the subclass inherits the properties of those classes as well. A subclass may redefine any of these properties for its own purposes, in which case the property of the superclass is no longer accessible.

Multiple inheritance occurs when a class inherits properties from two classes that are not connected to each other in the class hierarchy.

Polymorphism.   When the same message is sent to different objects, each can respond in kind because it has its own method with which to act on the request. In traditional languages, this is called *operator overloading* and must be implemented by extensive checking of data types. In object-oriented languages, an extensive typing facility is not needed because each object is the master of its own operations. For example, the message **close** might be sent to a file object or a window object with a different action resulting in each case. As another example, if the + operator is sent to a number object or to a string object, the result would be different in each case; the message is valid as long as a corresponding method exists within the class specification of number or string.

```
3 + 2           ⇒   5
'3' + '2'       ⇒   '32'
```

Once the methods are coded, implementation details may be ignored. This is closer to the way human thinking and problem solving is accomplished.

Dynamic binding.   In object-oriented languages, the association of an object with a property occurs during run time. Smalltalk is sometimes called a "typeless" language. It is this characteristic that facilitates the development of generalized data abstractions. For example, a definition of a stack need not worry about whether the contents of the stack will be integers, strings, or any other type data.

Garbage collection.   In procedural languages like Pascal, before a pointer is reassigned, the data object it was pointing to must be reclaimed using some sort of "dispose" statement. Of course, once a pointer is reassigned, the object to which it originally pointed is no longer accessible. One characteristic of object-oriented programming systems (made necessary because of dynamic binding) is automatic space reclamation by garbage collection techniques (e.g., reference counting).

13.3 STUDY PROBLEM #1: BUBBLE SORT PROGRAM

Fig. 13.1 lists a complete Smalltalk solution to the bubble sort problem of Chapter 7. This program does not reflect much of the object-oriented features of the Smalltalk language but is a fairly straightforward translation of the algorithm presented in Chapter

```
|infile outfile employees item limit  sorted temp printOut |
infile := DiskA file: 'NMPRSNEL.DAT'.
outfile := DiskA newFile: 'IDPRSNEL.DAT'.
printOut := Transcript " or Printer" .
employees :=OrderedCollection new.
item := infile nextLine.
[infile atEnd]  whileFalse:
        [employees add:  (OrderedCollection
                                with: (item copyFrom: 1 to: 9)
                                with: (item copyFrom: 10 to: 121)).
        item := infile nextLine.
        ].

limit := (employees size) - 1.
sorted := false.
[sorted] whileFalse: [
    sorted := true.
    1 to: limit do: [:r|
        ((employees at: r) at: 1)   ((employees at: r+1) at: 1)
        ifTrue: [
            temp := employees at: r.
            employees at: r  put: (employees at: r+1).
            employees at: (r+1) put:  temp.
            sorted := false
            ] "end ifTrue"
        ].  "end do r"
    limit := limit - 1.
    ].  "end whileFalse"

employees do:  [ :empRec |
    empRec do: [:field | outfile nextPutAll: field].
    outfile cr
    ].
outfile close.

printOut  cr;
    next: 20 put: Space; nextPutAll: 'Bubble Sort Report'; cr;
    next: 20 put: Space; next: 20 put: $- ; cr; cr;
    next: 5 put: Space;
    nextPutAll: 'Number of records read from input file -- '; cr;
    next: 10 put: Space; nextPutAll: 'NMPRSNEL File -- ';
    nextPutAll: employees size printString; cr; cr;
    next: 5 put: Space;
    nextPutAll: 'Number of records written to output file -- '; cr;
    next: 10 put: Space; nextPutAll: 'IDPRSNEL File -- ';
    nextPutAll: employees size printString; cr.
```

Figure 13.1   Bubble sort program, version 1

7. This ought to give us a feeling for the syntax of the language and enable us to compare it with other languages we have studied.

Let us remember, however, that Smalltalk is not a closed system. To use it is to change it. This does not mean that one has to be very careful of "breaking" it. It is just as easy to restore a previous version of the system.

A second version of the program employed a new method, **bubblesort:**, listed in Fig. 13.2. This new method was added to the instance methods of the built-in class **OrderedCollection**. Once added, this method becomes a part of the system and is not distinguished as an "add-on." The message protocol (external interface) of class **OrderedCollection** now contains the message **bubblesort**, which is used in the second version of the bubble sort program, listed in Fig. 13.3. Notice that the added message looks like any of the other (built-in) operations. The language has been changed to suit the user.

This is just a very small example of the power of Smalltalk and object-oriented programming. When you work in Smalltalk, you are not merely writing a program. With every problem-solving experience, you are designing (or, at least, customizing) your own personal programming language.

These and the other complete illustrations presented in this chapter were coded in Smalltalk/V and run on an IBM PC/XT computer.

13.4 DATA: TYPES, FILES, AND DATA STRUCTURES

Every Smalltalk data element—from the simplest to the most complex—is an object, an instance of a class. The class describes the organization of the object's private data and the kinds of operations to which such an object will respond. The class is itself an object and may receive messages corresponding to *class methods*.

Typing is dynamic in Smalltalk. The data types we are familiar with from other languages—integer, character, etc.—are all defined as classes. Instances of these classes may be assigned to variables dynamically without prior "type" declaration. Variables may be reassigned dynamically, to point to objects of a different class. For example, the assignment sequence

```
var := 'string'.
var := 10
```

is entirely legitimate in Smalltalk.

Constants

Literals. A literal may be an object of class **Number**, **String**, **Character**, **Symbol**, or **Array**. The appearance of the literal object implies the class to which it belongs.

A *numeric literal* may be of one of the subclasses of **Number**—**Float**, **Fraction**, or **Integer**. **Float** class objects contain a decimal point, for example, −127.5. Objects of class **Fraction** contain no decimal point but do have a negative exponent. Any other numeric literal would fall into class **Integer**.

A *nonnumeric literal* may belong to class **Character** or **String**. A **Character** literal is denoted by preceding it with a dollar sign, for example, $A. A **String** literal is

```
bubbleSort: keyPosition
        "My new method for anOrderedCollection"
        "Answers the receiver 'bubble sorted' in sorted order
        by the value stored in index keyPosition."
    | limit sorted temp  |
    limit := (self size) - 1.
    sorted := false.
    [sorted] whileFalse: [
        sorted := true.
        1 to: limit do: [:r|
            ((self at: r) at: keyPosition)
                  ((self at: r+1) at: keyPosition)
            ifTrue: [
                temp := self at: r.
                self at: r  put: (self at: r+1).
                self at: (r+1) put:  temp.
                sorted := false
                ] "end ifTrue"
            ].  "end do r"
        limit := limit - 1.
        ].  "end whileFalse"
    ^self
```

Figure 13.2   Method added to class OrderedCollection

enclosed within single quotation marks and is considered to be an indexed series of characters. This means that the individual characters are accessible by an integer index value.

An *array literal* contains an indexed series of other literals enclosed in parentheses and preceded by a pound sign. For example, #(yes no), #(10 20 30 40 50), #('A' 'B' 'C').

Named constants.   There are a few predefined "constants" in Smalltalk. Actually these are instances of classes that may be instantiated only once; they may not be reassigned to become instances of any other class. The object **nil** is the only instance of class **UnidentifiedObject**. Similarly, classes **True** and **False** (themselves subclasses of class **Boolean**) are allowed a single instance each, objects **true** and **false**.

User-defined constants.   The closest we come in Smalltalk to a true user-defined constant is the use of literal objects of class **Symbol**. Any object that is an instance of class **Symbol** is very much like a **String** (**Symbol** is a subclass of **String**) except that the characters in a **Symbol** object may not be changed. Every instance of class **Symbol** must be unique. A **Symbol** is denoted by preceding it with a pound sign, for example, #identifier or #yes.

Variables

In Smalltalk, a variable contains a pointer to an object, rather than the object itself. A variable may point to different kinds of objects at different times during execution. Thus,

```
|infile outfile employees item printOut |
infile := DiskA file: 'NMPRSNEL.DAT'.
outfile := DiskA newFile: 'IDPRSNEL.DAT'.
printOut := Transcript " or Printer" .
employees :=OrderedCollection new.
item := infile nextLine.
[infile atEnd]  whileFalse:
        [employees add:  (OrderedCollection
                            with: (item copyFrom: 1 to: 9)
                            with: (item copyFrom: 10 to: 121)).
        item := infile nextLine.
        ].

employees bubbleSort: 1.        "   added method "

employees do:  [ :empRec |
   empRec do: [:field | outfile nextPutAll: field].
   outfile cr
   ].
outfile close.

printOut  cr;
    next: 20 put: Space; nextPutAll: 'Bubble Sort Report'; cr;
    next: 20 put: Space; next: 20 put: $- ; cr; cr;
    next: 5 put: Space;
    nextPutAll: 'Number of records read from input file -- '; cr;
    next: 10 put: Space; nextPutAll: 'NMPRSNEL File -- ';
    nextPutAll: employees size printString; cr; cr;
    next: 5 put: Space;
    nextPutAll: 'Number of records written to output file -- '; cr;
    next: 10 put: Space; nextPutAll: 'IDPRSNEL File -- ';
    nextPutAll: employees size printString; cr.
```

Figure 13.3   Bubble sort program, version 2

the characterization of Smalltalk as a "typeless" language. There are three categories of variables: instance variables, shared variables, and temporary variables.

Instance variables make up the component parts of an object much like fields make up a record. Instance variables are unique for each object of a class and exist for the lifetime of the object. These are also called private variables, since they are not shared with any other object. They are available only to the object containing it. In order to gain access to an instance variable, a message must be sent to the object requesting the information. For example, in the expression

```
employee idNum
```

the message **idNum** is sent to the object employee, which then returns the value of its instance variable named **idNum**. The matching method for the message may look like this:

```
idNum
    ^idNum
```

Temporary variables are also private. Temporary variables may be *method temporaries*, *method arguments*, or *block arguments*. Method temporary variables are very much like the local variables in procedural languages. A temporary variable exists only for the duration of the activation of the method or block in which it is defined.

Shared variables are accessible to several objects and exist until explicitly deleted from the system. Shared variables are maintained in *pool dictionaries*, which are collections of entries consisting of a name and a value. Truly *global variables* are stored in the SystemDictionary called **Smalltalk** and are shared by all Smalltalk system and program objects. *Class variables* are shared by all objects that are instances of the class or its subclasses. Class variables are stored in a pool dictionary for the class. *Named pool dictionaries* provide limited global access to shared variables. The user specifies explicitly which classes are to have access to the variables stored in this sort of pool dictionary.

Smalltalk also provides, for each object, two *pseudovariables*, named **self** and **super**, which point to the object itself and cannot be reassigned. When **self** is the receiver of a message, the object's own message protocol is searched first for a match before the protocol of its superclass is examined; when **super** is the receiver of the message, the object's own message protocol is skipped. This is convenient when a superclass' method has been redefined for the subclass and one wishes to use the more general method.

Variable declaration. Variables need not be declared with regard to type. Instance variables must be named in the class specification. Temporary variables must be listed at the beginning of a method definition. The list is enclosed within vertical bars, for example: | i j k |

Implicit declaration. None is needed.

Initialization. Initialization of instance variables is done explicitly, usually when the new instance is created. For example, in the expression

```
SomeClass newOne
```

the message **newOne** might correspond to a class method coded as

```
newOne
        "Return a new object of the receiver class
         and initialize variables"
        ^(self new) initVars
```

where the **initVars** message invokes an instance method to initialize the new object's instance variables.

Built-in types. The data types of traditional languages—integer, real, character, etc.—are represented by classes in Smalltalk. In fact, type checking is rendered unnecessary in an object-oriented language since each object takes care of its own operations and will report an error if a message is received for which there exists no corresponding method.

```
Collection
    Bag
    IndexedCollection
        FixedSizeCollection
            Array
            Bitmap
            String
                Symbol
        OrderedCollection
            Process
            SortedCollection
    Set
        Dictionary
            SystemDictionary
```

Figure 13.4   Hierarchy of Collection subclasses

User-defined types.   All data types are represented by classes and are thus user defined. Even those classes that come built into the system (**String, Fraction**, etc.) may potentially be redefined because the source code is available to the user.

Structured Data

Smalltalk allows users a great deal of freedom to create and redefine any sort of structured data object. The class is an ideal data abstraction facility. A variety of "standard" data structures are built into the system initially. These may be redefined and added to by the user.

Records.   The Smalltalk system has no built-in record class. This is because *every* object is potentially a record. An object may contain private named instance variables that are equivalent to the fields in a record. These instance variables may be accessed only by sending a message to the object.

Collections.   Virtually all of the other data structures discussed in Chapter 4 may be represented by Smalltalk's class **Collection** and its subclasses. The hierarchical organization of many of the collection classes is listed in Fig. 13.4. Generally, the **Collection** class itself will have no instances. It is an *abstract* class that serves only to provide the common protocol for all its subclasses. Similarly, **IndexedCollection** and **FixedSize-Collection** are abstract classes.

Bag and **Set** are unordered collections, as opposed to **IndexedCollection** and its subclasses, which represent collections that are implicitly ordered and may be accessed by an integer index. **FixedSizeCollection** and its subclasses describe structures that are finite in size and cannot "grow." **Dictionary** object entries are accessible by key. Class **Bag** describes the protocol for an unordered collection, which allows and counts duplicate values.

Arrays. An instance of class **Array** is created by the message **new:** . For example, the expression

```
x := Array new: 27
```

sets up a 27-element array pointed to by the variable *x*. The individual elements may be accessed by the **at:** and **at:put:** messages. For example,

```
x at:3                    "returns the value stored in the 3rd ordered
                           position in the array x"
x at:j put: 20            "stores the value 20 in the jth ordered
                           position  in the array x"
```

Array elements may be any object and need not be homogeneous.

Strings. **String** is implemented as an array of characters with its own message protocol for string operations. A new instance of **String** may be created with the **new:** message or by assignment of a string literal to a variable. For example,

```
s := 'something in a string'
```

Lists. Linked lists may be implemented in Smalltalk using either class **Ordered-Collection** or class **SortedCollection**. See the illustration in Section 13.8.

Sets. Instances of class **Set** are unordered collections into which no duplicate values are accepted. The messages in the **Set** protocol include standard set operations such as a set membership test.

Abstract Data Types

Object-oriented programming in general, and Smalltalk in particular, implements the concept of data abstraction in a very elegant way. Abstract data types are defined as classes; variations may be defined parsimoniously as subclasses of other classes. The class definition contains named and indexed instance variables, the message protocol for interfacing with the rest of the system, and the methods for responding to those messages. These abstract data types along with their methods are "generic" since the instance variables need not be declared to be of any particular type or class. Values of the abstract data type are obtained by creating new instances of the class through which it is defined.

I/O File Structures

Accessing files on disk involves employing the protocols of two built-in classes: **File-Stream** and **Directory**. These provide messages for assigning, opening, closing, reading, writing, etc., to and from diskfiles. For example, the following message expressions were used in the bubble sort program:

```
infile := DiskA file: 'NMPRSNEL.DAT'.   "sets up a new FileStream
                                         called infile"
infile nextLine.         "reads from infile all
                          characters until a CR"
infile atEnd             "boolean test for end of file"
```

13.5 PROGRAM STRUCTURES

Program structure is the most obvious element in Smalltalk programming. Data structures are implemented by classes and control structures by blocks. Smalltalk's key program structure, the class, is an encapsulation of data, methods, and message protocol.

Programming in Smalltalk means defining classes. Fig. 13.5 contains a template for class specification. The specification includes

- a class name;
- a superclass, in order to indicate the position of the new class in the class hierarchy;
- a class type (pointer, word, byte), and whether the object can contain indexed instance variables;
- instance variable names;
- class variable names;
- any pool dictionaries the class will access.

For examples of class specifications see the illustrations in Section 13.8.

Class name:	<identifier>
Superclass:	<identifier>
Class variable names:	<identifier>
	<identifier>
	...
Instance variable names:	<identifier>
	<identifier>
	...
Class methods:	
method 1:	message-selector
	"comment"
	ltemporariesl
	expressions
method 2:	...
...	
Instance methods:	
method 1:	...
...	

Figure 13.5   Class specification format

The Program Text

Character set.   The Smalltalk character set contains the 52 upper- and lower-case alphabetic characters, the 10 numeric digits, the blank space and at least the following 23 special characters:

+	plus sign	<	less than sign	&	ampersand		
-	hyphen	>	greater than sign	|	vertical bar		
*	asterisk	=	equal sign	,	comma		
/	slash	\	backslash	.	period		
^	caret	:	colon	;	semicolon		
[ ]	square brackets	'	single quote	#	pound sign		
( )	parentheses	"	double quote	$	dollar sign		

Text formatting.   Smalltalk is a free-format language with all the usual enhancements to produce more readable source code. Since the source code for almost all of the system and program objects is available to the user, this should be examined before beginning to work with the language, in order to ensure conformity to text formatting conventions.

Free vs. fixed format.   Smalltalk text is totally free-format.

Indenting.   Indenting is allowed and encouraged.

Comments.   Comments, enclosed within quotation marks, are ignored by the compiler and may be inserted anywhere. The usual convention is for each method to contain at least one comment, at the beginning, stating succinctly what the method does and the object it returns.

Blank lines.   Blank lines may be used anywhere.

Punctuation.   The period (.) separates successive expressions, but it is all right to use one at the end of the last statement in a block or method. When messages are *cascaded*, the semicolon (;) is used as a separator. Cascaded messages are a series of messages to the same receiver object, in which the object is named only once. For example, in Fig. 13.6, the code in parts (a) and (b) produce exactly the same effect.

Single quotation marks delimit a string; double quotation marks delimit a comment. Parentheses, ( ), impose precedence on a series of messages. Square brackets, [ ], delimit a block. A colon (:) is used to indicate that a keyword message requires an argument.

Words

Some of the words used in a Smalltalk program are variable names and message selectors. Since Smalltalk is an extensible language—that is, it is meant to be "tampered" with—there are very few reserved words.

(a)

```
printOut cr.
printOut next:20 put:Space.
printOut nextPutAll:'Bubble Sort Report'.
printOut cr.
printOut next:20 put:Space.
printOut next:20 put:$-.
printOut cr.
printOut cr.
...
```

(b)

```
printOut cr;
  next:20 put:Space;
  nextPutAll:'Bubble Sort Report';
  cr;
  next:20 put:Space;
  next:20 put:$-;
  cr;
  cr;
...
```

Figure 13.6   Cascaded messages

Identifiers.   Identifiers are composed of combinations of upper- and lowercase alphabetic characters and numeric digits; the first character of the identifier must be a letter. For private data, like instance variables and temporary variables, the first character is a lowercase letter. For shared data, like global variables, class variables, class names, and variables in pool dictionaries, the first character is an uppercase letter. For example, the following identifiers were used in the bubble sort program described in Section 13.3.

employees	item	printOut
infile	empRec	outfile

Keywords.   Keywords in Smalltalk are identifiers created (or built-in) by the same rules as variable names. In the bubble sort program, the message keyword **bubblesort:** was added to the system. See the discussion of keyword messages in Section 13.6.

Statements

Smalltalk is not a statement-oriented language, like COBOL, in which one statement follows another in linear order. A method comprises a series of message expressions. The evaluation of message expressions is closer to the functional programming of LISP. Many of Smalltalk's built-in messages are discussed in Section 13.6.

Subprograms

Programming in Smalltalk involves creating classes and integrating them into the evolving Smalltalk system. Therefore, when we "run" a program in Smalltalk, we are actually running the entire system.

Types of subprograms. The structural units of the Smalltalk system are classes, methods, and blocks.

Internal subprograms. A *block* is an internal subprogram that may be considered akin to a compound statement or an ALGOL-type block. A block is enclosed in square brackets and contains a series of expressions separated by periods. A block is an instance of class **Context**. It may contain its own arguments; it may also *be passed* to a method as a message argument. The result returned from the block is the result of evaluating the last message in the block. Blocks are activated by the message **value** (or **value:** <arg>) and are crucial to the implementation of selection and iteration control structures.

External subprograms. *Class* specifications, along with their shared and private data and method descriptions, are Smalltalk's external subprograms.

Functions. All *methods* act like functions. They are invoked by messages applied to objects, and they return objects. *Class methods* are invoked by messages sent to classes. They are usually used to instantiate the class, for example: Array **new:** 100. Instance methods are invoked by messages sent to instances of the class, or to one of the object's pseudovariables, **self** and **super**. For example, the message **at:put:** corresponds to an instance method.

Sharing data. In Smalltalk, access to data stored in variables is determined by whether the variables are considered to be private or shared.

Shared variables. Global variables are maintained in the SystemDictionary called **Smalltalk** and shared by all objects in the Smalltalk system. Class variables are shared only by instances of the class in which they are defined and by instances of its subclasses. The variables stored in named pool dictionaries must be explicitly made accessible to instances in class specifications.

Private variables. Instance variables are private, accessible only to an individual object. Even different instances of the same class have different values for their instance variables. Method temporary variables are also private, with a lifetime limited to the duration of the activation of the method. Method temporaries are the most similar to the local variables of traditional languages.

Arguments. Method arguments and block arguments are typeless. For example, the familiar **at:put:** message corresponds to a method that may be passed any two objects as arguments. Of course, the code of the method clearly wants to work with an integer as the first argument, say, **at:** 3 **put:** 'X', although it will accept any object and attempt to work with it. In the following example, variable *j* is a block argument:

```
100 timesRepeat:
     [ :j | s := s + j]
```

Scope of variables.   Scope in Smalltalk is dynamic.

Subprogram libraries.   Since the entire system is continually open and subject to enhancement and evolution, it is unnecessary to maintain a subprogram library. A new class, once defined, becomes an integral part of the system, to be used at will just like an operator in a traditional language.

Brad Cox (1986) proposes the use of off-the-shelf modules called software ICs (integrated circuits), which may be easily customized using the principles of inheritance and polymorphism and integrated into an object-oriented programming system. Digitalk offers several Smalltalk/V "goodies" packs—sets of Smalltalk class specifications that may be added to the system problem solving in particular application areas, such as simulation, multiprocessing, and communications.

Program Abstraction

Once a problem is broken down into a hierarchy of objects, the "program" is simply the activity of these objects sending messages to each other. The need for program abstraction, therefore, is no longer terribly pressing. Within a class definition, the methods are program abstractions. They hide the "how" and allow other objects to send messages that simply indicate "what" is to be done.

Modular decomposition.   Modular decomposition in Smalltalk is based on a hierarchy of objects rather than the hierarchy of function described in Chapter 5. Methods are program abstractions, defining operations allowable on instances of a class.

Information hiding.   The object "wall" is a formidable one. There is no way that an object can arbitrarily access the private data of another object. It must request the information.

Self-Documenting Features

Smalltalk facilitates, although it does not guarantee, the production of self-documenting source code. The Smalltalk system is intended to continually change and grow as the user's knowledge and ability grow. The source code for virtually all system and program objects is available for examination, redefinition, and enhancement. In such an environment, the code had better be readable and maintainable. It is a good thing that methods are usually quite short. This is because each method does a very specific task.

We have seen that, in other languages, type declarations are part of the "enforced" program documentation. Since Smalltalk is a typeless language, we must be careful to choose descriptive variable names in general, and to consistently use argument names that are descriptive of the class of object we expect to receive as an argument. For example, although the following two method headers (for possible inclusion in class **String**) are equivalent, the more expressive argument in the second will make the entire method easier to read.

```
concatWith:  arg          concatWith:  aString
```

Finally, as with any other free-format language, the use of comments, indenting and blank lines goes a long way toward achieving the goal of self-documenting code.

13.6 CONTROL STRUCTURES

Messages passed to objects. This is the fundamental Smalltalk control structure. Everything else is an enhancement of this basic concept.

When an object receives a message, the object's own message protocol is first examined to determine whether it contains the message. If it does, then the matching method was defined in the specification of the object's class. If the message selector is not found, the system moves up a step in the class hierarchy and treats the object as if it were actually an instance of its superclass. If a match for the message selector is still not found, the system continues moving up the class hierarchy until it encounters a match or the root node (class **Object**) is reached. In the latter case, an error will result. This is why an object of a subclass may appear wherever an object of a superclass is expected.

An object can send messages to itself, for example, in coding a recursive method, by using one of the pseudovariables **self** or **super**. The difference between the two is, if an object sends a message to **super**, the class hierarchy is searched for a matching method beginning with the *superclass* of the object sending the message.

Operators

Operators are messages. Like any messages, they may be sent only to objects having matching methods—otherwise, an error results. In addition to the common operations listed below, every class of data has its own operations defined as methods. These would include operations on objects of class **String**, **Set**, **Bag**, **Dictionary**, etc.

Arithmetic operators. The arithmetic messages + (add), - (subtract), * (multiply), / (divide), // (integer division), and \\ (modulus) are matched by methods defined for **Number** subclasses **Float**, **Fraction**, and **Integer**.

Relational operators. The relational messages < (less than), <= (less than or equal to), = (equal to), >= (greater than or equal to), and > (greater than) are accepted by instances of class **Magnitude** and its subclasses. **Magnitude** is an abstract superclass that provides common protocol for its subclasses; these include the classes **Character** and **Number**.

Logical operators. The logical messages & (and), | (or), **not**, and the "short-circuit" messages **and:** and **or:** may be applied to objects **true** and **false**, the only instances of classes **True** and **False**, respectively.

Expressions

An expression denotes an object and may be a literal, a variable name, a message expression, an assignment expression, a return expression, or a block.

Message expression. The general form for a message expression is:

```
<receiver> <message-selector> <arguments, if any>
```

Here, <receiver> is an object for which the message-selector is appropriate. The entire expression denotes an object as well—that is, the object returned.

There are three kinds of message expressions: unary, binary and keyword. A *unary message expression* consists of the receiver object followed by a message selector. No arguments are expected or provided. For example: 27 **factorial**. A *binary message expression* consists of the receiver, the message selector, and an argument. For example, in the message expression 3 + 5, the receiver is the integer 3, the message selector is +, and the argument (passed to the receiver's method) is 5. A *keyword message expression* consists of a receiver and a keyword message with one or more arguments, evaluated from left to right. For example, xArray **at:** index **put:** newValue.

Assignment expression.   An assignment expression is an expression preceded by an assignment prefix. This is a scalar variable name and the operator := . Assignment to a variable denotes pointer assignment rather than value storage. In other words, the pointer to the object on the right-hand side is copied to the variable on the left-hand side. The object itself is not copied.

Return expression.   The general form for a return expression contains a caret (up arrow) followed by the expression to be returned to the sender:

```
^ <expression>
```

Precedence.   Evaluation of a series of expressions proceeds from left to right with unary expressions evaluated first, then binary expressions, then keyword expressions, then assignment expressions and, finally, return expressions. Parentheses may be used to impose an order of evaluation other than the left-to-right rule. For example, without parentheses, the following message expression would evaluate to 9 rather than the 11 expected from our experience with other, more traditional languages.

```
avg := 3 + 24 / 3
```

Block expression.   A block is an instance of class **Context** and its protocol was described in the previous section. A block contains a series of expressions enclosed within a pair of square brackets. It may also contain one or more arguments. A block represents deferred actions, and in this it bears a resemblance to the call by name of ALGOL. A block expression is evaluated with the message **value**. For example:

```
[i := i + 1. v := v + i. x at: i put: v] value
    "This expression is equivalent to the following two expressions."
buildArray := [i := i + 1. v := v + i. x at: i put: v].
buildArray value

[ :i | v := v + i. x at: i put: v]  "A block with an argument, i."
```

Control Messages

Control structures such as those for selection and iteration are implemented in Smalltalk using blocks.

Unconditional branch.   A branching instruction such as the "goto" is rendered unnecessary in a nonprocedural language like Smalltalk.

Selection. The messages **ifTrue:**, **ifFalse:**, **ifTrue:ifFalse:**, and **ifFalse:ifTrue:** may be applied to the objects **true** or **false**. The argument for any of these selection messages is a block expression. For example:

```
quant < 100                                        "null else block"
    ifTrue: [queue add: newCustomer]

quant < 100
    ifTrue: [queue add: newCustomer]
    ifFalse: [Transcript show: 'below limit']
```

In the second example, **Transcript** is a global variable referring to a window on the screen. If the receiver is false, the message "below limit" will be displayed on the screen.

Multiway selection. A case structure is not built into the Smalltalk language but can be easily added by the user.

Iteration. Iteration messages, like those controlling selection, also expect block expressions as arguments.

Test-before loop. Two messages that implement the test-before loop, **whileTrue:** and **whileFalse:**, are sent to a receiver block expression with another block expression as an argument. For example:

```
[inFile atEnd]
        whileFalse: [...]
```

With the **whileFalse:** message, the argument block is repeatedly evaluated as long as the receiver block, in this case [infile **atEnd**], is **false**.

Test-after loop. None is built into the system, but it may be developed by the user by following the pattern of the methods implementing the other iteration messages.

Indexed loop. Three messages that represent an indexed loop construct are the **timesRepeat:**, sent to objects of class **Integer**, and the **to:do:** and **to:by:do:**, sent to objects of class **Number** (a superclass of **Integer**, **Float**, etc.). These messages expect, as an argument, a one-argument block expression. For example, the following expressions are equivalent for initializing a 100-element array of counters:

```
100 repeatTimes: [ :i | counterArray at: i put: 0]

1 to: 100 do: [ :i | counterArray at: i put: 0]
```

Control over subprograms. The fundamental control mechanism in Smalltalk programs is this: A message is sent to an object in order to activate a method corresponding to the message selector.

Call. Method activation begins when the appropriate message is sent to an instance of the class (or subclass) in which the method is defined.

Return. A return expression, prefixed by the caret (^), returns execution from a block or method with the value of the expression.

Control over program execution. The Smalltalk system is always in immediate mode. Any selected piece of code may be run directly from the screen using menu commands.

Subprogram Control Structures

Object-oriented programming systems can be used to model a variety of control mechanisms. Not all Smalltalk systems conform precisely to Smalltalk-80 in this area.

Simple call. The simple call of Smalltalk involves the application of messages to objects *à la* the functional style of programming. When a message is sent to an object, the object responds by invoking the corresponding method.

Recursion. Recursion in Smalltalk involves the use of the pseudovariable self. For example, a method for computing a factorial would be:

```
factorial
      "Return the factorial of the receiver"
self <= 1 ifTrue: [^1].
^self * (self-1) factorial
```

Implicit call. While there is very little about Smalltalk that can be called implicit, there is a way to handle exception handling. Code for handling errors or exception conditions can be contained within block expressions and passed to methods as message arguments. For example, when searching a tree in order to delete a particular node, what if the node cannot be found?

```
tree    deleteNode:someKey
      ifAbsent: [ "an exception block" ]
```

Parallel processing. Parallel processing ought to be a natural feature of an object-oriented language, since it is often implemented with message passing. Smalltalk-80 supports multiple independent processes with its **Process** and **Semaphore** classes, but Smalltalk/V does not. This is one of the few areas where the two diverge.

Coroutines. Coroutines are not specifically supported but can be simulated.

13.7 PROGRAM DEVELOPMENT

Smalltalk is unique among the languages we have studied because the language definition specifically includes and even depends on a user-friendly, interactive, integrated environment. In fact, Smalltalk is a system for program development rather than simply a programming language. This system, by definition, relies heavily on a mouse as a pointing device and includes such features as: high-resolution graphics, multiple overlapping windows, textual and iconic menus, pull-down menus, and scroll bars that expand the virtual space of the display screen.

The Smalltalk environment itself is a program-development system. For example, there are certain windows, called *browser windows,* which provide for selective display of hierarchical information. Programming in Smalltalk is generally done at the Class

```
|masterFile transFile newMaster printOut |
masterFile := MaintainableFile is: 'IDPRSNEL.DAT' on: DiskA.
transFile := MaintainableFile is: 'TRANS.DAT' on: DiskA.
newMaster := MaintainableFile is: 'OOPS.DAT' on: DiskA.
printOut := Transcript.  "use Transcript or Printer"
newMaster
    update: masterFile using: transFile;
    close;
    printUpdateReport: printOut.
```

Figure 13.7 External messages from user, sequential file update

Hierarchy Browser window: adding new class specifications, setting up subclasses and abstract superclasses, adding methods to existing classes, redefining methods of existing classes. The Class Hierarchy Browser window displays selected class specifications, selected class and instance methods of those classes, the selected class message protocol, and the entire class hierarchy. Any code displayed may be changed, and the change is immediately compiled and saved.

This Browser window is a powerful program-development tool, but equally important is the accessibility of the source code of virtually all the objects in the system. This is important not only for making changes to the system but also for quickly and easily developing subclasses and methods that are somewhat similar to existing classes and methods.

There are specialized windows to assist in debugging, as well. When an error is detected during execution, a *walkback window* is automatically drawn on the screen, and this walkback window has a menu option that pops up a *debug window* for more information. Also valuable for debugging is the *inspector window* with which objects may be examined at any time, upon request.

13.8 MORE SAMPLE PROGRAMS

Figs. 13.7 through 13.9 contain the code necessary to implement the Sequential File Update, Study Problem #2, in Smalltalk. Certain assumptions were made: that the key field on each personnel record—identification number—is contained in the first nine characters of the record, files are textfiles, and the transaction code is the last character on the transaction record. These parameters can be changed by making changes to the *recordIn* and *transRecIn* instance methods of class *MaintainableFile*.

Study Problem #3 (Part A), the multiple lists creation program, is implemented by the objects and methods described in Figs. 13.10 through 13.15. Fig. 13.11 sets up a class Node. Instances of this class are nodes similar to the "extended record" pictured in Chapter 7, Fig. 7.16. Fig. 13.12 contains the definition, including instance methods, of class LinkedList, the master list of all nodes.

The three sublists all being similar in structure and function, a device was used so as to avoid as much repetition in these definitions as possible. Taking advantage of Smalltalk's inheritance feature, an abstract class called *SubLists* is created in Fig. 13.14.

```
FileStream subclass: #MaintainableFile
  instanceVariableNames:
    'errorList nChanges nErrors nDeletes nAdds nTrans '
  classVariableNames:
    'TransCode '
  poolDictionaries: ''
```

(a) Definition of class MaintainableFile

```
is: aString on: dD
      "Answer a new instance of the
       receiver on a DOS directory file called aString"
   ^self on: (File open: aString in: dD).
```

(b) Class method is:on:

Figure 13.8   Sequential file update

```
addRecord: record
      "Appends a record (anOrderedCollection of
      strings) to the receiver MaintainableFile"
   TransCode = $A
      ifTrue: [
          self writeFrom: record.
          nAdds := nAdds + 1.
          ]
      ifFalse: [
          nErrors:= nErrors + 1.
          self errorLine: (record at: 1)
              withError: 'not A'.
          ]

changeOrDeleteRec: record1 using: record2
      "Change or delete record1 from MaintainableFile
      using information in TransactionFile record2.
      A changed record (anOrderedCollection of strings)
      is appended to the receiver MaintainableFile."
   (TransCode = $C or: [TransCode = $D])
      ifFalse: [
          nErrors := nErrors + 1.
          self errorLine: (record2 at: 1)
              withError: 'not C or D'.
          self writeFrom: record1.
          ]
```

Figure 13.9   Instance methods, sequential file update (continued next page)

```
        ifTrue: [
            TransCode = $C
                ifTrue: [    "change the record"
                    1 to: record1 size do: [:i|
                        record1 at: i put: (record2 at: i)] .
                    self writeFrom: record1.
                    nChanges := nChanges + 1.
                    ]
                ifFalse: [
                    nDeletes := nDeletes + 1  "delete the record"
                    ]
            ]


errorLine: firstString withError: secondString
        "Set up line in error listing for output later
        in printed report. "
    errorList add: (OrderedCollection
                with: firstString
                with: TransCode printString
                with: (TransCode = ($ )
                    ifTrue: ['missing']
                    ifFalse: [secondString]) ).

initializeUpdate
        "These instance variables are initialized
        only once -- receiver is the new master file."

    nTrans := nErrors := 0.
    nChanges := nDeletes := nAdds := 0.
    errorList := OrderedCollection new


printUpdateReport: textStream
        "comment"
    | nOK |
    nTrans := nTrans - 1.
    nOK := nTrans - nErrors.
    textStream
        skipLines: 4;
        tab:15; nextPutAll: 'Sequential File Update'; cr;
        tab:13; nextPutAll: 'Personnel File Maintenance'; cr;
        tab:5; next: 40 put: $-; cr;
        skipLines:2;
        tab:14; nextPutAll: 'Total number of transactions = ';
            nextPutAll: nTrans printString; cr;
        skipLines:2;
        tab:7; nextPutAll: 'Transactions processed successfully = ';
            nextPutAll: nOK printString; cr;
```

Figure 13.9   (continued next page)

```
            skipLines:2;
            tab:2; nextPutAll:
                'The following transactions could not be processed '; cr;
            tab:2; nextPutAll: 'due to errors:'; cr;
            skipLines:2;
            tab:5; nextPutAll: 'ID Number';
                tab:3; nextPutAll: 'TransCode';
                tab:3; nextPutAll: 'Error'; cr;
            tab:5; next: 40 put: $-; cr;
            skipLines:2.
    errorList do: [ :line |
        line do: [ :field |
            textStream tab:5; nextPutAll: field ].
        textStream cr].
    textStream
        tab:5; next: 40 put: $-; cr;
        skipLines:4;
        tab:10; nextPutAll: nAdds printString;
            nextPutAll: ' records added to Master File.';cr;
        skipLines:2;
        tab:10; nextPutAll: nDeletes printString;
            nextPutAll: ' records deleted from Master File.';cr;
        skipLines:2;
        tab:10; nextPutAll: nChanges printString;
            nextPutAll: ' records changed'; cr


recordIn
        "Answer the next record (an Ordered Collection of
        strings) from the receiver MaintainableFile stream."
    | item |
    item := self nextLine.
    self atEnd
        ifTrue: [ ^item]
        ifFalse: [
            ^OrderedCollection
                with: (item copyFrom: 1 to: 9)
                with: (item copyFrom: 10 to: item size)].


transRecIn
        "Answer the next record (an Ordered Collection of
        strings) from the receiver transactionFile stream."
    |record|
    record :- self recordIn.  "use the same read code as for a master file"
    self atEnd ifFalse: [

        TransCode := record last last.
        record at: 2 put:
        ((record at: 2) copyFrom: 1 to: (record at: 2) size - 1)].
    ^record
```

Figure 13.9   (continued next page)

```
update: masterFile using: transFile
        "Produce a newMasterFile (the receiver)
        derived from masterFile updated with transFile.
        All are MaintainableFiles."
    | masterRec transRec |
    self initializeUpdate.
    masterRec := masterFile recordIn.
    transRec := transFile transRecIn.
    nTrans := nTrans + 1.
    [transFile atEnd] whileFalse: [
        (masterFile atEnd) ifFalse: [
            (transRec at: 1)   (masterRec at: 1)
                ifTrue: [
                    self writeFrom: masterRec.
                    masterRec := masterFile recordIn.
                    ] "end ifTrue  "
                ifFalse: [
                    (transRec at: 1) = (masterRec at: 1)
                        ifTrue: [
                            self changeOrDeleteRec: masterRec using: transRec.
                            masterRec := masterFile recordIn.
                            ] "end ifTrue = "
                        ifFalse: [ self addRecord: transRec ].
                        transRec := transFile transRecIn.
                         nTrans := nTrans + 1. ].

            ] "end ifFalse   atEnd "
            ifTrue: [ "that masterFile is atEnd"
                [transFile atEnd] whileFalse: [
                    self addRecord: transRec.
                    transRec := transFile transRecIn.
                    nTrans := nTrans + 1.]
                ]
        ].
    [masterFile atEnd] whileFalse: [
        self writeFrom: masterRec.
        masterRec := masterFile recordIn]


writeFrom: anOrderedCollection
        "Write a record (anOrderedCollection) as the next
        line of text to the receiver MaintainableFile."

    anOrderedCollection do: [:field |
            self nextPutAll: field].
    self cr.
```

Figure 13.9   (concluded)

```
      "external commands"
| printOut |
printOut := Transcript "Transcript or Printer".
(LinkedList create)
    buildLists: (DiskA file: 'NMPRSNEL.DAT');
    printMultipleSublists: printOut.
```

Figure 13.10   External messages from user, multiple lists creation

```
Object subclass: #Node
  instanceVariableNames:
    'id info1 info2 job loc dept name next nextJob nextLoc nextDept '
  classVariableNames: ''
  poolDictionaries: ''
```

(a) Class definition

```
new: aString
      "Answer a new node with
      instance variables initialized from aString"
   ^ (self new) initNodeInfo: aString
```

(b) Class Method new:

```
dept
      "Answer the department of the receiver"
   ^dept

id
      "Answer the id of the receiver"
   ^id


initNodeInfo: aString
      "initialize aNode instance variables from aString"
   id := aString copyFrom: 1 to: 9.
   name := aString copyFrom: 10 to: 30.
   info1 := aString copyFrom: 31 to: 92.
   job := aString copyFrom: 93 to: 100.
   loc := aString copyFrom: 101 to: 101.
   dept := aString copyFrom: 102 to: 105.
   info2 := aString copyFrom: 106 to: 121.
   ^ self


job
      "Answer the job of the receiver"
   ^job
```

Figure 13.11   Class "Node," multiple lists creation (continued next page)

```
loc
        "Answer the location of the receiver"
    ^loc

name
        "Answer the name of the receiver"
    ^name


next
        "Answer the node next in order."
    ^next


next: aNode
        "Set the node next in order to aNode."
    ^next := aNode


nextDept
        "Answer the node next in order after the
        receiver, on the deptlist."
    ^nextDept


nextDept: aNode
        "Set the node next in order after the
        receiver, on the deptlist, to aNode."
    ^nextDept := aNode


nextJob
        "Answer the node next in order after the
        receiver, on the joblist."
    ^nextJob


nextJob: aNode
        "Set the node next in order after the
        receiver, on the joblist, to aNode."
    ^nextJob := aNode


nextLoc
        "Answer the node next in order after the
        receiver, on the loclist."
    ^nextLoc
```

Figure 13.11   (continued next page)

```
nextLoc: aNode
        "Set the node next in order after the
        receiver, on the loclist, to aNode."
    ^nextLoc := aNode
```

(c) Instance methods

Figure 13.11   (concluded)

```
OrderedCollection variableSubclass: #LinkedList
   instanceVariableNames:
     'first joblist loclist deptlist '
   classVariableNames: ''
   poolDictionaries: ''
```

(a) Definition of class LinkedList

```
create
        "Answer a new (mult-)linked list."
      ^(self new) initLists.
```

(b) Class method create

Figure 13.12   Class "LinkedList," multiple lists creation

An *abstract class* is one that is not intended to have instances. It may be quite incomplete in its definition. Its sole purpose is to provide definitions for the common variables and methods of its subclasses. In this case, the subclasses of *SubLists* are the classes *Depts-List*, *JobsList*, and *LocsList*, defined in Fig. 13.15. This abstract class is pictorially represented in Fig. 13.16, in which a class is represented by a rectangle and an instance of a class is represented by ovals.

EXERCISES

1. Complete Study Problem #3 (Part B) in Smalltalk.
2. Do Study Problem #4 in Smalltalk.

SUGGESTIONS FOR FURTHER STUDY

Manuals.   For Smalltalk/V, the vendor's reference manual, Digitalk (1986), also contains a tutorial. The Smalltalk-80 standard manual is the set of books by Goldberg (1984) and Goldberg and Robson (1989).

Books.   Budd (1987), Cox (1986), Kaehler and Patterson (1986), Krasner (1983), Pinson and Wiener (1988), Shlaer and Mellor (1988), Tello (1989).

Chapters in Books.   MacLennan (1983), Chapter 14: "Object-Oriented Programming: Smalltalk," pp. 453–498; Horowitz (1984), Chapter 14: "Smalltalk" by T. Rentsch, pp. 395–419; Sebesta (1989), Chapter 15: "Object Oriented Programming Languages," pp. 456–483.

Articles.   Kay and Goldberg (1977); See the August 1981, May 1985, and August 1987 issues of *Byte* magazine.

```
add: aNode after: previousNode
        "Set up links to add aNode after previousNode
        in receiver list."
    self
        after: aNode is: (self after: previousNode);
        after: previousNode is: aNode.
    ^aNode


after: aNode
        "Answer node next in order after aNode"
    ^aNode next

after: aNode is: nextNode
        "Set links so nextNode is next in order after aNode."
    ^aNode next: nextNode

buildLists: aFileStream
        "Answer a multi-linked list created from
        data stored on aFileStream."
    | record aNode |
    record := aFileStream nextLine.
    [aFileStream atEnd] whileFalse: [
        aNode := Node new: record.
        " self insert: aNode."
        joblist insert: aNode inList: aNode job.
        loclist insert: aNode inList: aNode loc.
        deptlist insert: aNode inList: aNode dept.
        record := aFileStream nextLine.].
    ^self

findPosition: aNode startFrom: firstNode
        "Answer the targetNode after which insertion
        (or deletion) is to take place."
    | pNode targNode |
    pNode := self after: firstNode.
    targNode := firstNode.
    [pNode = nil] whileFalse: [
        pNode id  aNode id
            ifTrue: [pNode := nil]
            ifFalse: [
                targNode := pNode.
                pNode := self after: pNode].
        ].
    ^targNode
```

Figure 13.13   Insurance methods for class "LinkedList," multiple lists creation (continued next page)

```
first
        "Answer the first node in the list"
    ^first

first: aNode
        "Set the first node in the list"
    ^first := aNode

initLists
        "private - Initialize types of sublists."
    joblist := JobsList setUp.
    loclist := LocsList setUp.
    deptlist := DeptsList setUp.
    ^self


insert: aNode
        "Set up links to 'insert' aNode into its
        position in the receiver linked list"

    self isEmpty ifTrue: [^self first: aNode].

    (self first) id  aNode id ifTrue:
            [^self
                after: aNode is: self first;
                first: aNode].

    ^self add: aNode after:
        (self findPosition: aNode startFrom: self first).


isEmpty
        "Answer true if receiver linked list is empty"
    ^first isNil


printMultipleSublists: aTextStream
        "Output report for all sublists."
    joblist listNames do: [:name |
        joblist printSublistOn: aTextStream
            using: 'Jobtitle' using: name].

    loclist listNames do: [:name |
        loclist printSublistOn: aTextStream
            using: 'Location' using: name].

    deptlist listNames do: [:name |
        deptlist printSublistOn: aTextStream
            using: 'Department' using: name].
```

Figure 13.13   (concluded)

```
LinkedList variableSubclass: #SubLists
  instanceVariableNames: ''
  classVariableNames: ''
  poolDictionaries: ''
```

(a) Class definition

```
setUp
      "Answer a new sublist of type specified by receiver."
   ^(self new) initExternalPtrs
```

(b) Class method setUp

```
first: aListName
      "Answer the first node in the sublist
      specified by aListName."
   ^ first at: aListName


first: aListName is: aNode
      "Set the external pointer to the first node
      in the sublist specified by aListName
      to aNode."
   ^ first at: aListName put: aNode


initExternalPtrs
      "private - For the receiver sublist type, create a
      Dictionary to hold external pointers to its sublists."
   first := Dictionary new

insert: aNode inList: aListName
      "Set up links to 'insert' aNode into list aListName
      of receiver type."

   (self isEmpty: aListName) ifTrue:
      [^self first: aListName is: aNode].

   (self first: aListName) id  aNode id ifTrue:
      [^self after: aNode is: (self first: aListName);
            first: aListName is: aNode].

   ^self add: aNode after:
         (self findPosition: aNode startFrom: (self first: aListName))


isEmpty: aListName
      "Answer true if list aListName of receiver type is empty"
   ^(first includesKey: aListName) not
```

Figure 13.14   Abstract class "Sublists," multiple lists creation (continued next page)

```
listNames
        "Answer the collection of names stored in the
        dictionary instance variable of the receiver."
    ^first keys


printSublistOn: aTextStream using: aListHeader
                            using: aListName
        "Output results for a single sublist type."
    | pNode |
    aTextStream
        skipLines:5;
        tab:25; nextPutAll: 'Multiple Sublists';cr;
        skipLines:3;
        tab:20; nextPutAll: 'Listing for ';
            nextPutAll: aListHeader; space;
            nextPutAll: aListName; cr;
        tab:10; next:40 put: $-; cr;
        skipLines:2.
    pNode := self first: aListName.
    [pNode = nil] whileFalse: [
        aTextStream
            tab:10; nextPutAll: pNode id;
            tab:10; nextPutAll: pNode name; cr.
        pNode := self after: pNode
        ].
```

(c) Instance methods

Figure 13.14   (concluded)

```
SubLists variableSubclass: #DeptsList
    instanceVariableNames: ''
    classVariableNames: ''
    poolDictionaries: ''


after: aNode
        "Answer the next node in order on deptlist"
    ^aNode nextDept


after: aNode is: nextNode
        "Set the next node in order on deptlist"
    ^aNode nextDept: nextNode
```

Figure 13.15   Class definitions for the three sublists, multiple lists creation (continued next page)

```
SubLists variableSubclass: #JobsList
  instanceVariableNames: ''
  classVariableNames: ''
  poolDictionaries: ''


after: aNode
        "Answer the next node in order on joblist"
    ^aNode nextJob

after: aNode is: nextNode
        "Set the next node in order on joblist"
    ^aNode nextJob: nextNode




SubLists variableSubclass: #LocsList
  instanceVariableNames: ''
  classVariableNames: ''
  poolDictionaries: ''

after: aNode
        "Answer the next node in order on loclist"
    ^aNode nextLoc

after: aNode is: nextNode
        "Set the next node in order on loclist"
    ^aNode nextLoc: nextNode
```

Figure 13.15   (concluded)

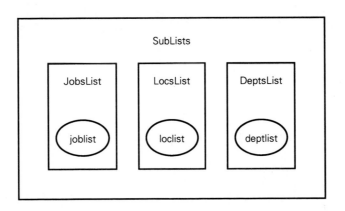

Figure 13.16   Abstract class sublists

PART 3

Other Programming Tools and Environments

INTRODUCTION

All languages are media for communication, computer programming languages even more so, because they provide a means for communication not only between humans and machines but also between humans and other humans.

Chapter 1 discussed the goals and some basic ideas underlying the study of programming languages. Part 1 of this textbook covered concepts common to many programming languages. Part 2 looked at specific languages in terms of their common structures. In order to attain the goals of Chapter 1, we need to do more than just look at the commonalities of programming languages and their individual attributes. We need to consider programming methodologies and tools, we need to consider modern programming environments, fourth-generation high-productivity programming tools such as integrated packages and query languages, and we need to consider the integrated applications development environment. These topics are important not only because of their widespread use in the programming function, but also because they continue to exert a critical influence over the design of new programming languages. It is also noteworthy that the integrated software systems discussed in Chapters 15 and 16 are frequently considered to be programming languages in their own right.

The chapters that follow may help to put Parts 1 and 2 into a practical framework and will, I hope, serve as a conduit toward creative term projects and lively discussions about some of the critical issues and important innovations in today's programming industries.

14

Program Design

The main thesis of this chapter can be summed up very succinctly: A good program is not an accident. Programming is not accomplished by luck, coincidence, or happenstance. Good programming is by design.

Programming by design requires some forethought with regard to the structure and outcome of the programming effort. What sort of software product will result? Who will use it? Is it expected to change over time? Programming by design encompasses a large variety of techniques that have been developed since the 1960s, beginning with modular programming up to the current interest in automated program design environments.

The material in this chapter constitutes a brief overview of the subject of program design. For more information on the material discussed, please refer to the sources listed at the end of the chapter.

14.1 WHAT IS A GOOD PROGRAM?

Before examining techniques for constructing a good program, it is reasonable to try to identify the species. Over the years, our conception of what makes a program "good" has undergone some radical changes. A case in point: FORTRAN programs were considered "good" if they produced efficient, executable code. While this is a valid objective, it is not sufficient today.

A good program does what it is supposed to do in the best possible way. Now, as a definition, this is altogether too vague, especially the part about "the best possible way." Several desirable program characteristics have been identified. A "good" program ought to be valid, readable, modifiable, efficient with regard to programmer time, and efficient with regard to storage space and processing time. These are general criteria that can be applied to any program. Other criteria may be more specialized and application dependent, such as the real-time constraints built into an on-line query system.

Criteria for Program Design

Validity. First and foremost, a program must be *correct*—that is, it should do what it is supposed to do without error. We can distinguish two kinds of validity, internal validity and external validity. *Internal validity* refers to the verifiability of the program. A program with internal validity meets the specifications and design goals that have been set down for it and does not contain "bugs." This is usually the objective when a program is tested for correctness. Of course, while a program may be proved to contain errors, it is impossible to prove that a program is correct.

External validity refers to the usefulness of the program. A program with external validity solves the problem that motivated its design in the first place. After all, there is no value in constructing a perfect program for the wrong problem. These two types of program validity can be expressed by the questions: Is the program right (internal validity)? Is it the right program (external validity)?

Readability. In addition to providing a means by which a programmer communicates instructions to a machine, a program ought to be understandable by human beings. This requirement becomes increasingly important as the programming function becomes increasingly more managerial and less technical. This changing role of programming may be seen in several trends: larger programming efforts, programming teams, auditing of programs, separation of analysis and design, maintenance programming.

Modifiability. There no longer exists the concept of a "throw-away" program. If it ever did exist, it was tied to the image of the lone scientist/theoretician, working out of a closet somewhere, who writes a long, unintelligible program in order to solve a terribly complicated mathematical problem and, once solved, the program is no longer needed. If this sort of programmer ever did exist outside of the collective imagination of the science fiction community, it was a short-lived existence.

The reality is that software is now treated as an asset of the firm that owns and uses it. Programs are no longer coded—they are *designed*. Programs are no longer executed—they are *implemented*. Programs are no longer "thrown away"—they are *maintained*. Maintenance programming accounts for the lion's share of a firm's programming effort. This means that most programming time is spent modifying programs as opposed to creating new applications. It is only sensible that some of that effort be put into a program right at the start to make it easy to modify later on.

Efficiency. It is indicative of the way that programming has changed over the last several decades that, while in 1954 the designers of FORTRAN put machine efficiency at the top of their list of requirements (although not before program correctness!), nowadays it comes last. This is not to minimize the importance of efficiency in programming. Efficiency considerations should permeate the entire programming effort. However, efficiency ought to be sacrificed in favor of modifiability or readability.

Efficiency concerns lie in two arenas: the human and the machine. If a program is *programmer-efficient*, then human time has been optimized; if it is *machine-efficient*, then CPU time and storage space have been optimized. Which would you suppose should have higher priority? Consider the following trends:

1. Computers are faster, more powerful, contain more storage space, and cost less.

2. Programs are larger, more complex, and take longer to write.

3. Programmers work slowly (due to 2) and cost a lot.

Given these trends, it is clear why programmer efficiencies have taken precedence over machine efficiencies.

In addition, there is the concept of an *elegant* program. This does not, as some would have you believe, apply to a program that employs clever tricks or to single-statement programs. (These are sometimes called "write-only" programs since that is all you can really do with them.) An elegant program goes beyond simply meeting the specifications. It is composed of *clear*, *simple*, *readable* code. It gets the job done in the best possible way.

14.2 THE WELL-WRITTEN PROGRAM

What does it take to write a good program? A measure of problem solving, skill, certainly. Beyond that, it is unclear.

If we look at people whom we identify as good programmers, we would find a host of different skills and, probably, very few common characteristics. One problem with this, of course, is that we might identify the good programmers incorrectly. Someone who works very hard on a project and lets you know about it may not be as good at the job as someone who works quickly, quietly, and efficiently—but the latter may appear to be someone who gets easy assignments rather than a good programmer. Beyond having problem-solving ability, then, what can we say about a good programmer? There is one common characteristic that comes up repeatedly—the ability to *communicate*.

The fact is that a person who is capable of writing English can write a program. And someone who is capable of writing *well* is capable of writing a good program. In fact, this has been identified repeatedly as a major factor in the design of a good program. According to some it is *the* major factor. The myth of the semi-illiterate hacker is just that—a myth.

Writing and Programming

How is writing a program similar to "just plain writing"?

Communication.   First of all, the primary activity in both writing and programming is the same. This activity is communication. Human beings use writing to communicate with each other, sometimes across vast distances, or over great spans of time. Similarly, a program is a medium of communication between programmer and machine, between programmer and programmer and, sometimes, between programmer and nontechnical personnel. The communication skills that you acquire in one spoken and written language can usually be transferred and put to good use when you communicate in another language. In other words, a good communicator has skills that transcend the syntax of any one particular language. The same is true for computer programming languages. A good programmer can communicate in FORTRAN as well as in MODULA-

2 or Ada because it is not the language that imparts this skill, it is simply an ability to communicate in a programming context.

Reading.   Many people think that to be a good programmer you simply start writing programs, using brute force if necessary to accomplish the task. The truth is more civilized. A good programmer, like a good writer, ought to begin by reading the work of others. This gives you a chance to see what is being done and, perhaps, adapt it to your own problem.

Keep it simple.   We have all seen written work that is unintelligible, but uses such nice big words and technical jargon that you think, "This must be good work." This syndrome is especially evident in student projects and articles in scholarly journals. This sort of work is designed to impress the reader so much that she will not bother reading it too critically. It is bad writing masquerading as good. On the other hand, we sometimes wrongly label a written work as bad if is it written simply, using clear language within a good organizational structure. We may think, "If I can understand it so easily, it must be trivial." This problem too has an exact counterpart in the realm of programming. An unintelligible program may impress us, while a simple and elegant one may appear to be "easy." As a writer or reader of programs, be careful of this pitfall.

Outline.   In Chapter 5, we saw that a control hierarchy chart representing a top-down program is strikingly similar to an outline. A composition, term project, or piece of fiction lacking a solid organizational structure is just as unreadable as a disorganized program.

Plan ahead.   In both writing and programming, you have to have a plan. You think ahead, not only when you make up the outline but also when you approach each new paragraph. This enables you to control the complexity of the product regardless of the complexity of the original problem. For example, the structured constructs—sequence, selection, iteration—with which we build programs help us to plan ahead in a formalized manner.

In fact, research in the area of cognitive behavior has shown that experts in many different fields—including writing and programming—store information in meaningful and relevant "chunks" (Simon 1974). Looking specifically at programming experts, Soloway and associates (1984, 1986) have shown that a program can be decomposed into a set of interrelated *goals*, and each goal is realized by a particular *plan*—that is, a chunk of programming knowledge.

Cohesion.   We all remember learning that a paragraph should contain only a single thought. Paragraphs, sections, and chapters share the requirement of program modules: They must be cohesive.

Esthetics.   In much written work, "white space" is important. It enhances the readability of the finished product even if it does not change its meaning. For instance, in "action" novels, there is often a lot of dialogue and short paragraphs. The page is more pleasing to the eye and you end up turning pages faster in keeping with the pace of the story. As another example, in print advertising, advertisements with a lot of copy are less likely to be read even if they provide valuable information. Similarly, in order to enhance program readability, we use a number of techniques that come under the heading of "esthetics." These include such devices as the use of blank spaces and blank lines, indentation, and the placement of borders around blocks of comments.

Read it through. Finally, just as you would ask a friend or colleague to review a piece of writing you have just finished—whether it is a composition, article, story, or novel—programmers submit their finished work to structured walkthroughs by a committee of their peers.

14.3 STRUCTURED PROGRAMMING METHODOLOGY

The term *structured programming* refers to a collection of programming techniques for implementing program and control abstractions in a hierarchical manner. The use of structured programming methodology in program design increases the likelihood of producing a program that is correct, readable, modifiable, and efficient. The techniques of structured programming may be used with any of the computer programming languages on the software ladder (see Chapter 2), from the lowest machine code to the highest machine-independent languages.

The term *structured programming* has come to represent different things to different people. We use it here to represent a body of techniques that may be applied to a large and complex program design task in order to produce programs that are logically manageable, well-structured, and easily tested for correctness. Structured programming methodology dictates that correctness be incorporated into the design of the program at the outset rather than having to "debug" errors out of it after the program has been completed.

As you have by now realized, a program is a conglomerate of data structures, program structures, and control structures. In fact, you could make the case that, in designing a program, the data structures are considered first, then the program structures, and finally the control structures. (This mirrors the organization of this textbook.) In fact, the data structures are considered first, but only in the broadest level of detail. Then as the program structure is refined over successive levels of detail, the design of the data structures is similarly refined.

Structured programming methodology encompasses three techniques:

1. the *modular* decomposition of programs into collections of modules, or subprograms
2. the *top-down* or hierarchical ordering of these modules
3. the use of *structured control constructs* at the detailed logic flow level.

The development of a program's structures utilizes the techniques of modular decomposition and top-down design to design a program in hierarchical levels of program abstraction. These techniques have already been discussed fully in Chapter 5. The statement-level control structures are drawn from the structured control constructs that are abstractions of control. These have already been discussed in Chapter 6. In order to pull these

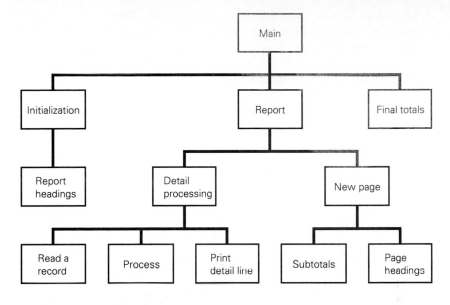

Figure 14.1   A report writer program

three techniques together under the umbrella of structured programming, we briefly review them here.

Modular Decomposition

Modularization of a program involves the identification, definition, and construction of relatively independent blocks of program code, called modules. These may be external subprograms, internal subprograms, or simply groups of statements within a program unit, in order of decreasing independence. Each module performs a clearly defined task and is characterized by a single entry point and a single exit point. Thus the module can represent a single action and is a means of building abstraction into a program.

Top-Down Design

Although modularization dictates that the program be decomposed into blocks of code, it doesn't say anything about how this decomposition ought to proceed. The top-down program-design technique assumes a modular program and organizes these modules into a hierarchical structure. Much like the outline you create before embarking on a term project, top-down design is characterized by stepwise refinement and delayed decision. An overview of a modular, hierarchical program is depicted in Fig. 14.1.

At any level in the hierarchy, the program can be regarded as complete and tested for correctness. We can do this by assuming an underlying abstract machine that contains operations corresponding to the lower level modules as yet uncoded. This is a boon to the management of complexity in programming but, of course, at the next level we are rudely awakened and forced to resume our coding. In this way, quite a bit of programming work is done while we defer lower level decisions to a later time. Of course, this design technique should not be used to justify procrastination—endlessly deferring critical decisions so that the abstract machine stays abstract.

Structured Control Constructs

Structured control constructs are statement-level control structures that may be described as either (low-level) stylized sequences of instructions or high-level language statements, each with a single entry point and a single exit point, which fall into one of the following three categories: simple sequence, selection, iteration. A construct is a building block. In this case, these are the building blocks from which the program is constructed, piece by piece.

The **goto** statement is not a structured control construct, and it is to be avoided as much as possible. Abstract control structures are more problem oriented and less procedural than the equivalent code using goto statements. These constructs facilitate the clear, natural expression of algorithms. Additionally, it is theoretically (and provably) possible to construct any program with only the three structured constructs mentioned and without a single use of the **goto**. However, there is no reason to be obsessive about it. Our main concern is with the readability and natural expressivity of the program. If the most natural way of expressing an algorithm is with a **goto** statement, then it is the one to use, but try *not* using it first. Forcibly removing a well-placed **goto** results in the same kind of cute programming tricks that characterized first- and second-generation programming and early FORTRAN programming; they were done then in the interest of machine efficiency.

Structured control constructs are control abstractions, just as subprogram units are program abstractions. The single-entry/single-exit requirement in both cases allows us to think in terms of a single action performed by a particular program or control structure. We use the Black Box model to visualize this abstraction. In fact, the "module" is central to this idea of abstraction. Fig. 14.2 illustrates this view of a module as any block of code. Thus, a program is a module; internal and external subprograms are modules. Structured control constructs, with the single-entry/single-exit characteristic, may be considered modules as well. Fig. 14.3 pictures specific control structures as Black Box abstractions.

The *simple sequence* construct is, as the name implies, the simplest construct. It consists of a statement followed by another statement (followed by another statement and so on):

```
statement1
statement2
statement3
...
```

Each of these statements may be a single executable statement (with the exception of the **goto** statement), a subprogram call, or another structured control construct. The compound statement is a language structure that implements the simple sequence construct, in the following way:

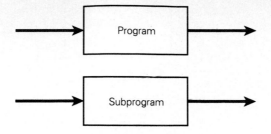

(a) Program abstraction

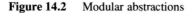

(b) Control abstraction

Figure 14.2   Modular abstractions

```
begin
      statement1
      statement2
      statement3
end
```

Simple sequence is the default control structure.

The *selection* construct is used when one wishes to choose from among two or more mutually exclusive alternatives. Selection may take the form of the **if/then**, the **if/then/else**, or the **case**. To choose between two alternative statements:

```
if (condition)
      then
            statement1
      else
            statement2
endif
```

A statement may be a single statement, a subprogram call, or a control construct. If, for example, more than one statement is needed in the "then" clause or the "else" clause, a simple sequence construct is used. Sometimes we only want to "do something special" if the condition is true:

```
if (condition)
      then
            statement
endif
```

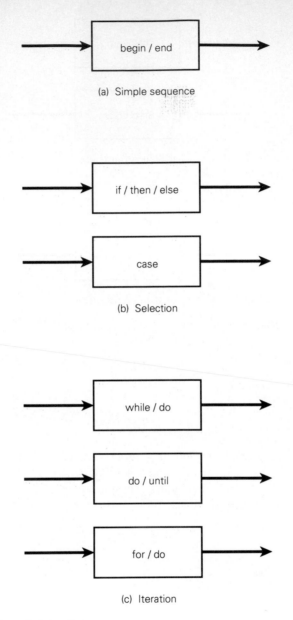

(a) Simple sequence

(b) Selection

(c) Iteration

Figure 14.3 Control abstractions

This is the control construct that typifies control-break processing, for example, end-of-page processing.

To select from among more than two mutually exclusive alternatives we can always use a nested **if/then/else**, in which the "else" clause contains another **if/then/else** construct. This was discussed earlier in the chapter and is just one of the ways in which we can combine these individual building blocks in order to produce a structured program. A **case** structure, when provided, does the same thing:

```
case SelectorVariable
      value1:                    statement1
      value2:                    statement2
      value3:                    statement3
      ...
      else:                      statement
endcase
```

Clearly, the **case** statement is not a critical one, but it assists in the natural expression of certain algorithms whose clarity might otherwise be masked by a large sequence of nested **if/then/else** constructs.

The *iteration* construct is used when a statement must be repeated. The only two forms of this construct that are theoretically necessary are the **while** and **until**. The **while** is used in situations where the test is to be done before entering the loop:

```
while (condition) do
      statement
endwhile
```

The **until** is used where the test is to be done after each repetition of the loop:

```
do
      statement
until (condition)
```

As usual, statement can be a single statement, a subprogram call, or another structured control construct. The difference between these two iteration constructs is, obviously, the position of the exit condition, the test for exiting the loop. The **until** construct will execute the loop at least once; with the **while** construct, the body of the loop may be bypassed completely if the condition is not met the first time into the loop.

A more general form of the iteration construct that is seldom used includes both of these constructs as special cases. Pictured in flowchart form in Fig. 14.4, it might be coded something like this:

```
do
      statement1
exitif (condition)
      statement2
enddo
```

Statement1 and statement2 are defined as above. At each iteration:

- statement1, or the first part of the loop, is executed;
- then a test on the exit condition is performed in order to determine whether to continue iterating or to exit the loop;
- then statement2, or the second part of the loop, is executed;
- and then control of execution returns to the beginning of the loop to start again.

This "test-in-the-middle" loop is sometimes called a *general loop* since any loop can be considered a special case. For example, a null (missing) statement1 reduces to a **while** loop and a null statement2 reduces to an **until** loop. From a syntactic point of view,

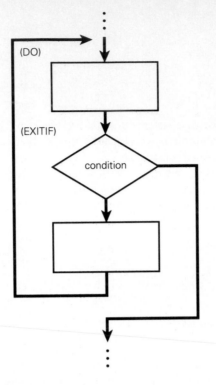

Figure 14.4 General loop

this construct is fictitious. Programming language designers steer clear of it because the **exitif** is too closely related to the conditional branch instruction (**if/goto**). In fact, when such a structure is needed, that is how it would be coded. (Some languages dress it up by providing an **exit** statement for early exit (branch) out of a loop).

Another iteration construct that is a variation of the **until** loop and, therefore, a variation of the general loop, is the *indexed* (or counting) loop. The indexed loop is characterized by an index variable that is incremented (or, sometimes, decremented) at each iteration and serves to move, or control, the loop.

```
for Index <- Initial to Final do
    statement
endfor
```

As mentioned earlier, this construct actually contains four well-defined parts:

* the *initialization* of the index variable is performed before the loop is entered;
* the *body* of the loop;
* the *incrementation* of the index variable, by the default value of 1 if an increment has not been specified on the **for** statement;
* and the *testing* of an exit condition, which compares the index variable against a final value.

This construct, though not theoretically necessary, is useful for code segments which, rather than being condition-controlled, must be repeated a certain number of times. This is the oldest form of the iteration construct.

These three constructs—simple sequence, selection, and iteration—can be nested to build any program. For example:

```
while (condition) do                         ==>iteration
    begin                                    ==>simple  sequence
        statement
        statement
        if (condition)                       ==>selection
            then
                repeat                       ==>iteration
                    statement
                until (condition)
            else
                begin                        ==>simple  sequence
                    statement
                    statement
                    statement
                end
        endif
    end
endwhile
```

Notice that this nesting of control structures still meets the single-entry/single-exit requirement. Of course, the smaller the modules in the program, the fewer levels of nesting necessary, and the more understandable the program code will be.

It is important to emphasize that the high-level language syntax elements discussed here are not prerequisites for the design and development of a well-structured program. You can program effectively in any programming language provided you are not bound by that language's built-in control abstractions. Every high-level syntax structure, from the **begin/end** compound statement to the **case** statement, can be coded using only low-level structures. The flowcharts presented earlier, in Chapter 6, attest to that.

14.4 SOFTWARE ENGINEERING

We have come a long way from the octal-coded programs and open subroutines of the 1950s. Computers are more powerful. Programs have become bigger and more complex. The technology of program design is aimed at managing this complexity.

Software engineering encompasses techniques for analysis, design, testing, validation, and maintenance of software. The discipline of software engineering can probably be traced back to the advent of structured programming techniques of the early 1970s.

Structured programming was a huge improvement over trial-and-error and spaghetti code. In fact, we can say that it has been a definite success. However, structured programming only goes so far. For very large and complex software systems, structured programming methodology breaks down. That is why other techniques have been developed, not to replace structured programming methods but to enhance them. These other techniques include data abstraction, information hiding, structured system analysis, database methods, database-centered fourth-generation tools (4GTs), object-oriented programming, editing environments, rapid prototyping, and automatic documentation. Computer-aided software engineering (CASE) techniques encompass and automate many of these methodologies.

All of these technologies, from structured programming to object-oriented programming and CASE, reduce complexity to human proportions. In doing this, some form of restriction is imposed on the programmer. Many of the newer methods take into account the fact that large programs are not simply created and then forgotten; rather they continue to go through a process of evolution and maintenance during the course of their useful existence.

Software Engineering Concepts

The following are some of the important concepts of software engineering. All share the same objective: reducing the complexity of the problem, thereby making the resulting programming task more manageable.

Modularity.   Modularity is probably the oldest software engineering concept, dating back to the early 1960s. It predates and provides a solid basis for the ideas of structured programming. High cohesion and low coupling are considered critical qualities for modules. Modularity was discussed more fully in Chapter 5.

Structure.   Modular programs may be structured in some way using one of a number of design methods—for example, functional decomposition, data flow, by data structure design, etc. The structure of a program is designed by specifying well-defined relationships among the modules. For example, the modules of a program may be related in a network of relationships or in a hierarchy—that is, a tree structure. A modular program constructed using *top-down design* results in a hierarchical structure. The resulting structure diagram is in tree form. Hierarchy is good at reducing the complexity of a problem, but not very good at encouraging "reusable code." This is because the rigid tree structure does not provide for common modules.

Information hiding.   When modules are well designed, they are relatively independent. They communicate with each other only through well-defined interfaces. A "user" module does not require access to all the implementation details—such as local variables, algorithms—of the "used" module. This unnecessary information may be hidden from the user, protecting the integrity of individual modules and reducing the confusion that comes along with too much information.

Abstraction.   All abstraction uses the concept of information hiding. Any abstraction allows one to ignore the tedious details (at least temporarily) involved in building a system and concentrate on the larger picture. Abstraction is the major concept used in *bottom-up design*: the construction of a large program by building layers upon layers of abstraction. As we have seen throughout this text, abstraction comes in many forms. As it relates to software engineering, we can consider data abstraction, program abstraction, and control abstraction.

Data abstraction involves the encapsulation and hiding of variables and operations needed to implement a data object. *Program abstraction* is the guiding concept underlying modularity. *Control abstraction* involves the use of high-level control structures—such as the selection and iteration constructs, monitors, coroutines, exception handlers, parallel processing—without concern for how they are actually implemented on a sequential machine.

14.5 COMPUTER-AIDED SOFTWARE ENGINEERING (CASE)

CASE products automate, and link together in an integrated environment, many of the tools with which programmers are already familiar—for example, compiler, debugging facility, editing environment, linker. In addition, CASE tools provide the programmer with an automated version of many of the structured methodologies of systems analysis and software engineering. Some CASE products go a step farther and generate the actual code based on the specifications of the software engineer.

There is such disparity among the different software products labeled CASE that a definition is impractical. There are sure to be a number of products that fall short of any definition. In general, the goal of all these techniques is to enable the software engineer to concentrate more effort on the processes of analysis and design and less on writing the program code—the reverse of the current situation in the industry. The idea is that if a problem is fully and correctly specified, the design specification ought always to produce a correct program.

CASE tools also assist in maintenance programming, an activity that continues as long as the program is in operation. For large, complex software systems this is as much a process of evolution as creation. Working in a CASE environment, the specifications are just as current as the program code since they must be modified in order to modify the program. The documentation, too, is always up to date.

Most CASE products are centered around a *repository* in much the same way that a 4GT (see Chapter 15) is centered around a database or an artificial intelligence language is centered around a knowledge base. A *repository* is a data dictionary, and then some. It contains definitions for every object in the system and for relationships among objects. It also keys these objects to the actual program code. Objects may be, for example:

- definitions for screen or printed reports;
- database schemata;
- structure charts;
- dataflow diagrams.

Reengineering is a concept that means that program design and modification are both made at the specification level. Thus, changes to the specification effect changes to the code. In addition, with reengineering, you can try "what-if" changes—that is, specify the change and let the system show you the effect of this change throughout the system. The word reengineering combines forward engineering with reverse engineering. *Forward engineering* starts at the specification and moves toward the implementation (the program code). *Reverse engineering* goes backward from the implementation level to find and modify the specification.

In addition, many CASE products also provide a number of personal and management tools, especially programming team management tools.

QUESTIONS FOR DISCUSSION

The following questions may require a fair amount of research in order to answer them completely.

1. What are some prevalent management techniques for managing the program design effort?
2. What are some of the problems and techniques of software documentation? Discuss user and technical documentation, printed manuals and on-line documentation.
3. What is prototyping, and how is it used?

KEY TERMS

The following list of terms presented in this chapter is a useful guide for studying.

abstraction	bottom-up design	control abstraction
data abstraction	information hiding	iteration
modularity	program abstraction	reengineering
repository	selection	simple sequence
software engineering	structured control constructs	structured programming
top-down design		

SUGGESTIONS FOR FURTHER STUDY

Sources. The following list of periodicals is a guide to sources for more and continuing information about the subjects of program design and software engineering. This list includes weeklies and monthlies, industry publications, and scholarly journals.

Byte	*Communications of the ACM*
Computer	*Computerworld*
Datamation	*Dr. Dobb's Journal*
IEEE Software	*IEEE Trans. Soft. Engineering*
Journal of Systems and Software	*PC World*
Software Engineering	*Software—Practice and Experience*

Books. Bishop (1986), Brooks (1975), Cohen (1983), Dahl *et al.* (1972), DeMarco (1979), Dijkstra (1976), Fairley (1985), Fisher (1988), Freeman (1975), Glass (1977), Gries (1978), Hanson (1986), Jackson (1975), King (1988), Liskov and Guttag (1986), Martin and McClure (1988), Weinberg (1971), Yeh (1977a).

Articles. Abbott (1987), Bergland (1981), Blum (1987), Bochmann (1973), *Business Week* (1988), Clark (1973), Darlington (1985), DeRemer and Kron (1976), Dijkstra (1968, 1972a), Glass (1988), Kernighan and Plauger (1974), Knuth (1974), Ledgard (1973), Ledgard and Marcotty (1975), Leventhal (1988), McCracken (1973), Margolis (1989), Merlyn and Boone (1989), Mikkilineni (1988), Nolan (1988), Parnas (1972a, 1972b, 1976), Ramshaw (1988), Simon (1974), Soloway (1986), Soloway and Ehrlich (1984), Tichy (1987), Wirth (1971a, 1974a), Wulf (1977), Yau and Grabow (1981), Yau and Tsai (1986).

15

Fourth-Generation
Productivity Tools

The programming languages, systems, tools, and methodologies of the fourth generation of software share a common feature: They are nonprocedural. Fourth-generation software was designed to solve some of the problems associated with programming in third-generation procedural languages. In general, the fourth generation is characterized by software that is considerably more data-centered; more specific to a problem area, less general-purpose; and further away from the level of the machine so that more work is done by the language processor or the system and less by the human user. Unfortunately, the term "4GL" (**4**th **G**eneration **L**anguage) has become a popular buzzword used to market many different types of commercial software products. This may help explain why there is probably no single definition of a fourth-generation language that will satisfy everyone.

15.1 OVERVIEW

What's in a name?   In this chapter, we refrain from using the term "4GL." This term is currently very popular in commercial data processing and appears on the label of just about any software product that maintains a database. This label was first applied in the early 1980s by James Martin (Martin 1982) to a particular kind of applications development environment composed of an integrated set of high-productivity tools. Unfortunately, Martin's definition of a 4GL does not take into account certain other fourth-generation software products that are closer to being languages, for example, PROLOG and Smalltalk. In this book, we use the closely alliterative term 4GT (**4**th **G**eneration **T**ool) to refer to those database-centered, integrated programming environments.

Nonprocedural programming. Everyone would probably agree, that fourth-generation languages and tools focus on *what* is to be done (i.e., they are nonprocedural) and can dramatically increase human productivity. This increase in productivity is accomplished by having the language instruct the computer by indicating to the computer the result desired, instead of listing all the steps that are needed to achieve this result. By shifting the task of controlling program flow to the software (i.e., automating many of the steps that would have to appear in a procedural language such as COBOL or FOR-TRAN), programs become much simpler to read and understand. This results in fewer errors, and debugging and maintaining programs becomes much easier.

Typically, procedural languages require many lines of code and are difficult and expensive to maintain. Debugging some complicated programs can often be a Herculean task, almost like finding the proverbial needle in the haystack. If we examine the typical procedural-language flowchart, we will find that most of it is an artifact of the computer programming process, concerned essentially with control of the program (e.g., loops). Only a small portion of the flowchart deals with real world equivalents and is results oriented so that it can be understood by nontechnical people. This ensures that errors will be much harder to detect and maintenance becomes much more difficult.

With procedural languages, programmers concentrate on the *how*. A program is essentially a step-by-step approach to how a task is to be accomplished. Nonprocedural languages, on the other hand, tell the computer *what* is supposed to be accomplished without detailing the steps that tell the computer how to carry it out. An analogy might help explain the difference between a procedural and a nonprocedural language. Suppose you wanted a young child to make scrambled eggs. You would have to list the steps:

1. Take two eggs from the refrigerator.
2. Take a bowl from the cabinet.
3. Break the eggs in the bowl.
4. Take out the frying pan.
   etc.

Many steps would be required and the likelihood of an error is greatly increased. Indeed, the scrambled eggs might very well contain eggshells since the instruction stating to throw the eggshells in the garbage was accidentally omitted. A procedural language works very much like a recipe—every step must be carefully detailed. A nonprocedural language is analogous to the way you would tell an adult to make scrambled eggs—a simple statement of "make scrambled eggs" would suffice. This statement of course would have to be predefined somewhere. But once it is defined, you would not have to go through the individual steps.

For example, suppose management wants to see sales plotted against advertising, and sales plotted against the price of the product, in order to determine if advertising and/or price has an impact on sales. This might result in a very long, difficult-to-read COBOL program, but might only require one line of code (looking very much like simple English) in a nonprocedural language.

```
PLOT = SALES WITH ADVERT PRICE
```

Clearly the mandate is for fourth-generation software to increase human *productivity* by making programming results oriented rather than procedure oriented, requiring less code than procedural languages by relying on predefined procedures and making intelligent default assumptions about what the user wants.

Characteristics of fourth-generation software.   Because fourth-generation software is results oriented, most are user friendly and easy to learn. Fourth-generation languages are essentially nonprocedural, although some may contain a procedural component. Most of the instructions are easy to understand, and even nontechnical employees can be taught to do some work with the language after only a few days of instruction.

In a nutshell, a fourth-generation language, system, or tool should have all or most of the following properties. It should be:

- Easy to learn, understand, and use, especially by (noncomputer) experts in the particular application domain for which it was developed;
- Data centered, especially around a database or a knowledge base;
- Maximizing human productivity rather than minimizing the use of computer time;
- Essentially nonprocedural and results oriented rather than procedure oriented;
- Provide results more quickly than a procedural language;
- Easy to debug and maintain;
- Able to improve the speed of application development.

Productivity tools.   Second- and third-generation programming tools consist largely of language processors. Today, even procedural language programmers have come to depend on a set of program development tools to enhance programming productivity. These may include an editor, a debugger, an on-line help facility, and CASE tools. Fourth-generation programming is performed against a backdrop of the trends toward integrated systems and environments that may include one or more language processors and program development tools, in addition to a number of packaged programs that promote increased programmer (or, often, user) productivity.

A *productivity tool* is a computer program or set of programs that speeds up the rate of application development, thereby increasing programmer output. Such a tool may be critical in helping data processing/MIS departments meet deadlines. In general, productivity tools are problem specific and not only encourage a timely development but also improve the reliability and maintainability of the finished product. Some of these tools include database management systems, query languages, natural language front-ends, graphics packages, spreadsheets, program generators, report writers, decision-support systems, and expert systems. They may be separate stand-alone packages or available as part of an integrated programming environment.

15.2 PACKAGES

As we saw in Chapter 2, the fourth generation began with packaged programs such as BMD to assist researchers in performing statistical analyses on a mainframe. Packaged programs, a set of programs or subprograms designed to solve a common problem encountered by a business or some other organization, were introduced. For a long while, such packages remained an important but small segment of the software industry.

Before the 1980s, most purchasers of computers were experienced programming professionals making decisions about large, costly systems. The need for nonprocedural, easy-to-use software was not very great. As the price of computers decreased and the number of personal computers proliferated, more and more nontechnical people purchased computers for personal use and for small business applications. The need for easy-to-use software products increased tremendously.

The phenomenal popularity of the microcomputer and its widespread use in homes, schools, and small businesses have influenced the design and introduction of a huge number of computer packages. Many of these packages are aimed at unsophisticated, nontechnical personal computer owners. Based on the common criterion that problem solving, rather than computer programming, is desired, these products were designed to solve one, or a few, typical problems. There are word processing packages, statistical packages, accounting packages, etc.

A major advantage of an off-the-shelf packaged software product is that a "road-tested" product is being purchased. The user can comparison shop and ask others how well the product performs. Many computer magazines rate various packages that are in the marketplace. Because of cost considerations and because it is immediately available, packaged software is a real boon for small firms and home computer users. Large companies, on the other hand, are not limited to off-the-shelf packages. A company can usually afford to have a package customized for in-house use. In that case the advantages of purchasing packaged software still apply. In addition, the documentation that comes along with these packages is often superior to that developed by in-house staff for the firm's own use.

A major disadvantage of the off-the-shelf package is that the user is not the same as the developer. The user may have some special needs that are not built into the package. After all, the user did not have any input into the design of the software. Many users have difficulty in finding software appropriate for their needs. This "make or buy" decision has been with us for a while but, more and more now, firms are using integrated packages and environments for their application-development needs.

15.3 INTEGRATED PACKAGES

Integrated packages evolved from the simpler, single-function packages. Companies marketing the simpler packages started combining different functions into a single software product. An integrated package contains several commonly used computing applications, which are integrated into one multifunction package designed so that the user can easily access the different functions. The term *integrated package* is applicable as long as two or more functions are combined. However, there are five applications that are often considered standard for the microcomputer-based integrated package: word processing, spreadsheets, database management, graphics, and communications. A report generator and a procedural or nonprocedural programming language may also be included. The individual elements of the integrated package are linked so that information can be easily shared and transferred among the components. A single command language for all components makes the package easier to learn. Often, the same menu structure is used for each application. Users can perform several activities concurrently, and the results of one application can be transferred to a second—for example, tables from the spreadsheet can be transferred to the word processor.

There are two approaches to the construction of integrated packages. One approach puts all the applications into one module. For example, Lotus Development Corp.'s Symphony® is an integrated multifunction package. The advantage of this type of integrated package is that it is usually easier to learn. However, because it is made to perform several different tasks, it may not be sophisticated or powerful enough to solve certain complicated problems.

A second approach treats the individual applications as building blocks. You can buy the individual components separately or together. They are made so that they fit together, and this allows a user to buy them one application at a time—a user might first buy the word processing package, later on the spreadsheet, and so on. This is the way, for example, Informix's Smart Software is sold. The advantage of this approach is that many more features can be added, and this type of integrated software can handle more complicated problems. However, this type of integrated package may be harder to learn.

The integration of single-function applications into a single package is consistent with the trend toward integrated applications-development environments rather than an individual programmer creating an individual program using a single language.

15.4 QUERY LANGUAGES

Query languages were developed in response to the great proliferation of databases in business. Managers did not want to be dependent on programmers using COBOL to query databases for them. Querying a database using a procedural language such as COBOL requires a skilled programmer and may take a great deal of time. Database management systems were developed for mainframes in the late 1960s. These included SystemR, INGRES, ADABAS, and ORACLE®.

To make databases accessible to people with minimal training, query languages were developed to be user friendly. Beginning in the early 1970s, formal query languages began to be paired with database management systems. For example, QUEL was developed for INGRES, SQL for SystemR, and NATURAL for ADABAS. Basically, query languages instruct the computer from which area in memory to select the data. However, many query languages contain various other features besides the ability to query a database. Many also allow the user to define the structure of the data, to manipulate and update the data, and to delineate security constraints for the data file. Formal query languages have highly stylized commands. They are easier to use than, say, COBOL, but they are still difficult to learn. The late 1970s saw the development of menu systems and the natural language front-end as a user interface to the query language. This type of product searches the user input for certain key words and then converts them into the syntax of the formal query language or even lower level computer instructions.

It should be noted that the better, easy-to-use query languages (including SQL) generally require that the data be stored as a relational database. With a relational database, a datafile is depicted as a table of rows and columns. The rows of the table contain records and the columns consist of fields. Any relationships among tables are defined in the data. Only one entry per column is allowed in a relational database. For example, each row might provide information about an employee of the firm; the columns would consist of such information as address, telephone number, job title, salary, etc.

QBE. One of the better known query languages is QBE (**Q**uery **by E**xample). It was developed in 1975 by Moshe Zloof at IBM, and it is relatively easy to learn. It is nonprocedural and utilizes a visual format. This makes QBE different from most query languages, which require that users query the database with English-like words and phrases. In QBE, the user is presented with a blank table and is required to insert the table name and relevant field names. QBE, in effect, helps the user structure the query by providing help and prompts. Because QBE uses a visual format, it is easier to learn and users are less likely to make mistakes.

SQL. Many other query languages were developed in the 1970s. However, SQL (**S**tructured **Q**uery **L**anguage), originally developed by IBM during the 1970s, is becoming the standard database query language. (The first commercial implementation of SQL was marketed by Oracle Corp. in 1979.) FOCUS, NOMAD, NATURAL, RAMIS, and many other 4GTs support SQL. However, it should be noted that SQL, even though it is becoming an international standard, is still only a relational interface language, and only provides a limited number of functions. SQL is not as easy to use as QBE. It can be used not only to query a database but also to define, manipulate, and update data.

INTELLECT. Another interesting fourth-generation query language is INTELLECT. It was developed in 1977 by Larry Harris, using artificial intelligence techniques. INTELLECT contains a knowledge base that deals with English grammar and methods to process the queries. INTELLECT uses natural language to access databases, so queries can be made in everyday English. In theory, end users that wish to use INTELLECT have nothing to learn. After the end user makes a query (e.g., "How many people in Florida own personal computers?"), the question will be "translated" and printed back into a more acceptable form. The end user is then able to check if the query was correctly interpreted before proceeding.

15.5 THE INTEGRATED APPLICATIONS DEVELOPMENT ENVIRONMENTS

The world of fourth-generation, high-productivity tools includes a particular kind of integrated programming environment that is not standardized but has generated much interest in the business computing community. In its own niche, this software product has been labeled a "full-function 4GL" but, while it *contains* a language (often more than one) it is more of an environment than a programing language. We call these products 4GTs (**4**th **G**eneration **T**ools) in an attempt to retain this distinction.

In the mid-1960s, Allied Chemical was looking for a language that was user friendly and easier to learn than COBOL. They hired Mathematica Inc., a consulting firm, to design a product for their use. In 1967, Mathematica delivered the first commercially available 4GT, RAMIS (**R**apid **A**ccess **M**anagement **I**nformation **S**ystem). RAMIS became so successful that a separate subsidiary was created (Mathematica Products Group) to further develop and market RAMIS, and in 1976, RAMIS II was introduced. RAMIS is currently being marketed by On-Line Software International, Inc. The major designer and architect of RAMIS, Gerald Cohen, left Mathematica in the early 1970s and teamed up with Peter Mittelman. Together they founded Information Builders, Inc., and in 1975 they introduced FOCUS, one of the most popular full-function 4GTs.

What Is a Full-Function 4GT?

Integrated packages are aimed essentially at personal computer users. Full-function 4GTs were originally aimed at mainframes. Because integrated packages were personal computer oriented, word processing became an essential component of any integrated software package. This was not the case with many of the full-function 4GTs, which were integrated but were originally mainframe products. However, the two models are quickly becoming less distinct and more like one another. It should be noted that the distinction between integrated packages and full-function 4GTs is disappearing. Most full-function 4GTs today have versions for personal computer users (e.g., PC/FOCUS®). This is similar to the problem we have in classifying hardware. The traditional classifications of personal computer, minicomputer, mainframe, workstation, and supercomputer are blurring. Indeed, many believe that the era of the mainframe computer is over. Personal computers and workstations can now perform jobs, such as handling the payroll for a large corporation, that used to require mainframes. Therefore, it should not surprise anyone that there should be similar problems in defining software.

Some full-function 4GTs are aimed at nontechnical end users; others are designed for programmer use.

Components of a full-function 4GT. The best way to determine whether a language is to be considered a full-function 4GT is by examining its features. Features that one might expect include:

- an intelligent, integrated *database management system*;
- a *data dictionary* and data definition language;
- a *query language* for querying the database;
- an environment for applications development including *a program generator*, which uses a skeleton program to produce a complete compiled application program from user-supplied detailed parameters of the specific application;
- a *report generator*, which generates a report-writing program from user specifications such as page numbers, subtotals, and headings;
- *graphics* generation and manipulation;
- a facility for *screen definition*;
- *decision support*, for answering what-if questions and to help in making decisions, including financial analysis and modeling, spreadsheet manipulation, and statistical and mathematical analysis;
- a procedural or nonprocedural *command language*.

A powerful full-function 4GT usually has the ability to handle all the programming requirements of an application with its own language. In some cases, however, the code is embedded in a third-generation language.

Software products that perform only one function, say, graphics generation and manipulation, might be very useful fourth-generation productivity tools, but a full-function 4GT should at the very least contain a database management system, a query language, and several of the above functions. A full-function 4GT allows users to build almost anything that could also be built with a procedural language such as COBOL.

Disadvantages.　　Much has been said about the benefits of fourth-generation productivity tools and full-function 4GTs. Some supposed disadvantages of full-function 4GTs include the following.

Lack of standardization.　　Every vendor offers a different type of product, and many of these products are incompatible with each other. This makes it more difficult to find programmers who are familiar with a company's own 4GT. This argument has some validity, but it should be pointed out that there is no standard third-generation language either. Knowing COBOL helps, but does not make you an experienced FORTRAN programmer. Despite the fact that there is no standard 4GT, there are similarities among RAMIS, FOCUS, and NOMAD, and a programmer familiar with one should not have too much difficulty learning the other. There is certainly at least as much similarity among the popular 4GTs as there is among the popular third-generation languages.

Interestingly, SQL (Structured Query Language), developed by IBM during the 1970s, is becoming the *de facto* standard relational database language.

Lack of computer processing efficiency.　　Full-function 4GTs usually require considerably more CPU time and disk space than third-generation languages. This is, of course, the direct result of trying to shift much of the programming burden away from the programmer to the software. 4GTs are certainly farther away from machine language than third-generation languages. Indeed, some question whether increasing human productivity and decreasing computer productivity can really be viewed as a savings. In defense of 4GTs, it does make sense to increase human productivity at the expense of computer productivity. After all, the cost of computer hardware and memory is dropping, whereas the cost of programmers is increasing.

It should also be noted that, in theory, there is no reason that fourth-generation software should not be as efficient, or even more efficient than third-generation software. It is true that fourth-generation software developers have been more concerned with making their software user friendly and adding capabilities than in improving performance. However, even today, there are a number of situations in which fourth-generation software has outperformed third-generation software. After all, third-generation languages have a weakness that can slow down their execution time: They require a large number of lines of code to carry out various applications, and each instruction then has to be compiled into a machine language instruction. With a 4GT, only a few lines of code are required to carry out the same task. In the future, one should expect to see fourth-generation software make great strides in processing efficiency and completely overwhelm their third-generation predecessors.

Limitations of full-function 4GTs in processing complex applications. For very complex applications, a programmer may be forced to use a third-generation language. It is certainly true that higher level languages will often eliminate options that were available with lower level languages. But this is usually necessary to ensure that the newer languages are easier to learn and easier to use. In fact, when third-generation languages were replacing second-generation languages, programmers complained about the loss of flexibility. Furthermore, as 4GTs improve, there is no reason that they should not eventually be able to perform as well as the third-generation languages (e.g., COBOL) that they are attempting to replace. However, currently there exist very complex applications that might require the use of a third-generation language. Because fourth-generation languages are essentially nonprocedural, rely on predefined procedures that do not always fit the problem at hand, and are nontechnical end user oriented, they will have to be somewhat less versatile than third-generation languages. Even with the addition of procedural tools to the 4GT will still be less adaptable than many third-generation languages. Thus, for special, complex situations, you might be better off with a third-generation language rather than with a 4GT.

Some Full-Function 4GTs

Let us briefly examine some of the fourth-generation integrated systems available that can be considered full-function 4GTs.

Focus. FOCUS (currently being marketed by Information Builders, Inc.) is a DBMS with an integrated nonprocedural query language. FOCUS was designed so that it can run on a mainframe or be used interactively on a personal computer (PC/FOCUS). FOCUS is used by both experienced programmers and relatively nontechnical end users. The entire FOCUS vocabulary consists of fewer than 100 words. The query and reporting functions in FOCUS use simple words such as COUNT, SUM, PRINT, and LIST. FOCUS includes the following:

- An integrated database management system;
- A query language;
- A report generator;
- Graphics capability;
- A financial modeling language;
- Statistical analysis;
- Data security (which enables management to restrict access to files or even values within a field).

The FOCUS database is built around the hierarchical data model rather than the relational model of, say, SQL's database. Thus, data stored in a FOCUS database should be hierarchical in nature or they will have trouble fitting into the more constrained approach. A relational database is more flexible. However, the hierarchical database means that FOCUS queries are much more natural and inherently user friendly than are those of a relational query language like SQL.

For example, the following is a sample FOCUS program that will create a tabular report from data stored in a file called EMPLOYEES. (The data set from Chapter 7 may be used for this exercise.)

```
TABLE FILE EMPLOYEES
PRINT ID AND NAME
BY JOBTITLE
IF DEPT IS 'MIS'
END
```

This set of commands will generate a report listing the identification number and the name of each employee at each job title in the MIS department. The following FOCUS query will produce a two-way table of average salaries in the MIS department, with job titles as row headings and locations as column headings.

```
TABLE FILE EMPLOYEES
SUM AVE.SALARY
BY JOBTITLE
ACROSS LOCATION
IF DEPT IS 'MIS'
END
```

Notice that the hierarchical nature of the data is not evidenced in the queries. The user need not know the technical details of how the data has been stored in the database. Note, too, that the commands are simple and English-like and that only a few lines of code are required to produce a report.

RAMIS II®.   RAMIS II (On-Line Software International, Inc.) is another leading full-function, fourth-generation language and database management system, similar to FOCUS. Indeed, there is a great deal of competition between the two. RAMIS II, like FOCUS, also has a version available for the personal computer (RAMIS II/PC). RAMIS II is designed to query databases, generate reports, and analyze data, and is aimed at the nontechnical end user.

RAMIS II contains various components to make it easy to use for both the novice and the expert. RAMIS II ENGLISH allows users to make queries in natural English. Its knowledge base, developed using artificial intelligence techniques, contains four dictionaries: a file dictionary which provides information about data in the database files; a general dictionary containing several thousand English words and phrases; a dynamic dictionary, which builds up a vocabulary as the system is used; and an application dictionary that contains a specialized vocabulary. This allows someone using RAMIS II ENGLISH to request information using their own technical business terms. Another component of RAMIS II, MARVEL, is a menu-driven report generator that can be used by novices.

NOMAD2.   NOMAD2 (currently being marketed by Must Software International) is a highly integrated, full-function, fourth-generation language that provides a database management system incorporating procedural and nonprocedural languages, a report generator, a graphics generator, a screen generator, and a decision-support component that allows the user to perform statistical analyses and financial modeling. In many respects it is similar to FOCUS and RAMIS II. However, it lacks compatibility with files created by various database management systems such as ADABAS and TOTAL. It is geared to both experienced programmers and nontechnical end users.

NATURAL.   NATURAL, and its companion product the database management system ADABAS, was developed by Software AG of North America, Inc. as a full-function, integrated fourth-generation language. It can be used on a mainframe or a personal computer. The NATURAL procedural language is somewhat complicated, and it is geared more to programmers rather than end users. To make it more user friendly, the menu-driven SUPER/NATURAL was introduced.

15.6 IS IT A LANGUAGE?

Fourth-generation programming is more than merely nonprocedural. It highlights the trend toward integrated systems and environments that may include one or more language processors, program development tools, and specialized packages.

On one branch of the fourth generation, we have a language like PROLOG. Programming in PROLOG is definitely nonprocedural—we state relations, and we can query this set of relations—but it is not defined in terms of an environment. However, the PROLOG processor itself is a pretty powerful tool supporting such complex mechanisms as backtracking (see Chapter 12). On another branch of the fourth generation, we have packages like BMDP, SPSS-X and other statistical packages that accept user commands as input to parameterize an internal skeleton program. Is SPSS a language? How about dBASE? We talk of "writing an SPSS program" or of "programming in dBASE." A SPSS program provides *input* to a system, which is itself a program.

What about RAMIS II? Is it a language or an integrated programming environment? If we maintain this language/environment distinction, then, what about Smalltalk, a programming language within an object-oriented environment (see Chapter 13)? What about C programming within a UNIX environment? What about maintaining a knowledge base using an expert system shell (see Chapter 16)? If RAMIS II is a language, what is a decision-support system? An expert system? Where do we draw the line?

One of the characteristics of the fourth generation is a blurring of the distinction between the language and its implementation; between a language like Smalltalk and its graphical user environment; between a language like PROLOG, which enhances productivity by relying on a hard-working processor to perform functions like backtracking and searching a knowledge base, and a system like RAMIS II, which enhances productivity by an integrated set of software components that operate on a database. This trend is illustrated by Fig. 15.1, which places software on a continuum of complexity.

The horizontal axis in Fig. 15.1 represents a continuum of software complexity from individual machine-level codes, through procedural languages, to languages embedded in integrated programming environments. The height of the curve represents a sub-

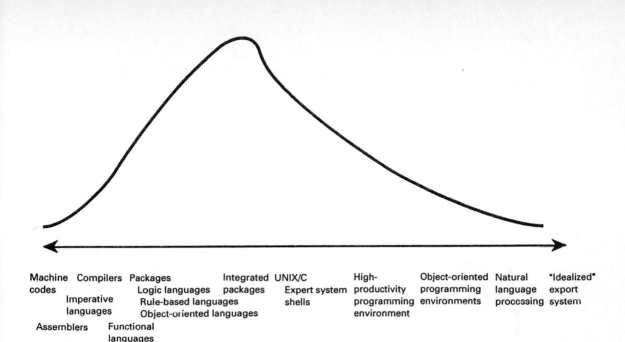

Machine codes	Compilers	Packages		Integrated packages	UNIX/C		High-productivity	Object-oriented programming	Natural language	"Idealized" export
Imperative languages		Logic languages Rule-based languages Object-oriented languages			Expert system shells		programming environment	environments	processing	system
Assemblers		Functional languages								

Figure 15.1   Continuum of complexity

jective evaluation of the relative frequency of use of the various types of software products.

Finally, to address the heading of this section: Is it a language? Perhaps, in the final analysis, the answer lies in the question.

QUESTIONS FOR DISCUSSION

The following questions may require a fair amount of research in order to answer them completely.

1. What are the advantages of a full-function 4GT over a procedural language such as COBOL?

2. What should a full-function 4GT contain? An integrated package aimed at personal computer users?

3. Under what circumstances should a company acquire a query language rather than a full-function 4GT?

4. Some experts denigrate 4GTs because they are inefficient users of computer hardware. Do you agree or disagree?

KEY TERMS

The following list of terms is a useful guide for studying the material presented in this chapter.

FOCUS	Full-function 4GT	integrated package
NATURAL (ADABAS)	NOMAD2	nonprocedural language
package	procedural language	productivity tool
programming environment	QBE	query language
RAMIS II	SQL	

SUGGESTIONS FOR FURTHER STUDY

Sources.   The following list of periodicals is a guide to sources for more and continuing information about the subjects of this chapter. This list includes weeklies and monthlies, industry publications, and scholarly journals.

Byte	*Communications of the ACM*
Computer	*Computer Language*
Computerworld	*Database Programming and Design*
Datamation	*IEEE Potentials*
IEEE Software	*IEEE Trans. Soft. Engineering*
Journal of Systems and Software	*PC World*
Software—Practice and Experience	

Books.   Baron (1986), Chorafas (1986a, 1986b), Martin (1982, 1985), Martin and Leben (1986a, 1986b).

Articles.   Bernknopf (1985), Blum (1987), Cobb (1985), David (1988), Misra and Jalics (1988), Sullivan-Trainor (1987), Van Hoeve and Engmann (1987), Verner and Tate (1988), Warren (1985), Wexelblat (1984).

16

Expert Advisors

The term artificial intelligence cannot be narrowly defined. It is, in fact, a broad conglomerate of many different areas of scientific endeavor. These include robotics, machine learning, vision systems, natural language processing, and knowledge-based systems. These diverse disciplines do share a common goal: In some sense, they all attempt to build a tool, in this case a computer system, that can mimic some small aspect of human behavior. Of course, in order to accomplish this goal the behavior itself must be well understood and clearly specified. In addition to encompassing a variety of endeavors, artificial intelligence research also brings together an amalgam of many disciplines that are quite different from each other. For example, computer science, linguistics, psychology, cognitive science, sociology, physiology, engineering, and operations research, to name just a few.

In recent years, the business and computing industries have expressed overwhelming interest in computer systems developed as expert advisors, to replace or assist an expert in performing a job requiring decision making. Of all the branches of artificial intelligence, expert systems is the one that presently has the most commercial appeal. (This may change in the next decade as neural nets gain support.) These systems have, in fact, become so popular that marketing and sales departments have been hard put to refrain from smacking the label "expert system" or "artificial intelligence" on every shrinkwrapped package that goes out the door.

Clearly it is important that we know what these expert systems are—and what they are not. And, from the perspective of this text, we would especially like to consider the programming languages and other tools that are used in developing these computer systems.

The treatment in this chapter is brief, not very technical, and necessarily superficial. It is intended as a starting point. For more information on the material discussed, please refer to the sources cited at the end of the chapter.

16.1 OVERVIEW

Expert systems come in many different sizes, shapes, and colors. They have been used in a variety of different fields for a variety of different purposes. Let us look at some characteristics that most expert systems ought to have in common.

Expert systems are primarily advisory systems. They provide information, or educated guesses, based on the data at hand, to assist a decision maker. They can explain the reasoning by which they came to a particular conclusion. They provide the decision maker with a convenient means of storing, maintaining, and accessing huge quantities of information including, for example, facts, rules, and probabilities associated with uncertain information. What's more, this quantity of knowledge is not by any means static. These systems can be easily and rapidly updated to reflect new information.

Some benefits typically associated with the use of expert systems include reduced decision-making time, improved decision making by nonexperts, better and faster training of new personnel, speedier communication of changes in information and/or procedures throughout the organization and, generally, improved information maintenance. Expert knowledge is not irrevocably lost when a human expert leaves the organization. Expertise in a particular domain is made more widely available and that of experts in different knowledge domains can be integrated into a single system. In addition, the expert system development process itself provides valuable information regarding how work actually gets done in the organization.

Expert systems have been used in medical diagnosis, geology, electronic diagnosis and maintenance, computer configuration, computer hardware design, computer repair, chemical engineering, military strategic planning, financial planning, accountancy, strategic product planning, and personnel training.

Typically, most commercial expert systems fall into one of several categories. They may be classified as advisory systems, decision support systems, planning/scheduling systems, or flexible/maintainable systems.

16.2 KNOWLEDGE ENGINEERING

Expert systems are often described as computer programs that can, within reason, mimic the expertise of a human expert in a particular domain and can, eventually, take the expert's place.

Some of the problems inherent in the use of human experts can be eliminated if a computer system can be shown to do as good—or at least almost as good—a job. Expert systems don't get sick, quit, or retire. They don't die taking their entire wealth of experience with them. In addition, a human expert is just one, unique individual who cannot be in two places at once. A machine can be duplicated and distributed to many remote locations, or the system can be accessed from many remote locations via communication networks. An expert system can be used to train new personnel so that human experts can spend time on more important endeavors.

Part of the problem of extracting knowledge from human experts is the difficulty in communication between the human expert and the software engineer developing the expert system. The increasing popularity and commercial use of expert systems have led to the evolution of a new discipline: knowledge engineering. The knowledge engineer is also an expert. This particular kind of expert captures another expert's knowledge and transforms it into a computer-usable form, the knowledge representation. This is a difficult enterprise. The expert usually starts off talking in generalities; the knowledge engineer must somehow bring the interview around to specifics about exactly what is done and why. Often, the expert himself does not know how or by what criteria he makes decisions. Sometimes the word "hunch" is used when in reality it may be a combination of rules, heuristics, and probabilities that are acquired with years of experience and not consciously invoked.

Since an expert system is a computer program, the system designer cannot begin to put it together without something that any program requires: an exact specification of what needs to be done. Typically, the programmer of the expert system is not the expert whose expertise is being modeled, and the expert cannot say exactly what the program needs to do. That is where the knowledge engineer steps in. Many techniques have been developed in order to elicit the most usable information from the human expert about the particular application domain. These range from following the expert around and observing to interviewing methods and questionnaire techniques.

One interesting technique uses the human expert to "simulate" a computer. The simulated computer is being used as an advisory expert system. The human expert is put behind a screen so that no subconscious, nonverbal cues pass between the expert and the user. Users, typically novices, approach this "computer" with a problem requiring expert knowledge. The expert asks pertinent questions, and the user answers each in turn. When the expert has obtained enough information, the "computer" advises the user how to perform the job. In this way the knowledge engineers expose precisely the information necessary to the decision maker. They may then ask the expert why he asked a particular question or chose a particular course of action. The expert will probably be better able to respond having gone through the exercise.

The knowledge engineer may already have enough information from this exercise alone to build a prototype system and begin the process of testing and refining it.

16.3 ELEMENTS OF AN EXPERT SYSTEM

There are four primary components of an expert system. These are illustrated in Fig. 16.1. First of all, and most important, there are the knowledge base and the inference engine, which maintain and provide access to the expertise. In addition, in order to provide for communication between the system and its users, there are the user interface and the explanation facility. These components differ widely from each other, and designers employ different tools and techniques in their development. These may include different programming paradigms or even different languages.

The Knowledge Base

The knowledge base contains a computer representation of the expert's knowledge and experience. Knowledge may be in the form of facts or heuristics derived from experience. A key element of an expert system is that the knowledge domain is separate from the control mechanism for solving problems (the inference engine). This means that the knowledge base can be easily modified to reflect new information, criteria, or proce-

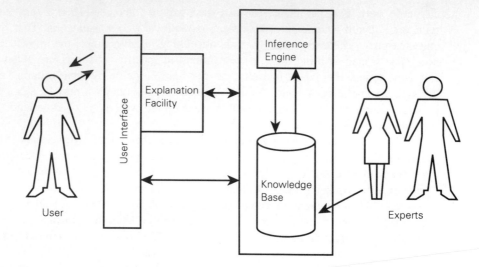

Figure 16.1   Components of an expert system

dures. Contrast this with the horror of maintenance programming typical of traditional procedural programming.

There are a number of forms for representing knowledge in an expert system. The form used should be the one most natural for the particular application. In particular, the knowledge base should be maintained in a form that is understandable to the human experts in that particular domain. After all, they will be primarily responsible for updating the knowledge base and for testing its performance against their own judgment calls.

Rules, sometimes called *production rules*, are the most widely used form for knowledge representation in expert systems. A set of rules, or if/then constructs, are matched against a set of facts. When a fact checks out, it causes the matching rule to "fire," and the indicated actions are executed. Rules may be relatively independent of each other and, then, the knowledge base is fairly easy to modify. The type of expert system called *advisory* is typically rule based.

Other knowledge representation methods are semantic nets and frames. In *semantic networks*, also called *associative networks*, *nodes* representing objects or events are connected to each other by means of *links* representing relationships. Thus, the knowledge represented by semantic nets is highly interdependent and more difficult to update than in a rule-base system. Still, this is a very flexible method for representing knowledge, and it is considered to be closely related to the way the human brain actually stores information.

One type of relationship typically represented in a semantic net system is a hierarchical relationship, sometimes called "is-a." This sort of relationship can be used to establish a hierarchy for property inheritance, thus saving space in storing the knowledge base. Nodes inherit properties from nodes that are higher in the hierarchy. Another sort of relationship, called "has-a," is used to describe an attribute of an object.

A *frame* is somewhat like a template that consists of slots waiting for values. Some slots may contain default values. Think of a frame as a questionnaire to be completed.

The slots may take on values in the form of rules, like attached procedures. Also, frames can be structured in a hierarchy. Therefore, the frames representation of knowledge is sometimes described as an integration of the rules and semantic nets methodologies.

The Inference Engine

The aim of an expert system is to mimic human reasoning and the inference engine is the component that contains the reasoning mechanism of the expert system. To relate it to a traditional imperative program, if the knowledge base contains the data structures, the inference engine contains the control structures.

In designing an inference engine, it is often feasible to design it so that it will work for more than one knowledge domain. The assumption is that although experts may claim expertise in different knowledge domains, they do at least one thing the same—they reason, with the domain of knowledge in the application. Of course, the better an inference engine fits one particular domain, the worse it will be for another. The more general the inference engine, the more domains it will be able to fit; however, it will not be the *best* fit for any one knowledge domain.

The inference engine is sometimes designed in two related parts, one for inference and one for control. The inference component, sometimes called the *interpreter*, examines facts and rules according to some principle of reasoning. The control component, sometimes called a *scheduler*, controls the order in which rules are to be applied and inferences made. The control structure of the inference engine can be described according to whether the reasoning mechanism is "backward" or "forward" and by the search strategy employed.

Backward vs. forward chaining. The order in which rules are examined by the inference engine is usually characterized as being either "backward" reasoning or "forward" reasoning.

Backward chaining starts with a solution and tries to prove it correct. Backward chaining systems are also called *top-down* or *goal-directed systems*. In this reasoning methodology, the system selects one hypothesis at a time and sets about trying to prove it. Each hypothesis, or goal, may consist of a number of subgoals, each of which must be proven in turn in order for the hypothesis to be proven correct.

Forward chaining starts with a premise and uses that as a starting point to search for a solution. Forward chaining systems are also described as *bottom-up*, *data-driven*, or *event-driven systems*. In this case, the system examines one item of data at a time, making what inferences it can from it. After analyzing some facts, the system may query the user for what other facts it needs in order to reach a conclusion.

These two reasoning methodologies have an analogy in the genre of fiction called mystery or crime fiction. The detective in these stories can begin with the facts and deduce from these the murderer, having no preconceived notion as to the identity of the evildoer. This is the Sherlock Holmes approach, and it follows forward reasoning. On the other hand, the detective can begin with a suspect—this is feasible when there are a small number of suspects—and try to reason backward and identify how the suspect committed the crime. This is the Lieutenant Columbo approach.

Of the two reasoning mechanisms, backward chaining is more efficient and is more commonly applied although the two may sometimes be combined. Backward chaining works better when the solutions are known, and there are not too many of them. Generally, forward chaining works better when the number of starting points is small relative to the number of possible solutions.

Search strategy. A search strategy is employed to search the knowledge base. The two alternative search strategies are depth-first and breadth-first.

Depth-first is the search strategy most commonly used. It is a search for greater and greater detail along a single search path to a possible goal before attempting to explore another goal. Queries that the system makes to the user are presented in a meaningful direction, going toward more and more detailed information.

The *breadth-first* strategy searches across rules on a particular level, eliminating those it can, before going to the next, more detailed, level. It does not commit the system to completely examine only a single goal before looking at any other goal. Questions to the user may appear to jump around in a totally random fashion.

The User Interface

The user interface is an interactive, often graphics-based component that facilitates communication between the machine and the human. It may use windows and menus. At any rate, it should be sufficiently user friendly so that users will be comfortable with the system. Ideally, the interface will mimic objects that they are already used to, such as particular paper forms. Developing this component may be the most expensive and time-consuming part of the expert system development process.

The interaction between the user and the expert system begins when the user presents a problem to the system. The system may then query the user for additional information. Finally, the system may make a recommendation to help the user solve the original problem.

The Explanation Facility

An important characteristic of an expert system is its ability to, on demand, justify its conclusions and explain the reasons for its queries. This is done by the component termed the *explanation facility*. This is certainly one feature that distinguishes a computerized expert system from a human expert.

The explanation facility communicates with the user in the language of the application domain, usually through the user interface. Sometimes the explanation facility is integrated into the user interface.

16.4 LANGUAGES FOR EXPERT SYSTEM DEVELOPMENT

Expert advisory systems have been developed in a large number of diverse programming languages. The oldest artificial intelligence language is LISP, designed in the U.S. in 1956 and, for a long time, the language of first choice in this country. PROLOG, designed in 1970 in France, has enjoyed strong success in Europe and, more recently, increasing popularity in the U.S. And, of course, a specialized language like OPS5 is well suited to building expert systems since it was designed especially for this purpose.

Still, general-purpose procedural languages are also used for expert system development (even COBOL). Recently, object-oriented languages like Smalltalk have become the subject of much intense and enthusiastic research in this area. Some experimental projects are under way that combine a number of programming paradigms—such as the object-oriented, access-oriented, constraint-oriented, logic, and/or production-system paradigms—into a single system for expert system development.

The trade-off is a familiar one. A language designed specifically for this application area (an "AI" language) will be a more natural medium for constructing the system. Programs will be coded more quickly and be easier to debug and maintain. On the other hand, expert systems are notorious for their vast memory and processor time requirements. A procedural language may be more efficient since its instruction set more closely resembles that of the underlying machine. Also, systems coded in such familiar languages as FORTRAN, Pascal, C, or Ada will be able to make use of a large body of routines and data sets residing outside the expert system.

16.5 EXPERT SYSTEM SHELLS

We have seen that an expert system will generally be designed with separate knowledge and control components. The control component, the inference engine, can often be designed to accommodate a large number of different knowledge domains. The expert system without its knowledge base is a reasoning system with nothing to reason about— it is an empty shell.

Like an AI language, an expert system shell is an expert system development tool. It contains everything an expert system needs except for the knowledge base. Since the user is expected to supply this knowledge base for a particular application domain, the expert system shell needs one further component—an interactive interface that may be used to build up the knowledge base. The user supplies the system with facts and rules in some natural form and the system converts this information to some internal representation.

The inference engine of the expert system shell will probably have a default reasoning mechanism and search strategy, but some allow these defaults to be changed by the user.

Expert system shells are among the most popular packaged software products. They also vary widely in capability, ranging in cost from under $100 to $100,000 and more.

16.6 FUTURE DIRECTIONS FOR EXPERT SYSTEMS

Expert systems are terribly popular commercial enterprises. Currently, one major problem with this type of programming involves its inefficient use of computer memory. This inefficiency is primarily due to the von Neumann architecture of most computers on which these systems are developed. Thus, the future of expert systems will include designing them as massively parallel systems over fifth-generation architecture.

On the software front, a major concern is that of designing systems that can learn from experience and update their own knowledge bases.

Neural nets are not really an artificial intelligence technique but an interesting development in computer architecture that has many applications in AI. Neural nets are based on the concept of massively parallel processors arranged in an interconnected configuration similar to the structure of neurons in the brain.

Finally, the research into multiparadigm systems promises to increase the potential of many large, complex software systems, including expert systems.

QUESTIONS FOR DISCUSSION

The following questions may require a fair amount of research in order to answer them completely.

1. How are expert systems different from decision-support systems? How are they the same?

2. What are the relative advantages and disadvantages of using AI languages like LISP and PROLOG to develop expert systems? Traditional languages like Pascal? C? Ada? What about expert system development tools such as shells?

3. How is expert system development different from developing, say, a database application? How are they the same?

KEY TERMS

The following list of terms is a useful guide for reviewing the material you learned about in this chapter.

backward chaining	breadth-first search	depth-first search
expert system shell	explanation facility	forward chaining
inference engine	knowledge base	knowledge engineering
reasoning mechanism	search strategy	user interface

SUGGESTIONS FOR FURTHER STUDY

Sources. The following list of periodicals is a guide to sources for more and continuing information about the subject of expert systems. Some of these sources are devoted exclusively to the subject of expert systems or artificial intelligence; others are general computer industry publications that regularly carry articles about expert systems. This list includes weeklies and monthlies, industry publications, and scholarly journals.

AI Magazine	*Artificial Intelligence*	*Byte*
Communications of the ACM	*Computerworld*	*Datamation*
Journal of Expert Systems	*PC World*	*IEEE Expert*

Books.   Charniak and McDermott (1985), Forsyth and Naylor (1985), Harmon and King (1985), Hayes-Roth *et al.* (1983), Jackson (1986), Sell (1985), Tello (1989), Van Horn (1986), Winston and Prendergast (1984).

Articles.   Abbott (1987), Basden (1983), Bender (1987), Bobrow *et al.* (1986), Coombs and Alty (1984), Fickas (1985, 1989), Fikes (1985), Firdman (1987, 1988), Harvey (1987), Keim and Jacobs (1986), Landry (1986), Maletz and Sandell (1988), Michaelson and Michie (1983), Williamson (1986).

A

Bibliography

A.1 BOOKS AND MANUALS

Adams, J. Mack, Phillippe J. Gabrini, and Barry L. Kurtz (1988). *An Introduction to Computer Science with Modula-2*. Lexington, Mass.: Heath.

Aho, Alfred V., Ravi Sethi, and Jeffrey D. Ullman (1986). *Compilers: Principles, Techniques, and Tools*. Reading, Mass.: Addison-Wesley.

Aho, Alfred V. and Jeffrey D. Ullman (1977). *Principles of Compiler Design*. Reading, Mass.: Addison-Wesley.

Anderson, T. and B. Randell (eds., 1979). *Computing Systems Reliability*. Cambridge: Cambridge University Press.

ANSI (1974). *American National Standard Programming Language COBOL*, ANS X3.23–1974, American National Standards Institute, New York.

ANSI (1981). *Draft Proposed Revised X3.23 American National Standard Programming Language COBOL*, Technical Committee X3J4, American National Standards Institute, New York, September.

ANSI (1988). *Draft Proposed American National Standard for Information Systems— Programming Language C*. American National Standards Institute, Document #X3J11/88–001, New York, January.

Backhouse, Roland C. (1979). *Syntax of Programming Languages: Theory and Practice*. London: Prentice-Hall International.

Bailey, T.E. and Kris Lundgaard (1986). *Program Design with Pseudocode*. Monterey, California: Brooks/Cole.

Barclay, Kenneth A. (1989). *C: Problem Solving and Programming*. Englewood Cliffs, NJ: Prentice-Hall.

Baron, Naomi S. (1986). *Computer Languages: A Guide for the Perplexed*. Garden City, New York: Anchor Books.

Barron, D.W. (1977). *An Introduction to the Study of Programming Languages*. Cambridge: Cambridge University Press.

Berry, R.E. (1984). *Programming Language Translation*. Chichester, England: Ellis Horwood, Ltd.

Bertsekas, Dimitri and Robert Gallager (1987). *Data Networks*. Englewood Cliffs, NJ: Prentice-Hall.

Bic, Lubomir and Alan C. Shaw (1988). *The Logical Design of Operating Systems*. Englewood Cliffs, NJ: Prentice-Hall.

Birns, Peter, Patrick Brown, and John C.C. Muster (1985). *UNIX for People*. Englewood Cliffs, NJ: Prentice-Hall.

Birtwistle, G.M., O.J. Dahl, B. Myhrhaug, and K. Nygaard (1973). *Simula BEGIN*. New York: Van Nostrand Reinhold.

Bishop, Judy (1986). *Data Abstraction in Programming Languages*. Reading, Mass.: Addison-Wesley.

Borland (1987a). *Turbo C Version 1.5, Additions & Enhancements*. Scott's Valley, Calif.: Borland Int'l.

Borland (1987b). *Turbo C Version 1.5, Reference Guide*. Scott's Valley, Calif.: Borland Int'l.

Borland (1987c). *Turbo C Version 1.5, User's Guide*. Scott's Valley, Calif.: Borland Int'l.

Borland (1987d). *Turbo Pascal Version 4.0, Owner's Handbook*. Scott's Valley, Calif.: Borland Int'l.

Borland (1988a). *Turbo Prolog Reference Guide, Version 2.0*. Scott's Valley, Calif.: Borland Int'l.

Borland (1988b). *Turbo Prolog User's Guide, Version 2.0*. Scott's Valley, Calif.: Borland Int'l.

Borland (1989a). *Turbo Pascal Version 5.0, Object-oriented Programming Guide*. Scott's Valley, Calif.: Borland Int'l.

Borland (1989b). *Turbo Pascal Version 5.0, Reference Guide*. Scott's Valley, Calif.: Borland Int'l.

Borland (1989c). *Turbo Pascal Version 5.0, User's Guide*. Scott's Valley, Calif.: Borland Int'l.

Brailsford, D.F. and A.N. Walker (1979). *Introductory ALGOL68 Programming*. New York: Wiley.

Bray, Gary and David Pokrass (1985). *Understanding Ada: A Software Engineering Approach*. New York: Wiley.

Brodie, Leo (1987). *Starting FORTH*. Englewood Cliffs, NJ: Prentice-Hall.

Brooks, Frederick P., Jr. (1975). *The Mythical Man-Month: Essays on Software Engineering*. Reading Mass.: Addison-Wesley.

Brown, Gary DeWard (1975). *FORTRAN to PL/1 Dictionary, PL/1 to FORTRAN Dictionary*. New York: Wiley.

Bryson, Susan M. (1982). *Understanding APL*. Sherman Oaks, Calif.: Alfred Publishing Co.

Budd, Timothy (1987). *A Little Smalltalk*. Reading, Mass.: Addison-Wesley.

Burks, Alice R. and Arthur W. Burks (1988). *The First Electronic Computer: The Atanasoff Story*. Ann Arbor, Mich.: University of Michigan Press.

Charniak, Eugene and Drew McDermott (1985). *Introduction to Artificial Intelligence*. Reading, Mass.: Addison-Wesley.

Chorafas, Dimitris N. (1986a). *Fourth and Fifth Generation Programming Languages*. Vol. 1: *Integrated Software, Database Languages, and Expert Systems*. New York: McGraw-Hill.

Chorafas, Dimitris N. (1986b). *Fourth and Fifth Generation Programming Languages*. Vol. 2: *Which UNIX? AT&T, IBM, and other Standard Bearers*. New York: McGraw-Hill.

Clocksin, W.F. and C.C. Mellish (1984). *Programming in Prolog*. Berlin: Springer-Verlag.

Cohen, Alan (1983). *Structure Logic and Program Design*. New York: Wiley.

Cooling, J.E. (1988). *MODULA-2 for Microcomputer Systems*. London: Van Nostrand Reinhold Int'l.

Cooper, Doug and Michael Clancy (1985). *Oh! Pascal!* New York: W.W. Norton.

Cox, Brad J. (1986). *Object Oriented Programming: An Evolutionary Approach*. Reading, Mass.: Addison-Wesley.

Dahl, O.J., E.W. Dijkstra, C.A.R. Hoare (eds., 1972). *Structured Programming*. New York: Academic.

DeMarco, Tom (1979). *Structured Analysis and System Specification*. New York: Yourdon, Inc.

Digitalk (1986). *Smalltalk/V Tutorial and Programming Language Handbook*. Los Angeles: Digitalk, Inc.

Dijkstra, Edsger (1962). *A Primer of ALGOL60 Programming*. London: Academic Press.

Dijkstra, Edsger W. (1976). *A Discipline of Programming*. Englewood Cliffs, NJ: Prentice-Hall.

Dybvig, R. Kent (1987). *The SCHEME Programming Language*. Englewood Cliffs, NJ: Prentice-Hall.

Ellzey, Roy S. (1982). *Data Structures for Computer Information Systems*. Chicago: Science Research Associates.

Elson, Mark (1973). *Concepts of Programming Languages*. Chicago: Science Research Associates.

Fairley, Richard E. (1985). *Software Engineerig Concepts*. New York: McGraw-Hill.

Feingold, Carl (1978). *Fundamentals of Structured COBOL Programming*. Dubuque, Iowa: Wm.C. Brown.

Feuer, Alan and Narain Gehani (eds., 1984). *Comparing and Assessing Programming Languages: Ada, C, Pascal*. Englewood Cliffs, NJ: Prentice-Hall.

Fisher, Alan S. (1988). *CASE: Using Software Development Tools*. New York: Wiley.

Forsythe, Richard and Chris Naylor (1985). *The Hitch-Hiker's Guide to Artificial Intelligence*. New York: Chapman & Hall.

Freeman, Peter (1975). *Software Systems Principles: A Survey*. Chicago: Science Research Assoc.

Gane, Chris and Trish Sarson (1979). *Structured Systems Analysis: Tools and Techniques*. Englewood Cliffs, NJ: Prentice-Hall.

Ghezzi, Carlo and Mehdi Jazayeri (1987). *Programming Language Concepts 2/E*. New York: Wiley.

Glaser, Hugh, Chris Hankin, and David Till (1984). *Principles of Functional Programming*. Englewood Cliffs, NJ: Prentice-Hall International.

Glass, Robert L. (1977). *The Universal Elixir and Other Computing Projects Which Failed*. Seattle, Wash.: Computing Trends.

Goble, Terry (1989). *Structured Systems Analysis Through Prolog*. Englewood Cliffs, NJ: Prentice-Hall.

Goldberg, Adele (1984). *Smalltalk-80: The Interactive Programming Environment*. Reading, Mass.: Addison-Wesley.

Goldberg, Adele and David Robson (1989). *Smalltalk-80: The Language*. Reading, Mass.: Addison-Wesley.

Goldstein, Larry Joel and Larry Gritz (1989). *Hands-On Turbo C®*. New York: Brady.

Gordon, Michael J.C. (1988). *Programming Language Theory and Its Implementation*. Englewood Cliffs, NJ: Prentice-Hall.

Gries, David (ed., 1978). *Programming Methodology: A Collection of Articles by Members of IFIP WG2.3*. New York: Springer-Verlag.

Griswold, R.E., J.F. Poage, and I.P. Polonsky (1971). *The SNOBOL4 Programming Language*. Englewood Cliffs, NJ: Prentice-Hall.

Grosshans, Daniel (1986). *File Systems: Design and Implementation*. Englewood Cliffs, NJ: Prentice-Hall.

Hanson, Kirk (1986). *Data Structured Program Design*. Englewood Cliffs, NJ: Prentice-Hall.

Harland, David M. (1984). *Polymorphic Programming Languages: Design and Implementation*. Chichester, England: Ellis Horwood, Ltd.

Harmon, Paul and David King (1985). *Expert Systems: Artificial Intelligence in Business*. New York: Wiley.

Harvey, Brian (1985). *Computer Science Logo Style: Intermediate Programming*. Cambridge, Mass.: MIT Press.

Hayes-Roth, Frederick, Donald A. Waterman, and Douglas B. Lenat (1983). *Building Expert Systems*. Reading, Mass.: Addison-Wesley.

Henderson, Peter (1980). *Functional Programming: Applications and Implementation*. Englewood Cliffs, NJ: Prentice-Hall International.

Hockney, Susan (1986). *SNOBOL Programming for the Humanities*. New York: Oxford University Press.

Hofstadter, Douglas R. (1979). *Godel, Escher, Bach: An Eternal Golden Braid*. New York: Basic Books.

Holt, R.C., G.S. Graham, E.D. Lazowska, and M.A. Scott (1978). *Structured Concurrent Programming with Operating Systems Applications*. Reading, Mass.: Addison-Wesley.

Horowitz, Ellis (ed., 1983). *Programming Languages: A Grand Tour*. Rockville, Maryland: Computer Science Press.

Horowitz, Ellis (1984). *Fundamentals of Programming Languages*. Rockville, Maryland: Computer Science Press.

Horowitz, Ellis and Sartaj Sahni (1983). *Fundamentals of Data Structures*. Rockville, Maryland: Computer Science Press.

IBM (1981). *IBM VS COBOL for OS/VS*. White Plains, New York: IBM Corp.

IEEE (1983). *Standard Pascal Programming Language*. ANSI/IEEE 770 X3.97, New York.

Iverson, Kenneth E. (1962). *A Programming Language*. New York: Wiley.

Jackson, M.A. (1975). *Principles of Program Design*. New York: Academic.

Jackson, Peter (1986). *Introduction to Expert Systems*. Reading, Mass.: Addison-Wesley.

Jensen, K. and N. Wirth (1984). *Pascal User Manual and Report*, 3rd edition. NY: Springer-Verlag

JPI (1988). *TopSpeed*™ Modula-2 User's Manual. Mountain View, Calif.: Jensen & Partners Int'l.

Kaehler, Ted and Dave Patterson (1986). *A Taste of Smalltalk*. New York: W.W. Norton.

Katzan, Henry Jr. (1972). *A PL/1 Approach to Programming Languages*. New York: Auerbach.

Kelley, Al and Ira Pohl (1984). *A Book on C*. Menlo Park, Calif.: Benjamin/Cummings.

Kemeny, John and Thomas Kurtz (1981). *BASIC Programming*, 3rd edition. New York: Wiley.

Kemeny, John and Thomas Kurtz (1985). *Back to BASIC: The History, Corruption, and Future of the Language*. Reading, Mass.: Addison-Wesley.

Kernighan, Brian W. and Dennis M. Ritchie (1978). *The C Programming Language*. Englewood Cliffs, NJ: Prentice-Hall.

Kernighan, Brian W. and Dennis M. Ritchie (1988). *The C Programming Language*. Englewood Cliffs, NJ: Prentice-Hall.

King, David (1988). *Creating Effective Software: Computer Program Design Using the Jackson Methodology*. Englewood Cliffs, NJ: Prentice-Hall.

King, K.N. (1988). *TopSpeed*™ Modula-2 Language Tutorial. Mountain View, Calif.: Jensen & Partners Int'l.

Knuth, Donald E. (1973). *The Art of Computer Programming*. Vol. 1: *Fundamental Algorithms*. Reading, Mass.: Addison-Wesley.

Knuth, Donald E. (1981). *The Art of Computer Programming*. Vol. 2: *Seminumerical Algorithms*. Reading, Mass.: Addison-Wesley.

Knuth, Donald E. (1982). *The Art of Computer Programming*. Vol. 3: *Sorting and Searching*. Reading, Mass.: Addison-Wesley.

Koffman, Elliot B. (1985). *Problem Solving and Structured Programming in Pascal*. Reading, Mass.: Addison-Wesley.

Koffman, Elliot B. (1986). *Turbo Pascal: A Problem Solving Approach*. Reading, Mass.: Addison-Wesley.

Korth, Henry F. and Abraham Silberschatz (1986). *Database System Concepts*. New York: McGraw-Hill.

Krasner, Glenn (1983). *Smalltalk-80: Bits of History, Words of Advice*. Reading, Mass.: Addison-Wesley.

Kroenke, David M. (1984). *Business Computer Systems: An Introduction*. Santa Cruz, Calif.: Mitchell Publishing.

Lazarev, Gregory L. (1989). *Why PROLOG? Justifying Logic Programming for Practical Applications*. Englewood Cliffs, NJ: Prentice-Hall.

Ledgard, Henry (1983). *Ada: An Introduction*. New York: Springer-Verlag.

Leler, William (1988). *Constraint Programming Languages: Their Specification and Generation*. Reading, Mass.: Addison-Wesley.

Liskov, Barbara and John Guttag (1986). *Abstraction and Specification in Program Development*. Cambridge, Mass.: MIT Press.

Loeckx, Jacques, Kurt Mehlhorn, and Reinhard Wilhelm (1988). *Foundations of Programming Languages*. New York: Wiley.

Loomis, Mary E.S. (1989). *Data Management and File Structures*. Englewood Cliffs, NJ: Prentice-Hall.

Lucas, Robert (1988). *Database Applications Using PROLOG*. Chichester, England: Ellis Horwood, Ltd.

McCracken, Daniel D. and William I. Salmon (1987). *A Second Course in Computer Science with Modula-2*. New York: Wiley.

MacLennan, Bruce J. (1983). *Principles of Programming Languages: Design, Evaluation, and Implementation*. New York: Holt, Rinehart and Winston.

Madnick, Stuart E. and John J. Donovan (1974). *Operating Systems*. New York: McGraw-Hill.

Marcotty, Michael and Henry Ledgard (1987). *The World of Programming Languages*. New York: Springer-Verlag.

Martin, James (1982). *Application Development Without Programmers*. Englewood Cliffs, NJ: Prentice-Hall.

Martin, James (1985). *Fourth-Generation Languages. Volume I: Principles*. Englewood Cliffs, NJ: Prentice-Hall.

Martin, James, with Joe Leben (1986a). *Fourth-Generation Languages. Vol. II: Representative 4GLs*. Englewood Cliffs, NJ: Prentice-Hall.

Martin, James, with Joe Leben (1986b). *Fourth-Generation Languages. Vol. III: 4GLs From IBM*. Englewood Cliffs, NJ: Prentice-Hall.

Martin, James and Carma McClure (1988). *Structured Techniques: The Basis for CASE*. Englewood Cliffs, NJ: Prentice-Hall.

Martin, Johannes J. (1986). *Data Types and Data Structures*. Englewood Cliffs, NJ: Prentice-Hall.

Metropolis, N., J. Howlett, Gian-Carlo Rota (eds., 1980). *A History of Computing in the Twentieth Century: A Collection of Essays*. New York: Academic Press.

Meyer, Bertrand (1988). *Object-oriented Software Construction*. Englewood Cliffs, NJ: Prentice-Hall.

Moore, John B. and Kenneth N. McKay (1987). *Modula-2: Text and Reference*. Englewood Cliffs, NJ : Prentice-Hall.

Morrison, P. and E. Morrison (eds., 1961). *Charles Babbage and His Calculating Engines*. New York: Dover.

Muldner, Tomasz and Peter W. Steele (1988). *C as a Second Language: For Native Speakers of Pascal*. Reading, Mass.: Addison-Wesley.

Nath, Sanjiva (1986). *Turbo Prolog: Features for Programmers*. Portland, Oregon: Management Information Source, Inc.

Nicholls, John E. (1975). *The Structure and Design of Programming Languages*. Reading, Mass.: Addison-Wesley.

Organick, Elliott I., Alexandra I. Forsythe, Robert P. Plummer (1978). *Programming Language Structures*. New York: Academic Press.

Philippakis, A.S. and Leonard J. Kazmier (1982). *Advanced COBOL*. New York: McGraw-Hill.

Philippakis, A.S. and Leonard J. Kazmier (1983). *Program Design Concepts with Applications in COBOL*. New York: McGraw-Hill.

Pinson, Lewis J. and Richard S. Wiener (1988). *An Introduction to Object-Oriented Programming and Smalltalk*. Reading, Mass.: Addison-Wesley.

Pratt, Terrence W. (1984). *Programming Languages: Design and Implementation*. Englewood Cliffs, NJ: Prentice-Hall.

Randall, B. (1973). *The Origins of Digital Computers: Selected Papers*. Berlin: Springer.

Reges, Stuart (1987). *Building Pascal Programs: An Introduction to Computer Science*. Boston, Mass.: Little, Brown.

Research & Education Association (1985). *Handbook and Guide for Comparing and Selecting Computer Languages*. New York: REA.

Russell, E.C. (1983). *Building Simulation Models with SIMSCRIPT II.5*. Washington, D.C.: CACI.

Sammet, Jean E. (1969). *Programming Languages: History and Fundamentals*. Englewood Cliffs, NJ: Prentice-Hall.

Schneider, Hans Jurgen (1984). *Problem Oriented Programming Languages*. New York: Wiley.

Schneyer, R. (1984.) *Modern Structured Programming*. Santa Cruz, Calif.: Mitchell.

Schwartz, J.T., R.B.K. Dewar, E. Dubinsky, and E. Schonberg (1986). *Programming with Sets: An Introduction to SETL*. New York: Springer-Verlag.

Sebesta, Robert W. (1989). *Concepts of Programming Languages*. Redwood City, Calif.: Benjamin/Cummings.

Sell, Peter S. (1985). *Expert Systems: A Practical Introduction*. New York: Wiley.

Sessions, Roger (1989). *Reusable Data Structures for C*. Englewood Cliffs, NJ: Prentice-Hall.

Sethi, Ravi (1989). *Programming Languages: Concepts and Constructs*. Reading, Mass.: Addison-Wesley.

Shammas, Namir (1988). *Introducing C to Pascal Programmers.* New York: Wiley.

Shaw, Alan C. (1974). *The Logical Design of Operating Systems.* Englewood Cliffs, NJ: Prentice-Hall.

Shelly, Gary B., Thomas J. Cashman, and Steven G. Forsythe (1987). *Turbo Pascal Programming.* Boston, Mass.: Boyd & Fraser.

Shlaer, Sally and Stephen J. Mellor (1988). *Object-oriented Systems Analysis: Modeling the World in Data.* Englewood Cliffs, NJ: Prentice-Hall.

Shumate, Kenneth (1984). *Understanding Ada.* New York: Harper & Row.

Smedema, C.H., P. Medema, and M. Boasson (1983). *The Programming Languages: Pascal, Modula, CHILL, Ada.* Englewood Cliffs, NJ: Prentice-Hall International.

Stein, Dorothy (1985). *Ada: A Life and a Legacy.* Cambridge, Mass.: MIT Press.

Sterling, Leon and Ehud Shapiro (1986). *The Art of Prolog: Advanced Programming Techniques.* Cambridge, Mass.: MIT Press.

Stubbs, Daniel F. and Neil Webre (1987). *Data Structures with Abstract Data Types and Modula-2.* Monterey, Calif.: Brooks/Cole.

Swartz, Ray (1989). *Doing Business with C.* Englewood Cliffs, NJ : Prentice-Hall.

Teft, Lee (1989). *Programming in Turbo Prolog with an Introduction to Knowledge-based Systems.* Englewood Cliffs, NJ: Prentice-Hall.

Tello, Ernest R. (1989). *Object-Oriented Programming for Artificial Intelligence.* Reading, Mass.: Addison-Wesley.

Tenenbaum, Aaron M. and Moshe J. Augenstein (1981). *Data Structures Using Pascal.* Englewood Cliffs, NJ: Prentice-Hall.

Tennent, R.D. (1981). *Principles of Programming Languages.* Englewood Cliffs, NJ: Prentice-Hall International.

Thomas, Pete, Hugh Robinson, and Judy Emms (1988). *Abstract Data Types: Their Specification, Representation, and Use.* New York: Oxford University Press.

Tobias, Jeffrey M. (ed., 1980). *Language Design and Methodology.* Proceedings of Symposium Held in Sydney Australia, September 1979. Berlin: Springer-Verlag.

Touretzky, David S. (1984). *LISP: A Gentle Introduction to Symbolic Computation.* New York: Harper and Row.

Tremblay, Jean-Paul and Paul G. Sorenson (1984). *An Introduction to Data Structures with Applications.* New York: McGraw-Hill.

Tsichritzis, Dionysios C. and Frederick H. Lochovsky (1982). *Data Models.* Englewood Cliffs, NJ: Prentice-Hall.

Tucker, Allen B. (1986). *Programming Languages.* New York: McGraw-Hill.

Van Horn, Mike (1986). *Understanding Expert Systems.* New York: Bantam.

Weinberg, Gerald M. (1971). *The Psychology of Computer Programming.* New York: Van Nostrand Reinhold.

Welsh, Jim and John Elder (1982). *Introduction to Pascal.* Englewood Cliffs, NJ: Prentice-Hall International.

Wexelblat, Richard L. (ed., 1981). *History of Programming Languages.* New York: Academic Press.

Wiatrowski, Claude A. and Richard S. Wiener (1987). *From C to Modula-2...and Back*. New York: Wiley.

Wiener, Richard and Richard Sincovec (1984). *Software Engineering with Modula-2 and Ada*. New York: Wiley.

Wilson, Leslie B. and Robert G. Clark (1988). *Comparative Programming Languages*. Reading, Mass.: Addison-Wesley.

Winston, Patrick H. and Karen A. Prendergast (eds., 1984). *The AI Business: Commercial Uses of Artificial Intelligence*. Cambridge, Mass.: MIT Press.

Wirth, Niklaus (1973). *Systematic Programming: An Introduction*. Englewood Cliffs, NJ: Prentice-Hall.

Wirth, Niklaus (1985). *Programming in Modula-2*. New York: Springer-Verlag.

Wooldridge, Susan (1973). *Software Selection*. Philadelphia: Auerbach.

Yeh, Raymond T. (ed., 1977a). *Current Trends in Programming Methodology. Vol. I: Software Specification and Design*. Englewood Cliffs, NJ: Prentice-Hall.

Yeh, Raymond T. (ed., 1977b). *Current Trends in Programming Methodology. Vol. II: Program Validation*. Englewood Cliffs, NJ: Prentice-Hall.

Yeh, Raymond T. (ed., 1978). *Current Trends in Programming Methodology. Vol. IV: Data Structuring*. Englewood Cliffs, NJ: Prentice-Hall.

Zarrella, John (1982). *Language Translators*. Suisun City, Calif.: Microcomputer Applications.

Zwass, Vladimir (1981). *Introduction to Computer Science*. New York: Barnes & Noble Books.

A.2 ARTICLES

Abbott, Russell J. (1987). "Knowledge abstraction." *Comm. ACM*, 30 (8, August), 664–671.

Abelson, Harold and Gerald Jay Sussman (1988). "LISP: A language for stratified design." *Byte*, 13 (2, February), 207–218.

Adelsberger, Heimo H., Udo W. Pooch, Robert E. Shannon, and Glen N. Williams (1986). "Rule based object-oriented simulation systems." In Paul A. Luker and Heimo H. Adelsberger (eds.), *Intelligent Simulation Environments*. San Diego, Calif.: Society for Computer Simulation, 107–112.

Allen, Keith R. and David J. Pokrass (1987). "Logic and functional programming." *IEEE Potentials*, 6 (3, October), 21–24.

Alpar, Paul (1987). "Structured expert system development." Working paper #87–04, College of Business Administration, University of Illinois at Chicago.

Althoff, James C., Jr. (1981). "Building data structures in the Smalltalk-80 system." *Byte*, 6 (8, August), 230–278.

Amarel, Saul (1988). "On the representation of problems in artificial intelligence." *Proceedings, International Conference on Computer Languages* (October 9–13), IEEE Computer Society, 168–176.

Amsterdam, Jonathan (1988). "Creating an adventurous language." *Dr. Dobb's Journal*, 13 (4, April), 18–39.

Anderson, Bruce (1988). "Object-oriented programming." *Microprocessors and Microsystems*, 12 (8, October), 433–442.

Anderson, Jim and Barry Fishman (1985). "The Smalltalk programming language." *Byte* (May), 161–165.

Arvind, A. and K.P. Gostelow (1982). "The U-interpreter." *Computer*, 15 (2, February), 42–49.

Ashcroft, E.A. and W.W. Wadge (1977). "Lucid, a nonprocedural language with iteration." *Comm. ACM*, 20 (7, July), 519–526.

Bach, William W. (1989). "Is Ada really an object-oriented programming language?" *Journal of Pascal, Ada and Modula-2*, 8 (2, March–April), 18–25.

Backus, John (1978). "Can programming be liberated from the von Neumann style? A functional style and its algebra of programs." *Comm. ACM*, 21 (8, August), 613–641. Reprinted in Ellis Horowitz (ed., 1983), *Programming Languages: A Grand Tour*, Computer Science Press, Rockville, MD, 146–174.

Backus, John (1980). "Programming in America in the 1950's—Some personal impressions." In N. Metropolis, J. Howlett, and Gian-Carlo Rota (eds.), *A History of Computing in the Twentieth Century*, Academic, NY, 197–273.

Backus, John (1981). "The history of FORTRAN I, II, and III." In Richard L. Wexelblat (ed.), *History of Programming Languages*, Academic, NY, 25–44.

Bailin, Sidney C. (1989). "An object-oriented requirements specification method." *Comm. ACM*, 32 (5, May), 608–623.

Balzer, Robert, Thomas E. Chetham, Jr., and Cordell Green (1983). "Software technology in the 1990's: Using a new paradigm." *IEEE Computer*, 16 (11, November), 39–45.

Baron, Naomi S. (1986). "The future of computer languages: Implications for education." *ACM SIGCSE Bulletin*, 18 (1, February), 44–49.

Barzel, Ronen and David Salesin (1986). "Patchwork: A fast interpreter for a restricted dataflow language." *Journal of Systems and Software*, 6 (3, August), 251–259.

Basden, Andrew (1983). "On the application of expert systems." *International Journal of Man-Machine Studies*, 19 (5, November), 461–477.

Batini, C. and S. Ceri (1985). "Database design: Methodologies, tools, and environments." Panel session. In S. Navathe (ed.), *Management of Data*, Proceedings of ACM SIGMOD 1985 International Conference on Management of Data. New York: ACM, 148–150.

Bellia, Marco and Giorgio Levi (1986). "The relationship between logic and functional languages: A survey." *The Journal of Logic Programming*, 3, 217–236.

Bellia, M., P.G. Bosco, E. Giovannetti, G. Levi, C. Moiso, and C. Palamidessi (1988). "A two-level approach to logic and functional programming." *CSELT Technical Reports*, XVI, 5 (August), 487–496.

Bender, Eric (1987). "The knowledge engineers." *PC World* (September), 172–179.

Bergland, G.D. (1981). "A guided tour of program design methodologies." *Computer*, 14 (10, October), 13–37.

Bernknopf, Jeff (1985). "A language by any other name...would not be COBOL." *Information Center* (October), 21–28.

Bic, Lubomir and Craig Lee (1987). A data-driven model for a subset of logic programming." *ACM Trans. Programming Languages and Systems* 9 (4, October), 618–645.

Blaha, Michael R., William J. Premerlani, and James E. Rumbaugh (1988). "Relational database design using an object-oriented methodology." *Comm. ACM*, 31 (4, April), 414–427.

Blum, Bruce I. (1987). "Evaluating alternative paradigms: A case study." *Large Scale Systems*, 12 (3), 189–199.

Bobrow, Daniel G. (1985). "If Prolog is the answer, what is the question? Or what it takes to support AI programming paradigms." *IEEE Trans. Software Enginnering* SE-12, 11 (November), 1401–1407.

Bobrow, Daniel G., Sanjay Mittal, and Mark J. Stefik (1986). "Expert systems: Perils and promise." *Communications of the ACM*, 29 (9, September), 880–894.

Bochmann, G.V. (1973). "Multiple exits from a loop without the GOTO." *Comm. ACM*, 16 (7, July), 443–444.

Bonar, Jerrey and Elliot Soloway (1983). "Uncovering principles of novice programming." *Proceedings, Tenth Annual ACM Symposium on Principles of Programming Languages*, January 24–26, Austin, Texas, 10–13, 84–88.

Booch, Grady (1986). "Object-oriented development." *IEEE Trans. Software Engineering* SE-12, 2 (February), 211–221.

Boom, H.J. and E. DeJong (1980). "A critical comparison of several programming language implementations." *Software —Practice and Experience*, 10, 435–473.

Borning, A.H. (1987). "Constraints and functional programming." *Proceedings, 6th Annual Phoenix Conference on Computers and Communications*, Feb. 25–27, Scottsdale, Arizona, IEEE, 300–306.

Borning, Alan, Robert Duisberg, Bjorn Freeman-Benson, Axel Kramer, and Michael Woolf (1987). "Constraint hierarchies." *OOPSLA '87 Proceedings* (October 4–8), 48–59.

Bover, David C.C. and Patty E. Brayton (1987). "Sorting techniques in logic programming." *Proceedings, IEEE Region 5 Conference*, March 9–11, Tulsa, OK.

Bozman, Jean S. (1989). "APL poised to move beyond its small, but loyal, coterie." *Computerworld* (October 2), 25–27.

Branquart, P. and P. Wodon (1988). "Algorithmic languages." *Philips Journal of Research*, 43 (3–4), 246–267.

Bray, Rick, Brian Fairless, Ross Gile, Susan Waller, Russell Maxey, and Daniel West (1989). "Comparing Modula-2 and C." *Journal of Pascal, Ada and Modula-2*, 8 (2, March–April), 27–29.

Breen, D.E., P.H. Getto, and A.A. Apodaca (1988). "An object-oriented programming methodology for a conventional programming environment." *Proceedings, Software Engineering '88* (July 11–15), IEE, 65–72.

Bruynooghe, Maurice, Danny De Schreye, and Bruno Krekels (1986). "Compiling control." *IEEE Symposium on Logic Programming*, 70–77.

Bulman, David M. (1989). "An object-based development model." *Computer Language*, 6 (8, August), 49–59.

Burns, James R. and J. Danell Morgeson (1988). "An object-oriented world-view for intelligent, discrete, next-even simulation." *Management Science* 34 (12, December), 1425–1440.

Business Week (1988). "The software trap: automate—or else." (May 9), 142–150.

Bylinsky, Gene (1988). "Technology in the year 2000." *Fortune* (July 18), 92–98.

Cagan, Martin R. (1986). "An introduction to Hewlett-Packard's AI workstation technology." *Hewlett-Packard Journal* (March), 4–14.

Carlyle, Ralph Emmett (1987). "Toward 2017." *Datamation* (September 15), 142–154.

Cashin, Jerry (1988). "More ways to say 'program': Why developers are exploiting C, Ada, Prolog and Lisp programming tools." *Software Magazine* (July), 31–40.

Celko, Joe (1987). "Data flow diagrams." *Computer Languages* (January), 41–43.

Cheatham, Thomas E., Jr. (1972). "The recent evolution of programming languages." In C.V. Freiman (ed.), *Information Processing 71*: Proceedings of the IFIP Congress 1971, Vol. I, North-Holland, NY, 298–313.

Chen, Weidong (1987). "A theory of modules based on second-order logic." *Proceedings, 1987 Symposium on Logic Programming*, IEEE, 24–33.

Chrisman, Carol and Barbara Beccue (1986). "Entity-relationship models as a tool for data analysis and design." *ACM SIGCSE Bulletin*, 18 (1, February), 8–14.

Cioch, Frank A. (1989). "The impact of object-oriented decomposition on procedural abstraction." *Journal of Pascal, Ada and Modula-2*, 8 (3, May-June), 48–55.

Clark, Keith and Steve Gregory (1986). "PARLOG: Parallel programming in logic." *ACM Trans. Programming Languages and Systems*, 8 (1, January), 1–49.

Clark, R. Lawrence (1973). "A linguistic contribution to GOTO-less programming." *Datamation*, 19 (12, December), 62–63. Reprinted in *Comm. ACM*, 27 (4, April), 349–350.

Clarke, Lori A., Andy Podgurski, Debra J. Richardson, and Steven J. Zeil (1989). "A formal evaluation of data flow path selection criteria." *IEEE Trans. Software Engineering*, 15 (11, November), 1318–1332.

Clarke, Lori A., Jack C. Wileden, and Alexander L. Wolf (1980). "Nesting in Ada programs is for the birds." *ACM SIGPLAN Notices* 15 (11, November), 139–145.

Clocksin, William (1987). "A Prolog primer." *Byte* (August), 146–158.

Coar, David (1984). "Pascal, Ada, and Modula-2." *Byte*, 9 (8, August), 215–232.

Cobb, Richard H. (1985). "In praise of 4GLs." *Datamation* (July 15), 90–96.

Cohen, Jacques (1985). "Describing PROLOG by its interpretation and compilation." *Comm. ACM*, 28, (12, December), 1311–1324.

Cohen, Jacques (1988). "A view of the origins and development of PROLOG." *Comm. ACM*, 31, (1, January), 26–36.

Cohn, Michael B. (1989). "Digesting nouveau programming." *Computerworld* (March 13), 21+.

Computerworld (1986). "History of computing." (November 3).

Computerworld (1989). "In depth: The IBM 360 turns 25." (April 24), 1, 81+.

Connell, N.A.D. (1987). "Expert systems in accountancy: A review of some recent applications." *Accounting and Business Research*, 17 (67), 221–233.

Cook, Steve (1986). "Languages and object-oriented programming." *Software Engineering Journal*, 1 (2, March), 73–81.

Coombs, Mike and Jim Alty (1984). "Expert systems: An alternative paradigm." *International Journal of Man–Machine Studies*, 20 (1, January), 21–43.

Cox, Brad J. (1984). "Message/object: An evolutionary change in programming technology." *IEEE Software* (1, January), 50–61.

Cox, Brad and Bill Hunt (1986). "Objects, icons, and software-ICs." *Byte*, 11 (8, August), 195–206.

Cuadrado, Clara Y. and John L. Cuadrado (1985). "PROLOG goes to work." *Byte*, 10 (8, August), 151–156+.

Cusack, E.L. (1988). "Fundamental aspects of object oriented specification." *British Telecom Technology Journal*, 6 (3, July), 77–81.

Danforth, Scott (1988). "Consistent choice narrowing—a new model for constraint based programming." IEEE, 595–604.

Danforth, Scott and Chris Tomlinson (1988). "Type theories and object-oriented programming." *ACM Computing Surveys*, 20 (1, March), 29–72.

Daniel, W.J.T. (1988). "Integration of rule-based and procedural code to obtain flexible engineering software." *Adv. Eng. Software*, 10, 2, 72–75.

Darlington, John (1985). "Program transformation." *Byte*, 10, 8 (August), 201–216.

Darlington, J. (1987). "Software development using functional programming languages." *ICL Technical Journal*, 5 (3, May), 492–508.

David, Michael (1988). "4GLs, 5GLs, and the database." *Database Programming and Design* (October), 42–49.

Dennis, J.B., G.R. Gao, and K. Todd (1984) "Modelling the weather with a dataflow super computer." *IEEE Trans. on Computers*. C-33 (7, July), 48–56.

DeRemer, Frank and Hans H. Kron (1976). "Programming-in-the-large versus programming-in-the-small." *IEEE Tran. Software Engireering*, SE-2 (2, June), 80–86.

Deutsch, L. Peter (1981). "Building control structures in the Smalltalk-80 system." *Byte*, 6 (8, August), 322–346.

Dewhurst, Stephen C. and Kathy T. Stark (1987). "Out of the C world comes C++." *Computer Language*, 4 (2, February), 29–36.

Dijkstra, Edsger W. (1968). "Go to statement considered harmful." Letter, *Comm. ACM*, 11 (3, March), 147–148.

Dijkstra, Edsger W. (1972a). "Notes on structured programming." In O.J. Dahl *et al.* (eds.), *Structured Programming*, Academic, NY, 1–82.

Dijkstra, Edsger W. (1972b). "The humble programmer." *Comm. ACM*, 15 (October), 859–886. Reprinted in D. Gries (ed., 1978), *Programming Methodology*, Springer-Verlag, NY, 9–22.

Dijkstra, Edsger W. (1978). "Correction concerns and, among other things, why they are resented." In D. Gries (ed.), *Programming Methodology*, Springer-Verlag, NY, 80–88.

Dologite, D.G. (1987). "Developing a knowledge-based system on a personal computer using an expert system shell." *Journal of Systems Management* (October), 30–37.

Doman, Andras (1981). "PARADOCS: A highly parallel dataflow computer and its dataflow language." *Microprocessing and Microprogramming*, 7 (1, January), 20–31.

Donaldson, James R. (1973). "Structured programming." *Datamation*, 19 (12, December), 52–54.

Doukidis, Georgios I. (1987). "An anthology on the homology of simulation with artificial intelligence." *Journal of the Operational Research Society*, 38 (8, August), 701–712.

Drabent, Wlodzimierz (1987). "Do logic programs resemble programs in conventional languages?" *1987 Symposium on Logic Programming*, 389–396.

Duff, Charles B. (1986). "Designing an efficient language." *Byte*, 11 (8, August), 211–224.

Ege, Raimund K. (1986). "The Filter—A paradigm for interfaces." Technical Report No. CSE-86-011 September 1986, Oregon Graduate Center, Beaverton, Oregon.

Ege, Raimund K. (1988). "Constraint-based user interfaces for simulations." *Winter Simulation Conference*, December 1988, San Diego, California, 263–271.

Ege, Raimund K., David Maier, Alan Borning (1987). "The Filter Browse: Defining interfaces graphically." *Proceedings of the European Conference on Object Oriented Programming*, Paris, France, June 1987, 155–165.

Eilbert, James L. and Richard M. Salter (1986). "Modeling neural networks in Scheme." *Simulation*, 46 (5, May), 193–199.

Eisenback, Susan and Chris Sadler (1985). "Declarative languages: An overview." *Byte*, 10 (8, August), 181–197.

Elfring, Gary (1985). "Choosing a programming language." *Byte* (June), 235–240.

Elmasri, R., J. Weeldreyer, and A. Hevner (1985). "The category concept: An extension to the entity-relationship model." *Data and Knowledge Engineering*, 1 (1, June), 75–116.

Ercegovac, Milos D. and Shih-Lien Lu (1983). "A functional language approach in high-speed digital simulation." *Proceedings, Summer Computer Simulation Conference*, July 11–13, Vancouver, Canada, 383–387.

Ercegovac, Milos D., Dorab R. Patel, and Tomas Lang (1983). "Functional language and data flow architecture." *Proceedings, Summer Computer Simulation Conference*, July 11–13, Vancouver, Canada, Vol. 2, 1007–1023.

Falkoff, Adin D. and Kenneth E. Iverson (1981). "The evolution of APL." In Richard L. Wexelblat (ed.), *History of Programming Languages*, Academic, NY, 661–673.

Faustini, Antony A. and Edgar B. Lewis (1986). "Toward a real-time dataflow langauge." *IEEE Software*, 3 (1, January), 29–35.

Feldman, P. and D. Miller (1986). "Entity model clustering: Structuring a data model by abstraction." *The Computer Journal*, 29 (4, August), 348–360.

Feuche, Mike (1989). "Object-oriented databases finding applications." *Management Information Systems Week* (April 10), 50–51.

Fickas, Stephen (1985). "Design issues in a rule-based system." *ACM SIGPLAN Notices*, 20, 7 (July), 208–215.

Fickas, Stephen (1987). "Supporting the programmer of a rule based language." *Expert Systems*, 4 (2, May), 74–87.

Fickas, Stephen (1989). "Design issues in a rule-based system." *Journal of Systems and Software*, 10 (2, September), 113–123.

Fikes, Richard and Tom Kehler (1985). "The role of frame-based representation in reasoning." *Comm. ACM*, 28 (9, September), 904–920.

Firdman, Henry Eric (1987). "How not to build an expert system shell." *Computerworld* (February 16), 57–61.

Firdman, Henry Eric (1988). "Expert systems: Are you already behind?" *Computerworld* (April 18), 99–105.

Flesher, Dale L. and Cindy Martin (1987). "Artificial intelligence." *The Internal Auditor*, 44 (February), 32–36.

Florentin, J.J. (1985). "New constructs in programming languages." *Computer Bulletin*, 1 (2, June), 10–13.

Foster, Ian T. and Anthony J. Kusalik (1986). "A logical treatment of secondary storage." *Proceedings, 1986 Symposium on Logic Programming*, IEEE, 58–67.

Gabriel, Richard P. (1989). "Using the common LISP object system." *Computer Language*, 6 (8, August), 73–80.

Gardner, Michael R. (1988). "Successes and limitations of object-oriented design." *Journal of Pascal, Ada and Modula-2*, 7 (6, November–December), 30–41.

Gaudiot, Jean-Luc (1986). "Structure handling in data-flow systems." *IEEE Trans. Computers* C-35, 6 (June), 489–501.

Gelernter, David (1988). "Getting the job done." *Byte* (November), 301–308.

Genesereth, Michael R. and Matthew L. Ginsberg (1985). "Logic programming." *Comm. ACM*, 28 (9, September), 933–941.

Gibson, Stanley (1989). "Software industry born with IBM's unbundling." *Computerworld* (June 19), 6.

Glass, Robert L. (1988). "Software design: It's all in your mind." *Computerworld* (November 7), 107–110.

Goguen, Joseph A. (1984). "Parametrized programming." *IEEE Trans. Software Engineering*, SE-10 (5, September), 528–543.

Goguen, Joseph A. and Jose Meseguer (1986). "Extensions and foundations of object-oriented programming." *ACM SIGPLAN Notices*, 21, 10 (October), 153–162.

Goldberg, Adele (1981). "Introducing the Smalltalk-80 system." *Byte*, 6 (8, August), 14–26.

Goldberg, Adele and Joan Ross (1981). "Is the Smalltalk-80 system for children?" *Byte*, 6 (8, August), 348–368.

Goodenough, John B. (1975). "Exception handling: Issues and a proposed notation." *Comm. ACM*, 18 (12, December), 683–696.

Grant, F.J. (1985). "Twenty-first century software." *Datamation*, 31 (7, April 1), 123–129.

Gries, David and Jan Prins (1985). "A new notion of encapsulation." *ACM SIGPLAN Notices*, 20 (7, July), 131–139.

Grimshaw, Andrew S. and Jane W.S. Liu (1987). "MENTAT: An object-oriented macro data flow system." *OOPSLA '87 Proceedings* (October 4–8), 35–47.

Griswold, Ralph E. (1981). "A history of the SNOBOL programming languages." In Richard L. Wexelblat (ed.), *History of Programming Languages*, Academic, NY, 601–637.

Guttag, John (1977). "Abstract data types and the development of data structures." *Comm. ACM*, 20 (6, June), 396–404.

Hailpern, Brent (1986a). "Multiparadigm languages and environments." *IEEE Software*, 3 (1, January), 6–9.

Hailpern, Brent (guest ed., 1986b). "Multiparadigm languages and environments: Guest editor's introduction." *IEEE Software*, 3 (1, January), 6–9.

Hailpern, Brent (guest ed., 1986c). "Multiparadigm research: A survey of nine projects." *IEEE Software*, 3 (1, January), 70–77.

Harris, Larry R. (1988). "When bigger AI isn't better." *Computerworld* (October 31), 79–83.

Harrison, Peter G. and Hessam Khoshnevisan (1985). "Functional programming using FP." *Byte*, 8 (10, August), 219–232.

Harvey, J.J. (1987). "Expert systems: present and future." *Computers and People*, 36 (January–February), 12–18.

Hausman, Bogumil, Andrzej Ciepielewski, and Seif Haridi (1987). "OR-parallel Prolog made efficient on shared memory multiprocessors." *Proceedings, 1987 International Symposium on Logic Programming*, Aug. 31–Sept. 4, San Francisco, IEEE, 69–79.

Hayes-Roth, Frederick (1985). "Rule-based systems." *Comm. ACM*, 28 (9, September), 921–932.

Henderson, P. (1986). "Functional programming, formal specification, and rapid prototyping." *IEEE Trans. Software Engineering*, SE-12 (2, February), 241–250.

Henderson, Peter B. and David Notkin (1987). "Integrated design and programming environments." *IEEE Computer*, 20 (11, November), 12–16.

Herath, Jayantha, Yoshinori Yamaguchi, Nobuo Saito, and Tochitsugu Yuba (1988). "Dataflow computing models, languages, and machines for intelligence computations." *IEEE Transactions on Software Engineering*, 14, 12 (December), 1805–1827.

Herriot, Robert C. (1977). "Towards the ideal programming language." *ACM SIGPLAN Notices*, 12 (3, March), 56–62.

Hickam, David H., Edward H. Shortliffe, Miriam B. Bischoff, A. Carlisle Scott, and Charlotte D. Jacobs (1985). "The treatment advice of a computer-based cancer chemotherapy protocol advisor." *Annals of Internal Medicine*, 103 (6, part 1), 928–936.

Hoare, C.A.R. (1972). "Notes on data structuring." In O.J. Dahl *et al.* (eds.), *Structured Programming*, Academic, NY.

Hoare, C.A.R. (1973). "Hints on programming language design." *SIGACT/SIGPLAN Sympoium on Principles of Programming Languages* (October). Reprinted in Ellis Horowitz (ed., 1983), *Programming Languages: A Grand Tour*, Computer Science Press, Rockville, MD, 31–40.

Hoare, C.A.R. (1981). "The emperor's old clothes." *Comm. ACM*, 24 (2, February), 75–83.

Hoare, C.A.R. (1986). "Mathematics of programming." *Byte*, 11 (8, August), 115–127.

Hoare, C.A.R. (1987). "An overview of some formal methods for program design." *IEEE Computer* (September), 85–91.

Hoare, C.A.R., I.J. Hayes, He Jifeng, C.C. Morgan, A.W. Roscoe, J.W. Sanders, I.H. Sorensen, J.M. Spivey, and B.A. Sufrin (1987). "Laws of programming." *Comm. ACM*, 30 (8, August), 672–686.

Hopper, Grace Murray (1981). "Keynote address." ACM SIGPLAN History of Programming Languages Conference, June 1–3, 1978. In Richard L. Wexelblat (ed.), *History of Programming Languages*, Academic, NY, 7–20.

Horning, J.J. (1979). "Programming languages." In T. Anderson and B. Randell (eds.), *Computing Systems Reliability*, Cambridge: Cambridge University Press, 109–152.

Horwitz, Susan and Tim Teitelbaum (1985). "Relations and attributes: A symbiotic basis for editing environments." *ACM*, 93–105.

Hull, M. Elizabeth C., Adib Zarea-Aliabadi, and David A. Guthrie (1989). "Object-oriented design, Jackson system development (JSD) specifications and concurrency." *Software Engineering Journal*, 4 (2, March), 79–86.

Ichbiah, Jean (1984). "Ada: Past, present, future. An interview with Jean Ichbiah, the principal designer of Ada." *Comm. ACM*, 27 (10, October), 990–997.

Ingalls, Daniel H.H. (1981a). "Design principles behind Smalltalk." *Byte*, 6 (8, August), 286–298.

Ingalls, Daniel H.H. (1981b). "The Smalltalk graphics kernel." *Byte*, 6 (8, August), 168–193.

Jacky, Jonathan P. and Ira J. Kalet (1987). "An object-oriented programming discipline for standard Pascal." *Comm. ACM*, 30 (9, September), 772–778.

Jenkins, Michael A., Janice I. Glasgow, and Carl D. McCrosky (1986). "Programming styles in Nial." *IEEE Software,* 3 (1, January), 46–55.

Johnson, W. Lewis and Elliot Soloway (1984). "Intention-based diagnosis of programming errors." Department of Computer Science, Yale University.

Jones, T. Capers (1984). "Reusability in programming: A survey of the state of the art." *IEEE Trans. Software Engineering*, SE-10 (5, September), 488–494.

Juris, Robbin (1987). "Look for smart systems." *Computer Decisions* (January), 36–39.

Kaehler, Ted and Dave Patterson (1986). "A small taste of Smalltalk." *Byte*, 11 (8, August), 145–159.

Kamath, Yagesh and Manton M. Matthews (1987). "Implementation of an FP shell." *IEEE Trans. Software Engineering*, 13, 5 (May), 532–539.

Kasif, Simon (1986). "Control and data driven execution of logic programs: A comparison." *Int'l J. Parallel Programming* 15, 1, 73–99.

Kavi, Krishna M., Bill P. Buckles, and U. Narayan Bhat (1986). "A formal definition of data flow graph models." *IEEE Trans. Computers*, C-35, 11 (November), 940–947.

Kay, Alan (1984). "Inventing the Future." In P.H. Winston and K.A. Prendergast, eds., *The AI Business*, MIT Press, Cambridge, Mass.

Kay, Alan and Adele Goldberg (1977). "Personal dynamic media." *Computer*, 10 (3, March), 31–41.

Keim, Robert T. and Sheila Jacobs (1986). "Expert systems: The DSS of the future?" *Journal of Systems Management* (December), 6–14.

Kernighan, Brian W. and P.J. Plauger (1974). "Programming style: Examples and counterexamples." *ACM Computing Surveys*, 6 (4, December), 303–319.

Kernighan, Brian W. and Dennis M. Ritchie (1988). "The state of C." *Byte* (August), 205–210.

Knuth, Donald E. (1967). "The remaining trouble spots in ALGOL60." *Comm. ACM*, 10 (10), 611–617.

Knuth, Donald E. (1972). "Ancient Babylonian algorithms." *Comm. ACM*, 15, 671–677. Also, Errata, *Comm. ACM* 19 (1976), 108.

Knuth, Donald E. (1974). "Structured programming with go to statements." *ACM Computing Surveys*, 6 (4, December), 261–301. Reprinted in Raymond T. Yeh (ed.), *Current Trends in Programming Methodology. Vol. 1: Software Specification and Design*, Prentice-Hall, Englewood Cliffs, NJ, 1977, 1–32.

Knuth, Donald E. (1984). "Literate programming." *The Computer Journal*, 27 (2), 97–111.

Knuth, Donald E. and Luis Trabb Pardo (1980). "The early development of programming languages." In N. Metropolis, J. Howlett, and Gian-Carlo Rota (eds.), *A History of Computing in the Twentieth Century*, Academic, NY, 197–273.

Kodosky, Jeff and Robert Dye (1987). "Graphical programing: A new visual language taps the virtual instrument metaphor." *Computer Graphics World*, 10 (2, December), 77–80.

Komorowski, Henryk Jan and Jan Maluszynski (1987). "Logic programming and rapid prototyping." *Science of Computer Programming*, 9 (2, October), 179- 205.

Konopasek, Milos and Sundaresan Jayaraman (1985). "Constraint and declarative languages for engineering applications: The TK!Solver contribution." *Proceedings of the IEEE*, 73 (12, December), 1791–1806.

Konstam, Aaron H. and Donald E. Wood (1985). "Software science applied to APL." *IEEE Trans. Software Engineering* SE-11, 10 (October), 994–999.

Korth, Henry F. (1986). "Extending the scope of relational languages." *IEEE Software*, 3 (1, January), 19–28.

Koschmann, Timothy and Martha Walton Evens (1988). "Bridging the gap between object-oriented and logic programming." *IEEE Software* (July), 36–42.

Kowalski, Robert (1979). "Algorithm = logic + control." *Comm. ACM*, 22 (7, July), 424–435.

Kowalski, Robert (1985). "The origins of logic programming." *Byte*, 10 (8, August), 192–193.

Kowalski, Robert A. (1988). "The early years of logic programming." *Comm. ACM*, 31 (1, January), 38–43.

Krajewski, Rich (1985). "Multiprocessing: An overview." *Byte* (May), 171–181.

Krasner, Glenn (1981). "The Smalltalk-80 virtual machine." *Byte*, 6 (8, August), 300–319.

Kull, David (1986). "Programming, not magic." *Computer Decisions*, 18 (September 23), 41–50.

Kurtz, Barry D., Donna Ho, and Teresa A. Wall (1989). "An object-oriented methodology for systems analysis and specification." *The Computer Journal*, 40 (2, April), 86–90.

Kurtz, Thomas E. (1981). "BASIC." In Richard L. Wexelblat (ed.), *History of Programming Languages*, Academic, NY, 515–536.

Lall, Roger K. (1986). "Development tools for expert systems copy human reasoning skills." *Computer Technology Review* (Fall), 25–27.

Landin, P.J. (1966). "The next 700 programming languages." *Comm. ACM*, 9 (3, March), 157–166.

Landry, John B. (1986). "Examining expert systems." *Computerworld* (July 9), 69–71.

Lane, Alex (1988). "Lint for the PC." *Byte* (November), 229–234.

Larkin, Timothy S., Raymond I. Carruthers, and Richard S. Soper (1988). "Simulation and object-oriented programming: The development of SERB." *Simulation*, 51 (3, September), 93–100.

Lassez, Catherine (1987). "Constraint logic programming." *Byte*, 12 (9, August), 171–174.

Lawlis, Patricia K. (1988). "Ada and software maintenance." *Conference on Software Maintenance* (October 24–27), IEEE, 152–158.

Ledgard, Henry F. (1973). "The case for structured programming." *BIT*, 13, 45–57.

Ledgard, Henry F. and Michael Marcotty (1975). "A geneology of control structures." *Comm. ACM*, 18 (11, November), 629–639.

Lee, Edward A. and David G. Messerschmitt (1987). "Synchronous data flow." *Proceedings of the IEEE*, 75, 9 (September), 1235–1245.

Leventhal, Laura Marie (1988). "Experience of programming beauty: Some patterns of programming aesthetics." *International Journal of Man–Machine Studies*, 28 (5, May), 525–550.

Lin, Engming (1986). "Expert systems for business applications: Potentials and limitations." *Journal of Systems Management*, 37 (July), 18–27.

Linowes, Jonathan S. (1988). "It's an attitude…object-oriented programming in conventional C." *Byte* (August), 219–224.

Liskov, Barbara and Stephen Zilles (1977). "An introduction to formal specifications of data abstractions." In Raymond T. Yeh (ed.), *Current Trends in Programming Methodology. Vol. 1: Software Specification and Design*, Prentice-Hall, Englewood Cliffs, NJ, 1–32.

Loucopoulos, P. and V. Karakostas (1989). "Modelling and validating office information systems: An object and logic oriented approach." *Software Engineering Journal*, 4 (2, March), 87–94.

Lubars, Mitchell D. and Mehdi T. Harandi (1987). "Knowledge-based software design using design schemas." *Proceedings, Ninth International Conference on Software Engineering* (March 30–April 2), IEEE, 253–262.

Luker, Paul A. (1989). "Never mind the language, what about the paradigm?" *ACM SIGCSE Bulletin,* 21 (1, February), 252–256.

McCarthy, John (1981). "History of LISP." In Richard L. Wexelblat (ed.), *History of Programming Languages*, Academic, NY, 173–183.

McCracken, Daniel D. (1973). "Revolution in programming: An overview." *Datamation*, 19 (12, December), 50–52.

McGregor, John D. (1987). "Object-oriented programming with SCOOPS." *Computer Language*, 4 (July), 49–56.

McKeeman, W.M. (1975). "On preventing programming languages from interfering with programming." *IEEE Trans. Software Engineering*, SE-1(1, March), 19–26.

MacLennan, Bruce J. (1985). "A simple software environment based on objects and relations." *ACM SIGPLAN Notices*, 20 (7, July), 199–207.

Madsen, Ole Lehrmann (1986). "Block structure and object oriented languages." *ACM SIGPLAN Notices*, 21 (10, October), 133–142.

Maleki, Jalal (1987). "VIVID, the kernel of a knowledge representation environment based on the constraints paradigm of computation." *Proceedings, 20th Annual Hawaii International Conference on System Sciences*, Jan. 6–9, 591–597.

Maletz, Mark C. and Henrik S.H. Sandell (1988). "Knowledge-based information systems: The merging of software engineerig and knowledge engineering." *Advances in Instrumentation*, 43 (Part 4), 1613–1623.

Mally, Casimir (1988). "Structure and generation of computer languages." *Proceedings, International Conference on Computer Languages* (October 9–13), IEEE Computer Society, 58–64.

Margolis, Nell (1989). "CASE fights to beat 'all talk, no action' image." *Computerworld* (January 2), 45–50.

Matthews, M. Haytham (1987). "PROLOG and C join forces." *Computer Language*, 4 (7, July), 34–44.

Merlyn, Vaughan and Greg Boone (1989). " CASE Tools: Sorting out the tangle of tool types." *Computerworld* (March 27), 65–70.

Mcycr, Bertrand (1987). "Reusability: The case for object-oriented design." *IEEE Software*, 4 (2, March), 50–64.

Michaelson, Robert and Donald Michie (1983). "Expert systems in business." *Datamation*, 29 (11, November), 240–246.

Mikkilineni, Rao V. (1988). "Potential use of the object paradigm for software engineering environments in the 1990's." *COMPSAC '88 Proceedings*, 439–440.

Miller, Edward F. Jr. and George E. Lindamood (1973). "Structured programming: Top-down approach." *Datamation*, 19 (12, December), 55–57.

Miller, William M. (1989). "Multiple inheritance in C++." *Computer Language*, 6 (8, August), 63–69.

Millikin, Michael D. (1989). "Object orientation: What it can do for you." *Computerworld* (March 13), 103–113.

Misra, Santosh K. and Paul J. Jalics (1988). "Third-generation versus fourth-generation software development." *IEEE Software* (July), 8–14.

Morgan, Carroll (1988). "Procedures, parameters, and abstraction: Separate concerns." *Science of Computer Programming*, 11 (1, October), 17–27.

Morgenstern, Matthew (1986). "The role of constraints in databases, expert systems, and knowledge representation." In Larry Kerschberg (ed.), *Expert Database Systems: Pro-*

ceedings from the First International Workshop. Benjamin/Cummmings, Menlo Park, Calif., 351–368.

Moskowitz, Leonard (1986). "Rule-based programming." *Byte* (November), 217–224.

Moskowitz, Robert (1987). "What's the truth about artificial intelligence today?" *PC Week* (September 29), 53–62.

Motteler, Howard E. and Carl H. Smith (1985). "A complexity measure for data flow models." *Int'l J. Computer and Info. Sciences* 14, 2, 107–122.

Naur, Peter (1981). "The European side of the last phase of the development of ALGOL." In Richard L. Wexelblat (ed.), *History of Programming Languages*, Academic, NY, 92–137.

Nelson, Greg (1985). "Juno, a constraint-based graphics system." In B.A. Barsky (ed.), *SIGGRAPH '85 Conference Readings*, San Francisco, July, 235–243.

Neufeld, M. Lynne and Martha Cornog (1986). "Database history: From dinosaurs to compact discs." *Journal of the American Society for Information Science*, 37 (4, July), 183–190.

Newquist, Harvey, III (1987). "Will the real AI language please stand up?" *Computer Language*, 4 (7, July), 58–59.

Newquist, Harvey (1988). "AI adapts to use of the vernacular." *Computerworld* (October 17), 82–83.

Nolan, Dan (1988). "Bad language." *Computerworld* (July 25), 67–71.

Nygaard, Kristen (1986). "Basic concepts in object oriented programming." *SIGPLAN Notices*, 21 (10, October), 128–162.

Nygaard, Kristen and Ole-Johan Dahl (1981). "The development of the SIMULA languages." In Richard L. Wexelblat (ed.), *History of Programming Languages*, Academic, NY, 439–478.

Obermeier, Klaus K. (1988). "Side by side." *Byte* (November), 275–283.

Ohran, Richard (1984). "Lilith and Modula-2." *Byte* (August), 181–192.

Orci, Istvan P. and Erik Knudsen (1987). "Knowledge engineering library—A Prolog-based toolkit for expert system design." *Proceedings, 20th Annual Hawaii International Conference on System Sciences*, Jan. 6–9, 385–391.

Ossher, Harold L. (1986). "A mechanism for specifying the structure of large, layered, object-oriented programs." *ACM SIGPLAN Notices*, 21 (10, October), 143–152.

Paige, Robert (1986). "Programming with invariants." *IEEE Software*, 3 (1, January), 56–69.

Parnas, D.L. (1972a). "A technique for software module specification with examples." *Comm. ACM*, 15 (5, May), 330–336.

Parnas, D.L. (1972b). "On the criteria to be used in decomposing systems into modules." *Comm. ACM*, 15 (12, December), 1053–1058.

Parnas, David L. (1976). "On the design and development of program families." *IEEE Trans. Software Engineering*, SE-2 (1, March), 1–9.

Parnas, David L. (1977). "The influence of software structure on reliability." In Raymond T. Yeh (ed.), *Current Trends in Programming Methodology. Vol. 1: Software Specification and Design*, Prentice-Hall, Englewood Cliffs, NJ, 111–119.

Pascoe, Geoffrey A. (1986). "Elements of object-oriented programming." *Byte*, 11 (8, August), 139–144.

Paseman, William Gerhard (1985). "Applying data flow in the real world." *Byte*, 10 (5, May), 201–214.

Patterson, William Pat (1988). "Brainstorming with a machine." *Industry Week* (April 18), 61.

Paul, Robert J. (1984). "An introduction to Modula-2." *Byte*, 9 (8, August), 195–210.

Perlis, Alan J. (1981). "The American side of the development of ALGOL." In Richard L. Wexelblat (ed.), *History of Programming Languages*, Academic, NY, 75–91.

Pintelas, Panayotis E. and Vasilios Kallistros (1989). "An overview of some software design languages." *Journal of Systems and Software*, 10 (2, September), 125–138.

Pitta, Julie (1988). "Now, whose desk do we put it on?" *Computerworld* (July 11), 1+.

Pountain, Dick (1988a). "Parallelizing Prolog." *Byte* (November), 387–394.

Pountain, Dick (1988b). "Rekursiv: An object-oriented CPU." *Byte* (November), 341–349.

Pratt, Vaughan (1983). "Five paradigm shifts in programming language design and their realization in Viron, a dataflow programming environment." *Proceedings, Tenth Annual ACM Symposium on Principles of Programming Languages*, January 24–26, Austin Texas, 1–9.

Radin, George (1981). "The early history and characteristics of PL/1." In Richard L. Wexelblat (ed.), *History of Programming Languages*, Academic, NY, 551–574.

Ramamoorthy, C.V., Atul Prakash, Wei-Tek Tsai, and Yutaka Usuda (1984). "Software engineering: Problems and perspectives." *Computer* (October), 191–209.

Ramshaw, Lyle (1988). "Eliminating go to's while preserving program structure." *Journal of the ACM*, 35 (4, October), 893–920.

Reddy, Ramana (1987). "Epistemology of knowlege-based simulation." *Simulation*, 48 (4, April), 162–166.

Reenskaug, Trygve M.H. (1981). "User-oriented descriptions of Smalltalk systems." *Byte*, 6 (8, August), 148–166.

Rehmer, Karl and Linda Rising (1986). "Teaching data abstraction in a beginning Pascal class." *ACM SIGCSE Bulletin*, 18 (1, February), 82–85.

Richmond, Alan (1986). "Software design by object-oriented functional layering." *Computer Physics Communications*, 41 (2,3, August), 377–384.

Ringwood, G.A. (1988). "PARLOG86 and the dining logicians." *Comm. ACM*, 31 (1, January), 10–25.

Robison, Arch D. (1987). "Illinois functional programming: A tutorial." *Byte*, 12 (2, February), 115–125.

Robson, David (1981). "Object-oriented software systems." *Byte*, 6 (8, August), 74–86.

Robson, David, Adele Goldberg, and the Xerox Learning Research Group (1981). "The Smalltalk-80 system." *Byte*, 6 (8, August), 36–48.

Rosen, Saul (1969). "Electronic computers: A historical survey." *ACM Computing Surveys*, 1 (1, March), 8–36.

Rosen, Saul (1972). "Programming systems and languages 1965–1975." *Comm. ACM*, 15 (7, July), 591–600.

Rosenthal, Donald A. (1986). "Transformation of scientific objectives into spacecraft activities." *Proceedings, Expert Systems in Government*, Oct. 22–24, McLean, Virginia, IEEE, 430–435.

Rothenberg, Jeff (1986). "Object-oriented simulation: Where do we go from here?" *1986 Winter Simulation Conference Proceedings*, 464–469.

Ruiz-Mier, Sergio and Joseph Talavage (1987). "A hybrid paradigm for modeling of complex systems." *Simulation,* 48 (4, April), 135–141.

Ryan, Jody L. (1988). "Expert systems in the future: The redistribution of power." *Journal of Systems Management*, 39 (April), 18–21.

Sammet, Jean E. (1972). "Programming languages: History and future," *Comm. ACM,* 15 (7, July), 601–610.

Sammett, Jean E. (1981). "The early history of COBOL." In Richard L. Wexelblat (ed.), *History of Programming Languages*, Academic, NY, 199–241.

Sanderson, D. Peter and Lawrence L. Rose (1988). "Object-oriented modeling using C++." *Proceedings, 21st Annual Simulation Symposium*, March 16–18, 143–156.

Schmucker, Kurt J. (1986). "Object-oriented languages for the Macintosh." *Byte*, 11 (8, August), 177–185.

Schwartz, Jules I. (1981). "The development of JOVIAL." In Richard L. Wexelblat (ed.), *History of Programming Languages*, Academic, NY, 369–387.

Schwartz, J.T. (1978). "Program genesis and the design of programming languages." In R. T. Yeh (ed.), *Current Trends in Programming Methodology*. Vol. IV: *Data Structuring*. Prentice-Hall, Englewood Cliffs, NJ, 185–215.

Seidowitz, Ed (1987). "Object-oriented programming in Smalltalk and Ada." *OOPSLA '87 Proceedings* (October 4–8), 202–213.

Selinger, P.G. (1987). "Database technology." *IBM Systems Journal*, 26 (1), 96–106.

Shammas, Namir Clement (1988a). "Ada comes to the Mac." *Byte* (September), 295–300.

Shammas, Namir Clement (1988b). "Object-oriented programming in Pascal." *Dr. Dobb's Journal*, 13 (1, January), 108–113.

Shammas, Namir Clement (1988c). "The BASIC revival." *Byte* (September), 295–300.

Shapiro, Ezra (1985). "SNOBOL and Icon." *Byte* (July), 341–349.

Shapiro, Leonard (1986). "Data design." *Byte*, 11 (4, April), 129–134.

Shaw, Mary (1980). "The impact of abstraction concerns on modern programming languages." *Proceedings of the IEEE*, 68 (9, September), 1119–1131.

Shaw, Mary (1984). "Abstraction techniques in modern programming languages." *IEEE Software*, 1 (4, October), 10–26.

Shaw, Mary, Guy T. Almes, Joseph M. Newcomer, Brian K. Reid, and William A. Wulf (1981). "A comparison of programming languages for software engineering." *Software—Practice and Experience*, 11, 1–52.

Sheil, Beau (1983). "Power tools for programmers." *Datamation* (February), 131–144.

Shepherd, Allan and Larry Kerschberg (1986). "Constraint management in expert database systems." In Larry Kerschberg (ed.), *Expert Database Systems: Proceedings from the First International Workshop*. Benjamin/Cummings, Menlo Park, Calif., 309–331.

Shortliffe, Edward H. (1987). "Computer programs to support clinical decision making." *Journal of the American Medical Association*, 285 (1, July), 61–66.

Simon, Herbert A. (1974). "How big is a chunk?" *Science* (February), 482–488.

Singh, Rajdeep (1989). "A survey of existing programming paradigms." Unpublished Masters thesis, Department of Statistics and Computer Information Systems, Baruch College of the City University of New York.

Soloway, Elliot (1986). "Learning to program = learning to construct mechanisms and explanations." *Comm. ACM*, 29 (9, September), 850–858.

Soloway, Elliot and Kate Ehrlich (1984). "Empirical Studies of programming knowledge." *IEEE Trans. Software Engineering*, SE-10 (5, September), 595–609.

Spohrer, James C. and Elliot Soloway (1986). "Novice mistakes: Are the folk wisdoms correct?" *Comm. ACM*, 29 (7, July), 624–632.

Sridharan, N.S. (1985). "Evolving systems of knowledge." *The AI Magazine* (Fall), 108–120.

Stahl, Bob (1988). "The ins and outs of software testing." *Computerworld* (October 24), 87–92.

Stairmand Malcolm C. and Wolfgand Kreutzer (1988). "POSE: A process-oriented simulation environment embedded in SCHEME." *Simulation*, 50 (4, April), 143–153.

Standish, Thomas A. (1984). "An essay on software reuse." *IEEE Trans. Software Engineering*, SE-10 (5, September), 494–497.

Steensgaard-Madsen, J. (1989). "Typed representation of objects by functions." *ACM Tran. Programming Languages and Systems*, 11 (1, January), 67–89.

Stefik, Mark J., Daniel G. Bobrow, and Kenneth M. Kahn (1986a). "Access-oriented programming for a multiparadigm environment." *Proceedings, 19th Annual Hawaii International Conference on System Sciences*, Jan. 7–10, 188–197.

Stefik, Mark J., Daniel G. Bobrow, and Kenneth M. Kahn (1986b). "Integrating access-oriented programming into a multiparadigm environment." *IEEE Software*, 3 (1, January), 10–18.

Stein, Jacob (1988). "Object-oriented programming and databases." *Dr. Dobb's Journal* (March), 18–34.

Stein, Richard M. (1988). "T800 and counting." *Byte* (November), 287–296.

Stevens, Wayne P. (1985). "Using data flow for application development." *Byte* (June), 267–276.

Stolfo, Salvatore J. (1987). "Initial performance of the DADO2 prototype." *IEEE Computer*, 20 (1, January), 75–83.

Strehlo, Kevin (1986). "Small talk with Alan Kay." *Computer Language*, 3 (1, January), 75–80.

Stroustrup, B. (1984). "Data abstraction in C." *AT&T Bell Laboratories Technical Journal*, 63 (8, October), 1701–1732.

Stroustrup, Bjarne (1986). "An overview of C++." *SIGPLAN Notices*, 21, 10 (October), 7–18.

Stroustrup, Bjarne (1988). "A better C?" *Byte*, 13 (8, August), 215–216+.

Sullivan-Trainor, Michael (1987). "Fourth-generation languages: The promise and the reality." *Computerworld* (November 9), S10-S15.

Sutherland, Ivan (1963). "Sketchpad: A man-machine graphical communication system." In *Proceedings of the Spring Joint Computer Conference*, IFIPS, 329–345.

Swaine, Michael (1988). "Parallel processing, object-oriented programming, and a reading list." *Dr. Dobb's Journal*, 13 (5, May), 100–118.

Sweet, Frank (1985a). "Lesson one: Durable doable databases." *Datamation*, 31 (August 15), 83–84.

Sweet, Frank (1985b). "Objects and events." *Datamation*, 31 (September 18), 152.

Sweet, Frank (1988). "Database directions." *Computerworld* (November 28), 85–89.

Tarnlund, Sten-Ake (1986). "Logic programming—from a logic point of view." *1986 Symposium on Logic Programming*, IEEE, 96–103.

Taylor, Dave (1987). "Languages: Past, present, and future." *Computer Language*, 4 (December), 57–62.

Tazelaar, Jane Morrill (1988). "In depth—parallel processing." *Byte* (November), 272–320.

Tello, E.R. (1984). "Basic to C." *PC Tech Journal*, 2 (4, October).

Tello, Ernest R. (1987a). "Object-oriented LISP on PCs." *Dr. Dobb's Journal*, 12 (5, May), 132–136.

Tello, Ernest R. (1987b). "Object-oriented programming." *Dr. Dobb's Journal*, 12 (3, March), 126–134.

Tello, Ernest R. (1987c). "Object-oriented programming." *Dr. Dobb's Journal*, 12 (11, November), 130–136.

Tello, Ernest R. (1987d). "Object-oriented programming in AI." *Dr. Dobb's Journal*, 12 (4, April), 146–150.

Tello, Ernest R. (1988). "Actor does more than windows." *Dr. Dobb's Journal*, 13 (1, January), 114–125.

Teresko, John (1988). "Making it simpler." *Industry Week* (April 18), 67–68.

Tesler, Larry (1981). "The Smalltalk environment." *Byte*, 6 (8, August), 90–145.

Tesler, Larry (1986). "Programming experiences," *Byte*, 11 (8, August), 195–206.

Tetewsky, Avram (1986). "Ada for conventional language programmers." *Computer Language*, 3 (12, December), 32–44.

Tetewsky, A. (1987). "The road to Ada tasking." *Computer Language*, 4 (August), 49–62.

Thompson, Bill and Bev Thompson (1988). "Topics in knowledge-based languages." *Dr. Dobb's Journal*, 13 (4, April), 40–49.

Thomsen, Kristine Stougaard and Jorgen Lindskov Knudsen (1987). "A taxonomy for programming languages with multisequential processes." *Journal of Systems and Software*, 7 (2), 127–140.

Tichy, Walter F. (1987). "What can software engineers learn from artificial intelligence?" *IEEE Computer* (November), 43–54.

Touretzky, David S. (1988). "How Lisp has changed." *Byte* (February), 229–234.

Treleaven, Philip C., David R. Brownbridge, and Richard P. Hopkins (1982). "Data-driven and demand-driven computer architecture." *Computing Surveys*, 14 (1, March), 93–143.

Tu, Hai-Chen and Alan J. Perlis (1986). "FAC: A functional APL language." *IEEE Software*, 3 (1, January), 36–45.

Udell, Jon (1988). "A C++ toolkit." *Byte* (November), 223–227.

Van Hoeve, Frans and Rolf Engmann (1987). "An object-oriented approach to application generation." *Software Practice and Experience*, 17(9, September), 623–645.

Van Horn, Mike (1987). "RuleMaster." *Byte*, 12 (January), 341–342.

Van Wyk, Christopher J. (1963). "A high-level language for specifying pictures." *ACM Trans. Graphics*, 1 (2, April), 163–182.

Verity, John W. (1987). "The OOPS revolution." *Datamation* (May 1), 73–78.

Vermeir, D. (1986). "OOPS: A knowledge representation language." *Proceedings, 19th Hawaii International Conference on System Sciences*, Jan. 7–10, IEEE, 156–157+.

Verner, June and Graham Tate (1988). "Estimating size and effort in fourth-generation development." *IEEE Software* (July), 15–22.

Vesonder, Gregg T. (1988). "Rule-based programming in the UNIX system." *AT&T Technical Journal*, 47 (1, Jan–Feb), 69–79.

Walker, Bill and Stephen Alexander (1986). "Data abstraction with Modula-2." *Dr. Dobb's Journal*, 1 (2, February), 62–64.

Warren, Carl (1985). "Latest languages link data to diverse tasks." *Mini-Micro Systems* (August), 135–142.

Warren, David H.D. (1987). "The SRI model for Or-parallel execution of Prolog—Abstract design and implementation issues." *Proceeding, 1987 International Symposium on Logic Programming*, Aug. 31–Sept. 4, San Francisco, IEEE, 92–102.

Wasserman, Anthony J. (1982). "The future of programming." *Comm. ACM*, 25 (3, March), 196–207.

Webster, Bruce (1985). "Methods: A preliminary look." *Byte* (May), 152–154.

Wechsler, Harry and David Rine (1988a). "Object oriented programming and its relevance to designing intelligent software systems." *Proceedings, International Conference on Computer Languages* (October 9–13), IEEE Computer Society, 242–248.

Wechsler, Harry and David Rine (1988b). "Object oriented programming (OOP) and its relevance to designing intelligent software systems." *Proceedings of the IEEE* (June), 242–248.

Wegner, P. (1976). "Programming languages—the first 25 years." *IEEE Trans. Computers* (December), 1207–1225. Reprinted in Ellis Horowitz (ed., 1983), *Programming Languages: A Grand Tour*, Computer Science Press, Rockville, MD, 4–22.

Wegner, Peter (1986). "Classification in object-oriented systems." *SIGPLAN Notices*, 21 (10, October), 173–182.

Wegner, Peter (1987). "Dimensions of object-based language design." *OOPSLA '87 Proceedings* (October 4–8), 168–182.

Wehrum, R. P., W. Hoyer, and G. Diessl (1986). "On some key features of Ada: Language and programming environment." *Computer Physics Communications*, 41 (2,3, August), 271–283.

Weisman, Randy (1987). "Six steps to AI-based functional prototyping." *Datamation* (August 1), 71–72.

Wells, Mark B. and Barry L. Kurtz (1989). "Teaching multiple programming paradigms: A proposal for a paradigm-general pseudocode." *ACM SIGCSE Bulletin,* 21 (1, February), 246–251.

Wexelblat, Richard L. (1984). "Nth generation languages." *Datamation* (September), 111–117.

Wiederhold, Gio (1984). "Databases." *Computer*, 17 (10), 211–225.

Wiederhold, Gio (1986). "Views, objects, and databases." *Computer*, 19 (12, December), 37–44.

Williams, Gregg (1985). "Debugging techniques," *Byte* (June), 279–289.

Williamson, Mickey (1986). "Expert System Shells: Design tools help MIS answer management's call." *Computerworld* (July 14), 51–57.

Wilson, Ron (1987). "Object-oriented languages reorient programming techniques." *Computer Design*, 26 (20, November 1), 52–62.

Winograd, Terry (1979). "Beyond programming languages." *Comm. ACM*, 22 (7, July), 391–401.

Winston, Patrick H. (1985). "The LISP revolution." *Byte*, 10 (4, April), 209–217.

Wirth, Niklaus (1971a). "Program development by stepwise refinement," *Comm. ACM,* 14 (April), 221–227. Reprinted in D. Gries (ed., 1978), *Programming Methodology*, Springer-Verlag, NY.

Wirth, Niklaus (1971b). "The programming language Pascal." *Acta Informatica*, 1 (1), 35–63.

Wirth, Niklaus (1974a). "On the composition of well-structured programs." *ACM Computing Surveys*, 6 (4, December), 238–259.

Wirth, Niklaus (1974b). "On the design of programming languages." *Proceedings IFIP Congress 74*, North-Holland, Amsterdam, 386–393. Reprinted in Ellis Horowitz (ed., 1983), *Programming Languages: A Grand Tour*, Computer Science Press, Rockville, MD, 23–30.

Wirth, Niklaus (1975). "An assessment of the programming language Pascal." *IEEE Trans. Software Engineering* (June), 192–198.

Wirth, Niklaus (1979). "The module: A system structuring facility in high-level programming languages." In Jeffrey M. Tobias (ed.), *Language Design and Programming Methodology*, Springer-Verlag, NY, 1–24.

Wirth, Niklaus (1984). "History and goals of MODULA-2." *Byte* (August), 145–152.

Wirth, Niklaus (1985). "From programming language design to computer construction." *Comm. ACM*, 28 (2, February), 160–164.

Wirth, Niklaus (1986). "Microprocessor architectures: A comparison based on code generated by compiler." *Comm. ACM,* 29 (10, October), 978–989.

Withington, Frederick (1987). "The mature intelligent computer." *MIS Quarterly* (March), 6–8.

Wulf, William A. (1977). "Languages and structured programs." In Raymond T. Yeh (ed.), *Current Trends in Programming Methodology. Vol. 1: Software Specification and Design*, Prentice-Hall, Englewood Cliffs, NJ, 1–32.

Yaeger, Judy (1989). "High-level-language selection: Improving productivity." *News 3X/400* (May), 29–47.

Yau, Stephen S. and Paul C. Grabow (1981). "A model for representing programs using hierarchical graphs." *IEEE Trans. Software Engineering*, SE-7 (6, November), 556–574.

Yau, Stephen S. and J.-P. Tsai (1984). "A graph-based software maintenance environment." *Proceedings, COMPCON 84 SPRING* (February), 321–324.

Yau, Stephen S. and Jeffery J.-P. Tsai (1986). "A survey of software design techniques." *IEEE Trans. Software Engineering*, SE-12 (6, June), 713–721.

Zaniolo, Carlo, Hassan Ait-Kaci, David Beech, Stephanie Cammarata, Larry Kerschberg, and David Maier (1986). "Object oriented database systems and knowledge systems." In Larry Kerschberg (ed.), *Expert Database Systems: Proceedings from the First International Workshop*. Benjamin/Cummmings, Menlo Park, Calif., 49–65.

Zeigler, Bernard P. (1987). "Hierarchical, modular discrete-event modelling in an object-oriented environment." *Simulation*, 49 (5, November), 219–230.

Zhong, YouLiang, Seirei Ishizuka, and Ryuichi Enari (1988). "Integrating abstract data types with object-oriented programming by specification-based approach." *Proceedings, International Conference on Computer Languages* (October 9–13), IEEE Computer Society, 202–209.

B

Glossary

Abstract data type. A programmer-defined data type that specifies a new domain as well as the operations that are allowed on members of that domain. Once defined, the abstract data type may be used like any other type, without regard for the details of how the type has been implemented. See *Data abstraction*; *Information hiding*.

Abstraction. Abstraction is the means by which we consider only such information as is relevant to the problem at hand, ignoring trivial details and unimportant facts. Abstraction models a chosen view of reality in which irrelevant objects or properties are ignored, making the model simpler and more appropriate as an object of study. See *Information hiding*.

Access-oriented programming paradigm. In this approach to programming, the access (storing or retrieving) of data objects from variable locations in storage can cause attached procedures to be invoked.

Access mode. The mode, or direction, of access from any particular file is determined by whether the file is to be used for input, for output, or both.

Activation record. A record, created at the invocation of a subprogram, that contains locally declared variables, subprogram parameters, a pointer to the executable subprogram code, and the return address for the next instruction in sequence in the calling program.

Actual parameter. *Argument*. When a subprogram is called, the name of the subprogram is followed by a list that corresponds in number and order to the parameters listed in the subprogram specification. The items in this list, the actual parameters, are specified by the author of the calling program and are the means by which information may be passed to or received from the subprogram.

Ada. A programming language for embedded computer systems that was designed according to specifications of the U.S. Department of Defense.

ALGOL. ALGOrithmic **L**anguage. A programming language that was developed to facilitate the communication of ideas among members of the international computing community. Its features include explicit type declarations, arrays with dynamic bounds, recursion, and nesting of program units. Versions include ALGOL58 (originally, IAL), ALGOL60, and ALGOL68.

ALGOL68. A much extended revision of ALGOL60, ALGOL68 is a huge, general-purpose language. ALGOL68 innovated the user-defined data type and the pointer type.

Aliasing. Aliasing occurs when two variables access the same storage location.

Anonymous variable. An unnamed storage location, such as that which holds the result of an evaluated expression.

APL. A Programming **L**anguage. An applicative, interactive, science-oriented language that assumes the array as the default data structure and features a nonstandard character set.

Applicative programming paradigm. See *Functional programming paradigm*.

Argument. See *Actual parameter*.

Arithmetic operators. Operators that act on numeric, computational data.

Array. An ordered collection of data elements all of the same type, usually fixed in size.

Assembler. A translator program that translates assembly language to machine language. There is a one-to-one correspondence between each assembly-language instruction and the corresponding machine-language instruction.

Automatic code generator. A general term to describe any system that accepts high-level specifications and outputs a machine-coded program.

Backward chaining. One way that rules may be examined by the inference engine of an expert system or rule-based system. In this reasoning mechanism, the system starts with a solution and then tries to prove it correct. See *Forward chaining*.

BASIC. Beginner's **A**ll-purpose **S**ymbolic **I**nstructional **C**ode. A high-level language designed to introduce students in nonscientific disciplines to computing. The major goal of the language was to simplify the user interface.

Batch processing. A type of processing environment in which there is no interaction of any sort with the executing program. User jobs are submitted in sequential batches.

Binary search tree. A binary tree that has been ordered for a binary search, a type of search algorithm that reduces the size of the data set by one-half at each iteration.

Binary tree. A type of tree in which each node has at most two descendants.

Binding. The association of a property with a particular unit of program code. For example, the binding of one or more attributes (such as location, type, or value) to a variable.

Binding time. The time when binding occurs for a particular association. It can occur before run time (early or static binding) or after run time (late or dynamic binding).

Black Box Model. A model governing abstraction. In this model, a set of inputs is mapped to a set of outputs. The model does not reveal *how* the transformation is implemented, only *what* it does.

Boolean type. A binary-valued data type, it may take on such values as (false, true) or (0,1).

Bottom-up design. A programming approach in which the programmer begins coding immediately, starting with some low-level subprograms that are well defined. This results in the construction of a large program by building layers on layers of abstraction. This approach, which often results in excessive concern with low-level details, may draw attention away from the larger problem. (See *Top-down design* for a different approach.)

Brackets. A matched pair of symbols or keywords that delimits a portion of code.

Breadth-first search. A search strategy employed to search the knowledge base of an expert system. It searches across rules on a level, eliminating those it can, before going on to the next, more detailed level. See *Depth-first search*.

C. A programming language developed at Bell Laboratories, used in coding the routines of the UNIX operating system. It was the first portable operating system. C facilitates the coding of low-level operations in a high level language.

Call by address. See *Call by location*.

Call by location. *Call by address. Call by reference.* The most widely used method of parameter passing. The calling subprogram passes the machine address of the argument to the subprogram. The corresponding parameter is a pointer variable that points to the location of the argument.

Call by name. A parameter-passing method in which the evaluation of each argument is deferred until it is actually needed during execution of the subprogram. Instead of passing a value to a parameter, a rule for evaluating the parameter is passed. Each time the parameter name appears in the text of the subprogram, it is "replaced" by the exact text of the argument.

Call by need. A parameter-passing method employed by functional programming languages. An argument is evaluated only when its value is needed and not immediately at the point of call.

Call by reference. See *Call by location*.

Call by result. A parameter-passing method that is used in the language Ada. Parameters are set up like local variables but are not initialized to any values in the main calling program. At termination, the values stored in the parameters are copied back to the corresponding arguments in the main program.

Call by value. A parameter-passing method in which parameters are set up as variables local to the subprogram and are initialized at invocation to the value of the arguments.

Call by value-result. A parameter-passing method that was used in ALGOL-W, it combines features of call by value and call by result. A parameter is declared and initialized as a local variable with initial value equal to that of the argument. When the subprogram terminates, the final value of the parameter is passed back to the argument.

Character type. A data type that takes on as value a single character, which may be alphabetic, numeric or a special character.

Class. A structure that defines the variables and methods for a set of objects that are instances of the class. See *Object-oriented programming paradigm*.

COBOL. **CO**mmon **B**usiness-**O**riented **L**anguage. Designed to meet the needs of the data processing community, COBOL is a language characterized by a heavy reliance on English, a record data structure, file description and manipulation facilities, and noise words for readability.

Cohesion. The degree to which each subprogram performs only a single function and all statements contained within that subprogram relate only to that function.

Compiler. A type of language processor that transforms an entire source program composed of high-level language statements into an object program consisting of machine-language executable code.

Compound statement. A program structure composed of a sequence of two or more simple statements, often delimited by a pair of matching keywords.

Computer abstraction. See *Virtual computer*.

Concurrent processing. See *Parallel processing*.

Constant. A data item that remains unchanged throughout the execution of the program.

Constraint-oriented programming paradigm. In this approach to programming, the programmer specifies a set of relations among a set of data objects. The constraint-satisfaction system then attempts to find a solution that satisfies the relations. A spreadsheet is an example of a constraint-oriented program. PROLOG is a special type of constraint-oriented language in that it satisfies logical constraints.

Control abstraction. A stylized, structured control construct that enables a programmer to think in terms of high-level concepts as opposed to low-level detailed instructions. For example, constructs of the parallel processing model of subprogram control.

Coroutines. Two or more subprograms that exert control over each other.

Coupling. The degree of relatedness of a subprogram to the rest of the program.

Critical region. In parallel processing, the section of code that contains the statements requiring access to a variable that is shared with other processes.

Data abstraction. A language facility that integrates the representation of a programmer-defined data object and the operations that may be performed on that data object into a single syntactic unit. Data abstraction is implemented by information hiding. The object in object-oriented programming is a data abstraction. The data models of database management systems are data abstractions, as are the models for knowledge representation in artificial intelligence applications.

Database. A logically interrelated set of data items, related to a particular application or environment, stored on a large-scale direct-access storage device.

Database management system. *DBMS.* Specialized software used to access a database. It is the software interface between the physical storage of the data and the use of the data in various applications.

Data-centered language. A data-centered language is one in which programs are developed by means of a formal specification of the data that is to be manipulated. See *Process-centered language.*

Data element. The most basic data entity, the building block with which complicated data structures and large databases are composed.

Dataflow programming paradigm. In this approach to programming, the flow of data through a network of operations is specified. Dataflow analysis determines dependencies between data, and the order of execution is in turn determined by these dependencies. The inherent parallelism in the algorithm is exploited. Dataflow programs are mainly intended to run on parallel-architecture dataflow machines, which are still, for the most part, experimental. The dataflow paradigm is one model of parallel processing.

Data hierarchy. The logical organization of data stored on permanent storage media such as magnetic tape. Related data items are organized into records and related records are organized into files.

Data structure. An organized collection of data objects subject to certain allowable operations.

Data type. A domain of data elements associated with a set of operations that act on those elements. Every programming language has some built-in data types.

DBMS. See *Database management system.*

Deadlock. When two parallel processes cannot terminate or continue because they remain indefinitely in a state in which each is waiting for the other.

Declarative programming. *Nonprocedural programming.* Declarative programming languages have a data-centered approach to programming and are concerned with *what* is to be done with the data rather than detailing *how* it is to be accomplished. This term is sometimes applied to a subset of nonprocedural programming languages in which programming is accomplished only by stating facts and assertions.

Delimiter. A symbol or keyword that separates pieces of program text. Delimiters provide the punctuation for the program.

Depth-first search. A widely used search strategy employed to search the knowledge base of an expert system. It is a search for greater and greater detail along a single search path to a possible goal before attempting to explore another path leading to another goal. See *Breadth-first search*.

Deque. **D**ouble-**E**nded **QUE**ue. A type of queue structure allowing for insertions and deletions at both ends.

Dimensionality. The number of dimensions, or directions, of an array structure.

Direct file. See *Relative file*.

Disabled condition. An exception that is not being monitored for occurrence.

Dynamic scoping rule. In dynamic languages, the scope of a variable is determined during execution time by the most recent occurrence and still active definition of that variable name.

Efficiency. A criterion used in evaluating a programming language and its implementation. Refers to the utilization of memory space and processing time.

Enabled condition. An exception that is being monitored for occurrence. When the condition occurs, it will *raise an exception*.

Entry point. The point at which execution begins when a subprogram is invoked.

Enumerated type. A user-defined type that provides for the enumeration (listing) of the domain of the type by the programmer.

Exception. An event that occurs unexpectedly, infrequently, and at random intervals, such as an attempt to divide by zero or a subscript that is out of range.

Exception handler. A subprogram, written by the programmer, that interfaces with the operating system and is invoked only when a specified "exceptional condition" (e.g., an attempt to divide by zero) is encountered.

Exit point. The point at which execution of the subprogram ends and control is returned to the calling program.

Expert system shell. A complete expert system without a knowledge base.

Explanation facility. One component of an expert system that can, on demand, justify its conclusions and explain the reasons for its queries. It communicates with the user in the language of the application domain, usually through the user interface.

Explicit control structure. A control structure that is imposed by the programmer over the default flow of control provided by the language.

Expression. A formula for computing a value, represented as a formalized sequence of operators, operands, and parentheses.

Extensibility. A criterion used in evaluating a programming language. An extensible language enables the programmer to define new language components which then become indistinguishable from the language's own built-in primitives.

External subprogram. A subprogram that is separate from the text of the program and may be compiled separately into an object module.

File. An organized collection of records related to a particular application.

File organization. The organization, in terms of a physical ordering, of the records in a file residing on secondary storage, implying the appropriate operations for accessing particular records.

File structure. The organization of data residing in secondary storage and subject to input/output related operations.

Fixed-format language. A language containing strict rules governing the arrangement of program text on a line.

Flowchart. A pictorial method of expressing program logic flow. Flowcharts are machine and programming language independent and allow programmers to focus on logic flow without having to worry about syntax.

FLOW-MATIC. A language designed in 1958 that used English words heavily and was geared to business data processing. It influenced the subsequent design of COBOL.

FOCUS. A full-function 4GT centered on a hierarchical database.

Formal parameter. *Parameter.* Specified in a subprogram, it is a data name place-holder that will be associated with a storage location on invocation of the subprogram. See *Actual parameter.*

FORTH. A language that combines features of both high-level and low-level programming. FORTH arithmetic is based on Reverse Polish notation and programs are constructed using functions.

FORTRAN. **FOR**mula **TRAN**slating System. The first high-level programming language, it is imperative and science oriented.

Forward chaining. A reasoning mechanism used by the inference engine of an expert system. This reasoning mechanism starts with a premise and uses that as a starting point to examine one item of data at a time and search for a solution. See *Backward chaining.*

4GT. **4**th **G**eneration **T**ool. See *Full-function 4GT.*

Fourth-generation software. *Declarative programming. Nonprocedural programming.* Fourth-generation software is results oriented, concentrating more on *what* is to be done rather than on describing in detail *how* to do it. It attempts to maximize human productivity rather than minimize the use of computer time, and it is often aimed at the nontechnical user in a particular application area. Some major trends in fourth-generation software include rule-oriented and object-oriented languages, packaged software, integrated packages, query languages, and integrated programming environments.

Free-format language. A free-format language has no fixed fields on the lines of program text. A delimiter is often used to indicate the end of a statement.

Full-function 4GT. A full-function 4GT (**4**th **G**eneration **T**ool), as well as being centered around a database, will generally have a query language, a report generator, a graphics generator, a facility for screen definition, the ability to do financial and statistical analysis, and it will often have its own procedural or nonprocedural language. FOCUS, NOMAD2, and RAMIS II are examples of full-function 4GTs.

Function. A value-returning subprogram—one that returns a single value to the calling program.

Functional programming paradigm. *Applicative programming paradigm.* In a functional programming language, a program is a function that is built up from smaller functions. Functional programming languages achieve results by the application of functions to arguments that may themselves be functions. They are expression oriented rather than statement oriented.

Generic function. A function whose type depends on the type of argument used at the point of call.

Global variable. A variable that is declared in the main program unit, remains in existence throughout the execution of the program and may be accessed in all program units.

Goto-less programming. In theory, all programs can be coded without the unconditional branch, using the structured control constructs of simple sequence, selection, and iteration. Some languages have eliminated the **goto** entirely.

Graph. A collection of nodes and edges. A graph is the most generalized data structure.

Hierarchy chart. A graphical view of the entire modular decomposition of a hierarchical program in which every subprogram is represented by a rectangle.

High-level language. A programming language that is problem oriented rather than machine oriented. It requires less detail and fewer lines of code than a low-level language because the language itself handles much of the detail work.

Identifier. A programmer-defined word that provides access to program and data entities.

Imperative. Statement oriented.

Imperative programming paradigm. A statement-oriented approach reflected in all the languages that have their roots in FORTRAN, COBOL, and/or ALGOL. A program is assumed to be a sequence of detailed statements to the computer defining how a task is to be accomplished. Imperative programming languages are characterized by variables, the assignment operation, and the iteration control construct.

Implicit control. A subprogram control construct in which a subprogram causes another subprogram to be invoked but does not call it directly, for example, an exception handler.

Indexed loop. A form of iteration construct that is used when it is desired to execute a code segment a countable number of times. An index variable is used to control iteration.

Indexed sequential file. A file stored sequentially on a direct-access storage device along with an index, which allows for direct access to a particular record in the file.

Inference engine. The expert system component governing reasoning.

Information hiding. A software engineering concept that a subprogram should have access only to the information that it requires. Any data it does not need to know should be inaccessible to it. Much irrelevant information is thus hidden from the user, protecting the integrity of individual modules and reducing the confusion that comes along with too much information.

Input parameter. Values that are input to, and operated on by, the subprogram.

Input/output parameter. Values that provide two-way communication between the calling subprogram and the called subprogram.

Integrated package. A multifunction package of programs containing several commonly used computing applications such as, for personal computers: word processing, spreadsheet, database management system, graphics, and communications. See *Package*.

Interactive processing. A processing environment characterized by interaction between the program and its human user during program execution.

Internal subprogram. A subprogram that is part of and contained within the text of the program, and compiled along with the program in which it is called.

Interpreter. A type of language processor that operates one instruction at a time, translating a high-level language statement and executing it immediately.

Iteration. *Repetition. Loop.* A control construct that enables repetition of the execution of a group of statements.

Iterative composition. See *Iteration*.

Job. A unit that interfaces with the operating system, it may contain several programs and subroutines to be linked together and/or executed in sequence.

Key. A data item that serves to uniquely identify a particular record.

Keyword. A word that is part of the built-in vocabulary of the programming language.

Knowledge base. One component of an expert system, it contains a representation of the expert's knowledge and experience.

Knowledge engineering. The process of capturing an expert's knowledge and transforming it into a computer-usable form.

Label. An identifier for a program statement.

Lexical scoping rule. See *Static scoping rule*.

Linked allocation. One of two ways in which storage can be allocated for most data structures. With linked allocation, each component is a node having two parts: one containing the original data element and the other containing a pointer to the next component. A structure that is allocated storage in a linked manner is a dynamic structure capable of change. Dynamic structures are ordered explicitly, each component containing within itself the location of the next item. See *Sequential allocation*.

Linked list. A dynamic list structure.

LISP. An interactive, functional programming language that is used widely in artificial intelligence. Some important features include the use of symbolic expressions as opposed to numbers, the "eval" function for interactive evaluation of LISP statements, and dynamic data structures.

List. An ordered sequence of components, which may themselves be lists.

Local variable. A variable declared within the confines of the subprogram specification, it is created when the subprogram is invoked and ceases to exist when execution of the subprogram terminates.

Logic programming paradigm. A rule-oriented programming approach. The programmer provides a description of a problem in the form of predicate logic statements. The system then is interpreted by a mechanism based on resolution logic. A logic program is composed of: a knowledge base, the program structure, a goal to be proved, and an inference mechanism. This approach does not attempt to deal with uncertainty and does not include an explainer facility as part of its definition. The prototypical logic programming language is PROLOG.

Logical operator. An operator that acts on Boolean data and is used in constructing conditions.

Logo. A language designed for teaching children mathematics. It is similar to LISP in that it relies on the use of functions and list structures. A distinctive feature of Logo is its "turtle graphics."

Loop. See *Iteration*.

Low-level language. A programming language that is machine oriented; i.e., it closely follows the built-in instruction set of the underlying computer. Assembly languages are highly machine oriented.

Machine code. The built-in instruction set of the computer, it is formatted in the binary or hexadecimal number system.

Message passing. A parallel processing model that simulates a distributed processing system and allows for the exchange of information among communicating processes.

MODULA-2. MODUlar LAnguage 2. A high-level language with facilities for system programming, it was intended for use in large-system software design and supports a high degree of problem decomposition and program abstraction.

Modular programming. An approach to software engineering in which a large program is designed as a collection of blocks of code. Each subprogram performs a single, clearly defined task and is characterized by a single entry point and a single exit point.

Modularity. The degree to which a program is composed of independent subprograms with clearly defined interfaces. See *Modular programming*.

Module. A block of program code. See *Subprogram*.

Monitor. A named subprogram containing a collection of parallel processes that share data.

Multilinked list. A list in which each component node contains two or more pointers and is able to reside on several logical lists simultaneously.

Mutual exclusion. A problem that must be considered when designing programs with parallel control. When two parallel processes must both be able to access a common resource (e.g., database), but this access must be limited in some way so that the data is protected from an unintentional loss of integrity.

Named constant. A word that identifies a constant and is protected from change.

N-S chart. Nassi-Shneiderman **chart**. A method of expressing program logic flow that can be viewed as a pictorial equivalent of pseudocode. A rectangular, nested flowchart that "forces" structured control constructs onto the algorithm. Like pseudocode and flowchart, it is machine- and programming-language independent, and allows programmers to focus on logic flow without having to worry about syntax.

NATURAL. A full-function 4GT that is associated with the ADABAS database system.

NOMAD2. A full-function 4GT.

Nonprocedural language. A language that focuses on the results that one seeks rather than laying out the necessary steps to get there. See *Declarative programming*, *Fourth-generation software*.

Numeric types. Data types that can accept arithmetic operations. These include integers, floating-point, fixed-point, and complex numbers.

Object-oriented programming paradigm. An approach to programming in which the organizing principle is the data object. The data object is an active entity asked to perform operations (called methods) on itself. A complex problem is viewed as a network of objects that communicate with each other by message passing that invokes these methods.

Object program. A machine-executable program produced as output from a compiler.

Operand. A component of an expression, an operand represents access to a data value and may be a constant, a variable name, a function reference, or another expression.

Operation. A single computer instruction; a type of simple subprogram.

OPS5. Official Production System, version **5**. A rule-oriented production-system language used in artificial intelligence.

Output parameter. An output parameter receives its value as the result of processing done within the subprogram. Its value is passed back to the point of call.

Package. A program or set of programs designed to solve a problem common to a large number of users—for example, statistical analysis or graphics.

Parallel processing. *Concurrent processing.* The concurrent execution of two or more subprograms called processes. They operate simultaneously, relatively independently, and may communicate with each other and share common resources.

Parameter. See *Formal parameter.*

Pascal. A narrowly defined, simple and elegant programming language designed by Niklaus Wirth in his opposition to ALGOL68. Pascal influenced the design of many subsequent languages.

PL/1. Programming Language/1. A general, multipurpose language developed by IBM that drew on concepts from several major languages including FORTRAN and COBOL. Some important features include multitasking, defaults, and explicit use of pointers and list processing.

Pointer. A reference to an unnamed data object.

Portability. A criterion used in evaluating a programming language. If a language is portable, then programs written in the language will work and provide similar results on many different machine/compilers; i.e., they will be machine independent.

Precedence rules. Rules that govern the implicit control over the operations within an expression.

Problem oriented. The degree to which a program can handle a particular problem or application area efficiently. For example, COBOL is particularly well suited for problems in business data processing; FORTRAN is especially appropriate for problems in the scientific areas. PL/1 is an example of a true general-purpose language, since it can handle any problem area as well as another.

Procedural language. A process-centered language. The primary objective of a procedural programming language is to express the individual detailed instructions that the computer will follow in order to accomplish its task. Languages differ in the degree to which they are procedural. See *Nonprocedural language.*

Process-centered language. A language that is concerned with the details of computing a solution and with the process of problem decomposition. *See Data-centered language.*

Processing environment. The degree to which the program interacts with its environment during execution time. Some examples of processing environments are: batch processing, interactive processing, and parallel processing.

Processing mode. The manner in which a file will be used—for example, batch mode or query mode.

Production-system programming paradigm. In this rule-oriented approach to programming, a program consists of a set of condition-action rules called productions. Production systems can handle uncertainty and are frequently used in the construction of expert systems.

Productivity tool. A program or set of programs that speeds up the rate of application development—for example, report writer, program generator, natural language front-end, graphics package.

Program abstraction. A relatively independent program unit for the processing of a specific task that may be called by another subprogram without the programmer needing to know exactly how the program abstraction accomplishes its goal, only what the function is that it performs. See *Abstraction*, *Information hiding*.

Programming environment. A set of tools that includes a programming language and serves to aid in program development. Some of the tools that may be contained within a programming environment, also known as a software development environment, include an editor, a linker, debugger, and an on-line help facility.

Programming language. A notation for expressing data structures and instructions for computing purposes.

Programming myopia. A condition characterized by dependence on one particular programming language.

Programming paradigm. An approach to programming. Most programming languages assume a particular programming paradigm as the major organizing principle. The most prevalent paradigm today is the imperative programming paradigm.

PROLOG. PROgramming in **LOG**ic. A logic-oriented language that is declarative rather than procedural. It is used in artificial intelligence including the areas of natural language processing and the building of expert systems.

Pseudocode. A nonpictorial method of expressing program logic flow. Pseudocode is machine and programming language independent and allows the programmer to focus on logic flow without having to worry about syntax.

QBE. Query By Example. A popular query language that is easy to use because it works with a visual format.

Queue. A list into which new items may be inserted at one end only (the REAR), and from which items may be deleted at the other end only (the FRONT).

Query language. A user-friendly language that usually accompanies a database management system and is normally powerful enough to allow for sophisticated programming of a procedural or nonprocedural nature. Examples are NATURAL for ADABAS, SQL , and QBE. PROLOG is sometimes considered a query language based on logical relations.

Raising an exception. This involves noticing that the exception condition has occurred, causing program execution to be interrupted or temporarily suspended, and the invocation of the exception handler.

RAMIS II. **R**apid **A**ccess **M**anagement **I**nformation **S**ystem **II**. The first commercially available, full-function 4GT.

Random file. See *Relative file*.

Readability. A criterion used in evaluating a programming language. The degree to which programs written in that language may be easily read and understood by humans.

Real-time processing. A processing environment in which external processes, such as physical objects, interact with and impose strict time constraints on the responses from executing programs.

Reasoning mechanism. The control structure of the inference engine of an expert system, which attempts to mimic the way people reason. Two reasoning mechanisms are backward chaining and forward chaining.

Record. A hierarchical data structure. An ordered collection of data elements not necessarily of the same type, each element identified by name.

Recursion. A programming technique in which a subprogram calls itself. See *Recursion*.

Recursive subprogram. A subprogram that calls itself.

Reengineering. A concept that program design and modification are both made at the specification level. Thus, changes to the specification effect changes to the code.

Reference. An evaluated variable name that provides access to data.

Relational operators. Operators that form conditions and can operate on virtually all types of data.

Relative file. *Direct file. Random file.* An unordered collection of component records stored on a direct access storage device in which each record may be accessed directly by location (absolute or relative).

Repetition. See *Iteration*.

Repository. An extended data dictionary used by CASE tools. It contains definitions for every object in the system and for relationships among objects. It also keys these objects to the actual program code. Objects may be, for example, definitions for screen or printed reports, database schemata, structure charts, dataflow diagrams.

Reserved words. Language keywords that are off-limits to the programmer and may not be used to denote programmer-supplied words.

Rule-based programming paradigm. See *Production-system programming paradigm*.

Rule-oriented programming paradigms. An approach to programming in which one may: specify facts and rules about objects and their relationships; query the system regarding these objects and relationships; combine facts to express them as a single rule; easily integrate new facts and rules into a program. PROLOG and OPS5 are rule-oriented languages that represent two divergent world views: the logic programming and production-system programming paradigms.

Scheduled call. A type of subprogram control used in event-oriented simulation programs. Control over some subprograms is managed by a timing mechanism (a subprogram that may be built into the programming language or coded by the programmer), and a subprogram is scheduled to be invoked at a particular activation time.

Scope of a variable. The portion of the program in which a variable name is associated with and accesses a particular value.

Search strategy. The technique used to search the knowledge base of an expert system. See *Depth-first search*, *Breadth-first search*.

Selection. A control construct that is employed when one wishes to choose among two or more alternative blocks of code.

Selective composition. See *Selection*.

Self-documenting. A criterion used in evaluating a programming language. The degree to which a program is self-explaining. Self-documenting techniques enhance the readability of a program.

Semaphores. A Boolean variable with two operations: wait and signal. It is used to control access to a shared resource in parallel processing.

Separator. A delimiter that indicates the end of one program entity and the beginning of the next.

Sequential allocation. One of two ways in which storage can be allocated for most data structures. With sequential allocation, a single block of contiguous storage locations is allocated for the structure. A structure-allocated storage in a sequential manner is incapable of change throughout its lifetime; it may be called a static structure. See *Linked allocation*.

Sequential file. A linear sequence of related records that may be ordered on some key field.

Sequential composition. See *Simple sequence*.

Set. A data structure of unspecified size containing an unordered collection of distinct values.

Side effect. A change to a global variable, occurring as the result of processing done in a subprogram.

Simple call. A highly constrained subprogram control construct that allows the calling subprogram to exert total control over the called subprogram.

Simple sequence. The simplest control structure and the default in imperative languages. Individual statements are executed one after another in the order in which they appear in the program.

Simple statement. A statement that contains a single action, for example, **ADD**.

SIMULA. **SIMU**lation **LA**nguage. A programming language for simulation applications. SIMULA67, the 1967 revision, was of a more general nature.

Smalltalk. The language that defines the object-oriented approach to programming. It is a language embedded within an environment. The environment is a user-friendly, interactive interface with multiple overlapping windows, graphical and textual menus, and a mouse for selecting and pointing.

SNOBOL. Stri**N**g **O**riented Sym**BO**lic **L**anguage. A string-processing language for formula manipulation.

Software engineering. The discipline of software engineering can be traced back to the structured programming techniques of the early 1970s. It includes techniques for analysis, design, testing, validation, and maintenance of software.

Source program. A program written in a high-level language and then input to the compile process.

SQL. **S**tructured **Q**uery **L**anguage. A query language that is becoming the standard way to communicate with relational databases.

Stack. An ordered set of items into which new items may be inserted, and from which items may be deleted at one end only (the TOP).

Static scoping rule. *Lexical scoping rule.* Every variable is accessible in the subprogram in which it is declared and to any subprogram nested inside of it—unless the same variable name is re-declared as a local variable in some inner subprogram—but is not accessible to any subprogram outside or surrounding it.

Static structure. A structure that is incapable of change throughout its lifetime.

Stepwise refinement. The consecutive specification of subprograms over several, progressively more detailed levels of abstraction. This process of stepwise refinement results in the modular decomposition of a program into a hierarchical structure.

Storage structure. What data structures become after being mapped to memory.

String. An ordered sequence of characters of dynamically changing size.

Strongly typed language. A programming language in which the types of all variables are determined at compile time. Usually includes rigorous type checking.

Structured control constructs. Statement-level control structures are either (low-level) stylized sequences of instructions or high-level language statements, each with a single entry point and a single exit point, which fall into one of the following three categories: simple sequence, selection, iteration. (The goto is not a structured control construct.)

Structured English. See *Pseudocode*.

Structured programming. A set of programming techniques for implementing program and control abstractions in a hierarchical manner. Its purpose is to make programs more readable, less error-prone, and easier to maintain. Three techniques in this category are: modularity, top-down design, and the use of structured control constructs.

Subprogram. A block of code that has a name, is relatively independent, and performs a specific task.

Subprogram call. The invocation of a subprogram.

Subprogram library. A collection of external subprograms that may contain such built-in functions and/or procedures as arithmetic functions, statistical procedures, searching/sorting arrays, etc. This allows programmers to build on rather than duplicate the work of previous programmers.

Subtype. This user-defined type allows for the specification of the domain as a subrange of another already existing type.

Symbol table. The symbol table maps program symbols such as variables with their properties such as type, size, and relative location.

Synchronization. A problem that must be considered when designing programs with parallel control. When concurrently executing processes attempt to communicate with each other, one process must wait for the completion of or a signal from another process.

Test-after loop. A form of iteration in which statements contained within the body of the loop will always be executed at least once regardless of whether the condition tested is true or false the first time around.

Test-before loop. A form of iteration in which statements in the body of the loop are iterated as long as a particular condition, which is tested before each iteration, is true.

Textfile. A stream of characters, separated into lines by an end-of-line character such as the carriage-return.

Top-down design. A structured programming technique in which a large, complex task is structured into a hierarchy of manageable subtasks. At each level in the hierarchy, low-level decisions and detail work are delayed to be performed later when work on a lower level will be considered.

Tree. A hierarchical collection of nodes and the branches connecting them. Each node may be considered the "root" of another tree.

Tree traversal. The process of "traveling" over the branches of a tree in such a way so that each node is accessed only once.

Typing system. A facility for defining new data types and for declaring variables to be of such types.

User-defined type. A data type that is defined by a programmer and provides a limited means for specifying the domain of a "new" type based on some other predefined type.

User interface. An interactive, often graphics-based system component that facilitates communication between the computer system and the human user.

Variable. A receptacle for storing data values.

Variable-length record. A record with a changeable number of repeated fields.

Variant record. A record that is allowed to have two or more variations.

Virtual computer. The abstract machine that the user sees and interacts with, for example a "COBOL computer." The same hardware with different sets of software can be transformed into different virtual computers.

von Neumann computer. The architecture on which most of today's computers are based. It uses a configuration in which the central processor is tied very closely to an internal memory unit containing a large number of unique addressable storage locations, which may be retrieved one at a time, and a one-word bus for transporting data between these two components. One instruction is executed at a time, in sequence.

Writability. A criterion used in evaluating a programming language, it refers to the degree of easiness to design, code, test, run, document, and modify programs.

C

Guidelines for Quality Term Projects

The following are some brief guidelines to help you in preparing for term research projects. These may be individual or group projects. Such activities are important to the development of your skills, knowledge, and confidence in your chosen area of study.

Written Papers

Papers must be typewritten and well structured with section and paragraph headers, footnotes, tables, and graphs. Aside from text, your paper should include a title page, a table of contents, and an annotated bibliography. In addition to using books as reference material, you must use very current articles from trade journals, scholarly journals, and conference proceedings. Make certain that you use plenty of footnote citations, referencing material that you have used in preparing your paper. The best papers reflect the author's own insight about the chosen topic and come to some sort of conclusion.

Oral Presentations

Oral presentations are an important learning device. You gain experience speaking in front of a group, this time a *friendly* group. Practice speaking comfortably. Do not read from a sheet of paper. Prepare a set of *brief* notes in keyword form on index cards as a memory aid.

Use the board sparingly as that takes away from your presentation time. Prepare photocopied handouts and/or overhead-projection transparencies in advance. All group members should be prepared to answer questions even if only one actually made the presentation.

Suggested Topics

The Ada programming environment	CASE tools
C programming in a UNIX environment	Computer crime
Data integrity, security, privacy	Decision support systems
Documentation techniques	Ethics and professionalism in CIS
Fifth-generation software?	Packages, integrated packages, and 4GTs
Programming in a 4GT: FOCUS (e.g.)	Programming paradigms
Prototyping in system development	The Smalltalk programming environment
Software development in the year 2000	

A project can also be built around a single programming language, or a group of related languages. Such a project might include some programming work (say, the study problems of Chapter 7) and demonstration of the results to the class. Make sure you relate the new language to other languages you have learned or that most of the class would know.

Where to Look

A convenient starting point for many of the topics listed above is the bibliography of this book. Consult the references at the end of the appropriate chapter. Also, a search of the following sources is certain to turn up current material.

ACM Computing Surveys	*ACM SIGCSE Bulletin*
ACM SIGPLA Notices	*ACM Trans. on Programming Languages*
Acta Informatica	*AT&T Technical Journal*
Byte	*Communications of the ACM*
The Computer Journal	*Computer Language*
Computerworld	*Datamation*
Dr. Dobb's Journal of Software Tools	*Expert Systems*
IBM Journal of Research and Development	*IEEE Computer*
IEEE Potentials	*IEEE Software*
IEEE Trans. on Software Engineering	*International Journal of Man-Machine Studies*
Journal of the ACM	*Journal of Logic Programming*
Journal of Object-oriented Programming	*Journal of Pascal, Ada, and Modula-2*
Journal of Systems and Software	*PC Week*
Proceedings of the IEEE	*Science of Computer Programming*
Software Engineering Journal	*Software—Practice and Experience*

Index

Internal validity, 483
Interpreter (inference engine component), 515
Interpreters, 56, 57
Interpretive routines, 15, 18
I/O
  See also File structures
  in C, 392
  in MODULA-2, 347
  parameters, 133
  in Pascal, 309
  in PROLOG, 431
Is-a relationship, 198, 514
Iteration, 9, 13, 163, 173–76, 177, 191, 269, 491–93
  in C, 401–2
  in COBOL, 273
  indexed loops, 174–75
  in MODULA-2, 356–57
  in Pascal, 314–15
  in PROLOG, 437–39
  in Smalltalk, 464
Iverson, Kenneth, 25

Japanese Fifth Generation Computer Systems Project, 33, 55, 417
Jensen, K., 138
Job, defined, 126
Jobs, Steve, 446
JOVIAL, 23, 27
Jump, 163

Kay, Alan, 33, 445, 446–47
Kernighan, Brian, 375
Key-to-address transformation methods, 104
Keyword message expression, 463
Keywords, 123–24
  in C, 391
  in COBOL, 264
  in MODULA-2, 345–46
  in Pascal, 308
  in PROLOG, 429
  in Smalltalk, 459
Knowledge base, 193, 194, 195, 513–14
Knowledge engineering, 512–13
Knuth, Donald, 13
Kowalski, Robert, 33, 418

Label (program element), 68
Language dependence, 5–6, 10
Language extension, 149
Language processors, 53–64
  compile process, 59–63
  types of, 55–59
  virtual computer, 53–55
Laning, J.H., Jr., 20
Large-scale integration, 14
Late (dynamic) binding, 58, 198, 449
Lazy (delayed) evaluation, 139, 192
Leaf node, 96
Learning curve for programming languages, 50
Length, string, 84
Lexical analysis, 59, 60
Lexical scoping rule, 131
Lexical type checking, 70

Libraries, subprogram, 129
  in C, 396
  in COBOL, 267–68
  in MODULA-2, 350–53
  in Pascal, 310–11
  in PROLOG, 432
  in Smalltalk, 461
Lilith system, 330
Linear data structures, 77, 84–96
  See also specific languages
  arrays, 74–75, 85–87
  lists, 73–74, 87–96
    deques, 90, 91
    linked, 75, 87, 89, 91
    queues, 90–91
    records, 91–96
    stacks, 89–90, 109–11, 160
  strings, 68, 73, 84
Linked allocation, 78
Linked lists, 75, 87, 89, 91
Linked storage allocation, 81, 82–84
Links, 514
LISP, 22–24, 31, 33, 35, 43, 58, 192, 418, 516
  lists in, 73–74, 82
  operators in, 157
  recursion in, 181
  string handling in, 84
LISP Machine, 55
List(s), 73–74, 87–96
  in C, 387
  in COBOL, 258
  deque, 90, 91
  linked, 75, 87, 89, 91
  in MODULA-2, 341–42
  multilinked, 91, 92, 228, 411–16
  multiple
    in COBOL, 285–93
    in MODULA-2, 367–73
    in Pascal, 323–28
    in PROLOG, 441–43
    in Smalltalk, 471–78
  in Pascal, 304, 323–28
  in PROLOG, 426, 441–43
  queues, 90–91
  records, 91–96
  in Smalltalk, 456
  stacks, 89–90
  tree represented as, 97
Literals, 65
  in C, 380
  in COBOL, 250
  in MODULA-2, 335–36
  in Pascal, 299
  in PROLOG, 421
  in Smalltalk, 451–52
Local variables
  in C, 394
  in COBOL, 267
  in MODULA-2, 349
  in Pascal, 310
Location, parameter passing by, 134–36
Logical (Boolean) data elements, 68, 257, 301
Logical (Boolean) variables, 72
Logical operators, 118, 157
  in C, 398
  in COBOL, 269

  in MODULA-2, 354
  in Pascal, 313
  in PROLOG, 435
  in Smalltalk, 462
Logical records in COBOL, 258
Logic programming paradigm, 45, 193, 195, 418
LOGLISP, 202
Logo, 28
Long integers, 380
Loop constructs, 13, 491–93
LOOPS, 202
Loops *see also* iteration
  test-after, 176, 177
  test-before, 175–76
Low-level programming language, 36
LUCID, 201

McCarthy, John, 22
Machine code, 14, 18, 19, 36, 40
Machine-code subroutines, 18
Machine dependence, 5
Machine language coding, 18, 19
Main module, 147
Main program, 126
Maintenance
  of files, 103
  of programs, 4
Mark and sweep method, 199
MARK I computer, 14
Martin, James, 498
Master files, 103
Master/slave relationship, 141, 178, 179
Match-select-execute cycle, 194–95
MATH-MATIC, 20
Mauchly, John, 19
Memory management
  in C, 376
  in MODULA-2, 331
  in Pascal, 299
  in PROLOG, 421
Message expression, 462–63
Message passing, 9, 186–87, 196, 197
Messages, 448
  cascading, 458
  in Smalltalk, 463–65
Metalogical rules, 418
Method arguments, 454
Methods, 45, 196–97, 448, 451, 460
Method temporaries, 454
Mitchell, Grace E., 21
Mittelman, Peter, 504
Mixed mode expressions in C, 398
Models, data, 106
Modifiability of program, 483
MODULA
  parallel processing in, 143
  parameter passing in, 136
MODULA-2, 28, 30, 38, 58, 70, 213, 329–73
  control structures, 354–59
    control statements, 355–58
    expressions, 354–55
    lack of **goto** statement, 167
    operators, 354
    subprogram control structures, 358–59
  data in, 331–44
    abstract data types, 65, 343

Text formatting, *cont.*
  in COBOL, 262, 263
  in MODULA-2, 344–45
  in Pascal, 307
  in PROLOG, 428–29
  in Smalltalk, 458
Textual units, 9
Third generation languages, 20–32, 40
Thompson, Kenneth, 29–30, 375
Time-sharing, 43
Timing routines, 182–84
Tokens, 60
Top-down (goal-directed) systems, 193–94, 515
Top-down (hierarchical) design, 145, 147–50, 487–88, 494
Transfer, 163
Transform, 7–8, 145
Transform algorithms, 104
Transistors, 14
Translators. *See* Language processors
Traversal of tree, 232–33
Trees, 96–98
  equivalence relation and, 78
  evaluation of expression in, 160
  of expressions, 159
  nested subprograms as, 132
  parse, 60, 61
  in PROLOG, 426–27
  syntax, 60
  traversal of, 232–33, 247
Triangular matrix, 85, 87
TurboPascal®, 295, 304
Turbo PROLOG, 417, 419
Two-way selection
  in C, 400
  in COBOL, 270, 271
  in MODULA-2, 356
  in Pascal, 314
  in PROLOG, 436–37
Type casting, 383, 398–99
Type checking, 69, 70
  in MODULA-2, 338
  run time, 200
Type transfer function, 350
Typing, 69–70
  See also Data structures
  in MODULA-2, 337–40
  in Smalltalk, 451

UCSD Pascal, 295
Unary message expressions, 463
Unary operator, 157
Unconditional branching, 163
  in C, 400
  in COBOL, 270
  in MODULA-2, 355–56
  in Pascal, 313
  in PROLOG, 436
Unconditional constraints, 200
Unification (PROLOG), 433–34
Unions in C, 386–87
UNIVAC, 14
UNIX® operating system, 29–30, 375
Unnamed (anonymous) variables, 73, 124, 134
until loop, 491, 492–93
User-defined constant(s)
  in C, 381
  in COBOL, 255
  in MODULA-2, 336
  in Pascal, 299
  in PROLOG, 421
  in Smalltalk, 452
User-defined types, 76, 108
  in C, 383–84
  in MODULA-2, 339–40
  in Pascal, 301–2
  in PROLOG, 422
  in Smalltalk, 455
User-defined words in COBOL, 262
User-friendliness, 2

VAL, 201
Validity of program, 483
Value, parameter passing by, 136–37
Value parameters, 310, 349
Value-result, call by, 136, 137
Variable(s), 65, 66–67, 190
  See also specific languages
  anonymous, 73, 124, 134
  bound, 421
  in C, 381–84, 394–95
  class, 197, 454
  in COBOL, 256–57
  declaration of, 256, 300, 336, 381, 421, 454
  free, 421

  generic, 386
  global, 130–31, 135, 267, 310, 349, 394, 454
  index, 66
  instance, 196, 197, 448, 453
  local, 267, 310, 349, 394
  logical (Boolean), 72
  in MODULA-2, 336–40, 349–50
  name of, 123
  numeric-type (computational), 71
  in Pascal, 299–302, 310
  private, 460
  in PROLOG, 421–22
  scope of, 130, 131–33
  shared, 454, 460
  in Smalltalk, 452–55
  static, 130
  subscripted, 74
  temporary, 197, 454
Variable-length records, 95–96
Variable parameters, 310, 349–50
Variant records, 94–95, 386
Virtual computer, 53–55
Virtual (logical), notion of, 68–69
Von Neumann, John, 13–14, 203
Von Neumann architecture, 14, 15–16, 32, 154, 190

Walkback window, 466
Warren, David H.D., 418
while/do loop. *See* Test-before loop
while statement, 491
WHIRLWIND computer, 20
Windows, in Smalltalk, 465–66
Wirth, Niklaus, 29, 30, 294–95, 330
Words
  in C, 390–91
  in COBOL, 262–64
  in MODULA-2, 345–46
  in Pascal, 307–8
  in PROLOG, 429
  in Smalltalk, 458–59
Writability of programming language, 46

Zierler, N., 20
Zuse, Konrad, 20